Brazilian-African Diaspora in Ghana

Ruth Simms Hamilton
AFRICAN DIASPORA SERIES

The Ruth Simms Hamilton African Diaspora series at Michigan State University Press presents the past and contemporary experiences of African people throughout the world, written by emerging and established scholars in various fields in the social sciences and humanities in pursuit of a reconceptualization of the historical global movements of African peoples. This series pays tribute to the life and legacy of Dr. Ruth Simms Hamilton, a pioneer in African Diaspora Studies, and builds on her seminal work and conceptualization of the African diaspora.

The series editors are particularly interested in innovative book length manuscripts grounded in scholarly research and inquiry that challenge both pre-existing and established notions of the African diaspora by engaging new regions, conceptualizations, and articulations of diaspora that move the field forward. In underscoring new frontiers and frameworks in the study of African descendants' lived experiences, the series presents new approaches to the production of knowledge on African diasporas. In keeping with the tradition of the field, the series is an interdisciplinary undertaking devoted to scholarship on the histories, political movements, institutions, cultures, intellectual discourse, ways of knowing, and identities of African and African descended peoples. Since the diaspora is based largely on movement, the transnational migrations of Africans throughout history and in contemporary times have complicated what it means to be black and or African depending on the political, economic, religious, geographical, and cultural context Africans find themselves. As a result, scholars are forced to confront the evolving realities and constructions of blackness and Africanness in a changing world. While much of the scholarship in the diaspora continues to focus on the Americas due to the enduring legacy of the middle passage and trans-Atlantic slave trade, in addition to these areas the editors encourage manuscript submissions that bring greater visibility to less studied but nonetheless critical areas of the Africana world. This includes internal diasporas within the African continent and African diasporas of the Indian Ocean, Pacific and European regions.

The series highlights the global experiences and dynamic dimensions of peoples of African descent. It maps their historical and contemporary movements, speaks from their radical (unique) narratives and explores their critical relationships with one another. By exploring Afrodescendents within their particular and broader sociocultural, historical, political, and economic contexts, it contemplates similarities, difference, continuity and transformation.

CO-EDITORS
Glenn Chambers, *Michigan State University*
Quito Swan, *Howard University*

EDITORIAL BOARD
Afua Cooper, *Dalhousie University*
Gerald Horne, *University of Houston*
Franklin W. Knight, *Johns Hopkins University*
Besi Muhonja, *James Madison University*
Cheikh Thiam, *The Ohio State University*
Robert Trent Vinson, *The College of William and Mary*

Brazilian-African Diaspora in Ghana

THE TABOM, SLAVERY, DISSONANCE OF MEMORY, IDENTITY, AND LOCATING HOME

Kwame Essien

Michigan State University Press • *East Lansing*

Copyright © 2016 by Kwame Essien

♾ The paper used in this publication meets the minimum requirements
of ANSI/NISO Z39.48-1992 (R 1997) (Permanence of Paper).

Michigan State University Press
East Lansing, Michigan 48823-5245

Printed and bound in the United States of America.

22 21 20 19 18 17 16   1 2 3 4 5 6 7 8 9 10

Names: Essien, Kwame, author.
Title: Brazilian-African diaspora in Ghana : the Tabom, slavery, dissonance of memory,
identity and locating home / Kwame Essien.
Other titles: Ruth Simms Hamilton African diaspora series.
Description: East Lansing : Michigan State University Press, 2016. | Series: Ruth Simms Hamilton
African diaspora series | Includes bibliographical references and index.
Identifiers: LCCN 2015299453| ISBN 9781611862195 (pbk. : alk. paper) | ISBN 9781609175047 (pdf)
| ISBN 9781628952773 (epub) | ISBN 9781628962772 (kindle)
Subjects: LCSH: Freedmen—Ghana—History. | Immigrants—Ghana—History.
| Africans—Brazil—Emigration and immigration—History. | Children of immigrants—Ghana—History.
| Ghana—Emigration and immigration—History. | Ghana—Colonial influence.
Classification: LCC DT511 .E87 2016 | DDC 966.700496081—dc23 LC record available at
http://lccn.loc.gov/2015041934

Book design by Charlie Sharp, Sharp Des!gns, Lansing, Michigan
Cover design by Erin Kirk New
Cover image of slave ship is used courtesy of Lorenzo Dow Turner papers,
Anacostia Community Museum Archives, Smithsonian Institution,
gift of Lois Turner Williams (ACMA PH2003.7064.279)

Michigan State University Press is a member of the Green Press Initiative and is
committed to developing and encouraging ecologically responsible publishing
practices. For more information about the Green Press Initiative and the use of
recycled paper in book publishing, please visit *www.greenpressinitiative.org*.

Visit Michigan State University Press at *www.msupress.org*

For my wife
Dzidzor
and our two daughters
Esi-Gyapeaba
and
Edinam Aba-Kraaba

Contents

List of Figures and Tables ix
Acknowledgments xi
Introduction xvii

PART 1. FROM BRAZIL TO GHANA: UNMATCHED FORTITUDE
AND LOCATING HOME

CHAPTER 1. Reverse Diaspora: Dissonance of Memory, Voyages
 of Hope, and Degrees of Return 3
CHAPTER 2. Historicizing the Returnee Presence in Gã *Mãŋ*: Challenges
 and Silences 31
CHAPTER 3. The Social History of Gã *Mãŋ*: Colonialism and Their Impact
 on the Brazilian-African Diaspora 51
CHAPTER 4. The Evolution of Land in Gã *Mãŋ* and Brazilian-African
 Diaspora: Paradox of Freedom and the Birth of Conflicts 91
CHAPTER 5. Escaping Slavery into Colonialism and Squabbles: How
 Colonial Projects and Internal Disputes Threatened Brazilian
 Land and Freedom 119

PART 2. CONTRADICTIONS OF RETURN: TRANSPORTING ATLANTIC TRADITIONS, SKILLS, AND CULTURES AND REFASHIONING IDENTITY

CHAPTER 6. (Re-)Creating Brazilian Slavery in an Enabling Environment: The "Ghost" of Slavery 153
CHAPTER 7. Contributions by the Brazilian-Africans and the Tabom: Impact on Ghana's History... 175
CHAPTER 8. Brazilians Together, Brazilians Apart: The Family Trees and the Process of Becoming Gã 195

PART 3. DIASPORA IN FULL CIRCLE: HOME IS GHANA, BRAZIL IS OUR MOTHER COUNTRY

CHAPTER 9. Fading Diaspora and Receding Memory: How the Brazilian Government and the Tabom Are Preserving the Brazil House and Crisscrossing the Atlantic in Full Circle 227
CHAPTER 10. Telescoping Lula's Unfulfilled Promise and the Implications of the Tabom's Visit to Brazil: A Hopeless Situation? 259
CONCLUSION 275

Notes 281
Bibliography... 337
Index.. 359

Figures and Tables

Figures

FIGURE 1. Map of coastal Accra... xviii
FIGURE 2. Brazil House xxiv
FIGURE 3. Francis Zaccheus Santiago Peregrino.................................7
FIGURE 4. Letter inquiring about Francis Zaccheus Santiago Peregrino............8
FIGURES 5A AND 5B. Emancipated Africans returning to Africa, 1888 13
FIGURES 6A AND 6B. List of some female and male slaves from Africa 15
FIGURE 7. Sozenja dos Santos, a Brazilian-Gã from Accra 53
FIGURE 8. Brazilian chief João Antonio Nelson with *Mãŋtsɛ* Tackie Tawiah
    and members of the Gã royal family 85
FIGURE 9. Land acquired for European residential area..........................97
FIGURE 10. Disputed land between João Antonio Nelson and colonial
    officials in Accra 109
FIGURES 11A AND 11B. Gã *Mãŋtsɛ* Tackie Tawiah and *Mãŋtsɛ* Nii Kojo
    Ababio IV 132
FIGURES 12A AND 12B. Disputed Brazilian lands between Brazilians
    and non-Brazilians in Accra.. 141
FIGURE 13. Copy of court case *Rashid Brimah & 3 Ors. v. Hadji M. B.
    Peregrino-Brimah*.. 143

FIGURE 14. Brazilian Olosun Mosque 185
FIGURE 15. Manyo Plange 189
FIGURE 16A. Ambassador Miguel Augustus Ribeiro presents his credentials
    to President John F. Kennedy... 191
FIGURE 16B. Harry Francisco Ribeiro 191
FIGURE 17. Azumah Nelson.. 192
FIGURE 18. Chief Justice Georgina Theodora Wood 193
FIGURE 19. The Nassu family tree, showing the relationship between
    the Lutterodt and the Peregrino/Peregrino-Brimah family trees........... 204
FIGURE 20. Peregrino House at Accra, Ghana................................ 205
FIGURE 21. The Mama Nassu-Lutterodt family tree 207
FIGURE 22. The Peregrino/Peregrino-Brimah family tree..................... 210
FIGURE 23. Elmina Castle.. 230
FIGURE 24. Luiz Inácio Lula da Silva and Tabom chief Nii Azumah V 231

TABLES

TABLE 1. Selected newspaper coverage of PANAFEST and Emancipation
    Day celebrations 47
TABLE 2. Brazilian/Tabom chiefs who were involved in disputes over
    Brazilian lands... 108
TABLE 3. Gã mãŋtsɛmɛi (kings and chiefs) who were involved in disputes
    over Brazilian lands that were presented in both colonial and
    native courts 133

Acknowledgments

My motivation for researching and writing about the life histories of ex-slaves and their descendants in Ghana came from my mother and grandmother, who shared stories about my great-great-uncle, Chief Andoh II. Chief Andoh II was the chief of Elmina, an important slave port in coastal Ghana, between 1884 and 1898. Stories about his interactions with Europeans in the area, the proximity of my family house to the Elmina Castle, slave routes from the hinterland through Elmina where millions of slaves were forced onto slave ships helped me recognize the importance of understanding my family's connection to colonial history and the legacy of the transatlantic slave trade.

In 1999, I visited the Boone Hall Plantation in South Carolina to gain a better understanding of the African experience in America. I could hardly contain my amazement at how similar the pictures of the plantation's slaves were to my own community members in Ghana. The images of horrors and heroic stories in the slave dungeons at Elmina and those of the Boone plantation intensified my insight. This experience awakened me to the reality of the historical connections between the people of Elmina and those of African descent in the Atlantic world, and ultimately, my interests in reverse migrations, focusing first on the history of African American expatriates, activists, and intellectuals who relocated to Ghana in the mid-twentieth century. It was during my search for archival materials about the African American experience in Ghana at the Public Records and Archives Administration Department (PRAAD) in Accra that I came across documents about the "Brazilians" in Ghana. This became

Acknowledgments

the beginning of my journey to various archives in search of transatlantic connections between Ghana and Brazil.

Starting in 2005, I received a number of fellowships and grants that enabled me to complete this book. These awards facilitated several visits for archival research in the United States, England, Brazil, Ghana, Nigeria, Italy, and Dominican Republic, as well as attendance to conferences in some of these areas. They include the Patrice Lumumba Graduate Research Fellowship, John Warfield Summer Research Fellowship, and Dolores Zohrab Liebmann Research Fellowship from the University of Texas at Austin (UT); the Pre-Doctoral Fellowship from the West Africa Research Association; and the Presidential Research Grant for Professional Development at Gettysburg College. I would also like to express my appreciation to faculty members in the history and the Africana studies departments at Gettysburg College for their motivation and for awarding me the Derrick K. Gondwe Fellowship. This prestigious award allowed me to complete my dissertation and the early stages of the manuscript. At Lehigh University, the Paul J. Franz Jr. Pre-Tenure Fellowship, the Gipson Institute Research Grant, and the Faculty Research Grant supported the final stage of the manuscript.

There are several people in Brazil, the United States, Ghana, Nigeria, and England who have played major roles in making this book, which began when I was a graduate student at the University of Illinois, Urbana–Champaign (UIUC) a success. After I completed my master's degree in African Studies, I decided to pursue a master's degree in Latin American and Caribbean studies to gain deeper insight into African diaspora history. It was during this turning point that my research agenda for this project gained momentum. I would like to extend my gratitude to Jean M. Allman and Merle Bowen at the Center for African Studies, as well as faculty members affiliated with the Center for Latin American and Caribbean Studies at UIUC for supporting during my master's degrees in African Studies and Latin American and Caribbean Studies. They not only expressed their interest in my research, but they funded my first Association for the Study of the Worldwide African Diaspora (ASWAD) conference in Rio de Janeiro, Brazil, in 2005. This was my first international conference and the beginning of my journey tracing the travel routes of enslaved Africans and the Tabom. It was at ASWAD that I interacted with great Brazilian scholars and activists including Abdias do Nascimento, who was a great inspiration to me, and Efo Anani Dzidzienyo of Brown University, who became one of my mentors. I benefited from Anani's wisdom in ways I cannot express. May the gods of our ancestors bless you richly. I also met historian Michael J. Turner of Hunter College, who walked up to me at the end of my presentation at the conference and said, "I'm proud of you for researching about the Brazilians in Ghana. Let me know if I could help in anyway." Michael, these stimulating words continue to echo after a decade. Thank you and

Acknowledgments

thank you once again. Your seminal work about the Aguda served as a foundation for my book.

From UT, I would like to show my sincere gratitude to Oga Toyin Falola, Juliet E.K. Walker, Jonathan C. Brown, James Denbow, Niyi Afolabi, and Akwasi B. Assensoh. I give credit to Edmond T. Gordon and Omi Osun Joni L. Jones at the John L. Warfield Center for African and African American Studies for funding the early years of my graduate studies at the history department. You gave me a precious opportunity to excel. My colleagues at UT—Saheed Aderinto, Matt Heaton, Tyler Fleming, Emily Brown, Lady Jane Acquah, Danielle Sanchez, and others—were very supportive of my work. I am thankful to two Brazilian graduate students, Silvia Lorenso and Andréia Lisboa de Sousa, for translating some of my documents.

The "Black Atlantics: An Urban Perspective, 1400–1900 Conference" in 2009 at UT allowed me to interact with two internationally renowned scholars in the field of African diaspora history, João José Reis of Universidade Federal de Bahia, Brazil, and Robin Law of the University of Stirling, Scotland. Sharing the conference space and listening to João and Robin was a rewarding and refreshing experience. When I sat in João's "Research Seminar in Latin American History, *Perspectives on Slavery in Brazil*" during his tenure as the 2006 Tinker Visiting Professor at UT, I was a little intimidated by his presence. However, after the first day of class, I realized that he was not only a brilliant scholar, but he also had a great sense of humor. Over the years, he has provided extensive feedback that shaped this book. Muito obrigado.

Milton Guran, Elisée Soumonni at the Department of History, Université Nationale du Bénin; James Sweet at the University of Wisconsin, Madison; and Kwasi Konadu at City University of New York were also very helpful. The feedback Roquinaldo Amaral Ferreira offered after my presentation at the West African Writers and Political Kingdom Lectures at Brown University was timely and useful to my manuscript. At Gettysburg College several of my colleagues in Africana studies and the history department, including Jen Bloomquist, Scott Hancock, Linus Nyiwul, Timothy Shannon, Abou Bamba, and Rebecca Barth, offered a wide range of mentoring and support for my research. Although I spent a very short time with my former colleagues at the University of Central Arkansas, Conway, I appreciate their support also. Bob Fullilove's comments on some of the chapters were also valuable.

I would like to thank all my colleagues at Lehigh University Africana Studies Program and the history department: James B. Peterson, Monica Miller, Susan Kart, Darius Williams, Imaani El-Burki, Monica Najar, Gail Cooper, Michelle LeMaster, Natanya Duncan, and especially William Bulman for taking time from their busy schedules to provide feedback on my book proposals and for reading chapters in the manuscript. Other scholars have helped me on my way. Seth Moglen, English department gave me incredible feedback on my proposals, which animated the central thesis of my manuscript, while Chief Edward P. Morgan, Stephanie Watts, Saladin Ambar, Kashi Johnson, Lyndon Dominique, Bruce Whitehouse, Vera Fennell, Christopher Driscoll, and others were great sources of motivation. Also, my sincere appreciation to Laura Chiles, of the dean's office, for assisting me with my research travel grants. My special thanks to Dzidzor Essien and Jacob Ruttle at the Library and Technology Services Lehigh University for helping me to create high resolution images for the manuscript.

The history department graduate seminar students and I have had important exchanges covering themes of slavery and memory. These dialogues shaped part of the concluding chapter. Sean, Everett, Karen, Cal, Sam, Blake, Jason, and Khalid, I appreciate your honest remarks. Friends, including Nana Akua Anyidoho, Augustine Tawiah, Abdulai Idrissu, Harry Odamtten, Thabiti Willis, Clifford Campbell, Lornette, Jeff Brown, and others were very supportive of my work. Herman Von Hesse, I am glad I can depend on you. Thank you for reading part of the manuscript and providing critical feedback, and for collecting and sharing numerous documents about the Tabom and your knowledge of Gã social history.

In Ghana, I owe several people my appreciation. First, I would like to thank Samuel Boadi-Siaw at the University of Cape Coast, Ghana, whose writings contributed greatly to the Tabom historiography. Samuel was very excited about my research. In fact, he recommended that I contribute a chapter to the *Back to Africa* anthology. The Tabom community embraced this study and granted me interviews and provided useful information. Nii Azumah V, the Tabom Chief; the late Elder George Aruna Nelson; Aishatu Nelson; the Peregrino-Brimah family; Chief Justice Georgina Wood; and her father, elder William Lutterodt were extremely generous. The Tabom people responded positively and critically whenever I needed their assistance. Their involvements in my research shaped the book in immeasurable ways. I would also like to thank Brazilian ambassador in Ghana Irene Vida Gala, Marco Aurelio Schaumloeffel, and the staff at the Brazilian Embassy in Ghana, Accra, for the information they provided to advance my manuscript. I also appreciate the support of Bright Botwe, Florence Titriku-Sakyi-Amah, and other archivists at the PRAAD for their patience in searching for requested documents. The various records they shared with me provided new dimensions that reinforced the originality of my book. My sincere gratitude also goes to Ebenezer Ayesu at the University of Ghana, Legon, for sharing some of his archival collections about the Tabom. To the staff at the Balme Library at the University of Ghana, Legon, I say thank you.

In Nigeria, special thanks to Chief David Richards, Elizabeth Ngozi Ojeh, and Oluwa Seun Adeniyi, who provided hospitality and facilitated my visit to the Afro-Brazilian community—the Brazilian Olusun Social Club and Brazilian Gees at Bamgbose,

Lagos, where I conducted a number of interviews with the help of Alhaji Ishmael. A word of gratitude also goes to Ademola O. Dasylva at the University of Ibadan, Nigeria, and Okpeh Okpeh at Benue State University, Makurdi, Nigeria, for offering similar support during my research at the National Archives of Nigeria, Ibadan. In England, I would like to thank my sister, Maame Efua Esson, and my friends Christopher Monney and Ama Biney for their assistance during my numerous visits to the National Archives in Richmond, Surrey, and the British Newspaper Library at Colindale.

This long list of acknowledgments would not have been possible without the outstanding mentoring by Thomas Jackson and Janine Jones at the University of North Carolina at Greensboro (UNCG). Thomas, thank you for your confidence in me and for teaching me how to use archives, starting with the William Henry Chafe Oral History Collection at the Duke University's David M. Rubenstein Rare Book & Manuscript Library. I am honored to be your student. I would also like to express my appreciation to the Gentrys, the Hammers, and all the parents of the students who rode my bus, when I was a school bus driver at Grimsley High School, Greensboro, North Carolina. Lornette Ratliffe, my bus supervisor, and Bernard Townsend gave me flexible work hours to allow me to complete my bachelor's degree at UNCG. Keith Abraham and Pete Cowan, I appreciate your unconditional support. Guy Tunstall, a veteran bus driver, was also very supportive of my graduate studies and research.

This book would not have been possible without my interactions with Alex J. Schwartz, senior editor at Michigan State University Press (MSUP). The moment we met at the MSUP booth, during the African Studies Association Conference in Baltimore in 2013, I felt something unique about Alex from other acquisition editors I shared my manuscript with. Alex was very stern and straightforward about his expectations, but he was graceful and full of humor. He was not only passionate about significance of my work and including it as part of the Ruth Simms Hamilton African Diaspora series. Alex also expressed deeper knowledge about reverse migrations than the other acquisition editors. In fact, his rich knowledge made it easier for me to articulate the significance of my study to the field. I also appreciate the confidence Glenn Chambers expressed about my manuscript. I am thankful to the anonymous reviewers for their insightful suggestions as well as the following MSUP staff: Anastasia Wraight, Annette Tanner, Julie Loehr, Lauren Spitzley, Terika Hernandez, and Elise Jajuga for their patience and unending support. Their critical insights and excellent critiques have shaped the manuscript in positive ways.

Finally, I am grateful to my family in Ghana and abroad for their patience and support. To my wife and daughters, I owe you a lot of family time after sacrificing many years to complete this manuscript.

Introduction

> Several hundreds had gone back to the shores whence they had been carried in chains and were moving inland to their old homes.
>
> —Christopher Fyfe, *A History of Sierra Leone*

Sometime during the 1820s, a group of liberated African slaves on a ship from Brazil arrived in Accra, Ghana (formerly the Gold Coast), to find a new *home* (figure 1). Their unmatched fortitude had an impact on their history thereafter. The ex-slaves' desire to move back across the Atlantic waters greatly inspired their descendants, the Tabom, who were born in Ghana from the nineteenth century on, to follow a similar trajectory toward Brazil. Although welcomed by Gã *Mãŋtsɛ* (Gã King) Tackie Komeh I, the leader of Accra (1826–56), the ex-slaves who survived slavery would find themselves under threat from British colonial officials, European Christian missionaries, and traders vying for control over the social, political, commercial, and religious spaces as well as land.[1]

This book is the untold story of these freed Brazilian-African slaves and the Tabom. Although this story is part of reverse migration history, until now the field lacked a full-length study providing a broad historical narrative focusing on this group of ex-slaves and the Tabom. Exploring the trajectories of their travels—the multiple routes to and fro across the Atlantic in search of their ancestral roots and connections—help underscore their continuing relevance to discourse on the African diaspora. As such, this study weaves their story into existing stories of other returnee communities in Ghana, and

Figure 1. Map of coastal Accra.

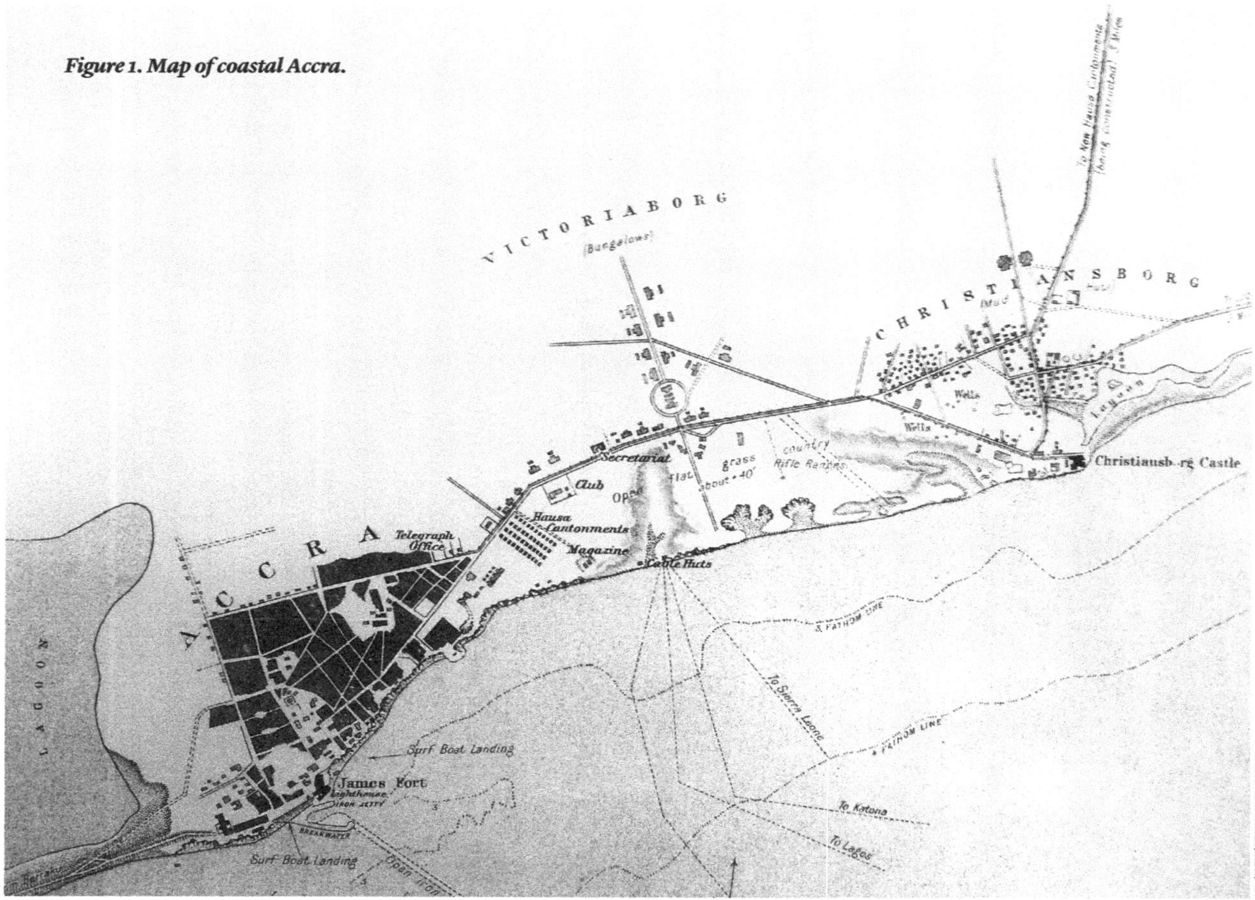

NATIONAL ARCHIVES, KEW, UK.

Africa in general. My book situates the role of historical memory and identity formations within the Brazilian-African diaspora, further contributing to ongoing diaspora and Atlantic discourse.

Covering the multigenerational journey of the ex-slaves from enslavement to their liberation and beyond, my book explores three stages of their transatlantic migrations: involuntary migrations to Brazil, reverse migrations back to Africa, and their descendants' visits to Brazil. In focusing on the plurality of their voyages from the New World to Africa and back to the New World, my book uncovers broader west-to-east and east-to-west journeys across the Atlantic. I expand the present perspective, while exploring trips of a second kind among the Tabom, who continue traveling from Ghana to Brazil seeking new links to their ancestral roots. It is in looking at the latter phases of this journey and its expanded view of reverse migrations that this work departs from the existing one-dimensional paradigm that traces journeys from the New World back to Africa.

Along the same path taken by João Antonio Nelson, who found a home in Ghana with his parents in the 1830s following emancipation, soon after colonialism other prominent Ghanaians, such as Georgina T. Wood, have crisscrossed the Atlantic. Wood, like other Tabom, traveled in 2011 to Rio de Janeiro, Brazil, to visit the former home of her Brazilian ancestors and to hold meetings with government officials.[2] Other claims about those who have visited Brazil are difficult to verify because there is insufficient evidence to support this assertion. Indeed, while it is true that some Tabom have traveled to Rio de Janeiro and Bahia/Salvador, or aspire to do so in the future, others, including the grandson of Chief João Antonio Nelson, Elder George Aruna Nelson, who died in 2009 at the age of ninety-three, could not fulfill that dream.[3] Whereas for some who left Brazil for Ghana, the search for home was an attempt to reconstruct their identity, driven by a yearning to connect to their ancestral roots, others were searching for places to live, driven by curiosity and survival. The story and history behind this complex phenomenon unravels, focusing significantly on how dissonance of memory informs and continues to shape the Brazilian-Ghanaian Atlantic narrative in preserving the past and locating a home.

The story of the ex-slaves slaves from Brazil and the Tabom is as fascinating as it is obscure, unlike the well-known histories of the "Aguda" (slaves that settled in Nigeria, Benin, and Togo), Americo-Liberians, the Sarro,[4] and other resettled communities of emancipated slaves in Angola, Upper Guinea, the Amazonia region of Brazil, and Jamaica.[5] As Silke Strickrodt rightly states, "there still are gaps in the historiography, [sic] one area that remain understudied is the Brazilian settlement in the coastal part of present-day Ghana."[6] The story of the ex-slaves and the Tabom remains largely unknown not only because of gaps in the literature but because of other factors affecting

Ghanaian socioeconomic and political culture that focus largely on the history of expatriates of African origins from North America and the Caribbean who now live in Ghana. Struggling to overcome these silences, the Tabom have made conscious efforts to move their marginalized ancestral history from the periphery of African diaspora historiography to the center of burgeoning transatlantic discourse.

Brazilian-African Diaspora in Ghana is deeply rooted in themes of slavery, identity formation, citizenship, contested spaces, and land disputes over what became known as "Brazilian land" in Accra. It is also the paradox of emancipation and colonialism. Abolition and colonialism were laced with inconsistencies: emancipated Africans survived slavery in Brazil, but they were threatened by colonialism in Ghana. As a number of scholars including Robin Law have observed, "At a more fundamental level it can be argued that the abolitionist project was in an important sense inherently imperialist, since it involved a proposed alternative course for the development of Africa, and thus implicitly asserted a supposed responsibility and right of Europeans to decide the future of the continent."[7]

In illustrating the experiences of the freed slaves and their offspring during and after abolition of slavery and British colonialism in Ghana, I follow the life stories of four members of the Brazilian-African diaspora: two came from Brazil and the other two were born in Ghana. They include João Antonio Nelson and Ferku (the only name used in the archives), and for the Tabom, George Aruna Nelson, a leading member of the Tabom community, and Georgina T. Wood, the current chief justice of the Ghanaian supreme court. I begin with the story of João Antonio Nelson, the three-year-old who arrived with his parents aboard a ship from Brazil. He was later selected as the second Brazilian chief or leader of the Brazilian-African diaspora in Accra and served from 1865 to 1900. Although he retained no memory of his earliest experiences under slavery, as an adult and Brazilian chief he was intensely aware of the threat to freedom posed by British colonialism. After the British enacted the Public Land Ordinance of 1876, they seized the land Chief João Antonio Nelson and his community inherited from their parents and used it for building British residential areas and for other colonial projects. Two decades later João Antonio Nelson helped lead a rebellion against the British colonial Compulsory Labour Ordinance of 1897 for which he and other leaders were jailed. João Antonio Nelson's experience in colonial Accra, marked by an illusion of freedom, shed light on the challenges the ex-slaves and Tabom encountered in colonial Accra. Besides their possessions, including land, the ex-slaves passed on memories of their experiences under slavery and their skills in farming to their descendants. At the advent of colonial rule, especially from the late 1890s, the Tabom demanded unrestricted control over the properties passed on to them. This led to many land disputes between them and British officials, as well as conflicts between the Tabom people and the Gã people and migrants in Accra. Other clashes were between members of the Brazilian-African diaspora over properties they inherited.

This study attempts to distinguish genealogy and generations: the first generation (1820s–1900), the second generation (1901–57), and the third generation (from 1957 on). This separation or the compartmentalization of the Brazilian-Africans and their descendants is in no way foolproof; such contingencies remain significant because it allows me to chronicle the history of the Brazilians by placing their account within a broader Ghanaian historical framework: the precolonial, the colonial, and the postcolonial periods. These three important periods, particularly the precolonial period, enable me to show how their history evolved over time. *Brazilian-African Diaspora in Ghana* begins in the precolonial period by explaining why the liberated Brazilian-Africans settled in Ghana, by tracing evidence of their contributions to Ghanaian societies, and by looking at how their descendants preserved and articulated their memory of Brazil.

For clarity, I use "ex-slaves," "Brazilians," "returnees," "liberated Brazilian-Africans," and "freed slaves" interchangeably in reference to the ancestors of the *current* generation—the "original" people who established the Brazilian-African diaspora in Ghana in the 1820s. The use of "Brazilians" carries a generic meaning that could also apply to Brazilians of European or other ancestries, which is why I prefer to use "Brazilian-Africans." Such an approach, the lumping of various Brazilian racial groups, overshadows the different layers of diversity among these groups. However, most references to the "returnees" in the archives refer to them only as "Brazilians." I supplement the usage of "Brazilians" with the use of "ex-slaves" although we lack evidence that all those who resettled in Ghana were once enslaved in Brazil. I employ "Tabom" specifically to describe children, grandchildren, and great-grandchildren of the first generation. The word "Tabom/n" comes from the Brazilian Portuguese word "tudo bom," which literally means "OK," "I am well/fine," or "everything is great." According to the late Elder George Nii Aruna Nelson and the Tabom *Mãŋtsɛ* Nii Azumah V, the Gã people derived the name "Tabom" after they heard conversations between the local people and the returnees who only spoke Portuguese when they arrived in Ghana. The early settlers repeatedly used "Tabom/n" to express themselves since they could not understand Gã, the language of the people of Accra.[8] However, the returnees were often identified as Brazilians during the precolonial and the colonial periods rather than being called "Tabom." Sometimes their offspring are identified as Tabom and Ghanaian-Brazilians, in particular because a large section of the group was born in Ghana and not Brazil, as in the case of the first settlers.[9]

Making a distinction between the old and new generations illuminates the identity of these groups that largely lived in three different colonial eras and under distinct

Introduction

historical conditions. Also, various generations interacted with both the Gã people and British colonial rulers in unique ways. This characterization becomes even more useful when examining how the identities of the early settlers evolved from one generation to the next, from Brazilians to Ghanaian-Brazilians—the Tabom people. The new generation was able to relate relatively easily with local cultures and values systems in comparison to the distant cultures of their forebears. This later shaped how some of them related to Brazil.[10] Also, "diasporan returnees" and "expatriates" will be used in describing returnees of non-Brazilian-African descent who migrated from the West Indies and North America to Ghana starting in the early twentieth century. They included Caribbean blacks and African Americans, all of whom share a common history of slavery and reverse migrations with the Brazilians. Indeed, the Brazilians arrived in Accra before the latter groups.[11]

My book points out the challenges in writing Brazilian-African diaspora narratives and recalls why most Ghanaians are not knowledgeable about the history of this returnee group.[12] It also speaks broadly to why the Tabom experience is located on the periphery of Atlantic and diaspora studies, scholarship about reverse migrations, and especially Ghanaian historiography, while other diasporic returnees (especially African Americans) in Ghana receive enormous attention and coverage.[13] In readdressing these transatlantic stories, various themes are revisited in the main chapters. The broad and recurring themes of *memory*, *dual identity*, and *audacity* help integrate various aspects of the Brazilian-African diaspora story. Against the shared background of these ideas, I reflect on the transformations of character of the Brazilian-Africans and purpose through changing predicaments, the multiple routes their ancestors took along their journeys traversing the Atlantic, different stages of migration and assimilation, and their determination and motivations along the way. The historical journeys of the Tabom are also viewed, in light of these themes, as an unending search for a lost homeland. Part of this is fantasy, as in the case of expatriates in Ghana. Responses to slavery and efforts to resist and combat exploitation and oppression largely determined the paths of return to Africa following emancipation in Brazil and the onset of British colonial rule in Ghana. Dissonance of memory shaped how some of the Tabom remembered their past especially with regard to land tenure as they protected Brazilian lands from intruders during bitter land disputes in colonial courts. In addition, dissonance of memory has directed the migratory behaviors of the Tabom historically and continues to shape their travels from Ghana to Brazil. As such, memory has powerfully affected and continues to influence the trajectory of Brazilian and Tabom history.

Several points delineate the book's major rationales: First, this book fills the void and provides a new dimension in our understanding of returnee communities, especially a new insight into the transatlantic reverse migration narratives. Second, another important purpose is to show the intersections of abolition and colonialism, including the ways the emancipated Africans contesting their freedom escaped from slavery in Brazil to colonial oppression in Ghana. I look at the apparently paradoxical nature of British policies as noted by Robin Law, simultaneously spearheading abolitionist movements in Brazil while setting up colonial enclaves and stringent ordinances within Africa.[14] Over time, such conditions shaped the experiences, identities, and consciousness of the ex-slaves and the Tabom. The third rationale, and one of this work's principle themes, is to document the role of freed slaves as agents of change and the quality of their social, religious, and technological contributions as they carried their skills and cultures back and forth across the Atlantic into Brazil and Ghana. In addition to their lasting contribution to Brazil's development via labor and other cultural exchanges, through reverse migration the ex-slaves significantly impacted the social history of Ghana from the precolonial period, importing aspects of Brazilian culture in such areas as borehole drilling (for extracting water), agriculture, and tailoring.

Reflecting on the contradictions of freedom—particularly the overlaps between their emancipation in Brazil and colonialism in Ghana—and that of return covered alongside a related crisis of identity among the Tabom, returnees' involvement in slavery is reexamined, along with how their role in the slave trade in Ghana (from the late 1800s) changed over the course of their history. Obvious contrasts in character are seen between contributions of the ex-slaves in Accra, their demonstrated defiance or audacity to rebel at one time, and their participation in the slave trade, concurrently, despite memory of the horrors of slave life in Brazil. The discussion (in light of these unifying themes) returns to tackle the failures of the members of the Brazilian-African diaspora in Accra to uphold the virtues of freedom they once defended, enslaving the local people instead.

Fourth, this book examines the significance and the fledgling relations between the leaders of the Brazilian-African diaspora in Ghana and the Brazilian government (the process of restoring Brazilian-African history in Ghana), situating their mutual exchanges within the broader transatlantic context with significance for discourses on global history, cultures, and commercial and heritage tourism in the twenty-first century. These mutual relations, for example, contributed much to the United Nations Educational, Scientific and Cultural Organization–funded restoration of the Brazil House,[15] which was formerly known as the "Warri House" and was opened for tourism on 17 November 2007, has satisfied part of the need (figure 2). The Warri House was built in 1835 by Mama Nassu, one of the first settlers in Jamestown or Otublohum, and is believed to be the first house built by the ex-slaves. It is not surprising that the Tabom played a major role in making this historical site visible. Such undertakings among the

Introduction

Figure 2. Brazil House.

Tabom leaders are influenced not only by their need to express both aspects of their dual Brazilian-Ghanaian identities but also by economic interests via tourism.

Theoretical and Methodological Perspectives and Relations to Existing Literature

The study of cross-cultural exchanges across the Atlantic/diaspora from the period of the Middle Passage is an evolving one. Historically, theories about the African diaspora in *reverse* are one sided: they cover involuntary and voluntary migrations from a narrow scope. Early works treat the history of slaves and emancipated Africans peripherally, focusing the narrative on Europeans. Africanists and Atlanticists alike have criticized this approach.[16] A recent wave of scholarship, including João José Reis's *Divining Slavery and Freedom: The Story of Domingos Sodré, an African Priest in Nineteenth-Century Brazil*, has moved the spotlight through the use of biographies focusing on the voices of "ordinary" slaves and emancipated Africans.[17] Although some authors have partially addressed this imbalance, others cover reverse migration by concentrating on the creation of returnee communities and identities on the African continent—particularly West Africa. Of the latter, most of the literatures shift attention to the Aguda people's stories. We can *reverse* these theoretical gaps by tracing multiple transatlantic travels that includes the Tabom story in wider diaspora conversation.

Geographically imbalances remain. Unlike existing works, particularly those with a unidimensional focus, I contend that the African diaspora in reverse includes the reciprocal connections to multiple destinations in Africa and the Atlantic world. The terms "the Atlantic world" and "the New World" will be used interchangeably in reference to communities in North and South America, Europe, and other areas in the world with ties to the Middle Passage. The running narrative in *Brazilian-African Diaspora in Ghana* stretches back and forth and meshes together the past, the present, and the future. Unlike much of the existing scholarship that examines reverse diasporas from the Atlantic world but restricts the analysis to a given geographical range in a linear sphere, my study is nonlinear in orientation. This study explores plans for additional movements by the Tabom back to Brazil, in cyclical motion. Thus, my book looks at the diasporas in reverse from multiple fronts and defines this phenomenon as continuing movement and relocation. In short, my book charts a new path that traces movements from multiple points. Besides historical memory, the plan to visit Brazil is shaped by the promise former Brazilian president Luiz Inácio Lula da Silva made to the Tabom people during his visit to Ghana in 2005. It is also based on a yearning to connect with an unknown distant ancestral *home*.

The African diaspora in reverse has copious tributaries that connect people of African descent through various oceans and land. Akin to the *sankofa* bird that moves its neck as if rotating toward multiple points, the Tabom history, like other diasporic experiences, stretches beyond historical timelines, multiple ancestral roots, diverse travel routes, cultural boundaries, geopolitical space, and transnational frontiers.[18] Historian Paul T. Zeleza describes this constant movement as "multiple belongings."[19] The *Back to Africa* anthology explicitly demonstrates how returnees, especially the Aguda people from Brazil and Cuba, who relocated to Nigeria and Benin, negotiated their identities and created their own communities in response to the challenges that they were confronted with in their new locales. According to Milton Guran, "in order to insert themselves in local society—given their diverse ethnic origins—the ex-slaves valorized their 'stay' in Brazil, as their only common element. It was as if slavery were taken as the starting point for a new life. Thus, it is exactly the culture acquired in Brazil that commanded the process [of assimilation or disassociation]."[20] I view identity formation as a fluid process altering and altered by internal and external factors as part of the broader transatlantic experience. Some scholars have located this continual movement of people of African descent to myriad slave sites in Ghana and have theorized how these returnees refashion and negotiate their identity as diasporan blacks at these sites, particularly how local Ghanaians identify with slavery and the slave sites.[21] Others, however, view these voyages by people of African descent as one in pursuit of strangers "who left behind no traces."[22]

Historically, the African diaspora in reverse has created fledgling ties between Africans who live on the African continent and those of African descent through their common experiences with slavery; it brings together issues about their shared genetic genealogy, converging and diverging memories of their ancestral past, their common identities and traits, as well as the cultural bonds they form through constant movements to Africa and other areas of the Atlantic world. These multiple trajectories allow scholars to study the common geographical and ancestral bonds between these groups and how descendants of African slaves fashion and refashion their identities over time.[23] The African diaspora in reverse also explores debates about citizenship, gender dynamics, and the role of diasporan blacks in globalization—especially how returnee communities in Ghana create, replicate, and "consume tourism" in their locales. Tim Coles and Dallen J. Timothy address similar issues about heritage tourism.[24] Kristin Mann's study of *Slavery and the Birth of an African City: Lagos, 1760–1900* also sheds light on how slavery shaped commerce and identity in tandem.[25] The Tabom history with slavery has also influenced their consciousness about the commercial benefits of sites of memories in their communities.

During my research, I examined archival materials from Ghana, Nigeria, Brazil, England, and Italy, in addition to conducting over fifty interviews since 2005 with the Tabom and non-Tabom in Ghana and London, England, as well as Aguda or Afro-Cuban returnees in Lagos, Nigeria. In general, my book is grounded in archival research about Africa and Brazil on both the local and transatlantic levels. It draws from colonial and missionary records, letters, abolitionist papers, Brazilian consular records, and British diplomatic and parliamentary reports on abolition and slave vessels, statistical data on voyages, newspapers, published accounts, and colonial administrative papers at the National Archives, London. Other sources include supreme/district and high court documents and land tenure records at the Public Records and Archives Administration Department (PRAAD) in Accra, as well as police/immigration passport records located in the Arquivo Público da Bahia, Brazil. I draw from *The Trans-Atlantic Slave Trade: A Database on CD-ROM* and other sources to examine the flow of Africans from one port or plantation to the other. Although these databases have some limitations, for example the original ethnicity, identity, or language group or the exact locations of freed slaves who landed in Accra in the early 1800s, the use of groupings like the "Minas" provide a micro reference and geographical point for narrowing this search to trace their ancestry and for statistical purposes.[26] Through a broad interpretive framework, I marry artifacts, archival, and other relevant records with oral history and life experiences of both the ex-slaves and the Tabom people.

I draw on thematic and methodological elements that run through other returnee communities and scholarly fields. My study thus employs an interdisciplinary approach by integrating diverse literature in history, anthropology, diaspora, tourism and heritage studies, and scholarship that emphasizes the importance of material cultures in my analysis. These interdisciplinary approaches not only allow me to bring multiple interpretations to bear but facilitate the processes of knowledge building through the use of existing literature and theories while at the same time extending my study to other academic territories that are yet to be explored (in relation to reverse migrations), especially in globalization, tourism, and the "performance" of African cultures at sites of memories.[27] Although I have relied on diverse sources, there is no easy way of identifying the origins of the returnees. For instance, some of the photographs I have collected from various archives about freed slaves who left Brazil for West Africa do not always provide information about the actual destination of all the freed slaves on board.

In terms of the timeline of their voyages back to Africa, there is no document or data I have come across that points to a specific date; therefore I use the 1820s as the beginning of their arrival specifically because the earliest document I know of in the archives at PRAAD refers to this date. The other reason is that a number of Brazilians who gained manumission returned to the Bight of Benin and possibly to Ghana prior to the 1835 slave rebellions in Bahia, Brazil.[28] The revolts led to other movements to the coastlines of West Africa.[29] I draw from records about migrations before and after the 1835 revolts. With this approach, I am able to account from the early 1820s through the demise of slavery in Brazil in 1888. I must add that, we are able to talk about these selected dates because there were intense conflicts over Brazilian land in Accra. Cursory references to these dates from the land disputes in colonial courts housed at PRAAD have not done enough to clarify the arrival dates of the ex-slaves, but it is worth considering.

Most of the documents I have examined especially at the National Archives of London, Kew Garden show that Lagos, Nigeria, was the destination of many of the returning ex-slaves partly because large amounts of slaves were captured from this area for transport to Brazil. Tracing the origins of the ex-slaves who settled in Ghana can be difficult, but some of these documents show that Brazil remained in the minds of most of these returnees after they returned to Africa. The growing bond between the governments of Brazil and Ghana in some ways transcends the horrific narratives that gave rise to the Middle Passage and to slavery and oppression in the New

World.[30] The importance of the Brazil House and other icons of material culture to the Brazilian-African diaspora and to Ghanaians—as well as their relevance for global heritage tourism, the study of World Heritage Sites, tourism studies, and discourse on Atlantic/diaspora history—is also essential. Besides their growing interest and connections to the Brazil House, the Tabom people desire to visit Brazil is important. I also explore what looks like a "dark cloud" that has become an obstacle hindering their plans to visit Brazil with a selected group from their communities.

There are other methodological challenges, especially inadequate secondary sources, in covering the history of the Brazilian-African diaspora in Ghana. Therefore, I use the body of work about the history of diasporan communities elsewhere to support my analysis. Through this approach, I employ an Atlantic historical framework, connecting historiographical works about returnees from Brazil, Cuba, North America, the Caribbean, and other geographical regions. In addition, I am aware of the challenges in depending on ethnographic approach to this kind of study. The various family groups I have interacted with do not have any documents like passports, birth certificates, and other tangible primary data about their great-grandparents or grandparents who came from Brazil. Also, with regard to other subjects or questions about why their ancestors settled in the Ghana, the older members of the community point out that the first generation resettled in Ghana because it was a safe haven compared with other coastal settlements in West Africa. According to some of the youth I have interviewed, the first generation chose Ghana because they knew how to find their homeland.[31] There are other entangled interpretations to this story. The narratives of George Aruna Nelson, who was ninety-one years old at the time of my interview, basically stated that the first generation settled in Ghana because there were opportunities for commercial activities after their status changed to freed slaves. Tabom *Mãŋtsɛ* Nii Azumah Nelson V looked at it from another angle and suggested that the first generation was mostly made up of Muslims who were captured from areas in Nigeria at the height of Islamization in northern Nigeria and therefore did not want to return to the same place.[32] The archival documents I have examined so far do not clearly answer these questions. Nonetheless, further interviews have clarified these entangled responses.

It is difficult to explore the gender roles of the community in the early generations. The history of Tabom women has been sidelined in the currently available narratives. The existing historiography and the interviews I have conducted over the years largely focus on males with little or no substantial information of the position of women in the migration and settlement processes. Specifically, most of the information talks about how the men organized their community to preserve the skills they brought from Brazil, how they distributed land that was offered by Gã mãŋtsɛmɛi, and how they participated in farming activities such as planting of mangoes that later contributed to the socioeconomic trading of the area.[33] In a few instances, women are mentioned when there is a discussion about the role of the *mãnyɛ* (queen mother) or when referring to the wife of a Tabom *mãŋtsɛ*. Gender components are more problematic when it comes to matters relating to inheritance. In terms of appearance, much is said about the ways the men among the first generation preserved their Brazilian cultural values by dressing in European suits and hats, but the appearance of women in this group is also placed on the fringe.

The situation, however, is not exactly the same in other places of returnee settlements in West Africa. Historian Lisa A. Lindsay and others have highlighted the activities of Aguda women in Nigeria.[34] However, the Tabom women are becoming less visible representations of the history of this current generation. At Swalaba, where the Scissors House was built in 1854 by ex-slaves with skills in tailoring, the Tabom women served as property managers. They collected rent and managed housing properties in the community. Unfortunately, they lost this economic control and their visibility after the building burned down during a fire outbreak.[35] The nomination of Georgina Theodora Wood as the chief justice of Ghana has somewhat elevated the image of women in the Tabom community. She was raised at Warri House now the Brazil House.[36]

As I bring attention to the overlaps with other reverse diaspora narratives, my book leans on broader discourses in African, Atlantic diaspora, and "Black Atlantic" history.[37] Existing scholarship on Brazilian-African returnees to Ghana is very thin, consisting of a journal article, two book chapters, my doctoral dissertation, a masters' thesis, and Marco A. Schaumloeffel's book, *Tabom: The Afro-Brazilian Community in Ghana* (2008).[38] Schaumloeffel was a Portuguese language instructor and attaché at the Brazilian embassy in Accra. His book was part of a joint project financed by the Ministry of Foreign Relations in Brazil and the Brazilian embassy to provide an overview of Afro-Brazilian history in Ghana. One of the goals was to cement Brazil's ties with the Tabom people. Mae-ling Jovenes Lokko's *Brazil House*, although very brief, is another significant addition.[39] All the existing studies are narrow in scope. Although they provide a good synthesis, they fail to engage academic debates and discourse in the field. *Brazilian-African Diaspora in Ghana*, on the other hand, follows aspects of this tradition but positions the story of the ex-slaves from Brazil and the Tabom alongside other reverse migration narratives of its ilk. Additionally, the story of Brazilian-African diaspora in Ghana overlaps with the "Back-to-Africa" movement funded by the American Colonization Society during the period of Reconstruction in America in the nineteenth century.

Overall, there is no major book that competes with *Brazilian-African Diaspora in Ghana* outside that of Marco A. Schaumloeffel's book, which gives a general overview of the Tabom story with an expressly political, or diplomatic, rather than academic impetus.[40] My book engages in a wider array of discourses and is broader in scope than Schaumloeffel's. There are also major methodological differences between the two books—for one thing my reference materials, the resources and research used in the construction of my book, are more extensive.[41] Although other literature contributes to the Atlantic/diaspora dialogue, they lack the necessary themes and adequate complexity required for any thorough treatment of this subject.

Brazilian-African Diaspora in Ghana contributes uniquely to the field in the following areas: It emphasizes multiple modes of migration—Africa to Brazil, Brazil to Ghana, and Ghana to Brazil—rejecting the one-dimensional perspective of transatlantic voyages between the Atlantic World and West Africa that is widely accepted by most authors, as in the case of the Aguda, Americo-Liberians, Sarro, and African American returnees. It focuses on both the slave narratives and diverse identities of emancipated Brazilian-Africans and their offspring. In addition, it examines memory of and migrations from Brazil as well as the origins of their settlements in Ghana. These themes have overwhelmingly been neglected in existing scholarship, which is heavily centered on the voyages from Brazil and Cuba to Nigeria, Benin, Togo, and Angola, as well as journeys from the United States, and the West Indies/Caribbean to Liberia and Sierra Leone. In addition, *Brazilian-African Diaspora in Ghana* uniquely addresses the connections between geographically disparate returnee communities in West Africa, an important notion that essentially all other concerned works have thus far failed to develop or appreciate. For instance, the stories of the Tabom and the Aguda are inextricably intertwined, and without this perspective one cannot fully understand the Tabom experience in Ghana. Placing the ex-slaves' and the Tabom's continuous travels between Lagos and Accra within the larger story of reverse migrations is relevant. In light of the conceptual segregation of narratives and the absence of works recognizing the importance of the ties between different communities of slave descent, this work reexamines existing literature, oral history and traditions, and the archival materials on both the Tabom and the Aguda in search of mutually informative themes.

The Tabom-Aguda regional historical ties to West Africa are not the only exchanges that shaped the Brazilian-African diaspora narratives in Ghana. Afro-Caribbean/West Indian and African American experiences influenced the Tabom story locally. For example, the strategic positioning of African American business owners and investors, who have made great progress in the tourism industry in Ghana by creating enabling environments, for instance comfortable spaces that allow them to fuse their grief over lost heritage with monetary gains, has impacted the Brazilian-African story.[42] This approach did not escape the Tabom leadership. I distinctively situate Brazilian-African diaspora history, especially the renovation of the Brazil

House, within the ongoing Brazil-Ghana international relations story and discourse about heritage/global tourism. The fledgling ties in areas of history, culture, politics, economy, sports, and heritage tourism hold together Brazil-Ghana Atlantic connections and dual identities. Brazil House sustains the memory as well as the legacy of the Brazilian-Africans and the Tabom.[43]

A reflection on the countless number of ships—like the one on the cover of the book—that crossed the Atlantic once or perhaps several times with slaves or ex-slaves raises several questions: Who were these emancipated Africans? What in the history of Brazil and Ghana permitted these historical connections between the two countries over a century after the demise of slavery in both locations? In terms of identity, how does the African diaspora contribute to the ways in which the people of African ancestry refashion their identity and their history? What are the gender dynamics in the creation of returnee communities on the African continent? How do scholars who study reverse migrations situate the role of tourism in the appropriation or commodification of African and diasporic identities? How do both local Africans and returnees consume and allocate features of tourism to show their links to transatlantic slavery and for economic benefits? What is the intersection between grief and financial gains in returnee communities? Put simply, who is entitled to resources generated via tourism around sites of memory or material culture and who is not: the returnees or the local people? These questions are important for framing the winding narratives associated with these journeys based on hope and memory, deeply housed in the psyche of the Tabom people.

STRUCTURE OF THE BOOK AND OVERVIEW OF THE ARGUMENT

The book consists of ten overlapping chapters arranged chronologically and thematically and is organized into three parts. Part 1, "From Brazil to Ghana: Unmatched Fortitude and Locating Home," is influenced by the courage and the perseverance the ex-slaves demonstrated when they boarded ships back to Africa. It begins by showing the origins of the first diaspora returnee community in Ghana and tracing the first leg of migrations from Brazil either directly to Ghana or to Nigeria and later to Ghana. It refers to three major driving forces in Brazil including manumission, the 1835 slave revolts in Bahia, and the demise of slavery in Brazil in 1888 that contributed to their freedom and reverse migrations. Chapter 1, "Reverse Diaspora: Dissonance of Memory, Voyages of Hope, and Degrees of Return," examines the role of memory in the reverse migration stories. I chronicle the history of Africans in Brazil, how they

Introduction

preserved African cultures, how returnees remembered Africa, and how all these historical factors contributed to their yearnings for a homeland. Chapter 1 introduces two more relevant points: the role of British abolitionists in securing the safety of emancipated slaves during their voyages, and conditions in Lagos that forced some of the returnees to seek a homeland and sanctuary elsewhere, like Ghana. The impact of slavery, abolition, and colonialism from the nineteenth through the twentieth centuries provides new avenues for reexamining the origins of the Brazilian-African returnee history in West Africa, especially using comparative study to explore continuity and change in the formation of these returnee communities and their identities in different locations. I assert that the transformations Africans went through in the New World or the dilution of African-Lusophone names did not only provide multiple identities or complicate their ethnicity and origins, but it has made it increasingly difficult to provide statistics and estimates of the population of individuals and various family groups that joined the voyages to Accra.[44] Chapter 1 also explains challenges in writing Tabom history using limited available sources.

Chapter 2, "Historicizing the Returnee Presence in Gã *Mãŋ*: Challenges and Silences," begins with the origins of the Brazilian-African diaspora in Accra and the various waves of migrations from the 1820s. I trace their arrival and the reasons for settling in Accra, particularly how the ex-slaves left Lagos, Nigeria, for Ghana and who these people were. A case in point is the archival records about the Aguda travels from Lagos to Accra and why the ex-slaves decided to settle in Accra amid the choices of other settlement locations in West Africa. Further, I explain why Gã mãŋtsɛmɛi offered hospitality and land to the newcomers and how the ex-slaves negotiated complex cultures and traditions in coastal Accra during settlement. Statistics about the actual number of returnees to Ghana are difficult to find. In part, the chapter posits that the waves of migrations from Brazil to different settlement locations in West Africa intertwine with each other: the Tabom story is buried deeply in the Aguda experience. Although the Aguda-Tabom interactions do not give us enough clues about their population in Ghana, the fluid and mutual exchange provides a base for exploring and tracing the travel patterns and the Tabom ancestral heritage.

Chapter 3, "The Social History of Gã *Mãŋ*: Colonialism and Their Impact on the Brazilian-African Diaspora," contextualizes the ex-slaves' paths of migration from Brazil to Ghana and from Nigeria to Ghana within the broader history of Ghana, particularly the social history of Gã *mãŋ*, Accra. I review the history of precolonial Accra in the 1800s and ultimately discuss how narratives about both the freed slaves and the Tabom fit within larger social, political, and cultural developments. This chapter also explores contradictory British policies that supported abolition in Brazil while maintaining an oppressive colonial presence in Accra, particularly the intersection of these policies with memories of enslavement among emancipated Africans as they negotiated colonialism's complex cultural and political institutions in the Gold Coast colony. In the context of the challenges the returnees encountered, I assert that expectations around abolition among emancipated Africans were never realized. After escaping slavery in Brazil, freed slaves journeyed with hope only to find new forms of oppression and servitude under British colonial rule in Accra. The chapter argues that the advent of colonialism was a watershed moment in Brazilian-African diaspora history in Ghana because the conditions it created hastened rebellions—freed slaves and local chiefs in Accra united in confronting their European colonizers. Here, I maintain that one cannot talk about Tabom history without explaining how Gã social history influenced Tabom identity before and during British colonial rule. They complement each other.

Chapter 4, "The Evolution of Land in Gã *Mãŋ* and Brazilian-African Diaspora: Paradox of Freedom and the Birth of Conflicts," examines how land in Gã *mãŋ* and the Brazilian-African diaspora evolved over time. I argue that the freed slaves from Brazil had a different ideology about family and communal relations than their descendants. I maintain that landownership (from gifts of land from Gã *Mãŋtsɛ* Komeh I) was indeed a blessing to most of the early settlers who perhaps owned land for the first time in their lifetime. The early generations of Tabom were aware of land to their ancestors especially the fact that most of them were exploited in various plantation systems in Brazil.[45] But over time, land tenure became a curse to the subsequent generations as disagreement over inheritance gradually created tension among them. This chapter begins and concludes with the nomadic life of Ferku, a freed slave from Brazil who first settled in Lagos and later moved to Accra to begin a marriage union with Yawah, another Brazilian who was born in Accra. It underscores Ferku's continues travels across the Atlantic as a metaphor for the Brazilian-African diaspora story in Ghana. Ferku's complex love story came to an end around the 1930s when he decided to relocate to Lagos in his old age but without Yawah. The fracture in their marriage, particularly the piece of land Ferku left Yawah that was entangled in land dispute, speaks to the complex ways in which the liberated Africans reconstructed their identity, negotiated the properties they owned, and managed the paradox of freedom in British colonial Accra from one generation to the next.

Chapter 5, "Escaping Slavery into Colonialism and Squabbles: How Colonial Projects and Internal Disputes Threatened Brazilian Land and Freedom," builds on the previous chapter, studying parts of the precolonial and early colonial history of Ghana from the 1880s through the 1950s. It examines how the freed slaves escaped slavery in Brazil but were confronted with colonialism later. I maintain that remembering their ancestors' enslavement in Brazil, and the rebellion by Chief Nelson against the Compulsory Labour Ordinance of 1897, made them hypersensitive toward any signs of exploitation, oppression, or manipulation by those who wanted to take the "Brazilian land" from them as land values soared—especially, as Accra transformed from a rural area to a commercial metropolis in the early 1900s. Chapter 5 delves into selected land disputes that weave through almost every layer of the Brazilian-African diaspora story in Accra, tying into conflicts between Tabom individuals, within Tabom families, between Tabom people and British colonial officials especially after the Public Land Ordinance of 1876, as well as those between the Tabom and Gã mãŋtsɛmɛi (Gã leaders) and migrants in Accra. In addition, I examine contemporary conflicts regarding ownership of and control over land/properties including the recent supreme court case *Rashid Brimah & 3 Ors. v. Hadji Peregrino Brimah*, the dispute between the Peregrinos and the Brimahs that began in 1998.[46]

Both chapter 4 and chapter 5 chronicle the genesis of land disputes within the Tabom community in tandem, especially the ways in which this tension created division and silences in their communities. The former draws from the social history of Accra, particularly stringent colonial land ordinances, whereas the latter uses supreme/district and high court documents and land tenure records at PRAAD to examine conflicts between various Tabom individuals and family groups, court disputes between the Tabom and Gã mãŋtsɛmɛi over Gã stool land, and lawsuits the Tabom brought against British colonial officials. Other disputes were between the Tabom and migrants in Accra over Brazilian land.

Part 2, "Contradictions of Return: Transporting Atlantic Traditions, Skills, and Cultures and Refashioning Identity," explores the degree to which free Brazilians participated in slavery both along the coast and within inland settler communities in the Gold Coast and examines contributions the early settlers and their offspring made to the social history of Accra from precolonial times. Chapter 6, "(Re-)Creating Brazilian Slavery in an Enabling Environment: The 'Ghost' of Slavery," raise questions about the paradoxes of return by juxtaposing returnees' contributions against their involvement in slavery in Ghana from the late 1800s and provide examples of other ex-slaves' involvement in slavery in other settlement locations in Benin and others.[47] The chapter also documents how enabling conditions in slave coasts in West Africa, particularly the degree to which slavery was entrenched in precolonial Accra, influenced returnees' interest in similar activities in their new environs. To put the returnees' involvement in slavery in a historical context, I include a synopsis of the long history of slavery in Accra that benefited Gã, Akwamu, Ashante and Fante leaders, missionaries, colonial officials, European merchants, and others in both inland and coastal territories of the Gold Coast.[48] I argue that the ex-slaves and the Tabom did not invent slavery along the coastal areas of Otublohum, Accra, or any other location; rather, they took advantage of opportunities already available to achieve power and economic advancement. The ex-slaves and some of the Tabom used slaves for domestic use. This had negative impact on the ways in which the Tabom associate or disassociate with this history. The role the ex-slaves played in enslaving Ghanaians at the latter stage of abolition, especially how these activities have tainted their image and story of freedom and how it has created silences among their descendants is relevant. I contend that this negative impact has made it increasingly difficult for some of the family groups to publicly showcase their Brazilian ancestry or participate in activities within their communities.

Chapter 7, "Contributions by the Brazilian-Africans and the Tabom: Impact on Ghana's History," explores various contributions by the Brazilians and their descendants from the precolonial period. The ways in which the ex-slaves imported various skills and knowledge in the areas of irrigation technology, agricultural production, and others was remarkable. Some of their offspring served in the British colonial regiment during World War II. Some prominent members of the Tabom served as ambassadors, professors, and church leaders. Others include Georgina Wood, the first female chief justice on the Ghanaian supreme court. Chapter 8, "Brazilians Together, Brazilians Apart: The Family Trees and the Process of Becoming Gã," explores how the Brazilians are together and how they are apart. It also restates the difficulties in tracing their ancestral origins and their population and tracks the evolution of the Brazilian-African diaspora in Accra and various family groups. I explore their history in regard to generational identity and cultural change. Not all family groups have openly provided information about their ties to Brazil, so the chapter selects three major family groups, the Lutterodts, the Peregrinos, and the Nelsons and charts their history with respect to the overriding themes of the book. In general, it covers parts of the precolonial and colonial eras of Brazilian-Tabom identity formation and transformation from the 1870s to 1950s. Themes such as class, religion, the relevant differences between the early settlers (freed slaves) and their descendants, as well as their complex assimilation into Gã and other cultures in Accra while simultaneously maintaining aspects of Brazilian identity are included in this chapter. There is evidence of receding memory because how these groups remember Brazil varies in depth and in breadth.

In contrast, part 3, "Diaspora in Full Circle: Home Is Ghana, Brazil Is Our Mother Country," emphasizes the Tabom peoples' yearning for Brazil and how that is informed by historical memory, and examines how the ex-slaves and the Tabom remembered, forgot, ignored, performed, and negotiated their ties both to Ghana and Brazil at different times and in different circumstances. This part begins with Chapter 9, "Fading Diaspora and Receding Memory: How the Brazilian Government and the Tabom Are Preserving the Brazil House and Crisscrossing the Atlantic in Full Circle," which builds on the previous chapters by weaving the past with the present and the future. This

Introduction

chapter examines the various ways the Tabom collaborated with the Brazilian government to restore their history to prevent the Brazilian-African diaspora from fading from historical memory. The Brazilian embassy in Accra acts as a bridge between the past and the present and has interacted with the Tabom community since the 1960s. This mutual relation goes beyond their shared cultures, history of enslavement, and exploitation during the Middle Passage. For instance, economic partnership between Brazil and Ghana cumulated in the Ghana–Brazil Chamber of Commerce and Industry that was officially opened on 13 April 2005 in Accra during Lula's visit to expand salt, sugar, paper, cocoa, shea-nut butter, and bauxite production and exports, and the exploration of further economic exchanges between the two countries in the twenty-first century. Additionally, the new Ghanaian government has awarded various road contracts to Brazilian firms as part of economic partnerships between the two countries.

This chapter also highlights the role of the Brazil House in global tourism, new challenges confronting various family groups over who should manage the Brazil House, and why the Brazilian Embassy in Accra has been entangled in this complex debate about inheritance, material culture, and the Tabom people's right to manage this ancestral landmark. It also provides a window for understanding the current state of the Brazilian-African diaspora: ongoing mutual relations between the Tabom people, the Brazilian government, and the Brazilian embassy in Accra, and the impact of the promise former Brazilian president Luiz Inácio Lula da Silva made to the Tabom people during his first visit to the community in 2005. Questions about why this promise has not been realized yet, why some of the members of the community could not achieve their dreams of visiting Brazil before their death, examples of those who have been able to visit Brazil, as well as the difficulty in tracing the stories of those who may have visited Brazil are important. Further, I discuss how their inability to visit Brazil during the 2014 World Cup soccer tournament added to their frustration.

In tying together various historical developments that have energized the Tabom base and sustained memory of a *home* in Brazil, part 3 illuminates promises former Brazilian president Lula made to the Tabom to enable Tabom leaders and a selected group to visit Brazil. This dream has not been fulfilled yet. However, individual efforts have kept the dream alive. Most importantly, the 2014 summer World Cup soccer tournament in Brazil, in which both Ghana and Brazil participated, raised new interests within the Brazilian-African diaspora as the Tabom and Ghanaian soccer fans in general prepared to travel to Brazil or watch this important historical tournament on their television sets in Ghana. Regardless of which team the Tabom embraced or supported, in part, we see evidence of some form of identity crisis in the Brazilian-African diaspora and the challenges that lie ahead in preserving, reconstructing, and disseminating their Brazilian and or Ghanaian heritage.

Chapter 10, "Telescoping Lula's Unfulfilled Promise and the Implications of the Tabom's Visit to Brazil: A Hopeless Situation?," reemphasizes and reevaluates the promise Lula made to the Tabom people, explaining attempts to arrange for the Tabom to visit during his tenure and why this has not been accomplished yet. I examine the impact on the Tabom people's plans to travel to the home of their ancestors. There are difficulties in identifying, verifying, and documenting claims about the Tabom people who have already visited Brazil on their own. I end with a synthesis of the biography of the late Elder George Nii Aruna Nelson, who was the oldest member of the Tabom community before his death, to trace how both the older members and younger ones remember Brazil and the frustrations associated with their dream to visit their distant ancestral homeland. A number of Tabom including Elder Nelson, who died on 5 April 2009 at the age of ninety-three daydreamed about Brazil, but he could not set his foot on the land on which his forebears were enslaved. Although there is evidence of receding memory of Brazil among the Tabom, some of Elder Nelson's offspring have shown steadfast interest in visiting Brazil as well.

PART 1

From Brazil to Ghana: Unmatched Fortitude and Locating Home

Chapter 1

Reverse Diaspora: Dissonance of Memory, Voyages of Hope, and Degrees of Return

> In every conceivable manner, the family is a link to our past, a bridge to our future.
> —Alex Haley

Enslaved Africans left Africa, but they never forgot their ancestral homeland.[1] It seems reasonable at this point to state that over time a portion of the enslaved Africans in the New World became disconnected from their heritage.[2] Due to their unmatched fortitude, most ex-slaves were determined to reconnect with their African roots.[3] When they joined various voyages back to the land of their ancestors they did not erase every memory or aspect of their Brazilian life after their resettlement.[4] Put differently, they returned to Africa "'Brazilianized,' 'Bahianized,' [and] 'Portugalized.'"[5] The same can be said of the evolving identity formation among the Tabom, the descendants of freed Brazilian-Africans in Ghana, who continue to think about Brazil, the land where their grandparents and great-grandparents were enslaved. Few Tabom people have visited Brazil. There are hundreds who aspire to do so but have not fulfilled this dream. The traditional Adinkra symbols *nkyinkyim* and *sankofa*, are two significant cultural motifs that help provide a context for this chapter, especially in terms of why enslaved Africans remembered their African heritage. The *nkyinkyim*, is an Akan Ghanaian Adinkra figure that literally means "twisting" or "dynamism"—the notion of constant movement from one location to the other. The *nkyinkyim* symbol carries an array of meanings and has cultural, political, and social value. In many Ghanaian cultures,

3

the symbol is sometimes used on top of a staff, a traditional vertical bar that is carried by a linguist, the chief's assistant. It is also used in clothing, jewelry, furniture, basketry, pottery designs, and building decorations. The *nkyinkyim* has a fluid character, but it lacks a common meeting point as it twists and turns. Culturally, it emphasizes that life is an endless passage. The *sankofa* symbol is another Akan Adinkra figure that literally means "going back for something you left behind"—it expresses the idea of returning to the past, to what is behind, as suggested by the neck of the *sankofa* bird stretching toward its tail feathers. *Sankofa* is used in ways similar to *nkyinkyim* in terms of its material and social significance. The *sankofa* bird is noted for not being content with a static position. Rather, it moves constantly in search of new and old territories. These cultural expressions help highlight the objectives of this book.

The common thread that runs through this rich traditional Ghanaian symbolism with respect to this study is the notion of an unending journey or continuous movement in a form of a "Z-path"—a triangulated route from several geographical points across the Atlantic. Some scholars characterize this trend as "circulatoriness and proliferation of departures."[6] This speaks to the rapid migration of returnees and the interwoven, but distinct, forms of mobility across cultural spaces, sites of slavery and historical memory, geographical boundaries, transnational connections, and homelands in Africa and the Afro-Atlantic world.[7] These continuous and overlapping trajectories signal a sense of being "here" and "there" as well as nostalgia for a known or imagined *home* and identity somewhere, either simultaneously or separately.[8] It also echoes an aspect of dual heritage, identity crisis, or double consciousness.

There are other Ghanaian cultural articulations from which we can draw. For instance, *worle heni worje*, a Gã expression that literally means "we know where we come from," is often used by the Tabom to express similar things to the Akan symbols.[9] Further, *worle heni worje* epitomizes the idea of belonging somewhere one knows or, in some cases, a place of imagination—sometimes based on stories passed from generation to generation. Taken together, *nkyinkyim*, *sankofa*, and *worle heni worje* are all entrenched in the notion of "return" and "belonging" to a place. This yearning for African and Atlantic roots has been described as going through an "experience of exile and cultural alienation [from the homeland] . . . real or mythic, that is rarely forgotten and with which one seeks to establish a new relation . . . This is achieved through complex blending of dream (utopia) and determination . . . An attempt to negate separation, restore ties and retrieve lost identity . . . A form of romance and longing, of moral obligation and loyalty . . . The notion of return serves as a unifying theme that raises a fundamental question about the relation to Africa [and the Atlantic world], a fragile relation that is constantly explored and rethought."[10]

As numerous court documents over land disputes show, the story of the Brazilian-Africans began in Gã *māŋ*, Accra, the capital city of Ghana where several returnees and their offspring created their new homes and preserved and reconstructed their identities over time. One of these documents, *Madam Sarah Clegg v. Emmanuel Drissu Cobblah*, refers to the liberated Brazilian-Africans as the "Brazilian community of Accra."[11] Memories of this place that were passed on from one generation to the next resonate throughout their story. This fluid exchange shows continuity and change between the two intertwining histories of the freed slaves from Brazil and their descendants, most of whom were born in Ghana.

The significance of the multiple paths across the Atlantic geography cannot be overstated. Indeed, in tracing these important trajectories, I am not suggesting that the Tabom people who have already visited Brazil or those who have plans to do so have given up their Ghanaian citizenship. Instead, they continue to find creative ways of highlighting both their Ghanaian identity and their "Brazilianness." The social and cultural history of precolonial Accra is important to the facilitation of settlements, especially the hospitality by the Gã people when the returnees were offered a gift of land by the Gã mãŋtsɛmɛi.[12] For the Brazilian-Africans, another avenue that provided uplift besides the gifts of land was the opportunity to hold prestigious titles such as mãŋtsɛmɛi (kings or chiefs). These prominent positions allowed them to serve in some cultural capacity as chiefs. The role of Brazilian chiefs in their communities was purposely created by Gã *Mãŋtsɛ* Tackie Komeh I, who reigned from 1826 to 1856. *Mãŋtsɛ* Tackie Komeh I welcomed the ex-slaves because he needed them to meet historical, cultural, economic, and social needs in Accra.

The common travel paths of the Aguda and the Tabom, particularly in the nineteenth century, allow us to understand the difficulty in reconstructing their narratives, especially the imbalance and limitations in the archives. In addition, internal factors in Brazil including slavery and abolition as well as external motivations, such as memories of Africa shaped returnees' interest in relocating to various locales in West Africa in an attempt to reclaim their heritage. A similar enthusiasm for reverse migration existed among other freed slaves from Cuba and North America, especially during the Back-to-Africa movement that was coordinated by the American Colonization Society (ACS)[13] and other philanthropic organizations in America and Europe.[14] The Brazilian-Africans left during chaotic periods, especially after some gained manumission, after a series of revolts, and at the peak of the abolitionist movement. Most returnees who traveled directly from Brazil or settled temporarily in Lagos (Onim) arrived in precolonial Accra in the early 1820s when tensions between the Gã people and the British were at a boiling point.[15] These interrelated factors were largely influenced by contradictions entrenched in Britain's larger vision for the freed Africans, and for Africans in general.[16] The transition from slavery to emancipation and, later, the enforcement of British imperialist projects created a stormy process that upset the returnees' dreams of freedom. In addition, the returnees' rejection of Brazil after their agonizing experience with slavery, degrees of memory retention especially as they grappled with varying features of identity formation, and yearning for new citizenship in Africa complicated their story. In Latin America as in other places of dispersal in the Atlantic world, these multifaceted historical developments drove the search for a *home* elsewhere. Radical abolition campaigns by the British especially in the early nineteenth century propelled and contributed to these stories of liberation in the Afro-Atlantic world, but these reforms had their limits.[17]

The epigraphic comment by Alex Haley reminds us, on the one hand, of the pivotal role of memory and family linkages in understanding the transatlantic experience. In his interrogation of the processes for assembling ancestral ties, historian Paul E. Lovejoy, on the other hand, states that "how are histories to deal with gaps in documentation and historical memory?" He raises questions about why there is such a wide or stark difference in the archives. Lovejoy asserts, "why is it that in some places there is a wealth of historical documentation, while in other places it is difficult to reconstruct the basic chronology of the past? . . . How did such constructions of knowledge and society affect those who were taken to the Americas as slaves?"[18] If there is a story to be told there should be data to support it, but that is not always the case. Although we have a general sense of the number of African slaves that were dispersed to various plantations in Brazil from the mid-eighteenth century, as illustrated by David Eltis,[19] it is difficult to trace how many left the shores of Ghana and to quantify their reverse migrations to Ghana.

There are several unanswered questions including how many slaves were taken from Ghana, the number of emancipated slaves who returned to Ghana, and whether these returnees or their ancestors were actually from this location. The basic chronology included here attempts to historicize the origins of freed slaves who made Ghana their new home in the early nineteenth century—a situation H. W. Von Hesse refers to as "Tabon conundrum."[20] The limited literature about liberated Africans and their descendants in Ghana is not solely the result of a lack of archival sources or of shortcomings in the various archival holdings, as Lovejoy posits.[21] Rather, historians have failed to reconstruct the story of transatlantic communities in Ghana based on the documents available. Though I do not have all the answers as I venture into this historical territory, I draw from a variety of sources including correspondence in private collections within the Tabom community such as a letter the Peregrino-Brimah family shared about one of their ancestors, Francis Zaccheus Santiago Peregrino, who left Accra sometime in the late 1890s to travel to England. He continued to the United States and later to South Africa where he become a journalist (figures 3 and 4).[22]

Figure 3. Francis Zaccheus Santiago Peregrino.

In explaining the cross-cultural interactions and exchanges between the Aguda (returnees in Nigeria, Benin, and Togo) and the Brazilian-Tabom who crisscrossed Lagos and Accra, I assert that not all returnees who settled in a particular town, village, or region in West Africa were originally from that location. Even so, family networks and trading activities between the Aguda and the Brazilian-Tabom from the early nineteenth century through the twenty-first century reveal lasting historical and cultural bonds between these two groups. My findings reveal that the returnees were of diverse backgrounds. Over time, assimilation into local cultures somewhat overshadowed or blurred their transatlantic heritage.

Reverse migrations from either Brazil, Cuba, or North America to West Africa overlapped in many interesting ways. There is ongoing debate about why, when, and how returnees commuted back and forth or moved from the Bight of Benin, an important region for commerce and slavery in Africa.[23] Although there are important differences in routes of return, these transatlantic journeys share much in common. In their reverse migrations from the North American and West Indies side of the Atlantic, most of the freed slaves located to either Liberia or Sierra Leone, as ACS documents show.[24] A similar reverse migration path is recorded by Solimar Otero and others, who trace the Yoruba-Cuban return and the Yoruba-Brazilian Aguda stories. In *Afro-Cuban Diasporas in the Atlantic World*, Otero notes that some of the enslaved Africans in Cuba maintained mutual contacts with their relatives in Lagos. In fact, their memory of a motherland in Africa was similar to how their distant relatives in Lagos felt about Cuba.

Manu Herbstein
Consulting Engineer
P.O. Box C697, Accra, Ghana • Tel (233 21) 773978 • Fax (233 21) 774283

9 June, 1993

Chief Amida Peregrino-Brimah,
P. O. Box 3182,
Accra.

Dear Chief Peregrino-Brimah,

I am trying to find some information about Francis Zaccheus Santiago Peregrino (1851-1919) whose photograph appears on the enclosed photocopy, where he is described as "editor of the South African Spectator, published in Cape Town from 1900". I surmise, from your surname, that you must in some way be related to him; and I wonder whether any recollection of him has come down in your family history. I have your name and address from the Accra telephone directory and I shall get in touch with you by telephone shortly. I thought it best to send you the photograph in advance, rather than just phone you out of the blue, as it were.

I have a description of Peregrino as "a talented, if a little eccentric, West African journalist from the Gold Coast, who had lived in both England and America before making his way to South Africa in 1900."

Elsewhere he is described as follows:

"Early Coloured educationalist and journalist. Born in Accra, in what is now Ghana, he was of Ashanti origin and lived for a while in England, where he married. During the 1890s he came to Cape Town, set up the 'Progressive Institute' with himself as principal, and in 1899 published a Short History of the Native Tribes of South Africa. In 1906 he started the first newspaper for the Coloured people, which he continued till his death."

I know also that Peregrino was a friend of Sol T. Plaatje, the distinguished South African journalist, novelist and first secretary of the African National Congress; and that in 1903 Plaatje stayed with Peregrino for a month at his home in the Cape Town suburbs.

He is not mentioned in Prof. K. A. B. Jones-Quartey's books on the history of the press in Ghana and it may well be that he left this country as a relatively young man, before starting his career in journalism. Since he was evidently a pioneer in the fields of both education and journalism, a full generation before Dr. Aggrey, I am sure that his "rediscovery" would be of interest to many Ghanaians. My own interest arises from the fact that I am a South African who has lived in Ghana for many years and that. Cape Town, where Peregrino lived and worked for the last 20 years of his life, is my home town.

Yours sincerely,

Manu Herbstein

M.I. Herbstein, BSc (Eng), DIC, FIStructE, MICE, MGhIE
Chartered Civil and Structural Engineer

Figure 4. Letter inquiring about Francis Zaccheus Santiago Peregrino.

According to Otero, "Yoruba culture so deeply influenced Cuban national identity, this kind of performance behaved as a mirror of sorts, in which the Cubans and the Yoruba in nineteenth-century Lagos found a piece of themselves reflected due to this shared mythological and religious cultural context."[25] There were marriage unions between the Afro-Cuban freed slaves and Yoruba people and others between Sarro and Yoruba people in Lagos from the nineteenth century.[26] However, the histories of the Aguda (from Brazil) and the Tabom are largely explained in narrow terms. At times in these narratives, people who are involved in transatlantic crossings are presented as not having any viable ties, or they are sometimes portrayed as belonging to distinct historical groups even though in fact they share deep-rooted points of intersection. In general, the Brazilian-Tabom history is buried within a broader historiography of returnee communities on the Bight of Benin involving movements by Afro-Brazilians and Afro-Cubans.

The study of cross-cultural interactions and exchange across the Atlantic diasporan world from the period of the Middle Passage continues to evolve.[27] Earlier works placed the narratives of slaves and emancipated Africans on the periphery while the story of Europeans claimed the central position. This approach has been criticized by Africanists and Atlanticists alike.[28] While more recent literature has partially addressed this imbalance, other contributions seek to cover reverse migrations by concentrating mainly on the creation of Atlantic diasporan communities and identities on the African continent—particularly in West Africa. Much of the emergent literature related to West Africa shifted attention to the account of the Aguda. Here, I not only emphasize multiple reverse migrations from Brazil or settlement communities in West Africa, I also highlight the significance of emerging migrations by the Tabom people from Ghana to Brazil in the twenty-first century.

(RE)THINKING THE SILENCES IN THE BRAZILIAN-AFRICAN DIASPORA

Silences embedded in the Brazilian-African diaspora story are shaped by the problem of imbalances in the archives. The gaps serve to remind us of other situations elsewhere. As Lovejoy articulates, there is wealth of historical evidence in some archives while others are emaciated. Relevant literature and ethnography lend some insight into the Brazilian-African diaspora story.[29]

Challenges and obstacles that interfere with conducting archival research are just part of a larger problem. Michel-Rolph Trouillot makes the same point more critically in *Silencing the Past: Power and the Production of History*, where he remarks that some historical voices are strategically selected while others are intentionally silenced and systematically erased to illuminate other paradigms.[30] Another work that addresses other challenges in exploring archives and how scholars negotiate this complex process is Jacques Derrida's *Archive Fever*, which examines different dimensions of archival holdings in shaping historical memory.[31] Derrida's notions of space and memory and their relation to archives resonate in Terry Cook's *Controlling the Past* and other such works that explore the complexities of archives.[32] In *Processing the Past*, Francis X. Blouin Jr. and William G. Rosenberg outline similar challenges and imbalances in exploring various archives.[33] Trouillot's assertion that some historical events are strategically selected or left out is indeed true in the case of reverse migrations from either Brazil or Cuba to West Africa. Particularly in the fact that there is more study about the Aguda than the Tabom in Ghana, this imbalance is not necessarily because of insufficient data in the archives for documenting the latter story. In part, this is due to the fact that scholars have not made enough attempts to document the history of the Brazilian-African diaspora in Ghana.

There are other ways of exploring archival sources, improvising and charting new academic paths for piecing together different dimensions of historical memory. I draw from ordinary stories using a "bottom-up" approach. In her analysis of liberated Africans in Sierra Leone, Suzanne Schwarz asserts that "micro data about individuals gathered through nominal linkage can also contribute to an analysis of wider issues including the nature and experience of freedom in the context of slave trade abolition."[34] Schwarz's approach complements recent works that rely on the stories of "ordinary" slaves. The problem is not just about reverse migrations in West Africa. As Roquinaldo Ferreira rightly relates in his study of returnee communities in Angola, little work has been done on Brazilian returnee communities in Angola compared to areas in West Africa.[35] Ferreira's recent work, *Cross-Cultural Exchange in the Atlantic World*, as well as works by James H. Sweet, such as *Domingos Álvares* and his meticulous study of Christian and Muslim slave converts including Domingos, Carlos, Cesário, and Diego, have all contributed to new ways of readdressing these lapses.[36] João J. Reis, writing on Domingos Pereira Sodré a Nagô, a (Yoruba) priest in nineteenth-century Bahia, and other authors fill some of the methodological gaps as they trace the life histories of these individuals using their biographies.[37]

Being faced with limited archival documents, I chose to follow the footsteps of Schwarz and the others I have mentioned earlier.[38] In addition, I depend on ethnography—specifically, the memory of the Tabom people. The biographical study of Ferku (the name used in the collections at the Public Records and Archives Administration Department, or PRAAD) in order to show not only his shared ties with family or ancestors he left behind in Brazil but also how his multiple links shaped his identity and nomadic lifestyle as he traveled back and forth to Accra and Lagos. I examine closely both the similarities and the differences between the holdings at PRAAD and at national archives in Nigeria (Ibadan in particular) that speak to the Tabom and Aguda story in terms of family ties. A question that particularly intrigues me is whether the returnees who relocated to Ghana were originally from there or were just freed slaves in search of a home. Such questions only add to the ambiguity entrenched in the archival documents, especially sources relating to slavery, abolition, return, identity formation, and citizenship issues. The need is to locate documents that show linkages between emancipated Africans who relocated to one settlement community or another. Such would enable us to know if the Aguda and the Tabom shared common historical connections. Broadly speaking, part of the answer lies in how we use the available documents at PRAAD as a lens to explore other migration patterns or ancestral connections to multiple transatlantic locations. Besides Ferku, whose nomadic travels between Accra and Lagos are visible at PRAAD, there are a number of freed slaves who fit into the category of Tabom-Aguda connections and exchanges. They include those who also visited their relatives and friends and sometimes traded between Accra and Lagos selling beads and other goods.[39]

In the case of Ghana, I draw from a number of archival holdings at PRAAD to establish that a large portion of returnees in Accra were mainly Aguda-Yoruba people who left Lagos to find new places of settlement in British precolonial Accra because of their long tradition of commerce along the Nigeria–Gold Coast Atlantic corridor. A segment of their population joined the exodus for their safety when they found out that some of the freed slaves who settled in Lagos were being reenslaved and taken back to the New World.[40] Yet for others, it was their interest in spreading their Islamic faith that motivated their journeys.[41] Some of these Aguda people intermarried with both the Tabom and non-Tabom people in Accra. The constellation of relationships created new transatlantic connections to communities in Accra and stabilized activities especially between these returnees and the local people as both Aguda and Tabom crisscrossed the Nigeria–Ghana Atlantic waters. To gain a clear picture of the settlement patterns in West Africa of the emancipated slaves from Brazil and Cuba, and to fully understand the Tabom-Aguda experience in Ghana, one must compare the holdings at PRAAD and others at the Archives Nationales in Porto-Novo, Benin, and at the Nigerian National Archives in Lagos and Ibadan as well as explore the existing literature and oral histories. Otherwise, we cannot understand the overlaps between these two returnee groups. Although such academic expeditions can be murky, they will enable us to hear the voices of the Yoruba and Aguda people through their legacy.

Although they were once viewed as *strangers* in Accra, the records at PRAAD show they were not aliens but active players who contributed immensely to the history of Ghana from precolonial times.

Tracing the Names of the Returnees

I know of no database that clearly provides evidence of slaves who were taken to Brazil and later joined voyages back to the Gold Coast after gaining their freedom. Indeed, in my later discussions I depend on scanty documents at PRAAD that include statements by the Tabom about the arrival of their ancestors from Brazil. The following family names appear in the archival records and through interviews with the Tabom people: Plange, Sokoto, Nasu/Nassu, Nelson, Aruna, Peregrino, Maslieno, Fiscian, Ribeiro, Manuel, Nakpala, Damburka, Abdulamas, Vialla, Zuzers, and Morton. However, it is difficult to know if these returnees were actually from the Gold Coast or were onboard ships that docked in Lagos (figures 5a and 5b). Important holdings available at the Brazilian embassy in Accra and other Brazilian government institutions, such as Ministère des Relations Exterèrieres (the Ministry of External Relations), have also shaped my research. One major project—*Letters from Brazil* by Carlos da Fonseca, which contains photographs, personal documents, and more than four hundred letters that were exchanged between the offspring of freed slaves in Ghana, Nigeria, Benin, Togo, and Brazil—has been exhibited in these countries.[42] This project was originally initiated by the Sociedade Protertora dos Desalidos (Society for the Protection of the Disenfranchised) in Salvador da Bahia, Brazil, in 1832. The collection of letters provides a broad coverage of family history and especially traces the migrations of former slaves from Brazil to West Africa. It also shows the origins of their homes in Brazil as well as cross-cultural interactions and exchanges that highlight the sense of transatlantic kinship. Examples of these letters include one from Professor Cyril Fiscian, a Tabom, that reads: "It gives me great pleasure to send this message of peace and goodwill to my brothers and sisters in Brazil and look forward to the day when I shall see you all."[43] A letter from a member of the Da Costa Aguda family in Lagos maintains that "the descendants of the Da Costa family extend their greetings to the Da Costa's in Brazil. Our address is 151 Bangbose, Island Lagos, Nigeria."[44] Another letter from Maglore da Piedade, an Aguda from Porto-Novo, Benin, relates, "Dear relatives from Brazil, we are the da Piedade of Porto-Novo. Sorry for the unusual way in which we communicate. We would like to always correspond with you. Greetings to all Brazilians and to our relatives [in Brazil]."[45]

Figures 5a and 5b. Emancipated Africans returning to Africa, 1888.

"Letters from Brazil" is a significant source for understanding part of the Tabom and the Aguda story. These selected letters exemplify the value of sources not deposited in any major traditional archival house. Further, it provides a lens for tracing the origins of the returnees, especially in the Aguda case. The same cannot be said, however, for the Brazilian-African diaspora in Ghana, though most of the correspondence embedded in this project shows that Afro-Brazilians in particular were able to trace their families in Lagos and other areas. Moreover, most of the Aguda people have had a long exchange with their relatives in Brazil, dating from the late 1800s.[46] With several photographs of the original settlers from Brazil in "Letters from Brazil," one can draw from these photographic narratives memory that covers a wide range of class, gender, and age groups. The Tabom story, which was also part of the project, shows the opposite: no clear evidence of their family members in Brazil or photographs of their ancestors besides the ones displayed at the Brazil House in Accra. The sample letters from the Tabom included in "Letters from Brazil," which was organized in various returnee communities in Nigeria, Benin, and Ghana, basically show that the Tabom's greetings were just part of a ritual to show their involvement in the exercise: they lacked any substance in terms of connecting to the Afro-Brazilians in Brazil who participated in this exercise. Part of the disconnection between the Tabom and their distant relatives is due to fact that they have not been able to travel to Brazil to see these family members, in contrast to those Aguda who have been to this distant location several times since their arrival in the 1800s. Because the long years of assimilation into local Ghanaian cultures led to the disappearance of Brazilian-Portuguese names, their Brazilian heritage was made all but invisible in Ghana.

The stark difference in the literature concerning the Aguda and the Tabom is based largely on variation in the archives as well as on the records at Kew that include the names (African and Brazilian), ethnicity, and age groups of the slaves from Nigeria (figures 6a and 6b), which have provided sufficient markers for scholars to trace numerous family groups that joined waves of voyages from Brazil to Lagos and other locations.[47]

Scholars who have used the Arquivo Público da Bahia and other archival depositories elsewhere have contributed to the study of reverse migrations focusing mainly on the Aguda story. These works draw from birth and baptism certificates, passport records, police and immigration reports, passenger ship records, and others.[48] In one of Lisa E. Castillo's works, which is grounded heavily on archival data, she was able to trace the travel paths of freed slaves between Lagos, Nigeria, and different slave ports in Salvador, Bahia, Rio de Janeiro, and Pernambuco. In each of these stories Castillo is able to connect family names spanning a generation or more. This includes freed Nagô or Yoruba Africans such as Elisa do Bomfim, Bamboxé Obitikos, Eduardo Américo Souza Gomes, and others who traveled back and forth across the Atlantic

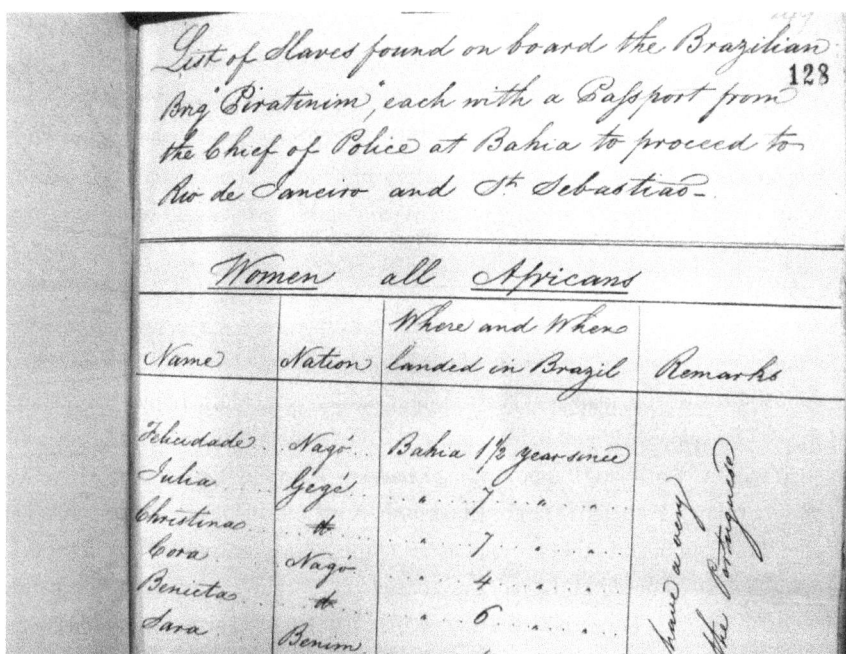
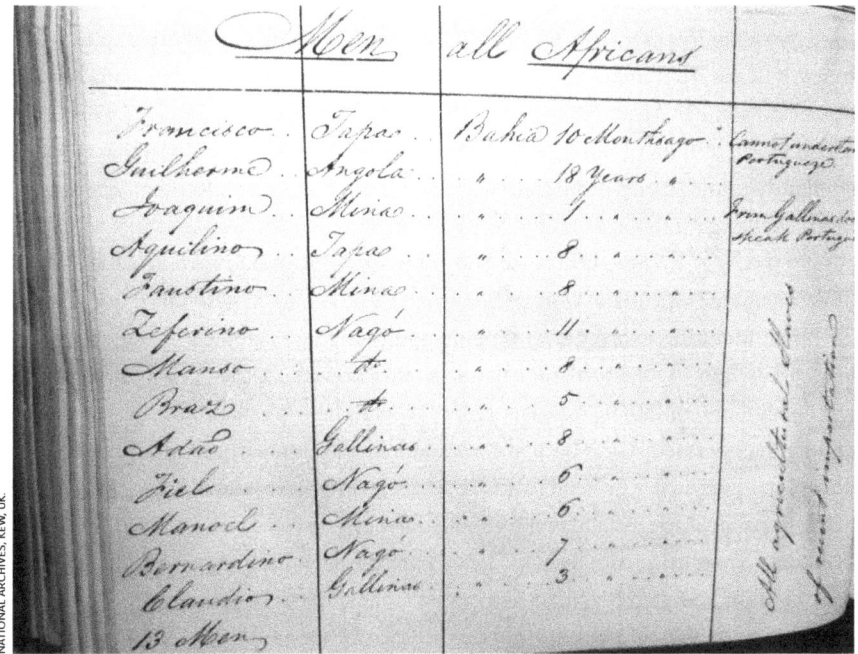

Figures 6a and 6b. List of some female and male slaves from Africa. FO 84/920, 127-28.

waters.⁴⁹ Other literature shows that the Nagô people's travels across the Atlantic were so frequent that it seemed as if these distant locations were close to each other. Besides traveling to visit family members or for trade, a large group of Nagô religious leaders, especially those who remained in Brazil, used these travel paths as some kind of pilgrimage to charge their "religious battery" in Onim (Lagos) so they could learn how to perform extraordinary divination in candomblé, *xangô*, and other religious rituals in Brazil.⁵⁰

Although they had adopted Brazilian-Portuguese cultures and Christian names, these emancipated Africans also retained their Yoruba names, for example Bamboxé Obitikos. Other names of freed slaves have been documented in other sources. They include João da Rocha, Juan des Castro, Sabina da Silva, and Maria Louisa Machada;⁵¹ Maria da Conceicao, Manoel B. Moreira, and Constancia Maria do Rosario;⁵² as well as João Balbino Cardoso (Ifagbohũ), João Baptista (Omoniyi), Theodora Maria de Alcantara (Ajayi), Francisco Marcos (Ifagbũmi), Anna Cardoso Santos (Morohũkeji), Paola Maria (Ainã), and others who negotiated their Brazilian and Yoruba identities simultaneously as noted in the work of Lorenzo D. Turner.⁵³ Some of Turner's rich collections, labeled "Lorenzo Dow Turner papers" and housed at the Anacostia Community Museum Archives, Smithsonian Institution, include a photograph of slaves on a slave ship from Bahia, Brazil, to Lagos and other unknown destinations in West Africa as shown in figures 5a and 5b. One of the documents with his handwriting states, "En route to Lagos from Bahia after the abolition of slavery, some of them were born in Brazil and some in Africa."⁵⁴

It seems as if there was not much fun or activities in the Gold Coast that merited similar dynamic stories or migrations back and forth to Brazil. In other words, it is more challenging to explore the stories about Brazilian-African diaspora as in the case of the Aguda. There is no such body of work at PRAAD to chronicle the origins of emancipated Brazilians who settled in Accra or Ghana in general or to examine how their identities evolved over time. In addition, these significant records at Kew lead researchers to statistical information about those who settled in Lagos, but not to any documents containing travel patterns to Ghana. The Brazilian-Portuguese names among the liberated slaves both at Kew and in the "Letters from Brazil" project are obvious. However, it is difficult to find Brazilian-Portuguese names among the stories of the Brazilian-Africans and of the Tabom that have survived for over a century. Basically, due in part to the paucity of evidence available, it is currently not possible to trace the origins of liberated Brazilian-Africans in Ghanaian public archives.

In terms of their identity, it is not easy to trace the names, which come in all shapes and forms, of those Brazilians and Tabom who settled in Ghana. The names of the early Brazilian settlers were mainly of Brazilian-Portuguese roots. This includes João

Antonio Nelson (Nii Azumah II), who reigned as Brazilian chief from 1836 to 1900.[55] Besides serving as Brazilian chief, João Antonio Nelson was an herbalist. He also owned his business selling beads.[56] Those who were born in the Gold Coast to Brazilian and Ghanaian or Nigerian parents typically used a combination of Brazilian, Ghanaian, Yoruba, and Muslim names, but over time most of these names were displaced by local ones or were fused into Yoruba or Islamic names. For instance, part of the Peregrino family uses "Brimah" (following Peregrino) to show the Yoruba-Muslim-Brazilian connection or identity that emerged through their paternal lineage. According to archival sources and the great-grandchildren of Fatima Okpedu (a Brazilian-African) and Chief Brimah, this cultural intermingling and exchange occurred after the marriage union between them, especially as Brimah was a devout Yoruba Muslim merchant who traveled back and forth between Lagos and Accra.[57]

There are other Tabom names that are mixed with European ones. The Lutterodts, who trace their ancestry via Mama Nassu, a Brazilian who is believed to have been one of the leaders who joined the first wave of migrations to Accra, have a corrupted name that is perhaps derived from a Lutterodt who is believed to be a European immigrant to Accra in the mid-1800s. Unlike the Peregrino-Brimah ties that combine Brazilian-Yoruba influences, in the case of the Lutterodts, the European name overshadows the Brazilian. But this does not suggest that the Lutterodts are disconnected from their Brazilian origins. According to Elder William Lutterodt, the oldest person among the Lutterodts, he is proud of his Brazilian heritage not only because his great-great-grandparent built the house that became known as the Brazil House but because of the significance of his Brazilian-Ghanaian-European identity to the reconstruction of Brazilian-Tabom history.[58]

As the complexity of the Peregrino and Lutterodt names shows, most of these Brazilian names faded after more than a century of integration into local Nigerian and Ghanaian cultures. It is becoming increasingly difficult to trace Brazilian names in the archives in Nigeria, Ghana, and Brazil because of the period of metamorphosis driven largely by Yoruba, Gã, and European influences and other shades of cultural dilution. As a result, Brazilian-Lusophone names are now mixed with either Yoruba-Nigerian, Gã/Akan-Ghanaian, Muslim-Christian, or European names. My efforts to trace the origins of the Brazilian returnees in Brazilian archives using some of the names they used in Accra have proven difficult. Specifically, I provided Lisa Castillo, an archivist at Arquivo Público da Bahia, with the following dominant Brazilian names in PRAAD records and in oral traditions with the hope that they could be traced via the repository in Bahia or other archives in Brazil: Manyo Plange, Mama Sokoto, Mama Nasu/Nassu, Abiana Nelson, Alasha Nelson, and family names associated with the Arunas, Peregrinos, Maslienos, Fiscians, Manuels, Nakpalas, Damburkas, Abdulamas, Viallas,

Chapter One

Zuzers, and others popular in the Brazilian-African diaspora. According to Castillo, the identities of the returnee communities in West Africa have evolved from one generation to the other. She added it is difficult to trace these names in police reports or archival sources mainly because of assimilation and changes to the names over time. Most of the names the Tabom inherited over the years are similarly difficult to find because of the many years of assimilation. Castillo concluded that although there are documents at the Arquivo Público da Bahia covering a long list of police reports about freed slaves who left Brazil voluntarily or were deported to West Africa between 1835 and 1837, none of them included the names I provided.[59]

National archives at Accra and at Ibadan as well as at the Arquivo Público da Bahia are not the only collections that helped facilitate the reconstruction of Brazilian-African diaspora narratives in Ghana. British archival collections at Kew provide sufficient correspondences between British abolition officials in Brazil and in Nigeria for tracing the travel patterns of the freed slaves from major ports in Bahia and Rio de Janeiro to Lagos.[60] These documents, including British parliamentary and abolitionist papers such as those in figures 6a and 6b, provide detailed tables of family groups on board captured slave ships, information on various naval patrols, as well as the slaves' gender, names, ages, and identities.[61]

The repositories at Kew are broad in scope, well organized, and allow researchers to trace migration paths and transatlantic experiences from Africa to the New World and back again. A number of scholars have relied on these records.[62] It is fairly easy to trace the origins of the Aguda returnees because of the abundance of data at Kew and other repositories. There are several letters by British abolitionists regarding the conditions of slaves from Lagos, particularly the difficulty in settling them back in Lagos and other areas after their liberation. Pierre Verger's voluminous work in particular draws heavily from British parliamentary records, Brazilian consular reports, and others currently deposited at Kew. The Foreign Office (FO) and Colonial Office (CO) documents in the National Archives provide a good lead that includes tables and statistics for exploring the number of slaves that were transported to Brazil from the late eighteenth century and slave routes—their places of origin/capture and where the slaves were settled in Brazil. Other documents include details about slave ships and naval patrols, names of ship owners, slaves and their owners, the goods that were transported alongside humans, details about police records and passports that were issued to the liberated Africans, where the freed slaves resettled in Africa, correspondence between African chiefs and abolitionists, and so on.[63]

My efforts to trace the genealogy of the liberated Brazilians and Tabom in Ghana have not been easy owing to the complexity of the archives. The records at PRAAD and other repositories in Ghana are insufficient; all that they possess are the scanty records included herein. But the archives in England, Brazil, Ghana, Nigeria, and Benin are not the only repositories for exploring the Aguda and Tabom stories. Evidence concerning other aspects of the Middle Passage experience is deposited elsewhere. Lorenzo Dow Turner's collections at the Anacostia Community Museum and others, which include both papers and photographs, offer insight into stories of freed slaves from Brazil who relocated to Africa. Some of these sources reveal the life stories of the slaves, and one includes a photograph of Sozenja Ana dos Santos, a slave woman who, according to Turner, was a former resident or "citizen" of Accra. In Bahia, she played a major role in preserving and teaching African cultural performances such as candomblé, a religious tradition mixed with Africa and Brazilian cultural practices.[64]

Another challenge in tracing the origins of the Tabom is the variation in archival holdings for the study of returnees in Ghana and other areas in West Africa. My numerous visits to Kew had one central goal—to excavate data about liberated African slaves who left Brazil to what was then the Gold Coast. However, my trips to Kew were not very helpful. They provided the same result as my explorations of other archives. There are numerous documents about freed slaves who resettled in Lagos or other towns in Nigeria, with maybe a skeletal reference to slaves from the Gold Coast or "Mina" slaves. In the case of slaves destined for Lagos, the documents I found follow narratives about the systematic process of abolition, negotiations that took place between British abolitionists, Brazilian government officials, and British consulate officials in Lagos, specific names of slave owners, the identities of particular slaves, and the names of the slave ships that carried them across the Atlantic involuntarily. The involvement of African chiefs and kings in slavery is also covered broadly in the documents housed at Kew and in colonial newspapers.[65]

Brazilian authorities and various chiefs and kings in Lagos in particular harnessed slavery, but sometimes they reluctantly facilitated abolition. There was a clash of interests. Those who endorsed slavery complicated the matter, but despite their intransigence abolitionists stood firm. Although the broader goal of British abolition was to end the exploitation of the Africans in Brazil, their involvement in abolition also aimed at articulating their religious piety in preparation for grandiose civilization missions later. To accomplish this daunting task, British abolitionists had to ensure the safety of those relocating to the land of their ancestors. For example, the Earl of Clarendon, in a letter that circulated at the British consulate in Lagos on 28 December 1853, emphasized the importance of protecting people he described as "self-emancipated" Africans. They consisted of about 130 families from Brazil who escaped from mines and plantations.[66] The archival document is silent about the laws regarding escaped slaves, and it does not mention the names of these slaves; moreover, it is not clear whether some of them shared the same history and family bloodline with returnees who relocated to Accra later. However, these archival documents show that some were Yoruba returnees from Egba in Nigeria who gained manumission together with their wives and children. In Lisa Earl Castillo's work about passport records and police reports, she makes note of a larger number of returnees who were determined to be reunited with the people and the communities they or their ancestors were forced to leave behind. The letter details how these slaves spent their own savings to buy their freedom.[67]

For abolition to succeed there was a need for collaboration and alliances across the Atlantic waters and on land. First, the British took the lead by signing anti-slave trade treaties with European leaders and with the freed slaves who held various positions of power especially in Liberia.[68] The abolitionists also worked closely with various African chiefs along the Bight of Biafra to suppress and eventually abolish slavery.[69] Some chiefs were given gifts and even paid large sums of money to influence them.[70] African chiefs benefited immensely from the attention they gained during this time. While British authorities were busy giving out gifts and money to the chiefs, Portuguese authorities also exploited this mutual exchange. A letter from Benjamin Campbell that was sent to Senhor Marcos Borges Ferras on 25 July 1851 notes that Portuguese merchants undermined efforts by the British authorities as they also established closer ties with African chiefs to continue slavery.[71] In both situations, the chiefs were the major beneficiaries. Second, although British authorities consulted naval commanders assigned to various vessels on high-seas patrols, this was not always the case. Actions against the slave trade varied—some having broad implications and others narrower effects;[72] some involving treaties signed by both the British and other European powers and others promoted by the British Parliament acting alone. The Act of Parliament 51, for instance, mandated that British naval patrol agents report illegal vessels to abolition officials in order to prosecute the offenders.[73] Also, the Convention to the Treaty of 22 January 1815, in particular, was signed for the purpose of preventing European subjects from being involved in illicit slave traffic.[74] Documents that were circulated in Brazilian, Spanish, and Cuban diplomatic posts demanded unconditional commitment to emancipation laws.

British authorities who orchestrated the abolition campaign in the early to mid-nineteenth century had a daunting task of enforcing grandiose abolition laws and treaties across the length and breadth of the Atlantic world, especially on rural plantations and in urban centers.[75] The Brazilian General Assembly passed legislation on 7 November 1831 to end slavery, but the practice continued.[76] Brazilian authorities, elites, and those who had a major vested interest in slave labor, especially in the Brazilian port city of Salvador, Bahia, occasionally ridiculed British abolitionists. Hollanda Cavalcanti, a senator from Pernambuco, another slave enclave, was completely against abolition, and he was not the only one who benefited from slavery. Several Brazilian politicians became an obstacle to abolition. Some refused to grant permission to British Naval patrol to inspect ships suspected of transporting slaves into Brazilian ports. Others protected slave merchants including Manuel Pinto. British citizens in Brazil, including Jonathan Dixon, a merchant in São Paulo owned several slaves and also did not support attempts to end this illegal activity.[77]

To avoid delays and overcome interference and distractions, it was important for the British to speed up their abolition efforts. There were numerous emancipation proclamations, declarations, and alliances between the British, Brazilian authorities, the Spanish royal family, Cuban leaders, and influential individuals, groups, and institutions across the Atlantic world. In the face of opposition, these entities sought to enforce abolition laws from the early nineteenth century. During this time, negotiation and debate over abolition varied among these groups; correspondences were lengthy and filled with details about agreements and disagreements. Among these were letters circulated by the British Parliament to expedite abolition. To speed up the process, British authorities enforced various policies including the creation of programs in Lagos to accommodate skilled liberated Africans in Brazil who were interested in returning to their ancestral homeland to begin a new life. During this time they issued passports to these returnees and provided other incentives.[78] While the British were busy issuing passports, the Bahian government also gave out passports to Africans on the Island of São Tomé to relocate to Bahia, Brazil, to replenish skilled labor needs. Most of these immigrants boarded the Portuguese ship *Conceição*.[79]

The process of enforcing and sustaining freedom for the freed Africans was beset by inconsistency, contradictions, and other entanglements. Historically, slavery and emancipation actually shared a common trait: abuse. Reports by abolitionists make clear that British authorities and consuls in Brazilian ports could not assure the safety of the returnees from one port to the other or from the land of capture to the land of bondage or dispersal. The policies the British introduced to ensure their safety were necessary and effective, but they were marked by exploitation of the emancipated Africans from the beginning of the voyages back to Africa. Burdened with anxiety and uncertainties about where to seek sanctuary after they had experienced varying degrees of exploitation in the plantations, the freed Africans became victims of abuses again, this time on slave ships that were supposed to guarantee some form of safety. In reference to Portuguese ships, one correspondent states that the liberated Africans "receive the worst treatment and [were] not free from the risk of being landed against their will at Whydah [Benin] or some other places where they would immediately be seized, reduced to slavery again and their property on board the vessel became the property of the Portuguese Captain."[80]

Others suffered after they landed in West Africa.[81] Some reports showed that over 569 slaves were tightly packed side by side with goods on a schooner, *Henriqueta*, that left the ports of Bahia to travel to Lagos. In addition, a number of passengers were starved on the long voyages to Lagos, while others lost their money and properties on the ship.[82] A letter from the British consulate in Lagos describes how ship owners and captains harassed, abused, and intimidated returnees after they had paid their passage for the voyage. In one such incident, slaves who paid for their passage back to Lagos on the Portuguese ship *Emillia* were abandoned in Dahomey, Benin, which later became a French territory, with no one holding the ship owners accountable for the crime.[83] Another report spoke forcefully against the robbing of slaves by ship captains.[84]

CLANDESTINE ACTIVITIES AND CHALLENGES WITH RETURN

There were a number of ways to elude the abolitionists. Sometimes operators of foreign vessels used clandestine strategies to cover up abuses and exploitation in their efforts to prop up slavery. Most of these ships were determined to escape British monitoring systems both on land and on sea.[85] A letter dated 28 August 1821 acknowledges that a Portuguese ship, controlled by Captain Ian Francisco, played a dual role in both stabilizing slavery and facilitating the process of return. Francisco, who was engaged in some form of indirect barter trade and owned an African slave named Don Antonio, entered a port in Pernambuco, Brazil, with a cargo of salt and other goods. During the same trip, there were more than fifty captured African slaves on board. Plans were discovered whereby the ship captain was to proceed with public auction of the slaves to buy more goods for resale in Africa. According to Royal Navy records, "The case of the Negroes brought here [to Brazil] . . . and advertised probably for sale is a flagrant breach of law and Treaty."[86] However, efforts by British Royal Navy officers to stop the ship proved futile, as did efforts to gain the help of African chiefs in minimizing the number of captured slaves in their territories and alleviating the misery of the freed slaves. On 20 April 1842, a correspondence between British consul Robert Hesketh and the Foreign Office expressed frustrations with ship captains who used the flag of the United States of America to cover up illegal slavery activities.[87] Another letter from British Minister Hamilton to the chargé d'affaires in Rio de Janeiro states that, "slave dealers not only feel confident of perfect security under American flag, but also now exultingly put aside all the cunning disguises under which they have neither commenced the illegal voyages to Africa."[88]

Members of the returnee population embarked on journeys to Africa after saving money for many years to purchase their freedom.[89] Some of these voyages were also paid by various associations or the communal groups they were members of. According to Pierre Verger, one of the emancipated groups paid about £1,200 to free about seventy slaves.[90] The freed Africans were aware that freedom was tenuous, and for that reason they did not want to burn the bridge that connected them to the abolitionist groups that could help facilitate their travels and secure their safety. Abolitionists, for their part, did not turn their backs on the freed slaves, although the provisions they made could not meet all the needs and expectations of the returnees. The letter from Campbell to Lord Clarendon shows a response to a request the emancipated slaves made to the Earl of Clarendon, governor of the colony, for their safety after they had landed in Lagos with nowhere to go and with no support system to enable them to settle appropriately. The response by the Earl of Clarendon showed British officials' interest in providing security for the returnees:

> My protection of those Africans who having purchased their emancipation from slavery in Brazil have settled in Lagos . . . as it armed me with the authority to interfere on behalf of 230 of these self-emancipated Africans lately brought to Lagos from Rio Janeiro and Bahia in the Portuguese vessel *Linda Flor*.[91]

Most of these freed slaves described in Clarendon's correspondence sought permission to settle in Lagos rather than other areas along the Bight of Benin mainly because they wanted to remain close to the watchful eyes of abolitionists and consulate offices in Lagos. Others did so because of evidence of a larger returnee population in Lagos compared to other potential places of settlement. Besides providing security, the abolitionists paid the passage of those who could not afford it. Upon arrival, the returnees were required by law to obtain permission for passage from one settlement location to another to prevent their being recaptured by slave traders. In part, these laws were created to deter the freed slaves from engaging in slavery of other returnees. The British abolitionists were not required to assist the returnees in identifying which cultural bloodline, family groups, or communities in Africa their ancestors belonged to prior to their capture. Clearly, the fact that the earlier involuntary migrations were spontaneous made such a task problematic. In leaving slavery behind, the lives of emancipated slaves were further complicated by just how and what they remembered about their ancestral past, as the journeys back to Africa created both opportunities and obstacles.

Archival collections at Kew help bring attention to the hardships freed slaves endured as they wrestled with simultaneous change and continuity. Trapped between two foreign places, the returnees had to make swift decisions. They had to choose between Brazil and Africa. Their limited options in Africa during the early stages of returnee settlements in West Africa, especially problems with assimilation, compelled some to return to Brazil, their former place of enslavement. Pierre Verger describes the lives of various families who embarked on these journeys back to Brazil.[92] These ambitious travels and stories of resilience and resistance did not occur in isolation, nor were they confined to the period of the Middle Passage. They continued after abolition. Lisa A. Lindsay explains how Juan des Castro's family made similar arrangements to get back to Brazil. In Castro's case he jogged between Brazil and Lagos, shipping tobacco and jerked beef from Brazil and using his tailoring skills to make extra money whenever he was in Lagos.[93] Others found new ways to continue engaging in transatlantic commercial activities after the demise of slavery in Brazil in 1888. As the literature on the Aguda shows, most of these returnees invested heavily in business ventures trading in palm oil, tobacco, and other crops.[94] Lorenzo D. Turner, in his study of ex-slaves who arrived in Lagos in 1909 via Las Palmas and the Canary Islands, notes that some of these freed Africans were comfortable crisscrossing the Atlantic between Lagos and Brazil. According to Turner,

> They would carry to Africa such Brazilian products as tobacco, sugar, dry salted beef, and cachacha, a drink made from sugar cane. On their return, they would bring to be sold in Brazil such African products as kola, nuts, palm oil, black soap, pepper, beads, baskets, straw, dippers, parrot feathers, beans, pomade, mattresses, cowries, drums and a cloth used as a sash by women and called in Portuguese panno da costa.[95]

By the dawn of the nineteenth century, the efforts by individual slaves, family groups, and British abolitionists had made a great impact on migrations both ways across the Atlantic. The overlapping interests of these groups resulted in various voyages being undertaken from Brazil across the Atlantic in *search* of a *home* in West and West-Central Africa. Some of these freed slaves settled comfortably in Lagos as traders while others sought various opportunities to contribute their skills and refashion their identities.[96] In the case of North America, the Back-to-Africa movement, which was orchestrated by the ACS and philanthropic groups, allowed freed blacks from the United States and the West Indies to relocate to Liberia and Sierra Leone in particular. Efforts in this direction began at the outset of the abolition movement and continued through the post–Civil War period known as Reconstruction. On the one hand, ACS papers and ship records provide ample documentation for scholars to trace both the America-to-Africa and Caribbean-to-Africa reverse migration experiences.[97] The Brazil-to-Africa story involving Ghana, on the other hand, is partly nested within the Aguda account.

As British abolitionist and parliamentary papers show, the Aguda account established points of dispersal and embarkation in Lagos, where some of the subsequent migrations to Ghana originated alongside direct-from-Brazil migrations to Ghana.

Even considering the sizable ACS collections, the statistical data on voyages as well as the abolitionist papers, Brazilian consular records, and British diplomatic and parliamentary reports on abolition at Kew cannot be matched. For the study of reverse migrations from Brazil to Lagos, newspapers, photographs, and police/immigration passport records can also be found in the Arquivo Público da Bahia, Brazil, and on *Trans-Atlantic Slave Trade: A Database on CD-ROM*. It is important to note that the imbalance in migration records for Lagos vis-à-vis other areas, especially Ghana, is due in part to the fact that more slaves were originally taken from Nigeria than from Ghana.[98] The large quantity of documents housed at Kew concerning emancipated slaves returning to Lagos dwarfs the scanty holdings about migrations to Ghana located elsewhere.

It is evident in a number of precolonial and colonial documents that freed slaves who were taken back to Africa did not necessarily return to their homes of origin. However, in some situations returnees navigated back to where they or their ancestors were captured, as we see in the case of Afro-Cuban Yoruba people who relocated to a known homeland in Lagos.[99] Memories of a distant place, as faint as they may have been, enabled the enslaved Africans to retain aspects of their African cultures that aided communal unions to form solidarity.[100] In *Recreating Africa*, we learn that the creolization process, or the fusion of African cultures into New World ones and vice versa, did not occur immediately. Rather, African slaves preserved their cultures for long periods of time. In fact, in Brazil African cultural practices were so potent that one Catholic priest articulated to his flock that during times of trouble, "their [Brazilians'] only hope for survival was consulting with an African diviner/healer."[101] In *The Akan Diaspora in the Americas*, Kwasi Konadu provides evidence that Akan slaves from Ghana also preserved their cultural practices, which are still visible in spiritual centers (*terreiros*) in Brazil today. In fact, Carnival songs including "Negrice Cristal" show evidence of Akan cultural consciousness in Brazil.[102] By and large, such awareness and determination to retain a connection to their African roots contributed immensely to the later search for locations in Africa where they had been captured.

A letter from a British official named Hudson, which was addressed to Lord Stanley, regarding the protocol for transporting freed African slaves in Brazil shows that West Africa was not returnees' only destination. The slaves, who were referred to as a "Body of freed Congo and other negroes," were transported back to Cabinda (a Portuguese colony), in southwestern Africa.[103] Cabinda became part of Angola in 1956. Such settlements beyond West Africa raise more questions than answers regarding reverse migration patterns. It is likely that most of the freed slaves returned to these areas because they were familiar with the geographical terrain. Their long history of movements to multiple locations after their return, however, reshaped their migratory paths. My visit to the Brazilian Quarter and Cuban Lodge in Lagos, Nigeria, the epicenter of major Portuguese- and Spanish-speaking returnee settlements, shed more light and confirmed earlier findings. According to Muneer Akolade, a resident of the area, the Brazilian-Africans and Yoruba-Cubans who are known as the Aguda people in Nigeria, Benin, and Togo had close contacts with their relatives in Dahomey, Whydah, and other locations on the coastline, but most of them relocated to the Gold Coast to settle permanently.[104] Catholic missionary records at the Pontificia Universitas Urbaniana on the premises of the Vatican in Rome also provide insight into early settlements in Nigeria. References from court cases that are currently housed at PRAAD in Accra also show evidence of the frequent movements of Brazilian merchants and returnees in the Gold Coast that helped them to forge strong bonds.[105]

Home Sweet Home: Imagination, Memory, Return, and Identity

Memory and identity must be considered together. Memory, which could be authentic or an illusion, has played a critical role in relations between people of African descent and the continent of Africa since the end of slavery.[106] It was the power of memory that aided voyages back to specific communities in Africa. Anthropologist Pilar Riaño-Alcalá argues that "memory as a cultural practice is a bridge between the individual and the collective that facilitates processes of identity construction" and preservation.[107] Indeed, memory not only influences identity formation but has a great deal of effect on how people preserve their skills, religion, and various cultural practices. Literature on memory covers both the Middle Passage and the period of emancipation. For instance, as Michael A. Gomez notes in *Exchanging Our Country Marks*, and as Judith A. Carney rightly asserts in *Black Rice*, the transatlantic experience was a frontier for showcasing cultural practices, traditions, skills, and diverse innovation.[108] Edda L. Fields-Black makes a similar argument in *Deep Roots*.[109] Some of these traditions, skills, and aspects of African survivalism within dispersed slave groups motivated various enslaved populations, including maroon slave communities, to navigate complex oppressive systems during their quest for freedom.[110] And as freed Africans they brought both what they had preserved and what they acquired from their New World experience back to their settlements in Africa to make contributions to their development.

Slave revolts and other forms of resistance to slavery did not guarantee emancipation. Neither did freedom movements and emancipation campaigns that surfaced especially in the late nineteenth-century Atlantic world disappear after slavery ended in Brazil in 1888. Although there is evidence of ethnic pride or memory of a homeland somewhere in Africa among the Brazilian-African returnees, the majority of freed slaves had two main battles: maintaining a distinct African identity in the New World, and re-creating, upon their return to Africa, a new identity encompassing their New World socialization or based on racial/cultural mixture—that is, creolization. Whichever way one evaluates this complex evolution, it is obvious that the notion of freedom, the emancipated slaves' ideation, their interest in refashioning their identity, and especially their determination to return to a *home* where most of them had never been all collided on the historical stage. In the case of the returnees in Ghana the emergence of British colonialism in the early nineteenth century redefined their freedom, their sense of belonging, and later their exclusion.

In terms of emancipated Africans' reverse voyages of hope, Kim D. Butler establishes that memory of a "hostland and homeland" interweaves on many levels.[111] Similarly, W. E. B. Du Bois underscores how memory and identity intertwine. He simplifies the metaphor this way: "Two souls, two thoughts, two unreconciled strivings, two warring ideals in one dark body, whose dogged strength alone keeps it from being torn asunder."[112] Other dispersed slave populations, like the former African slaves in Brazil, carried their skills and cultural practices to the Afro-Atlantic world via involuntary migrations, as several works have shown. But although they left Africa, Africa never left them. In addition, African slaves in Brazil, especially the older ones, who retained their memory of a home in Africa imagined this distant location and finally relocated to Africa before their deaths.[113] Although there seems to have been a fluid transition from Brazil to the Gold Coast, what is striking is that the older returnees preserved such aspects of their Brazilian identities as how they dressed and use of the Portuguese language. For the early settlers, they remained "Brazilians" most of their life in the Gold Coast, but their offspring—both those who were brought from Brazil and those who were later born in the Gold Coast—gradually assimilated into local cultures.

These closely related experiences and transitions from the early nineteenth century inform us about how the history of the Tabom who were born in Ghana interlocks with their ancestors' experiences in various plantations or sites of slavery in Brazil. In analyzing evidence of double consciousness among the older generation of settlers, it is crucial to explain how this had ripple effects on their offspring decades later. In part, I contend that the experience with Brazilian slavery influenced the identities of their offspring in many ways: those born Ghanaians, but who zealously claimed a Ghanaian identity as well as a Brazilian ancestral connection; those influenced by

Ghanaian values and cultures but who tirelessly incorporated memories of a Brazilian past; and those living in Ghana who forged a relationship with Brazil. It is through these multiple retention paths that the Tabom people refashioned their dual identity as Brazilian-Ghanaians. How do the back-and-forth linkages, memories of a *home*, and overlapping identities that Du Bois conceived in terms of an identity crisis contribute to the story of the returnees and their offspring? To answer this question, it is important to widen the scope of this transatlantic dialogue in ways that not only cover reverse migrations to Ghana but also include new travel trends by the Tabom to Brazil, in order to make connections between the stories their ancestors passed on to them over time.

Besides linking constellations of memory in order to map out migratory paths from and to Brazil from several angles and to gain a deeper insight and appreciation for returnees' transoceanic voyages, it is imperative to explore and compare these experiences with various other circum-Atlantic reverse migrations that emerged from similar circumstances throughout the Spanish, British, and Portuguese spheres of the Afro-Atlantic world.[114] Memory and the notion of return both served as links between Africa and the Atlantic world as emancipated African slaves from Brazil in particular continued their long tradition of migration to the Bight of Benin, and later to the Gold Coast in the early 1800s—after settling first in Lagos.[115] Although some of these returnees were convinced that their selected destinations could meet their yearning for a home, there is no evidence that their ambitious dreams became reality. There was, however, another twist to the journey home as the newcomers and the local people interacted. Tensions developed in part because the returnees who converted to Christianity embarked on efforts to spread their newfound faith.

For most of the returnees, a "homecoming" did not automatically unite them with the local people, given their separation by time and space for decades if not centuries. Neither was it easy for their offspring to navigate a journey back to Brazil later. However, many of the freed slaves, in their determination to return *home* to Africa, overcame the negative perceptions, uncertainties, and challenges that they encountered. Later, some had to deal with the reality of rejection by various communities upon their return. Memory of a homeland that was passed on from one generation to the next shaped the returnees' knowledge of Africa and informed connections to a distant family group somewhere. In the Brazilian reverse migration story, the negotiation of history, space, and culture is very complicated. The rejection and sense of "not belonging" or fitting into local value systems felt by Brazilian-Africans is partly due to the disconnection that was created both during and after the Middle Passage experience, especially the unique identities and cultures that emerged on both sides of the Atlantic over time. Further, the journeys of peoples of African ancestry who left Africa and came back after many years contributed to how local people viewed or responded to the returnees.

The point of departure was obvious: Africans and their descendants who remained on the continent were not well informed about the transatlantic experience, and most of the returnees, for their part, were not very knowledgeable of their "distant relatives." Further, both groups had varying experiences with racism, slavery, and various levels of exploitation and prejudice. This mutual ignorance influenced how these two groups perceived each other. Whereas returnees felt some sense of entitlement or belonging to communities on the African continent because of their involuntary dispersals and the horrors of the transatlantic passage, their hosts or those they left behind in Africa saw them as coming from another country beyond the boundaries of the continent, as evidenced by the fact that returnees often were unable to speak local languages.

On the one hand, the contention and differences that were created by the long period of separation between the two groups were aggravated by misperceptions, and the situation was made worse by the fact that each group tended to project a sense of superiority over the other. Moreover, some returnees who might have sustained their pride in African cultures while in the New World could not relate well to the cultural practices in their new environs. In fact, the Christians among them in particular often viewed African practices as backward or inferior to Western ones. Some of these returnees were convinced that their social and religious experiences in Brazil planted them more closely to a civilized European culture than their ancestors who were never enslaved, or remained in Africa.[116] For their part, Africans on the continent could not always differentiate some of the returnees from Europeans and other foreigners because of their prejudices toward the local people. Other historical forces also shaped the ways in which these two groups related to one another. There is no agreement on remembrances and effects of the Middle Passage, both direct and indirect, particularly of the horrors of the transatlantic slave trade. As far as some of the Ghanaian population is concerned, especially from the twentieth century, their understanding of the discourse of the Middle Passage and particularly the significance of the slave castles and forts on their coastline is largely about their relevance to commercialization and global capitalism.[117]

There are other factors that help explain the varied attitudes and outlooks. Antônio Olinto in *Casa da Agua* (*The Water House*) asserts that nostalgia about home and the reality of rejection shaped early contacts between returnees and local people in Nigeria.[118] The reality of rejection goes beyond cultural differences, what sites of memories mean to both groups, and unique historical conditions that have shaped people of African descent on each side of the Black Atlantic. Identity politics, or how diasporan Africans in the New World and continental Africans see themselves or present their stories, also varies widely. For all its horrors, the Middle Passage, which encompasses a complex series of voyages and trajectories, opened up doorways for cultural, religious, social, and racial mixing—creolization—but in it also created a spectrum of multiple definitions of what it means to be "African" or "Black," particularly where freed slaves had to settle to reconstruct their identity—either in Brazil or in Africa. The search for *home* was daunting, frustrating, and confusing for some. Nonetheless, this daunting task was a rewarding venture for others. Several freed Africans including one Oshifékuédé who was captured in Omaku in Ijebuland, Nigeria, and others like him preferred to remain in Brazil while those I have discussed in this chapter joined dangerous voyages back *home*.[119]

There is a stark difference between the collections at Kew and other archival collections covering reverse transatlantic migrations, these records do converge on various grounds. An example of such convergence occurs where the stories of some African slaves who gained freedom here and there on their own intersect with the role abolitionists played in ending slavery for others across the entire Atlantic world. Abolitionists were active in developing strategies for relocating or facilitating the process of settlement, particularly in West Africa and including the areas that became known as the Bight of Benin and the Bight of Biafra (Bight of Bonny). The complex forms of reverse migration from Brazil to different destinations, from Lagos in the east to Accra in the west, share striking features with their migratory trajectories. But they share different paths too. In the case of Kew, the constant activities of British officials with respect to their efforts to end slavery and provide safety for a large group of emancipated Africans who were determined to return to the African continent resulted in the creation of a large volume of data.[120] But the same cannot be said about PRAAD and other archives in West Africa where fewer returnees relocated.

Chapter 2

Historicizing the Returnee Presence in Gã *Mãŋ*: Challenges and Silences

It appears that as far back as the thirties [1830s] a ship load of Africans were landed from Brazil and after they were land [sic] the Gã chiefs gave them land to build on the town Accra and also bush land to cultivate. These lands were divided among the Brazilians.

—Chief Justice Crampton Smyly, 1915

In pursuing the dream of reverse migration, the ex-slaves sought to create a new community in Gã, Accra, to fit their imagination and to meet self-gratifying needs. It is however not clear how many of these new settlers made it to Accra or whether they or all their ancestors were originally citizens of Ghana prior to their enslavement. Reasons for the waves of migration and their initial interactions with Gã mãŋtsɛmɛi that ultimately led to their settlements in Accra are documented. The social history of Accra, particularly their long history of hospitality to newcomers, was a major factor that facilitated the returnees' choice of Accra. Through this generosity, the ex-slaves were gradually introduced to Gã cultural practices. It was through this systematic integration that the returnees were able to select their own leaders to serve as Brazilian chiefs—and later, Tabom chiefs.

Broadly speaking, Brazilian-African voyages to the then Gold Coast followed two major trajectories. They included travels from Brazil to Ghana and stopover destinations at West African locations, particularly Nigeria.[1] Travels to Ghana did not end there, for upon settlement in Accra, a number of returnees continued to travel back and forth to Nigeria, where some had landed before they relocated to Accra. Efforts by the Tabom to visit Brazil show a new form of migration beyond the ones from the New World back to Africa. Other levels of migrations between multiple places exist. Historian Paul T. Zeleza describes this constant movement and idea of endless mobility as "multiple belongings."[2] In "Unfinished Migrations," Tiffany Ruby Patterson and Robin D. G. Kelley explain the extent of voyages along the coast of Africa within the diaspora. They reframe the transatlantic debates with emphasis on the significance of continuity between slave trade from Africa to the New World and reverse migrations. Like Patterson and Kelley, Zeleza is convinced that the African diaspora is a "state of being and a process of becoming, a kind of voyage that encompasses the possibility of never arriving or returning, a navigation of multiple belongings."[3] Zeleza believes that the African diaspora must extend even beyond the "Black Atlantic," because the diaspora embodies multiple diasporas and conjunctures.[4] According to Kim D. Butler, the transatlantic crossings and cultural blendings have no end. Butler elucidates historical factors that gave rise to other forms of reverse movements. She also relates that transnationalism and recurring voyages enable people of African descent to "articulate their rightful share as citizens of nations they helped create" and in some cases to find a homeland they left behind or sometimes imagined.[5] Similar to the aforementioned assertions, Michael J. Turner provides an important insight into the genesis of former Afro-Brazilian slaves' mobility along the Bight of Benin. Turner describes the various ways the returnees organized as communities, how they negotiated their presence vis-à-vis local residents, contesting for space and power as well as commercial monopoly, and how they moved back and forth along various rivers in West Africa. He depends on ship records and documents to determine the number of Afro-Brazilians (Aguda) who traveled to and from Africa. According to Turner, "Afro-Brazilians who were able to leave Brazil in the period between 1850 and 1875 had been able to make the greatest financial progress and economic success on the African coast."[6] The success of returnees along the Bight of Benin did not depend on one particular enterprise. They engaged in legitimate trading especially in Whydah, Benin.[7]

Antônio Olinto's remarkable piece also provides fascinating imagery about journeys to an ancestral homeland and a dramatic account of a Brazilian family that joined the voyage from Brazil to coastal territories in Africa, particularly Lagos, to connect with their roots in Nigeria.[8] In the last two decades, other scholars have underscored different stripes of reverse migrations, including voyages from the Caribbean, North America, and South America. These returnees settled in Liberia, Sierra Leone, Benin, Togo, Nigeria, and Ghana. Yet these works have not fully explored all the returnee communities. Existing literature often limits its scope to communities that developed in Benin, Togo, and Nigeria, underplaying other viable aspects tied to Ghana's

Afro-Brazilian history. The study of returnees' arrival in West Africa from the end of the nineteenth century provides insights and reveals the levels of acculturation or assimilation in their new and former places of settlement. In the case of Ghana, the Brazilian presence had an impact socially and culturally in Gã *mãŋ* (Gã state). Other scholars have also acknowledged the Brazilian presence and its religious significance to Ghanaians' history. For example, in *Making the Town: Ga State and Society in Early Colonial Accra*, British historian John Parker asserts that "these ex-slaves and their descendants, while retaining a distinct identity based largely on the continuing adherence to Islam, became recognized as a part of Gã community."[9]

In general, migrations to Accra were driven by several forces, including commerce, the enslavement of the local people, and the desire to acquire land. The long history of movements to Accra, which became the precolonial capital in 1877, especially Otublohum, an *akutso*, or quarter, of Kinkã, had an intrinsic value to returnees' migration trajectory as well as both coastal and inland Brazilian migrant communities from the 1820s on. In drawing from these parallels, it is vital to underscore how the history of settlements and resettlements in Accra overlapped with existing Gã traditions. For instance, on the Gã side, "it is said that being strangers themselves, the Otublohum people did not hesitate to invite slaves from Brazil who [were] deposited on the coast of Accra to join them."[10] The challenges the returnees encountered and how they negotiated their return culturally, economically, socially, and religiously after their agonizing experiences on Brazilian plantations deserve attention. I categorize the returnee populations into two groups, the coastal and the inland settler communities, to highlight their unique characteristics. Both coastal and inland settler groups did not forget where they had come from, and neither were they interested in remaining in one fixed location. This difference had an impact on their settlement patterns, particularly on the ways in which they reconstructed their identities.

The Significance of Accra to Brazilian Settlement

Several coastal towns in Ghana facilitated commerce, mission work, and Brazilian-African settlements and created cross-cultural interactions and exchanges between foreigners and the local people. Correspondence between Portuguese and British consul officers in Rio de Janeiro and Lagos shows that several Africans who gained their freedom but decided to stay in Brazil found jobs working on merchant ships. *Emillia*, one of these ships, sailed between different ports in Brazil and Lagos using Cape Coast as a stop point for filling their water reservoir. Cape Coast also served as an important trading post.[11] Other ships landed on the coastline of Gã mãŋ, Accra, Elmina, and Winneba, very important European trading posts. Accra meant different things to strangers and migrants who interacted with the area. Europeans in particular benefited from their settlements in Accra as they carried out commercial activities, propagated Christianity, and especially established various colonial posts. One reason the Brazilian-Africans chose Accra as their settlement destination in West Africa was the importance of this location in their memory. While some were convinced that their ancestors were originally captured from the Gold Coast, others chose Accra because they were too old to remain in Brazil.

The availability of land was another driving force. There was plenty of virgin land in the area for the very few people who lived there. A Basel missionary, Henry Wharton, who arrived in June 1845, reported that the population of coastal Accra was about seven thousand.[12] For those who never inherited land in Brazil, they were looking for the opportunity to own land before their demise. Landownership was later tied to the Brazilian-African and Tabom identity. Wharton continued that Accra was "full" of wild animals, including hyenas and pythons, that threatened the lives of humans and animals alike.[13] Other Europeans shared their experiences about Accra and painted a different picture of the area. An 1899 account by H. Debrunner, another Basel missionary, which was published in German in pamphlet form by the Basel Mission in 1954, states,

> We are in Accra, the most important city of the Gold Coast.... There is a lively traffic on the street from Accra to Christianborg. Bicycles, one, two, ten, twenty are ridden by Africans and Europeans. Smart little chariots, drawn by small African horses move up and down the street. People want to enjoy the sea breeze of the evening.... There again is a group of traders... having a cigarette in the corner of the mouth and swinging a stick with silver decorations lazely in their hand.[14]

These two missionary reports bring attention not only to the stark differences in coastal Accra but to the transformation that took place in this area before the turn of the twentieth century. Part of this transformation could be attributed to the changes that occurred after British colonial officials moved the capital of the Gold Coast from Cape Coast to Accra, the new seat of the colonial government in 1877.[15] On the one hand, Wharton's experience emphasized Accra's dangers, which did not present the town as a promising site for settlement. However, ex-slaves from rural Brazil were unlikely to find the wildlife that dominated the landscape of Accra very threatening because of their own interactions with wild animals on sugar or coffee plantations. There is another dimension to the bustling lifestyle of coastal Accra that dominates the second description by Debrunner. His characterization of Accra at the twilight of the nineteenth century draws attention to similar activities that prevailed in some areas in Brazil, especially urban locations where some of the returnees might have lived during their servitude. Debrunner's description also points to fledgling trading activities and entertainments that drew people from diverse class and social backgrounds to coastal Accra. It is likely that returnees, especially the merchants in the upper echelons, found Accra conducive for their environmental, economic, and social needs.

In terms of the trading networks that Debrunner points to, British scholar Robin Law also reveals that the Gold Coast, and Accra in particular, was an important destination for Brazilian returnees mostly because of its potential for trade and settlement.[16] With its coastline ideal for fishing and mercantile activities and the remote, inland region good for farming, these two natural features accommodated the skills of the Brazilian returnees and shaped their historical accounts over time. In Accra, the Brazilians combined commercial activities and an agrarian lifestyle to aid their patterns of settlement and as a means of survival. Transformations that occurred within the coastal and rural communities in the early 1800s were largely influenced by the availability of land and conditions of land tenure. Besides the topography, the breeze from the Atlantic Ocean together with access to a large body of water attracted Europeans and their maritime trading networks, along with migrants and ex-slaves to Otublohum and other major nearby locations such as Osu, a well-known Danish settlement and trading post.[17] Otublohum also has important shrines for the Gã *wulomo* (spiritual leader) and religious priests in Accra. The spiritual and cultural component of the Gã *wulomo* provides a tangent that touches on the formation of Brazilian and Tabom identities. The spiritual elements in Otublohum fostered and influenced the establishment of the Tabom quarter during Brazilians' gradual process of assimilation into local cultures. This integration was done in tandem with mutual engagements between the Brazilians and the Gã mãŋtsɛmɛi, as well as the Brazilians' hostility toward Britain's colonial system for introducing various ordinances that threatened their freedom and landownership.[18]

Accra was an important location in Ghana's history for other reasons. For example, European colonial officials, missionaries, and explorers who visited the Gold Coast in the late nineteenth century had positive things to say about the busy urban center that had transformed gradually from a rural landscape. Around the 1890s, a British colonial official described Accra as "the best provisioned town on the coast" with emphasis on the Ussher Fort area where the first generation of returnees settled.[19] Further, not only was Accra characterized as the "epicenter of an older Gã world,"[20] some who visited this place described Accra as a "sleepy old-fashioned, haphazard sort of place, an ordinary West Coast trading town firmly rooted in the customs and traditions of the past."²¹ Accra would later become the seat of the postindependence Ghanaian government.²²

Accra was not new to European merchants, missionaries, and colonial officials. Due to constant competition between Europeans and Gã leaders for land, commercial monopoly, and revenue collection, coastal Accra was divided into several European districts. The creation of Dutch Accra, English Accra, Danish Accra, and other districts from the eighteenth century ensured some kind of European monopoly over commerce particularly along the coastline. Other districts included the Tabom quarter, a subdivision of Otublohum quarter.²³ In other words, although Accra belonged to the Gã mãŋtsɛmɛi and the Gã mãŋbii (citizens), the constant commercial interactions and exchanges between Europeans and the Gã mãŋtsɛmɛi dating back to the seventeenth century led to some kind of mutual agreement that enabled Europeans to establish trading posts in specific areas along the southeastern coastline.²⁴ Europeans treated these social spaces as their personal property. These demarcations were necessary to maintain a level of peace and to keep strangers and migrants in the area within defined spaces to minimize tension, especially among diverse groups seeking refuge or opportunities there. The returnees made their mark during the early period of settlement but without controversy.

One may wonder how the Europeans perceived the returnees. The Dutch, the British, and the Danes knew about the Brazilian migrations to Accra. They mainly viewed the Brazilians through the lens of slavery and abolition. Governor Edward Carstensen's diary reveals his disdain for slavery. He believed that slavery along the Bight of Benin humiliated and threatened the local people, but he condoned slavery that was perpetuated by the Danes, particularly their plantations in the West Indies. The British were also aware of migrations along the coastal belts of the Bight of Benin and its implications to British colonial projects. Constant correspondence between British colonial officials in the Gold Coast colony and Lord Frederick J. D. Lugard, the British official who designed the system of indirect rule in Nigeria, attest to the pivotal role of colonial Accra to Britain's imperial imagination. Land tenure was a priority to the British. Colonial ordinances, particularly those relating to land tenure, did not make any exceptions or provide any form of immunity: anyone who lived in the Gold Coast colony, including emancipated Brazilians, had to abide by colonial land policies. This affected land the Gã mãŋtsɛmɛi gave to the returnees, "Brazilian land."

The geographical region around Accra, where Gã leaders offered Brazilian-Africans land, was once called the *jwɛiamli* or *koowie* (bush) because it was farther away from *nshɔna* (coastal) areas and towns.²⁵ It is no surprise that most of the descendants left their remote communities in the *jwɛiamli* temporarily or permanently to relocate to the *nshɔna*, where diverse groups settled. They returned immediately because they felt threatened by others who trespassed on Brazilian land.[26] Most Brazilian-Africans who joined the exodus to Accra lived within the coastal population near Swalaba, a collection of households in Otublohum—the two main areas of initial returnee settlement. The cultural significance of Otublohum to early Brazilian-African settlements and the ways in which the town shaped aspects of Brazilian-Africans' history and identities cannot be overemphasized. In some ways, Brazilian-African identities were constructed, expressed, represented, and interpreted around Gã and Otublohum sociocultural norms as well as land tenure. Other returnees established various social networks with residents around business centers in Accra. It was through these processes of intermingling, especially marriage, that the second generation assimilated and eventually became immersed within the broader cultures within Accra, especially the traditions of the Gã people.[27]

The first settlers also married local spouses, especially among the Gã and Akan people. These mutual unions fused local names with Brazilian ones. Some of the names of the returnees were also influenced by their Muslim faith. They included Mahama, Aishatu, and others. However, there is no evidence to suggest that the first generation assimilated into local cultures to the extent their descendants did. There are other interpretations to the choice by Brazilian-Africans of Accra over other locations. Oral traditions establish that the Brazilians were familiar with the coastline of Africa because some of the returnees were captured as slaves from such areas and were determined to return *home*. Some Brazilians who were employed by Portuguese merchants and worked on ships or vessels that sailed across the Atlantic Ocean to Accra shared their experiences about the city. Demand for water-drilling technology and water provisions for ships in coastal Accra also created a need. Some of the returnees joined the exodus to Accra in the mid-1800s because of their interest in contributing to the improvement of the water quality in the area. Poor water and sanitation conditions in Accra during this period, particularly the health crisis they created, buttress this argument.

WAVES OF MIGRATION, TIME OF ARRIVAL, AND RETURNEE POPULATION

There were numerous reverse migrations from either Brazil directly to Accra or after a temporary stop in locations such as Lagos, Whydah, and others along the Bight of Benin. Unlike reverse migrations from various ports in Brazil to the Bight of Benin from the nineteenth century that are easy to trace in archives such as the National Archives at Kew, it is problematic to trace settlements from Brazil to Accra. Various explanations about the waves of migration exist, with the number of waves of migration fluctuating between two and four.[28] Parker attributes the migrations in part to efforts by the returnees to spread Islam. Roger Gocking's analysis, on the other hand, offers useful insight but shifts to another dominant faith, Christianity. According to Gocking,

> The second wave of Brazilians who came in the 1840s and 1860s were from a more privileged strata of Brazilian society. Most of them were Christians, and they entered Accra primarily as merchants. . . . They intermarried with other members of this elite, and their children branched out into occupations other than trading. . . . The Ribeiros married into the Cleland family, a prominent Accra family, and also into the family of the famous Methodist missionary Thomas Birch Freeman.[29]

For my analysis of the timing of arrivals, I focus on three closely related documents at the Public Records and Archives Administration Department (PRAAD) in chronological order.[30] They are mainly from the land disputes in British colonial courts. The first, a testimony by Isaac Cobblah Fiscian, a Tabom, does not say where his grandfather originated from in Brazil or the age of his parents, but it shows that "the late Aruna was one of the Brazilians who migrated to the Gold Coast in or about 1826."[31] The second confirms the 1830s time frame by relating that "it appears that as far back as the thirties [1830s] a ship load of Africans were landed from Brazil."[32] The third provides more details about the returnees. In it, Chief Nelson notes that "sometime in the year 1836, Brazilians landed in Accra. They came in one cargo ship . . . there were seven elders among them namely Mama Sokoto and others." He continues by saying by the Gã king Komeh I gave them land, which "remained the property of the Brazilian community."[33] It is believed that these early settlers received a vast area of land that remained the property of the Brazilian community as a whole and was not deeded to individuals. Part of the court land disputes I have discussed in this book challenged this notion of gifts of land to the community rather than to individuals.

With respect to the time line of slave rebellions in Brazil and the returnees' arrival in the Gold Coast, the documents do not say whether the last group returned after the 1835 revolts in Bahia, Brazil, a year earlier.[34] It is likely that a great portion of the returnees relocated around this time. In addition to archival information about the key dates 1826, the 1830s, and 1836, these three records also provide evidence that freed slaves embarked on a cargo ship to Ghana. Furthermore, their unique characteristics inform us about the complexity of the voyages to Accra, as well as land tenure and land distribution practices there. Most important, these archival documents mention the names of the elders, leaders, and other travelers who arrived at different times. These names are useful for exploring the different family groups that constitute the

"Brazilian family tree"—the "original" settler group of returnees in the early 1800s.[35] The various names they brought from Brazil and the ones they took on in Accra also contribute to the reconstruction of a "Tabom family tree" in the formative years of the second generation from the early 1900s. Due to scanty information in the archives about this subject, it is difficult to quantify the number of returnees from one generation to the next.

Ghanaian historian Samuel Quarcoopome, one of the early scholars who tackled this subject, posits that the migrations began in the 1830s.[36] Another Ghanaian historian, Samuel Boadi-Siaw, suggest that their settlements were established between 1829 and 1836, but does not explain how many waves of migration there were.[37] The joint work of Alcione M. Amos, a Brazilian, and Ebenezer Ayesu, a Ghanaian, mainly draws on these two prior scholars. Unlike Quarcoopome and Boadi-Siaw, Amos and Ayesu include the migration of another Brazilian family, the Costas, to Accra in 1838.[38] Marco Aurelio Schaumloeffel, a former Brazilian language instructor at the Ghana Institute of Languages and a former staff member at the Brazilian embassy in Accra, also draws on the work of these scholars.[39] These varying dates have influenced and complicated statistics about the population of the early settlers. Brazilian-Africans may have followed additional, different migration pathways that are as yet unknown. Although it is established that they arrived during a tumultuous period in the history of Accra, as Gã leaders fought with other local groups and later with Europeans for power and territory,[40] there is no substantial evidence that points to the returnees' involvement in these conflicts. Also, there is no proof that the Brazilians fought with other groups in the Gold Coast, probably owing to their small population size.

Contestation over the Population of Brazilians in Gã Mãshi

Brazilian migrations to Ghana spanned a wide period approximately between the early nineteenth century and the turn of the twentieth century. Although it is feasible to create a rudimentary ancestral tree for these groups, it is not easy to quantify with any certainty the actual population of Brazilian-Africans and their ancestors. Part of the reason is that the Brazilian-African diaspora in Accra is not a homogeneous community. In order words, the spontaneous journeys make it difficult to tabulate the exact number of travelers. The Tabom are unsure of the exact number of returnees who established settlements in Accra. The various family stories and lineage serves as a starting point for a projection.

Dissonance of memory and inconsistency in tracing the trajectories of reverse migrations resonated in other facets of the Brazilian-African diaspora. For those who settled in the Gold Coast the population size of the original settler group is relative; it depends on whom you talk to and what they know about their past, or on which historical data and oral tradition you choose to consider. Accounts of the early settlers range between five, six, or more family groups. Some relevant findings at PRAAD show that the actual group of people who arrived between 1830 and 1835 was six or more families, but they include no mention of how many other people accompanied each family group. Three of these archival documents help underscore the complexities of identifying the exact number of settlers in Accra. In the first document, Fiscian argues that his grandparents arrived in 1826.[41] Another show that they arrived on a ship but does not say who was on board or how many individuals there were. It does, however, state that these returnees received gifts of land. In addition, there were seven elders including Mama Sokoto. Unlike Nelson's court testimony that points to seven elders, Fiscian highlights Aruna, one of his ancestors. Scholars who have examined Dutch and Danish records are also uncertain about the population of the ex-salves. W. F. G. Derx—a Dutch official at Elmina, a bookkeeper, and a judicial officer—was vague in one of his reports to the Dutch parliamentary commission, which was created in 1853. According to Derx, "under our possessions [on the coast], we can point to few manumitted [slaves], outside of a community of perhaps *forty* persons of both sexes with their children at *Accra*, which people arrived from Brazil, and were granted permission to settle at that place. They had purchased their freedom using their own resources."[42] Clearly, such records also leave gaps in our reconstruction of the early Brazilian population, but they show that the Brazilians arrived on different ships at different times with different vision.

It has not been easy looking for archival documents about the population that arrived in the Gold Coast. However, there are various statistics about returnees who settled in Lagos and other areas. Local and colonial newspapers in Lagos, especially the *Lagos Times*, *Lagos Standard*, and the *Weekly Times*, provided broad coverage that chronicled the arrivals of the ex-slaves.

The newspaper coverage also highlighted other aspects of their stories including the ships they boarded in Brazil, the health conditions of those on board, marriage ceremonies between the returnees and other returnees or with local people, religious ceremonies and rituals within their new communities, and announcements about obituaries and burial services. For instance the *Lagos Times* announced the death of one returnee, M. J. de Santa, a merchant who traveled on a ship known as *Africano* but died on his way back to Lagos after his honeymoon in Brazil.[43] The store owners and merchants advertised their goods while they also reported burglary and thefts to warn other store owners of what to expect from their customers. Other newspaper announcements reminded the returnees of ceremonies to celebrate Brazilian emperor Don Pedro II's birthday. Statistics provided by Sir John Glover, a British abolitionist, regarding liberated Africans who settled in Lagos between 1871 and 1886 were also printed.[44] The data included here is limited in many ways, but they provide important information useful for my analysis.

The problem is not only about not knowing how many returnees arrived in Ghana. Uncertainty also exists around how many Tabom people there are in Ghana. Although the Tabom communities grew in size from the early 1900s after the demise of most of the early settlers, it is difficult to determine their exact number. One reason is that not all descendants identify with the Brazilian story or heritage; many basically do not know exactly where in Africa they were captured and when they arrived in the Gold Coast as well as where their parents lived in Brazil.[45] Thus there remains uncertainty about the size of the descendant population today. The Tabom chief Nii Azumah V, while acknowledging that the actual population of the Tabom people today is not known, suggests that approximately two million people are descendants of Afro-Brazilian slaves in Ghana.[46] Intermarriages between the local people and the first generation and improper documentation by the Ghana Statistics Service have complicated the matter. The number provided by the Tabom chief could be less because the Gã people, the ethnic group that welcomed the ex-slaves in the Gold Coast, comprise 8 percent of the current population of Ghana. Since the Tabom community forms a fraction of the Gã population, my conclusion is that their current number is around five hundred thousand. In my assessment, based on archival documents examined so far, there were about six hundred to seven hundred Brazilian returnees in Accra by the end of the 1800s. Part of my analysis is also drawn from existing statistics covering the precolonial eras. First, the population of Accra in the precolonial era is inconsistent; second, other factors for this estimate are based on evidence of polygamous marriage practices among the returnees. To provide additional insight, a number of the descendants rely heavily on the expression *wɔ wokumɛi fa*, a popular phrase in the Gã language that translates as "our ancestors or the branches of our family tree are uncountable."

WƆ WOKUMƐI FA

The *wɔ wokumɛi fa* expression characterizes the difficulty in quantifying the number of returnees in the nineteenth century. In addition, the number and names of the original settlers are relative; they depend on which family group you talk to and what they know about their past. Sometimes the number is exaggerated by people in Accra who claim they are of Brazilian descent to showcase the significance of the Brazilian presence and how they are connected to this history. Unfortunately, there is conflicting information about the number of Brazilians who were given Gã stool land in Accra after their arrival in the early 1830s. Narratives about the acquisition of land and the activities of Brazilian farmers, however, do not offer any concrete information about the size of these returnee groups. In addition, the descendants are unsure of the precise number of Brazilians who established their communities in Accra over time. As in the case of some other population groups with distant ties to the past and faint knowledge about their ancestral roots, the social lives of their descendants were shaped more by their environments and the conditions into which they were born and raised in the Gold Coast than by their distant heritage.

Although oral traditions and the interviews I have conducted have not provided simple answers to the inquiry regarding the number of Brazilians who migrated to the Gold Coast in the early 1800s, more information may yet be derived from the sources at PRAAD. The following names provide some knowledge of the early settlers: Mama Nassu, Aruna, Maslini, Nakpala, Damburka, and Abdulamu.[47] Nonetheless, very few family groups have established their ties to the early settlers. A good number of them have no knowledge about the origins of their Brazilian heritage. Another court case, *Peter Quarshie Fiscian v. Nii Azumah III*, between two descendants provides a list of a different group of returnees.[48]

Reciprocal Exchanges: Gã Stool Land for the Newcomers and Gifts from the Brazilians

The precise population and the number of ships that transported the freed slaves to the Gold Coast might never be known, but there is some certainty about other aspects of their story. Brazilian-Africans' identity construction or reconstruction was influenced in part by an attempt to turn their former oppressive conditions in Brazil into a more promising future. Their determination to succeed was not only shaped by fantasy about a home in West Africa or by motivations to join tentative exoduses to Accra after first settling in Lagos. Key aspects of their identities and those of their descendants were shaped by landownership. A number of works have shown the significance of land in Ghana from the precolonial era especially to strangers and migrants. In Accra, land tenure was often linked to the accumulation of wealth and territory. This created competition between migrants, immigrants, missionaries, colonial rulers, and other interested parties who contested fiercely for power and economic control.

Accra in particular and the Gold Coast in general have had a long history of European settlements and fierce competition that drew different groups together and pushed others apart. Gã leaders long contested with European powers, beginning with the Portuguese in the fifteenth century and including the British, Swedes, and Danes, for control over land and trading posts, especially along the coastline.[49] Colonial documents also demonstrate that land tenure in Ghana was not only tied to chieftaincy, inheritance, and colonial ventures. Access to land in some ways guaranteed one's social, economic, and political power at a given point in time. As former slaves, a portion of the returnee population, especially those who did not have any means of acquiring land in Brazil, had a strong desire to do so in Ghana. Those who had farming skills were determined to put the talents they cultivated on Brazilian plantations to good use. This was similar to what their ancestors had done, in reverse, when they preserved their skills, cultures, languages, and religious faith in order to survive the harsh life of plantation or urban slavery in Brazil.[50] There is no single answer to explain what motivated Gã *Mãŋtsɛ* Tackie Komeh I to offer such a vast area of land to the Brazilian returnees. On the one hand, it is believed that Gã leaders gave returnees Gã stool land because they were convinced the ex-slaves were members of the Gã population who had been sent into bondage in exile—involuntarily. On the other hand, court testimonies by descendants show that *Mãŋtsɛ* Komeh I provided the land as a gesture of good will and friendship between the local people and the Brazilians to stabilize the base of the Brazilian-African diaspora in Accra. A reference by Elder George Nii Aruna Nelson and evidence that was provided by plaintiffs and defendants in various court cases between 1885 and 1964 establish that the land was located around Fonafor Valley and Akwandor—which is part of modern-day central Accra near Accra Polytechnic, the Examination Council of Ghana, the National Archives of Ghana (now PRAAD), Tudu, Adabraka, and part of the Accra-Nsawam Road around Kwame Nkrumah Circle.[51] Still others have drawn attention to a gift of land that the Brazilians received from Ashong Djamawoh, the Korle spiritual leader of a small coastal town in Accra.[52] There is insufficient evidence to support the Djamawoh story.

Cultural factors provide a lens for explaining how gifts were exchanged in the past. The Gã people had a long history of providing hospitality to *gbɔi* (strangers), *nyanyemɛi* (friends), and even their *henyɛloi* (enemies). Returnees in particular were at the right place at the right time to benefit from this long-held Gã tradition. Besides cultural factors, other social traditions contributed to this exchange. For instance, interactions between the Gã people and foreigners in the area resulted in mutual exchanges, such as barter trading. Barter trade between inland communities and coastal

Chapter Two

dwellers consisted mostly of the exchange of rubber, cocoa, and palm oil from the inland people for umbrellas, caps, lamps, kerosene, and other goods from the coastal group.[53] The hospitality the Gã mãŋtsɛmɛi gave to the freed slaves was influenced by a number of factors. Brazilian merchants who crossed paths with the Gã *mãŋtsɛ* and the Gã *mɛi* (Ga people) established mutual friendships that included reciprocal gifts. Court documents at PRAAD provide insight into the lives of the first generation and clearly show the exact exchanges between the Brazilian returnees and the Gã mãŋtsɛmɛi. However, the dates of the exchanges are not known. The giving of gifts that were exchanged between the two groups was based on mutual understanding and interests. Like Gã *Mãŋtsɛ* Komeh I and Gã traditions, the Brazilians had a custom for showing appreciation, *apreciação*, for good deeds. They did not speak Gã fluently, or probably could not say a word in Gã, but they improvised somehow. In addition to the generosity that the Gã *mãŋtsɛ* bestowed on the returnees, the Brazilians also presented gifts in order to reciprocate the Gã leaders' generosity. According to a court account, the Brazilians "gave presents of brass calabashes, copper calabashes, clock and drinks."[54] The Gã people were familiar with calabash, which are often made from a plant. A calabash is used as a drinking cup and for pouring libations (a traditional ritual). What is striking about the gifts from the Brazilians is the kind of calabash they offered to the Gã leaders. Perhaps the Gã leaders appreciated this gift even more because of the decorative ornamentation or the materials that were used to coat the calabashes. One could assume that the Gã leaders could not resist accepting the clock and the drinks in addition to the calabashes because of their "foreign" appearance. However, this may not be the case considering the long history of contacts between the Gã people and Europeans, especially after centuries of cross-cultural interactions and exchanges along the coast. Land was indeed an important asset for the freed slaves, but other possible opportunities existed for stabilizing the Brazilian-African diaspora in Accra.

The second major gift of resources to the Brazilians besides land was the opportunity Gã *Mãŋtsɛ* Komeh I extended to the newcomers to select their own leaders as Brazilian mãŋtsɛmɛi. The Gã word *mãŋtsɛ* also means "owner of a community"; hence, besides taking on a leadership role, Brazilian returnees received authority and responsibility to manage their own sociocultural affairs. This title enhanced Brazilian-Tabom and Gã norms both historically and culturally.

The leaders of Accra who had a long history of interactions with strangers and migrants who visited or settled in their communities were familiar with the complexity associated with the settlement process of newcomers to their vicinity. They therefore saw the need to encourage the ex-slaves to put various leadership structures in place to facilitate settlement. The freed slaves from Brazil were the only newcomers in Accra who got such special treatment. It is against this backdrop that the titles of "Brazilian chief" and, later, "Tabom chief" were initiated or created within the Brazilian-African diaspora in Gã *mãŋ* from 1836.

WHY AND HOW THE BRAZILIANS BECAME CHIEFS: THE TABOM QUARTER AT OTUBLOHUM

Narratives about the formation of the Brazilian-African diaspora in Ghana did not develop in isolation. Part of their story was influenced by local cultural practices after Gã leaders offered them land for settlement. The role of Brazilian chiefs was supposed to establish a point of reference for unifying the community of returnees to facilitate the process of settlement. However, in the end, it created tension among various family groups who either did not see any need to unite or did not desire to share social space with other returnees, or who were not offered land in Accra, or who were denied the opportunity to select members of their own groups as leaders of the Brazilian-African diaspora. The main reason for the initiation of the first Brazilian chief, Nii Azumah I, who reigned from 1836 to 1865, was to solidify the friendship that developed between the returnees and the Gã leaders and to forge future ties. Another goal was to provide a forum to help the Brazilian colony assimilate gradually into Gã cultural systems and to bridge the gap between Gã people and the Brazilians, especially to encourage the returnees' participation in *homowo* festivals. *Homowo* celebrations unite the Gã people and their neighbors, so it was expected that such cultural festivities could help create similar bonds with the Brazilian-African returnees who had made the Gold Coast their new home.

Although the Brazilian-Africans made great strides in their transition into a new culture and environment, it was their reception by the Gã mãŋtsɛmɛi that made life much easier. For instance, the initiation of Brazilian chiefs and gifts of land to the Brazilian returnees convinced them that they could settle permanently in Accra. This strategy also opened doors for other waves of Brazilian migrants to the area by the 1860s. Despite the generous gifts granted to the Brazilians, the returnees' memories were still plagued by the horrific experiences they endured as slaves in Brazil. And when the British colonial systems emerged in the Gold Coast, they perceived a major threat to their freedom. Because of their small population size, which was somewhere around one hundred by the mid-1800s, and the language barriers they faced, the first generation of returnees encountered limitations as they interacted and negotiated with the local Gã people. The influence of the returnees was thus lessened, but they

Chapter Two

made various contributions via their agrarian communities and were able to forge ties with various Gã leaders when it came to rebelling against the colonial system. The returnees' involvement in the uprising after the Compulsory Labour Ordinance of 1897 was introduced marked a significant turning point in Ghanaian history in terms of Brazilian-Gã anticolonial nationalism. There is no trace of this in the existing historiography, however.

Gã *Mãŋtsɛ* Komeh I gave the Brazilians land mainly for settlement, to enable them to continue their farming traditions, and for sustenance. In this way, and with parcels of land on the side, the Brazilian-Africans became convinced that they could make a new home in Accra. Another objective for the selection of the returnees as chiefs was to place them in positions of authority so they could attract more Brazilian-Africans along the Bight of Benin to resettle in Accra, to invest in the economy for revenue purposes, and to create diverse Brazilian-African communities—a kind of "melting pot" of returnees in Gã *mãŋ*. This strategy opened doors for other Brazilian-African migratory waves as additional freed slaves moved to become part of the diaspora in the Gold Coast in the late nineteenth century. Brazilian merchants also joined the bandwagon hoping to accumulate wealth. The constant traffic and travel routes back and forth between Lagos and Accra solidified *Mãŋtsɛ* Komeh I's vision of a cosmopolitan town. This innovative idea, which fit well into the dreams of the freed slaves, attracted them to a place where they were free to use their skills and practice their varying religions.

The vision of the Gã *Mãŋtsɛ* Komeh I, who sought to tap the skills and wealth of the merchants among them who had experience trading between the Bight of Benin and areas in Brazil after emancipation, had a broad, lasting impact. British colonial officials were aware of the relevance of this transatlantic commerce, which is why they also expedited the abolition process to benefit from these dynamic commercial routes. Other scholars have revealed the significance of these trading activities to the history of both abolition and British colonial conquest in West Africa.[55] Komeh I's vision to improve his town by drawing from the expertise of the returnees shaped other developments including the expansion of Accra from a rural to a cosmopolitan town.[56] This strategy was replicated by Ghanaian leaders more than a century later in mobilizing diasporan Africans and their resources. The adoption of this scheme, which began during the administration of Kwame Nkrumah, Ghana's first president, and continued into the twenty-first century, attracted a large number of African Americans and Afro-Caribbeans who invested heavily in annual diaspora festivals such as the Pan-African Historical Theatre Festival (PANAFEST) and Emancipation Day celebrations (table 1). The Ministry of Tourism and Diasporan Relations, for instance, was created to serve the needs of diasporan Africans and expatriates who have relocated to Ghana.[57] Local and foreign media outlets have given substantial coverage to this vibrant development

Table 1. Selected newspaper coverage of PANAFEST and Emancipation Day celebrations

NEWSPAPER	TITLE OF NEWSPAPER ARTICLE	DATE OF PUBLICATION
		2001
Ghanaian Times	"5th Panafest Emancipation Launched"	10 July, p. 1
Spectator	"Panafest Enhancing Pan-African Ideals"	6 July, p. 8
	"Panafest—A Global Fraternity of Culture and the Past"	6 July, p. 8
	"Pan Africanist Poetry on Ghana Launched"	6 July, p. 8
		2002
Spectator	"Ghana Marks Emancipation Day"	31 July, p. 17
	"Slavery Days Remembered"	3 August, p. 3
Mirror	"Panafest Fever Grips Cape Coast"	30 July, p. 27
	"Calypso King at Dubois Anniversary"	30 July, p. 27
		2003
Times	"Emancipation Day Is Here Again"	26 July, p. 5
Mirror	"Panellists from Cape Coast Express Views on . . . Panafest and Emancipation Celebration"	2 August, p. 29
		2004
Times	"Emancipation Day Celebrations—Bridging the Gap between Africans at Home and those in the Diaspora"	5 July, p. 1
	"Emancipation Day to Cover All Slave Routes"	10 July, p. 12
		2005
Times	"Ghana, Jamaica to Build on Historical Ties"	15 July, pp. 1, 3
No issue		**2006–2007**
		2008
Times	"President Participates in Emancipation Carnival"	4 August, p. 1
		2009
Times	"A Visit to Manso Ancestral River"	3 August, p. 1
	"Nkrumah Centenary Special . . . 100 Years Ago Today"	21 September, p. 1
	"Let's Go Back to Study Nkrumah's Manifesto"	21 September, p. 21
Spectator	"Public Holiday to Honour Nkrumah: Is It Worth Celebrating?"	26 September, p. 23
No issue		**2010**
		2011
Graphic	"Time for Africans to Mobilise against Diseases, Hunger and Poverty—Veep Says at Launch of PANAFEST"	26 July, p. 33
	"Africa Must Unite—to Give Life to Nkrumah's Vision"	22 September, p. 1
No issue		**2012**
		2013
Mirror	"Sketches Herald Panafest—AU Celebrations"	27 July, p. 1

that has enhanced the history of diasporan communities in Ghana. In the end, it has lit a new path for engaging in a broader global conversation. This tradition continues in Ghana as local chiefs and queens also find creative avenues including the provision of varying incentives to attract diasporan Africans to Ghana.[58]

Mãŋtsɛ Komeh I's strategy, which was implemented from 1836, also proved useful to the British. Basel missionaries from Switzerland and Germany who began Christian evangelism in the Gold Coast had a similar approach to British officials, as Basel missionaries also invited Caribbean blacks to the Gold Coast in the mid-1800s to promote a similar agenda.[59] In fact, it is similar to practices by local chiefs in the past. Since the 1980s, local chiefs have depended on this strategy to create varying enabling environments to promote tourism for revenue purposes and to provide jobs at various locales.[60] In reverse, the inflow and outflow of returnees as well as the publicity they generated has gained a great deal of attention from the current Brazilian-African leader, Nii Azumah V, and the Brazilian embassy in Accra and contributed to the opening of Brazil House for tourism.

The fact that Gã mãŋtsɛmɛi had an enormous impact on their communities and on gbɔi alike posed a threat to British imperial projects. The British colonial authorities regulated the power of the Gã leaders and interfered with traditional customs in the area, which stifled the influence of the Gã leaders for a while. British restrictions thus weakened these leaders, making Brazilian-African chiefs all but invisible in broader Gã society. This had a ripple effect on Gã-Brazilian and British relations. Despite the stern restrictions, Brazilian-African chiefs were able to work closely with Gã leaders to anchor their freedom and protect their inheritance. Not all strangers or migrants who visited or relocated in coastal Accra were offered this hospitality and opportunity to flourish. The Brazilian returnees were the only migrant group from the New World who became part of the Gã paramountcy, or traditional council, later in the nineteenth century. These returnees were offered social and cultural space in which to operate, and they managed the affairs of the Tabom quarter with the assistance of Gã leaders. This created an opportunity for the returnees and their children to practice the farming and irrigation techniques they brought with them, refashion their identity, and follow their diverse religious observances. In the end, they were able to establish a vibrant presence in Gã *mãŋ*, beginning in the Tabom quarter, the epicenter of the Brazilian-African diaspora.

The opportunity the freed slaves were granted enabled them to make their own decisions about how to manage their affairs. During the early stages, they sought to promote their interests and sustain their Brazilian lifestyle within this diaspora enclave. Their acceptance into the area and their settlements were influenced mainly by the history of the descendants of the Gã and the Akwamu people who had earlier gained similar attention in that location when they sought sanctuary during warfare in their territories. Other foreign groups in the area included the Alata people, who are believed to be from Yorubaland in Nigeria. Yoruba migrants, traders in particular, had a long history of settling along the coastline of what became the Gold Coast colony in the early 1800s before the arrival of the returnees from Brazil, but none of these migrant groups had a quarter named after them as in the case of the Brazilians. There is limited documentation about the Tabom quarter, but oral history can supplement this scarcity. This drawback may be attributed to the small spatial area they occupied in Accra as well as their small population size in the early settlement period. However, it is likely that the returnees had a special place in the heart of Chief Kwaku Ankrah, the Otublohum leader who introduced the early settlers to the Gã *Mãŋtsɛ*, Komeh I, in the mid-1800s. It was after this important meeting that they had the opportunity to select their own leaders.

One cannot properly examine the history of Brazilian-Africans in Ghana, especially the selection of Brazilians as chiefs, without exploring how they intertwined with Gã cultural institutions and British colonial rule. Indeed, the role of the Brazilians in Gã society, which evolved as a result of the friendships between leaders of the Brazilians and Gã *mãnstɛmɛi*, left an enduring mark. This association also served as an important feature of the Brazilian-African diaspora in Accra as its population also encountered negative aspects of British imperialism, such as land exploitation and racism. The Gã paramountcy, which has roots in Akan cultural traditions and systems of governance, shares a number of things in common with the Brazilian-Africans' story. For example, culturally Gã mãŋtsɛmɛi are selected by the *dzase*, a group of elders who assist the king or chief during his tenure in office. Gã leaders are selected mainly through their family lineage. Gã customs allow succession from different lines—a kind of rotation that stretches across the length and breadth of different wings of the Gã paramountcy.[61] The procedures for appointing Brazilian chiefs and Gã chiefs follow a similar cultural pattern, except that Brazilian chiefs come from only one family line, the Nelson *we* (family). According to *Mãŋtse* Nii Azumah V, the current Tabom chief, these directives are sacred rules that were laid down by their ancestors and therefore will remain unchanged.

Another bifurcation within the Gã-Brazilian chieftaincy traditions is the level of freedom Brazilian or Tabom chiefs enjoyed during the precolonial period. Prior to British rule, the Gã people selected their leaders without the interference of Europeans. However, from the mid-1800s the British Crown demanded advance notification before Gã people were allowed to congregate to select a chief. Without the rubber stamp of the British, the work of *dzase* did not amount to anything; they could select anyone they wanted to lead them, but the British had the last word. Brazilian or Tabom chiefs were beyond the reach of colonial monitoring systems. Indeed, as Gã leaders, Brazilian chiefs also remained on the periphery. In some ways, the selection of Brazilian chiefs did not go through the same level of scrutiny as the selection of Gã mãŋtsɛmɛi.[62] The British monitored the selection of new Gã leaders in order to undermine any attempts to select radical citizens who might plot against the colonial apparatus.

In terms of *homowo* cultural celebrations, colonial censorship affected both the Gã people and the Brazilians. Also, the Gã people and the Brazilians shared other things in common during these festivities. The mãŋtsɛmɛi in both constituencies performed similar rituals: they were accompanied by the elders of the royal palace; they dressed in white clothes and warlike attire; they ate the same kind of food for the festivities, *kpokpoi/kpokple* (corn meal cooked with red oil); and they made merry with drumming and dancing in major streets in Accra. These two groups share other cultural things in common. When Brazilian chiefs were selected, they would go through the same cultural purifications—being confined in a room for a number of days to prepare them to inherit the stool, the traditional throne of a Tabom *mãŋtsɛ* (or in the Western sense, the crown).[63] The Tabom people have adopted both Gã and Akan names because of their long history with intermarriages—Brazilian-Gã-Akan unions as well as assimilation with other migrant communities, including the Yoruba traders and merchants who settled along the coastlines of Accra. By and large, Tabom customs were deeply entrenched in broader Gã traditions; they interlocked on many levels.

Other forms of exchanges between the ex-slaves, the Tabom and Gã mãŋtsɛmɛi as well as the social history of Accra shaped their history and identity over time. For instance, the initial show of hospitality by the Gã *mãŋtsɛ* in conveying a vast area of land and the selection of Brazilians and their descendants as chiefs enabled returnees to preserve a Brazilian-African diaspora for a long period of time. They created new communities and identities to contest with others over their inheritance. Most important, they became property owners in Accra. However, this original generosity came with a price. A number of Brazilians became involved in slavery for domestic use and for monetary gain.[64]

Chapter 3

The Social History of Gã *Mãŋ*: Colonialism and Their Impact on the Brazilian-African Diaspora

Naa, be ko mba;
Oshwila, be ko miiba;
Beni abo ado, dzee nɛkɛ abo ade
Dzeng ko bamba.
Lo, a certain time is coming
Oshwila, a certain civilization is coming
When the world was created, it was not like this
A certain world will come.

—Gã song

The epigraph is a Gã song that characterizes part of the perceptions of the people who lived in Accra. Newcomers to Accra comprised local migrants as well as foreigners—missionaries, colonial officials, merchants and traders from Holland, Denmark, Britain, Syria, Lebanon, and Brazil, among others. Those from Brazil were mainly emancipated Africans who were in search of a new homeland in Gã *mãŋ* at a time when British colonial officials enforced stringent ordinances to regulate and eventually control Gã land. This was characterized as "the systematic and study erosion of African traditions [that] continued as the authority of local kings, chiefs and headmen [were stripped] of their power to govern."[1] During this turbulent time various bills were introduced. The *Gold Coast*

Methodist Times reported on "a Bill intituled an Ordinance to regulate administration of public land and to define certain interest therein."[2]

Gã and Brazilian-African histories are unique in many ways, but they are inseparable and intertwine on many levels.[3] Their interplay provides an insight not only into the ways the social history of Gã *mãŋ* or other historical developments in the area complement aspects of the freed slaves' reverse-migration story, but also into the connections of these narratives to the larger story of British colonial rule from the nineteenth century.

The history of the Gã people connects with the Brazilian returnees' story on many fronts. The social history of the Gã *mãŋ* began in the thirteenth century, whereas the Brazilian-African diaspora in Accra occurred at the dawn of the nineteenth century. Both the Gã people and the liberated Brazilians had a long history of migration and resettlement across West Africa. The Brazilian-African diaspora in Accra emerged within a Gã diaspora that was established about six centuries before the arrival of the freed slaves. Therefore, the history of the Brazilian-African diaspora would be incomplete without an account of its overlap with the general history of Accra and with the histories of multiple migrations, the transatlantic slave trade, abolition, and colonialism in general. These important currents pulled together the history and the destinies of the Gã and the ex-slaves who shaped Atlantic narratives.

Scholars including Kwasi Konadu and Lorenzo D. Turner provide useful information about the Akan and the Gã people, who were among the enslaved Africans taken to the New World. According to Konadu, slaves who were dispersed to St. John after they were captured in the early eighteenth century from their Gã homeland (Accra) participated in slave revolts in the Caribbean.[4] For his part, Turner reveals the life history of Sozenja dos Santos, an ex-slave Brazilian-Gã woman who lived in Bahia in the early 1800s (figure 7). Her parents were from Accra.[5] None of the documents I have come across show any family ties between the members of the Brazilian-African diaspora in Accra and dos Santos. It is possible that none of her family members reconnected with their Gã ancestral roots after their freedom.

The Brazilian-Africans' interactions with authorities in Brazil prior to their voyages back to West Africa and tensions between the Gã people and Europeans in Accra in the precolonial period mutually reinforced each other. Over time, this overlapping development and consciousness set the stage for some kind of alliance between the Gã people and the Brazilians to rebel against the European presence, in particular colonial ordinances. The social history and way of life of the Gã mãŋtsɛmɛi (kings and chiefs of Accra), who became the "owners" of Accra, are entrenched in long-held traditions and customs that required them to render hospitality to both local people and outsiders, most notably to *gbɔi* (strangers, visitors, or guests), especially

Figure 7. Sozenja dos Santos, a Brazilian-Gã from Accra.

new migrants.⁶ However, historical developments among the Gã *mãŋ* or Gã mãŋbii (Gã nation or people), especially their extension of hospitality to newcomers, had consequences. As the Gã mãŋtsɛmɛi offered land to their guests and opened up their doors they became vulnerable as their authority was undermined; enduring cultural systems and traditional practices and the power of Gã leaders were challenged by the European imperialist project. The Gã leaders were not very successful in protecting their territories, cultural traditions, and social institutions especially in the eighteenth and nineteenth centuries. According to John Parker, Accra was never the same after foreign interference shook its cultural foundations and as "Gã townspeople struggled with outside forces and with each other to retain control over the center of their urban civilization."⁷ In the process of extending hospitality to the newcomers, especially Europeans, Gã mãŋtsɛmɛi became victims of the colonial order. "Reclaiming" Accra from the control of outside forces was a daunting task. It required Gã mãŋtsɛmɛi and all Gã mãŋbii both young and old to rise up to defend its territories, land, and other forms of inheritance for posterity.

The critical role of Gã mãŋtsɛmɛi in Gã cultural traditions or affairs is crucial in understanding the lasting effects of colonial rule in Gã societies, particularly how British rule stripped Gã mãŋtsɛmɛi of their power, their responsibility as the rightful leaders of the Gã mãŋbii, their cultural pride, and the opportunity to fulfill their responsibilities to their ancestors and gods without any interference. The cultural symbolism of Gã mãŋtsɛmɛi to the survival of Gã *mãŋ* cannot be over emphasized. The cultural symbolism is embedded deeply in the meaning of their title: "*mãŋtsɛ*" (singular) and "mãŋtsɛmɛi" (plural). Mãŋtsɛmɛi is derived from three words: *mãŋ*, *tsɛ*, and *mɛi*. The Gã word "*mãŋ*" represents the entire community or nation, "*tsɛ*" literally means owner or head, and "*mɛi*" is for a group of people. Put together, the word mãŋtsɛmɛi epitomizes the notion that those who are selected to lead the Gã *mãŋ* are the owners and the heads or leaders of the Gã nation—meaning they had a responsibility to preserve past cultural traditions and continue these norms during their tenure or lifetime. The advent of colonialism made this impossible.

Besides the essence of mãŋtsɛmɛi to the social history of Gã *mãŋ*, the acceptance of *gbɔi* and the inability of the mãŋtsɛmɛi to prevent other guests from settling in their societies also had a lasting impact on the host as well as local migrants, particularly members of the Brazilian-African diaspora in Accra. *Gbɔi* in Gã *mãŋ* often introduced their culture and assimilated into Gã societies in tandem.[8] The hospitality Gã mãŋtsɛmɛi offered to their *gbɔi* is part of a long tradition that was in line with the warm reception their ancestors had enjoyed from the people in the area when they first settled there in the thirteenth century. Based on this history, Gã leaders felt compelled to extend similar generosity and to preserve this rich tradition. In the nineteenth century Gã leaders had no problem extending gracious acceptance to Brazilian-Africans and expatriates from Europe, Asia, and the Middle East as well as to various local migrants, especially the Akwamu people from the mountainous regions in southeastern Ghana and other ethnic groups who moved to their territories to trade and to seek refuge during war.[9] The social history of Accra is significant to this study in numerous ways. First, the Atlantic coastline of Accra was vital for transatlantic commerce, trading networks, missionary ventures, the establishment of colonial posts, and slavery activities.[10] Second, it was a contentious site for enforcing and resisting European imperialist agendas.[11] For the people of Accra and the Gã mãŋtsɛmɛi, although colonial rule interfered with long-held Gã traditions that operated within the local culture, the arrival of the British in particular offered the Gã *mãshi* (nation or Accra proper) an ideal environment for trading and for revenue collection as well as showcasing and sustaining Gã cultural practices side by side with resistance against imperialism.[12] Third, Accra was a perfect place for Brazilian settlements for various reasons. Indeed, a number of liberated Brazilian-Africans including Sozenja dos Santos trace their ancestral origins to this location. Fourth, Brazilian returnees used the complex social and cultural dynamics of Accra to reconstruct their identity. For example, the hospitality *Mãŋtsɛ* Tackie Komeh I (ruled 1826-56) extended to the ex-slaves, which included gifts of land, enabled them to establish the Brazilian-African diaspora, to continue their agrarian practices, and to express their opposition to British land ordinances that demanded Brazilian land for colonial projects.[13] Finally, the returnees viewed this resistance as an extension of their previous revolts against slavery in Brazil. Put differently, the Brazilian returnees saw colonial rule as a threat to their freedom from slavery as well as to the gradual friendships they developed with the Gã people.

The impact of the social history of Accra and colonialism on the Brazilian-African diaspora provides an understanding of mutual exchanges between the two groups. Nineteenth century Gã social history shaped the origins of Brazilian land. The British Crown, on the other hand, was indifferent toward local customs. Colonial land ordinances such as the Public Land Ordinance of 1876, redefined land tenure in terms that served to complicate the matter—especially for land owned by the Gã people or the Gã mãŋtsɛmɛi, including stool land (sacred land for only members of the Gã royal family) and property owned by liberated Brazilians.[14] For the latter group, they included gifts of land former Gã *Mãŋtsɛ* Komeh I gave to the ex-slaves, which became known as "Brazilian land." Furthermore, these overlapping chapters also facilitate our understanding of the complex role of Gã *Mãŋtsɛ* Tackie Tawiah, who ruled from 1862 to 1902. It also reveals contradictions in Gã-Brazilian relations. For instance, in terms of his relationship and interactions with the freed slaves, Gã *Mãŋtsɛ* Tawiah worked side by side with Brazilian chief João Antonio Nelson, who led the Brazilian-African diaspora from 1856 to 1900, during the process of assimilation and as the freed slaves resisted colonial rule. Gã *Mãŋtsɛ* Tawiah later appeared in colonial court to challenge members of the Brazilian-African diaspora over the boundaries of Brazilian land and Gã stool land.[15]

Several literatures about the impact of colonial rule, the enforcement of ordinances, new judiciary systems, and resistance to changes in landownership provide important insight about resistance. The creation of new judiciary systems sought to set the tone for new power relations between the colonizer and the colonized population. For instance, British officials' creation of the supreme court in 1853 sought to undermine existing systems of authority. This was resisted on many fronts. Public agitation led to widespread protests and made colonial subjects more conscious of the effects of colonial rule. This compelled a number of the elite to engage in public debates, and in doing so it created new awareness about the systematic erosions of the authority of Gã mãŋtsɛmɛi. Some of the criticism was visible in newspapers such as the *Gold Coast Chronicle*. These reports characterized the waning powers of the leaders and the rate at which colonial intrusion threatened their future survival. They described this as "wholesale confiscation of the lands and the chiefs and the people [as well as] a wholesale subversion of all their ancient rights."[16]

According to Mary McCarthy, the supreme court basically applied

> the principles of British law only without reference to the Native law. . . . It was not long before Africans [and their leaders] were summoned to the Supreme Court and tried under the basis of British law. . . . The systematic and study erosion of African traditions continued as the authority of local kings, chiefs and headmen [were stripped] of their power to govern.[17]

Maintaining and sustaining a traditional lifestyle, cultural practices, and norms that were passed on from one generation to the next was not an easy task. If anyone in the Gold Coast colony was frustrated by the threat that European colonists posed and by the ordinances that characterized their presence, it was the kings, queen mothers, and chiefs who had a divine obligation to protect the land and the customs their ancestors had passed down to them. In Accra,

> The chiefs were also unhappy about the extent to which the ordinances empowered the [colonial] government to interfere in their affairs. . . . There was dissatisfaction and confusion about the legal position of chiefs vis-à-vis the government, about the customary position of the Head of the paramount chiefs and the minor chiefs . . . and about the de facto position of the educated elite with its self-appointed responsibility to assume leadership.[18]

Gã mãŋtsɛmɛi and other local leaders could not find any easy formula and solution for containing the threat of colonial rule. However, there was no indication that the Gã *mãŋ* compromised their values and beliefs under British colonial rule especially in the nineteenth century. The people of Accra did not surrender. A common adage among the Gã mãŋbii was "Gã nyo ekpakpa dzi mŋni enŋ kɛ ha amãŋ"—meaning a true Gã citizen is the individual who is patriotic and fights to defend his community and culture. In other words, "to fight in defense of the town (*mãŋ*) was a vital element in the process of becoming Gã."[19] The Gã mãŋbii in general were committed to these nationalist ideals. The Brazilian-African returnees who were welcomed to Accra valued and respected the Gã people's determination to protect their heritage. In fact, the founding fathers and mothers of the Brazilian-African diaspora in Accra took a similar position to preserve their Brazilian-Portuguese identity in areas of language, in the way they dressed, and in how they preserved their religious faith, whether Christian or

Muslim.[20] In this respect, it is important to add that the ex-slaves did not subscribe to or show any commitment to Gã cultural norms during their early days of settlement, but this changed somewhat when British colonial rule threatened landowning members of this diaspora group. Basically, the freed Brazilians showed some allegiance to the Gã *mãŋ* when it served their self-interest.

For the liberated Brazilians, their understanding and interpretation of land tenure differed from that of the Gã mãŋbii and Gã *Mãŋtsɛ* Tawiah. While the ex-slaves were committed to the idea of challenging colonial land ordinances, they were mainly occupied by the need to preserve Brazilian land. In other words, while challenging British officials' intrusion on their family properties, they resisted pressure from Gã *Mãŋtsɛ* Tawiah who later claimed it was wrong for his predecessor, Gã *Mãŋtsɛ* Komeh I, to give out sacred Gã stool land. The Brazilians also prevented trespassers from their land. They did so while also self-confidently protecting their Brazilian identity, especially during the early stages of their settlement in Accra in the nineteenth century, and negotiating their new dual identity as Africans—that is, Brazilian-Africans.

NIGBƐ GÃ MƐI JƐ? THE ORIGINS OF THE GÃ PEOPLE AND THE GÃ DIASPORA

Prior to the development of the Brazilian-African diaspora there was a vast open savannah that later became known as "Gã" or Accra. The Akan people in Ghana call this area *nkrang*. In fact, the name "Gã" was coined from *loebii*, a Gã word for a large army of ants. Since *gã* is a category of ants, the word was used to describe the migrations of the ancestors of the Gã people to the coastal area that became one of the epicenters of precolonial commerce, the capital of the Gold Coast in 1877, and an area of modern Ghanaian urban sprawl. In that sense, Gã or *gã gã*—the mobility of ants—was synonymous with the exodus of a large body of people who relocated individually or in groups to Accra.[21] This name was introduced by the early people in the area to describe the first migrations of the Gã people to the coastline sometime between the twelfth and thirteenth centuries.[22] In modern terms, the sociopolitical, cultural, and economic dynamics of Accra could be characterized as a melting pot because of the kinds of people attracted to it in the past and those the city continues to attract to the area, the cross-cultural interactions and exchanges it generates, as well as the various activities that bring various cultures in the area together.

Gã has other meanings. The Gã mãŋbii, or people, are a coastal minority ethnic group in southern Ghana who speak a language called Gã. From the sixteenth century

Chapter Three

on, the Gã people depended on the sea and the coastal land as a meeting point with Europeans and other merchants.[23] Sometimes, the Gã people acted as middlemen who traded in palm oil, slaves, and other goods, both foreign and local. Officials of the Dutch West India Company in particular interacted with these intermediaries and with the Gã mãŋtsɛmɛi at different points in time to gain a monopoly over trade and to build forts along the coast, in order to ensure their visibility and economic security in Accra.[24] Part of the mutual agreement included the use of the "Note System" that involved a kind of annual or biannual payment in monetary form that merchants paid to local kings and chiefs as a form of taxation to guarantee a temporal space for European settlement so as to carry out both commercial and religious agendas.[25] In some cases, Europeans gave out gifts to local chiefs to solidify friendship bonds and to sustain mutual trade as well as ensure future relations and exchanges.[26] Danish settlers used gifts to the chiefs as a way to compete with the English and other Europeans. They included gifts on special occasions such as the New Year's feast to local chiefs who met the needs of the Danes. Some of these gifts included "1 Danish flint lock, 6 cables, 1/8 barrel of gunpowder . . . 1 knife 8 dam, 1 piece of lead 25 dam, 1 bar of iron, 1 quart of gin, 120 dam [and others]."[27]

An exchange of gifts was not a new phenomenon in interactions between the Gã mãŋbii and their guests. When the emancipated Brazilian-Africans arrived in Accra, they also presented "brass calabashes, copper calabashes, a clock and drinks" to their hosts.[28] As the gifts and the reciprocal responses gained currency, so did the problems that came with them. For the Gã mãŋtsɛmɛi and the mãŋbii their interactions and exchanges enhanced commerce, but they also created vulnerability in the face of expanded European settlements in coastal Accra from the sixteenth century. Rural-to-urban migrations to Accra and political changes in the country in the postindependence period also complicated these interactions and exchanges and weakened the influence of the Gã people on the coast. For instance, they have lost a large portion of their land and have become a microethnic group that is embedded in macromigrant communities dominated by Akan people, the largest ethnic group in Ghana.[29]

Nigbɛ Gã mɛi jɛ in the Gã language means "where do the Gã people come from?" Researchers are not the only ones interested in this inquiry. Sometimes the Gã people themselves raise similar questions about their roots, and there is Gã folklore that underscores this important question. There are multiple ways of tracing the history of the Gã people and of analyzing differing interpretations about their origin. For instance, Gã oral traditions claim that the Gã people moved from Nigeria. Others suggest that they came originally from Mesopotamia via Benin and Nigeria after Muslim jihads in the thirteenth century.[30] Other studies show that the Gã people originated from Bonny, Nigeria, and other areas in western Sudan in the fourteenth century.[31] Another interpretation notes that they were originally from Akwamu and had stronger ties to the people of mountainous areas in the Eastern Region of Ghana. Some colonial accounts even suggest that the Gã people originated from Sarne, a town near Niger.[32] In her analysis of the origins of the Gã people, Margaret J. Field maintains that they were part of "families of refugees fleeing in separate parties 'from Tetetutu and other Benin parts' [in West Africa]."[33] It is also supposed that the Gã people of Hebrew ancestry migrated from Abyssinia or Upper Egypt,[34] or that they relocated to Accra to escape oppression under King Akpo of Dahomey.[35] The debate about the origins of the Gã people continues. One of the most dominant theories about their origins states that the Gã people migrated from a location between the rivers of Ogun and Kwara.[36] Carl C. Reindorf, an important historian in Gã history, asserts that the ancestors of the Gã people "immigrated from the sea" and arrived on the coast one group after the other.[37] Regardless of the outcome of this debate, it is clear that the Gã people shared a history similar to the reverse migrations and movements of the Brazilian-African returnees. That is one of the reasons why Gã leaders allocated specific areas for their guests.

The creation of various migrant communities was part of the hospitality Gã mãŋtsɛmɛi extended to many newcomers. Irene Odotei-Quaye asserts that the *akutsei* (districts) consisted of Gã people and aliens and "was the residence of slaves and laborers of the English company in Accra; ... the descendants of these laborers and slaves continued to serve the British company" from the eighteenth century.[38] Brazilian returnees navigated complex traditions in Accra. Sometimes they conformed to or participated in Gã traditions, but other times they showcased their Brazilian identity in the way they dressed and the use of the Portuguese language. The inclusion of the emancipated Brazilians in the Gã paramountcy (a wing of the Gã political institution) facilitated the process of their social and cultural integration. For instance the Tabom quarter, or *akutso*, which was located at Otublohum, where many of the Brazilians settled, became an important historical landmark in the history of both the Gã people and the Brazilians.[39] The Brazilian-African diaspora emerged gradually after the Tabom quarter became a home or a sanctuary for new Brazilian returnees.

THE GÃ PARAMOUNTCY AND THE TABOM QUARTER

The Gã paramountcy, which comprised the cultural institutions and the areas and towns (*mãjii*) that formed the Gã sociopolitical system that existed before colonial rule in Ghana, included a religious wing. It was divided into seven districts: Otoblohum, Akumaji, Abola, Gbese, Sempe, Alata, and Asere. Also the Gã people spread across the following coastal towns in the south: Nungua, Teshie, Osu, Labadi, Tema, and Jamestown. The Gã paramountcy had a *wulomo*, a priest who was responsible for dealing with matters of spirituality and of fetishes in Accra. Otublohum was believed to have been founded by Otu Ahikwa, an Akan warrior whose ancestors fled Denkyira (a region of central Ghana) with his troops and migrated to Accra in the 1700s to seek refuge along the coast.[40] The Otublohum Divisional Council was composed of Pokoase, Dzan-man, and Afiama, and the Tabom quarter refers to one of the areas in Accra where freed Brazilian slaves settled upon their arrival in the 1820s. The Tabom quarter was created in the mid-1800s specifically for Brazilian settlements and to meet part of the needs of the Gã mãŋbii.[41] The acceptance and integration of the Brazilians into the Gã paramountcy and their settlement patterns marked an extension of the long history of hospitality in Accra that included divisional town councils.[42]

The Tabom quarter appointed delegates to the Otublohum chief's court for social and cultural activities. The *akutsei* also served the needs of individuals and the Brazilian-African diaspora in general.[43]

Otublohum also related to the Gã paramountcy and Gã social history through other channels. These included the selection of heads of families to the chief's court from the Nii Kofi Apenteng *we* (family), Denson *we*, Asafoatse *we*, Dzase *we*, and Nii Oto Din *we*—all of whom continue to use the Gã language as a medium of communication. The freed Brazilians were part of this local establishment, but in terms of the use of Portuguese language by the Brazilians, it is not clear how the early Brazilian settler groups selected heads of family or leaders in individual family groups except evidence that they had one leader for the Brazilian-African diaspora (Brazilian/Tabom chiefs) in a given time period from 1836.[44] There is insufficient information to explain how the Tabom quarter interacted with the Otublohum Divisional Council linguistically during the early stages of settlements from the 1820s. It is likely that the early Brazilian settlers played a more minimal role in the chief's court than did their descendants who became Gã and participated in Gã customs and festivals such as *homowo* from the twentieth century. *Homowo* literally translates as "hooting or making fun of hunger" after the end of a famine or dry season.

The Otublohum people have a mixture of Gã and Akan origin besides the freed slave quarter. The "Otublohumites" include descendants of the Akwamu people who intermarried with Gã people and adopted aspects of Gã culture including language.[45] Most of the Akwamu people migrated to Accra to trade or to serve as a volunteer labor force during wars. The Akwamu people settled permanently after years of assimilation and accommodation to both Gã and Akan cultures. They adapted their customs in terms of funeral rites, food harvest celebrations, and diverse festivals.[46] The Akwamu people's assimilation into Gã societies was gradual. Despite the scale of their migration, the Gã people were able to dominate the Akwamu people mainly because of their larger population size and the advantage they possessed owing to their having settled in the area over a longer period. Indeed, the small size of the Gã *mãshi* and its limited population did not erase Gã nationalism. In fact, the *mãshi* continued to uphold long-held cultural norms and collectively defended Gã societies.

Gã Nationalism

The roots of Gã nationalism predate uprisings during the tenure of British rule from the nineteenth century. The Gã mãŋtsɛmɛi mobilized their people not only to maintain their sphere of authority, but also to sustain their traditions, political consciousness, and pride in Gã identity. The Gã mãŋbii are one among many minority groups in Ghana whose territories were threatened by the influx of migrants, especially those from rural areas seeking to establish coastal settlements to meet economic needs in particular. Like other coastal inhabitants, the Gã people had to protect their coast, land, and customs for posterity's sake. Some of these preservationist or defensive measures were conducted peacefully, but others were carried out via warfare. During this turbulent time in their history, the Gã *mãŋ* lost some of their battles, but they prevailed in a number of these conflicts. For instance, they defeated the Ewe people (from the Volta region) in the Accra-Anlo War of 1784.[47] The Asante Empire was a powerful system that controlled most societies in the Gold Coast.[48] Also, although the Asante people were highly respected and feared by both Europeans and local groups, who characterized them as the "Masters of the coast land from Elmina to the Volta, of the mountainous countries of Akwapim and Akim between the coast and Ashante," the Gã people fought the Asante after they invaded Accra in 1826. A year later, the Gã *mãŋ* fought with the Ewe people again in the Bame War of 1827.[49]

Conflicts between the Gã mãŋbii and other ethnic groups continued for centuries through the nineteenth century. The earliest time line in the archives I have come across shows that the liberated Africans arrived in coastal Accra in 1826, a turbulent period in the region's history.[50] However, there is no substantial evidence that points to the freed slaves' involvement in these local conflicts. Also, there is no proof that the Brazilians fought against other groups in the Gold Coast, as others have suggested.[51] The small size of the Brazilian-African diaspora population in the early nineteenth century, which numbered about seventy to seventy-five by 1836,[52] and evidence of constant movements to and from Otublohum and the Tabom quarter as well as back and forth to Lagos to visit family members would have made engaging in such conflicts very difficult.⁵³ Indeed, if the opposite is the case the returnees' involvement in local conflicts would have added some dimension to their story during the early periods of settlements in Accra.

The Gã people not only fought against local people, they resisted foreign intrusion, particularly by the British. The formative years of British colonial rule occurred after more than a century of warfare between other Europeans and the Gã mãŋtsɛmɛi over control of Accra's coastal commerce. In addition, Gã leaders perceived British intrusions on Gã traditions and culture as an insult to their gods or ancestral spirits, an insult to their authority as the mãŋtsɛmɛi of Gã *mãŋ*, and particularly a threat to the future of the Gã *mãshi* and their Gã heritage. The colonial presence infringed upon the land traditions and practices of other cultural groups, too. British colonial officials' lack of consideration for traditional norms was an extension of a wider imperialist policy that spread across the length and breadth of the globe. This gigantic and ambitious imperialist vision began in the Americas, Asia, and elsewhere centuries before the British set their permanent tents along the coast of Accra.⁵⁴ In the case of Ghana, long-held traditional customs and practices that were older than the whole time span of British colonial conquest were set aside or dismissed. Indeed, regardless of the determinations by Gã leaders to establish their authority, Europeans rarely sought permission from Gã leaders before establishing a settlement or their ordinances. The consensus among colonial officials was that the best way to control their colonial subjects was to imagine a problem for their subjects and enforce radical policies that did not require any feedback from the local people or knowledge of existing local traditions.⁵⁵ As S. K. B. Asante asserts,

> There was a universal concept of ancestral ownership of basic property. Land, then, was an ancestral trust enjoining the holders of property to discharge the following social functions in their use of property: 1) first and foremost to uphold the honour of the ancestors; 2) to promote the prosperity of the kingroup; and 3) to ensure the security of generations unborn, insuring them against poverty and destitution.⁵⁶

The advent of colonialism and colonial officials' failure to honor existing Gã and Akan traditions and their inability to explain colonial ordinances to their colonial subjects were not the only problems: the British provided conflicting explanations about their involvements in local affairs.⁵⁷ Sometimes, as in the case of indirect rule—a blueprint for colonialism—the British selected whatever could aid colonial administration or distract the colonial subjects. Their strategy included the use of the educated elite as instruments of hegemony.⁵⁸ These educated elite were often referred to as "Government men" in colonial newspapers.⁵⁹ Furthermore,

Colonial rule set the terms of debate, and created some of the contradictions that helped to keep it going. In the mid-1890s, officials in the Gold Coast Colony proposed that *waste land* be declared the legal property of the Crown because they could manage it better.⁶⁰

The suggestion was vigorously opposed by African intellectuals and merchants, who sought to protect their own future access to and control over land by arguing that there was no such thing as "waste land" in the colony. All land belonged to "the natives" who were represented by their chiefs.⁶¹ Sara Berry's inclusion of the response by the intellectuals and merchants does not necessarily suggest that they were the only ones who stood up against the Crown for making claims to land that belonged to the people. The Brazilians also held that the land was not only for the "natives" or the Gã people but also belonged to the newcomers or immigrants in Accra.

Public protests largely sent one strong message to the British Crown: Gold Coast land does not belong to the queen of England as the officials articulated.⁶²

The concept of ownership is relative in the sense that what one society perceived as the processes for achieving land tenure meant something entirely different to another society. Berry's analysis of the response of the local people to the characterization of the inheritance of the people of the Gold Coast as a "waste land" speaks to the prejudices and apathy of the Crown toward African customs, diverse traditions, and social systems in general. Other Gã traditions energized their willingness to protect their sovereignty.

WƆ DIƐŊTSƐ WƆ SHIKPƆŊ NƐ

In addition to the notion that "Gã nyo kpakpa ji mɔni nɔɔ kɛ hãã emãŋ," which means a devoted Gã citizen is the one who fights for the Gã nation, there were other traditions that served as a stimulant, reminder, and reinforcement for Gã consciousness. One such tradition is entrenched in the expression "wɔ diɛŋtsɛ wɔ shikpɔŋ nɛ"—from a Gã patriotic song that means this land (Gã land) or territory belongs to us. Also, it is a Gã expression that is intended to send a warning signal to foreigners that they have no right to trespass on or claim these lands. Moreover, it reinforces Ghanaian cultural pride and the belief that the Gã people have the right to take their lands back from anyone who seized them or who made laws that changed local traditions and value systems associated with land tenure. This important message of ownership and cultural pride transcends Gã norms. The nationalist song is typically played on Ghanaian national

Chapter Three

television in the evenings to end daily programs. In this context, each evening the song reminds Ghanaians to be proud of their Ghanaian heritage and continue to resist foreign rule and of the need to pass this message on to future generations.

The idea of ownership permeates this important expression and the lyrics that gained enormous attention in colonial Accra. However, the age of "wɔ diɛŋtsɛ wɔ shikpɔŋ nɛ" and where it resonated does not merely imply that visitors and foreigners in precolonial Accra danced to the tune, embraced these expressions, or stored the message in their memory. Indeed, at the height of the British colonial conquest and the introduction of colonial ordinances, this important song did not have any impact on British imperialism. But the message it conveyed influenced landowning members of the Brazilian-African diaspora in Accra. "Wɔ diɛŋtsɛ wɔ shikpɔŋ nɛ" reminded the Gã *māshi* that they had a responsibility to protect their ancestral heritage, but that did not mean that the emancipated Brazilians had to give up Brazilian land to satisfy their host. There were other contentions and differences between host and guest. Freed Brazilians were involved in disputes with Gã *Māŋtsɛ* Tackie Tawiah over Gã stool land or land belonging to members of the Gã royal family. In a number of court proceedings, in particular the case *Tackie v. Nelson*, the freed slaves and their offspring argued that the land that became known as Brazilian land was given to them by Gã *Māŋtsɛ* Tackie Komeh I, *Māŋtsɛ* Tawiah's predecessor, and therefore could not be taken from them. Several archival documents confirm that the disputed land was indeed a gift from *Māŋtsɛ* Komeh I, but this evidence did not prevent a clash between *Māŋtsɛ* Tawiah and the Brazilians.[63]

One can examine and reflect on the social history of Accra from other, overlapping angles. The history of the Gã people, especially interactions between their leaders and the liberated Africans, extended beyond land disputes between them. Both groups benefited from trading activities and cross-cultural interactions and exchanges that took place in Accra. The Gã people also benefited from commercial and religious activities or various ventures between them and foreigners who traveled to or settled in Accra, especially as "Accra emerged in the seventeenth century as one of the many trading entrepôts on the Gold Coast of West Africa that served as links between the expanding Atlantic economy and the African interior."[64]

Precolonial Gã mãŋtsɛmɛi, who played a pivotal role during the early interactions and confrontations with the British, were selected mostly through a specific Gã *weku*, or family lineage. The selection process was sometimes organized by *jaase*, elders from various Gã family groups. Conflicts between Gã mãŋbii from the postindependence eras, especially in matters over inheritance and land disputes, have complicated Gã history.[65] Besides honoring their ancestors, they had other responsibilities with important cultural, spiritual, and social implications. Part of the social job description of a Gã *māŋtsɛ* and the chiefs who assist him was to create an environment for promoting trading in Accra to generate revenue and create jobs for their people, to settle disputes, to preserve Gã cultural traditions, and to protect and promote the interests of the Gã *mãshi*. Other leaders in the Gã *akutsei*, within the Gã paramountcy, played important roles in challenging British rule. Basically, Gã leaders had to confront foreign threats while remaining calm enough to promote commerce. These mãŋtsɛmɛi were strategic in their approach and were able to lead without jeopardizing their economic interests or partnership with both foreign and local traders.[66]

The Gã *mãŋ* have had a long history of resisting and rebelling whenever they felt threatened by outside forces. They fought with local people including the Akwamu, the Asante, the Fante, and the Ewe ethnic groups to control land and trading posts in the coastal area. Other groups also flexed their muscles as they pursued other interests. Like the Gã, the Fante and the Asante clashed numerous times for similar cultural and social reasons as well as in competition for political and economic space.[67] Europeans, too, became entangled in local conflicts. In fact, they had no qualms in fanning flames of conflict.[68] In some situations, the Dutch and other Europeans employed a divide-and-rule approach, and in doing so they assisted one local group to defeat another to achieve a particular end.[69] These ethnic groups did not always need an outside provocation; both the Fante and the Asante, for example, turned against each other and against Europeans whenever they deemed it necessary for commercial benefits.[70]

When Europeans waged local battles, they usually were vying for space to settle and for monopoly over trade. Such contests for power were the order of the day. During this chaotic time, the British and the Dutch clashed over territory along the coast of Accra and other areas where they both sought to build forts to exert their political and economic authority and influence. The Danes and the English disagreed over how to dominate the people of the Gold Coast. The former were successful in forming an enabling environment that created a level of trust between local chiefs, but this mutual agreement allowed the British to gain the upper hand especially over commerce and resources. The Danes were understandably unhappy with this development. According to the Danish governor Edward Carstensen,

> The English reap the benefit of the Danish communications, while Denmark carries the burden of a costly administration.... The chiefs of these towns are paid by Denmark, peace and order in the country is maintained by the Danish government, but gold and the palm oil of Akim and Akwapim is received by the English.[71]

Carstensen's diary (recorded from 1842 to 1850) reveals unequal partnerships and rewards between Europeans and the local people. These uneven exchanges reflect broader inequalities that shaped contacts between Gã leaders and Europeans from the precolonial period. Other conflicts were caused by disagreement over how to manage European forts, especially disagreements over trading networks and how to end slavery.[72]

The transatlantic slave trade and Western imperialism share much in common; therefore, those freed from slavery faced the threat of colonialism, which compromised the inalienable rights of the newcomers to Accra. The construction of forts and castles along the coastline of Ghana both as trading posts and as European residences to facilitate colonial rule dates back to the fifteenth century when the Portuguese built the Elmina Castle in 1482. Part of the reason for building a fort was to send a signal to other Europeans to keep away from a particular trading territory or post.[73] More than a century later, these trading posts were used as dungeons for holding enslaved Africans as they awaited transport.[74] These trading posts also served as places of religious worship for European missionaries and later as temporal holding cells for Ghanaian chiefs who were either sent into exile or otherwise removed from their communities for resisting British rule.[75] Gã and Asante kings, chiefs, and queen mothers who rebelled against foreign rule were subject to this treatment. The threat of exile occurred around the same time colonial rulers formulated ideas including indirect rule and notions that colonial subjects needed some form of protection from Europeans to improve their religious and social conditions.

Protect or Colonize?

Sending mixed messages to colonial subjects about the importance of foreign intervention and influences permeated the colonial psyche. There was an illusion that the introduction of foreign models including the notion of "protectorate" could guarantee submission or would be embraced with little resistance.[76] Europeans' use and application of the word "protect" or "protectorate" was problematic from various angles. Indeed, the very concept of protectorate raised more questions than answers. For instance, who was protecting whom? By whose authority? Why was this protection necessary, and who benefited from the arrangement? Prior to the official establishment of the Gold Coast as a British protectorate, the Gã people broke their old cordial relations with the Asante Empire and formed an alliance with the British in the early 1820s.[77] This friendship did not last, however, as they became subject to the partitioning by which Europeans carved the Gold Coast colony into more manageable pieces to lessen tensions between the colonizer and the colonized. Among these bifurcations was the division of the Northern and Southern Protectorates in the Gold Coast that accompanied introduction of the system of indirect rule. The notion of the protectorate was itself contradictory and troubling in other ways. First, it was designed purposely to serve British interests. Second, as the name implies, it was presented by the English Crown as a benevolent policy to "protect" the people of the Gold Coast. Ultimately, colonialism became an extension of servitude. Projects such as the creation of the protectorates established the ground for British colonial rule by the dawn of the twentieth century.

Criticism of the contradictions in the idea of protectorate resonated in colonial newspapers, which were ironically provided by colonial officials as an outlet for the masses to express their views on various subjects. This public medium also enabled colonial officials to evaluate the responses of colonial subjects to a particular policy or ordinance. One article in the *Gold Coast Echo* challenged this notion and exposed the double standard:

> Sir, we are called the Protectorate people and our country is called a "Protected" Territory at the same time that is styled the "Gold Coast Colony." . . . Let anyone speak [against the concept of protectorate] and the Governor can imprison or transport the offender, without trial. . . . These things are done in the name of England, and Lord Knutsford says [he] will listen to no complains.[78]

Colonial structural policies affected cultural practices also. In one newspaper report, a local commentator accused the colonial government of eating with both hands—meeting the needs of the British Crown and exploiting the colonies at the same time but pretending as if that was in the best interest of the people of the Gold Coast.[79] Clearly, aspects of colonial agendas were in opposition to the needs of the people of the Gold Coast. By offering a form of social media for the oppressed to voice out their frustration, colonial newspapers including the *Gold Coast Independent* reported that "while the agitation lasted they [British authorities] were able to gauge the intensity of the feeling" against colonial ordinances.[80] Although there was criticism from the grassroots, the British protectorate gained ground in the early 1900s when the entire Gold Coast became a British colony. Despite a degree of tolerance for the colonized population's expression of their frustrations or other feedback via newspapers, an exchange of letters and telegraphs between colonial officials and the English Crown showed hostile responses. These correspondences confirmed that the British were very concerned about the influences of Gã and Asante leaders, especially given how local cultural traditions and norms threatened British rule.[81] The British needed other systems to defuse confrontations with the local people, one that could be achieved through existing local systems.

Chapter Three

Indirect Rule and Colonial Ordinances

Indirect rule, as the term implies, involved a basic shift from rule of colonial subjects directly by Europeans as colonial officials to a system that depended heavily on local leaders as vehicles for carrying out colonial projects. Indirect rule was the invention of Lord Frederick J. D. Lugard, a British official who spent most of his time in Nigeria from 1914 through 1919. Lugard proposed a system for carrying out colonial agendas by tapping into existing forms of local traditions. Lugard's system of governance became a model for colonial rule elsewhere in Africa and throughout the British Empire. Lugard replicated ideas that existed but were not implemented prior to his tenure. According to Amon Nikoi, Charles S. Solomon, a former British administrator in the Gold Coast, warned decades before Lugard that

> No attempt should be made to govern the country except through the selected chiefs of the people who are open to the best influences and whom the people will implicitly obey. . . . In fact, the country must be ruled and governed by a native element and Great Britain can easily assist and guide it by laws and regulations—the fruit of ages of experience, engrafted onto and merged with such existing native system and methods the people may desire to keep and follow.[82]

It is uncertain whether Solomon held in high regard existing local African institutions or was just interested in how to manipulate local systems to enhance colonial rule. Another declaration by King George V suggests that the colonies were not mature enough to take care of their internal affairs and that Europeans therefore had to come to their rescue. The king stated, "It will be the high task of all my Government to superintend and assist in the development of these countries for the benefit of the inhabitants and the general welfare of mankind."[83] In addition, a pronouncement by Joseph Chamberlain, a British colonial official, summed it up this way: "We develop new territory as Trustees for Civilization, for the commerce of the world."[84]

The implications of these statements are many. A dominant notion was that the colonies could not survive on their own and therefore needed redemption or foreign intervention at various levels. It is clear that Solomon had a vision that was based on some form of mutual agreement between the colonized and the colonizer, but there is no indication here that local chiefs embraced this system or how their future should be envisioned by outsiders. Indeed, the subsequent references by King George and Chamberlain reinforce the notion that people in the colonies were considered uncivilized but they had resources that were highly valued. The justification for colonial intrusion in Africans' sociocultural and political affairs was intended to establish a gradual systematic transition into civilization and progress using the Europeans' formula. For the British, the application of indirect rule and implementation of colonial ordinances in the Gold Coast were necessary for stability in the colonial sphere. The common view that local cultural traditions were uncivilized practices was perpetuated in many other arenas. Missionaries in particular served as organs for propagating this ideology. As Governor Carstensen's diary shows, both the Danes and the English welcomed missionaries to their various places of settlements in the Gold Coast with open arms not necessarily because they shared the same religious faith. Rather, the presence of the missionaries aided in providing opportunities for civilizing the local people.[85] According to Carstensen, "Denmark has declared that she will stay in Africa for the sake of the Africans, then private charity will help a Christian mission still in its honourable undertaking."[86] There were series of discussions among colonial officials in the *Gold Coast Independent* regarding the white man's burden to save colonial subjects from their evil practices.[87]

The colonial systems' dependence on local resources and a selected few to advance was a strategic choice. In other words, although colonial rulers frequently had no regard for existing local practices or in some situations characterized them as backward, they were selective in what they rejected and what they considered acceptable. The local people, especially the educated elites and the chiefs who signed up to serve as agents for colonial rule, had a daunting task and the responsibility to act as instruments and liaisons for the colonial administration. What was intended to enhance existing traditional institutions, as Solomon suggested, instead stifled these communities' development: the majority of the local population and their leaders became spectators. The imposition of foreign laws gradually weakened existing social order and altered local lifestyles.

There were other broader objectives for introducing indirect rule. This does not mean that the British were missing in action in the process of carrying out and completing their imperialist agenda. First, the indirect approach allowed the British to promote their colonial agenda behind the scene. Second, indirect rule lessened tensions between colonial officials and the local people. Third, indirect rule was a cheaper form of governance because it allowed the British to spread or concentrate their resources and manpower across the various territories they took over while the local leaders and elites did the dirty work. Fourth, some of the educated elite and local chiefs in particular who served as go-betweens used indirect rule as a platform to regain the authority and respect they had lost as a result of colonial rule.[88] As middlemen, both the elite and the chiefs used this bridge to self-serving purposes whenever the opportunity presented itself. For the most part, the educated elite were not concerned about the needs of the general population. After rubbing shoulders with colonial officials—enjoying a taste of Western lifestyles such as dressing in suits and after traveling to England to pursue higher education—the select few served as representatives and the voices of the colonial machinery.[89] Fifth, indirect rule gave the chiefs who embraced it the opportunity to amass wealth and make financial gains outside the surveillance of colonial officials or without close scrutiny. For some of these chiefs who volunteered or played the role as agents, they used the occasion to provide their self-serving version and interpretation of local customary laws and practices—thereby gaining "exclusive control of land and labor."[90] In general, indirect rule satisfied the needs of the British Crown, colonial rulers, some local chiefs, and others who volunteered to serve as instruments for carrying out colonial schemes.

Throughout the period of indirect rule, British colonial officials strategically selected local partners to fulfill colonial projects. As stooges of colonial rule, local chiefs became often unwitting instruments for gauging how colonial subjects would respond to various oppressive ordinances. Acting both as spectators and as referees, colonial officials were able to regulate and manipulate chiefs. For instance, in the process of carrying out colonial assignments, British officials ignored rifts between local chiefs and the people so long as they did not pose a threat to imperial projects. However, the colonial officials who performed the roles of judge and prosecutor intervened in various activities whenever there was a conflict of interest. As Kathryn Firmin-Sellers maintains,

> The institutions of the colonial state did not provide for the systematic resolution of such disputes. Under indirect rule, the British chose to delegate substantial advisory and administrative responsibility to the Colony's traditional rulers. But fearful that the chiefs might turn on them, the British denied chiefs the opportunity to influence policy making directly, and stripped the chiefs of the coercive powers.[91]

Others who opposed this foreign ideology also paid dearly for their opposition.

Gã Resistance and Repercussions

From the seventeenth century European powers worked side by side to reshape coastal Accra to fit European cultural imagination and capitalist goals. The Gã people were very generous and took good care of their visitors, but such was not always the case as they became increasingly threatened by various European intrusions. *Mãŋtsɛ* Tackie

Tawiah and other Gã leaders who ruled before and after him were mindful of the meaning of the slogan "wɔ dɛntsɛ wɔ shikpɔn nɛ." They did not accept interference by strangers, especially colonial rulers and European missionaries, among others. There was a tug-of-war as Europeans responded forcefully to maintain control. Gã *Mãŋtsɛ* Tackie Tawiah complained bitterly about British settlements in Accra and the failure to respect local protocols. Local leaders frowned on the treatment they had to endure in their interactions with colonial officials and questioned why they had to bow to Europeans in public settings. Gã *Mãŋtsɛ* Tawiah remarked that the British Crown took possession of vast areas of Gã land without any consultation.[92]

Although there were some forms of negotiations, most European settlements were accomplished through force and via violence. The creation of "Dutch Accra,"[93] "English Accra," and other European enclaves underscored Europeans' determination to carve out a piece of Accra for themselves by any means necessary.[94] During this important historical time, the English and the Portuguese built or rebuilt James Fort in 1576; the Dutch built Fort Creyecoeur (meaning "broken heart") in 1642, which is now called Ussher Fort. Both forts were situated along the shores of Otublohum, which later became the first location of Brazilian-African settlements. The Swedes built the Christianborg Castle in 1657, which the Danes took over in 1661. The Portuguese, too, later controlled the castle, changing its name to St. Xavier Fort in memory of the famous Jesuit missionary. The building was the seat of the current government of Ghana until 2013. The latter castle sits in close proximity to a variety of important business edifices in what was British and Dutch Accra.[95] Responses to British imperialism were swift, but they differed. During this tumultuous time there were numerous local strategies aimed at reinforcing Gã autonomy.

Resistance by the Gã people also compelled the Europeans to explore other options or approaches. On some occasions that suited their collective interest, the British and the Dutch worked closely among the Fante and the Asante, who were once enemies of the Gã people.[96] These two European nations later formed an alliance with the coastal Fante rather than the Asante to facilitate colonial projects from the coast to the hinterland.[97] The British preferred the Fante, whom they perceived as the lesser of two evils—they were more accommodating of Europeans than were the Asante.[98] The Fante also preferred an alliance with the British rather than the Asante people partly because the Asante often sold the Fante into slavery after a major battle.[99] To resolve this fear, the Fante state and their leaders provided various forms of assistance to the British as long as that guaranteed British protection for the Fante people against Asante attacks.[100] Most inland dwellers in Ghana characterize the Fante people as traitors because of the close relations their ancestors had with Europeans along the coast. However, the Fante did not always compromise their position or integrity. Sometimes they revolted against the British.[101] Violence, atrocities, and humiliating treatment of local leaders were common. In one confrontation between King Bonsu II and the Dutch, the leader of the Afutu people was destooled (removed from office) and exiled. His humiliation reminds us of coastal opposition and its consequences. Gã *Mãŋtsɛ* Tawiah and Asante King Prempeh I were also exiled. King Badu Bonsu II suffered a worse fate, for he paid dearly with his life. He was murdered by the Dutch, and his severed head was only returned to the royal family in Ghana in July 2009 after being displayed in a Dutch Museum for over 171 years.[102]

The Danes, the Dutch, and other Europeans who embarked on colonial conquest and Christian missionary ventures also managed to settle along the coast with or without the approval of Gã leaders. The colonialists put in place strategic policies to support European missionaries and merchants in ways that would enlarge the European footprint.[103] During this time, broader European agendas were entrenched in racist notions of civilizing the "uncivilized" Africans to save them from their barbaric customs. Carstensen characterized this as an "honourable undertaking."[104] Other Europeans created the self-serving impression that they were "protecting" local Africans from other forms of European influence. In doing so, the British established their own version of freedom, part of which permeates the chain of ordinances they enforced. After many years of fierce competition between Europeans in the Gold Coast, the British gained the upper hand, and they energized the colonial base with drastic measures and punishments including exile.[105]

THE THREAT AND IRONY OF EXILE

The notion of exile was foreign to local kings and chiefs until they suffered the consequence for rebelling against European rulers and the systems they put in place. The threat of exile was real. Prior to the use of exile as a form of punishment, local people who revolted against their leaders often faced harsh punishments, such as banishment from a particular town or village, imprisonment, or death. For these kings, chiefs, or leaders their authority represented a unique symbol of power; they believed they held sacred positions and that their authority commanded a great deal of respect from their citizens. The fact that Europeans had the audacity to challenge the authority of these local leaders (most of whom were perceived as divine rulers) with a threat of exile was inconceivable. Although meddling by foreigners in local traditions and value systems was a taboo, such interference gained considerable traction. Therefore, these local leaders had to reclaim their respect and honor in order to maintain their integrity or not to offend the gods of the land, as well as to fulfill the responsibilities their forefathers entrusted in them.[106] Further, they had to do so to sustain the respect and confidence of their subjects or followers. Besides the aggressive tactic of exile, the British had a notorious reputation for embarrassing local leaders and creating panic among the Gã populace throughout the Gold Coast. Heavy fines were imposed on Gã chiefs and other local rulers who disobeyed British authority (including Brazilian chiefs). In some situations in Accra, those who refused to pay the fines were arrested and imprisoned.[107]

In addition to Gã *Mãŋtsɛ* Tawiah's humiliating experience, there were other consequences especially in the late 1880s and early 1900s. Chiefs who prolonged conflicts with the British as Tawiah did were also sent into exile to intimidate them and to send a stern signal to others. They included Asante King Prempeh I, queen mother Yaa Asantewaa, and members of the royal family who prevented the British from taking away the "Golden Stool"—a symbol of Asante nationalism, identity, and pride.[108] The leaders paid the price as they were expelled from their own land to the Seychelles Islands.[109] The Cape Coast Castle, which once served as a trading post and later became a dungeon for holding slaves prior to their dispersal to the New World as well as a Christian chapel for European missionaries, was also the seat of the colonial government.[110] Still later it was used as a transit point for holding chiefs who opposed the British as they were prepared for exile in Sierra Leone or the Seychelles as in the case of queen mother Asantewaa and King Prempeh I. Those who were exiled in Holland by the Dutch suffered similar humiliations.[111]

Gã *Mãŋtsɛ* Tawiah in particular had no qualms about resisting British rule and motivating his Gã constituency into action. Though small in stature, he was a major threat to the British. He was incarcerated at the Elmina Castle from 1880 to 1883. Gã *Mãŋtsɛ* Tawiah, who had a spontaneous personality as well as a chameleon-like character, was isolated from his community for about three years. After his exile at Elmina, the old man became more radicalized.[112] The Gã *mãŋtsɛ* developed his own way of confronting the British. Sometimes he ignored them; other times *Mãŋtsɛ* Tawiah responded when it was convenient for him. As a form of resistance, he regulated and used his limited residual authority at the onset of British rule. As they did for Asante leaders and their people, influence and popularity gave *Mãŋtsɛ* Tawiah a platform for mobilizing the Gã people. This heightened concern among British officials, who sought to strip the Gã *mãŋtsɛ* of his power and influence. However, because of *Mãŋtsɛ* Tawiah's popularity and the outbreak of local revolts following his incarceration, British officials were unsure of what to do with him when he was released from captivity in 1883.

During the late 1880s it became increasingly difficult to coerce Gã *Mãŋtsɛ* Tawiah to bow to British policies even after his three years in isolation. Of course, having survived exile in his old age, he had little motivation to yield to the British. The British, meanwhile, clung to the hope that Tawiah's demise would be soon. The *Gold Coast Echo* published an article quoting a statement by a British commissioner who reminded other officials that the *mãŋtsɛ* did not have long to live. He believed that divine intervention would end the Gã ruler's reign. According to the newspaper report, "King Tackie was a live king [sic] and that when it pleased the Almighty God in his mercy to remove him. It will then be a question to decide whether the government would allow his place to be filled or not."[113]

British officials had other qualms with the Gã *mãŋtsɛ* as he challenged and established his authority (limited) as the rightful leader of the Gã *mãŋ*. Although the British did not always get along very well with the Gã mãŋtsɛmɛi, they relied on these local leaders to facilitate long-distance transportation. During the nineteenth century the major means of transporting goods and people over long distances across the hinterland and forest regions was carrying them on some kind of hammock carried by humans. Sometimes slaves performed this backbreaking task alongside long-distance travels selling various goods for their owners.[114] In the case of colonial Accra, *Mãŋtsɛ* Tawiah did not have slaves at his disposal to do such work. Of course, he could have improvised or made some kind of arrangement. The British were very irritated by *Mãŋtsɛ* Tawiah's seeming apathy. An angry outburst expressed by Sir Matthew Nathan, one of the governors epitomizes his frustration with the Gã *mãŋtsɛ* for his lack of support for British colonial projects, particularly his refusal to assist colonial officials during the governor's long expedition to the Asante Kingdom. This journey took a number of days by road from the coast in the south to the interior in the north. This was during the final stage of the British-Asante War at the turn of the twentieth century. According to Nathan,

> The first twenty miles of my march was through Accra country under Mãŋtsɛ Tackie whose power for any useful purpose has practically disappeared. He no longer has a court in which to sell justice at Accra and so has no revenue. He also has no powers of punishment and so no means of making his nominal subjects obey him. He is an old man with the recollection of great former importance and of an influence extending over all the Gã-talking people and he naturally resents the new order of things and is not inclined to assist the government that has brought it about. He declined to help with carriers for the Kumasi relief expedition.... When I asked Tackie for carriers for this journey he gave me four.[115]

Nathan's irritation illustrates how the British and the Gã *mãŋtsɛ* interacted when the British had control over the Southern Protectorate or the coastal and southern half of the then Gold Coast. It also explains how the British relied on or used local mãŋtsɛmɛi as vehicles for colonial projects during indirect rule and direct rule. Nathan's extensive comment underscores the limited powers of the Gã *mãŋtsɛ*, the significance of the *mãŋtsɛ* to the Gã people, the king's apathy, and his indirect ways of resisting British rule.

Mãŋtsɛ Tawiah fought some of his battles with the British on his own, but he had a large constituency of supporters who also challenged colonial rule. Most of the kings mobilized their communities on various fronts to show solidarity with him. Gender roles that were fluid during the anticolonial resistance enabled Gã women in particular to become a formidable force. They were very active locally and domestically, but that did not prevent them from positioning themselves nationally at the forefront of anticolonial uprisings. These women were aware of the constraints on Gã men and how their leaders were stripped of their power. For instance, when the British introduced the Town Council Ordinance of 1896 to give the British more control of local affairs in Accra, especially municipal taxation, Gã women made their voices heard. When the male leaders were contemplating when to challenge the Town Council Ordinance or were intimidated by the threat of being exiled like *Mãŋtsɛ* Tawiah, Gã women registered their grievances. One of their statements read: "Our Chiefs and Headmen and general male population have become enervated and demoralized.... They are afraid to speak their minds."[116]

The women of Accra had no problem showcasing the weakness or the limitations of their men in public forums, but they were not the only ones who responded. A few years after Gã women took to the street, Yaa Asantewaa, the queen mother of Ejisu in Asante, revealed similar problems encountered by Asante men. These men either were not courageous enough to oppose British rule or had been weakened by the British over time. Yaa Asantewaa, in one of her famous speeches, declared that if men were too weak and fearful to stand against the British to defend the Asante Kingdom, the women would.[117] Gã women took to the streets of Accra to demand change. Neither their public outcry nor their resistance resulted in the Gã women being arrested or punished, but subsequent protests did. The involvement of the Gã women in rebellions shows that they complemented their men in the ways they resisted colonial rule. Other migrants in various *akutsei*, or quarters, who witnessed the climate of revolts took advantage. At the zenith of Gã colonial resistance in the nineteenth century, the Brazilians were drawn into the series of rebellions.

Conflicts between the Gã mãŋtsɛmɛi and the British had ripple effects. Most of the conflicts between the British and the Asante Empire stemmed from disagreements over slavery, colonialism, and the future of the Gold Coast—especially after the British made desperate attempts to take the Golden Stool in order to present it to the queen of England.[118] This was intended to symbolize British dominance over the Asante people.[119] However, the dominant reasons British officials articulated privately was that they were keeping the most important treasure of the Asante people safe at the Cape Coast Castle, an important seat of the colonial system, so that it would not be destroyed.[120] Not all British colonial officials supported the treatment of the Asante people. For instance, a dispatch from Governor Nathan who was once frustrated by *Mãŋtsɛ* Tawiah's failure to provide carriers for long journeys later admitted various unjustifiable actions against the Asante people. He stated:

> I should say that the real origin of the uprising is the profound dislike on the part of the chiefs and leading people of Asant to British rule. The dislike is not unnatural. We take away from them all they care about and give them in place conditions of the life which have no attraction to them.[121]

Earlier on, the British wanted a peaceful resolution between them and the Asante people after the British were defeated numerous times.[122] Despite British officials' interest in resolving tension between the Crown and the Asante Empire, the British were very adamant. They braced for war and persisted in aggressive campaigns until they conquered the Asante Empire in 1901. It was after this defeat that the entire colony—both the Southern and Northern Protectorates—came under British control. Tension that developed between Gã leaders and British officials over power and political space lingered until the demise of British rule when Ghana gained her independence on 6 March 1957.

In the early 1870s through the 1880s, the British deliberately provoked Gã and Asante leaders in particular to justify punitive reactions that followed afterward. British officials, most notably Governor Ussher and George Cleveland, threatened *Mãŋtsɛ* Tawiah constantly. The British perceived the removal of *Mãŋtsɛ* Tawiah as a vital step in their endeavors as they prepared to establish a lasting sphere of political control in Accra three years after the Gã territory became the new capital of the Gold Coast colony.[123] *Mãŋtsɛ* Tawiah did not have to be worried about the British alone. His time in exile led to divisions within the Gã leadership and communities, especially disputes over Gã land or trespassing on lands under the king's control.[124] This includes the conflicts between a segment of the Brazilian-African population and Gã *Mãŋtsɛ* Tawiah over land tenure, for example *Tackie v. Nelson*. Indeed, when the *Mãŋtsɛ* returned to Accra to take his throne again on 9 March 1883, the Gã people gave him a red-carpet reception in Accra.[125] Correspondence between colonial officials, the British Crown, and the Gã leaders from 19 September 1892 shows British apprehension concerning large public gatherings that were held by *Mãŋtsɛ* Tawiah for various cultural ceremonies, including the swearing of the oath of allegiance by new chiefs to the king.[126] Danish governor Carstensen expressed similar suspicions about the ability of Gã leaders because of the fear that such gatherings could spark anticolonial revolts.

CUTTING OFF THE HEAD OF THE BOISTEROUS MONSTER IN THE PRECOLONIAL GÃ MÃŊ

Cutting off the head of dynamic colonial policies was not accomplished overnight. Conflicts between various local leaders and the British were very similar. In Accra in particular, some of the tensions were sparked by attempts by the British to weaken the power and influence of Gã leaders and to control commerce as well as revenue after Gã *Mãŋtsɛ* Tawiah was in exile. Culturally, the British did so by regulating Gã cultural festivities and by passing and enforcing ordinances such as Native Jurisdiction Ordinance of 1883 that stated that it was criminal offense for "natives to conspire to undermine and usurp the authority of Paramount Chief [those who supported colonial rule],"[127] and the Native Administrative Ordinance of 1927, among others. Both regulations sought to tighten the colonialists' hold on their subjects and limit local cultural practices while projecting positive views about European cultures and Christianity. In general, colonial officials had roller-coaster ties with local chiefs and the educated elite in the colonies. When it served colonial needs colonial officials had no qualms. However, colonial officials were irritated by lack of cooperation by their subjects, particularly resistance led by local chiefs who were committed to the needs of their societies. The colonial government did not hide their frustration. As one comment in the *Gold Coast Independent* relates about this "betrayal,"

> To return to the Native Administration Revenue Ordinance, a great responsibility is being thrown on the shoulders of the Chiefs, who are being called upon to be responsible wholly or in part for its introduction.... What [we] should not lose sight of is the unanimity with which they co-operated with their people in opposing the Income Tax proposal when it was put forward by the Government.[128]

The role of local chiefs during and after the advent of colonial conquest was indeed pivotal to the success or failure of colonialism. In the case of the Gã *mãntsɛmɛi* they were very consistent with the opposition to colonial rule. Indeed, they as other local leaders negotiated with colonial officials in ways that could maintain a level of agreement. However, for revenue collection in Gã societies, Gã *mãntsɛmɛi* did not compromise. Regardless of the tensions between Gã people and foreigners, Gã *mãntsɛmɛi* protected their people and their economic interests. At the same time, they ensured that a safe climate was created along the coast to advance trading with locals and foreigners.[129]

In part the motivation for revolting against colonial ordinances was not that they infringed on the freedom of the colonial subjects but that colonial rulers did not make any constructive efforts to explain the ordinances' significance to Accra, especially to those who could not read and write.[130] Moreover, they failed to address the problems associated with confusion over the details about the ordinances as well as their broader implications for stability in Accra. Gã leaders took drastic action. For instance, in January 1895 Gã mãntsɛmɛi submitted petitions to colonial officials and demanded explanations for all colonial ordinances including the poll tax that was introduced three decades earlier, in 1861. Their main objective was to call for the repeal of the law because in their opinion such taxation was illegal and counterproductive to the growth of Accra and Gã cultural norms.[131] Taxation was opposed on every level because the colonial subjects did not see they had any social and political obligations or commitments to the British Crown.[132] Other chiefs complained after a number of protesters were killed and their towns destroyed for staging uprisings.[133] In general, colonial ordinances undermined long-held social practices that elevated mãŋtsɛmɛi as the legitimate leaders of their societies.

These policies pitched citizens of a particular colony against the colonial machinery and sometimes against local rulers who embraced the laws. This would not have been possible without the assistance of a number of chiefs and the educated elite who served as instruments of colonial rule and sometimes as interpreters of the ordinances. Issues of interpretation or lack thereof complicated colonial ordinances. In Accra, Gã chiefs, most of whom were not familiar with the English language, had to depend on local elites for interpretation. In other engagements, these chiefs prolonged one meeting after another with colonial officials until they had enough understanding of the complex policies. In the process of serving as a bridge between the local leaders and colonial officials, the educated elite gained enormous visibility and access to all those who were affected by the colonial presence during the period of indirect rule.[134] The impact of colonial rule on the educated elite, especially on their interactions with Europeans, was huge. According to Samuel S. Quarcoopome,

> Africans who became educated and wealthy by virtue of activities began to look down on the traditional political setup. They sought to express their education and wealth in terms of political power. They condemned the traditional apparatus of government as outmoded and competed fiercely with the chiefs for political leadership.[135]

Not all the educated elites embraced indirect rule or contributed to its implementation; others established organizations such as the Aborigines' Rights Protection Society (ARPS) to oppose colonial rule.[136]

In addition to colonial ordinances covered so far, the British also interfered with Gã cultural traditions such as the *homowo*, an important celebration that is still practiced in the twenty-first century.[137] During this festival, the Gã *mãŋtsɛ* sprinkles *kpekpei*, a kind of corn meal mixed with red oil, as a sign of abundance.

It is not clear if or how the Brazilians were restricted during *homowo* celebrations as the various *akutsei*, including the Tabom quarter, celebrated with the Gã mãŋbii.[138] The Tabom people are still active participants in this annual festivity. By the end of the nineteenth century colonial restrictions on Gã cultural festivals compelled Gã mãŋtsɛmɛi to seek permission from British governors before they selected leaders in Gã *mãŋ*. Post-*Mãŋtsɛ* Tawiah Gã mãŋtsɛmɛi were more law-abiding than *Mãŋtsɛ* Tawiah who had a long history of rebellion. During the period of British rule from 1901 these Gã leaders put up little resistance as colonial rule gained extra traction. In a meeting between Sir Matthew Nathan, *Mãŋtsɛ* Okaidja, and others, the Gã leaders proposed the selection of new Gã mãŋtsɛmɛi to perform different social roles.[139] In the colonial era, whenever the Gã people gathered or prepared for any cultural occasion they created a level of anxiety.[140] During this time, the British forbade the Gã people from drumming and participating in other forms of merrymaking. In Gã traditions and other cultures in Ghana drumming is used to transmit messages. Echoes or sounds of drumming were also an indirect way of mobilizing the Gã *mãŋ* for both cultural festivities and revolts. This form of communication and the colossal gatherings it could generate were foreign to the British. Therefore, colonial policies did not often accommodate these customs because of the perceived threat they posed to British domination. The British characterized this particular channel of communication as an uncivilized practice. Yet, to resolve this problem and to minimize the anxiety it engendered, the British sought to manipulate conditions and terms for celebrating this important festival in various areas within the Gã paramountcy. British Ordinance 35 (1878) specifically stated conditions for cultural expressions and rituals for all Gã communities or towns although these rituals formed an integral fiber in *homowo* celebrations. As the ordinance clearly stated, "It shall be unlawful for any person, without permission ... of [a] Governor or District Commissioner to assemble for beating any drum, gong or other instrument or dancing."[141]

Enforcing colonial ordinances to regulate Gã cultural practices was a daunting task. When colonial officials were unable to implement these laws they introduced curfew to minimize drumming and singing in the streets of Accra. Part of these laws was included in the Criminal Code. One of these codes declared that there will be severe punishment for any colonial subject in any town who,

> After being warned to desist shouts or blows any horn or shell, or sounds or plays upon any musical instrument, or sings or makes any other loud or unusual noise ... in any Town, without a license in writing from the Governor or District Commissioner ... between eight o'clock at night or six in the morning.[142]

There were other ways of silencing and restricting the Gã leaders. A letter from John Maxwell, the acting secretary of Native Affairs, to the governor expressed such sentiments. Maxwell was characterized as "a more aggressive imperialist of the 1890s mould with little patience for dissenting African opinion."[143] His hostility undermined Gã nationalism. Maxwell later denied a request by the Gã mãŋtsɛmɛi to gather or perform rituals that were needed for various cultural ceremonies.[144] In general, the British set the terms of their relationship with the Gã people.

The Gã *mãŋ* was not the only cultural group whose practices were altered or stifled. The Fante state also suffered similar humiliation. In their case, British officials and their policies prevented the Fante people from performing funeral rituals and activities that in the past lasted for over a week. The British argued that such lengthy funeral rituals did not enhance social development. In 1858, Governor B. Pine introduced new laws to honor the dead. The major problem was that these funeral policies introduced different forms of discrimination for the dead based on class. Pine summed up the funeral policies this way: "Funerals for important chiefs could last for only three days, two days for lesser chiefs and one day for a private person."[145]

In general, the British were successful in their approach (especially in the case of the Gã *mãŋ*), which they continued after the demise of Tawiah. Frustrated by rejection and constant British manipulation of Gã customs, subsequent Gã leaders also had to ask for approval. A letter from Gã *Mãŋtsɛ* Tackie Obili (ruled 1904-19), who succeeded *Mãŋtsɛ* Tawiah, petitioned the governor to approve various issues in Gã courts. They included the following: "1). Grant of personal interview to the Gã *Mãŋtsɛ* by the governor periodically. 2). Power to be given to the Gã *Mãŋtsɛ* to compel the attendance of witnesses etc. at the court."[146] The fate of another petition for permission to begin drumming in preparation for *homowo* festivals that was sent a year before is not known.[147] It is uncertain if any of these petitions were approved. Moreover, the Home Office in London went beyond concerns about the power of the Gã *Mãŋtsɛ*. They were largely concerned with how periodic gatherings by the local people during Gã festivals could create social spaces for resistance against the British.[148]

Rewards for "Good" Behavior

Although the British regulated and controlled the affairs of Gã leaders, they could be reasonable at times. They "rewarded" Gã *Mãŋtsɛ* and chiefs for "keeping order" or for behaving as the British expected them to. Colonial newspapers, including the *Gold Coast Chronicle* spread this message to its reading audience to show a positive side of colonial officials and to attract local chiefs to support colonial agendas.[149] British officials at one point or the other tended to reward local chiefs monetarily. They paid Gã chiefs and others in the Gold Coast colony who successfully carried out their duties to enhance colonial rule. Gã leaders often played to the tune of the British to keep peace in order to create suitable conditions for organizing their followers secretly to rebel against colonial laws at the appropriate time.[150] It is uncertain if the Brazilian chiefs were also paid to carry out colonial projects. I have not come across any archival document that shows that Brazilian chiefs and the freed slaves who settled in the Tabom quarter also needed permission to organize their communities. Such information is important to our understanding of proximity in Gã–British–Brazilian relations.

A memo from a meeting between the British governor and commissioners reminded British officials to be mindful of ways to motivate the Gã leaders. One such letter read:

> Gã *Mãŋtsɛ* Tackie came to see me yesterday.... He desired to hold custom for certain fetish priests [Gã spiritual leaders].... I told him that this was a long custom and that in ordinary circumstances I should not permit it to be held.... But as the town has been quiet and orderly during the Yam custom [one of the customs Gã people inherited from Akan migrants] and during the period for which I had acted as Governor and as my period of service was coming to an end I would ask a favor to grant his application.[151]

In any case, Europeans were successful in manipulating the local people, but these Europeans would be the first to admit that they had their share of these battles.

The roller-coaster relations between colonial officials and their subjects, especially chiefs, defined the terms of the friendship or hostility between them. In Accra, sometimes, the Gã *mãŋtsɛ* and his elders went the extra mile to present gifts to British officials to express their willingness to maintain peaceful ties with the British, but that did not improve relations between the two. In fact, the British kept the Gã leaders at a reasonable distance to ensure that there was a clear distinction between the two groups in their quest to establish, reinforce, and sustain British authority. Another memorandum by Francis Growther, a British official, to Gã *Mãŋtsɛ* Tawiah underscored this boundary by emphasizing that "both the Excellency and Lady Roger are precluded by the Colonial Office Regulations from accepting presents and that therefore your proposal in this connection ... cannot be entertained."[152] This was after *Mãŋtsɛ* Tawiah presented gifts to the British official and his family.

Exchanges and interactions between colonial officials and the Gã state also had enormous impact on other immigrants in Accra. The actions and reactions of the colonial system and Gã mãŋbii shaped the narratives of liberated Africans who made

Gã *mãŋ* their new home. The arrival of the freed slaves from Brazil complicated the fact that the newcomers to Accra had just overcome a major confrontation with servitude in Brazilian plantations: they had to start over again, this time contending with a colonial political system that had gained unrestricted momentum by the end of the 1800s.

FREEDOM AS MYTH IN COLONIAL ACCRA

Traditions prior to and during Gã-British colonial relations remind us of the complexity in articulating transatlantic encounters in Accra between the Gã people, the British, and members of the Brazilian-African diaspora. It would be erroneous to assume that abolitionists' interest in canvassing for the demise of slavery in Brazil could guarantee that the liberated Africans could see their freedom overnight. The story of British abolitionist projects and imperialism are two diametrically opposed phenomena. In other words, the fact that the British Crown and many parliamentarians were actively involved in the abolition movement from the late eighteenth century does not suggest that the aspirations of enslaved Africans and their kinfolk in Africa were taken into consideration. However, the British government as well as philanthropic and religious groups devoted ample resources, manpower, and energy to acting as the voice of enslaved Africans—an important intervention and accomplishment that was largely limited to the Brazilian side of the Atlantic.[153] Metaphorically speaking, the British helped quench the fire that had ignited slavery and led to its expansion in Brazil, but at the same time added fuel to the fire of imperialism in the communities where slaves had originally been captured, particularly the very locations in which some of the Africans later resettled after their emancipation. As we shall see, this complicated historical dance—opposing slavery on the one hand, while embracing imperialism or tolerating it on the other—meant that abolition ironically became a catalyst for new forms of oppression under colonialism: it generated hope for some and despair for others simultaneously.

In the case of Brazilian slaves who gained manumission in the early 1800s or those who were deported to Africa after the infamous 1835 slave revolts in Bahia, they arrived as the British colonial project was getting under way.[154] It is important to examine the transition from abolition in Brazil in 1888 (when some of the enslaved African population gained freedom) to the time the Gold Coast officially became a British colony and gained stable traction by the dawn of the twentieth century.[155] Thirteen years after slavery was abolished in Brazil, notions of freedom for the ex-slaves fell prey to calculated plans for new forms of oppression under imperialism. Regardless of what time period one focuses on, it is obvious that the British Crown and its imperial apparatus took the measure of Africa and its people and acted to calibrate their future to meet the needs of imperialism. Looked at from another angle, the involuntary migrations of Africans into the New World during the transatlantic slave trade, their inclusion in plantation slavery systems, and lack of protection for the freed slaves during colonial rule were all part of a broader plan. As it turned out, British policies denied Africans who remained on the continent and those who joined them after emancipation their fundamental sovereign rights and their humanity. Indeed, the shared struggle and experiences of the Gã people and the freed slaves from Brazil created a consciousness for resistance.

COMMON STRUGGLE CREATED UNITY AND REVOLTS

The European presence posed a major threat to the power and integrity of Gã leaders and to the survival of the Gã *mãŋ* in general. The development of these fragile and hostile relations between Gã mãŋtsɛmɛi and Europeans occurred at a time when the Brazilian-Africans were also seeking attention and a safe refuge to begin a new life in Accra. Indeed, the freed slaves arrived at the onset of colonial rule. This coincidence underscores the contradiction of freedom and exploitation under colonialism. Most importantly, the emancipated Africans were not ready to give up the freedom they had gained in Brazil either by means of manumission, through successful slave rebellions, or after the demise of slavery in Brazil in 1888.[156] There were other striking overlaps. Returnees' long history of movement and migration interested the Gã leaders not only because they possibly shared common ancestral ties but because they both suffered under European oppression and exploitation. These examples and others show the historical cords that bound these two distant groups together across the Atlantic. Clearly, there was a mutual interest that connected the Gã *mãŋ* and the Brazilian-Africans. They had to find ways to create a close-knit relationship based either on kinship or on a common struggle for the freedom to control their land and to sustain their identity and cultural norms.

The interactions among the Gã mãŋbii, the Fante, the Asante, and the Ewe people as well as the Europeans were based on fluid but sometimes contentious exchanges that allowed them to act as friends by day and enemies by night. Although the Gã and the Asante people did not get along, their leaders united on some levels to resist the common threat of British oppression, much as the British and the Dutch cooperated to facilitate European imperialism. Something even more far-reaching would change the path of colonial and Brazilian history later. When the British enacted the Compulsory

Chapter Three

Labour Ordinance (CLO) of 1897, which demanded that local laborers carry British officials on long journeys and for colonial projects, Agyemang Prempeh I, the *Asantehene* (king), and Gã *Mãŋtse* Tackie mobilized their constituencies to rebel against the law.[157] This revolt came after *Mãŋtse* Tawiah returned from exile. Obviously, the heart of the old Gã *mãŋtse* had become hardened during his exile, and he therefore he did not care too much what the British thought of him. Gã and Asante leaders' common struggle with British oppression also stimulated other forms of resistance, part of which appealed to newcomers in Accra.

Gã and Brazilian returnee histories intertwine on a number of levels. Clearly, one cannot talk about the social history of Accra without taking into consideration its impact on the Brazilian returnees' story. As in the case of the Gã–Asante alliance, a similar kind of solidarity emerged among Gã leaders and those who led the returnee community. This unity fueled revolts against the British. For example, Brazilian chief João Antonio Nelson, who formed an alliance with local leaders, was arrested in 1897 with other Gã chiefs (figure 8). They were fined £25 for opposing the CLO. Nelson had arrived with his parents aboard a ship from Brazil at age three. He was later selected as the second Brazilian chief in Accra and ruled from 1865 to 1900. This shows that early Brazilian settlers were not spectators in colonial Accra; nor were they apathetic about British oppression. The Brazilian-Africans contributed to anticolonial nationalist consciousness in Ghana and were trailblazers in the drive to resist colonial rule.

Consistent with the imprint of colonial subjugation in other areas under British colonial hegemony, the distribution of power in Accra was uneven and was enforced strategically.[158] As elsewhere, Gã leaders and the British wielded differing degrees of power and influence. The Brazilian returnees held only minimal power during the nineteenth century. They were basically below the bottom rung of the power ladder, and their presence seldom exerted any pressure on the British to alter their colonial agenda in any major way; in a few cases, the British trespassed on or seized Brazilian land for colonial projects. However, both the British and the returnees had one thing in common: the determination to acquire wealth in the Gold Coast through every possible means.

While the Gã authorities and subjects had to engage both the British and the Brazilians in ways that would contain the two outsider groups, they had no effective means of monitoring them; as a result, the British in particular pursued colonial rule aggressively, and for their part, some of the ex-slaves themselves became involved in the enslavement of local people. Here we see evidence of unity between Gã leaders and Brazilian chief João Antonio Nelson, but there is a twist to the story. Despite evidence that Chief Nelson and *Mãŋtse* Tawiah formed an alliance to resist the CLO, there was tension between them. As if in a vicious cycle, the Gã *mãŋtse* contended with the

Figure 8. Brazilian chief João Antonio Nelson with Mãŋtsɛ Tackie Tawiah and members of the Gã royal family.

returnees and their descendants over land tenure. According to various court records, Gã *Mãŋtsɛ* Komeh I gave part of Gã stool land, which was supposed to be reserved for members of the Gã royal family, to the emancipated Brazilians.

There are several intersections between Gã leaders' determination to protect their territories and traditions, the arrival of the liberated Brazilian-Africans, and British colonial rule in Gã *mãŋ*. In a similar way, the fusion of narratives about the Gã mãŋbii, the Brazilians, and the British brings attention to the long history of landownership and disputes in the social history of Accra. The present difficulty in understanding land tenure is not limited to a particular time period in the past.[159] This chapter does not suggest that both British colonial authorities and the freed slaves took land belonging to the Gã mãŋbii illegally or that these two groups unified to exploit their host, the Gã mãŋbii. Rather, the ex-slaves disliked the British because colonial rule threatened the freedom they had gained after their enslavement in Brazil; in particular they opposed the use of colonial land ordinances to take Brazilian land. Perhaps the British disliked the returnees or saw them as trouble makers because of their long history with revolts in Brazilian plantations. The broader colonial agenda of the British involved multiple land seizures not only to complete colonial projects but also to raise revenues for the British Crown. For the ex-Brazilian slaves they did not have any interest in exploiting the Gã *mãshi*, much less the opportunity to do so. Their only interest was in protecting their inheritance in land. The freed slaves' response to both Gã *Mãŋtsɛ* Tawiah and

Chapter Three

the British was influenced in part by their history of servitude in Brazil, where most of the Africans were not allowed to own land or had to contend with new land policies after their freedom.¹⁶⁰

The freed slaves faced another dilemma. At the height of colonial rule, especially following the enactment of colonial ordinances such as the Public Land Ordinance of 1876, laws limited the rights of Gã leaders and the Gã mãŋbii to make claims to any land within new or redrawn colonial boundaries. *Mãŋtsɛ* Tawiah protested. For the Brazilians and their offspring, they wanted to ensure that the new land policies did not threaten land they received from Gã *Mãŋtsɛ* Komeh I, although legally; under new ordinances that land was also included in colonial boundaries.¹⁶¹

In the process of comparing Gã–Brazilian–British relations and interactions, other distinctions should be made concerning colonial agendas, the conditions in Accra, and how the liberated Brazilians navigated their way around the Brazilian-African diaspora. Obviously the Brazilians did not exploit Accra as the British did. For instance, dispatches between British officials and the Home Office in London show that the British transported a large quantity of silver and other minerals from the Gold Coast to England.¹⁶² There is no evidence that the emancipated Brazilian-Africans in Accra were there for the same reasons as the British. Nor have I found any evidence that says the colonial agenda was the same as the returnees' interest in relocating there. Like the Tabom chiefs and members of the Brazilian-African diaspora, they had restricted access to resources.¹⁶³ The Brazilians acquired a good portion of land in Accra and made substantial profits via commercial activities, while yet other freed Brazilian slaves benefited from both domestic slavery and the sale of slaves that were later transported across the Atlantic world.

Tension between the British and the people of the Gold Coast, especially the rivalry between the British and the Gã people or between the British and the liberated Brazilians on the local level, was not the only palaver or problem. On the national level other groups protested against the whole idea of colonial rule, in particular the ways in which colonial ordinances undermined local developments, cultural practices, and institutions. One such group was the ARPS. Whereas a portion of the educated elites were allies of the British who played a major role in the colonial administration and enforced colonial projects, others led local protests to challenge British rule. These included the leaders of the ARPS, which was established by a group of elites in 1897 to advocate for the rights of the people of the Gold Coast.¹⁶⁴ ARPS was successful in their radicalism and their agitation because they operated as a national organization that heavily drew its strength from the grassroots with powerful rhetoric that emphasized the idea that Africa was for Africans. They demanded immediate amendments to colonial ordinances that elevated long-held local cultural norms and traditions over

British models.¹⁶⁵ In the end, ARPS was able to convince colonial officials to withdraw the Land Bill.¹⁶⁶ According to David Kimble, the emergence of ARPS as a major force on the national stage was timely. It was an extension of the Mfantsi Amabuhu Fekuw (Fante Governing Society, an anticolonial movement).¹⁶⁷ One of the core manifestos of ARPS stated that colonial subjects were good enough to define their own destiny. The group also declared that "the principle of Trusteeship with respect to the lands of the people of the British West Africa by Government has been overdone. . . . The average British West African is quite capable of controlling and looking after his own interest."¹⁶⁸

Whereas Gã *Mãŋtsɛ* Tawiah evoked notions of rights to Gã sovereignty, other non-Gã societies, including Fante and Ashante leaders, also made their views visible. For instance, on the forefront of Fante nationalism, leading figures including John Mensah Sarbah declared that Fante cultures and customs did not need any refinement. Sarbah asserted that "the African social system has been built up gradually . . . so as to meet its own special requirement, and consequently should not be recklessly tampered with."¹⁶⁹ Sarbah's proclamation echoed the voices of victims of British colonial rule. In fact, it epitomized the dreams and aspirations of the Gã mãŋbii, the Brazilian-African diaspora, and colonial subjects in general. Other provoking responses of this kind, which resonated widely, defined British colonial encounters in Ghana from the nineteenth century.

The social history of Gã, Accra, most notably series of stern colonial policies impacted and weakened the authority of Gã mãŋtsɛmɛi and threatened long-established Gã cultural traditions. In addition, the freedom and properties the emancipated Africans acquired in Accra from the early 1800s was a significant watershed moment in the social history of Accra during the colonial days. In general, their settlements in Accra reveal a paradox of freedom and return to an ancestral homeland that was under grave sociopolitical turmoil by the dawn of the nineteenth century. Accra was a highly contested colonial space. Indeed, Gã mãŋtsɛmɛi did not accept the colonial system that successfully used local leaders and the educated elite to promote colonial agendas. Colonial intervention and the enforcement of ordinances concealed under what became known as the Lugardian Principle of Indirect Rule, which was achieved after the scramble for Africa by the end of the nineteenth century, subverted and weakened existing local institutions and cultural practices over time.¹⁷⁰ Europeans' scramble to create colonies in Africa also bears a striking resemblance to the competition between European powers for trading posts prior to and during the era of the transatlantic slave trade. During this time, Europeans drew artificial boundaries within communities, societies, and clustered cultural groups to form separate countries. The scramble for Africa, particularly British colonial rule in Ghana, would not have been possible without the role of European merchants, missionaries, and later local educated elites who in one way or another accelerated the process of colonial rule.[171]

Other newcomers were in Accra to do precisely the opposite. These included the liberated Brazilians who were in search of a permanent place to call their new home. Gã *Mãŋtsɛ* Komeh I's advice to the ex-slaves to select their own chiefs and leaders to lead the community bridged the gap between them and the Gã people. This facilitated the cultural integration of the emancipated Brazilians into larger Gã cultural systems. The strategic plans of Komeh I were also meant to attract more Brazilian-Africans who settled along the Bight of Benin to relocate to Accra for economic reasons.[172] Another motivation was to foster leadership within the Brazilian community that would join forces with Gã leaders in their quest to sustain Gã traditions and resist British rule. The Brazilian returnees settled in Otublohum where they established the Tabom quarter during their early years of settlement to begin a Brazilian-African diaspora—a community of freed slaves and their offspring. Through this process, the Brazilians were integrated gradually into both the cultural and the sociopolitical institutions of the Gã people by the end of the 1800s.

The emancipated Africans' systematic assimilation into colonial Gã societies by the end of the nineteenth century provided a firm base that shaped how they saw themselves and the ways in which they related to their hosts over time. Their partial integration also facilitated the governing of the Brazilian-African diaspora in Accra by Brazilian chiefs who served as mãŋtsɛmɛi, the representatives of the Brazilian community, as well as go-betweens for the community and Gã leaders. By the early twentieth century, this partial integration created a platform for permanent assimilation by their offspring, the Tabom. During this significant turning point in the social history of Accra, the freed slaves and their descendants clashed with both the British colonial authorities and *Mãŋtsɛ* Tawiah over what became known as Brazilian land.

Studies about the early years of Accra and the British colonial presence show that *Mãŋtsɛ* Tawiah was a controversial figure and a leading voice in campaigns against British rule and policies that exploited the subjects of the colonies. *Mãŋtsɛ* Tawiah was an influential actor and a formidable advocate against colonial intrusion in part of the area known in present-day Ghana as the Greater Accra Region. In the early decades of colonization, the British controlled the Southern Protectorate, which included Accra and other coastal towns. When the British defeated the Asante people in the Northern Protectorate in the Yaa Asantewaa War of 1900–1901, the entire Gold Coast officially became a British colony.[173] Similar to the relations between the British and the Asante chiefs, encounters between the British and *Mãŋtsɛ* Tawiah were so tense that the British sent the king into exile. The goal was to prevent the Gã people from further revolts against the colonial apparatus.[174]

Oral traditions from my interviews suggest that the Brazilians fought alongside the British during the British-Asante Wars.[175] These traditions also claim that the freed slaves supported the Gã people during the Gã-Akwamu Wars in the late 1800s through the early 1900s. There is insufficient evidence in the archives and oral tradition to support this assertion. However, ample evidence shows that the ex-slaves joined forces with Gã mãŋtsɛmɛi in other ways for mutual benefits. What is obvious is that the returnee's arrived beginning in the 1820s when Gã leaders and the British were in total disagreement over the role of the British and Europeans in managing sociocultural and political activities in precolonial Accra.[176] Gã mãŋtsɛmɛi therefore had a daunting task to defend their cultures and their land, inspire Gã nationalism, and oppose foreign rule in Accra simultaneously. In the process of accomplishing this overwhelming task, Gã leaders set the stage for degrees of uprisings. The Brazilians witnessed the friction between Gã leaders and British officials, and at the appropriate time they also joined the bandwagon to defend their rights. In fact, both Gã territories and the Brazilian-African diaspora became contested sociocultural sites of power particularly as colonial officials in Accra, missionaries, migrants, and expatriates of diverse hues sought to carve out permanent settlements in coastal Accra to establish a permanent colonial footprint, to establish church missions, to acquire land, to expand commerce, and to take advantage of fledgling mining opportunities.[177] This intrusion made landowning Gã people and the freed slaves alike uncomfortable.

Contradictions inherent in Gã states' right to self-determination, freedom associated with emancipation, abolition, and colonialism as well as the ways in which the ex-slaves' freedom from Brazil coincided with the introduction of colonial ordinances in Accra from the early nineteenth century had enormous impact. For instance on one hand colonial policies, especially land ordinances, threatened the Gã political and cultural institutions.[178] On the other hand this threat had ripple effects on landowning Brazilians and their offspring. In addition, in terms of the social history of Accra there is an irony in the hospitality Gã *Mãŋtsɛ* Komeh I extended to the ex-slaves, particularly the ways in which the gifts of land created tension between Gã *Mãŋtsɛ* Tawiah and the freed slaves after Tawiah inherited from Gã *Mãŋtsɛ* Komeh I. This paradox is significant to the Brazilian-African diaspora experience in Ghana, particularly during the land disputes between the ex-slaves and others.[179]

Besides fulfilling the dream of the ex-slaves who were able to own land perhaps for the first time, the hospitality *Mãŋtsɛ* Komeh I extended to Brazilian returnees allowed the freed Africans to complete part of the notion of a return to an African homeland that most enslaved Africans envisioned in Brazil but few were able to experience. A permanent dwelling place, such as the Tabom quarter and other pockets of land they acquired later in other areas in Gã *mãŋ*, enabled the returnees and their descendants to travel from one location to the other. Indeed, it also allowed them to construct and reconstruct their identities and establish the first Brazilian-African diaspora in Accra.

Chapter 4

The Evolution of Land in Gã *Mãŋ* and Brazilian-African Diaspora: Paradox of Freedom and the Birth of Conflicts

> It appears that as far back as the thirties [1830s] a ship load of Africans were landed from Brazils where they were taken from the Niger. After they were landed [sic] the Ga chiefs gave them land to build on in the town Accra and also bush land to cultivate.... Lands were divided up amongst the Brazilians by their headman Sokoto and the land in dispute forms a portion of the land known as Mama Nassu's land.
>
> —Chief Justice Crampton Smyly, 1915

The epigraph covers part of the diaspora exchange that took place after the ex-slaves from Brazil arrived in Gã *mãŋ* in the 1830s. Gã *Mãŋtsɛ* Tackie Komeh I (king of Accra) later gave the returnees gifts of land that was often referred to as "Brazilian land." The tradition of allocating personal land to newcomers was common in other areas. Historian Michael J. Turner, in his study of freed Brazilian slaves who settled in Benin (the Aguda), shows a similar practice by the local chiefs.[1] Clearly, in Accra as in other places land tenure formed an integral part of the returnees' identity formation and the processes of settlement or assimilation. Part of the epigraph also shows the ways in which land traditions within the Brazilian-African diaspora were used for farming practices after their arrival. Two leaders in the community, Mama Sokoto and Mama Nassu, supervised Brazilian land, but as life in their communities evolved, the Brazilian chiefs, the leader of the Brazilian-African diaspora, or colônia de Brazileiros (colony of Brazilians)[2] distributed and protected Brazilian land from non-Brazilians. Multifaceted issues relating to land acquisition, distribution, and transfer after the demise Sokoto and Nassu emerged and created tension within the Brazilian-African diaspora, from one generation to the next.³

After the demise of the early settlers, an old man in the colônia de Brazileiros who had inherited part of the Brazilian land decided to cross the Atlantic Ocean one more time. Before paying for his voyage to Lagos from Accra, he passed on his portion of land to the love of his life. The story of the marriage between this man known as Ferku, a freed slave from Brazil, and his bride Yawah, whom he married after he came to Accra from Lagos in the late 1800s, provides a good reference point for understanding the evolution of Brazilian-African diaspora in Accra. The story of their union helps explain the irony of return, the dissonance of inheritance, the multifaceted nature of land tenure and ownership, and how divisions over Brazilian land created ripple effects in Brazilian-African communities in British colonial Accra. The complex marriage union between Ferku and Yawah and their love story, especially the way it ended, mirrors other unforeseen interactions and tension between landowning ex-slaves and their offspring, as well as the effects of stringent colonial policies.⁴ Both Ferku's nomadic transatlantic lifestyle and his marriage ended abruptly when he decided to spend the rest of his life in Lagos. The piece of land Yawah inherited from her husband then became entangled in colonial courts that were established to address land disputes. As the case *Yawah v. J. E. Maslieno* demonstrates, part of this problem was caused by avarice and exploitation by some of the members of the Brazilian-African diaspora.⁵ Other aspects of this dispute also epitomize larger differences among various generations in the Brazilian-African diaspora in Accra as the younger generations of the Tabom sold most of the farmlands they inherited.

The ex-slaves from Brazil (the first generation) had a different ideology about family and communal relations than those who came after them. I also show how this sense of harmony evolved into conflicts that had ripple effects over time. Perhaps because of their shared struggle and experiences with oppression on plantations in Brazil and the fact that most of them had not owned land there, the first generation banded together. However, the chapter critiques the impression that the returnees created a separate community in the areas that the archives characterize as bush and did not interact much with the coastal people. In fact the Brazilian-African diaspora began on the coastline of Accra, Tabom quarter, and later spread to the interior.⁶ These were a dynamic group of returnees who moved back and forth between places. Conversely, the demise of the early settlers had an enormous, transformative impact on the subsequent history of Ghana. For instance, the Tabom people's assimilation into Ghanaian societies beginning in the late 1800s weakened communal activities and led to the obscuring of their ancestral history over time. These differences not only assist in the construction of a chronology of the returnee community, but they provide a path for our understanding of the distinctions between the first generation and their offspring. The Tabom trace their roots through either *naabi* or *kyerbi*, Gã words that mean matrilineal lineage and patrilineal lines, respectively. This matter of inheritance is important because it shows how gender lines were constructed and how power and space were also allocated within the Brazilian-African diaspora. These traditions were influenced in part by Gã cultural practices.

One cannot discuss transformation in the social history of Accra from the 1800s without taking into account overlaps in the Brazilian returnee narratives during the early period of emancipation as well as the impact of British colonial ordinances that were implemented at the peak of colonialism. Landownership for most of the Brazilians and their descendants solidified their sense of liberty, security, and power; therefore, the advent of colonial policies, particularly the Public Land Ordinance of 1897 that regulated all lands in Gã societies, was a nightmare.[7] Indeed, the Brazilian-Africans were not the only ones who were affected by colonial ordinances. For the Gã people and their leaders, their lives were not the same after they extended hospitality to the ex-slaves at the onset of abolition in Brazil, as well as to European missionaries, traders, and colonial officials.[8] The continuum of the transition from the demise of slavery in Brazil to the imposition of colonial rule in Accra shows a striking paradox of freedom and its denial, as evidenced in the Brazilian-African diaspora narratives.

Colonial rule and the series of ordinances the British introduced were not specifically targeted toward any particular group of liberated African returnees. However, in the end, as demonstrated in court disputes over Brazilian land, colonial policies affected the lives of these former slaves and their offspring throughout the colonial period and even after the demise of British rule in Ghana on 6 March 1957. Examples of several key ordinances associated with landownership enable us to situate the ripple effects in the social history of Accra.

Gã Land Traditions and the Genesis of Brazilian Land: Ferku's Reverse Dilemmas

It was a common saying among the people of the Gold Coast (now Ghana) that "land belongs to a vast family of whom many are dead, a few are living, and a countless host are still unborn." Local traditional norms in regard to land tenure were highly valued and passed on from one generation to the next. This changed after Gã mãŋtsɛmɛi (kings and chiefs of Accra) welcomed *gbɔi* to Accra. The interplay between existing land policies (practiced by the colonized) and the new ordinances (enforced by the colonizer), such as the Public Land Ordinance of 1876, as well to destoolment (replacement) of local chiefs who did not support colonial agendas, had a momentous impact on the people of the Gold Coast from the nineteenth century.[9]

The social history of the Gã mãŋbii, the original inhabitants of the area, shows that from the fifteenth century on, they contested with the English, the Portuguese, the Swedes, the Danish, and other Europeans for control over land and trading posts especially along the coastline.[10] Competition between European powers eventually led to British colonial rule in the early 1900s. During this watershed moment in Ghanaian history, the colonial rulers not only annulled existing local laws that allowed the local people and their guests to own pockets of land with no external influence; they invented and imposed their own ordinances and land policies. British colonial rule created sociopolitical bifurcation and several levels of problems for landowning individuals, families, groups, and societies when it ignored long-held religious, cultural, and institutional definitions of land tenure and distribution. The enforcement of colonial policies heightened after the capital of the Gold Coast Colony was moved from Cape Coast to Accra in 1877. The British Crown was determined to reform Gã societies to fit the British and Western imagination. The ambitious colonialists' agenda and laws affected the freed Brazilian slaves and their offspring, who had to depend on colonial courts and native courts (established by the colonial rulers) to reclaim gifts of land they received from Gã *Mãŋtse* Komeh I from those who had taken them illegally from the late 1800s.

Land was in such a great demand in Gã *mãŋ* that those interested in it paid huge sums of money for it.[11] Residents of Accra, especially Europeans and expatriates, needed land for such purposes as expanding their businesses, housing workers, or establishing missionary schools.[12] Writing to his family in Switzerland in the early 1900s, a missionary from Basel had this to say: "We are in Accra, the most important city of the Gold Coast. . . . There is lively traffic on the street of Christianborg. . . . There is a group of traders [here]."[13] Landownership was often key to one's identity construction and determined how much economic power one held. Access to land typically guaranteed one's social, economic, and political uplift and influence. As Kathryn Firmin-Sellers notes, "The rise of land values prompted Europeans and indigenous actors alike to work to redefine customary land tenure."[14] This redefinition of customary land laws shaped the ways in which landowning individuals and family groups could respond to the drastic changes brought by colonial rule.

Literature on land tenure in Accra during the colonial era in part examines the traditions that were in place prior to colonial rule in an effort to show the points of convergence and divergence.[15] Land in most Ghanaian societies is seen as a sacred space or landscape originally belonging to ancestral spirits and gods. However, the idea of using land to meet the needs of the *oman* (the Akan word for the entire community) was accepted together with its spiritual importance. The revered sacred value of land as well as its sociocultural relevance does not mean that land—as an ancestral resource passed from generation to generation—was not allocated to those who needed it for farming, housing, and so on.[16] Rather, this long-held custom mirrors the notion that land cannot be controlled by an individual or a particular institution. Nor can citizens of a particular community be alienated from land that belonged to the village and the people. According to S. K. B. Asante, "Land was the sanctuary for the souls of the departed ancestors.... [This] concept of landownership [was] thus bound up with the cult of ancestral worship."[17] Asante asserts that the value of land to most Ghanaian social groups and cultures meant that efforts were made by these societies to apportion land to people for a definite time period after which these mutual agreements allowed some form of exchange to the mutual benefit of both parties.

Precolonial Ghanaian societies were tied closely to the land because of the wealth it represented and the ways it enforced a communal lifestyle and agrarian activities such as farming and herding. Asante maintains that "an absolute sale of land ... was therefore not simply a question of alienating realty, [but] notoriously, it was a case of selling a spiritual heritage for a mess of pottage, a veritable betrayal of ancestral trust, an undoing of posterity."[18] However, people who lived prior to British rule in Ghana did not necessarily embrace the cultural wisdom of this idea that the sale of land was literally connected to the sale of a sacred heritage or ancestral trust. Land sales existed alongside land disputes for centuries before the advent of colonial land ordinances in the nineteenth century. Chiefs and heads of families depended on spiritual forces as evidence of land transactions; in some situations these local institutions of power exchanged land legally for money on mutually beneficial terms.[19] But when the British arrived and colonial projects such as the Stool Property Protection Ordinance of 1940, which required local chiefs to seek permission from colonial officials before giving out land, gained momentum everything changed—rights to landownership gradually became a myth.[20]

Increasing migrations to Gã *mãŋ* and other forces fused different cultures and belief systems in ways that complicated land tenure. For instance, population growth and increasing demand for land in Accra as it gradually transformed from a rural landscape to an urban one contributed to this shift. Migrations, especially of farmers who settled in Accra to plant and cultivate their products to contribute to fledgling economic activities along the coast, helped sustain the agrarian lifestyle; these farmers searched for land and paid large sums for it thus creating a bubble of supply by those who sold or rented temporal pockets of land by legal and illegal means.[21] The court records show that in some situations, Brazilian land was sold to the highest bidder or to the buyer who was determined to pay more.[22] Samuel S. Quarcoopome's study of the impact of urbanization on Gã *maashi* provides insights regarding the changes in Accra and how existing tensions between various groups vying for economic opportunities, power, and social mobility were heightened.[23] The advent of colonialism in particular changed the dynamics of power and ownership from communal affair to centralized institutional arrangements through which colonial officials exploited landowning individuals or groups by appropriating the right to seize, restrict, and regulate communal properties for the benefit of colonial ventures as noted in figure 9.

In line with their long history of conquest and empire building around the globe, the British endeavored to acquire resources from their colonies, motivated in part by the notion that African societies did not know the significance of the resources in their backyard, that they were uncivilized and therefore needed guidance, and thus ignored local traditions about land tenure that stood in their way. In addition, colonial ordinances were foreign to the people of the Gold Coast, who had attained a different level of education: the British attempt to articulate these laws to an entire population of non-English speakers led, not surprisingly, to chaos. As C. K. Meek's study *Land Law and Custom in the Colonies* relates:

> Confusion has been caused by the supposition that the sale of land was a new-fangled idea unknown to native customary law. It has also been assumed that native law is necessarily ancient custom and is therefore incapable of providing [for the British] the security of tenure demanded by modern conditions.... There is a political danger in allowing individuals to become owners of "freehold," without owing any allegiance to the local Native Authorities.... If "Indirect rule" is to continue to be a cardinal principle of British policy in tropical Africa, it would appear to be essential that local Native Authorities should remain the ultimate "owners" ... since the "ownership" or control of land lies at the root of all African conceptions of government.[24]

Meek basically draws attention to contradictions in the ways that imperialist strategy sought to destabilize fluid existing practices that had freely allocated portions of land without any major restrictions. The whole concept of imperialism was marked by both economic benefits and prejudice, which motivated the calculated efforts to strip African societies of the gains they had made in fostering a level of trust and accountability between the masses and their various leaders. Colonial policies had enormous impact on various societies and cultures in the Gold Coast, especially Accra, which became a hub for local migrants and foreigners alike.[25] Now Ghana's capital city and the seat of government, Accra not only attracted foreigners; it was also home to formerly enslaved

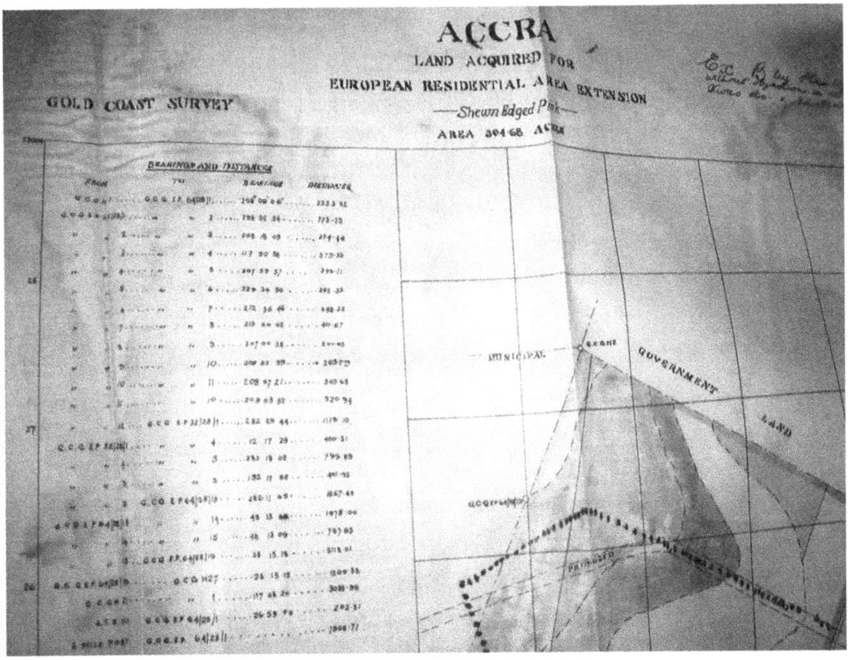

PUBLIC RECORDS AND ARCHIVES ADMINISTRATION DEPARTMENT, ACCRA, GHANA.

Figure 9. Land acquired for European residential area.

Africans from Brazil who were welcomed by the local chiefs who settled some of them in an area that became known as the Tabom quarter where some the returnees were given land.[26] Brazil has a long history with Ghana that dates back to the transatlantic slave trade. Lorenzo D. Turner's collections include photographs and stories of slaves in and from Brazil that tell the story of Sozenja dos Santos, who was originally from Accra. Dos Santos did not return to her homeland after the end of Brazilian slavery in 1888. She died in Bahia around 1905.

As dos Santos, other freed Africans did not return to Africa not only because they did not see any meaningful ties to the continent or had no memory of a homeland besides Brazil. Some did not immediately join voyages to Africa due to the fact that there were a number of economic opportunities including petty trading and farming in Brazil. Ex-slaves such as Antonio José Dutra later became wealthy through various trading ventures. Although some did not see any hope for a new life in Africa, a number of them made it home to Africa safely and intermarried with the local people. In the mid-1800s a man by the name of Ferku joined a group of liberated Brazilian-Africans on a voyage to Lagos. He later relocated to Accra, where other returnees were living. His resettlement, as others, however, coincided with the arrival of British colonial rulers. The colonial system being imposed on the Gold Coast bore the same hallmarks of oppression and exploitation that Ferku and others had escaped just decades earlier. The love story between Ferku and Yawah who were married in Accra also speaks to the ways in which an emancipated Brazilian passed on his land to his wife before he left her in Accra to settle permanently in Lagos somewhere in the early 1900s. However, the court case of *Yawah v. J. E. Maslieno* does not provide sufficient narratives to explain how Yawah was able to defend the wealth her husband entrusted to her care.

The involuntary migrations that began along the coastline of Gã *mãŋ* and other areas on the African continent in the seventeenth century as enslaved Africans crossed the Atlantic to plantations in Brazil and other destinations in the Americas and continued full circle back to Gã *mãŋ* encompasses a larger transatlantic narrative that is entrenched in abolition narratives. Abolition projects sparked a sense of hope for newly liberated Africans, many of whom then joined waves of reverse migration to an imagined homeland in places like Accra in the early 1800s.[27] However, the entrance of British imperialism onto this diaspora stage in Accra startled the freed slaves who had dreamed of a new peaceful life there void of an oppressive European imprint. Indeed, abolition and imperialism both were strategically designed to intrude into the lives of or cause interruptions to specific societies and groups of people. For instance, British involvement in slavery, abolition, and colonialism had a lasting impact on the lives of the freed slaves and the Gã mãŋbii who did not foresee the continuation of foreign meddling in their lives, cultures, and societies. The new forms of intrusion altered existing traditions especially with regard to land tenure. In many ways, the advent of colonial rule in Ghana, which gained momentum during the arrival of the emancipated Africans from Brazil, reminds us of the paradox as well as the intersections between freedom, imperialism, and its implications to landownership in Accra, which shaped the story of returnees such as Ferku.

It is believed that Ferku married and had children in Lagos before relocating to Accra in the Gold Coast colony in the 1870s to begin a new life. In Accra, Ferku's marriage union with Yawah lasted about twenty years. It is not clear if they had any children. However, there is important information concerning their marriage during the latter stages of their time together. As Yawah tells it, "Her parents hailed from Brazil. Her father's name was Aruna and her mother's was Fatuma. Ferku engaged and married her according to Brazil customs."[28] There is uncertainty about what aspect of Brazilian customs she was referring to, but besides polygamous marriage and the ex-slaves' preference for large family size, which is attributable to the need for extra labor hands in agrarian communities, most of the early settlers maintained their Brazilian culture. This was evident in their clothing, especially the elite among them who dressed in suits and hats, as well as their use of the Portuguese language in Lagos, Accra, and other areas.[29] In terms of religion, a portion of returnees sustained their Muslim and

Christian faith, which they later spread in various settlements. Yawah and Ferku's religious background is not known.

Yawah's marriage to Ferku, a man much older than she, was also not unusual among freed Brazilian slaves in Accra. It is believed that Ferku was among the early settlers who farmed on the land Komeh I, king of the Gã *mãŋ*, gave to the Brazilians. Besides their age difference, Ferku and Yawah had contrasting personalities and interests. For instance, whereas Ferku had lived in Accra for nearly five decades, he spent part of his time traveling back and forth to Lagos trading and visiting his extended family; Yawah, who was also of Brazilian-African ancestry, did not adhere to the tradition of the returnees who kept moving from one place to another. She spent much of her time in Accra assisting her father, Aruna, who was a trader.[30] The major challenge Ferku and Yawah encountered was not their age difference or the fact that he was born in Brazil and she in Accra or even that their lives were shaped by different experiences of socialization, upbringing, and cultural values. Rather, their major problem was the decision of where to spend the rest of their life: Accra or Lagos? Unlike other emancipated Africans and their children who kept traveling back and forth across the Atlantic, Yawah was basically not interested in relocating. This decision would define their future, especially how Ferku used his share of the land he acquired.

Ferku could not convince Fatuma, Yawah's mother, to persuade her daughter to join him in his routine trips to Lagos, in part because he could not change the fact that Yawah was very close to other members of the Brazilian community in Accra and the local Gã people as well. Like other descendants who were born in Accra, it is likely that she assimilated deeper into the local Gã culture from her childhood. However, Ferku had other plans that were colored by his memory of Lagos. Ferku's decision to move to Lagos permanently put his marriage and relations with extended family members, especially Yawah's parents, to the test. Ferku had to reach some kind of arrangement to guarantee that his absence would not affect Yawah's future in a major way. Her court testimony reveals other details about their relationship, in particular the compromise and the mutual terms of their separation. According to this story,

> Ferku was old before he married Yawah, and when [he] was about to leave for Lagos, he told Yawah's mother that he may not likely return back again to Accra as he is old and the only thing he can do for his wife as a gift was the land now in dispute ... the portion of land he has sold same to one Kwartei Asanti to defray his expenses to Lagos.[31]

One may wonder what plans Ferku had regarding his land before his disagreement with his wife about where to spend the rest of their life. Perhaps he was honest about his intentions, but how Yawah inherited the land raises some doubts and shows that that the land allocation was an afterthought. Ferku had to improvise to create a peaceful atmosphere before his last journey across the Atlantic. Perhaps, considering the history of legal and illegal land sales in the Brazilian community, Ferku might have sold part of this land before relocating to Lagos with Yawah. It is also possible that Ferku planned his departure long before, with or without his wife's knowledge or approval. He may even have used the land he transferred to Yawah or Asanti to please them and at the same time to avoid illegal possession by British officials who used new ordinances to take over private lands for colonial projects.[32] And the British might not have been the only ones Ferku was concerned about. It is likely that he knew about other indigenous actors such as migrants, expatriates, missionaries, the Gã mãŋbii, and other colonial subjects.

In retrospect, the emergence of Asanti as the owner of a portion of Ferku's property in the court document raises important questions about Ferku's decision prior to his departure to Lagos around the age of seventy-five. First, there is uncertainty about the main reason why Ferku decided to relocate to Lagos after living in Accra for about two decades. Like other older liberated Africans who made dangerous return voyages from Brazil to various locations in Africa in order to be buried in their ancestral homeland, Ferku might have not been from Accra but might have desired an eventual burial in his homeland of Lagos.[33] Part of the answer lies in the irony of such attempts at return, the fact that the idea of a home outside Brazil as well as Accra was a fantasy. Ferku faced the reality of disappointment after crisscrossing between Lagos and Accra on many occasions. In short, he had no immunity against new land laws after his liberation from Brazilian slavery. For her part, Yawah was left with a piece of land that was in dispute.

The court case *Yawah v. J. E. Maslieno* shows that Ferku easily assured both Yawah and her mother that his wife could depend on the land she inherited. There is no evidence that Ferku intentionally set up a contentious situation for Yawah regarding her ownership rights in the land. Yawah had to contest with indigenous actors such as Asanti and other Brazilians like Maslieno who took advantage of Ferku's absence to exploit her. The limited role of the Brazilian chief in monitoring and ensuring that such misunderstanding did not occur contributed to this. Broadly speaking, the dispute between Yawah and Maslieno, as well as the limited influence of Brazilian chiefs and confusion over their role characterized land disputes in the Brazilian-African diaspora from the late 1800s through the twenty-first century.

UNFORESEEN CLASHES BETWEEN FREEDOM, IMPERIALISM,
EXPLOITATION, AND LAND TENURE

Ferku's story should not be treated in isolation. There were similar experiences in the creation of other returnee settlements elsewhere. Discourse about the journeys of liberated Brazilian-Africans who joined voyages of hope to an imagined homeland must not only address the multifaceted experiences of the returnees as they crisscrossed turbulent Atlantic waters from Brazil to West Africa but also highlight the irony of return. The paradox of return reveals complex problems the ex-slaves encountered within their new settlement communities in Lagos, Benin, Togo, and the colônia de Brazileiros in Accra, as well as areas in Angola.[34] Antônio Olinto's *Casa da Agua* (*Water House*), which draws from the life histories of individuals or groups of returnees, helps us appreciate and understand the dual challenges emancipated Africans encountered:[35] on the horizontal level (within local communities of settlements) and on the vertical plane (institutional dictates, especially colonialism in Accra). For Brazilian-African slaves their problems began as they prepared to take their first steps after gaining manumission or after abolition of slavery in 1888.

Correspondence between British abolitionists, Brazilian authorities, and the Portuguese Crown reveals disturbing hurdles that slave owners, ship owners, and cartels placed in the way of the newly freed slaves. A letter from Benjamin Campbell to Lord Clarendon states that such hindrances were unacceptable. However, the long-distance correspondence did not alter the future of the freed slaves in any major way.[36] There was a series of clandestine activities both in Brazil and in various locations in Africa where slaves were taken.[37] In another correspondence, it was reported that some ship captains abused the freed slaves on their ships and stole the money some of the slaves had saved or the property they carried aboard the ship. Other ship owners lied to the freed slaves, taking the money they paid for their travel back to Africa and abandoning the helpless Africans on unknown islands or locations far from their destinations.[38] The *Gold Coast Echo* and other colonial newspapers covered part of the reverse migration story. On 5 November 1888, perhaps immediately after the formal abolition of slavery in Brazil, a report from Abeokuta, Nigeria, stated that, "Out of about 265 emigrants, the passengers of three vessels, who landed in Lagos, it appears that not one [of the returnees] escaped with any of their property save the clothes which they clad."[39]

The challenges the freed slaves encountered in Brazil prior to their return to Africa resemble those they had to deal with locally upon arrival. For instance, in Lagos and other areas local African chiefs and slave merchants sought an alliance that facilitated the reenslavement of the returnees.[40] One such chief was Akintoye, whose reign of

Chapter Four

terror drove the citizens of his community and returnees alike away from his region.[41] A number of freed slaves who settled in Lagos later relocated to Accra or other locations in West Africa to avoid reenslavement. There is insufficient evidence to show that Ferku was among the liberated Africans who left Lagos for Accra out of fear of being reenslaved; however, it is possible that he was part of the wave of freed slaves who moved to Accra to benefit from the hospitality Gã *Mãŋtsɛ* Komeh I extended to the ex-slaves. There were, however, obstacles for Ferku and other returnees for achieving or establishing their new identity from the nineteenth century.

Ferku's Diaspora Experience: Implications of His Freedom and Colonialism

Ferku's story, which stems from his nomadic involuntary and voluntary migrations across the geography of the African diaspora, especially the piece of land he gave to Yawah that later became entangled in court disputes, epitomizes other struggles and challenges African slaves in Brazil encountered with regard to their proximity to land. Brazilian sociologist Gilberto Freyre in *The Masters and the Slaves: A Study in Development of Brazilian Civilization* asserts that the strict established boundaries on Brazilian plantations were mainly meant to maintain a wide boundary between the slave and the master. In addition, he explores the structural binaries between *casa grande* (the big house) and *senzala* (the slave quarter). According to Freyre, the *casa grande* served multiple purposes: the home of the masters, a fortress, a bank, a cemetery, a chapel, a hospital, a school, a convent, a charity giving shelter, an orphanage, and a kitchen.[42] It is against this backdrop that the allocation of land and social space were constructed in Brazilian history.[43]

This practice that existed on many plantations in Brazil demanded free labor from slaves while simultaneously denying them any access to land.[44] As the literature on land tenure in Brazil shows, slaves had a minimal chance of acquiring land or any form of property. Part of the reason was that most of the land was used to demand free labor from the slaves to meet high economic needs.[45] Stuart B. Schwartz's seminal examination of slaves in Brazil, *Sugar Plantations in the Formation of Brazilian Society*, emphasizes the pivotal role of land to economic activities in the sugar region of Bahia and other areas. According to Schwartz, "The distribution of slave ownership in Bahia was related to the land usage of the region. . . . The districts of southern Recôncavo devoted primarily to subsistence farming of manioc [cassava] for local markets."[46] For most slave owners, free slave labor was important, but their main interest was in acquiring large areas of land for accumulating wealth. The latter was a priority over providing comfortable living spaces for the enslaved Africans or what the slaves could own as personal properties.[47] In fact, in many plantations "the slave was an item of movable property."[48] However, this does not imply that enslaved Africans never had the opportunity to own land in Brazil. Brazilian historian João José Reis has shown that emancipated Africans including Domingos Pereira Sodré, a Nagô priest, owned properties including slaves in Bahia in the nineteenth century.[49]

Besides Bahia and Recôncavo a number of major cities in Brazil made major economic strides in slavery activities. "Rio de Janeiro was the conduit of a significant volume of domestic and international trade … and was far and away the busiest slave port in the world in the nineteenth century."[50] Numerous other Africans managed to own land. Those who gained manumission included Antonio José Dutra, a freed African slave who became very rich after his freedom. He owned his own slaves and a barber shop in Rio de Janeiro. Dutra and others who gained their freedom prior to abolition in 1888 decided not to return to Africa. Part of the reason was that he owned vast tracts of land, lived comfortably, and thus did not encounter such hardship as other slaves did.[51] Unlike Dutra, who lived a life of luxury and had a stable future, other slaves who managed to purchase small pockets of land to improve their deteriorating living conditions in Rio de Janeiro did so based on conditions that they remained faithful to their owners and fulfilled rigorous back-breaking labor duties.[52]

Staying permanently in Brazil or returning to Africa was not a guarantee that such a decision could change the life of the liberated African. It was a game of chance that could go any direction. To be safe, a portion of the freed slave population made Brazil and Lagos, Nigeria, their dual home. These were mainly traders who were engaged in large-scale goods transfer including palm oil, dry meat, beads, and other items between these two Atlantic locations.[53] Pierre Verger's book, *Trade Relations between the Bight of Benin and Bahia from the 17th to 19th Century*, traces the evolution of trade between Brazil and the Bight of Benin over a century and examines commercial activities by slaves and freed Africans. The trading posts or sites as Verger describes served as a bridge for linking the two commercial Atlantic coastlines. However, fierce competition between Europeans for controlling trading posts in order to gain monopoly created tension. According to Verger, "The loss of São Jorge da Mina [Elmina Castle in Ghana] in 1637 contributed to disruption of the Portuguese economy and brought about a complete reversal in the principles governing commercial exchanges between the entire kingdom and its entire region of the African coast."[54]

The story Verger articulates extended beyond Brazil and the Bight. A number of returnees in the Brazilian-African diaspora in Gã *mãŋ* followed similar trading trajectories as they moved between Brazil, Nigeria, and Ghana in the nineteenth century selling goods including beads.⁵⁵ Yawah's father, Aruna, who also arrived from Brazil, continued the commercial traditions but he mainly focused on trading posts within Ghana.⁵⁶ In the case of Ferku, he does not say if he also traded along the coastline of Brazil and West Africa, neither does he reveal that he was a farmer. Commercial activities shaped some of these migratory paths, but other persons crossed the Atlantic for other reasons. There were a number of freed slaves who were so old by the time they joined the exodus back to Africa that as some have suggested, they were looking forward to returning to be buried in their ancestral homeland.⁵⁷ If Ferku falls within this category of returnees, then the land he owned in Accra would be his main treasure, but Lagos was supposed to be his resting place after his death.

Ferku's life in Brazil, as well as those of other returnees who became part of the colônia de Brazileiros, is not covered in the various works that speak about the African diaspora experience in Brazil, Accra, and Lagos. I am unsure of his experience in Brazil. But we know that in Accra those who owned Brazilian land, perhaps for the first time, valued these estates and protected them for posterity. At least they were not under any pressure from their former slave masters in Brazil or there was no condition attached to their land. According to the late elder George Aruna Nelson, Brazilian land was a symbol of power and prestige for most returnees and their descendants because of the role it played in the formative years of their history in the Gold Coast. For Nelson's ancestors and others who had limited access to land in Brazil, landownership in Accra was the dream of a lifetime. They used the land for farming and digging wells and for building tailoring shops and housing for rent.⁵⁸ For the returnees, possessing land was a reward for those who took the risk of crossing the Atlantic from Brazil to Ghana in search of freedom, land, and a homeland as well as the reconstruction of their dual identity. Over time, this exciting dream was shattered by colonial rule and stringent land ordinances.

If the properties Ferku gave to Yawah generated different levels of tension between those he left behind in Accra, British conquest as an imperialist project created even more problems from its inception in Accra in the early 1800s. Like the story about the conditions of Brazilian land in the wake of colonialism, there were other chaotic results from the exchanges and interactions that occurred after the Gã mãŋbii offered hospitality to newcomers to their coastal towns from the sixteenth century.⁵⁹ For instance, the intersections between the newly arriving emancipated Brazilian-Africans and British colonial officials all vying for social space, land tenure, and economic opportunities in the early 1800s complicated the story of emancipation and imperialism. Over time, the cross-cultural interactions and exchanges between the two groups of newcomers and their hosts, the Gã mãŋbii, created degrees of impediments that framed and redefined the social history of Accra.

The evolution of the transatlantic experience began and spread along the coastline of Gã *mãŋ* from the seventeenth century. The transatlantic journey created the infamous Middle Passage that continued during the period of abolition in the early nineteenth century and ended in Gã *mãŋ* where it began by the turn of the twentieth century. For the emancipated Africans who crisscrossed the Atlantic, their experience was marked by stories of hope, skepticism, contention, contradictions, betrayal, and courage. When the freed slaves returned to Gã *mãŋ* the horrific experience of slavery was fresh in their minds, but they were determined to advance or focus on their future so they tolerated and gradually embraced Gã cultures and traditions. They perceived various pockets of land that were allocated to them as a sign of a promising future. But their quest for self-determination did not last very long. The self-gratifying agendas of the British colonialists in particular showed no regard to local traditions, placing Gã social and cultural norms at the periphery.[60] By restricting Gã mãŋtsɛmɛi, migrants, and particularly the returnees from the right to decide what to use their land for, colonial officials made these groups more aware of insecurity in land inheritance. Colonial land policies undermined existing forms of land exchange and acquisition, and to sustain this radical reform colonial officials halted existing local policies and replaced them with their own.[61] The arrest of land in the Gold Coast colony left a lasting imprint on the Brazilian-African diaspora as well.

Prior to these major effects on landowning returnees, other transformations among the descendants fractured land use for farming purposes. These changes occurred around the time colonial rule and ordinances were gaining momentum by the end of the 1800s. The introduction and implementation of land titles, for instance, was necessary for British colonial officials to regulate existing local boundaries, acquire sufficient land for colonial ventures, and most important, raise taxes for the Crown. Colonial subjects complained about multiple taxes that were imposed on them.[62] From the fifteenth century and even earlier the Gã mãŋtsɛmɛi had their own ways of sustaining the Gã paramountcy through some form of taxation and mutual agreements between royal families and the citizens who owned land.[63] The British were aware of the long-held land traditions in Gã *mãŋ*, but they were strategic in their approach to avoid dialogue with local leaders and landowners to prevent delays in implementing colonial projects including taxation. Indeed, the ex-slaves and their offspring were not mere spectators: unwilling to be exploited again after their freedom from slavery in Brazil, they were unwilling to give up Brazilian land and neither were they inclined to pay taxes on properties they had inherited. The resilient position of the Brazilians and their offspring resonated in the streams of court disputes.

Chapter Four

The Complex Character of the Land Disputes and the Road to Court

The land disputes were of varying texture. On the one hand, they were shaped by the land traditions of Gã *mãŋ* that were sanctioned by Gã mãŋtsɛmɛi and allowed people to own land. On the other hand, they were influenced by complicated colonial ordinances that restricted land tenure. For instance, conflicts over Brazilian land were presented within a colonial framework presided over by lawyers, judges, and local chiefs from the Gold Coast as well as Sierra Leone who were trained by colonial officials. Most hearings took place after the British brought their major colonies in West Africa under one legal umbrella and began using similar ordinances to enable more efficient coordination of land disputes. In the case of the Brazilian-African diaspora in the then Gold Coast, the differences between colonial ordinances and existing land transfers became a murky area as colonial representatives sent mixed signals about the roles of Brazilian chiefs and the heads of individual Brazilian families. At times these chiefs were accorded high respect and power to use their authority as chiefs in court to assist with various proceedings pertaining to land. On some occasions, their traditional authority—including the ability to use their power to settle or make decisions about land issues within the Brazilian-African diaspora—was placed on the back burner, as in the case of the proagrarians versus the nonagrarian groups. During these turbulent times, various developments created two main groups of descendants with starkly different ideas about what had to be done to maintain unity or keep family groups apart.

Proagrarian Activities and the Position of Brazilian Chiefs

The proagrarian viewpoint endorsed the basic idea that because practically all the freed slaves who were given Brazilian land were farmers, all Brazilian land should be used only for farming purposes or to house the families of farmers.[64] Proagrarians embraced the Akan concept of *oman*—that land is for the community, not the individual. Brazilian chiefs were the advocates for articulating this tradition or lifestyle. When disputes arose, the parties had to appear in colonial courts for a judgment or some kind of settlement.

There have been five Brazilian chiefs since 1836.[65] Not all those who served in this prestigious capacity became entangled in contentious land issues or appeared in court to testify. According to a number of archival records, the Brazilian chief João

Antonio Nelson (known also as John Antonio Nelson and Nii Azumah II), who led the community from 1856 to 1900, arrived with his parents from Brazil at the age of three. Some of the documents about Brazilian land had his name printed on them, which indicated that he owned portions of this property (figure 10). It is also possible that his name on these properties shows the degree to which Brazilian chiefs controlled Brazilian land in Gã *mãŋ*. There is evidence showing that Chief João Antonio Nelson appeared in court, as did his successors, to testify about the boundaries of Brazilian land. However, ample evidence shows that Brazilian chief Nii Azumah III, who served the Brazilian-African diaspora from 1936 to 1961, appeared at least on three occasions to defend forcefully and articulately the vision of his ancestors. Nii Azumah III (Edward Pedu Nelson) was a witness to a number of court cases because most of them occurred during his tenure (table 2). The chiefs were vocal and exerted their authority whenever the opportunity presented itself. For instance, in one testimony Nii Azumah III proclaimed that "the land remained the property of the Brazilians [collectively]" but not for individuals.[66] In this case, the chief became fixated on his convictions based on his authority and on his commitments to the entire Brazilian colony. In another court appearance, the chief testified that "land granted to Brazilians has not been apportioned to groups or families, or heads of such groups or families and that the whole land is vested in him as chief of the Brazilians." According to the court record, he had "distributed and shared Brazilian land among [the Brazilians]."[67] In all the cases, the Brazilian chiefs did not give credence to the authority of the Gã mãŋtsɛmɛi or to the colonial administration in deciding the fate of Brazilian land. The chiefs consistently challenged any attempts to distribute Brazilian land, and according to Nii Azumah III, even when there was a need to split up a tract of land, descendants could not do so on their own. Rather, the chiefs, as they also stressed, were by and large the only ones with the "divine" right to sell or divide land among the descendants. Nii Azumah III held that he was entitled to "sell or grant portions of said land [and not any descendant]."[68]

If Nii Azumah's public pronouncement is accurate, it means that members of the Brazilian-African diaspora who passed on land they inherited to other family members did so illegally. Such provocative claims by the Brazilian leader deepened existing divisions in the community, and the notion that only these chiefs could decide how the rest of the population should use their inheritance in land was contested in court.

Members of the Brazilian-African diaspora had two battles on their hands; in terms of Brazilian land the nonagrarian group in particular was confused about who was on their side. Basically, they could not differentiate between the threat of colonial ordinances and claims by Brazilian chiefs. To begin with, not every member of the Brazilian colony acknowledged the authenticity of their leadership or regarded the

Table 2. Brazilian/Tabom chiefs who were involved in disputes over Brazilian lands

BRAZILIAN/TABOM CHIEFS	TENURE	COURT CASE	CLASSIFICATION
João Antonio Nelson (title, Nii Azumah II)	1865–1900	Tackie v. Nelson	Interfamily land dispute
Edward Pedu Nelson (title, Nii Azumah III)*	1936–1961	Nii Azumah III v. Larikie Aruna and Kankle Kofi	Interfamily land dispute
Edward Pedu Nelson (title, Nii Azumah III)	1936–1961	Peter Quarshie Fiscian v. Nii Azumah III	Intrafamily land dispute
Edward Pedu Nelson (title, Nii Azumah III)	1936–1961	Isaac Cobblah Fiscian v. Henry A. K. Nelson and Sohby Baksmaty	Intrafamily land dispute
Edward Pedu Nelson (title, Nii Azumah III)	1936–1961	Afua Nelson (on behalf of herself, Abraham K. Nelson, Mercy Nelson, Grace Nelson, Marian Nelson, and Lydia Nelson) v. S. Q. Nelson	Intrafamily land dispute

*Edward Pedu Nelson (title, Nii Azumah III) appeared in both colonial and native courts more than any Brazilian/Tabom chief to deal with matters relating to Brazilian land and other issues.
Source: Public Records and Archives Administration Department, Accra.

chiefs as their legitimate spokesmen. These leaders were neither trusted, well known, or accepted by many of the descendants. Part of the reason was that the Brazilian-African diaspora was not a homogeneous community, so one would not expect them to think along the same lines. The chiefs' audacious claim that they were the only ones who knew about their history with landownership fueled tension within the community. Of course, the Brazilian chiefs as the members of the Brazilian-African diaspora had their flaws. Although publicly a chief would express commitment to the whole community, privately he might favor one family group over another. Brazilian chiefs often found creative ways to draw followers from various family groups, but they did not always succeed in this daunting task. They were despised by some but supported by others. An advocate for proagrarian activities supported the Brazilian leader, and in the case of *Madam Sarah Clegg v. Emmanuel Drissu Cobblah* the witness related, "all Brazilian settlers who originally farmed on any portion of the land granted to the Brazilian community continued the farming during their lifetime, and on death their respective successors continued cultivation by farming."[69] This information points to evidence of continuity in agrarian activities but does not say whether other activities besides farming took place on Brazilian land.

Although Brazilians in the interior did not all live together on the same farmland, their agrarian lifestyle often allowed them to interact in common spaces or on adjoining land. The same cannot be said of the population that incorporated other professions or used farmland for housing or rental purposes within the same geographical area. In

The Evolution of Land in Gã Maŋ

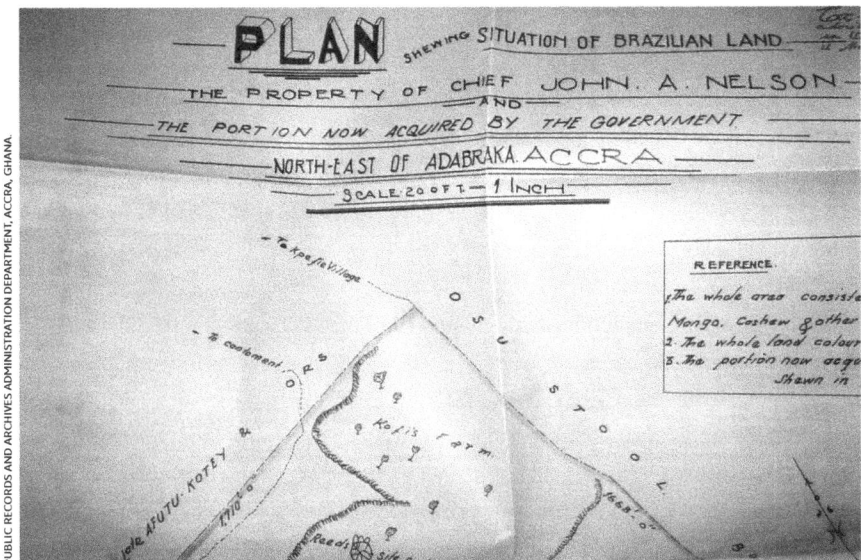

Figure 10. Disputed land between João Antonio Nelson and colonial officials in Accra.

one court hearing, Benjamin Addison, a descendant, asserted in his description of the land in his community, especially where his family lived, that "this area [in question] now, has become a building area." The gradual shift from farmland to residential area began in the early 1900s as new migrants sought land for settlements in locations that were later under dispute. Addison maintains that this change opened up new forms of interaction among descendants who lived mostly with their aged parents in remote areas of Accra; they began to interact with the general population, some of whom desired to own land.[70] The incorporation of other professions into Brazilian societies led to other forms of integration and exposure to outsiders. This shift was made mainly to ensure that descendants gained some level of prestige and wealth—something that was available in urban areas but was often unavailable in an agrarian location or in the *jwɛiamli*, or bush area.

Another group among the proagrarian descendants was flexible with their position. They had no qualms with the way things were done, so long as these changes benefited most of the descendants rather than just a small group. In other words, contestation over land or disagreement over whether to abandon farming practices for other professions was not always about how much space one could occupy or protect for posterity's sake. It was also about who did or did not benefit from the money the Brazilian-African properties produced. In another court case, Madam Yawah defended the communal customs that were promoted by her ancestors.[71] Yawah later pointed out that she did not have a problem with the new order or lifestyle that was introduced by some among the descendants. For her, the problem with the new arrangement was mainly that only a few individuals amassed wealth at the expense of other family members. Yawah was of the opinion that "J. E. Maslieno has been receiving rent from the tenants of the building on the property in dispute and his [sic] been enjoying it alone."⁷² It is not clear if Maslieno gave part of the money to all those who complained about his behavior.

The role of Brazilian chiefs—that is, how they were challenged by Brazilians like Maslieno or questioned about who benefited from the sale of Brazilian land—was not the only problem that emerged during the disputes. There also were complex interpretations as to the role of *weku yetsoi*, the family heads. Witness accounts, like that by Charles E. Reindorf, a medical practitioner who bought a piece of land from Maslieno, suggest that although the Brazilians had a chief who was known or acknowledged by some members of the community as the one responsible for land matters, other land transactions were carried out with the approval of heads of family. In the case of Fiscian and Maslieno, they often ignored this traditional protocol and appointed themselves, concurrently, as the leaders of the Aruna family. These two individuals, the self-appointed land agents, got along very well when it served their self-interest, but they opposed each other whenever either was unable to have control over a land sale.⁷³

Nonagrarian Activities

Those who supported the idea that Brazilian land was to be used solely for farming purposes did not waver in their assertion that their ancestors did not sell parts of the land to other Brazilians, Ghanaians, or those with no ties to the Brazilian story. The nonagrarian group, for its part, focused mainly on the use of Brazilian land for rental purposes or as real estate for sale. They also held firmly to their view. Indeed, their line of thinking was in direct opposition to the notion of a communal relation in land. This group not only challenged the idea of Brazilian land for farming alone, but believed in individual ownership for specific family groups. Whenever it became necessary to take a stand, they condemned the idea of communal land. Descendants with such convictions held that their ancestors approved the use of farmland for building houses for rent or for selling portions of land they had inherited to members of the Brazilian colony or to non-Brazilians. They did not believe that Gã *Mãŋtsɛ* Komeh I gave the land to the settlers all at the same time or on just one occasion—the implication being that a series of land gifts were made to different settlers at different times or waves of settlement. In this way, they ensured that the debate was framed around the establishment of *independent* Brazilian or Tabom family structures and not a Brazilian family structure with a single *collective* identity, leader, culture, and profession. Others held that Brazilian land was rather a gift from a priest in Gã *mãŋ*.[74]

Members of this constituency made their positions loud and clear in the court hearings. For instance, one of the disgruntled descendants also added in the *Madam Sarah Clegg v. Emmanuel Drissu Cobblah* case that, "No, it is not true that when the Brazilians were given the land together it was not given to them as one group; they were five groups. Yes, the five groups together constituted the Brazilian community."[75] This public statement identifies multiple family groups that had ties to the emancipated Brazilian-African slaves. Not only did the descendants who ascribed to this practice oppose the notion of collective ownership; they challenged the idea that they were a homogeneous group. The implication was that the early settlers who were given the land were not from the same family lineage or came from the same location in Brazil; therefore their offspring saw nothing wrong with selling "Brazilian land" to other descendants, the Gã people, Ghanaian migrants, Syrians, Europeans, or other expatriates. Thus, they drove a deeper wedge between various family groups and Brazilian chiefs who challenged such "illegal" sales. The polemics between the proagrarian and nonagrarian descendants, which took a number of interesting turns, had a lasting impact and extended beyond the confines of the Brazilian colony, as remembered in the Tabom's stories.

Maslieno was one of the descendants who claimed that Brazilian land was not meant to be used collectively and that individual families had the option to use it for their own interests. A self-appointed leader of the community, he was very adamant, forcefully challenging his opponents. In fact, Maslieno got into a number of land disputes with other descendants and even with a Brazilian chief. He felt a sense of ownership, entitlement, and unrestricted right to a Brazilian land heritage that included properties supposedly inherited by him and his siblings. He did things his own way while making various demands in court. According to Maslieno, "I am exclusively entitled to the whole of the rents collected and that I make this affidavit in support of a motion for directing the District [commissioner] to turn over the whole of the rents collected on house Nos. 137 and Nos. 138 block 6 to me."[76]

The lawsuits show that some descendants went after other members, such as the Maslieno and Ribeiro families, who claimed to be the only voice for the Brazilians. Descendants also challenged go-betweens or land agents who sold farmlands to outsiders and those who built on these farmlands or rented Brazilian properties as housing and stores to expatriates, the Gã people, and migrants in Accra. The price of houses on Brazilian land varied depending on their size and on who rented them.

Moreover, the price for stores and housing differed from one location to another. In 1931 small store rooms cost £1.10 per month, a bedroom went for £1.00 per month, and a chamber (bedroom) and a hall about £3.10.[77] In my interview with members of the Maslieno family in Accra, Madam Elizabeth Maslieno, the eighty-five-year-old daughter of J. E. Maslieno, shared stories of how Maslieno spent most of his time in court to protect their properties and very little time with his children.[78] She was not, however, aware of relations or family ties between her father and other members of the Brazilian-African diaspora. In addition to the proagrarian and nonagrarian debate, other features of the quarrels ranged from intraconflicts (those among Brazilians) to interconflicts (those between Brazilians and non-Brazilians).

Intraconflicts and Interconflicts

Court records for cases between 1889 and Ghana's independence in 1957 typically begin with details about how the descendants sought to reclaim lands that were legally or illegally sold to both Brazilians and non-Brazilians. The documents also explain how the older generation amassed wealth through farming and other activities and detail the kinds of crops they cultivated both for sustenance and for sale in the market. These included cashews, foodstuff as cassavas, and mangoes.[79] It is believed that the freed slaves brought some of these crops from Brazil. The litigious clashes over land shared a lot of characteristics despite their stark differences. For example, cases brought before the Supreme Court of the Gold Coast, the Eastern Judiciary public lands division, and the native courts often alleged the defendants had trespassed, squatted, or illegally claimed lands, which the plaintiffs objected to. Although it was easy to get rid of the squatters who used virgin lands, the opposition often came from people who were able to prove their family ties to the Brazilians and those who had some support from Brazilians as caretakers or middlemen who sold the land to them. Their main message about the land they inherited from their forefathers was that it was theirs and no one else's. The defendants held on to their claims based on fragile evidence of multiple transfers and purchases from members of the Brazilian community, mostly without a land title or deed. Other disputes were created after the British colonial government took over some of these contested lands for social infrastructure such as roads and government buildings or for other public use, with or without the consent of the original owners.

The court disputes were not resolved easily. Besides confusion over the role of Brazilian chiefs and the fact that there were no clearly marked boundaries and *legal* documents to support various claims, other problems were created by misunderstanding

The Evolution of Land in Gã Mãŋ

about the ordinances or their clarity as well as the legal systems that were put in place. For instance, the judges, although trained by the colonial officials to carry out land ordinances, could not engage the defendants and plaintiffs in ways that communicated their understanding of land bills and colonial policies. In addition, the use of translators was very helpful because most of those involved in the conflicts could not understand some of the court procedures, particularly the legal terms involved. In some situations, the ways in which expatriates and local migrants in Accra competed for Brazilian land generated multiple disputes and heightened existing tensions.

OUR/THEIR TRADITIONS: THE SHIFT TO A RENTAL AND LAND-BASED ECONOMY

The land disputes between the freed slaves and their descendants were shaped primarily by two opposing sets of memories and ideas: on the one hand, it was held that their story and identity in colonial Accra was based on an agrarian lifestyle and the farming skills they brought from Brazil; and on the other hand, it was believed that agrarian practices were irrelevant to their new identity in their new locale. The polemics were also shaped by arguments over what professions the coastal settlers practiced compared with those of the remote inland settlers. The descendants who did not follow or remember what had happened during their ancestors' lifetimes were not alone in departing from their past traditions. Not even the descendants who took over their family land after the demise of the early settlers devoted all of their time and energy to farming traditions. Aware of other locations of settlement, especially Otublohum and other areas in Accra, and the opportunity to interact with the growing migrant settler communities, they often found ways of sharing their time between these two areas. Descendants who were carried away by the attractive incentives of a lifestyle outside the bush spent little time in agrarian communities. In fact, some were away for so long that upon returning to visit, they found they did not even know where their family land was located.

During court appearances, those in this latter category had problems explaining who their parents' farming neighbors were. These descendants registered their protest whenever they traveled back to these farmlands to evict intruders or when they joined litigations, but their memories were often blurred. In one such instance in court, Mary Adisa Cobblah provided details about her family's agrarian lifestyle during her childhood. She asserted: "I myself used to farm on this land. It is about 40 years ago since I last farmed."[80] Four decades was quite a long time to be away from one's family roots and identity tied to land and farming. In contrast, offspring who spent a lot of time on the farmland and accepted farming as a lifestyle did not encounter problems identifying the boundaries of their farmlands. Cobblah's testimony shows how descendants who preferred to live in the city treated land that they inherited and how their attitudes toward farming converged or digressed from those of their ancestors. Indeed, rural and urban/coastal settlements were two different worlds.

City or coastal life was more economically rewarding than life in the interior or farming areas.[81] In a way, life in fledgling urban colonial Accra in the early 1900s created a platform for descendants to explore other options shaped by cross-cultural experiences and interactions with foreigners or new migrants. Life in urban areas or along the coast was beneficial in terms of the skills descendants could acquire compared to the restrictive isolation of the agrarian lifestyle. In the early 1900s, as a good portion of their offspring abandoned rural areas and focused on renting urban or coastal properties, they received financial support from other relatives from the Bight of Benin, particularly Nigeria, to begin their new ventures. Some of those who moved to the city also received support to pursue higher education. This included individuals who were funded by wealthy family members in Lagos to acquire an engineering degree abroad.[82] Additionally, migrations to urban and coastal Accra fostered other forms of upward mobility. For some men including Cobblah (the only name used in the archives), a Brazilian and perhaps a relative of Mary Cobblah, life in the city opened a door such as service in the colonial army in the 1930s. Indeed, his commitment to the army did not prevent him from returning to his family's land to protect it from trespassers who were mostly of non-Brazilian descent.[83] Their transition to the city was facilitated by caretakers who protected their land while they were away.

The Role of Caretakers in the Rural and Urban Areas

Caretakers played a pivotal role in the transformation that took place in various Brazilian communities. In the history of land tenure in colonial Accra, caretakers were often seen as the central points of contact, especially in situations where a particular piece of land was left unattended for a period of time.[84] In a number of court cases, descendants noted that the choices they made between sustaining farming practices or continuing new professions as tailors, dressmakers, or coastal traders, especially in Otublohum and Swalaba, were based on having caretakers' help. The defendants claimed that it was challenging or impossible to commute regularly from distant rural locations to urban Brazilian settlements.[85] To avoid having to travel back and forth, most descendants who had closer ties to agrarian communities sought the service of younger family members who remained on their farmland and had no present intention of relocating elsewhere. At times they hired non-Brazilians. In some situations, descendants paid caretakers to groom the land until they were able to return. As migrations to Accra soared, so did the price of land; and as trespassing and illegal land sales became common in these areas, caretakers occasionally sold some of the land under their care.[86] Arrangements between "absentee" descendants and the caretakers they hired were often unreliable and contributed to the shift from land-based traditions to a rent-based Brazilian economy as well as to new identity formations as assimilation became the dominant norm during this period. Over time, these movements to the coast and the city played a vital role in the changes that occurred in Brazilian-African diaspora in Gã societies.

The introduction of land-based rental properties and evidence that some Brazilians preferred urban lifestyles to agrarian practices was not facilitated by descendants' decisions alone. Non-Brazilians who encroached or had access to Brazilian lands legally or illegally were either unaware of or unconcerned about the need to protect features of the Brazilian presence in these isolated areas. As one witness claimed in court during his settlement in the area: "I saw cassava, ground-nuts and mango trees on the land. ... I destroyed some of the cassava trees."[87] Descendants themselves created some of these problems, and if they would not do more to protect their heritage, who would? It is obvious that new occupants of the land did not share the same values as the ex-slaves and their descendants who had invested in the preservation of Brazilian land and agrarian traditions. Descendants became vulnerable from two additional fronts as they devoted less time to the farming traditions of their forebears. By gradually embracing other professions, they planted themselves deeply in Gã culture or opened their culture to outsiders, particularly along the coast. And by doing so, they created an opening or pathway for outside interference. Regardless of which way one examines these trends, both cases created divisions rather than unity and shaped the connections between land and Brazilian-African identity. Indeed, by involving outsiders in Brazilian land, descendants opened their communities up to disruption and interference that resulted in other series of court cases from the 1920s through the 1960s.

The gradual shift from an agrarian to a rental- and land-based community lifestyle was not embraced by all descendants. A segment of the population continued to preserve their farming identity, with its long-standing traditions within the area, while others blazed new pathways. This occurred in the inland farming territories, the coastal areas of Otublohum and Swalaba, and some areas in the city of Accra. In essence, descendants who remained in agrarian communities modified Brazilian farmlands through construction of buildings for rent while also adopting new identities and occupations. Those who traveled outside this area traded in beads, while others learned tailoring and dressmaking.[88] The multiple migratory pathways crisscrossing different geographical spaces in Gã *mãŋ* were very helpful to some of the members of the Brazilian-African diaspora. A number of descendants also moved away from farming regions to pursue education in Accra or traveled back and forth from inland farming areas to the Bight of Benin.[89] In 1894, George Akwetey Nelson in his old age advised his son to pursue higher education rather than doing menial work in the agrarian community so he could save enough money to meet their needs.[90]

Ferku, a freed slaves' nomadic life started after he left Brazil to settle in Lagos and later to Accra to begin a marriage union with Yawah, another Brazilian who was born in Accra. His endless travels were a metaphor for the Brazilian-African diaspora story in Ghana. Ferku's complex love story concluded when he decided to relocate to Lagos in his old age but without Yawah, who chose to remain in Accra. As described in the case *Yawah v. J. E. Maslieno*, although Ferku left his wife a piece of land, the property was consumed by land disputes among the Brazilians and their offspring, the Tabom. The fracture in their marriage speaks to the complex ways in which the liberated Africans reconstructed their identity and contested their freedom and land in British colonial Accra. Ferku's ability to move between Lagos and Accra provides an insight into the fluid but multifaceted Brazilian-African diaspora story in Ghana. Although there is evidence that British colonial ordinances often superseded existing traditions about land tenure around the same time Ferku relocated to Lagos, there is no indication that he gave up his land to his wife for fear that it might be subject to a mendacious British land grab.

Historically, since the freed slaves arrived in Accra at different times and in different groups with distinct family stories, they lived as a separate returnee group within the larger Gã society. The Brazilians might not have known about Ferku's situation in terms of the complications after he left the land for his wife. However, over time they became more conscious about the impact of British land ordinances. This awareness resonated in the colônia de Brazileiros or the Brazilian-African diaspora in Accra in various locations in Ghana. Tracing the life history of Ferku is quite challenging, but one thing is obvious: he not only crossed the Atlantic from Brazil to Lagos, but he moved back and forth between Lagos and Accra in an ambitious exploration. Unlike other freed slaves, Ferku was fortunate enough to have left Brazil sometime in the 1860s, but this does not mean that his journey to freedom was without trouble just because he came to Accra. In fact, like the local people in Accra he, too, had to contest and contend with British colonial policies. Details of Ferku's early life in both Lagos and Accra are not known—only that he relocated in the late 1800s and interacted with Yawah and her family prior to his departure to Lagos in the late 1920s. However, while information about his background is very limited in the archives and among his offspring, his story has broad implications and touches major themes concerning the life of freed slaves and their descendants in Accra. Ferku and Yawah left an indelible mark in ways that enable us to track the multilayer forms of reverse migrations crisscrossing the Atlantic.

Ferku's decision to leave Brazil shaped many aspects of the Brazilian-African diaspora narratives. For instance, his memory of his homeland in Africa, especially his interest in traveling from Lagos to Accra, shows the unending trajectories of the Atlantic voyages. Silences about his extended stay in the Gold Coast colony and the nuances in his experience speak to other challenges in tracing the life stories of freed slaves in Accra from the nineteenth century. In general, Ferku's life, which forms a core of reverse diaspora stories, mirrors a constellation of memory as well as the efforts of ex-slaves to refashion their identity on their own terms as they searched for a place they could call home outside Brazil. Most significantly, Ferku's interactions with other returnees and their family networks allow us to understand various aspects of inheritance, especially landownership and transfer and the transformation that occurred after the early settlers passed on their properties of land and their agrarian skills to their descendants. In a broader sense, the lives of Ferku and others in Accra interconnected with numerous developments in Gã *mãŋ*, particularly the transformation that took place as the British Crown and colonial officials implemented the Public Land Ordinance of 1876, the Native Jurisdiction Ordinance of 1883, and the Compulsory Labour Ordinance of 1897.[91] The marriage of Ferku and Yawah, for example, emphasized various aspects of the diaspora encounter in Accra. Other couples in the returnee community in Accra managed transatlantic relationships and complicated interactions. The stories discussed in this chapter embody a larger problem associated with landownership, inheritance, and how assets that the former slaves owned or inherited were distributed and contested over time.

Land dispute in Accra's Brazilian-African diaspora was very complicated. In court, land disputes took different twists and turns. The intrafamily conflicts included disputes between the members of the Brazilian-African diaspora, and the interfamily conflicts pitted the Gã mãŋtsεmεi, members of the Gã royal family, and the Gã people against the returnees and their offspring. Other interfamily disputes included those between the Brazilians/Tabom and migrants or between the Brazilians/Tabom and Europeans, British colonial officials, missionaries, as well as Lebanese merchants.

Land disputes were clearly and sharply marked by two camps: the proagrarian advocates who believed Brazilian lands were for communal use, and nonagrarian activists who opposed the former. The chiefs who positioned themselves as "referees" had a responsibility to maintain some degree of order and a responsibility to pass on to the younger generations the traditions of unity that were practiced by their ancestors.

The Brazilian chiefs who became instruments for the Brazilian-African diaspora were largely successful in protecting land that they inherited as they rearticulated the dreams of their ancestors. The role of the Brazilian chief was complicated by debates over rental- and land-based economic practices that in some ways opened up a door for foreigners and local migrants alike to trespass on Brazilian land. The Brazilian chiefs were largely not acknowledged by both British officials and various family groups within the Brazilian-African diaspora for varying reasons.

In general, interactions between the leaders of Accra, the ex-slaves, and British colonial officials were not mutually exclusive. They were deeply intertwined, so their overlaps should be acknowledged rather than treated separately. By involving newcomers temporarily or permanently in the social affairs of Gã mãŋbii, the foreign presence shaped and reshaped the social history of the Gã *mãŋ*. For example, the foreigners and the local people who took Brazilian land illegally did so as land acquisition was becoming a necessity in Accra, a coastal fishing post that was gradually transformed into an urban landscape during the advent of colonial rule. Indeed, the ex-slaves and their offspring were not the only ones affected by colonial ordinances. Gã traditions and colonial records demonstrate that land tenure was tied to chieftaincy, inheritance, and colonial ventures that threatened Brazilian land and the dreams of the returnees. Some of the conflicts that erupted within the Brazilian-African diaspora over a century ago have had lasting consequences on the younger generations.

Chapter 5

Escaping Slavery into Colonialism and Squabbles: How Colonial Projects and Internal Disputes Threatened Brazilian Land and Freedom

> The [Brazilian] family fortune . . . was taken by Town Authorities under the Town Ordinance . . . for the purpose of widening or constructing the road that now exists.
> —Mary Afua Nelson, 1931

The Tabom people sustained and articulated their memory of "Brazilian land" when they appeared in colonial courts to defend their rights to the land that had been passed on to them. Landownership was indeed a blessing to most of the ex-slaves from Brazil and perhaps owned land for the first time. But over time it became a curse to the subsequent generations as disagreement over inheritance gradually created lasting tension among them. Prior to internal land disputes, colonial intrusion arrested social gains within the Brazilian-African diaspora and in broader Gã societies.

Selected court documents about land disputes shed light on the contentious polemics about the uses of Brazilian land—whether for farming or for sale. Indeed, some of the Tabom held on to the agrarian traditions of their parents and grandparents, but this does not mean that the ancestors were a homogeneous group or that all the descendants were farmers or had to use the gift of land only for agrarian purposes. Lawsuits that were brought before colonial and local courts show aspects of unity among the first generation. Part of the land documents also offer a backdrop for understanding gradual shifts within the Brazilian communities during the transition from the first-generation settlers of the early 1900s to subsequent generations.

British colonial policies threatened land owned by members of the Brazilian-African diaspora, especially their freedom to own these properties and the strategic ways in which colonial authorities confiscated Brazilian land for colonial projects. I explore the protectiveness toward Brazilian land displayed by landowning members of Tabom communities, who inherited land from parents or grandparents after the demise of colonial rule. Memory played a central role in the creation and the articulation of the origins of Brazilian land in Accra especially when the members of the Brazilian-African diaspora testified in court during land disputes to make claim to these properties.

The narratives of the emancipated Africans including conflicts over Brazilian land are contextualized within the broader social history of Accra, particularly the impact of British colonial rule and its implications on the arrival of the liberated Brazilians. In addition, a large number of court disputes over land were colored by the dissonance of memory. Dissonance of memory, especially variations in the evidence that was presented in court, reminds us of the possibility that some testimonies were tainted or were enhanced to accord with particular vested interests.[1] While not disputing the Brazilians' former ownership of particular tracts of land, one tribunal expressed surprise over the ability of their offspring "to narrate what happened 100 years ago."[2] The fact that a segment of the Tabom population remembered their ancestors being denied landownership in Brazil during their servitude made them hypersensitive toward any signs of oppression, exploitation, and manipulation by those who wanted to take the Brazilian land from them. The returnees and their offspring responded the same way to those who placed legal obstacles in the way of their preserving what land they had inherited. Indeed, various ordinances and deeds orchestrated by British colonial officials, including the Public Land Ordinance (PLO) of 1876, threatened the very freedom the ex-slaves enjoyed and the gifts of land from Gã *Mãŋtsɛ* Tackie Komeh I. The fact that the Brazilian-African community thrived after slavery while remaining vulnerable under British colonialism shows how inconsistent was the experience of freedom and how complicated the notion of return to an imagined homeland.

The descendants' ability to remember what was passed on to them from one generation to the next was indeed impressive. It was this tenacity that allowed them to challenge those British colonial officials who relied on a decree from the Crown to take part of the Brazilian land to advance colonial projects. The descendants' remarkable memory about details of this land is juxtaposed with their harnessing of past events. For instance, while it is true that the older Brazilians (early settlers), as well as some of the Tabom, were able to remember details about Brazilian land in court testimony, this memory allowed the contemporary generation to dwell on stories that were passed on to them to continue disputes over their family properties. Ongoing conflict between the

Peregrino and Brimah children over land and other properties in the court case *Rashid Brimah & 3 Ors. v. Hadji M. B. Peregrino Brimah* provides an insight into the dark side of the complicated history of colônia de Brazileiros or the Brazilian-African diaspora in Ghana. The conflicts provide a backdrop for the complex exchanges, polemics, and fractured relations that took place at the turn of the twentieth century.

As Accra went through various changes from the eighteenth century, the history of the allocation of and access to land took on spiritual, cultural, and legal turns. This historical dimension together with colonial conquest gave rise to the establishment of a colonial supreme court and native courts to settle disputes and to introduce land titles to establish lines of legal ownership. Based on the long history of intricate land tenure in Accra, intrusion by outside forces, tension between the Gã people and European settlers, and concerns about losing Gã stool lands to outsiders, such as colonial rulers, one might assume that Gã leaders would not accept new settlers.[3] However, the Gã *Mãŋtse* Komeh I did not close his doors of hospitality to the emancipated Brazilians who began arriving in the 1820s and kept coming in the 1830s; to assist the returnees, the Gã king allocated a sizable area of land located around the Fonafor Valley and Akwandor, near central Accra and close to the Adabraka community, to them—Brazilian land. The land was likely given between 1826 and 1856 during the reign of *Mãntse* Komeh I.

In the early period of Brazilian-African settlement, the freed slaves and the Tabom did not express any interest in creating communal communities or make any major attempt to do so. So they became easy targets for exploitation by outside forces. Even though there is no evidence that these returnees initiated any collective mobilization program or sociocultural activities that enabled them to socialize in the nineteenth century, the evidence that the British colonial officials meddled with Brazilian land generated panic and struck a highly sensitive emotional nerve that provoked spontaneous responses to the crisis. The threat reminded the Brazilians of their servitude in Brazil and raised the specter of their being stripped of their rights to determine how to use their properties. The insecurity associated with colonial ordinances, the reality of exploitation, and the threat of losing their freedom reshaped individual, family, and communal consciousness. In general, it evoked new forms of assertiveness from the late nineteenth century on.

Colonialism and the introduction of colonial ordinances had a giant impact that did not affect the Gã people alone. The antagonism that had bubbled up among the native population after the implementation of the PLO of 1876, the municipal ordinances that followed, and especially the ruthless policies that gave surveyors the green light to destroy buildings owned by citizens of the colony resonated far and wide. For the liberated Africans and their families, especially those who depended on their farmland and rental houses for sustenance or financial survival, their frustration spilled over and transformed into a flood of solidarity within the community. That is to say, although the members of the Brazilian-African diaspora in Accra did not see themselves as one unit or necessarily formed close relationships, they needed to bond together to lessen the insecurity. In general, the threat of the British colonial presence to their new freedom infused a sense of solidarity among them. Their leaders in particular became more conscious of the implications of colonial rule and more concerned for the future of the community.[4] The timing was perhaps too late for the members of the Brazilian-African diaspora as colonial rule rapidly stifled long-held land traditions. Land disputes among the emancipated slaves and their offspring were not caused by colonial ordinances alone but by inward tension partly generated within the Brazilian-African diaspora.

Eradicating Long-held Land Traditions and the Origins of Land Disputes

British colonial officials through the sets of ordinances and deeds they imposed on their colonial subjects interfered with local land practices or held them in contempt. The legal barrage they unleashed gained uninterrupted momentum in the late nineteenth century. These ordinances include but were not limited to the Native Jurisdiction Ordinance of 1883, the Native Prisons Ordinance of 1888, the Stool Property Detention Act of 1904, and the Native Administrative Ordinance of 1927, all of which were introduced strategically to cripple the authority of the Gã mãŋtsɛmɛi and other chiefs in the Gold Coast colony.[5] The introduction of land titles accompanied the passage of these ordinances. Taken together, the imposition of foreign legal concepts undermined and finally eliminated long-held local practices partly because of "widespread confusion in the matters of titles to land."[6] Although this process lasted for nearly a century, even today the acquisition of legitimate land titles and deeds in Ghanaian societies remains a problem.

Land titles and deeds were colonial inventions—part of the land policies that were enforced after the British created institutions like native courts and schemes such as indirect rule.[7] Local chiefs and landowning individuals or family groups did not foresee the extent of British colonial intrusion, and therefore they did not make provision to suit colonial expectations, standards, and policies of the native courts, which would become a key instrument for the implementation of colonial projects. As a result, descendants who petitioned the courts for the right to keep their land, property, or other forms of inheritance that they claimed were passed on to them attempted to explain that their forebears were not bound by any laws before the emergence of colonial rule, especially such policies requiring owners to possess titles for the land they owned. According to a court account by Henry A. K. Nelson, who inherited land from his father, "When the Brazilians arrived each family did not carve ownership of a portion of land by occupation out of the common land of the Brazilian community. Mere cultivation of cassava on another's land does not create title or effect title."[8] The symbolism of land title was of great importance to the ex-slaves and their offspring. Those who inherited Brazilian land legally or illegally, however, faced a double dilemma. First, most of the descendants did not have any legal documents to prove the validity of their claims because their ancestors were not offered official land titles, yet like any other subject of the colony, they were not exempted from colonial land legislation. Second, it took the British quite a while to set up their colonial apparatus to deal with such legal complications. This process was delayed partly by responses from the leaders of the Aborigines' Rights Protection Society (ARPS), which was established by the educated local elite, that challenged the British Crown and colonial authorities for exploiting and imposing their will on their colonial subjects.[9] Disagreements between the British and the Gã mãŋtsɛmɛi stifled these efforts as well.[10]

Aspects of the court clashes over Brazilian land highlighted the significance of having a land title or deed. But possession of such was not easy to achieve since in the precolonial era it was not a common practice and the changes occurred only after the colonialists arrived. The impact of land titles and property rights on Gã traditions during the colonial era underscores how these important accounts shaped and reshaped Brazilian history in Ghana from the nineteenth century. In the precolonial period, kings, local chiefs, and heads of families dispensed land by word of mouth in the presence of witnesses or by making reference to, and performing rituals evoking the authority of, ancestral spirits.[11] In other words, the Gã mãŋtsɛmɛi had their own way of allocating land prior to the advent of British colonial rule. This non-Eurocentric approach among the Gã *mãshi* allowed the Gã mãŋtsɛmɛi to allocate Gã stool land (land belonging to the Gã royal family). In the precolonial era, the approach by the Gã mãŋtsɛmɛi succeeded in the sense that it allowed allocation of any kind of land to anyone in Accra without scrutiny by foreigners. The granting of pockets of land by Gã *Mãŋtsɛ* Komeh I to the liberated Brazilian-Africans in the 1830s is a typical example of how local leaders effectively dealt with land tenure. This approach did not survive under the new British regime as the colonialists introduced the use of land titles as the only legitimate claim to a piece of land. Regulating landownership and demanding land titles in colonial Accra were implemented many decades after *Mãŋtsɛ* Komeh I gave the ex-slaves land. By enforcing land ordinances it became increasingly difficult for the Gã chiefs to relate to their neighbors or to foreigners in their community in terms of how they shared their wealth and carried out Gã traditions of hospitality, specifically land in British colonial territories.[12] This rich tradition changed at the height of colonial rule as British officials confiscated Brazilian land for colonial projects.

CONTRADICTIONS OF FREEDOM: SEEK YE FIRST BRITISH COLONIAL PROJECTS

British colonial agendas did not arrest long-held Gã land tenure practices alone: they bore a hallmark of forms of exploitation that largely forced colonial subjects to seek the interest of colonial agendas first. In the case of the evolution of the Brazilian-African diaspora in Accra, British colonial policies reveal levels of contradiction of freedom. In other words, the emancipated Africans left Brazilian slavery behind but relocated into colonialism.[13] The hospitality that Gã *Mãŋtsɛ* Komeh I extended to the liberated Brazilian-Africans, especially the enormous gift of land, facilitated their settlement in Accra. However, British abolitionists' contributions to the freedom of the enslaved Africans did not carry much weight beyond Brazil. The abolitionists kept a close eye on the freed slaves to ensure that the freedom they were granted could be protected in the long term, but their mission and vision were inadequate. For instance, a letter from Benjamin Campbell to Lord Clarendon on 4 May 1854 claimed:

> My protection of those Africans who having purchased their emancipation from slavery in Brazil have settled in Lagos . . . it armed me with the authority to interfere on behalf of 230 of these self-emancipated Africans lately brought to Lagos from Rio de Janeiro and Bahia in the Portuguese vessel *Linda Flor*.[14]

However, there is no evidence that their safety was guaranteed. Actually, there is no indication that the British Crown and Parliament, which supported abolitionist projects, had made any plans to protect the freedom of the African slaves who resettled in their ancestral homelands. The arrival of the Brazilians, which coincided with the advent of British colonial rule, made this dream impossible.[15] In Ghana, the liberated Africans and their offspring had every right to protect the Brazilian land they had received as a gift, but they could not escape the reach of the colonial ordinances. Put differently, the yearning of freed slaves to tie their freedom directly to landownership in Accra was short lived.

In court, the descendants had ways of remembering the experiences or the stories their ancestors passed on to them especially means to shield against outside intrusion and thus ensure control of their properties. Their memory of their ancestors' history of exploitation in Brazil and the revolts that preceded their freedom permeated their robust testimonies. The Tabom in particular were aware of their ancestors' servitude and especially of Chief Nelson's revolt against the Compulsory Labour Ordinance (CLO) in 1897 in Accra. In general, because most of the Brazilians did not respect the authority of the colonial rulers, especially in matters relating to their land and inheritance rights, they were not occupied with polemics and debates over issues such as land titles that Brazilian mãŋtsɛmɛi acknowledged were new to them. Most of the populations were more interested in negotiating and navigating through the colonial court system in order to win their own cases—in particular to avoid taxes on land—than in preparing legal documents to protect their properties in the future. Although they were conscious of the legal threats to their survival as a people of Brazilian ancestry, their vision was very narrow—it literally remained within the borders of Brazilian land or the Brazilian-African diaspora in Accra. Their inward-looking or introverted attitude, which centered largely on Brazilian-Tabom interests, was not similar to colonial agendas that sought to please only the British Crown and its imperialist ventures.[16]

The returnees were threatened by the British colonial presence, particularly the series of land policies, laws, and ordinances that were introduced beginning in the 1870s. Lieutenant Governor Charles Cameron Lee in his correspondence with the Legislative Council of Her Majesty Queen Victoria declared,

> Lands required for the service of the Gold Coast Colony, by and with the advice and consent of the Legislative Council thereof, as follows—(I) This Ordinance may be cited as The Public Lands Ordinance of 1876; (II) The Ordinance shall extend to the whole of the Gold Coast Colony and Protected Territories and Protectorate of Lagos.[17]

These directives were meant to give the British officials the authority to gain access to and control of every visible space within the protectorate and the Gold Coast colony. The PLO of 1876, among others that Lee endorsed, was the beginning of trouble for those who owned land in the Gold Coast colony. As Lee's declaration articulates, the ex-slaves were free in the sense that they were no longer under the watchful eyes of their Brazilian plantation owners; but the fact that they had escaped slavery did not guarantee their freedom under British colonial rule. Put in another way, colonial rule did not provide any form of immunity for the freed slaves who returned to colonial Accra: British policies did not discriminate or make any distinction between the returnees and those who were never enslaved. Part of the reason why Brazilian chief João Antonio Nelson joined Gã mãŋtsɛmɛi to protest against the CLO of 1897 was largely in response to the British officials' confiscation of Brazilian land that he was in charge of.

The PLO of 1876, which contributed to the loss of part of Brazilian land, was not the only policy that gave the green light to confiscate land in Gã *mãŋ* and other areas. Other reforms had significant impact in the Gold Coast colony. Another correspondence by Governor Sir William B. Griffith spelled out other details about policies for the colony. These policies, established in the 1880s, included British colonial municipal ordinances that clearly stated that the local municipal councils, "shall have power to acquire movable and immovable property for the purpose of carrying into effect the provisions of the Ordinance but the Council shall not mortgage, alienate or lease any immovable property without the consent of the Governor in writing."[18]

In the 1870s, as power devolved to the municipal-level building inspectors, the use of force in carrying out ordinances increased. Not only did municipal ordinances permit colonial officials to take over properties owned by the local people without any negotiation, beginning in the 1880s they also granted surveyors the power to demolish or alter any local structures that obstructed colonial projects.[19] This is one of the examples of colonial laws that directly affected the Brazilian-African diaspora. Some of the ex-slaves reported cases of British intrusion on Brazilian land and the destruction of their properties to Brazilian chief João Antonio Nelson and the various family heads that were the leading voices of their communities. The reporting of threats of colonial intrusion on Brazilian land did not resolve the communities' anxiety over the ordinances. At this time the freed slave communities were not unified. During the mid-nineteenth century colonial policies made some exceptions that gave the Brazilians and the subjects of the colony the opportunity to contest colonial ordinances. One such land policy stated that the interest of the landowner should be considered first.[20]

Part of these flexible colonial ordinances made considerable provision for the subjects of the colony to volunteer their lands or advertise their interest in selling them to colonial authorities in colonial newspapers such as the *Gazette* and the *Gold Coast Independent*—the major outlet for announcing land sales and for enforcing new colonial policies.[21] Some Brazilians also used the *Gazette* to warn the public about the dangers of purchasing Brazilian land from other members and nonmembers of the Brazilian-African diaspora in Accra. The major problem was that most colonial subjects were illiterate and therefore unfamiliar with the ordinances' details and their implications for traditional landownership policies. The lack of knowledge would later lead to efforts by the educated elite (who did not accept indirect rule) to demand reforms to the land ordinances. One such group that played an instrumental role in these protests was the ARPS, which was established in 1897 to oppose the Crown Lands Bill of 1896 among other legislative actions. The British Crown characterized the ARPS as a "menace of its imperial policy."[22]

There are numerous examples of British colonial intrusion on Brazilian land. Indeed, the ordinances were like a brushfire that swept through any available space that was marked for colonial projects, including territories of the Brazilian-African diaspora in Accra. The British were not concerned about who owned a particular tract of land; after all, the Crown gave colonial officials the green light to take what they needed to enhance colonial rule. However, there were exceptions to this stringent order. According to C. K. Meek, "in the Gold Coast Colony the land rights of the people are not qualified by any claim of proprietorship on the part of the Crown, and if land is required by the Government for public purposes it is obtained by voluntary agreement or through statutory procedure."[23]

A number of local chiefs and individuals made various arrangements to provide land to colonial officials voluntarily to meet particular needs, but in general, changes in the ways in which personal properties should be used were troubling for the landowning population. To the colonial apparatus, it was as if there was no such thing as private property, although they made efforts to negotiate their interest in colonial land with local leaders in some of these cases. Everything was fair game to be seized for public use, except what those who served the Crown and the few other Europeans in the Gold Coast colony possessed.

Certainly, landowning members of the Brazilian communities—who had either received land directly from Gã King Komeh I or inherited land from their parents, grandparents, siblings, or other family members—took advantage of the newspaper outlet to warn people interested in Brazilian land. Although ample evidence shows that British colonial officials did not tolerate local land practices, the colonial power did not act without at least *some* consideration such as paying compensation for some of the land they seized. Some of the Brazilian land was used for constructing public streets and government buildings and for European residential areas.

AFTER THE BRITISH CONFISCATED BRAZILIAN LAND: COMPENSATING THE BRAZILIAN-AFRICAN DIASPORA

After British colonial authorities confiscated Brazilian land, the returnees were not assured of any reparation of any kind. However, some of the witnesses in court testified that they were given some compensation. Compensation for members of the Brazilian-African diaspora did not follow a linear path. It was unpredictable until the negotiation process was complete. British officials often did everything possible to make reference to a particular colonial ordinance or paid little money for any Brazilian land partly because colonial ordinances gave them the power to do so. One Brazilian made reference to colonial policies when he stated that "the family fortune... was taken by Town Authorities under the Town Ordinance... for the purpose of widening or constructing the road that now exists."[24]

In the first place, the Brazilians had no regard for colonial policies because the policies did not serve their needs. In most of these court cases, the party with the best bargaining skills won. This made the compensation process tedious and lengthy. Sometimes the compensation was based on the location of the land and other times on the size of the land. In cases where the boundaries were difficult to determine because of complex factors including multiple ownerships to a particular piece of land, the different landowning Brazilians exploited this opportunity by prolonging the negotiations until they were given sufficient money. In one court proceeding, *Thomas A. Hammond v. Isaac Fiscian and Titus Glover*, Zuzer Maslieno, a Brazilian, testified that in 1895 British colonial officials demanded his family land for colonial projects, to which the family objected. Armed with legal instructions embedded in colonial policies and with the approval of both the governor and the supreme court, the British officials were able to take part of the Maslienos' family land without their approval. The Maslienos were later compensated after they won a lawsuit that was filed years later.[25] In another case, a Brazilian was paid £1,650 for the use of his portion of Brazilian land for colonial projects.[26]

For the case *Mary Afua Nelson v. Samuel Quarshie Nelson*, one of the intrafamily disputes, the case was about disagreements between members of the Nelson family over how much they should be compensated after their family house was demolished and the area used for colonial projects. In court, one of the witness pointed to a map showing his family land and expressed that

> The portion of my [family] property earmarked for demolition and pointed out that [the] Government had valued it at £1,077.... I am claiming £1,500.... I would stick to my figure and if possible I would prove to him [the judge] that the building is worth what I claim... I told them [the court] that I will not accept [any amount] less than £1,500.[27]

In this case as others, negotiations for settlement continued for a long period of time. Finally, colonial officials gave up and paid £1,500. This was an indication that stringent colonial policies had a flexible side to them.

There were many examples of British colonial intrusion on Brazilian land that the Brazilians and their offspring used for agricultural purposes. Court records show that "in about 1931, when the Government acquired a portion of the larger area granted for European Residential Area, and the area acquired took in a portion that had been cultivated and under the control of the plaintiff's family, the then family head Frank Ribeiro claimed the compensation."[28] The amount is not stated in the court document. In the case of *J. E. Maslieno v. J. A. Nelson* on 16 November 1945, supreme court documents note that the colonial government took a portion of Brazilian land for building streets, but there is insufficient information to show what happened thereafter.[29]

In addition to the British officials, the people of Accra also had a special interest in acquiring Brazilian land despite the problems associated with such transactions and the cost for compensating the owners. Although members of the Brazilian-African diaspora won most of the court cases, they increasingly became frustrated with unresolved disputes between different family groups over boundaries of their land as well as the frequency of intrusions by outsiders. For example, on 4 February 1938, the *Daily Echo*, a colonial newspaper, strongly warned the public against purchasing land from any member of the Brazilian community. Another notice that was referred to in court declared:

> Any person or persons negotiating for purchase acquisition, lease, mortgage or otherwise of any portion of the said property, comprised within the limits described below with any person or persons other than Frank Joseph Ribeiro of Adabraka, Accra, the authorized representative of the Lawrence family of the Brazilians, does so at his or her own risk, peril or loss.[30]

COLONIAL OFFICIALS TO EXPATRIATES: NEW DESIRE FOR BRAZILIAN LAND AND PROPERTIES

Compensation from colonial officials was not the only option for making profit from Brazilian land. Around 1945 some members of the Brazilian community made as much as £2,100 for selling portions of land either legally or illegally.[31] It is imperative to note that the changes associated with agrarian society and land-based rental practices in the Brazilian-African diaspora coincided with important historical developments such as the strategic migrations of European merchants and other expatriates to the Gold Coast during the precolonial period. Their major goal was also to amass wealth and to prop up colonial ventures. Since coastal Accra was not very developed in the early 1900s, some of these investors and entrepreneurs sought private land, affordable housing, and stores to rent for their business activities. Like British colonial officials who used Brazilian land for their projects, these expatriates also became attached to properties belonging to the Brazilians.

Brazilian land was very attractive to expatriates and other diaspora communities alike. These diverse communities benefited immensely from Brazilian land. Syrian merchants in particular leased land from the Brazilians because of its strategic location in what later became the central trading center in Accra. In one such transaction, a Syrian paid three different sums of money—£55, £50, and £10—to three Brazilians, but the record does not detail the terms of this exchange.[32] Black entrepreneurs from the West Indies who traded in Accra also rented rooms from the Brazilians.[33] Most freed Africans from the West Indies who migrated to the Gold Coast did so mainly to support Christian mission work that was initiated by Basel missionaries, the Moravian church, and others. Other foreigners, including Lebanese and European merchants, also paid large sums of money for Brazilian land. They included merchants who bought empty bottles and used them for marketing their mineral water products.[34] These traders gained access to buildings managed by both inland descendants and those close to urban Accra. Such transactions generated new land disputes between diverse migrants and the Brazilians.

Some of these conflicts over Brazilian land were also caused by foreigners who either did not want to pay for the land they were given by the Brazilians or could not afford to pay them. A number of Europeans who rented buildings belonging to the Brazilians did not honor their promises. They stayed in these building for many months without paying because their businesses did not flourish as they expected. According to one court report, "the first European who took the house resided for five months at £209 . . . having failed in his business he went away without paying anything."[35] It was difficult for the Brazilians to track down these expatriates because they moved from one coastal location to another in search of business opportunities elsewhere.

British officials were not the only enemies of the freed slaves and the Tabom. There were other self-made enemies within their own camp who sought to take over land allocated to a particular family group or the entire community for personal use. Debates within the Brazilian-African diaspora over what I characterize as proagrarian and nonagrarian traditions regarding how to use Brazilian land was another major source of conflict. Intraconflicts and interconflicts that were presented in colonial and native courts shook the foundations of Brazilian landownership and in some ways threatened the future of the Brazilian-African diaspora. Whereas colonial policies became the central instrument for carrying out new land policies, memory was the key for defending Brazilian land as the court dealt with an avalanche of cases.

Avalanche of Court Cases: Remembering What Happened One Hundred Years Ago

In order to examine the avalanche of conflicts over land, and thus show how these disputes produced such devastating outcomes, we must focus on selected court cases and oral histories. Unfortunately for the local people, some of the witnesses whose testimony was called for were either too old to appear in court or had already died before this turbulent time in the history of Brazilian-Africans in Accra.[36] However, the large number of descendants who did testify reveals the degree to which the land disputes affected the returnee colony. In general, land tenure and conflicts had an enormous impact on the Brazilian-African diaspora. Some who testified described their motivations for traveling back to their communities. One witness noted, "I heard about the suit.... I know that litigation affected all Brazilian families that owned land North of Farrar Avenue, where the land in dispute is situated."[37]

Court documents about the land disputes outnumber every other type of information available concerning this legal history in part because of the attention these court cases gained after the Brazilians demanded compensation from British colonial officials as well as the emergence of a stream of land disputes.[38] These cases, in tandem with other sources of information including oral history and traditions, tell us how properties were allocated to the Brazilians and how they were transferred to the next generation. In addition, court records show how other migrants, like the Brazilians, contested various forms of property as they also appealed to courts to grant access to land that they had purchased from the Brazilians. The complex nature of the litigations often led to other forms of lawsuits. Plaintiffs and defendants who were unsatisfied with verdicts by the Supreme Court of the Gold Coast filed for appeals or took their cases to a native court or public tribunal.[39]

Ripples in a Brazilian Pond: Zigzag Tales, Contesting Freedom, and Land Tenure

The ripple effects spread far and wide in the Brazilian community, generating other problems that would later push the conflicts beyond its confines. Intrafamily disputes that included chains of lawsuits and countersuits over land that was sold legally or illegally to members and nonmembers of the returnee communities permeated other social territories as well. Descendants not only fixated on how to prevent other

Chapter Five

Figures 11a and 11b. Gã Mãŋtsɛ Tackie Tawiah (left) and Mãŋtsɛ Nii Kojo Ababio IV (right), who were involved in disputes over Brazilian land.

Ghanaians of Brazilian descent from gaining or claiming Brazilian lands; they also stood up against anyone and everyone who threatened their efforts to protect their inheritance, even contesting with Gã mãŋtsɛmɛi at one point or another. After a decade of confrontation with British officials in matters that threatened his life, his throne, and the Gã *mãshi* in general, Gã *Mãŋtsɛ* Tackie Tawiah appeared before a court to defend his right to Gã stool lands, a humiliating and frustrating experience for a Gã king of his caliber. It is not certain if he was aware of the boundaries of all the gift of such royal land *Mãŋtsɛ* Komeh I, had offered to the returnees. *Mãŋtsɛ* Tackie Tawiah hardly expected a confrontation with the returnees' descendants just sixty years after the land was granted. Nii Kojo Ababio IV also had to intervene in the dispute (figures 11a and 11b). A synthesis is provided in tables 2 and 3 to underscore the role of both Gã mãŋtsɛmɛi during their tenures.

Mãŋtsɛ Tawiah, one of the most powerful Gã kings, did not tolerate colonial rulers. For this reason, he was a threat to Governor Ussher and George Cleveland, who attempted to coerce him to abide by colonial ordinances. *Mãŋtsɛ* Tawiah was exiled for his strong stance against foreign interference in Gã *mãŋ*.[40] He returned from exile more resolute than before to complete the battles he started earlier against his adversaries. As a result, during his tenure especially when he was exiled there was high level of distrust between the Gã king and the Brazilians partly because of the lack of communications between the two groups during this chaotic period in Gã social history. As

Table 3. Gã mãŋtsɛmɛi (kings and chiefs) who were involved in disputes over Brazilian lands that were presented in both colonial and native courts

GÃ MÃŊTSEMEI	TENURE	COURT CASE	CLASSIFICATION
Tackie Komeh I	1826–1856	His name was mentioned in all cases regarding who gave Gã stool land to the Brazilians	Both intrafamily and interfamily land disputes
Tackie Tawiah	1862–1902	*Tackie v. Nelson*	Interfamily land dispute
Kojo Ababio IV	1891–1938	*Yawah v. J. E. Maslieno**	Intrafamily land dispute
Tackie Obili	1904–1919 and 1932–1944	*Yawah v. J. E. Maslieno*	Intrafamily land dispute
Tackie Yaboi	1919–1929	*Yawah v. J. E. Maslieno*	Intrafamily land dispute
Ayi Bonte	Served temporarily when Tackie Obili was destooled (removed from his throne) in 1919	*Yawah v. J. E. Maslieno*	Intrafamily land dispute

*Yawah v. J. E. Maslieno lasted for many years, and the case was presented in both colonial and native courts partly because of the complication with the evidence that was provided. As noted above, four Gã mãŋtsɛmɛi were involved until it was settled in Yawah's favor.

Source: Public Records and Archives Administration Department, Accra.

the Brazilian chiefs were in court to settle land disputes both within their communities and against outside intruders, the fatigued *Mãŋtsɛ* Tawiah made his case before the supreme court and native tribunals to demand portions of land. In *King Tackie v. Robert Nelson* he testified that it was not true that all the land Brazilian and the Tabom was given to them by *Mãŋtsɛ* Komeh I.[41]

KING TACKIE V. ROBERT NELSON (TAIWO)

In the case of *Tackie v. Robert Nelson* (no. 1432) in 1892, the rift was between King Tawiah and two members of the Nelson family, Robert Nelson and G. A. Nelson. It became evident that the boundaries of the land in dispute were not very clearly demarcated and did not have land titles. The Nelsons, according to Brazilian-Tabom traditions, were the only family group that could be selected as Brazilian-Tabom chiefs. In carrying out these traditions, the Brazilian chiefs believed they alone had the right to give out Brazilian land. In his capacity as a Gã king, Tawiah wanted to reclaim stool land for the royal family and Gã people. In opposition, Brazilian-African descendants presented one witness after another to establish that these disputed lands belonged to their forefathers. For instance, a member of the Aruna family reported that, "My father, Dangana farmed the area in dispute. He belonged to the Nii Aruna family of the Brazilian community. My father died 42 years ago. When I grew up my brother and I used to accompany my father to farm on the area in dispute."[42] In this case, the Brazilians provided several witnesses including older parents, some of whom were present when the land was given to them. Gã *Mãŋtsɛ* Tawiah was present when these witnesses established their claim to Gã stool land based on memory and their interactions with *Mãŋtsɛ* Komeh I. Others testified based on their own experiences when they used these pockets of land for various use. *Mãŋtsɛ* Tawiah could not say the same but speculated about what Gã stool land was supposed to be used for—not as a gift to outsiders.

This court case had another twist. According to Ghanaian customs, a king or chief does not speak in public directly to the audience because of his authoritative position.[43] Royal announcements are the work of the king's linguist, or *okyeame* (modern-day public relations officer). In the case of *Tackie v. Nelson*, however, King Tawiah had to speak for himself because British colonial authorities intentionally amended this cultural protocol in ways that allowed them to usurp or enforce their authority. British colonial ordinances created a bifurcation in power dynamics intended to frustrate Gã leaders and other colonial subjects who objected to British rule. King Tawiah's frustration with these British tactics is evident in the correspondence between the Gã mãŋtsɛmɛi and the British Crown.[44] The Brazilians were aware of how vulnerable King Tawiah had become by the height of the promulgation of colonial ordinances. In *Tackie v. Nelson*, the king was fighting multiple battles. On the one hand, he was dealing with British officials who had stripped him of his authority as the legitimate king of Gã *mãŋ* and humiliated him in exile; were it not for this colonial impediment, he could have easily taken over all the areas of Gã stool land King Komeh had given to the ex-slaves from Brazil. On the other hand, King Tawiah was also contesting "sacred" land that was supposed to be for members of the Gã royal family but had been handed over to a group of freed slaves, whose offspring were now determined to protect it. Not only that, the freed Brazilians, most of whom were in their old age at the onset of the land dispute in the late 1890s, challenged King Tawiah.

Broadly speaking, King Tawiah had to face directly some of the early recipients of the land. Although most of these settlers were very old by the 1890s, they showed up in court to ensure that their offspring were not exploited again as they had been in Brazil. Their offspring had been told over and over again that the gift of land was made to their ancestors long before King Tawiah's reign. Thus, as far as they were concerned, it was Brazilian land and not Gã stool land anymore. Indeed, a dissonance of memory among various family groups came out in the court testimony. Nonetheless, most of the descendants had a legitimate argument. They believed they were entitled and were proud to hold onto this family treasure. Further, it is vital to add that the liberated slaves and their children had a great deal of respect for the cultures of the Gã people, but they did not feel attached to Gã cultures. Rather, they saw themselves as a separate community within a larger Gã society. This period in the history of the Brazilian-African diaspora was a crucial turning point in their identity formation.

Tackie v. Nelson, which occurred three years after *Mãŋtsɛ* Tawiah returned from exile in Elmina, had yet another twist. King Tawiah had to depend on members of his royal court to defend his right to determine the boundaries of Gã stool land. One of the elders in the king's court suggested that conflict with the Brazilians escalated because the descendants took advantage of the absence of the Gã *mãŋtsɛ* and took over extra land that was not originally included in the gift to their ancestors.[45] The court documents suggest that some form of settlement ended this crisis with *Mãŋtsɛ* Tawiah. Indeed, Tawiah's personality allowed him to maneuver his way through conflict. A brilliant leader, he possessed unique skills in negotiating with the local people and foreigners alike. He had a roller-coaster relationship with the emancipated Brazilian-Africans and their descendants that allowed him to operate fluidly. For instance, although Chief João Antonio Nelson shared family ties with the Nelsons who contested with *Mãŋtsɛ* Tawiah, there is no evidence that he appeared in court or participated in this case. However, five years after the land dispute with the Nelsons, *Mãŋtsɛ* Tawiah was arrested again, this time along with Brazilian chief João Antonio Nelson and other Gã mãŋtsɛmɛi, for opposing the British CLO of 1897.[46] It is such twist and turns that complicated Gã-Brazilian relations.

NII AZUMAH III V. LARIKIE ARUNA AND KANKLE KOFI

The land dispute between the three individuals Nii Azumah III, Larikie Aruna (both members of the Brazilian community), and Kankle Kofi was also presented to the Supreme Court of the Gold Coast, public lands division. In this second interfamily conflict (no. 769/48) Aruna, the plaintiff, sued Brazilian chief Nii Azumah III (who ruled from 1936 to 1961) for interfering with land sales (which Aruna sold to Kofi). The lawsuit demanded £25 in damages for Kankle Kofi, whose land was seized by the chief and later sold to another person. Aruna claimed that the elders of the Aruna family approved the transaction, because they did not need the chief's approval for allocating part of the land of their ancestors to Kofi, a non-Brazilian. This case in particular underscores nuances in the authority of a Brazilian chief. The Brazilian community was divided over this issue. Most members of the Nelson family, the only group from which chiefs are appointed, gave their support to the Brazilian chief, Nii Azumah III, whereas others, including members of the Plange family who traced their lineage through the *naabi* (matriarchal lineage), supported the Arunas. The Plange families trace their roots to Adsuma Maryamu Matta, a prominent Brazilian who also joined the exodus to Accra.[47]

Although inconsistencies frequently arose in the evidence provided by some heads of family groups, owing to intricate arguments about who selected them to their position, colonial courts and policies placed value on the input of family leaders in the court proceedings because most of these leaders were normally older people. It was believed that they had lived long enough to know more about their family history. Therefore, social issues were determined through this lens. Prior to the judgment, Nii Kwei Kuma II, the judge, questioned why there were no high-level representatives from the Nelson family to prove that they had Chief Nelson's approval. Also, the judge pointed out that "no elder of the Brazilian community who made him [Aruna] the head of the community called to prove that the land in dispute was vested in him during his election and installation as advanced by him."[48] The judge also reprimanded the Brazilian chief for not showing any documents and land titles to the court as justification for taking over Kofi's land on behalf of the entire Brazilian community. In fact, the judge was suspicious of the witnesses from the Plange family for presenting his cousins, instead of neutral members from other family lines. This request was, however, inconsistent with the other court cases because there was no such question about the presence of neutral family members to confirm any evidence. The assumption by the judge was that all the descendants shared common family roots or that they were supposed to know more about each other. But their migration patterns to Accra show that despite their shared story of slavery in Brazil, the Brazilian-African diaspora was made up of various groups of freed slaves with diverse blood lineage.

In the later proceedings, the judge reminded the court that colonial policies and native courts that were established by the British share some things in common: both recognize the significance of land titles in lawsuits. This point may have been overstated because there is no indication that the various ordinances and institutions that were created by the British Crown had a major impact right at the outset. Based on this argument, Nii Kwei Kuma II, a local Gã chief who represented the native court, found Nii Azumah III guilty and ordered him to pay Aruna for the land. This is one of the few examples where the court found a Brazilian chief guilty. It shows that colonial officials did not recognize the role of the Brazilian chiefs. These leaders had very limited authority within the Brazilian-African diaspora.

ISAAC COBBLAH FISCIAN V. HENRY ASUMAH KWAKU NELSON AND SOHBY BAKSMATHY

Along with defending Brazilian land from outside intruders, the ex-slaves and the Tabom, also guarded their inheritance and sued other Brazilians who attempted to steal or trespass on their properties. One such case was presented by Isaac Cobblah Fiscian, the great-grandson of the late Aruna and the leader of the Aruna family, against Henry Asumah Kwaku Nelson and Sohby Baksmathy; it concerned a piece of property located at Akwandor in Accra and was presented to the Supreme Court of the Gold Coast, public lands division. Fiscian claimed that his family controlled the land after it was allocated to the Brazilian community, and thus the court should have prevented other Brazilians from having access to the area. Nelson and Baksmathy, in their defense, argued that Akwandor land was part of the property that was given to the entire Brazilian community, and that therefore the court should rule on their behalf.[49] What is fascinating about this case is that whereas the plaintiff pushed for total control of the land, the defendants attacked the standing of Fiscian, arguing that he had no respect or authority among his own people and therefore could not bring such a lawsuit. The court records show that Nelson's father, G. A. Nelson, owned a piece of the land in the Akwandor area that he converted from farmland to a garden. The difference between farmland and garden was not clear in this case, but one interpretation was that G. A. Nelson got permission from one of the family members to use the land as a garden to grow flowers instead of using it for planting mangoes and crops for sale on a large scale, as most Brazilians did in this area.[50] Samuel Quarcoopome's study confirms the agrarian activities in describing the role of the Brazilian farmers in creating a forest of mango tree plantations in old Accra.[51]

A closer look at the case shows that the land dispute was far more complex than an argument over what was planted. This other dimension had to do with buildings that were erected legally, or illegally, by the Nelsons on the land. To strengthen his case, Nelson stated that his father built a house for the family and later handed it over to his children. The Nelsons also challenged claims by Fiscian that he witnessed the erection of the building in the 1920s and was aware of its sale in 1945 in the same area. After a lengthy exchange, the court ordered the defendants to provide documents including land titles and deeds to prop up their claims of ownership. The judge then ordered a clerk and a land surveyor of the Deeds of Registry in the Gold Coast to clarify how the Nelsons transferred the building to Baksmathy, the second defendant. The testimony by the town engineer showed that although the building was transferred legally, there were safety concerns about the durability of the materials used on the project and the fact that the building extended beyond its original boundary. These minor infractions violated colonial codes, which by this period had grown unbearable. Based on colonial policies, the Nelsons as others were bound by the ordinances and therefore were at fault. However, the Brazilians elevated their rights to protect their properties over colonial ordinances. In this case, the town council therefore ordered the demolishing of the building, though the demolition was not carried out for reasons unknown.[52] There is a paradox here: Brazilians including Fiscian had no regard for colonial ordinances. Yet in this case it was those very ordinances that ended up deciding the case in his favor.

Fiscian, the carpenter, described his confrontation with intruders on his family land that began in the 1920s. According to the court records, the dispute with the defendants persisted for almost twenty years because the lawsuits were taken to both the native courts and the supreme court in an attempt to reach a settlement.[53] Such lengthy litigation would require significant resources, time, and money to sustain. For the last court case in 1945, Fiscian was pressed to push for a quick resolution, because Nelson was in the process of completing yet another project on the disputed plot. What provoked Fiscian was the news that Nelson had already sold the new project to Baksmathy—meaning Fiscian now had two battles on his hands.

There were other interesting ironies about this case. For instance, Fiscian could not seek help from the lawyer Bossman, a man known for winning court cases, because Bossman was married to Nelson's daughter. Bossman also could not take the case because both Fiscian and Nelson families intermarry with the Bossman family. But the complications did not end there. Fiscian and the court found out that Nelson hired his son-in-law, Bossman, to prepare documents for transferring the building to Baksmathy. In this case, Fiscian felt betrayed by his old friend Bossman. Nelson therefore needed some kind of intervention on his side. Memory played a pivotal role later in this tangled dispute as he shared his childhood experience. Nelson explained to the court that in the 1890s he lived with his father, who plowed a large area of land where he lived and planted cashew trees and cultivated cassava. According to Nelson, he and his siblings requested land from his father, which he used to build a house in 1922; he later rented it out.[54] Nelson noted that Fiscian had moved to coastal Accra during that time, and therefore he had no knowledge of what occurred in the bush area in dispute. According to Nelson, his conflict with Fiscian started when Fiscian and the town council complained about his plans to put up new buildings on the site his father gave him and escalated when he gave his property to Baksmathy, the second defendant. Fiscian challenged claims by the Nelsons that they had land beyond the area where Nii Azumah I (Brazilian chief from 1836 to 1865) built his first and only house. He also disputed the argument by the Nelsons that they acquired most of the land through a will passed on by Nii Azumah I.[55]

In his closing statement, N. A. Ollenu, the counsel for the defendant, underscored the contradictions in Fiscian's testimony, especially the authenticity of his role as leader of the Aruna family. This conclusion was based on a lack of evidence or support by any member of the Aruna family to confirm his position. Ollenu was convinced that the Nelsons had clearly shown that none of the property in question was owned by any individual family in the Brazilian community, such as the Arunas. Ollenu accepted Brazilian traditions that gave the chief authority to make decisions about land with very little opportunity for the Aruna family to respond. Ollenu also supported the Nelsons' claim that the original Brazilian land was not divided among the family heads. Before Judge Caussey read the final verdict, he stated that long years of land disputes in the Brazilian community had left both psychological and physical scars on most of the Brazilians, who spent over two decades contesting with the Nelson family over land. Judge Caussey added that the Nelsons had taken advantage of new colonial policies about land title to avoid future harassment by the Arunas or other interested groups. Although the judge could not accept evidence that the late Nelson provided the land to his children in 1915, he was convinced that his son used the land to build another house in 1922 for rental purposes. The judge concluded that the Fiscian family should have challenged the Nelsons much earlier when they started their project. Finally, he ruled on behalf of the Nelsons and ordered Fiscian to pay all fines.[56]

The outcomes of the court cases oscillated like a pendulum. Fiscian filed an immediate appeal on the basis that the judge had failed to prove that the Arunas were not the rightful owners of the Akwandor land. This case continued for many years, but the judgment was not reversed.[57]

J. E. MASLIENO V. J. A. NELSON

Cases of intrafamily conflict were widespread. The *J. E. Maslieno v. J. A. Nelson* case (no. 77/1950), between J. E. Maslieno, who claimed he was the leader of the Aruna family, and J. A. Nelson from the Nelson family was also presented before the Supreme Court of the Gold Coast, public lands division. The litigation was about an allegation of trespassing on Brazilian land and the question of who had the right to live on the land. The plaintiff, Maslieno, sued Nelson for £25 in damages for trespassing on his land and for selling it later to a man named Pinnock without Maslieno's approval. Prior to the final judgment in the case, representatives from the court were sent to the site, which is believed to be the current location of the West African Examination Council, the Ministry of Information, the National Archives of Ghana (PRAAD, Accra),

Chapter Five

and the Young Women's Christian Association in central Accra. This visit established that the location was part of the original land that the Gã mãŋtsɛmɛi allocated to the Brazilians. Other details by the court suggested that not all the descendants owned part of it, especially the Nelsons. As the record shows,

> Although according to the statement the defendant is a chief for the Brazilians but his father had no land allotted him likewise the plaintiff himself consequently the defendant failed to show his father's portion or his own.... The Councilors were satisfied that the spot where the defendant sold to one Pinnock was portion of plaintiff's father's land in his charge and therefore decided that the defendant had committed a trespass and the land must go back to the plaintiff with damage of £10.00.[58]

In short, Nii Azumah Nelson III was found guilty of trespassing.

YAWAH V. J. E. MASLIENO

The *Yawah v. J. E. Maslieno* case revolves around the story of Ferku, whose love story says a lot about the ways in which Ferku and other returnees navigated complex migratory routes from Brazil to Nigeria and later to Ghana in search of the ideal location for settlement. *Yawah v. J. E. Maslieno*, which began in colonial courts but ended in native courts that were established by the British as an alternative to colonial courts, demonstrates the complexity of the legal system during the colonial period. It also shows how gender roles within the Brazilian-African diaspora were skewed and how the educated members exploited the noneducated members. Further, it reveals evidence of deceit and cover-up as men like Maslieno gained influential positions in their communities.

In this case, which happened after Ferku left Accra for Lagos and gave his share of land to his wife, Yawah, Maslieno took advantage of Ferku's absence. He influenced Yawah to hand over her property so that Maslieno could rent it to those who were interested. The court record shows that Yawah's parents raised Maslieno when he was a child, therefore his request was welcomed with open arms. It is not clear if Maslieno was able to sell part of the land to non-Brazilians. What is obvious in this case was that it was tossed between colonial courts and native courts. During this process Gã mãŋtsɛmɛi including Yaboi complicated matters when he questioned the validity of Yawah's story. In fact, he, as Gã *Mãŋtsɛ* Tawiah, did not accept Gã *Mãŋtsɛ* Komeh I's decision to give Gã stool land to the Brazilians. What is also missing in this court

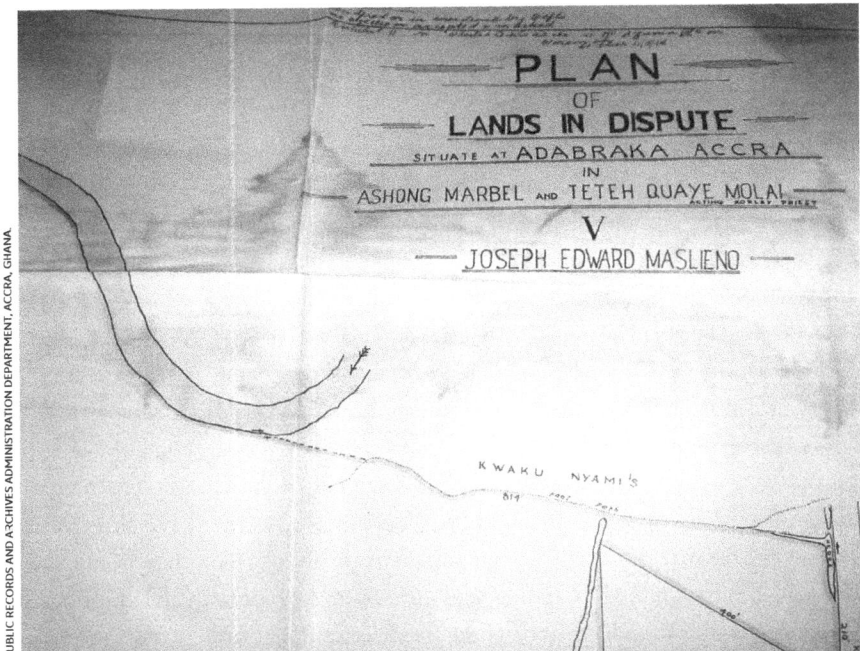

Figures 12a and 12b. Disputed Brazilian lands between Brazilians and non-Brazilians in Accra.

narrative is that it is not clear if the case went back to the colonial court. What we know is that *Yawah v. J. E. Maslieno* ended in favor of Yawah after another Gã *mãŋtsɛ*, Ayi Bonte, challenged Gã *Mãŋtsɛ* Yaboi by confirming the authenticity of Yawah's land inheritance. It became clear that Maslieno exploited Yawah because she was old and was illiterate—in other words, vulnerable.[59] Besides the fact that there was evidence to support Yawah's property claim, Gã *Mãŋtsɛ* Ayi Bonte took into consideration the fact that Yawah was much older than Maslieno, and in Gã tradition Maslieno was supposed to honor her, not steal from her.

There was a wide spectrum of court cases relating to Brazilian lands in Gã *mãŋ*. They include but are not limited to *Plange v. Brazilians, Millers v. Victoria Van Hein, Nassu v. Basel Mission, Jemima Nassu v. Basel Mission Factory and Victoria Van Hein, Nelson v. Ammah and Aruna, Luttrodt St. Yawah v. Maslieno, Nelson v. Nelson, Nelson v. Amisah, Mattier v. Aryichoe, Nii Anyetei Kwao v. Nii Azumah III, Frank Ribeiro and Hashem Noshie*; and *Ashong Mabel and Tetteh Quaye v. Joseph Edward Maslieno* (figures 12a and 12b). There is insufficient documentation of some of these court cases.

Ripples into the Twenty-First Century: The Ghosts of Chief Brimah and Fatima Okpedu Return

The Brazilians made tremendous strides in resolving land disputes, but this does not mean they no longer hold grudges against each other: ripples from the conflicts did not vanish suddenly; unresolved past problems still affect following generations after over a century. In fact, pockets of leftover arguments over land still remain in Accra, and ongoing disputes continue to rage in the halls of the Supreme Court of Ghana. One recent public land dispute between the descendants of Chief Alhaji Brimah and Madam Fatima Okpedu has reopened old wounds. This complicated matter falls under both intrafamily and interfamily conflicts. Brimah was a devout Yoruba Muslim and a businessman who left Nigeria for Accra in the late 1800s. Works about early Muslim settlements in Accra provide insight concerning Brimah and his contribution to commercial activities in colonial Accra.[60] A document written by members of the Peregrino-Brimah family about their grandfather, Brimah, also shows how he migrated to Accra and contributed to trading activities. Brimah supposedly fell in love with Okpedu, who is believed to be one of the freed slaves from Brazil—a member of the Peregrino family. The court case, an interfamily conflict that began in the 1980s, gained substantial attention in various communities. The lawsuit (no. FAL/1040/10) was filed by the plaintiff, Rashid Brimah, and three others against the defendant, Hadji M. B.

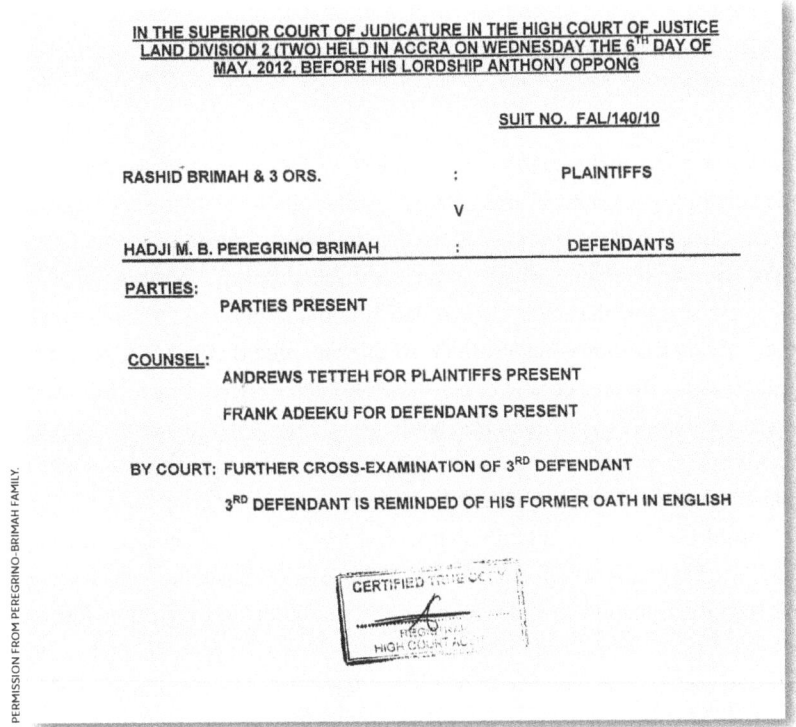

Figure 13. Copy of court case Rashid Brimah & 3 Ors. v. Hadji M. B. Peregrino-Brimah.

Peregrino-Brimah. Both parties share the same grandparent, Chief Alhaji Brimah, who died in the 1940s and left a number of properties for his offspring (figure 13).

One of the central issues about the court case is disagreement over Okpedu's status as a slave or a freed person by the time she started her union with Chief Brimah. One group (the Peregrino-Brimah) believes that Okpedu was a freed slave from Brazil before her marriage to Chief Brimah, so her offspring deserve to inherit the properties she acquired from her union with Brimah. But her stepchildren claim that she was rather a slave in Accra with no Brazilian heritage at the time and was a concubine of their grandfather Chief Brimah; therefore she was not entitled to any wealth after the death of Chief Brimah. In court, the latter group insisted that slaves could not inherit properties. What is problematic about this claim is that there is no evidence that some of the returnees became slaves in Accra after their emancipation. Looking at it from another angle, what they seem to be suggesting is that Okpedu was not a Brazilian returnee but an ordinary slave in Gã *mãŋ* who happened to have been married to Chief Brimah.

Chapter Five

The Significance of the Court Cases and Their Complications

There is sufficient evidence to show that the Gã *Mãŋtsɛ* Komeh I gave the Brazilians land in multiple geographical areas. Based on this argument and the conclusions that emanated in some of the court cases, the disputes were contested over multiple locations of Brazilian settlements in Accra. What is striking about *J. E. Maslieno v. J. A. Nelson* this court case is that the evidence provided by both Maslieno and Nelson contradicts aspects of oral traditions and written records that argue that the first generation of returnees were offered free land by Gã *Mãŋtsɛ* Komeh I.[61] According to the narratives, the returnees were not provided free land during their first interactions with the Gã king. Instead, they requested an isolated land to dig wells to provide them with fresh drinking water, because most of them had infections and stomach problems after they were introduced to water in Otublohum, their first location of settlement along the coast.[62] The Brazilians called water drilling in this area "Mungatabu," which according to oral traditions means "we have found water."[63] It is not known if this is a Brazilian-Portuguese word, a local Gold Coast word, a common word from the Bight of Benin, where the returnees often visited, or a word derived from a combination of terms. After they were offered the land the returnees introduced well-drilling techniques.[64] Another testimony showed that Brazilian land was offered by Ashong Djamawoh, the Korle priest of a small coastal town in Accra. The witness claimed that the gift form Djamawoh was located in the "middle of two roads."[65] Yet another statement by Isaac Cobblah Fiscian emphasized that Brazilian land was given by Chief Nii Ankrah of Otoblohum.[66] Although the dominant claim pointed to Gã King Komeh I, my inquiry shows that multiple pockets of land were given to the freed slaves at different locations at different time periods by different Gã leaders.

There are some similarities in the oral traditions and existing literature about how the liberated Africans were offered land by the Gã chief. However, archival records from the court cases suggest that the Brazilians were offered land by the Gã chief to reciprocate various gifts including a clock the Brazilians brought to the chief and the royal family during their frequent interactions along the coast.[67] Another interpretation by the late Elder George Aruna Nelson, who was the oldest member of the Brazilian-African diaspora in Accra during our interview in 2008, was that the Brazilians acquired the land because of their skills in tailoring.[68] The dominant theory is that the returnees who were able to afford to travel along the Bight of Benin for trading purposes had regular contact with leaders of Gã traditional areas, especially those in the Otublohum area, which is why they were given land to settle in Accra. In my opinion, the long history of migrations from Lagos to the Gã traditional area created a solid platform for the allocation of Brazilian land and the creation of the Brazilian-African diaspora in Accra.

Dissonance of memory was a major feature in the court proceedings. This was acknowledged by one of the judges when he declared that "there is no dispute that the Brazilians once owned [land] in that vicinity but what baffles the Tribunal's comprehension is ... [how] the defendants are able to narrate what happened 100 years ago."[69] Contrary to this assertion, there were other features that complicated court proceedings as the parties took the stand. Although they went to great length to provide the court with historical evidence supporting their claim to the land in dispute, there was lack of clarity about the information they provided and the knowledge court officials had. In fact, even some of the witnesses who claimed to be part of various Brazilian families had somewhat little knowledge of their own history. As the descendants aired their dirty laundry in public courts, non-Brazilians exploited the situation and attempted to prove their blood ties to freed slaves and especially the Brazilian-African diaspora.

The question some of the judges raised in court was to inquire about who was an authentic Brazilian and who was fake.[70] In the early 1900s, especially after the demise of the early settlers, a number of counterfeit Brazilians who aspired to associate with the Brazilian history to gain access to land adopted innovative strategies to meet these goals. As court records show, some local people took advantage of land disputes to claim ties to the Brazilian family tree because the name "Brazilians" had become a buzz word that was synonymous with land acquisition, amassing properties, and court disputes.[71] Indeed, those with true ties to the Brazilians were able to show their heritage in some cases, while others created fraudulent stories with the goal of gaining access to resources, especially land at Akwandor and other isolated areas in Accra.[72] In one such court appearance, the judge challenged the authenticity of claims about ties to Brazilian-African diaspora in Accra when he noted "some twenty people calling themselves, children, grandchildren, and descendants of Aruna [one of the early settlers]."[73] The judges had no easy way of monitoring or differentiating Brazilians and non-Brazilians after many years of intermarriages especially between the younger generations and the people of the Gold Coast. A similar trend emerged in the mid-1940s as the second generation had to challenge other local people who trespassed on Brazilian lands.[74] This thread of inconsistency and deceitful claims runs through other narratives in the Brazilian-African diaspora.

Isaac Cobblah Fiscian's case against Henry Asumah Kwaku Nelson and Sohby Baksmathy is problematic. The details provided by Fiscian not only chronicle the history of the first-generation Brazilians and the various families that form the branches of the Brazilian family tree, but it brings to the fore how colonial projects interfered with Brazilian property in the Gold Coast. Some important details were revealed in court that provide additional insight into the geographical location of Brazilian land. For instance, Fiscian talks about the ways in which the British colonial rulers took some of the land for constructing roads, lanes, and other social projects for colonial ventures. His account of land allocation extends beyond the geographical boundaries of Adjabang Valley, Fonafa Valley, and Kibbi-Accra road, where oral tradition confirms that the Gã chief allocated land for the Brazilians. It is possible that the freed slaves purchased additional land after they received gifts of land from Gã mãŋtsɛmɛi.

The distinct characters of various Brazilian family groups that were involved in the land disputes speak to the variation in the stories they presented in court. As a descendant of Brazilians, Fiscian's childhood account of growing up in the 1920s suggests a shift of paradigm—from one that highlights a sense of unity among the first generation, especially those who were offered free land by the Gã chief, to one that debunks this idea and establishes a discourse of individualism and tension among the first generation. During one of his cross-examinations Fiscian affirmed that Mama Sokoto and Azumah were the first leaders of the Brazilian community. Sokoto is believed to have migrated from Nigeria.[75] Also, Fiscian's report emphasized the various skills of his ancestors from Brazil especially in farming—although he could not tell whether his great-grandfather, old man Aruna, had farmlands or was a farmer. Like other descendants, Fiscian also confirmed that he sold part of the land his family inherited to descendants of both Brazilians and non-Brazilians legally and illegally.

Fiscian's testimony also transcends oral tradition and written records when he points out to the court that the first generation did not cluster within a given space after they were allocated the land. Rather, Fiscian debunked the notion of communal relations. Fiscian forcefully argued that Brazilian settlers in the mid-nineteenth century promoted values of individualism and competition.[76] Fiscian's analysis challenges existing accounts that largely speak otherwise, especially the claims by the Brazilian chiefs in the court records. Another element that stands out in his testimony was Fiscian's emphasis on other returnees who moved to the Gã traditional area during this period. He stated that there were a number of West Indians from the Caribbean who rented rooms from some of the houses that were contested by the Brazilians. These West Indians may include migrants and technicians that British officials invited from the Caribbean region.[77] Their presence in Accra embodies the success of Gã mãŋtsɛmɛi in attracting diverse groups of migrants to their area. Fiscian also talked about the first generation's involvement in slavery when he explained how Mama Sokoto could not transfer property to the slaves she owned. However, what was missing in Fiscian's detailed version was his ability to tell exactly where each member of the first generation settled and farmed. Fiscian's account contradicts the Nelsons' and others' in the sense that he was convinced that only the Arunas used Amusadai land. These specific answers could have enhanced the courts' understanding of the complex nature of land dispute in the area, particularly the boundaries. There are other testimonies that shed a light on the history of the first generation. The account by Henry Asumah Kwaku Nelson, like Fiscian's, provides other significant information and challenges in narrating the Brazilian story.

Court proceedings also differed. For Fiscian's account he limited the number of early settlers, while the testimony by Nelson in particular raises the number to between seventy and seventy-five returnees during the first wave of migration. During his court appearance on 14 April 1919, Henry Nelson notes that they included Mama Sokoto, but he does not say where the settlers arrived from, Brazil or Nigeria. In addition, although Fiscian argued that the first-generation Brazilians did not have a communal relation on the land, Nelson stated otherwise. He debunked the idea of a decentralized Brazilian community in Fiscian's testimony. According to Nelson, "the land was not apportioned between them. They shared the land together. A particular family did not settle in a particular spot."[78] However, Nelson does not mention Otublohum as the original area of settlement as others seem to suggest. In fact, Nelson told the court that he spent most of his time at Swalaba, near Otublohum, where oral tradition and written records show that the returnees built the Scissors House.[79]

Nelson's account also provided a clearer picture about inheritance, especially properties that were accumulated by the Brazilians outside the contested land. He added that his father left his children with houses at Swalaba and Kokomlemle before his death. Also, Nelson's account provided more information about the size of the plots some of the Brazilians owned. He claimed his father had four plots about one hundred by one hundred feet each at Akwandor that were divided among his siblings—H. A. K. Nelson, Maama G. Nelson, and Kobina Nelson—and his cousin G. R. Lamptey. There is insufficient evidence suggesting that women in the Brazilian community also inherited land. In some ways, Nelson's details about the size of the land contradict his earlier account that Brazilians did not have a separate demarcated land—the idea that all land belonged to everyone or could be used for multiple purposes (agrarian activities). In fact, Nelson's specific description rather supports Fiscian's claim that each Brazilian family sought after its own interest.

The case between Fiscian and Nelson also opened up discussion about how the Brazilians amassed property outside Akwandor. Ellen Ashong Nelson, the mother of Nelson, testified that when her husband was alive, he cultivated his land and planted corn, cassava, and other farm products. She told the court that the husband gave his portion of the land to his children and acquired other wealth outside the Brazilian community.

Chapter Five

The exchanges in court underscored the fact that chiefs within the Brazilian-African diaspora did not have jurisdiction over Brazilian land. The verdict also underscored the fact that chiefs within the Brazilian community did not have jurisdiction over other families with ties to the Brazilians. What is striking about the winding Brazilian-Tabom tales is that some of the exchange in the court cases contradicts aspects of oral traditions and written records that argue that the first generation of returnees were offered free land by Gã King Komeh I on one occasion.[80] Specifically, one witness suggested that different returnees received gifts of land at different times.[81]

There was an irony with the story of reverse migration. The freed slaves who found a new place to call home in Accra with a yearning to control their own land were obstructed by British imperialism and clashes within the Brazilian-African diaspora, especially after the demise of the early settler generation. The gifts of land Gã leaders made to the emancipated Brazilian-Africans in the 1830s allowed most of them to own land, possibly for the first time. This vast area of land, which was a blessing to the earlier generation, became a curse among their descendants over time as it led to conflicts and divisions. Part of the problem was that the descendants adapted Brazilian traditions that promoted communal agrarian activities that they did not care too much about. Over time, they became more involved in a culture of land sales for commercial purposes. The nonagrarian lifestyles were new to most of the older members of the Brazilian-African diaspora. Indeed, the early settlers were mainly concerned with landownership because they remembered their servitude in Brazil. To protect their integrity some of the ex-slaves and the Tabom relied heavily on memory to defend their inheritance. However, those who were born after the mid-twentieth century in Ghana differed on this issue because of their limited knowledge or memory about their ancestors' experiences both in Brazil and in colonial Accra. In contrast, during the early periods of settlement in the 1820s dissonance of memory among the descendants, their varying degrees of socialization, and ultimately their deep assimilation into Ghanaian cultures shaped the ways they handled the possession of lands their ancestors passed on to them. An understanding of this complex and interesting dynamic can be approached via the archives and through oral history.

Ample archival evidence at PRAAD and elsewhere shows that the ex-slaves received a vast area of land as a gift from Gã *Mãŋtsɛ* Komeh I. However, we cannot overlook doubts that were raised by members of the Gã royal family regarding the exact size and locations of Brazilian land. About five decades after *Mãŋtsɛ* Komeh I gave the ex-salves land in Accra, *Mãŋtsɛ* Tackie Tawiah the new Gã leader had to defend some areas of land he claimed belonged to the Gã citizens and not the Brazilians. In the court case *Takie v. Nelson*, *Mãŋtsɛ* Tawiah declared that some area of "land belongs to my stool" but not the Nelson family or the Brazilians.[82] *Mãŋtsɛ* Tawiah was not the only member of Gã *māshi* who had a problem with the legitimacy of some areas of land ex-slaves and the Tabom claimed to be part of Brazilian land. The children and grandchildren of *Māŋtsɛ* Komeh I also argued that part of the Brazilian land was actually land Komeh gave to his daughter Na Korley. The descendants of *Māŋtsɛ* Komeh I asked the court to take the land from the Brazilians, but there is no evidence that the court granted their demands.[83] Clashes over Brazilian lands caused by the bitter land disputes in both the colonial supreme court and native tribunals that began in the late 1890s and continued into the twenty-first century reveal degrees of litigations.

Ripple effects from the squabbles never quite abated. Still other contentions over land and property emerged in the late twentieth century. Additionally, in the twenty-first century there are contentious issues related to the selection of leaders for Brazilian colonies and management of historical landmarks. The initiation of colonialism and the laws that accompanied them affected both the hosts and the guests in Accra and reshaped the social history of the Gã people in ways that left a lasting impact. The triangular relationship between the Gã people, the Brazilians, and the British became even more complex thereafter. Similarly, the ripple effects in the Brazilian-African diaspora remind us of the paradox of freedom and the intersection between emancipation and colonialism.

In locating a homeland after Brazil–Ghana transatlantic crossings and in reconstructing a lost identity, the returnees were also faced with complex challenges of protecting their properties. British colonial rule was not to blame for all the problems the Brazilians and their offspring encountered from the 1800s: the various individuals and family groups of the Brazilian-African diaspora in Accra contributed to these problems. The descendants provoked each other, cheated members of their communities, and made enemies within their camps. Decades of land disputes almost eroded the gains the early settlers made from the period of settlements, and divisions among the various family groups have made the Brazilian-African diaspora in Ghana invisible.[84] Some leaders of their community, individuals, and institutions such as the Brazilian embassy in Accra have collaborated with other interested groups to preserve fading aspects of the Brazilian-African diaspora from the margins to the center of burgeoning transatlantic history and global tourism. As a result of ongoing transformation in their story, a number of descendants, the Tabom, have crisscrossed the Atlantic to connect with their Brazilian roots while others have also expressed their interest to pursue these journeys for posterity's sake.

PART 2

Contradictions of Return: Transporting Atlantic Traditions, Skills, and Cultures and Refashioning Identity

Chapter 6

(Re-)Creating Brazilian Slavery in an Enabling Environment: The "Ghost" of Slavery

Dutch Accra has for a long time been the residence for several slave trade agents especially immigrated Brasilian negroes who have correspondents in Vay and Popo. ... Three months ago two negroes were thus caught in Ningo [near Accra]. They were to have been brought to the lower coast by a Brasilian negro.

—Governor Edward Carstensen

The ex-slaves and the Tabom have made a significant impact in Ghanaian society since they began arriving in the 1820s. Paradoxically, as stated in the epigraph, not all the returnees or their descendants engaged in productive ventures in the Gold Coast.[1] The enabling environment others created made it very convenient for the newly liberated Brazilians to replicate slavery as they had known it in Brazil.[2] As was also the case of returnees who settled elsewhere, some freed Africans imitated their oppressive plantation owners and engaged fully in slave-trading activities in the Gold Coast.[3] David Eltis and others have also shown that "British subjects owned, managed and manned slavery adventures."[4] British colonial officials on the other hand paid slave owners large sums of money for their slaves and used them to fight wars against the Asante Empire from the mid-nineteenth century. After completing this war mission, they returned slaves to their owners.[5] When it was convenient for British officials, they treated slaves who escaped (after they were "borrowed" from their owners) as committing a criminal act.[6] These illegal and inhumane activities were condoned not only by colonial officials, but also by Gã mãŋtsɛmɛi, local people, merchant groups, and missionaries, among others. They all contributed to a cycle of events that eventually created avenues for the Brazilian returnees to exploit others for profit. As the *African Times*, a colonial newspaper, publicized, members of the Brazilian returnee communities made enormous profits from the sale of slaves.[7] However, the archival documents I have examined are short on statistical details. There are no numerical figures showing how much money the Brazilian settlers generated from these illegal activities. Nonetheless, there is ample evidence that returnees' involvement in "small-scale" slavery dating back to the early 1800s contributed to the overall expansion of the transatlantic slave trade.

Brazilian-Africans' slavery activities on the Gold Coast cannot be compared to those that took place in Nigeria, Benin, and elsewhere, including the slavery practices that existed in the Gold Coast prior to the arrival of the returnees. The present author's findings have not yet led to any case confirming that a Brazilian returnee in the Gold Coast was arrested by the British for participating in slavery within British territories. But as I have attempted to show, their paths crossed nonetheless, especially as British colonial officials seized Brazilian land for colonial projects. This overview represents an effort to piece together and provide a chronology for the Brazilian-Africans' involvement in slavery in the Gold Coast, based on scanty documents and oral history, in order to start a conversation that can build on this analysis.

The ex-slaves who settled in Accra did not invent slavery in Ghana; rather, they took advantage of opportunities already available to practice slavery in an environment conducive to the institution.[8] Those involved spun the wheels of slavery to meet their personal needs. As the archives and colonial newspapers relate, the enslavement of Africans by returnees was quite common in other West Coast regions of Africa.[9] The cross-cultural interaction and exchanges between the freed slaves, migrants, expatriates, Europeans of various backgrounds, and the Gã people shaped the Brazilian-African diaspora from the early nineteenth century. To provide a broad narrative about the Brazilian-African diaspora, it is paramount to show the interactions between the Brazilians and all their neighbors. For it is through these multiple lenses that we can place the history of reverse migrations in proper historical perspective—inclusive of the social history of the Gold Coast. In the end, the decisions and choices the earlier settler groups made also influenced the lives and the identities of their offspring over time.

Numerous scholars have raised important historical questions about the participation of local Africans and community leaders, especially chiefs, in the slave trade.[10] This growing body of literature does not ignore the role of Islamic merchants and local African kings and chiefs, nor does it deny the extent of Europeans' involvement in slavery and how it escalated the slave trade. The implications of slavery on both the local and continental levels are also relevant. Brazilian-Africans were involved in these inhumane ventures, and Brazilians and their European counterparts crossed paths as slavery activity within the Gold Coast reached its zenith, especially at the twilight of the nineteenth century when the British intensified their campaign to end the slave trade.[11] Other Europeans who acted as the moral compass in the Gold Coast stood up against slavery.[12] Nonetheless, they found it highly difficult to eradicate these illegal practices. Returnees' involvement in slavery, which entwined with existing local practices, had consequences on their communities, especially on how descendants thought of and related to the actions of their ancestors. As a result, ties between the current generation and their Brazilian heritage are complicated, especially in terms of their apathy about the matter.[13]

The history of involvement in slavery activities by the ex-slaves is significant in helping to explain why the Brazilian family tree was "broken" as well as why the branches became weaker and the leaves withered over time. Some of the descendants are just not interested in discussing their Brazilian heritage. This dark side of their history has been characterized as the most horrific era in African, African diaspora, and Atlantic history.[14] Although there are archival sources and other literature about this contentious subject, during my interviews some descendants would deny this or express no interest in engaging in conversation about it. They find themselves in an awkward situation. They find it difficult to admit to the practice of slavery by their ancestors, perhaps for fear that they might be perceived as endorsing these acts. Put another way, this precarious position requires degrees of denial on the part of the offspring of the returnees who engaged in slavery. While some interviewees simply have limited knowledge about the subject, others appear to be wracked by guilt about the early settlers' participation in slavery. Moreover, various traditions in Accra in the nineteenth and early twentieth centuries served to cushion returnees' self-reproach or justify their actions as just part of the culture of that era.

A handful of archival records show that some of the freed slaves and their descendants sold their female slaves, used some of them for domestic work, and married some of these slaves. Their intimate relations with those they enslaved raise more questions about the genealogy of both the Brazilian and the Tabom family trees.[15] In general, Brazilians' involvement in slavery activities has tarnished the image of the community. Yet the stain left by their enslavement of local people has not erased the enormous contributions members of the Brazilian-African diaspora have made to Ghanaian history.

Chapter Six

CONTRADICTIONS OF ABOLITION

We can draw parallels between Brazilian-Africans' actions in the Gold Coast and in other places they settled. For instance, the returnees in Lagos in particular were highly regarded and not seen as trouble makers. In 1877, British governor Alfred Moloney described those he interacted with as "represent[ing] an orderly, industrious and respectable portion of this community and set[ting] generally a good example as citizens."[16] Similar to Moloney's assessment, a number of liberated Brazilian-Africans who made the Gold Coast their new home made positive impacts. Part of the returnee population took advantage of several appealing opportunities that were offered to migrants and strangers to help improve the communities in Accra. Unlike those involved in human trafficking, those with the skills to do so engaged in commerce, in trade back and forth between Brazil and various business centers such as Lagos. In addition, others applied skills they learned from Brazil to farming and well-drilling. Evidence of the Brazilians' dark history shows not only how pervasive slavery was in the Gold Coast but how tumultuous were the depressing conditions. Slavery during this historical period reflected the instability in the area, and it was entrenched in a culture of exploitation, violence, and inhumanity.

The epigraph at the beginning of this chapter shows the impact of slavery in the Gold Coast. Danish governor Edward Carstensen's diary echoes conflicting attitudes toward slavery activities by freed slaves and how that impeded abolition efforts. Missionary's recollection, reinforces the fact that Europeans too benefited heavily from these illegal activities while indicating how a dark cloud of guilt overshadowed the image of missionaries in addition to the liability of slavery for the propagation of the Christian gospel. The statement by Carstensen signals a warning about the role of Brazilian returnees in slavery in coastal Ghana. On the one hand, he reveals his double standard. The Danish governor points to the illegal activities of the Brazilian returnees, but what he fails to say was that the ex-slaves were basically reproducing the same inhumane practices that the Danes themselves were also involved in as they enslaved Africans in the Gold Coast and transported them on Danish ships, including the *Christianborg*, to Danish plantations in St. Croix, St. Thomas, and other islands in the West Indies.[17]

Thorkild Hansen's insightful trilogy—*Coast of Slaves*, *Ships of Slaves*, and *Islands of Slaves*—not only dispels myths that the Danes were more tolerant of abolition than other Europeans. The work also provides broad chronology detailing Danish investments in slavery in the Gold Coast from the mid-seventeenth century. Danish criticism of others who were involved in slavery was very striking when one considers the fact that the number of slaves they transported to the West Indies between 1671 and 1733 was about 5 percent of the total number of slaves that were taken from the Gold Coast. A report by Joseph Wuff, a Danish lawyer and missionary, shows his disdain for slavery. Wuff claim that the Danes did not give up slavery easily: they maintained their monopoly on the illegal trade for an extensive time to sustain their inhumane plantation activities in the West Indies.[18] The first Danish slave ship is believed to have sailed from the coastline of southeastern Ghana to St. Croix with about 457 slaves.[19] In the early eighteenth century the Danes sold some of their slaves to the Portuguese and the French based on some kind of mutual agreements between them.

Besides Christianborg Castle in Accra, about 1,500 slaves were taken from Danish forts such as Kongensteen in Ada, Fredensborg in Ningo, Augustaborg in Teshie, and others to the West Indies. It is estimated that by the early 1840s, the Danes transported over one hundred thousand slaves to their plantations in the West Indies. During this time, Danish slavery activities were so effective that it almost depleted part of the coastal population especially around the Volta basin. According to a report by one of the Danish ship captains, "a hundred years of intensive trade . . . thinned the population near the coast, the slaves had to be fetched further way [inland]."[20] As in the Gold Coast, the Danes treated their slaves on their island plantations brutally. In fact, Danish plantations were characterized as the "crematorium that not only devowed the increase in population, but as in the case of St. Croix, yearly burnt up a supply of 575 new slaves."[21] The decision by some of the emancipated Brazilian-Africans to prop up slavery was similar to the attitudes of the Danes and others. However, there were some differences. I resolve this dilemma between their involvement in slavery and their positive contributions by reconciling both. The returnees were not a homogeneous group and therefore cannot be lumped together. Although these ex-slaves might have shared similar convictions at times, they behaved and operated differently based on their unique backgrounds and distinct experiences. The heterogeneity or shades of diversity among them shaped their perceptions and socialization, particularly how they perceived slavery. Not all returnees contended with the meaning of being enslaved, especially its inhumane dimensions, as well as the significance of their own liberation and its implication for the survival of the individual and the community in general. Most of the freed slaves in the Gold Coast were there to chart their own paths and destiny, and they had legitimate reasons to do so. However, as did Wuff and other Europeans who opposed slavery, some of these ex-slaves from Brazil also opposed slavery in the Gold Coast after they settled there. Nonetheless, those returnees who enslaved local Ghanaians upset the conventional dynamic of slavery/emancipation as they replicated the same oppression they had ultimately revolted against in Brazil.

Although David Eltis's slave voyages database has aided various researchers seeking to understand the Brazilian-African diaspora in Ghana, I have come across no record that categorizes the freed Brazilian slaves into groups or explains when each was enslaved. Simply put, it is extremely difficult to trace their origins and the approximate number of the returnees who enslaved the local people. However, I have not found any statistics or evidence that sheds a light on the nuances of motivations for enslaving the local people or the number of returnees who were involved. Some of these returnees may have desired a connection to their distant African heritage, yet they ended up causing harm to the very culture groups they embraced or identified with. How can we explain this contradiction?[22]

There might not be any definitive answer for this historical conundrum, but there are a number of theories that provide an insight. Brazilian scholar Florestan Fernandes has declared that "slavery had been a destructive experience for Brazil ... which had left deep wounds and scars in the Brazilian psyche."[23] These psychological impacts, as Fernandes explains, might have had an influence on Brazilian returnees to West Africa. It is possible that their traumatic experience in the New World led to their enslaving local people. Stories about returnees in other areas in West Africa who became involved in the enslavement of local people for fear that they and their family might also be recaptured fit well into Fernandes's theory, and thus could help explain why those who settled in the Gold Coast gradually became involved in slavery. My analysis about the different migratory paths of return emphasizes that these were mutually exclusive stories that occurred at different locations of settlement. In other words, they are striking stories that could either converge or stand on their own in a given time period or situation. In general, conditions in the Gold Coast facilitated slavery.[24]

ENABLING SLAVERY ENVIRONMENTS AND THE IMPACTS ON THE RETURNEES

The enabling environments others put in place made it more convenient for the liberated Africans to re-create slavery. Brazilian slavery in the Gold Coast, which covers a small portion of the larger narrative, emerged alongside other flourishing trading networks around the period of abolition. In coastal Accra, in particular, the culture of slavery benefited a lot of people and major institutions. Slaves were exploited and manipulated by several people and institutions in the Gold Coast including European chartered companies and wealthy women.[25] One Anna Lutterodt who was married to George Lutterodt, a Danish merchant and government official, also owned slaves.[26]

Lower-class women often became victims of Gã and European slavery projects. In some cases, local women were tricked into marriage and later sold into slavery. War captives suffered a similar fate.[27] Most of these slaves served as laborers and recruits during warfare, while others performed various domestic roles. Gã chiefs and other local leaders joined in, forming alliances with chartered companies and supporting slavery in diverse ways. Gã leaders and British officials promoted and protected their interests at the same time. Both groups were implicated in the slave trade, and for that reason neither could speak with moral authority against the illegal activities by the liberated slaves from Brazil.

African kings and chiefs, European colonial officials and missionaries, merchants of all kinds, and some of the local population each played roles in creating an enabling environment for sustaining slavery. The relentless efforts by chiefs to ensure their visibility in transatlantic commercial exchanges and to earn profits in trade shaped slavery.[28] At times, legitimate trade between Europeans and African chiefs that involved the exchange of cash crops such as rubber, cocoa, and palm oil for umbrellas, caps, lamps, kerosene, and other goods gradually shifted to the sale of human beings. On one occasion, an African chief promised to provide human beings as part of the barter trade.[29] It is not clear if this was the result of negotiation between the parties involved or was initiated solely by the chief. The chief made a huge request: "We want three things from you, and we shall give you three things for it: we want guns, gunpowder and rum—and we shall give you men, women and children."[30] Notorious slave merchants including João de Oliveira, Domingo Martins, and others such as local chiefs traded palm oil alongside human cargo.[31] The possibilities that one could be captured in any given time at any location and exchanged for goods created panic and suspicions in most slave societies in Africa.

Relationships among individuals and family members of the returnee communities particularly complicated matters, for a person might be enslaved by family members, neighbors, or close associates at any time. Maria's account in *The Water House* (*Casa da Agua*) shows that her uncle sold her into slavery in Abeokuta, in southwest Nigeria, sometime in the mid-1800s. The volatile nature of African societies affected by slavery created conditions that were especially vulnerable for freed slaves like Maria who embarked on return voyages.[32] Further, during the abolition movement in the nineteenth century, panic about reenslavement was common among both returnees and the local Africans.[33] A number of the emancipated Africans who were fearful of the level of disorder and insecurity in their communities left Lagos, Dahomey (Benin), and other areas so that they would not be enslaved again.[34] As slavery in these African communities became common and the slow pace of abolition continued, fears and suspicions among the people increased.

Enslavement perpetrated by family members, as in Maria's story, was not the only problem. Some of the local people in the Gold Coast became suspicious of foreigners because of the involvement of missionaries in the slave trade, as precolonial Basel missionary records show.[35] Some missionaries benefited enormously from slavery activities in Accra and nearby areas. For example, Andre Riis depended on his slaves for labor. Riis's involvement marred the image of the Basel missionaries from Germany, Switzerland, and other parts of Europe. Despite threats by church leaders to expel him from the mission society, Riis did not budge.[36] Widespread negative attitudes toward foreigners not only impeded abolition but also made it difficult for European missionaries to carry out evangelism effectively. As one missionary observed,

> The centers of the black people are independent and free, one cannot, even so, forsee the lot reserved for missionaries who first go to evangelize, especially today when the Negroes are angry with the white men from whom they suffered so much, especially having seen their children stolen in such numbers. Betrayed a thousand times, it cannot be presumed that they will receive any missionary, until they recognize them as such.[37]

The British campaign to end human enslavement within the British Protectorate in coastal regions along the southeast was not all that vigorous. The British Royal Navy provided vessels across various sections of the Atlantic to suppress slavery and ultimately end it.[38] However, their efforts toward the north, in the area of the Ashante Kingdom by the turn of the nineteenth century, had a peculiar meaning to Brazilian-African history.[39] In fact, antislavery campaigns extended beyond the Gold Coast, intended to weaken any form of slavery in any area where the British set up colonial posts. The British had to contend with former residents of Brazil who had established strong ties with slave merchants and chiefs in Africa.[40] The most crucial region was the Bight of Benin, most notably the French territory of Whydah, where notorious slave merchants such as the Brazilian Francisco "Chacha" de Souza and his ally Gezo, the king of Dahomey (r. 1818–58), created their own enterprises to increase the transportation of "human cargoes" to the New World.[41]

Robin Law's study of Chacha, the well-known Afro-Brazilian slave trader, makes a significant contribution to our understanding of this situation. Chacha, who left Brazil around 1800 and settled in Badagry in the early 1800s,[42] had similar fledgling slavery networks run by Domingo Martinez and other slave merchants in Porto Novo, just to mention a few. Chacha owned a number of slave ships, including the *Attrevido*, which transported hundreds of slaves from Whydah to various ports in Brazil.[43] He married a local woman and was later given the title of chief in Ouidah. José Cerqueira Lima, a Brazilian merchant, also owned thirty ships traveling regularly between Rio de Janeiro,

Bahia, Para, Pernambuco, and various ports in West Africa and made a fortune.[44] A front-page story in the *African Times* had this to say: "The slave trade agent of the late Lima has renewed the slave trade vigorously. He is paying fifty dollars per head."[45] Chacha's strategic assimilation into the local culture empowered him and provided protection for his illegal acts.[46] In spite of his notorious past, he is acknowledged by some as one of the noble Brazilian returnees. Chacha's descendants continue to celebrate his life. To others, his disreputable slavery activities overshadow his other legacy. As we shall see, the fact that a number of returnees in other settlement areas were involved in slavery after their freedom does not take the blame away from the local inhabitants who invested heavily in slavery. Put in another way, slavery in Accra predated Brazilian-Africans' settlements in the area.

European Colonial Officials and Slavery

Several entities, including British and Danish officials, chartered companies, missionaries, chiefs, and local people, participated in slavery, but they were willing to participate in ultimately ending slavery. Generally, each group responded to the abolition movement differently. The polemics that were generated during this chaotic time reveal double standards in addressing these issues. My inquiry has not uncovered any evidence that slavery by returnees or within the early Brazilian-African diaspora posed any imminent threat to British antislavery campaigns as in other areas along the Bight, such as Whydah, Lagos, and remote areas where slavery was rather intense.[47] The effects of slavery on the local population were generally more brutal than in the "isolated" cases within Brazilian-African communities in the Gold Coast. This appraisal in no way suggests that British colonial officials ignored slavery by Brazilians in the Gold Coast and other areas. They enforced stern abolition policies forcefully across the dominant slavery regions, which included coastal and hinterland areas, especially within the Ashante Kingdom and Dahomey, a French territory where it was practiced on a much larger scale.[48]

The British are generally credited for campaigning vigorously for abolition.[49] However, they underestimated the challenges for ending slavery.[50] British sources reveal the extent to which the question of abolition was discussed, but they engaged in debate far less about slaves owned by the British in various locations in West Africa. For the British to be effective in conveying moral and religious messages against slavery, they had to clean their own house first. Ending slavery especially along the Bight of Benin was a daunting task partly because of its long history with the transatlantic slave trade.[51] In some cases, slaves who were freed in the Gold Coast were recaptured by other merchants. A letter from Reverend W. Locker, a British missionary, to other missionary organizations in England states that British antislavery campaigns were not very effective because a number of freed slaves were being taken abroad again—after their emancipation.[52]

The British condemned slavery in the strongest terms as they intensified their abolition campaigns along the Bight of Benin in particular from the 1800s, but these efforts could not prevent a number of freed Africans from Brazil and Cuba from carrying out slaving activities in West Africa.[53] In fact, British demands during this time that Europeans stop investing in slavery fell on deaf ears. Letters circulated by British missionaries show that a Henry Robbin, a British man, was arrested and put on trial in Abeokuta, Nigeria, for buying slaves.[54] The attitude of some British officials also complicated the situation when they ignored slavery activities within their own administrative circle. In the *Gold Coast Echo*, a resident of Cape Coast blamed British officials for sustaining slavery and exposed their double standard: "When the Governor is charged with buying slaves, anything [he says] is sufficient and satisfactory explanation. Will the Governor be satisfied with the same excuse if made by any private person who shall follow his example and buy slaves?"[55] In addition to the concerns by the local people in Cape Coast, the travel diaries of T. B. Freeman, a British colonial official, show that he also criticized slavery, which he witnessed in the region during his expedition to Dahomey.[56] There were other reports in the *Gold Coast Echo*, but none of this put an end to slavery. Clearly, financial interests often outweighed any others. The British lacked the moral authority to prevent anyone associated with the Crown or the colonial institution itself from indulging in inhumane practices. Despite their inability to manage these complex structural mechanisms all at once, the British were able to put some strategies in place to disseminate messages promoting abolition far and wide.

British missionary Reverend Locker and the citizens of the Gold Coast were not the only ones who rebuked the British for their insincerity or their tortoise-like or token approach to ending slavery. The diary of Danish governor Carstensen adds accusations of its own. According to Carstensen, "Even the English themselves are seen possessing numerous owned slaves."[57] Some of these allegations were unconvincing because there is ample evidence that the British played a leading role and invested more heavily in abolition in their colonies than any other Europeans. Fierce competition for power between European nations fueled some of these allegations.

Revisiting Carstensen's diary is paramount. In one of his letters he states that "Danish authorities cannot prevent Negroes from being carried to non-Danish territory and there be sold."[58] In part it suggests that Danish authorities were limited in their efforts to end slavery. Carstensen's letter of 15 November 1847 states further that they provided more protection for slaves than the British, but there is ample evidence that they were not innocent in fueling slavery activities. The Danish also invested heavily in slavery both in Africa and in the West Indies. For instance, the Danish slave ship *Laaburg Gallei* arrived on the African coast of Cabo Verde (Cape Verde) in 1723 to begin this illegal activity. In the eighteenth century approximately forty-one thousand slaves were transported on various Danish vessels. Other Danish ships carried Danish-African names to symbolize their particular experience with Africans or the locations where they enslaved Africans. One such ship name was *Kogen af Ashanti*, which alluded to the experiences of Danish merchants and their competitors, the Ashante Kingdom. Danish ships were not the only space for sustaining slavery; the Danes' old forts that still stand on the coastline of Ghana boosted both commerce and slavery. Archaeological remains on the southeastern coastline show evidence of Danish involvement in slavery. These sites include Christianborg in Accra (formerly used as the office of Ghanaian presidents), Fredensborg, which was located at Ningo, Pridstensteen at Keta, and Kingensteen at Ada. One of Thorkild Hansen's works shows that slaves were transported from the Gold Coast to St. Croix to increase labor in Danish plantations. Some of the slaves were transported through these forts.[59]

MISSIONARIES AND SLAVERY

The involvement of a wide range of people and groups in slavery added new momentum to the slave trade. The missionaries were largely expected to have higher ethical standards. Missionaries' involvement in slavery therefore upset long-held notions of religious piety within the walls of the Christian church. The participation of Christians in the abuse and exploitation of the very people they sought to evangelize and save from what they often characterized as backward and uncivilized cultures raises important questions. If the bearers or ambassadors of the Christian faith did not uphold human rights, respect, and dignity for all diverse groups, who would? Returnees who were engaged in slavery took advantage of the situation. The Danes' mission work in precolonial Ghana in the nineteenth century was undermined by their involvement in slavery to the point that some African parents who had sent their children to be educated in mission schools withdrew them from these boarding schools for fear that the Europeans might enslave their children. In some cases, "the children ran away from the school at Akropong [in eastern Ghana].... They thought that the missionaries would put them into chains. But the missionaries were able to convince parents and guardians to send the boys to school again."[60]

The *Digest of Articles in Basel Missionary Periodicals* and records from 1828 to 1851 show that the Danish government worked closely with missionaries to propose alternative forms of trade after abolition. In making these provisions, the Danes created agricultural plantations in the area now known as the Akwapim mountain range. These plantations produced cotton, coffee, and various fruits.[61] While the survival of these plantations depended solely on slave labor, the Danes built roads that connected farmland to isolated towns in the area where Christian missionaries wanted to expand their work. In 1836, Andreas Riis, a pioneer of the Basel Mission campaign who owned eight slaves, created a private plantation that depended on slave labor in the Abokobi area in the Eastern Region of Ghana. Such plantations were typically managed by freed African slaves from the West Indies who were relocated to the area by missionaries to proclaim the gospel.[62] One of the rationales for enslaving the people at Abokobi and other areas was that slaves would benefit immensely from being introduced to Christianity. Some Danish officials and missionaries hailed this alternative approach, but others were completely opposed. For some of the missionaries, the Basel Mission's involvement in slavery had a lasting impact on their work in propagating the gospel. Swiss and German missionaries were also affected by "lack of Christian morality" that Europeans displayed during this time.[63]

It is evident that the benefit of enslaving Africans did not meet the broader needs of the missionaries. Dr. Paul Isert, a German botanist and physician who witnessed atrocities against slaves during his tenure in the Gold Coast from 1783 to 1786, spoke against slavery perpetuated by the Danes.[64] In general, the Basel Mission did not condone missionaries owning slaves, but they supported efforts to convert these slaves and baptize them.[65] Occasionally, the Basel missionaries made attempts to get rid of slavery activities within missionary posts completely. In some cases, they expelled wayward missionaries.[66] A letter from the Basel Mission to Riis asserted, "it is against the very principle of missionary work. The plantation shall not be worked by slaves—rather, sell it at a loss."[67] Another correspondence from the Basel Mission committee meeting on 13 July 1845 concluded that the best way to discourage Riis from sustaining the plantation was to "take over the plantation from Riis, not as a farm to be worked by slaves, but as a shelter for missionaries traveling between Akropong and the coast."[68] The second decision in particular was very useful. Basel missionaries, including Reverend Johannes Zimmerman, used these plantations "as a place of rest when they traveled in the night through the Akropong mountains."[69] Other pronouncements by the Basel Mission show how they took drastic actions to establish a distinction between the leadership, on the one hand, and wayward missionaries like Riis who had a mind of their own or supported slavery, on the other. Two emotional reports illustrate how the Basel Mission opposed these illegal activities. The first states broadly:

> All these Christian nations were trading in slaves [in the Gold Coast]. Sometimes people were just simply stolen and sold secretly to the Europeans—they had secret cells for these. Heartbreaking scenes occurred when slaves were shipped. These were dark times indeed ... [we] found it difficult to plant Christianity in the sandy soil of the Accra plains. We must not forget that the mortgage of the blame of slave trade laying on Christians.[70]

The next reprimands some of the missionaries for their involvement and declares:

> Oh how much trouble the question of slavery has already caused.... How many moral dilemmas it has already placed me in, so that last year I hardly knew what was what. ... It will take generations to bring about true abolition of slavery.... Experience has proved this convincingly; we had to expel the majority of slave holders because they were inwardly too lazy. If however, our Christians are too weak, then we must admit this and work towards other communities; communities which bow to the law of the spirit of freedom. Thus I conclude that our liberation of slaves reveals the shortcomings of our communities and us missionaries.[71]

In addition to chastising one of their own, a number of missionaries expressed concerns about the condition of slaves and intervened in various ways to alleviate their suffering. On 20 August 1848, a letter by Frederiksgave Schiedt, a missionary, reveals abuse of slaves by their captors who mainly used them for labor. In one particular instance, missionaries made some kind of a deal with slave merchants to free these slaves after they were baptized. An attempt to baptize a slave named Lumate in Accra failed, but his life was saved by Danish authorities, who later set him free.[72] Thorkild's analysis of Carstensen's diary states that "for every slave the Danes freed, hundreds slipped through the net."[73] Additionally, Basel Mission records also point out that runaway slaves sought refuge in Prampram, a coastal area, while those who could not escape were sold to Dutch officials to serve as laborers in Java-Buatrine trade posts.[74] Although missionaries' involvement in slavery stained their religious reputation and undermined the effectiveness of their religious message and piety, it was the final stage of abolition and British colonial rule in the early 1900s that finally paved the way for Christian missionaries to reclaim their voice, their sense of direction, and their influence in the Gold Coast. This was carried out in a more aggressive manner during proselytization campaigns in coastal Accra.

Danish officials were well positioned to uncover what the British hid behind the curtain. Governor Carstensen in particular had an ambitious strategy to end slavery.[75] Besides criticizing the British, he viewed abolition as a gateway for justifying colonization, the propagation of Christianity, the expansion of Danish commercial interests, and especially for perpetuating racist notions that Africans needed civilizing. Basically, as the mutual exchanges between African chiefs and Europeans came under siege during abolition, "the old slave trade tribute to the chiefs had to be replaced with systematic civilizing work done by [Danish] missionaries."[76] Carstensen was convinced that Africans could not survive through their own efforts, or achieve a civilized status, or attain enlightenment, without the help of Europeans, particularly missionaries. The Danes did not get on very well with the British after many decades of disagreements over commerce and colonization in the Gold Coast. However, in the mid-1850s, the Danes sold the Christianborg Castle—a symbol of Danish presence in the Gold Coast—to the British for £10,000 after they lost their influence in the area.[77]

Governor Carstensen had other allies for carrying out the Danes' vision. He depended on the Basel Mission from Switzerland to begin civilizing projects and suggested a mass migration of Africans (from the African continent) to the West Indies so they could be exposed to the Western way of life. This goal was, however, marred by contradictions of another kind. At one time, both British and Danish officials had praised the Back-to-Africa movement, which was mainly organized by the American Colonization Society in part to spread Christianity in Africa. These journeys across the Atlantic were largely motivated by the poor conditions of slaves after manumission, the threat of slave revolts, the abolition campaigns under way in the Atlantic world, and the freed slaves' yearning to reconnect with their African heritage. One British official used the Back-to-Africa movement to Liberia as well as other voyages from the Caribbean to Sierra Leone as a model for ending slavery in West Africa. In his diary Carstensen makes reference to a British citizen by name, Buxton. The governor embraced Buxton's grandiose strategy for civilizing Africans by relocating them elsewhere. According to Carstensen, Danish plantations in the West Indies could be used to civilize Africans by focusing on a select group to carry out this ambitious experiment. Carstensen laid out the basics of the project in a letter: "A plan for a united and forceful joint effort must be made and followed. The work of civilization to be based particularly on cultural establishment, young people (mulattos and negroes) are to be sent to the West Indies to learn how to grow sugar cane, tobacco and other tropical growths."[78] Carstensen stated later that "the negro will learn, beyond the sea, that in Africa he can be independent and active, that there he has a wide scope to make use of the knowledge and capacities the influence of civilization gave him."[79]

The declarations by Carstensen reflected a similar ideology in the nineteenth century that facilitated the European presence in Africa and that ultimately opened the way for justifying colonial rule. In addressing broader questions about the morality of abolition, it would be misleading to ignore the intersection between abolition and colonization: the latter depended heavily on the former to begin new forms of European exploitation.[80] To create an enabling socioeconomic and political environment for facilitating a transition to colonization, Europeans worked both sides of the Atlantic to carry out their self-gratifying vision for Africa. The British and Danish officials envisioned an African population that in their view could be enlightened by a civilized freed-slave population who were already exposed to Western cultures in the New World during their enslavement. That way, the initial dirty work would be done by people of African ancestry and not by Europeans. In fact, the Danish later developed another plan that could serve the civilizing mission and capitalist interests simultaneously. This strategy plan was to ship part of the African population from various locations in Africa to settle in Liberia and Sierra Leone where Europeans and their American counterparts had experimented with the settlements of ex-slaves and made considerable progress. They also aspired to select some returnees to play leading roles in enforcing European projects on the African side.

The British were successful in this latter endeavor: they relocated skilled Africans, including engineers, post managers, medical doctors, and others, to the Gold Coast from the early 1800s to facilitate colonial conquest.[81] The Basel Mission followed a similar approach when they transported several black missionaries from the West Indies to facilitate Christian conversions in the Gold Coast around the same time. In one of Carstensen's letters to officials in Copenhagen, Denmark, on 15 November 1847, he relates that the exchanges should begin from West Africa where Europeans had a strong presence. In his efforts to solidify his argument, Carstensen predicted that if this mission is carried out, "civilization will give the Barbarian, superstitious negroes ideas brought with them from Africa, will gradually disappear."[82] Carstensen was not alone in this ambitious racist endeavor. Benjamin Campbell, who played a leading role in British abolition, expressed similar sentiments in his correspondence with the British Consul Office in Lagos. Campbell believed that freed slaves who did not convert to Christianity were not only an obstacle to the broader civilization mission, but their uncivilized state was also a hindrance to colonial rule.[83] Carstensen and Campbell's vision for ending slavery and for creating a "safe" platform for colonial ventures is profound.[84]

The idea of modeling or reinventing a new enlightened society in Africa is not the problem here. What is disturbing in his projection is twofold: first, abolition is not mainly linked with moral guilt but was tied to a broader civilizing mission that began with Danish territories along the Guinea coast; and second, whether slavery should be abolished or not, Africans needed to be exposed to Western ideals as a prelude to enlightenment. In fact, these liberated Africans were free only in the sense that they were no longer serving their slave masters on Brazilian plantations. However, their freedom would still be restricted for the self-gratification of Europeans as Carstensen envisioned it. His agenda had other implications. A segment of the Basel Mission embraced or shared his racist outlook, and in their own ways they sought to carry out this prejudiced vision in the name of offering salvation. One such missionary report recounts, "I remember how the children in Africa grow up like wild beast.... We go in order to give a good example to the people in Africa and to teach them how a Christian should live."[85]

The common interests of Europeans like Buxton and Carstensen overlapped with the story of the returnees from South America, North America, and the Caribbean in West Africa in the 1800s. In the case of black Americans from North Carolina who were financed by the American Colonization Society and the Quakers, some of these returnees formulated and internalized notions of racial superiority over the Africans before they even set foot on the ships that transported them to Africa.[86] Claude A. Clegg III traces these contentious stories of settlements from the 1820s. Clegg states that black Americans who left North Carolina and other Southern states replicated the very racial oppressive systems they endured in the United States when they resettled in Liberia.[87] James T. Campbell's study of "emigrationist fever," which was led by Paul Cuffe and a number of bishops from the African Methodist Episcopal Church, and which attracted freed slaves mostly from Newport, Baltimore, Philadelphia, and other northeastern cities, promoted a similar vision to improve conditions in Africa.[88]

RE-CREATING BRAZILIAN SLAVERY IN THE GOLD COAST AND THE TRAJECTORY OF ENSLAVEMENT

Accra was the epicenter for transatlantic commerce as well as religious propagation. Accra and other coastal towns were not only the nexus for legitimate trade, but with their long history with the transatlantic slave trade they were the site of flourishing slavery networks along the wide vibrant coastline. Liberated Africans from Brazil returned to Africa to reconnect with their African roots, to establish their own communities, to reconstruct their identities, and for some to work closely with slave merchants to make profit. These slave agents were aware of the grave consequences of these inhumane activities, but they continued it during the abolition period from the mid-1800s on.[89] Brazilian-Africans became involved in slavery on a number of fronts. This includes freed slaves who were employed on European ships that engaged in slavery along the Bight of Benin prior to the abolition of slavery in Brazil in 1888. Besides these, others who relocated to the Gold Coast involuntarily or voluntarily became aware of the economic benefits of the trade on the local level. Some of these returnees were determined to continue efforts to undermine the abolitionist campaigns. In general, slavery in the Gold Coast was conducted contemporaneously with similar activities in Benin, Togo, and Nigeria as returnees engaged in local, regional, and international human trafficking.

Whether Ghana became a sanctuary for slaves who were escaping from slave dealers along the Bight of Benin or not, or served as a corridor for capturing slaves, it is also true that returnees had other motives. Along the coastline of Accra in particular, Brazilians created their own slavery enterprises on a lesser scale. Their lucrative ventures did not escape the watchful eyes of Europeans in the area who monitored movements by travelers to and from the Accra coast. For example, a letter by Edward Carstensen states that "Dutch Accra has for a long time been the residence for several slave trade agents especially immigrated Brasilian negroes."[90] Besides the warning by Carstensen, which in fact contradicts Danish slavery activities in the same areas and beyond, there were other concerns. Christiaan Ernst Lans, a Dutch official, also raised similar concerns when he rebuked Otublohum *Mãŋtse* Kwaku Ankrah for allowing the Brazilians characterized as "not the best bunch of people" due to their involvement in slavery in the area.[91] Accra was not the only place in Ghana where Brazilians captured or sold slaves. As others also relate, "It was reported that members of the returnee community controlled a flourishing trade in slaves from Krepi [northwestern Ewe land], who were 'readily bought' as farm workers." Some of the early settlers engaged in slave-trading activities in other locales such as Ada, Keta, along the southeastern coast, and along the banks of the Volta River, where family groups such as the De Souzas settled.[92] For those returnees who were part of the Brazilian-African diaspora, a number of court documents also show that the descendants of the returnees also had other questionable contacts with slaves.

An article in the *West African Herald* stated that British authorities sought to arrest Geraldo, "a former servant of Lima, a Portuguese slave dealer" who resided in Keta (a coastal town), in the Volta Region of modern Ghana, for enslaving Africans and for obstructing antislavery campaigns.[93] Another article in the *African Morning Post* reported that slavery activities and public auctions persisted in Ghana even in the 1930s. According to the article, "A young lady was sold publicly for £15. It is said that she became a *persona non grata* and was hooted by her fellow villagers."[94] It seems like this young lady was rejected by either her family or her community for reasons not clearly stated in this newspaper report.

During the transatlantic slave trade, most of the slaves who were captured were needed for labor in the New World. This pattern continued in the Atlantic world as slaves were moved from one location to the other.[95] In returnee communities along

Chapter Six

the Bight of Benin, a large percentage of those enslaved by the returnees were sold for monetary gain. In contrast to the stories about Chacha containing estimates of the wealth he accumulated via slavery activities,[96] there is no direct evidence I can point to about the precise monetary rewards attained by the members of the Brazilian-African diaspora who were involved in the enslavement of the local people in the Gold Coast. However, in their case, the Brazilian returnees did not always use slaves as laborers or sell them to other people. In fact, some of the Brazilians and their descendants had married their slaves, odonkor. In most Ghanaian societies, odonkor, the word for slave, is not entertained in daily discourse because it connotes a position of inferiority as well as the idea of an outsider or foreigner from a lower class.[97] They often later integrated the slaves into their families through marriage. As one of the archival documents reads, "Oldman Asuma bought Nahfio's mother and lived with as husband and wife and they begat two male children. . . . Yawanukpe's mother was also bought by Mama Nassu [a leader among the first settler groups]."[98] Asuma was not the only Brazilian who had children with their slaves.[99]

Evidence of sexual intimacy between Brazilian-Africans and their slaves certainly complicates the history of the returnees. It is a taboo to be associated with the odonkor population.[100] Considering the origins of this word and its cultural implication, it is understandable that the Tabom took a neutral position in our interviews. Broadly speaking, sexual unions between members of the Brazilian-African diaspora and the odonkor epitomize another aspect of Brazilian-Africans' assimilation into broader Ghanaian society in the nineteenth century. This means that tracing the DNA of Brazilian-Africans extends beyond just attempting to track their origins from their locations of capture prior to being taken to Brazil.[101] My argument here is that Ghanaians of Brazilian heritage can trace their ancestry in several ways: via their Brazilian roots, their lineage with captured slaves (especially odonkor, within the African continent either from Ghana or from nearby territories), as Ghanaians, or the combination of these identities.[102] Put directly, some Tabom carry the genes of odonkor. The evidence not only shows that physical intimacy took place between returnees and slaves who were captured in various regions. But the reactions to this evidence by certain descendants—their opposition to having an open dialogue—points to problematic Ghanaian cultural interpretations of slavery. Court proceedings show how the Brazilian-Africans used some of the slaves they purchased from various areas in the Gold Coast to perform domestic chores.[103] In one of my interviews with Nii Azumah V, the Tabom chief made references to what he witnessed as a child regarding his contacts with odonkor. The current leader of the Brazilian-African diaspora added that some of the slaves cooked, did laundry, and had other household responsibilities. .[104] This practice of involving odonkor in domestic affairs was in line with existing traditions in Ghanaian society.

Some of the archival documents I have found point out that slaves who were owned by the returnees could not inherit property because of their status as slaves. Other findings show that although slaves in the Brazilian-African diaspora were constrained in many ways, they had some rights to inheritance and were treated with a degree of respect.[105]

Impact of Slavery

Slavery in general had an enormous impact on African societies and shaped the ways in which people of African descent on both sides of the Atlantic relate to and identify with their African heritage—and each other. Besides the deep psychological impacts of enslavement, as Fernandes points out, Brazilian-Africans' involvement in slavery in the Gold Coast not only fueled aspects of the transatlantic slave trade in its final stages, but their investment complicated ties between the returnees and their descendants, especially when one examines how the Tabom perceive their identity and ancestral heritage. This consciousness has contributed to levels of silence about slavery in their history. Considering the cultural structures of the society they developed, such as that around the meaning of odonkor, their attitude toward the dark side of their heritage deserves attention. Basically, most people in Ghana do not want to have any association with slavery or discuss their family members' involvement with slaves in the past. It is a taboo and disgrace at the highest level. In fact, it is unacceptable to ask about the ancestral origins of kings, chiefs, or queen mothers because of the fear that tracing their royal roots might reveal that they or the family members they inherited from were once slaves. This is based on the fact that slaves who served in royal palaces from the fifteenth century were later selected as *nifa hene* and *benkum hene*, the Akan words for leaders in influential positions. Some actually became kings or chiefs, or attained other positions of power. The effects of such silence regarding the reconstruction of the Brazilian-African experience, especially the steady process by which members of the younger generation distance themselves from their Brazilian roots, or identify as Ghanaians, has obscured information that could be useful to a clear understanding of their history.

The Brazilian-African diaspora in Ghana was an eclectic community that consisted of liberated Brazilians who had varying reasons for returning to their ancestral homeland. The settlement of the Brazilian-Africans was complicated by the fact that they arrived during a tumultuous time in the history of the Gold Coast. It was during these chaotic times that some of the returnees found comfortable niches to participate in slavery. Some who came to the Gold Coast proved unable to resist the temptation of selling other Africans into slavery, including people with whom they shared similar physical and historical ties. Even so, those who practiced slavery were not the only guilty parties. We also know that the arrival of the early settlers happened around the same time Gã mãŋtsɛmɛi, the people of the Gold Coast, Europeans, missionaries, and merchants among others were heavily involved in slavery. This twist of fate together with the hospitality Gã leaders extended to the returnees, especially gifts of Gã stool land, attracted more returnees.[106] This generosity not only opened up doors for the establishment of the Brazilian-African diaspora in coastal Accra. While others took the opportunity to participate in flourishing slavery activities in the area, conditions in the Gold Coast enabled some returnees to contribute the skills they had brought from Brazil. The ex-slaves were generally well positioned in their new environs. Despite the advantages they had over other non-Brazilian African settler groups in Accra, some of the returnees were psychologically scarred by their experiences as slaves in Brazil.

The "ghosts" of slavery haunted the emancipated Africans wherever they set up their tent: having escaped from slavery in the New World, many fell into another form of slavery in progress in the very place they called *home* in Africa. Their exposure to slavery activities in their new environs challenged how they viewed their own freedom from slavery. Indeed, those returnees who participated in slavery in the Gold Coast were certainly responsible for their own actions, but other factors that most likely influenced their involvement should not be separated from this story. It is equally important to note that problems with reenslavement of Africans by slave merchants, local chiefs, colonial officials, and missionaries had tremendous implications.[107] What happened in one place had ripple effects in other resettlement communities. As in other settlements elsewhere, some of the returnees became "spectators" in the Gold Coast, whereas others jumped on the bandwagon and participated fully in these illegal activities. The returnees ultimately took advantage of an enabling culture that tolerated slavery. These developments occurred around the time Europeans of different backgrounds in the Gold Coast—British colonial officials, philanthropists, and religious groups such as the Basel Mission—were struggling with how to address the infamous "slave question," debating, negotiating, and contending with what to do with the slaves they or people within their institutions owned in the Gold Coast from the late 1800s.

The story of slavery by members of the Brazilian-African diaspora in Ghana touches on several provoking tangents. First, it would be misleading to assume that slavery activities by the ex-slaves from Brazil during the abolition period in the Gold Coast had nothing to do with the region's social history; rather, their involvements were enabled by actions of local people and of foreigners who set the stage for and condoned these illegal acts. The arrival of the Brazilians coincided with British officials' gradual transformation of a slavery system into a colonial system that threatened the freedom the returnees had gained in Brazil. Historical conditions in Brazil had a major impact on slave narratives. Over time, the British realized that abolition was a more complex and demanding task than they had anticipated. The British denounced slavery in the strongest terms but could not stop the activities of those, including Europeans, who chose to perpetuate slavery. Britain's commitment to abolition contributed immensely to the demise of the transatlantic slave trade. Criticism of the inability of the British to provide protection for slaves must be considered in the narratives. However, the British made greater strides toward ending slavery than other Europeans.

A portion of the returnees might have relocated to Ghana purposely to make a profit through the enslavement of the local people. Broadly speaking, the various activities that took place in Ghana created a scenario appropriate for strangers, migrants, and all kinds of travelers to the area to benefit from. The enabling environs devised by the Gã people and Europeans served as an impetus for slavery activities in the nineteenth century. According to one report by the Dutch West India Company, a chartered company, "Accra is always a good place of good gold and sometimes plenty of slaves."[108] Further, oral evidence and numerous archival documents in various locations highlight the impact of slavery during this era. A number of colonial newspapers reported that the enslavement of Africans by chiefs and perhaps returnees was very common both in the Gold Coast and in other regions of West Africa. Reverend Carl Christian Reindorf, who was of both Gã and Danish lineage, did not turn a blind eye to clandestine activities by Gã mãŋtsɛmɛi, particularly Mãŋtsɛ Kwaku Ankrah, the chief of Otublohum (Dutch Accra) who facilitated Brazilian-African returnees' settlement at the Tabom quarter. Reindorf notes that "slaves were sold at night and Ankrah had them in charge till a slaver [merchant] arrived, and poor creatures were shipped in darkness to avoid detection by the English and Danish government."[109]

It is a fair question to ask: Why should an enslaved population mimic a dehumanizing practice and inflict similar pain and violence on a society with which some of them claimed they shared similar ancestral history, kinship, or bloodline? In general, the paradox about freed slaves' involvement in slavery in Africa generates more questions than answers. In Ghana, their marriage to odonkor especially provided another window for understanding their ancestral composition, particularly how that shaped the memory of the Tabom people. Although odonkor normally refers to slaves who were captured from the hinterland or the northern territories of the Gold Coast, their origins could in fact be traced to any location because of how widespread slavery activities were across the geography of the African continent.[110] This association between odonkor and marginalization or rejection shows up in present social and cultural discourse on the part of many Tabom people, who are uncomfortable with the possibility of historical connections between their grandparents or great-grandparents and odonkor; hence their reluctance or negative attitude toward questions about this controversial subject is characterized as "positively cloaked in impenetrable silence."[111] Decades of land disputes and the Brazilians' involvements in slavery almost eroded the gains the early settlers made. This unpleasant historical experience that was created mostly by the early generations encompasses a dot on a vast canvas in the Brazilian African diaspora story. The ex-slaves and the Tabom made incredible contributions to the social history of Gã *mãŋ*, and to Ghana in general.

Chapter 7

Contributions by the Brazilian-Africans and the Tabom: Impact on Ghana's History

Returning to Africa, they brought the novelties that they learned on the other side of the Atlantic; the cultivation of mangoes, of cassava and beans; irrigation techniques, the knowledge of carpentry, architecture, and tailoring. The returnees also brought the Brazilian way of life. In the way they speak, in their festivities, in their cooking, and in all the cultural manifestations, we see a little of Brazil.

—President Luiz Inácio Lula da Silva, 2005

The idea that Africans left Africa but Africa never left them is not only true when one examines how African slaves preserved their skills as well as their identities and cultures in the New World;[1] the same case can be made for freed slaves who traveled back to Africa with creolized cultures and their unique skills.[2] The enabling environment that various interest groups created in Ghana created a convenient space for more activities than the ex-slaves' enslavement of the locals. It also enabled the returnees to contribute to their new environs in positive ways. In the epigraph, former Brazilian president Luiz Inácio Lula da Silva acknowledged part of the contributions by the returnees from Brazil. Lula's observation was not new. Some of the Tabom people are aware of this and have made this public. As one of the descendants related during a court appearance, "our ancestors also contributed decisively to the growth of the social life in Accra ... for example, the wearing of European style clothing and the use of kerosene."[3]

Chapter Seven

In their interrogation of the differences between transnational and transcultural connections to old communities and new communities in the case of reverse migrations or travels back to Haiti, Nina Glick Schiller and Georges Fouron forcefully argue that a clear distinction should be made between the role of ancestral ties, yearnings to visit the homeland, and the involvement of returnees in social developments.[4] Schiller and Fouron are not the only ones to make these observations. At the pinnacle of abolition in the early nineteenth century, European colonial officials in West Africa did not necessarily welcome the idea of settling freed African slaves in areas they claimed as part of their imperial possessions, but they acknowledged the usefulness of these settlements to colonial ventures especially when the end of slavery could accelerate imperial agendas. This notion was embraced by several colonial officials. In an attempt to create a cohort of skilled returnees in the Queens Colony of Lagos, Benjamin Campbell pursued liberated Africans with various skills to join voyages back to their ancestral homeland. First, on 18 June 1887, the *Lagos Observer* quoted Campbell stating that "the repatriation of mechanics and trained cultivators of the soil is especially desirable and should receive general encouragement . . . and will be admirable, valuable and necessary centers for the diffusion among their less developed country men in Yorubaland of enlightenment and civilization."[5] Campbell also sought to establish profit-making private shipping companies including Destemido, a Portuguese firm, to facilitate this grandiose plan.[6]

Like Campbell, Alfred Monoley, a British Governor in Lagos, contended that returnees were "an orderly, industrious and respectable portion of this community . . . generally a good example as citizens."[7] Moloney's account does not describe all returnees who made it back to Africa, but it does describe the character of most of the freed slaves. Both visions also bring attention to Governor Carstensen's prudent remarks about the liberated Brazilians who settled in Accra to enslave the local people.

Many of Carstensen's diary entries show he had a high regard for the Africans' role in the success of Danish plantation systems that had produced sugar, coffee, and other plantation products, especially how the ex-slaves could improve their conditions in their motherland. Carstensen relates that "the African from the West Indies and America form crowds of good workers, . . . by returning to Africa, to where they would take knowledge and ideas, from which only the independence and progress of Africa can be expected."[8] The governor's fascinating interpretation of the significance of the freed slaves was largely based on their many years away from the African continent. However, he also criticized some returnees, "immigrated Brasilian negroes," for their involvements in slavery in Dutch Accra.[9] Carstensen's observation was valid, but these freed slaves form a very small part of the story of return; the returnees who settled in Accra did more than participate in the enslavement of the local people. During his tenure as a governor, Carstensen ignored these other valuable contributions by members of the Brazilian-African diaspora in Ghana.[10] *Mãŋtsɛ* Nii Azumah III, offers a sharp contrast to Carstensen's finger pointing. According to *Mãŋtsɛ* Nii Azumah III, the liberated slaves did more than participate in slavery in the Gold Coast (reverse slavery). He remembers the contributions of his ancestors "to the growth of the social life in Accra."[11]

Evidence regarding contributions by members of the Brazilian-African diaspora, which has been marginalized, is pivotal to the reconstruction of the social history of Gã *mãŋ* and the Gold Coast in general. Despite challenges of language barriers and assimilation during the early periods of settlement, the returnees formulated various plans by negotiating settlements and engaging with the local people. I dwell on the varying contributions by the newcomers, especially their activities on the local and national levels. These include how Brazilian chiefs worked side by side with Gã *mãŋtsɛmɛi* to revolt against the British Compulsory Labour Ordinance of 1897, their agrarian practices, their techniques in well-drilling, and their skills in tailoring. The Tabom people also followed in the footsteps of their forebears by contributing to reforms during and after the precolonial period. In general, these important contributions are not acknowledged in Ghanaian and transatlantic historiography.

Two Ghanaian adages communicate important related ideas concerning returnees' attitudes after settlement. First, *Kɔ ne oha* is a common Gã expression that means "take and give." In some ways, it conveys the idea that you or your family does not only have to benefit from a particular social activity but also has to contribute in some way to your environs. This norm is indeed a noble idea. However, in some respects, *Kɔ ne oha* embodies a contradictory idea that most Gã people frown upon. It is embraced and hailed when it has to do with giving back to those who assisted you in your time of trouble. In this context, it is seen as an alternative way of expressing your appreciation and providing resources for others to enjoy. However, it can also refer to situations in which one exploits his or her community and later finds a way to compensate members of the community to justify his or her previous action. Another cultural expression that speaks to this binary is the Ghanaian expression *okumfu dumfu* from the Akan language that literally means "one who destroys and builds in tandem." Both *Kɔ ne oha* and *okumfu dumfu* warn against individuals or groups of people who take advantage of bad situations. Some may seek out opportunities, and some may create negative situations to justify their actions. In general, such people are seen as attentive to their surroundings. Both adages suggest that some people will not respond to an immediate problem because they believe they can give back later.

My use of these cultural analogies does not suggest that the contributions of the ex-slaves were based on guilt or were shaped by a desire to redeem a dark side of their ancestral history. Most of those who indulged in slavery did so through their own volition and did not necessarily have any direct ties to those who aided in improving conditions in the Gold Coast. These adages do not imply that the returnees contributed to various endeavors to offset a section of their population's history of slavery. In other words, their contributions were not an attempt to redeem the image of the Brazilian-African diaspora for the sins or crimes that were committed by a few members who indulged in slavery. Rather, these terms are used to juxtapose contradictions in return and the complexity of their reverse migrations.

Transferring Skills from Brazil

The contribution of Brazilian chief João Antonio Nelson is a lens for establishing the origins of anticolonial nationalism before the turn of the twentieth century—after which colonialism gained additional momentum and traction. The returnees' opposition to British rule predates the forms of opposition that emerged in the early 1920s and 1930s. Put in another way, João Antonio Nelson's revolt against the Compulsory Labour Ordinance of 1897 is one of many examples of Brazilian-Africans' contributions to precolonial Accra many decades before prominent Ghanaian nationalists were born. The absence of this account from historiography reveals the narrowness of other approaches to the study of national history from the colonial period. Aside from rebellions and negotiations to topple British rule on 6 March 1957, these limited accounts tend to showcase the pioneering role of Dr. Kwame Nkrumah and other "founding fathers" and "founding mothers" who participated in various Pan-African conferences in an attempt to instill black consciousness and pride at the international level.[12] The story of João Antonio Nelson, a torchbearer of anticolonial nationalism in precolonial Accra, and other Gã *mãŋtsɛmɛi* as well as other local chiefs and kings who were arrested and imprisoned challenges these one-dimensional histories of precolonial nationalism.

The ex-slaves excelled in other areas. In Brazil, the agrarian lifestyle was so closely knitted with slave identity to the extent that some slaves did not want to be associated with it after emancipation because of its ties to exploitation. The returnees who settled in the Gold Coast were not bothered by this kind of stigma. Their agrarian lifestyle, which dated back to the time when African slaves were forced to work on plantations across Brazil, did not end there. They carried their agrarian skills with them on their voyages back to Africa. A number of researchers have shown that returnees who settled along the Bight of Benin continued this tradition. Some of the reports noted that the returnees "brought to Africa their taste for cassava meal, guava sweets, Brazilian foods

[and] Brazilian ways."[13] Those in agrarian communities in Accra did the same. Both oral traditions and archival documents about land disputes in the Brazilian-African diaspora provide insight into their agrarian tradition. It includes the introduction of farm products such as cassava, a carbohydrate called *mandioca* in Brazil, *bankyi* in the Akan, and *dwade* in the Gã language. A tradition holds that this important crop was introduced around the late 1800s after returnees were provided with a vast area of land. If this theory is true, it implies that the planting of cassava began in the south, especially Accra where most of the returnees settled, and spread into other regions in Ghana. However, the abundance of cassava outside the Greater Accra region and the proximity of Accra to the Atlantic coastline seem to suggest that the crop spread into Accra through rural–urban trading. The evidence I have provided shows that returnees did not abandon this rich tradition after Gã *Mãŋtsɛ* Tackie Komeh I offered them land in Accra. According to historian Samuel Quarcoopome, Brazilians shaped farming in some areas in Accra, especially the planting and cultivation of fruits like mango and other farm products.[14] A good portion of the second generation followed the footsteps of their ancestors, but there is little evidence that the current generations will continue these agrarian practices.

During the precolonial era, Brazilians contributed to trading activities along the Bight of Benin. Other freed Brazilians traveled between the coastline of West Africa and major trading ports in Brazil. In terms of Otublohum, coastal Accra, Brazilian merchants contributed to the maritime trade and revenue that was controlled by Gã *mãŋtsɛmɛi* prior to the introduction of the Native Jurisdiction Ordinance and the Compulsory Labour Ordinance.[15] They also spread their skills in tailoring and cloth-making, which formed part of their identity. Further, the returnees used their technological knowledge to improve the quality of drinking water in the area.[16]

WATER CRISIS AND SANITATION IN ACCRA: THE RACE TO MAKE CONTRIBUTIONS

A wide range of transatlantic factors forms the basis for the freed slaves' movements from Brazil to Accra, including their temporary stops in areas like Lagos before relocating to Accra. Narratives about the Brazilian-African diaspora would be deficient without showing the ways in which the diaspora is closely knitted with Europeans' colonial conquests, efforts to spread Christianity, and other radical attempts to inject foreign values systems into the Gold Coast. In the precolonial period, the returnees, the British, and European missionaries did not seem to share the same vision in Accra

Chapter Seven

despite their common interest in trading, spreading their faith, and enslaving the local people. However, natural and man-made disasters made cooperation possible. Additionally, some of the problems the British encountered in Accra, especially poor water conditions, created an environment that facilitated the returnees' contributions. It also allowed these distant groups to work side by side together. These three different entities played monumental roles in resolving water crises in the Gold Coast. On the Brazilian side, a tradition holds that the Brazilians called water drilling in this area "Mungatabu," which means "we have found water."[17] Indeed, the search for clean drinking water was a priority to strangers, migrants, expatriates, and, especially, the Gã *mãŋ*.

Returnees with skills in drilling wells also found abundant land to spread their technology and took advantage of avenues to teach the local people water-drilling technology. Unlike the abundant records in the archives about the involvement of the British and missionaries in resolving the water crises in Accra, most of the evidence on the Brazilian side is based on the limited data present in court documents about land disputes. I supplement this limitation with oral traditions. According to the late Elder George Nelson, his grandparents became very visible in Accra because of their skills in well-drilling. There are no traces of these skills among the younger generations. Even so, most of the interviews I have conducted with different members of the Brazilian-African diaspora share the story. "Letters from Brazil," a project funded by the Brazilian government, shows how those who settled in Lagos also contributed their skills in well-drilling.

Prior to public interactions between the British and the returnees, the British had expressed grave concerns about sanitation problems in coastal Accra. These problems, which were made public later, began in the early 1800s and continued into the twentieth century. In his reports about the conditions in the Gold Coast from 1900 to 1910, British official Sir Gordon Guggisberg remarks,

> Throughout the country no sanitation worthy of the name existed. In Accra the capital and in all the coast towns the conditions were very bad. The conservancy system was primitive in the methods obtained for the disposal of refuse which today would be absolutely taboo. The water supply which is of the first importance in the tropics was rain-water collected from the roof in storage tanks. The tanks were frequently dry and foul water from polluted wells was often sold as much as 6d per gallon.... The native quarters consisted of dark ill-ventilated mud hovels crowded together, ideal foci for epidemic diseases. The merchants lived over their stores surrounded by unsanitary native compounds. Government officials lived in bungalows made in England brought out and re-erected outside their towns.[18]

Colonial ordinances and reports raised concerns about poor environmental conditions in Accra. While some of these reports stated that European residential areas were clean, others pointed out that conditions elsewhere were a "standing menace to the health of the community at large."[19] Newspaper reports reinforced the importance of a healthy and sustainable environment in Accra to colonial agendas.[20] Like the returnees, the British officials also dealt with problems of unhealthy water conditions for their own benefit. The British provided "two reservoirs . . . with a total capacity of 45 million gallons," and they opened the Victoriaborg Reservoir in 1888.[21]

The British introduced wells in some areas to curb the water situation, but this was inadequate. Later, the opening of pipe-borne water systems from the Densu River in 1888 alleviated the problem. Water conditions in colonial Accra got better in the early 1900s after the Accra Town Council Bill and a form of revenue system was introduced in coastal towns to improve clean water in the area. Despite colonial officials' response to the water crisis the problem persisted alongside segregated water systems and residences that favored the upper class and European housing projects. The use of prefabricated building materials in particular enabled colonial officials to settle on any land they preferred either temporarily or permanently to shield them from unhealthy environs.[22] These interactions between the Brazilians and the British were short-lived and did not extend beyond solving the water crisis in colonial Accra. Nonetheless, land disputes created tensions after British officials took part of the Brazilian land for colonial projects. The British paid substantial amounts of money as compensation in court to settle this conflict.

There were other positive stories about the Christian missionaries beyond their involvement in slavery in the Gold Coast. Missionaries had their own solution to the water and sanitation crisis. Like oral history in Brazilian communities, archival sources at the Public Records and Archives Administration Department, British colonial documents, and Basel Mission records that were compiled by Reverend H. Debrunner provide an insight into water conditions in Akropong and areas in Gã territories. Most of these areas were known as the bush or forest regions because of their distance from the coastline and their remoteness to vibrant activities in urban Accra. According to one mission report in 1862, the people of Abokobi (the blessed center of missionary activity), the Akwapim hills, and the Accra plains walked hundreds of miles in search of water during the dry season.[23]

Those who dug holes in nearby swamps gained access to pockets of water. Residents in this area, however, depended on missionaries to resolve their problems through religious rituals like prayer as well as technology. Although the latter provided good results, the Basel missionaries preferred the former; their prayers served as a vehicle for spreading news among the locales that the Christian God was powerful and could be depended on to provide drinking water. They often made references to the Old Testament, particularly Isaiah 43:20, and repeated the verses over and over to the local people.[24] The Bible reference states, "The beast of the field will honor Me, The jackals and the ostriches, because I give waters in the wilderness and rivers in the desert, to give drink to My people, My chosen."[25] The missionaries had a simple message: God will continue to provide clean water in the desert and the wilderness. It is not clear how many local people were converted through the missionaries' prayers. However, the Basel Mission's innovative technological approach gained attention. For instance, in December 1857, Basel missionaries provided a sixteen-foot shaft and metal ladders that allowed people in Akropong and Abokobi to have access to good drinking water. These metal shafts and ladders, which were constructed in Europe and shipped to various missionary posts, lifted people up and down and lowered their buckets deeper into the soil.

Searching for good drinking water during those days was a daunting task. The operation of this equipment from Europe shows that the composition of the top soil strata, which contained iron and about seventy feet of clay-strata and large rocks, made it difficult to dig for water. These obstacles, however, did not prevent the missionaries and the locals from quenching their thirst. On 20 August 1858, Reverend Reid and other missionaries reported that they were able to find fresh water in some areas from the hills of Akropong toward coastal Accra. As one of the letters explains, the missionaries invested heavily in this venture not only to please the local people and reaffirm their faith but also for their own survival. According to one of the letters,

> Reverend Reid went down into the shaft in the distinct hope to reach water soon. Indeed, they had not to dig far till the first drops came, then more, and more fresh clean water.... There was great joy after the discovery to the extent that the Catechist even filled a bottle with the precious liquid and hurried in his joy and traveled to Christianborg [Castle] to bring water to the missionary there. It was a great day indeed and many [offered] the prayers of thanksgiving addressed to God on this day.[26]

This back-breaking approach somewhat solved the crisis.[27] According to the missionary records, the celebration did not last very long as other natural disasters disrupted the joyful atmosphere. The earthquake of 1863, in particular, impeded the search for water. Indeed, the missionaries did not give up hope as their water containers ran dry each day. Unstable conditions created other urgent needs for water. Dehydration and malaria infections were common among European communities, and residents required access to water to sanitize and reenergize those who were affected.[28] It was a race against nature because of the rate at which people were affected.

Basel missionaries from Switzerland, Germany, and other areas in Europe therefore made the search for water their most important task besides propagating the gospel. Access to healthy water remained a top priority as missionaries brought their family members to live with them. Other newcomers arrived to establish Christian mission schools as part of their broader religious and civilizing goals. These new arrivals also prioritized education in various mission posts. In 1859, Reverend Hect reported that about twenty-six boys were enrolled in missionary schools at Abokobi. These classes were conducted in both Gã and English and were devoted to the teachings of the Christian Bible and prayers. Concerns about the health needs of teachers and students in these missionary schools remained a top priority, too. In addition to dehydration and malaria, bad drinking water created guinea-worm infections and cholera, which threatened everyone. There was panic among European communities. This anxiety was very necessary because by 1844 over one hundred Danish missionaries and colonial officials had been killed by various diseases including malaria and fever.[29] To curb this lingering problem, the Basel missionaries, like the British colonial officials, built huge water tanks, but another earthquake in 1872 destroyed their work.[30]

There were other ways of improving water conditions in the Gold Coast besides well-drilling by the Brazilians, British colonial officials, and missionaries. Historian Sandra E. Greene talks about the introduction of similar innovations in Anlo, a coastal town in the Volta region of Ghana in 1840. According to Greene, Baeta, a Portuguese who settled in a town called Akoto, constructed a number of wells. These wells were not necessarily intended for local consumption, but instead for Portuguese and Cuban slave ships that landed in the area.[31] Considering contacts between Brazilians and the Portuguese in the past and the evidence of technological transfers, it is possible that well-drilling was a common feature in the interactions between slaves and their Portuguese plantation owners, hence returnees' interest in transporting these skills upon their return. Although wells are still common in small towns and villages in some areas in Ghana today, standing pipes have taken over this technology in Accra and other locations.

BRAZILIAN AND TABOM RELIGIOUS CONTRIBUTIONS

In addition to improving the physical well-being of their new neighbors, the ex-slaves never forgot their faith and the importance of sharing their spirituality with others. These faiths include Islam, Christianity, and *shango*, all of which are believed to have been carried over to or from Brazil.[32] Their decision to evangelize brought them closer to Europeans again; missionaries, in particular, welcomed freed slaves as Christian "brethren." The Muslims among them, however, had little or nothing to do with Europeans during this time. In general, the Brazilian returnees made varying religious contributions that are worthy of attention. Religion was also featured in broader conversations and exchanges. Several scholars have underscored the ways in which African slaves, especially those from Nigeria, carried their Islamic faith to the New World and later back to Africa. Slaves from other areas including Angola also preserved their cultures and other traditional norms.[33] The African slaves practiced Islam alongside the African religions and cultures. The latter had enormous impact on white slave plantation owners who depended on slaves to perform various forms of divination to help them find stolen items in the plantations and protect them from evil deeds. Those of Catholic faith in particular relied on African slaves as well. According to Sweet, "Catholic priests acknowledged African religious powers . . . priests advised whites that their only hope for survival was consultation with an African diviner/healer. . . . Catholic priests conceded that exorcisms and other church remedies were no match for African spirits."[34] João José Reis explains how slaves contributed to the uprisings of Bahia in the 1830s when he analyzes the systematic and strategic processes by which Nagô (Yoruba) Africans planned and executed the 1835 *Males* (Muslim) slave revolts.[35] Upon settlement, Brazilian-Africans carried elements of the religious traditions they took from Africa and the faiths they acquired in Brazil. Those who settled in Nigeria, Benin, and other places became vehicles for the propagation of a particular faith. For instance, Muslims who returned to Nigeria built the Brazilian Olosun Mosque in Lagos (figure 14).

The number of returnees who arrived in the Gold Coast as Muslims or Christians is not known. There is no evidence that suggests that the freed Brazilians built any major mosque that has survived over a long period of time as in the case of those who settled in Lagos.

Although the first generation of returnees preserved some elements of their Brazilian heritage, such as their Muslim identity, their descendants were consumed by local Ghanaian and Western cultures and were increasingly likely to let their Brazilian identity weaken after the death of the older generation.[36] With the rapid spread of Christianity, particularly Protestant movements at the peak of colonial rule in the late nineteenth century, it was likely that some of their offspring would be attracted to Christianity. During one of my interviews in Accra it was revealed that most Tabom either became Christians or embraced Islam while growing up. The Muslims among them worshipped with other Ghanaians in mosques that have been built for followers in the community or had their own private places of worship on their compound.[37] My visit to the Brazilian Olosun Mosque on King Street, Lagos, Nigeria, which was built

Figure 14. Brazilian Olosun Mosque.

by Brazilian returnees in 1865 and was rebuilt by their descendants in 1966, confirmed how former slaves preserved the faith they had carried back to Africa. According to Muneer Akolade, the Aguda people in Lagos and other areas along the Bight of Benin not only safeguarded their faith but converted people in Lagos and its surrounding neighborhoods.[38] Other places of worship including the Alabayun Mosque, the Tairu Mosque, and the Salvador Mosque were built by other Aguda returnees in Nigeria.[39] Other sites of worship have been identified by studies about the returnees in Benin. It is possible that some of the slaves who were repatriated to the Bight of Benin after the revolts made their way to the Gold Coast, not only to spread their Islamic faith but to be part of the new Brazilian Muslim diasporan returnee communities in Accra. The work of these "Muslim evangelists" contributed immensely to Brazilian and Tabom religious identities as they sought various opportunities to convert the local people to Islam. In Ghana returnees continued practicing as Muslims without any restrictions. The Islamic faith of the early settlers set them apart and made them visible. According to Parker, "the arrival of the Tabons from Brazil in 1836 [a year after the uprising] represented the first influx of Muslims in Accra."[40]

Religion was a significant part of the reverse migration story. Brazilian-Africans were not the only ones to enter the race to win "pagan" souls on the African continent.

Narratives about the other returnees elsewhere are also key to understanding how religion shaped identity within the African diaspora. The recent work by Gibril R. Cole, *The Krio of West Africa*, provides an important insight into the origins of the Krio diaspora in Nigeria. Liberated Africans in Sierra Leone who became known as Sarro Christians were also guilty of this prejudice. These agents of civilization and modernity were determined to save their kinfolk from what they believed to be idolatry. African religious worshippers were not the only victims of this intolerance. Cole relates that "the arrival of the Saro and Aguda Muslims in the Lagos area led to complications between Islam and Christianity,"[41] as these two religious groups competed fiercely with each other for religious domination.

Historian Michael Turner contends that emancipated Brazilian-Africans who settled in Benin felt the effects of these prejudices, as they created rifts between the returnees and the indigenous people. In fact, the problem did not begin in Benin. Religious piety contributed to tension between slaves and ex-slaves who shared different faiths (Christians, Muslims, and African traditional religions) in Brazilian slave societies. As Reis articulates, Muslim Nigerian slaves in Brazil (Nagô), particularly the trailblazers of the 1835 Muslim slave revolts in Bahia, ridiculed slaves who adhered to Catholicism in Brazil. They made mockery of the Christians among them, especially those who used the rosary as part of their prayer rituals. The rift that developed in Brazil took a new turn after freed slaves crossed the Atlantic back to Africa and affected the other forms of division and prejudices that emerged. In the case of Nigeria, Cole asserts that religious tension crossed boundaries as competition for conversion increased. British officials exploited this competition to their advantage: it fed right into their vision of using both returnee groups to civilize the local people to prepare them for colonial rule. Nonetheless, the British preferred the Sarro Christians because most of them spoke English and were familiar with European values. It was easy to use them to serve in various colonial public positions.[42] The ex-slaves' involvement in spreading Christianity in particular was a tradition the returnees, especially the Catholic converts, carried with them from Brazil. Despite widespread mistrust in most societies about the returnees, especially those who were prejudiced against the local people due to their religious practices, Brazilian-African Christian returnees became torchbearers in propagating the Christian faith in Lagos. Their piety facilitated the expansion of Christianity in West Africa in the early nineteenth century as they forged ties with Catholic missionaries.

Returnees of Catholic faith who resettled in West Africa later joined various missionary efforts mainly because of their religious convictions and sense of duty, but not necessarily because they felt superior to Africans. One missionary record relates: "The missionaries who make up the team on the Niger are almost all Negroes from

Sierra Leone."⁴³ In some cases, Catholic missionaries trained ex-slaves to help with evangelistic programs because they believed that since the returnees shared a similar heritage and race with the local people, their participation would make evangelism easier. Moreover, there were other emancipated slaves who volunteered to spread the gospel without missionary influence. The interactions between the ex-slaves and the missionaries enhanced the spread of Christianity. Further, Christian missionaries who faced difficulties evangelizing the people along the coast of Lagos depended on these devout returnees. For example, Padre Antonio, a freed slave from Brazil, was one of the leaders who were actively involved in the conversion of the local people. He and others established a Catholic church to facilitate mission work in the area.⁴⁴ Michael J. Turner's analysis of freed Brazilians who were involved in the conversion of Africans in Benin and Lagos claims that it was a gradual process. Whereas the emancipated Brazilians' settlements and assimilation into local African communities took a long period, the ex-slaves' involvement in the proselytization of Africans in particular made them visible and a force to reckon with. According to Turner, as go-betweens for propagation of Christianity especially among the coastal dwellers of Lagos and key locations in Benin, "the Afro-Brazilians constituted a willing audience for the missionaries as they had experienced Catholicism in Bahia [and other areas in Brazil]. . . . The Bresilien Catholics expressed delight at the missionaries' arrival and the respect with which they regarded the priests were genuine emotions, in part because the Bresiliens were able to realize certain pragmatic as well as spiritual desires from their newly established missions [and their role in evangelism]."⁴⁵ In general, Afro-Brazilian returnees' investment in spreading Catholicism was so pervasive in their places of resettlements that they not only overshadowed other returnees of Muslim faith but the word "Aguda" became directly linked with Catholicism.⁴⁶

Christianity, like Islam, also had an important presence within returnee communities in West Africa. In Ghana, there is no evidence I am aware of that shows religious bickering between Brazilian-Tabom Muslims and Christians as in the case of Nigeria and other returnee settlements in areas of West Africa. Missionary groups from various corners of the earth, especially Europe and the Caribbean, made enormous contributions to the spread of Christianity in the Gold Coast. As missionary records show, returnees who became known as the Aguda people in Nigeria and Benin became a vehicle for establishing and propagating Christianity in these locales. Similar to their forebears, who invested heavily in spreading Islam in Accra, the Brazilians facilitated the propagation of the Christian gospel. In fact, the Brazilians were visible within the Protestant churches in Ghana and played prominent roles in both the Anglican and Methodist churches.⁴⁷ The selection of Rt. Reverend Kojo Aruna Nelson (from the Nelson family) as the provost of the Cathedral of the Most Holy Trinity (1963–77) and the assistant bishop of the Anglican Church of Accra (1966–77) may have influenced members of the community to convert to Christianity.[48] And His Very Reverend Emmanuel Issah-Modulpe Peregrino-Brimah (from the Peregrino-Brimah family group) became a Methodist minister in the 1990s.

Although some of the returnees from both Brazil and Cuba were Catholics, there is no evidence of their visibility in the Gold Coast—as in the case of those of Anglican and Methodist faith. It is possible that most of the early settlers were Muslims. Perhaps the subsequent generations were influenced by Protestants from the late nineteenth century. In contrast, most of the Aguda settlers in Nigeria, Benin, and other areas carried their Catholic faith and were involved in various Christianization missions in these areas. In Lagos, the freed Africans not only showcased their Catholic faith, returnees like Joaquim d'Almeida built a chapel in 1845 and dedicated it to Senhor Bom Jesus da Redem São in memory of their former place of worship in Bahia.[49]

Islam occupied a central part of the Brazilian returnee identity and ideation in the nineteenth century. Adherents of Islam and Christianity lived in harmony in the Brazilian-African diaspora. However, the returnees did not compromise their religion despite the dominance of local religions and the emergence of Christianity along the coast, which was orchestrated as part of larger colonial and commercial projects in the early 1800s. According to Nii Azumah V, a good number of descendants embraced Christianity in the early 1900s because of the strong Christian missionary presence in colonial Accra. Yet that transition could not erode their Muslim identity.[50] From the 1930s onwards, the tradition of using Islamic names continued in spite of descendants' conversions. This practice has indirectly preserved the Tabom's Muslim identity in the form of their Islamic middle names, which include Mama, Salami, Abiana, and Azumah, which are all corrupted forms of traditional Islamic names. Names such as Mama or Mahama, Aishatu, Abdulahi, and Aruna are typically associated with Hausa or Muslims in Ghana and are very popular among the Tabom. What is striking about these names is that whereas the Tabom Christians often use names that are traditionally regarded as Muslim, the Tabom Muslims do not use names from the Christian Bible or European names. In an interview, Nii Azumah V is reported to have stated that, "I am called Abdulahi, but I am a Christian."[51] This is an indication that Islam had enormous impact on the Tabom identity—more so than Christianity. Interactions with Tabom Muslims in both Accra and Lagos as well as my participation in the burial service of Elder Nelson in a Christian church provide useful insights. Islam and Christianity are not the only faiths within the Brazilian-African diaspora. Other less popular religious practices tied to both Brazil and other areas in the diaspora also exist.

The Tabom embrace other religions besides Islam and Christianity. Aspects of their religious identity such as *shango*, which is believed to have been preserved since

Figure 15. Manyo Plange, a Brazilian veteran of British colonial army during the British-Ashanti War expedition of 1895. Image displayed at Brazil House.

they arrived in the Gold Coast, are still practiced. But this practice is not very popular. According to the late Elder George Aruna Nelson, this religious ritual, which was passed on by the first generation, is still practiced by some members of the community.[52] Unlike the Islamic and Christian rituals, *shango* practices are not common or visible in public space.

SERVING IN THE BRITISH COLONIAL ARMY AND TABOM AUTONOMY AFTER THE FALL OF COLONIALISM

Several citizens of the Gold Coast including the Tabom people fought in the world wars.[53] E. Addey Plange, also referred to as Manyo Plange (figure 15), a senior army officer, and Henry Plange, both served in the colonial army in the Ashanti Expedition of 1895 during the British-Ashanti War.[54] Others served in the colonial regiment that the British created to defend England and its allies during the world wars. A number of court documents, including *Akua v. Nelson*, clearly show that some descendants were drafted into the British colonial army around 1939. In response to a question about where he was during the early stages of a land dispute, Enoch Cobblah Codjoe responded forcefully that, "yes, I also went to the 1939-1945 War."[55] Codjoe, who served in World War II, mentioned that his family lost their land after he left to serve abroad. Upon his return in the late 1940s, he sued to reclaim the land his Brazilian ancestors entrusted into his family's care. The war veteran was able to make a convincing case about his family's inheritance. There is no evidence that he enjoyed any privileges for his service.

The Brazilian returnees' contributions did not end with the history of precolonial and colonial Accra. In the postindependence era the Tabom people served as diplomats, politicians, government ministers, church ministers, educators, tailors, entrepreneurs, and sports icons. It is also not clear how the descendants in general participated in nationalist movements or Pan-African projects to end British rule in the Gold Coast. The story about Francis Zaccheus Santiago Peregrino's involvement in the Pan-African movement adds to Nelson's contribution to colonial revolt and nationalism. It would be interesting to know how the community as a whole became involved in nationalist rebellions and protests, especially during the imprisonment of Nkrumah at Ussher Fort Prison between 1947 and 1951 for his radicalism and opposition to British rule. The prison is located next to Brazil House at Otublohum and Swalaba, Accra, where it is believed that the Scissors House was established by Brazilian returnees with skills in tailoring.

The period between the 1950s and the demise of Nkrumah's government in 1966 was another pivotal moment in the Tabom chronology. Ghana's independence on 6 March 1957 opened a new niche for expatriates, returnees, and their descendants from the African diaspora to contribute in one fashion or the other—especially diasporan returnees from the United States and the Caribbean. The former were invited by *Osagyefo* Nkrumah to contribute in various ways to postindependence nation-building reforms.[56] They consisted of intellectuals, engineers, medical doctors, activists, and others who served the new nation of Ghana in incredible ways.[57] This process was part of a long tradition that was initiated by the Gã *mãŋtsɛmɛi* and British colonial rulers as they "exported" the skills of diasporan blacks in one colonial region to the other (particularly the Caribbean/West Indies) to stabilize their interests.[58] The Tabom people made their presence known after the demise of British colonial rule, particularly in the 1960s. They participated in social and economic activities similar to other diasporan returnees with Pan-African orientations. For instance, Elder George Aruna Nelson, who was trained at the Scissors House, asserted that he was employed to make suits for Kwame Nkrumah because of his skills in tailoring.[59] The Tabom have made a lot of progress in the tailoring industry. Other successful African-Brazilians include Alfred Morton and Isaac Morton, whose businesses have flourished in Accra, as well as descendants who have occupied different positions in both private and public institutions as educators, entrepreneurs, and in other roles.[60] The late Dr. Cyril Fiscian was a professor at the University of Ghana. Fiscian traces his ancestry through his grandfather Nathaniel Kassum Fiscian who died in 1992 at the age of eighty-two years. It is not clear if his grandfather was born in Brazil.[61] Two other Tabom people served

Figure 16a. Ambassador Miguel Augustus Ribeiro presents his credentials to President John F. Kennedy in the Oval Office, White House, Washington, DC, 25 April 1963.

Figure 16b. Harry Francisco Ribeiro, a prominent lawyer and relative of Miguel Augustus Ribeiro.

Chapter Seven

Figure 17. Azumah Nelson, three-time World Boxing Council featherweight boxing champion and later a lightweight boxing champion. Image displayed at Brazil House.

in Kwame Nkrumah's government: Dr. Alfred Morton was Nkrumah's physician, and Miguel Augustus Ribeiro served as the first Ghanaian ambassador to the United States during the tenure of John. F. Kennedy (figure 16a). One of his family members, Harry Francisco Ribeiro, who was born in Accra in 1873, was a prominent lawyer in Accra (see figure 16b).

From the mid-1960s through the late 1970s, there were a number of tumultuous events in the Ghanaian political and economic landscape. When Nkrumah was overthrown by the military, Ghana experienced other changes in government.[62] The Tabom continued to play a dominant role in Ghana's sociopolitical scene when Ambassador Ribeiro was replaced after the fall of Nkrumah's regime. Political and economic instability gave rise to the June 4th Revolution of 1979, which was led by Flt. Lt. Jerry John Rawlings, a former president of Ghana. During the 1980s, at the height of the revolution, three things stood out in the Tabom community. First, in international sports, Azumah Nelson, "the terrible warrior," a third-generation Brazilian from the Nelson pedigree on the Brazilian family tree, became a three-time World Boxing Council featherweight boxing champion and later a lightweight boxing champion (figure 17).

Nelson began his journey in the world of boxing in 1984 and became a national and world hero when he defeated Wilfredo Gomez from Puerto Rico. Nelson's victory gave Ghanaians something to celebrate during the revolution years. Public solidarity was visible, especially within the Brazilian-African diaspora. Students and young people were also attracted to Nelson because of his charisma and youthful image. He retired in 1997. While Nelson became famous in the boxing arena, his uncle, the late Sam Nelson, became the deputy minister of sports in the mid-1980s.[63] A striking event

Figure 18. Chief Justice Georgina Theodora Wood, the first female chief justice of Ghana. Image displayed at Brazil House.

that coincided with the ascendency of both Rawlings and Nelson was the economic stability in Ghana in the 1990s. During Rawlings's tenure as a democratically elected president from 1992 to 2000, political stability improved a number of sectors of the country's economy, including tourism. This created a suitable platform for the Tabom community to showcase other positive elements within their communities besides Nelson's victory. For instance, as the country made strides in the area of tourism, there were increasing demands and interest in tourism within Tabom communities in Accra—hence, the opening of Brazil House in November 2007.

Another important event was former president Lula's historic visit to the Tabom people. Finally, successful political transitions in Ghana gave the Tabom new opportunities to contribute their skills to the legal and democratic processes. Former Ghanaian president John Kofi Agyekum Kufuor selected Georgina Theodora Wood, a Tabom, as the first female chief justice of Ghana in 2007 (figure 18). The chief justice's job is the highest position occupied by any Tabom or any female in Ghanaian history. Wood traces her ancestry through the Lutterodt pedigree on the Brazilian family tree. In my interview with the chief justice, she noted that she was born at the Brazil House (formerly the Warri House), which was built by her great-great-grandfather, Mama Nassu.[64] The story about this important historical landmark and others reshaped the history of the Brazilian-Africans, especially the drive to enhance tourism in the Tabom communities. Her father, William Lutterodt, was ninety-two years old during my interview. He was extremely proud of his daughter's achievement during our interaction and he facilitated my meeting with the chief justice.[65]

Chapter 8

Brazilians Together, Brazilians Apart: The Family Trees and the Process of Becoming Gã

It is a fact that none of us here present has ever visited Brazil but that is not important. . . . We continue to consider Brazil as our mother country. Mr. Ambassador [Dantas], as you are the legitimate representative of a country we consider . . . as our mother country.

—Nii Azumah III, 3 April 1961

There was continuity and change in the Brazilian-African diaspora in Accra as the history of the first generation came to an end by the early 1900s. Differences between the first settlers and their descendants, particularly how their historical memory facilitated the fashioning of identities, shaped the lives of the subsequent generations. The Brazilian family tree used in this chapter refers to the original group or older generation of settlers who were offered land by Gã leaders sometime in the mid-1830s.[1] The Tabom family tree, on the other hand, depicts the genealogies of new generations. There are shades of diversity embedded in the narratives of returnees and their offspring, notably notions of double consciousness—the ways in which they identify either as Brazilians, Tabom, Ghanaians, or a combination of any of these classifications.

Members of the Brazilian-African diaspora were together at one time but were apart at another time. The evidence by members of the Nelson and Dangana *weikumei* (families) during their court appearances over land issues reveal differences between the family groups that form part of the Brazilian and Tabom family trees. One statement

Chapter Eight

notes that "there is no Brazilian custom in Accra different from the Accra custom; the custom applicable to the Brazilian is the Accra or Gã custom in all matters."[2] These statements also provide vital insight into the synopsis of identity formation within the Brazilian-African diaspora in Accra. Whereas a segment of their population evidences aspects of memory of Brazil—the location where some of their ancestors were born, and a place only imagined by their descendants—others also showed a level of loyalty to Gã traditions and customs. The epigraph presents a one-dimensional focus on Brazil. The statement by Brazilian chief Nii Azumah III, who led the community from 1936 to 1961, demonstrates his commitment to the notion of Brazil as his "mother country," an assertion that continues to resonate among the current generation. This important reminder also shows how Brazilian chiefs, who were selected only from the Nelson *we*, preserved their Brazilian past.[3]

Nii Azumah III's public announcement was made during a ceremony to welcome the first Afro-Brazilian ambassador to Ghana, Raymundo de Souza Dantas, to their community in 1961. Dantas was appointed by former Brazilian president Jânio Quadros. It has been more than fifty years since the chief made this comment. The Tabom who have visited Brazil have solidified Nii Azumah III's proclamation of Brazil as a mother country. In contrast, one of the Tabom relates the differences between the generational groups. In this particular reference the author establishes her close ties to the Gã people: "I am a Gã woman of the Brazilian community."[4] Here, she indicates the overshadowing of Gã customs and culture as well as the disconnect most descendants experience between a place or a *home* where they were born and where they have never been.

Various transformations continue to shape identities within the Brazilian-African returnee community. The Tabom people identify differently with Brazil. Their understanding of their past, especially of how their ancestors navigated their experience in colonial Accra, shaped the complex process of *isolacao* (isolation) and *assimilar* (assimilation) particularly through their interactions with their hosts—at the Tabom quarter. Not only that, while some of the early returnees settled in isolated forest regions, founded by their family members and friends in the mid-nineteenth century, others settled and resettled along the coast.[5] It was in this new phase of their history that they immersed gradually, and later deeply, into Gã culture and traditions.

To understand how the history of the Brazilian-Africans evolved from the precolonial period, it is vital to appreciate the diversity associated with the Brazilian-African and Tabom stories that emerged either together or apart. There were distinct features between the first and second generations, some of which were the effects of the transformation that enslaved Africans went through from their time of capture somewhere on the African continent and when they were carried into slavery in Brazil.[6]

The cultural and religious socialization they underwent in Brazil also had its effect as they returned to Africa. In Lagos and other places of settlement, the returnees continued practicing their faith, particularly Islam and Christianity. The Tabom embraced Islam, the dominant religious faith of the early settlers, and later Christianity and local religious practices. Other transformations that occurred after their resettlement, such as interaction with local cultures, had enormous impacts over time. For others in Accra, it was the transformation from an agrarian lifestyle to renting and selling their houses and family land and participating in urban economic activities in the early twentieth century that were important. These transformations and others are significant for understanding the complex socialization, identity formation, and cultural nuances in the Brazilian-African diaspora.

There were several watershed moments, particularly the changes that took place at the turn of the twentieth century. This was a major point of departure from traditions established by the earlier returnees to those shaped by the emerging generations. The ex-slaves and the Tabom people constructed and displayed their identities multiple ways. The strategic and interchangeable choices, the competing memories and challenges the Brazilians and their descendants encountered as they negotiated their Brazilian and their Ghanaian ancestral heritage contributed to their double consciousness.

The sense of dualism the two groups experienced, based largely on overlapping identities, is pervasive, especially among the descendants in terms of their memories of Brazil. The Tabom people passionately claim an identity based on their Ghanaian experience as well as their Brazilian ancestral ties: though born in Ghana, they make us aware of their simultaneous historical relationship with Brazil; though influenced by Ghanaian cultural traditions and value systems, they diligently integrate what they remember about their Brazilian heritage. In an interview with the late George Aruna Nelson, the ninety-one-year-old Tabom elder passionately expressed his desire to visit Brazil to merge the history of his forebears with his own.[7] Indeed, the elder and others may have settled in Otublohum and other areas in Accra where their forebears settled, but they daydream about ancestral roots in Salvador, Bahia, and other locations in Brazil.[8] How do the "push and pull" factors previously described contribute to the notion of a return to Brazil? As "flexible actors," some of the Tabom continue to enjoy the taste of two worlds: Ghana and Brazil.[9] They express this duality particularly through the way they think, how they envision their past, or what their fantasies about Brazil consist of.

The multidimensional angles for framing their sense of self, particularly the winding ways they connect with their ancestral past, are a potent force in their narratives. The fact that several freed slaves were determined to return to a *home* where they had not been before did not mean they all shared those feelings about Africa. While some of the liberated Africans were unsure of their future in Africa, particularly how to adjust to their new environment, the early Brazilian-African settlers in Accra did not necessarily feel that way. Most of them were conscious of who they were and how they should adjust to their new life. They did so by emphasizing either their dual or their singular identity. Put another way, some saw themselves as Africans first or as people who were forced into bondage. Others viewed themselves as Brazilians by birth after living in Brazilian plantations most of their life. Their children and subsequent generations sometimes embraced a Brazilian past when it was convenient, while at other times they rejected their Brazilian heritage or minimized it. Yet in some situations they welcomed their dual Ghanaian and Brazilian identities. Attitudes expressing both choices can be found among various family groups.

Memory played a pivotal role upon their return, just as memories of Africa sustained them during their lives in the New World. In Brazil, their oppressive conditions coaxed them into some form of "code switching," especially in terms of their conversion to either Islam or Christianity in order to survive.[10] Narratives of the reverse migrations between Brazil and Ghana reflect the emergence of the Brazilian-African and Tabom-Gã identities. The experience and knowledge of these two distant locations divided by the waters of the Atlantic continue to shape their memory of the Middle Passage experience. The early Brazilian-African settlers in Accra and their descendants were aware of how remote these two geographical locations were from each other. Returnees were mindful of their identity first as enslaved Africans. But many of the freed slaves maintained aspects of their "Brazilianness" in terms of how they spoke, how they dressed, what skills they possessed, and what religious faith they had upon arriving in Accra. This diversity within the returnee population was key to determining where they settled or where they preferred to live—either along the coast or in inland farming areas to amass wealth, acquire land, and continue with their individual or collective professions.

While there is a linear way to determine how the Brazilians came together at one point and apart at others, particularly during their early period of settlement in the nineteenth century, it is not clear if or how they created a unified community or pockets of communities during this time. What is certain is that over time each generation carved its own character and identity—they were not a homogeneous community. The generational difference shows how they were together and apart in a given historical period. A sizable number of liberated Africans from Brazil and their offspring sought various ways to make sense of their past, and in doing so they reconstructed their identities taking into consideration their ties to both Brazil and Ghana. It is imperative that we reconstruct their varying experiences with these two Atlantic locations by telling their stories through the lens of the waves of migration, the settlement processes, their identity formation, and especially the ways in which the narratives of each family tree converged at a given time and diverged during other historical periods.

THE BRAZILIAN AND TABOM FAMILY TREE: THE FIRST GENERATIONS, 1780S-1900

Brazilian-African migrations to the Gold Coast spanned a wide period from approximately the end of the eighteenth century to the late nineteenth century. Although there is evidence that a number of former slaves returned to West Africa in the late 1780s after manumission, information at the Public Records and Archives Administration Department (PRAAD) confirms that they arrived in Ghana beginning in the 1820s. Narratives about the origins of the Brazilian family tree fall within this time frame. To argue for the notion of a Brazilian family tree is not necessarily to assert that all freed slaves who came from Brazil were from the same bloodline. In fact, "family tree" is used in this book to identify various populations within larger diverse groups.[11] Although it is feasible to create a form of ancestral tree with "branches" for the diverse groups, it is not easy (or perhaps even possible) to quantify the Brazilians in the actual returnee population: some of their ancestors are not known.

In the nineteenth century, there may have been returnees who shared close kinships. Others, though, were likely friends from the same plantation or the same neighborhood and may not have interacted the same way when they arrived in the Gold Coast. Or returnees might also have been strangers who were merely traveling on the same ship either directly from Brazil or from the Bight to Gã *mãŋ*. The various waves of returnees included some who desired to reconnect to their roots and others who were in search of opportunity in a new place.[12] Both on the coastline and in inland locations in Gã *mãŋ*, Accra, branches of the Brazilian family tree sprouted up in different locales and expanded in different directions from generation to generation, as returnees refashioned their identities or expanded their communities, creating new cultures as they went. As a result, they did not form a cohesive ancestral structure during their (re)settlement. In fact, there has not been any effective system in place to graft all Tabom groups into a single Brazilian family tree since the nineteenth century, partly because of decades of intermarriage and other ways of integrating with local cultures.[13] It is thus a truly daunting task to trace the ancestral origins of the Tabom people. This difficulty is compounded by the inconsistency and limited data in the documentation of their origins.

There are both similarities and differences between the experience of the Brazilian-African diaspora compared to other reverse migration stories, such as in Liberia (Americo-Liberian), Sierra Leone (Sarro), Nigeria, Benin, and Togo (Aguda), among others. In the case of Ghana, distinct characteristics are discernible among the offspring of Brazilian-Africans that might not be found in other returnee communities. For instance, the Tabom people do not always openly welcome other Tabom people just because they share a common history. Sometimes the Tabom relate to other Ghanaians of Brazilian ancestry as strangers, as people they know nothing about or with whom they have had no contact. A recurring theme in my interviews and over the decade of interactions I have had with members of the various branches of the Tabom family tree is a lack of awareness of all the branches that make up the Brazilian family tree. Some Tabom express apathy about their history and about these connections. Even where others' existence is acknowledged, there is rarely any sustainable dialogue between the disparate groups. Specifically, the Lutterodts, Peregrinos, Nelsons, Fiscians, Ribeiros, and others may have heard of other Brazilians or Tabom people, but they lack the kind of shared experiences that might make these shared ancestral ties to the Middle Passage, and to the period of enslavement in Brazil, significant. The Lutterodts and the Peregrinos (from the Peregrino-Brimah lineage) are the only family group that I know of that have confirmed they share a common ancestor, Mama Nassu, a central figure in the Brazilian-African story. In short, it will be misleading to expect close-knit relationships and a significant degree of interaction and exchange among descendants in the Brazilian, Tabom, and Gã communities.

Unlike *homowo* celebrations, an annual festival that brings the Gã mãŋbii, the Tabom, and other surrounding communities together, these diverse Tabom family groups do not have any particular activity that brings them together to celebrate their Brazilian past.[14] This apathy has roots in the decades of land disputes over inheritance as well as in the stringent selection process for choosing new Brazilian chiefs, among other causes.

The Tabom Family Tree

The first generation of emancipated slaves returning to what is now Ghana had no intention of assimilating into local cultures.[15] Several things changed after their demise. Unlike the early settlers, most of the Tabom people immersed themselves deeply into local cultures and "became" Gã people or citizens of Accra so they could live lives tied to a particular place and thus no longer experience an abstract, rootless identity.

Broadly speaking, the process of "becoming Gã," or assimilating into Gã customs, did not happen overnight. Rather, a series of complex negotiations had to occur before this important stage of Brazilian, Tabom, or Ghanaian identity could be reached. The idea of the Tabom family tree is important to the reconstruction of Tabom identity and the process of becoming Gã. As with other aspects of Tabom history, tracing the genealogical branches has proved difficult mainly because they themselves were inconsistent in tracing their origins and documenting their transatlantic travels. Simply put, the Brazilian tree, which originated in South America, was transplanted along the Bight of Benin. Over time, it spread to the coastline of Accra where new branches formed. In Ghana, the Brazilian family tree then expanded through childbearing.[16] The Tabom family tree grew in similar fashion.

The members of the Tabom family tree on which I focus after a number of interviews include the Lutterodt, Peregrino, Nelson, Ribeiro, Morton, and Fiscian families. These distinct groups have *wei yetsoi*, individual heads of families. The head or headman, or *caboccer* in Portuguese, is a tradition their Brazilian-African ancestors passed on to them. For instance, Ezekiel Fiscian was the head of the Fiscian family, Liliki acted as the head of the Aruna Yawafio family, and Ambah Fatuma was also the acting head of the Aruna Dangana family in the mid-1900s.[17] In a number of court cases, the Tabom people defended their claims to ownership of a particular land parcel that was passed on by their parents by making reference to a particular head of family. As a descendant in one of the court disputes stated passionately, "[We are] children, grandchildren and descendants of Aruna [one of the original settlers]."[18]

The few women heads of families include Sarah Clegg who became the head of Lawrence family. The Fiscian family traces their ancestry through the Abdulamu lineage,[19] whereas the Dangana map their lineage via the Aruna family.[20] Other family lineages are more difficult to trace owing to lack of access, apathy, and other factors. These family groups are excluded in my analysis.

The heads of various groups were not more powerful than those selected exclusively from the Nelson bloodline, but they too exercised considerable power.[21] Micro family networks focused on individual family groups, but the position of the Nelsons represented a macro jurisdiction that indirectly gave that one family unit a mandate to represent all Ghanaians of Brazilian descent, especially in social, cultural, and public functions. The Brazilian family branches that I have listed multiplied and expanded the Brazilian population decade after decade. However, since the early 1900s, when the schism over land occurred, descendants have not been able to unite or interact in any major ways with extended family members with ties to the first generation. The Tabom chiefs whose work is to bring the different family groups together have not been successful in this endeavor for various reasons. In one court case, the tribunal had its own challenges in depending on the Tabom chiefs to settle their problems privately. The court declared that some of the friction that emerged was "a matter between members of the same family"—a reminder that, like any other community, there were internal struggles within the Brazilian population that complicated not only their ancestral linkages but also efforts to settle disputes among them both privately and publicly.[22]

In addition, disagreements and silences within the community after the demise of the first generation have made it difficult, if not impossible, to piece together how subsequent generations with a long history of assimilation were connected at various levels to the original settler groups or the Brazilian family tree. In other words, it is becoming increasingly difficult to talk to other Ghanaians who are part of the Tabom family tree. With the exception of the Lutterodts, Nelsons, and Peregrinos, descendant groups have been mute or have provided only limited access to the information needed to reconstruct Brazilian-African history inclusive of all family units in Ghana. Other researchers provide a different perspective on this "winding" family tree.

Significance of the Family Trees

The Brazilian and the Tabom family trees could prove significant in aiding scholars in pinpointing the exact locations where Africans were taken captive before they were dispersed to various locations in the New World. They could also help in determining destination sites for reverse migrations back to Africa. This data could supplement other information available, for instance in the *Trans-Atlantic Slave Trade Database*, in ways that could improve existing estimates of the returnee populations.[23] In addition, these names and their origins could provide a base for tracing their ancestral origins and connections in Brazil as well as their first points of settlement on the Bight of Benin. Similarly, genealogists could establish continuity and change in the ancestry of family groups or between various generational cohorts. A recent study of the origins of returnees has depended on DNA testing and other scientific methods.[24] This innovative methodology for tracing the origins of people of African ancestry could be applied to the Brazilian-African diaspora. The family trees might also help clarify contentions concerning claims of ties to Brazil.

STUDY OF SELECTED BRAZILIAN AND TABOM FAMILY GROUPS

The history of the Brazilian-African diaspora is not about one particular family group or how much a particular entity contributed to the reconstruction of their history. Rather, like a tree it is made of several parts, and each component contributes to the growth of the community. Also, these separate family units are like branches standing on their own but sharing the same roots. It would be misleading to focus on one particular family group (*we*) or use their experience to paint a broad picture of the entire community. Nonetheless, based on evidence that the core roots of the Brazilian story could be traced through Mama Nassu, a well-known symbol, I draw from his ties in my representation of the community. Several family groups claim that Nassu was their grandparent or share family ties with him, but not all these distinct family groups acknowledge others who make similar claims. The only exception is the Lutterodts, who have revealed the common ties between them and the Peregrinos via Nassu; they share a common family heritage through different branches of the Nassu family tree. The Lutterodts, for instance, make reference to the Brazil House, the house Nassu built. The Lutterodts lived in Nassu's house until they handed it over to be used as a tourist site in 2007. The Peregrinos share ancestral ties with Nassu's relative Adjuma/Adsuma meaning "Friday" in Hausa (figure 19).[25] The Peregrinos trace their lineage via Adjuma, who is sometimes referred to as Matta. In the words of A. R. Gomda, a journalist who has covered part of the Brazilian and Tabom story in Ghana over the years, "When Mr. Lutterodt [Elder William Lutterodt] turned up for the funeral of the late Chief Amida Peregrino-Brimah who died on 10th January 1998, he was attending the funeral of his cousin."[26]

It is important to underscore the fact that although both the Lutterodts and the Peregrinos trace their Brazilian heritage from a common source, they also share other heritage through intermarriages with the Gã and Akan people as well as via Europeans and Yoruba migrants in the Gold Coast. This has not only enlarged their distinct family trees but has also complicated the Brazilian-African diaspora narrative. Most importantly, the fusion of their history with other cultures reinforces the central tenet of my book: that their reverse migrations are tightly laced with other cultures and historical developments.

Limitations in reconstructing the narratives of the liberated Brazilians and their offspring are due not only to inadequate archival materials but also to silences within the community. Despite a generally aloof attitude among many family groups, a number of families have been vocal and involved in my research. Their support helped transcend the wide gap from more than a century of disunity. They have been tenacious

Chapter Eight

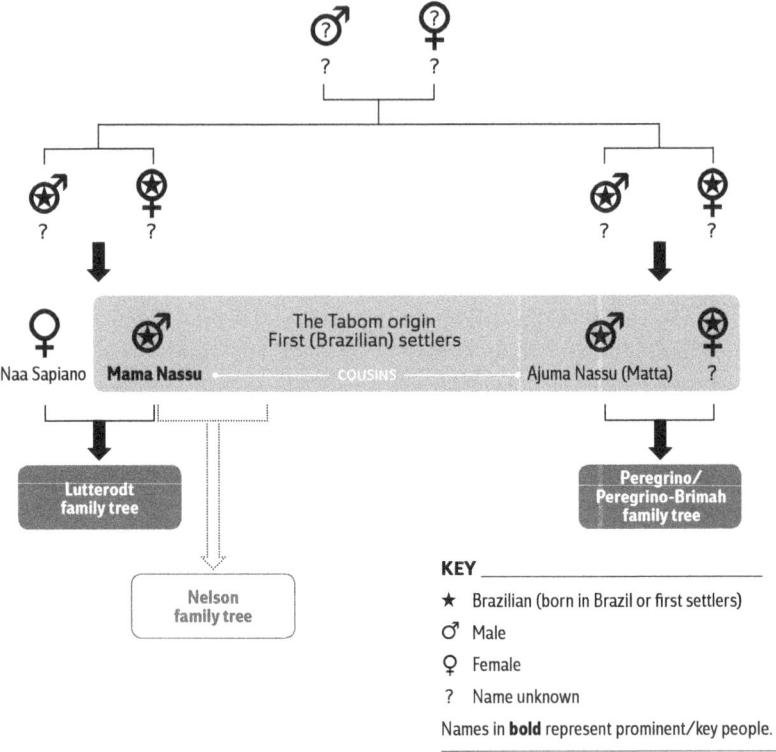

Figure 19. The Nassu family tree, showing the relationship between the Lutterodt and the Peregrino/Peregrino-Brimah family trees.

in piecing together fragments of their history, motivated by a concern to document their history for posterity. They have told me their stories and shared with me important private family documents, including photographs and letters. Due to limitations in the data about the overall Brazilian-African diaspora, just these three family groups are discussed: the Lutterodts, the Peregrinos, and the Nelsons.

I am not claiming that the entire history of the Brazilian-African diaspora hinges on these selected family groups. However, the stories of these three families are both similar and unique, and each has made major contributions not only to the social history of Accra but in the case of the Peregrinos to the Pan-African movement at the height of the black anticolonial, antisegregation, and antiapartheid period from the 1950s.[27] Another reason why the three groups stand out among others is that their story is tied to three major historical sites of memory in the Brazilian-African diaspora in Accra: the Brazil House, which was renovated on 17 November 2007, for

Figure 20. Peregrino House at Accra, Ghana.

tourism purposes; Peregrino House (figure 20), which is located near Mokola, the heart of commercial activities in Accra; and the Scissors House, which was destroyed by fire in 2007.

There is ample evidence to show that other family groups have ties to Brazil, but they do not have any particular ancestral reference points that clearly define their lineage or explain their roots.

THE LUTTERODT *WE*

The Lutterodts trace their Brazilian roots to Mama Nassu, a farmer who is believed to have arrived in Accra in the 1830s. Nassu played a key role in the allocation of Gã lands to the Brazilians for farming and housing because of his friendship with Gã mãŋtsɛmɛi. Nassu is referred to as the captain, the flagbearer, or the leader of the early settlers. He was, however, not a Brazilian chief. Nassu's ceremonial flagbearing responsibilities meant that he had to perform certain cultural rituals that required the use of a flag to demonstrate the group he was part of. In my interview with Elder William Lutterodt he described Nassu as the central pillar for understanding his family history. Nassu, he said, was very industrious and did not depend on anyone to provide his needs.[28] That is one reason why he built the edifice now known as the Brazil House. Nassu's decision provided not only a place for his family to call their own but also a comfortable environment to entertain guests who traveled to Accra. It is possible that Nassu's house, although containing a huge compound and plenty of rooms, was not very visible to the public during his lifetime. Over a century later, his house has made his descendants and the neighborhood where the house is located more visible to tourists. Without this historical landmark there would not have been a large permanent feature to solidify evidence of Brazilian-Africans in the area.

Elder William was about ninety-two years old during our interview, but he had a sharp memory and provided details about each member of the Lutterodt's family tree. He stated that Nassu married a Gã woman named Naa Supiano and bore a daughter named Naa Kyarcha. This meant that Chacha or Kyarcha was among the first generation of the Tabom. After her marriage to Nii Otu, who was of Gã origin, she bore five children including Adelaide Amponsah, William Lutterodt's mother (figure 21).

Lutterodt later had six children, among them Georgina T. Wood, the chief justice of Ghana. Elder Lutterodt is not ashamed to say that his father's "Lutterodt" lineage gradually overshadowed his mother's Brazilian bloodline. He states that "My children, I named them after my father . . . so all my children are Lutterodts. We named them after my father's tradition . . . Asini [Gã tradition]."[29] However, he later emphasized that part of the reason for using the Lutterodt name was not only because he inherited it from the patriarchal lineage but also because his father, Alfred Theodore Lutterodt, was of both European and Gã descent. Therefore, he needed to preserve his father's name for posterity. The Lutterodts never forgot their great-grandparents. It was through their memory of their ancestral linkage to Brazil that they contributed immensely to the renovation of the Brazil House for tourism.

Since Nassu's death in 1874, the Brazil House has undergone series of changes. After Nassu's demise Kofi Acquah, Amponsah's brother became the manager of the Brazil House. Elder Lutterodt contends that "my uncle [Acquah] was the one who renovated the house. Then my mum took over and we lived there."[30] According to Lutterodt, his grandmother and uncle took care of the property until the 1940s, when Acquah left Accra for a town called Warri in modern-day Nigeria. Thereafter, some family members relocated to Nassu's house while other rooms were rented to non-Brazilians to raise money to maintain the house. Elder Lutterodt also maintained that some of the rooms were rented to merchants in the area who used them as storage facilities for their goods. Amponsah did not leave Nassu's house when her brother traveled to Nigeria. Indeed, Acquah did not remain in Warri for the rest of his life; he returned about a decade later to live in Nassu's house until his death. When he

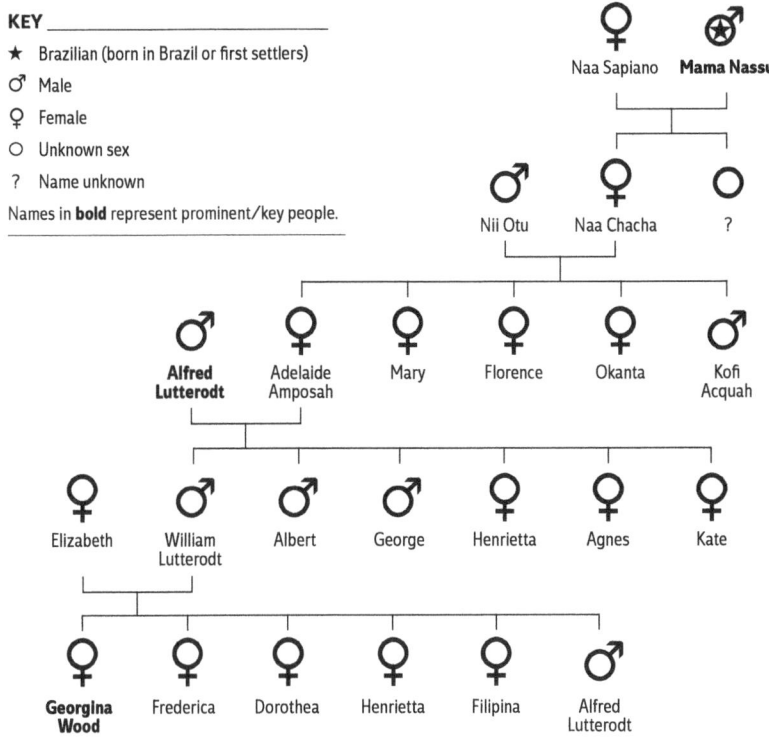

Figure 21. The Mama Nassu-Lutterodt family tree.

returned to Nassu's house, Acquah named the property "Warri House" to symbolize his long trip to Warri.

Those who lived in the Warri House, like their ancestors, kept moving from one location to the other. Elder Lutterodt, who later became a postmaster during the colonial period, was posted to different regions of the Gold Coast to work in newly established post offices. He moved his large family back and forth, which gave them the opportunity to see other areas besides the coast of Accra. As both Lutterodt and his daughter Wood stated in our interview, his parents and siblings were raised at the Brazil House until her late teen years, when Elder Lutterodt moved the family off the coastline of Otublohum to a more urban environment in mainland Accra as these new areas took on cosmopolitan shape. One of the reasons for relocating was overpopulation along the coastline.

My first visit to the Warri House in 2005 and my first visit to the refurbished Brazil House two years later were quite striking, especially when I compared the fragile concrete-and-wooden structure and disorganized and crowded compound of the Warri House to its current state. There were plenty of justifiable reasons for this transformation. Years of misunderstanding between the tenants and the caretaker of the property, Elder Lutterodt, created tension between the two groups in part because the tenants did not take good care of the property. The Brazilian government and embassy, UNESCO, the Ghanaian government, the Lutterodts, and the Tabom Chief Nii Azumah V had competing interests in Warri House, though not necessarily because they were concerned about the rapid disappearance of evidence of Brazilian-African presence in Ghana. They responded aggressively, in part, because of the ways in which heritage tourism had gained uninterrupted momentum during the twenty-first century. This occurred against the backdrop of Ghana's rising position as the most visited heritage site in West Africa, particularly with regards to sites of memory associated with the Middle Passage and the transatlantic slave trade. Put in another way, several parties involved in the story of the Warri House saw its potential to tourism, especially revenue collection to improve the Tabom community or at least give them some visibility after their communities were placed on the margins of heritage tourism for over half a century.

In general, the ways in which Elder Lutterodt and his children preserved the Warri House for posterity paid off as they agreed to work closely with others who had expressed vested interests in their inheritance. After years of negotiations between the Lutterodt family, who were represented by Elder Lutterodt and his son Dr. Alfred Lutterodt, a medical practitioner in Canada,[31] and the interest groups mentioned above, there was a consensus that the Warri House should be reconstructed to attract tourist and local visitors. Their bold decision was not only to raise revenue but to make the Brazilian-African diaspora story as visible as other diasporan narratives in Ghana.

After this decision, their biggest challenge was the relocation and compensation of current tenants, many of whom were from varying backgrounds, and some of whom were adults who had been born at the Warri House. Although there is no doubt that the Lutterodts owned the property, it was not easy to move these residents out of the property without giving them advance notice. With the exception of the Lutterodts, no interested parties or other Tabom family groups provided any money to compensate the tenants. In the words of Elder Lutterodt, "My son, the doctor, sent us twenty million [Ghana cedis, the local currency] and we shared it among the people in the house. We said we didn't want any trouble."[32] Clearly, no one group can claim to be carrying the burden of preserving their heritage alone. Indeed, we can make a similar case for Tabom Chief Nii Azumah V, who performs several cultural roles without getting financial support from other Tabom people. By and large, as important as it is to highlight the small and large contributions of members of the Brazilian-African diaspora to the unearthing of their long-buried transatlantic story for public consumption, the Lutterodts must be applauded for their selfless acts. It is important to underscore their pivotal role not only in protecting their family history but in financing this important project and sharing their public property with the Tabom people and the general public. In addition to allowing the Warri House to be converted to the Brazil House, the Lutterodts donated an old padlock that is believed to have been used to lock the main entrance to the compound of the Warri House for decades. This was handed over to the Brazilian embassy. The padlock is also an embodiment of their willingness to share their private fortune with the public to showcase the Brazilian and Tabom presence in Ghana. This padlock also personifies the fluidity of the reverse migration story, the umbilical cord between Brazil and the Tabom, and the fact that their history is ongoing. Without the sacrifice of the Lutterodts, there would not have been anything as visible as the Brazil House. Elder Lutterodt concluded that his family has knowledge of activities at the Brazil House and that they are still key players in the daily affairs of the property.

The Peregrino and Peregrino-Brimah *Wei*: Pan-Africanism and the Yoruba-Brazilian Factor

The Peregrino family tree extends beyond those included in this book and is covered in two parts in order to emphasize their differences. The first is framed around the story of Pan-Africanism, whereas the second is grounded within broader Yoruba-Brazilian interactions and diaspora in Ghana. As figure 22 shows, the Peregrino trace their roots through Ajuma Nassu (Matta), Mama Nassu's cousin, and later, via intermarriages, between the returnees and the people of Accra.

Pan-African literature does not often devote much coverage to the impact of returnees and their descendants in Ghana. Unlike the American African legacy in Ghana, much is not known about the Brazilian-African or Tabom role in Pan-African endeavors, especially between the precolonial and colonial history of Ghana. Put differently, there is no major record of Brazilian-African returnees' involvements in Pan-Africanism on a national or international scale except the case of Marika Sherwood's work, the *Origins of Pan-Africanism*. The journey of Francis Zaccheus Santiago Peregrino, a descendant of a liberated Brazilian-African who is believed to have been born in Accra in 1851 (figure 3) is worth mentioning here. In fact, his son, Francis J. Peregrino, also contributed immensely to Pan-Africanism.[33] Peregrino's ancestors navigated various paths across the Atlantic from Brazil to Ghana; he on the other hand followed a similar transatlantic trajectory from Ghana to England, to the United States, and later to South

Chapter Eight

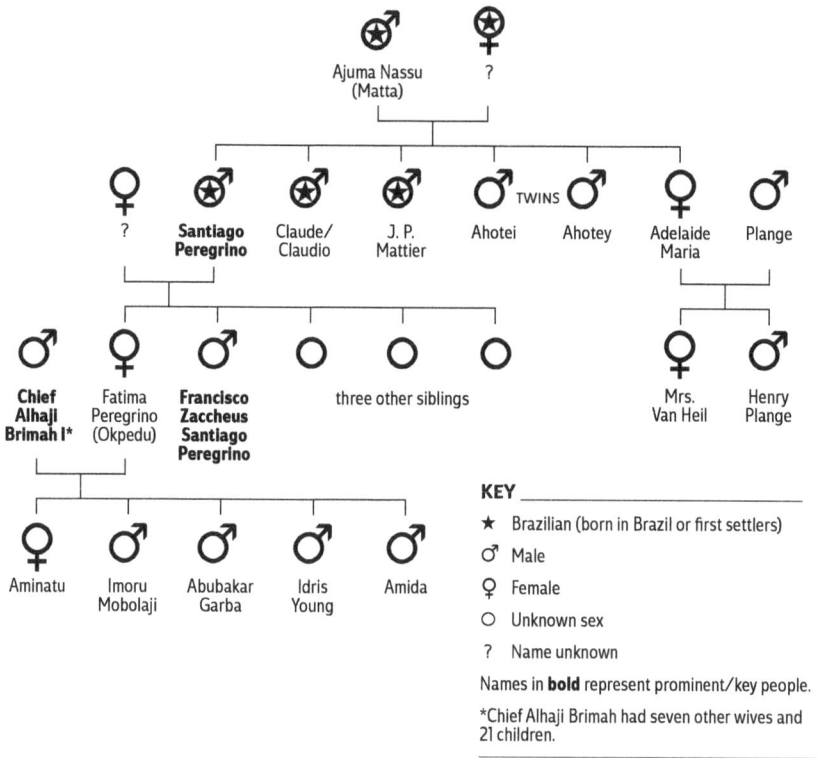

Figure 22. The Peregrino/Peregrino-Brimah family tree.

Africa. The Peregrinos' voyages from the late 1800s were outstanding, pivotal, and striking in the sense that they occurred at the climax of Pan-Africanism. In England Peregrino was a steel worker, but in Albany and Buffalo, New York, he published the *Spectator*, a monthly newspaper.[34] It is believed that Peregrino's interaction with Henry Sylvester Williams, one of the founding fathers of Pan-Africanism, enabled the two to join forces to support various struggles of South African blacks during the apartheid era. Part of their collaboration extended deeper into larger problems that black people encountered with racism and colonialism across the globe. The interaction and Pan-African alliance Peregrino and Williams developed were beyond their shared ancestral African heritage. Their collaboration and partnership shaped the organization of the conference in London from 22 to 24 July 1900. Marika Sherwood's analysis of the second Pan-African Conference in London points to myriads of speakers, both men and women, including W. E. B. Du Bois and Anna Jones, a black American educator from Wilberforce University, Ohio, as well as the Caribbean, among others.

The second Pan-African Conference in London did not end ties that were established between the two. Both the elder Peregrino and Williams returned to South Africa in 1901 after the conference to serve as vehicles for spreading Pan-African rhetoric. The two brought fresh hope to both the black diasporan community in Cape Town and local black South Africans at a time when the Boers (Dutch settlers) had waged war on black people in the country. Peregrino continued his work as a publisher. He became the editor of the *South African Spectator* while Williams pursued a profession in law where he came face-to-face with deep-seated racism of varying magnitude. Both Pan-Africanists used the newspaper and the court of law to demand freedom and expose human rights violations. They also showcased Europeans' illegal seizure of native lands.[35] Perhaps this was influenced by the problems of land tenure in colonial Accra or the effects of British colonial land ordinances on Brazilian land prior to his journey abroad. It is held that Peregrino in particular played a monumental role in the struggle against apartheid in the early stages.

Peregrino was indeed a man of multiple talents. In South Africa he published a short history of the native groups there. Manu Herbstein, a South African engineering consultant in Accra, describes Peregrino as "a talented, if a little eccentric, West African journalist from the Gold Coast."[36] According to a number of Tabom people who trace their lineage through the Peregrino-Brimah line, they are proud of the role played by Francis Zaccheus Santiago Peregrino in the Pan-African movements.[37] Besides the Peregrinos, there is no major account of returnees who became active in Pan-Africanism. The situation was similar among the Tabom people: besides their contributions to postindependence Ghanaian societies, they did not play any major role nationally, regionally, or continentally in sustaining or spreading Pan-Africanism. In the few examples where they did participate in Pan-Africanism, Ghana's historiography did not capture this narrative alongside Nkrumah's involvement.

Other Tabom who identify as Peregrino share a history not only with Brazil but with the Yoruba people of Lagos, Nigeria. In the supreme court land dispute *Rashid Brimah & 3 Ors. v. Hadji M. B. Peregrino-Brimah* part of their story is also framed around disputes over land and properties that these two groups inherited. The creation of a Yoruba diaspora and Brazilian-African diaspora in colonial Accra is important for understanding the common ties that existed between freed slaves from Brazil and Yoruba migrants who left Nigeria to begin a new life elsewhere. Some of these Nigerians and Aguda who plied the Atlantic waters did so to join other family members or friends, to expand trading activities, or to spread their religion in the Gold Coast. Intermarriage between Brazilian-Africans and Yoruba travelers blended these groups in ways that solidified the dream of the Gã mãŋtsɛmɛi to create diversity in coastal Accra. It also increased diversity within the Brazilian-African diaspora. Some marriage unions were with other foreign migrants, including European missionaries, merchants, and possibly colonial officials. A few examples, including the love story between Ferku and Yawah, show the intertwined nature of Brazilian-Tabom-Ghanaian identity. Over a century of intermingling, assimilation, and acculturation facilitated the formation of various identities.

Yoruba migrations to Ghana date back to the eighteenth century when Nigerians traveled in large numbers to settle in coastal Ghana. Some relocated to seek jobs at Sekondi, a port city and an important center for commerce.[38] Their arrival happened around the same time the liberated Africans began landing from Brazil and as the British were establishing colonial rule. For instance, colonial officials regulated their colonies in ways that facilitated Britain's interests across the African continent. At other times, the British took advantage of available labor in various locations to prop up colonial ventures. Part of this labor force that became known as the "Alata" people, made up of Nigerian immigrants, served colonial labor needs in Accra. This tradition of moving colonial manpower around extended beyond West Africa.[39] These policies were not limited to transporting black bodies, skills, and manpower within the African continent. Efforts by other colonial systems to force Africans, including newly liberated slaves, to the West Indies to work in plantations scared many local people and the returnees alike.[40] The creation of Alata towns around Otublohum by some of these immigrants at the turn of the twentieth century enabled a convenient environment for marriage unions between Brazilian-Africans and Yoruba immigrants. This includes the prominent Yoruba Muslim merchant, Chief Alhaji Brimah, also known as Butcher. His remarkable contribution to the establishment of Islam as well as his entrepreneurial skills have received considerable attention in academic circles.

The investment in Accra by Brimah, a wealthy, devout Yoruba man, cannot be ignored. In "Settling in and Holding On: A Socio-economic History of Northern Traders and Transporters in Accra's Tudu, 1908–2008," Samuel Aniegye Ntewusu provides lengthy discussions about Brimah's interactions with the local people. Ntewusu's work draws from colonial documents that place Brimah in the center of urban development in Accra.[41] Brimah's other achievements include the expansion of the suburbs of Accra. Chief Brimah was not only a devout Muslim; he was also a shrewd investor who knew how to navigate the complex colonial system without creating unnecessary trouble for himself as an outsider. Indeed, the chief was not valued by his offspring alone; he was respected by both Gã mãŋtsɛmɛi and British colonial officials for the way he used his multiple talents to help meet the needs of colonial Accra. The special treatment or attention Chief Brimah received was not entirely unique in Gã social history. Gã mãŋtsɛmɛi had a long history of creating comfortable and convenient environments for their *gboi* (visitors) and strangers who were in Accra, especially those with skills and money to contribute to revenue collection. According to Gã mãŋtsɛmɛi, Brimah's interactions with the colonial system were based on mutual understanding between them—particularly, his close friendship with Gã *Mãŋtsɛ* Tackie Tawiah.[42]

Faced by the growing migrant population and increasing body of religious groups and leadership tension among the Fulani, Hausa, and Yoruba migrants in colonial Accra by the end of the nineteenth century, it was important to find one person, Headman to represent the migrants to keep peace and to facilitate development in Gã *maashi* and colonial Accra. Gã mãŋtsɛmɛi had a long history of providing hospitality to strangers and migrants to their area, not only because they themselves were once accepted to this area or because they understood that a peaceful environment was conducive for social harmony, but because it was useful for generating revenue, particularly among merchants who settled in Accra. On the other hand, British colonial ordinances sought to monitor newcomers in the area to avoid any outside threat. Further, the Danes, the Dutch, and the English guarded the various districts they created along the coastline of Accra and were very interested in those settled in the area to protect their varying interests.[43] Gã King Tackie Tawiah interacted with Chief Brimah several times and was pleased with him. Unfortunately, King Tawiah died a few days after expressing his unconditional support for Chief Brimah. A close aide of King Tawiah provided insight about Tawiah's understandings of Brimah as the ideal leader. *Asofoatse* Kojo (captain of the Gã paramountcy) states that the late King Tawiah had no reservation about selecting Chief Brimah as the headman of the diverse migrant community because of his positive influence in the area.[44]

With recommendations from Gã mãŋtsɛmɛi and various colonial officials, Chief Brimah was selected as headman of the Muslim community on 1 July 1909 after he competed with various leaders among the Hausa and the Fulani community. He was chosen, in part, because of his involvements in various trading networks and his social and religious leadership qualities. Europeans in the area did not have a problem with newcomers who were not a threat to them. The British officials were in support of any religious groupings that could improve the lives of the people of Gã *mãŋ* and provide a peaceful atmosphere to enhance colonial projects. Interactions between Chief Brimah and colonial officials show how visible he was in colonial space. One of the letters by Major Hebert Bryan, the acting British governor, after he received a delegation from the Mohamedan community confirms this:

> I am glad to have an opportunity of seeing you here today. I understand that it is the wish of the Mohamedans in Accra to have Alhaji Brimah as the Headman. . . . I have known Alhaji Brimah for over five years now and I believe he will make a good Headman for the Mohamedans [religious sect who were part of the Muslim community].

He is a rich man and will be able to help materially in the upkeep of the mosque.... He will be able to help the poorer members of the Mohamedan community.[45]

The selection of Chief Brimah as the leader of the Mohamedan community was vital not only to the successful expansion of colonial ventures in Accra but also to the mobilization of various migrant groups that competed with each other over religious leadership as well as for commerce. In the biography of Chief Alhaji Brimah I, Dr. Alhaji Farouk Brimah, former deputy minister of environment, science, and technology in Ghana in the late 1990s and one of the great-grandsons of Chief Brimah, provides details about Chief Brimah that are absent in other literature about the devout Yoruba Muslim migrant. Born around the late 1820s in Illorin (now part of Kwara State in Nigeria), Chief Brimah became wealthy at an early age through selling cattle. He relocated to the Gold Coast around 1870 to trade. According to Brimah, his grandfather "was known to have supported generous causes by giving cash or kind. On every Friday, he was providing food, money, clothing and other gifts to the poor."[46] It is possible Chief Alhaji Brimah was not just performing a religious obligation, but his big-heartedness gained him enormous popularity among both Gã mãŋtsɛmɛi and British colonial officials.

In general, Alhaji Brimah left an indelible legacy. His tenure brought a level of understanding and cooperation among various religious and ethnic migrant groups. Moreover, he was successful in expanding local migrant businesses and establishing trading towns like Cow Lane. Chief Brimah's tenure lasted less than a decade; he died on 4 May 1915. He left behind twenty-six children from several wives including Madam Fatima Okpedu, who was a descendant of a freed slave from Brazil. As noted in the case *Rashid Brimah & 3 Ors. v. Hadji M. B. Peregrino-Brimah*, some of his grandchildren (from different mothers) were entangled in property disputes that lasted for many years. These properties are located at Knutsford Avenue, Okaishie, and Central Accra. In my last interview with A. Olowun Toyin Peregrino-Brimah, he noted that the case ended in favor of the Peregrino-Brimah children because they had sufficient evidence to show that they were the rightful owners of the properties in dispute.[47]

Love stories involving Brazilian-Africans and local people went beyond the romance between Chief Brimah and Okpedu, which unfortunately did not end well. A number of Yoruba people besides Brimah also engaged in lasting marriage unions. According to the members of the Peregrino family (Peregrino-Brimah), their great-grandparents established other contacts in both Lagos and Accra that enabled their family to flourish over time.[48] The disputes over properties that Brimah and Okpedu left for these descendants have ruined their common family ties and destabilized their history. The Yoruba factor is significant in other discourse about the Brazilian and Tabom family trees in Ghana. There are other members of the community who have strong ties to other Yoruba migrants in Accra and in Lagos. According to Segun Peregrino, the marriage union between his grandparents has left a schism between their descendants, who continue to fight over the properties they inherited; nevertheless, the marriage between his grandparents left an enduring legacy that has allowed members of the Peregrino family group to keep both their Brazilian and their Yoruba names and cultures as they maintain lasting relations with their relatives in Lagos—their other *home*, where they travel occasionally.[49] In general, the history of cross-cultural interactions and exchanges between the Brazilian-Africans and other groups in the Gold Coast, especially with the Gã people, provides a fluid intersection for the transformation of their story. Put another way, as the descendants of the freed slaves planted themselves in local Gã cultures in the early 1900s, they "became Gã" through the way they self-identified and via their worldview.

The Mama Nassu and Mama Sokoto Factor

Among the other leading figures in the Brazilian returnee narratives are Mama Nassu and Mama Sokoto, whom many view as the founding fathers of the Brazilian-African diaspora in Accra. It is uncertain if they arrived at the same time, but both names appeared in several court documents regarding disputes over Brazilian land. The case *Jemima Nassu & org v. the Basel Mission & another* states that "lands were divided up amongst the Brazilians by their headman Sokoto and the land in dispute forms a portion of the land known as Mama Nassu's land."[50] Several family groups, including the Lutterodts, Peregrinos, and Nelsons, have established their ancestral roots to these individuals, who are believed to have been present when the early settlers were given gifts of land by Gã mãŋtsɛmɛi in the mid-1800s. Other family groups claim they are great-grandchildren of Nassu. However, collectively they do not seem to have answers as to why they do not share the same blood ties with other family groups who also claim Nassu as their great-grandparent. Indeed, it is possible that all these family groups share an ancestral lineage with Nassu mainly through bloodline. They do not seem to know more about Sokoto, and the records at PRAAD are also lacking. Some stories about Sokoto portrayed him in a negative light. Sokoto, like other ex-slaves, is believed to have owned a slave.[51]

On the one hand, considering the popularity of Nassu in narratives about the Brazilian-African diaspora and all his achievements, it is possible that some of these family groups do not have any actual ancestral ties to him but just want to claim an association with this figure for self-gratifying reasons. On the other hand, it is also possible that all of the groups have ties to Nassu but do not want to admit any evidence of common blood ties with other descendant groups with whom they do not want to associate. Such contradictions complicate the reconstruction of complete Brazilian and Tabom family trees in Ghana, resulting in inconsistencies when one compares the relationships of particular family groups that share the same family name. For instance, the Peregrinos in Accra do not embrace or acknowledge all other Ghanaians of Brazilian heritage that have the same name, despite their common genealogical origins. It is also possible that not everyone with a Peregrino name has any ties to the Brazilian-African diaspora narratives.

Unlike discourse about the Aguda in Nigeria, Benin, and Togo where names such as Da Rocha, Da Silva, and others whose ties to Brazil are somewhat established,[52] it is frustratingly difficult to resolve questions about the Brazilian-African diaspora in Ghana. Ghanaians with similar family names make claims to a Brazilian heritage on the basis of their Brazilian-Portuguese names. However, there is no easy way of verifying this.

Azumah Nelson We: The Role of the Brazilian and Tabom Chief

The flagbearer position is not the only role played by a particular family group. The selection of the freed Brazilians from the Nelson family as mãŋtsɛmɛi, literally translated "the owners" of the Brazilian-African community, to manage the affairs of the Brazilian-African diaspora did more than just set the stage for forging ties and attracting more settlers to Accra. Cross-cultural interactions and exchanges between Gã leaders and returnees groomed the Brazilians and their descendants to serve in various leadership capacities, which also aided the adjustment period. It is likely that Brazilian chief João Antonio Nelson, whose stool title was Nii Azumah II—the longest-reigning Brazilian leader, who ruled from 1865 until 1900—had a robust and fruitful engagement with the Tabom quarter. Nelson, who was born in Brazil in 1826 and arrived in Otublohum at the age of three, assimilated quite easily into Gã cultural norms at an early age. He was one of the few early settlers who attained such leverage among the returnees. Although it is possible that he played a vital role in the social history of Accra, it is not clear whether Nelson identified as a Brazilian, as did most of the settlers who arrived around the same time. On the one hand, based on a photograph of Nelson with Gã leaders, in which he appeared in a European-style suit and hat, one might say he leaned toward his Brazilianness. On the other hand, his long years in leadership of the Brazilian-African diaspora likely enabled him to showcase a dual identity. It is more likely that Chief Nelson spoke the Gã language after his long stay in Accra and his interactions with the people in Gã *mãŋ*. In general, the role of Brazilian and Tabom chiefs was different from existing local ones and left a mixed legacy.

Brazilian chiefs were not very visible during their interactions with the larger Gã communities and with British colonial officials. Besides their limited population size, there were other obstacles. Unlike Gã mãŋtsɛmɛi, who battled constantly against foreign intrusion and manipulation, Brazilian chiefs did not have the same power or authority because they were selected purposely to lead or operate within the jurisdiction of the Brazilian-African diaspora. The entire Brazilian-African community was subject to both colonial ordinances and laws established by the Gã paramountcy, or territories under the Gã king or stool. It is imperative to add that members of the Nelson family who served as Brazilian or Tabom chiefs were not the only ones with limited power in colonial Accra. Even the Gã mãŋbii, the original owners of Accra, were restricted by the colonial presence, particularly by such laws and ordinances as the Native Jurisdiction Ordinance of 1883, which was enforced by the British to weaken the capabilities of Gã kings and chiefs to collect and use revenue without British interference.[53] This policy threatened various profit-making ventures among the Gã leadership in Accra. The creation of the Tabom quarter at Otublohum and especially the selection of the returnees as chiefs showed that the Brazilian-Africans were no longer seen as foreigners. At a point in time they became part of the Gã paramountcy and were active in Gã society culturally, socially, commercially, and religiously.[54] However, the stark differences between the function of the Gã mãŋtsɛmɛi and the Brazilian mãŋtsɛmɛi cannot be overemphasized. There were varieties of chiefs in Accra. Brazilian chiefs were seen as *gboi* chiefs—that is, "visiting" or "honorary" chiefs.[55] The structure of Brazilian "chieftaincy" was different from that of the local chieftaincy in that they were not chiefs in the traditional Ghanaian sense. In addition to their unique roles, the Brazilians were leaders who acted as ceremonial chiefs, or *mãŋtsɛmei ni bɛ hewalɛ*, a Gã expression that translates as "chiefs with limited authority."

In essence, the returnees were characterized as *mãŋtsɛmɛi ni bɛ mãŋbii*—leaders without much power or subjects—but they were somewhat involved in Gã affairs despite their limited power. According to Elder George Aruna Nelson, members of his family who served as Brazilian chiefs and some returnees ruled part of Accra in the late 1890s. The elder implied that his ancestors were selected by the Gã leaders to lead the community because of their skills in tailoring, the way they dressed and "behaved" as Europeans, as well as their knowledge in drilling wells.[56] In my assessment, there is no proof that this story occurred in the history of the Gold Coast before or after the capital of the Gold Coast colony was moved from Cape Coast to Accra in 1877. Even if this was the case, the elements Elder Nelson referred to would not have had any major effect on why such a decision was made by the Gã leaders. The elder was likely referring to the elites among the Brazilian returnees who gained favors or respect among the Gã mãŋtsɛmɛi—members of the Brazilian-African diaspora who played prominent roles in Gã society in the early history of Accra, including members of the Ribeiro family.[57] As Roger S. Gocking has emphasized in his analysis of coastal communities in the Gold Coast, the Ribeiros used their wealth to negotiate marriages with prominent families from Accra.[58]

Brazilian and Tabom chiefs acted as the intermediaries between the Gã paramountcy and the Brazilian-African diaspora. Although they could not operate on the national scene, the authority of the Brazilian chiefs allowed them to settle disputes in their local communities, involve themselves in domestic issues of various kinds, and promote good relations with the people of Accra. Their responsibilities included ensuring some level of unity among the various families in order to showcase their shared Brazilian heritage. However, nearly a century of land disputes and factions led to fractured ties and heightened tensions between various family groups and placed their vision of harmony on the back burner. The role of the Nelsons in the Brazilian-African diaspora to some extent made the returnees visible among their people. Their general invisibility in broader Ghanaian society and their relevance to members of their communities in particular, however, remain problems in the twenty-first century, although Tabom chiefs have made huge efforts to reverse this trend.

The fact that the role of the Nelson chiefs has been overshadowed does not suggest that their broader involvement in the social history of Accra or Ghana is irrelevant. Clearly, the selection of Brazilians and their descendants as chiefs has had a lasting impact. Six members of the Nelson *we* have served since 1836: Nii Azumah I, who ruled from around 1836 through 1865; Nii Azumah II, between 1865 and 1900; Nii Aruna I, between 1900 and 1926; Nii Azumah III, about 1936–61; and Nii Azumah IV, from 1961 through 1981. The first two Brazilian chiefs were born in Brazil. There was a break in this tradition between 1981 and 1997, because of tension over the selection of a new Tabom chief. The current Tabom chief was selected in 1998.[59] Part of the public outcry in this instance occurred in 1981 after the death of Nii Azumah IV. Tensions escalated during preparations to select a new leader as other family groups challenged the long tradition of selecting mãŋtsɛmɛi from only the Nelson family group. Due to disagreements among the families, the stool remained vacant for eighteen years.[60] This contentious period lasted until 1998.

Nearly two decades of squabbling did not bring any different result: once again, another member of the Nelson family was selected to lead Ghana's Brazilian-African diaspora. His coronation title was Nii Azumah V. He has made important contributions to the community, such as his collaboration with the government of Brazil and the Brazilian embassy. This led to the renovation of the old Brazil House for tourism in 2007.

In addition to the cultural symbolism, Brazilian chiefs had other social responsibilities such as protecting Brazilian properties like land for posterity. During their court appearances, they mainly established the authenticity of Brazilian boundaries and challenged attempts by some descendants to claim land for individual family groups. In one of the court disputes, Brazilian chief Nii Azumah III, whose tenure occurred at the peak of the land disputes, proclaimed that "land granted to Brazilians has not been apportioned to [individual] groups or families or Heads of such groups or families."[61] Such public declarations were pervasive. In this particular case, the Brazilian chief sought to explain the original intentions of the first generation and their determination to create communities as a way of uniting the settlers and their descendants. However, a number of descendants held other views that challenged the notion of maintaining a communal society or preventing individual descendants from claiming pieces of the land their family inherited for particular uses. In this case, not only was the chief's main interest the promotion of unity, but he used this occasion to flex his political muscle. Nelson chiefs did more than just protect Brazilian lands from trespassers; in colonial courts, they demanded compensation from British colonial officials who took away Brazilian land for colonial projects.[62] Over time, mutual contacts and exchanges between the Gã people and the Brazilian-Africans, especially in the social history of Accra, served as a foundation for integrating the newcomers into Gã cultures.

Becoming Gã: The (Re)making of Brazilian-Tabom Identities

Gã traditions in particular and Ghanaian cultural practices in general overlap in other ways with respect to the Brazilian-Tabom story. Shared cultural traits are significant because they support the argument in this book that the narratives about the Brazilian returnees' presence in colonial Accra are incomplete without highlighting how Brazilian-African and Tabom cultures are closely linked with Gã/Ghanaian cultural traditions. Current generations lean more closely toward a Ghanaian identity and cultural practices than did their forebears. In "becoming Gã," those who adopt these cultural traits show the differences that existed between the first generation and subsequent ones, especially how acculturation or the borrowing of Gã culture by their offspring gave way to their deeper integration into local cultures. This does not totally mean that all Tabom people forgot about all that their Brazilian-African parents or grandparents passed on from one generation to the other. For instance, during the visit by Raymundo de Souza Dantas, first Brazilian ambassador to Ghana, in 1961, the Tabom who were present at a ceremony to welcome Dantas sang "Viva Iálá," a popular Bahian song, to welcome Idoline de Souza Dantas, the ambassador's wife.[63] Aspects of Brazilian cultures could not survive. Various changes that emerged in the Brazilian-Tabom story took on other forms in the postindependence era as descendants became even more involved in Ghanaian society. In general, the defining moment facilitated assimilation, especially after the demise of the early generation.

Copious outstanding ingredients sustained the Brazilian-African diaspora in the initial stages, stabilized their identity construction and reconstruction, and united the early settlers in the 1830s. This included the Gã mãŋtsɛmɛi selection of Nii Azumah I (Azumah Nelson), a leading member of the Brazilian returnees, as the community's first chief or official leader in 1836. As Gã customs demanded, the Brazilian elder was presented with a traditional stool to symbolize the local people's acceptance of the returnees into the Gã traditional area. The returnees, especially those from the Nelson family who accepted these prestigious positions, adjusted to their new environment. The initiation also symbolized the Brazilian chiefs' liberation from slavery and ascension to a new throne as the first *mãntsɛ*. His title as ruler was Nii Azumah I.[64] The initiation of the first Brazilian chief epitomized the cross-cultural fertilization and the "birth" of identity formation, which evolved over time. Although there is ongoing debate and disagreement about the one-dimensional process for selecting the Tabom *mãntsɛ*, this tradition of enstoolment has become a vehicle for uniting the Tabom community and for providing recognition of their presence in Ghana. On the whole, Gã-Tabom identities demonstrate the open-mindedness and wisdom of the returnees who accepted the advice by *Mãntsɛ* Tackie Komeh I to be part of the Gã paramountcy.

In terms of the growth of a vibrant diaspora, there have been both achievements, such as the selection of leaders, and failures, such as ongoing disputes over land, since the passing of the first generation of Brazilian-Africans. These changes underscore my assertion that there are differences between the traditions and cultural values of the returnees and their offspring. Part of the transformation began by the mid-nineteenth century when the early settlers married local people in Accra.[65] These unions knit the two groups together. Further, this had a momentous impact on their descendants, the Tabom, by the turn of the twentieth century. As Gã people, the Tabom celebrated *homowo* and embraced other Gã cultural practices. Like other ethnic groups in Ghana, the Tabom also use alcohol for various cultural rituals.[66] According to Ghanaian custom, practically for all ethnic groups, citizens do not talk to the chief directly. Communication is always done through the chief's spokesperson. This protocol is to maintain the structure of power and respect for the chief. During my first interview, Nii Azumah

V followed this custom. I spoke to the chief through an ɔkyeame (linguist), the chief's spokesman. The ɔkyeame's responsibility is to repeat in his own language the guest's message to the chief. During the interview, the linguist instructed me to present a bottle of schnapps (alcoholic drink), which was used to pour a libation.[67] This ritual helped pave the way for me to reconstruct Brazilian-Tabom history.

The history of the Brazilian-African diaspora shows that although the members share a similar heritage, they are not a homogeneous group. Their arrival in Accra, illustrates their complex processes of settlement in West Africa. They did not all live in the same location in Brazil, and there is no evidence that their voyages were coordinated from one shipping port or embarkation point. Furthermore, there is no evidence that all the returnees who boarded ships to Accra were from the same family or knew each other in Brazil. It is certain that the newcomers differed in terms of ethnicity, race (phenotype), religious faith, class, and profession. It is also clear that the liberated Africans and their offspring shared similar traits but also had some differences. Like other population groups from diverse class or social backgrounds who settled in Accra, the liberated Brazilian-Africans were also confronted with divisions along various lines. While part of the Brazilian population embraced education and invested heavily in commerce, both of which sustained class and social status, others devoted most of their time to continue various agrarian practices they brought from Brazil. In addition, both the older and younger generations created a social class system within their communities that made it easy for the wealthy class to disassociate themselves from the working class. For instance, most educated people, and merchants in particular, established connections with the upper echelon of colonial society—missionaries, Europeans, and wealthy expatriates that assembled in precolonial Accra from the mid-1800s. This stark binary created clearly marked lines that remained for a long time in their history. In his assessment of the history of the Brazilian-African diaspora, Roger S. Gocking relates that

> the second wave of Brazilians who came in the 1840s and 1860s were from a more privileged strata of Brazilian society. Most of them were Christians, and they entered Accra primarily as merchants. . . . They intermarried with other members of this elite, and their children branched out into occupations other than trading. . . . The Ribeiros [a Brazilian family] married into the Cleland family, a prominent Accra family, and also into the family of the famous Methodist missionary Thomas Birch Freeman.[68]

Besides the distinction Gocking provides, wealthy returnees, especially the merchants, identified as Europeans. They wore suits and hats and enrolled their children in European-run schools, while children of poor returnees and those who were not interested in Western education attended Islamic schools in their communities. Other Brazilian-Africans could not afford to put their children in schools and lived on the social periphery in remote areas where they invested their energy in farming in order to provide a level of economic security for their posterity. Some of these Brazilian-Africans thrived planting fruits such as mango all around Accra.[69]

Not all the Brazilian-Africans in the lower class invested in farming but sought alternative options to elevate their social status. It is important to add that Brazilian-Africans with no formal education generally ensured that their children and grandchildren became educated so they could in turn serve their parents in some capacity, especially in their old age. Some of the descendants relocated to urban or coastal Accra, where most commercial activity occurred, to acquire education or some level of skills and to interact with the diverse migrant population there. One descendant asserted that he traveled to the Bights (the Bight of Benin) in 1920 to learn engineering with the support of his parents, who were farmers.[70] Of course, not all members of later generations were interested in traveling abroad. Most stayed with their parents in the agrarian communities. Due to class disparities and other issues in the Brazilian-African diaspora, the second generation (those who were born from the mid-nineteenth century) in particular became entangled in various legal disputes over land in some areas of Accra. Other community divisions resulted from matters having to do with representation and leadership as various family groups challenged the validity of selecting leaders only from the Nelson family line. It is not clear whether the first waves of returnees were faced with similar challenges. We know, however, that the early settlers had different ways of dressing or identifying with Brazilian or Portuguese cultures.

Brazilian Bii Atale kɛ Amɛ Gbɛɛ

Brazilian clothing (*atale*) and their names (*amɛ gbɛɛ*) deserve some attention. Most of the early returnees appear in photographs wearing European-style attire, which set them apart. Not all the descendants adopted European-style clothes, hats, and costumes, even though most of their ancestors did so upon initial settlement in the Gold Coast. Some preferred to wear clothing that primarily expressed their Islamic or Christian faith. Others wrapped clothes loosely around their bodies. The use of European clothing was common in British colonial Accra more than a century before the arrival of the Brazilian returnees.[71] For example, a number of Tabom family photographs taken between 1835 and 1900 show the first Brazilian mãŋtsɛmɛi, who were born in Brazil, wearing suits as they performed their duties as Brazilian chiefs. Subsequent leaders who were born in Ghana dressed in local Ghanaian clothing both privately and when accompanied by an ɔkyeame to serve as a go-between for the chief and his guests. Even if the early Brazilian settlers wanted to identify with European outfits, over time their descendants did something different with their attire. Sometimes they wore local outfits. The contrast between the two groups shows a gradual process of assimilation. The transformation embodies the stark diversity in the Brazilian-African diaspora from the top down and the bottom up.

I have not come across any photographs of wealthy Brazilian-African women in Accra. It is widely held that on a few occasions, they would adorn themselves in European-style clothing, especially the wealthy class. The project "Letters from Brazil" provides a wide spectrum of photographs depicting the appearance of freed Brazilian women in Nigeria, Benin, Togo, and other locations.

Inheritance and Gender

Another area in which returnees from Brazil and their offspring experienced differences in customs is inheritance.[72] Inheritance among the Tabom people follows the traditional customs of Gã people. In terms of gender roles, past Gã traditions, like the practices of others in Ghana, had a degree of balance though cultural practices often favored males. Men, as sons, take the role of leaders of the family upon the death of their father or mother (when the father is already deceased), and they often use the properties they inherit to provide basic needs of the family. In some cases, the brother of the deceased parent takes care of the family when there is no male heir. Men who assumed a position of responsibility for a family are also required to take care of the widow.[73] It is not clear how or what form of practices took place among the first group of Brazilian-African returnees in Accra. In general, women were not assigned the role of responsible heir because of their status in the broader society.

In situations where a will was not made, especially in the early 1900s, descendants and various family members would gather around the father on his sick bed to ask questions about his properties and how they should dispose of them. During this emotional time, the one who was sick was also asked if he or she owed anyone money or any form of debt, or had other things to talk about. When possible, children also made their final requests of their dying parents. This custom was important to avoid future disputes or litigation after their deaths. For instance, during George Akotey Nelson's final days, one of his children, who had become immersed in Gã culture, asked his father to disclose a private transaction between them. He asked in Gã, "Ata negbɛ nsika lɛ yɔ?" This translates: "Father, where is my money?" Apparently his son had given him some money to keep, so he wanted to ensure that the transfer was settled or clarified in the will the father left behind to his brother, S. Q. Nelson.

Tabom Queen

In terms of the gender dynamics within the Tabom community from the early 1900s, women had power. Property in Brazilian-African communities could be passed on to either males or females, but male inheritance dominated this process. Brazilian women owned tracts of land and served as female family heads. They included Madam Yawah. Tabom women also served as landlords or proprietors. For instance, at the Scissors House women were responsible for the collection of property rent. According to *Mãŋtsɛ* Nii Azumah V, women in the community used such money partly to prepare for *homowo* festivities.[74]

A lot is known about the role of Brazilian-Tabom mãŋtsɛmɛi, who served as chiefs from 1836, but not much is known about the role of their women who held similar positions of power—*mãŋnyɛ*, a Gã word that literally means "a female leader of a community or society." In most Ghanaian cultures a king or chief works hand in hand with a queen mother, who plays various roles in their communities. In the Asante Kingdom in particular, a queen mother (or *ohemaa* in the Akan language) is owner of the nation. The story of Yaa Asantewaa, the queen mother of Ejisu who fought against the British in the late 1800s to oppose colonial rule, is one of the best-known accounts of Ghanaian women in the anticolonial nationalist struggle.[75] The Asante Kingdom is not the only location for tracing the influence of women. Women have occupied prominent positions of power in Gã history as well. According to Harry N.K. Odamtten, oral tradition reminds us of a great Gã female king, Naa Dode Akabi, whose story resonates in popular Gã songs.[76] In the case of the Tabom, women who serve as *mãŋnyɛ* have been given very little visibility; the focus is mainly on men from the Nelson lineage who have played this prominent role as Brazilian chiefs for more than a century.

PART 3

Diaspora in Full Circle: Home Is Ghana, Brazil Is Our Mother Country

Chapter 9

**Fading Diaspora and Receding Memory:
How the Brazilian Government and the Tabom
Are Preserving the Brazil House and Crisscrossing
the Atlantic in Full Circle**

> Once upon a time, Brazil had gone to Africa in search of slaves. Over the last five decades, Brazil has been traversing the African continent in search of trade and other relations... couched in terms of emphasizing historical and cultural links and ideas.
> —Anani Dzidzienyo

There are numerous continuities and changes in the Brazilian-African diaspora story. They include stories about the origins of mutual cultural ties between Brazil and the Tabom people and the ways in which these ties contributed to the Tabom people's strategic position in the tourism industry. Leaders of the Brazilian-African diaspora, individual members of the community, and institutions like the Brazilian embassy in Accra collaborated with other interested groups to preserve fading aspects of the Brazilian-African diaspora. Their ultimate goal was to move their history from the margins to the center of a burgeoning transatlantic history and global tourism for posterity. As a result of ongoing transformations in their story, a number of Tabom people have expressed their deep desires to visit Brazil, and others have already crisscrossed the Atlantic to connect with their Brazilian roots.

Memory facilitated ties between the Tabom and the Brazilian government and created innovative ways for the Tabom people to rebrand their history for economic reasons and for posterity. For instance, the Brazilian government and the embassy in Accra played a central role in pushing the tourism wheel as they worked closely

Chapter Nine

with the Tabom leadership and others to fill the void in heritage tourism in Ghana. To understand this winding process, it is significant to revisit the sacrifice the Lutterodts in particular made to set the wheel rolling—converting the "Warri House" to Brazil House for tourism. Differences between how the returnees and their offspring connected to Brazil at diverse historical periods using the opening of the Brazil House as a backdrop provides an overview of the growing historical, cultural, and economic partnerships between the two countries on both the local and national levels. However, past problems and the different levels of silence and challenges have hindered the growth of the Brazilian-African diaspora in Ghana.

It is a great disservice to tell the history of the freed Brazilian slaves and their offspring in Ghana without showing the ways in which it overlaps with other stories. In several parts of the book, I have provided a transatlantic perspective on the intersections, influences, and overlaps in the narratives of other ex-slaves from Brazil and Cuba who settled in different locations. Furthermore, the impact of the social history of the Gã *mãŋ*, British colonial officials, missionaries, and strangers and migrants in the Gold Coast on the Brazilian-African diaspora, beginning in the nineteenth century, were very essential. The narratives of other returnees from North America and the Caribbean also shaped the history of the Brazilian-African diaspora. This includes how African American businesspeople have made great progress in the tourism industry because of the advantages they have enjoyed due to the Ghanaian government's one-dimensional approach to tourism.[1] This narrow approach excludes the Tabom people from showcasing their ties to the Middle Passage or sites of memory.

The Tabom people can be characterized as a diasporan returnee community whose story has been placed on the margins for a variety of reasons. In fact, the Tabom have lived longer in Ghana than any other returnee group from North America or the Caribbean, but in the tourism sector their story has been overshadowed by newcomers from the diaspora. Returnee communities in Ghana, especially African Americans, have been fairly successful in navigating and positioning themselves in spatial spheres of tourism. Some of these returnees own guest houses, hotels, and motels and operate car rental and travel tour agencies that facilitate tourism. At these sites of grief they simultaneously shed tears and make monetary gains.

Over the years, the Tabom people, especially the Lutterodt family, whose ancestor Mama Nassu built what was known as the Warri House and is now known as the Brazil House, have become more aware of this one-sided approach. This new consciousness has energized the Tabom base. Part of this interest enabled the Lutterodt family and the Tabom leaders to work closely with the Brazilian embassy in Accra to place the Tabom story at the forefront of tourism in Ghana. On some levels this recent undertaking in the community, which resulted in the repairs to and the official opening of the Brazil House on 19 November 2007, was influenced by those who identified the deteriorated state of the Warri House and those who recognized its potential for profit-making via tourism. This edifice is a symbol of return, not only by Mama Nassu, the owner of the house, but by all the returnees. As Luis Fernando de Andrade Serra, the former Brazilian ambassador to Ghana, rightly stated during the opening ceremony, the construction of the house was part of a larger vision beginning a fresh life among their hosts, the Gã people.

The showcasing of their history has been shaped by various forms of performance, appropriation, and commodification—all of which sought to generate profit from symbols of slavery. For the Tabom people, the performance and commodification of the history of their ancestors from Brazil is about more than their leaders' and their community members' strategic showcasing and selection of which identity they prefer (Brazilian, Ghanaian, or Brazilian-Ghanaian). Rather, I borrow from Paulla Ebron's understanding of performance and the commodification of African heritage and their connections to the Middle Passage to explain these strategic choices.[2] Despite the public performance and display, beneath the surface there is evidence of receding memory among the Tabom when one examines uncertainties about what the meaning of Brazil House and a Brazilian heritage means to a portion of their population. Some kind of holistic innovation and motivation was therefore necessary or justifiable to resurrect the fading Brazilian-African diaspora. The rationale behind the repairs to and the opening of the Brazil House are good examples of how the Tabom people, like other returnees in Ghana and the Ghanaian government, have taken advantage of sites of memory and spaces of mourning such as Elmina and Cape Coast Castles in order to amass wealth and to raise revenue through the tourism industry.

The African diaspora extends beyond the New World, and the multiple reverse migrations from Africa to the New World and back to Africa are significant, especially how these multiple trajectories have shaped Tabom history in the twenty-first century. Most significantly, we can begin another conversation and draw attention to the importance of the Brazil House, including its intersection with Tabom people's visit to Brazil, its relevance to the survival of their history in Ghana, and its implications to Brazilian, Ghanaian/African, and African diaspora historiography. The renovation of the Brazil House for tourism has generated a different degree of excitement in the Tabom communities and made them more visible. Nonetheless, the Tabom people are not only interested in the money they will generate from tourists who visit the historical site at the heart of their community. Rather, they are reacting to decades of institutional neglect of their community and their history with the transatlantic slave trade. Put another way, the Ghanaian government's neglect of sites of memory in the Brazilian-African diaspora that are of equal historical significance as other landmarks on the

Chapter Nine

Figure 23. Elmina Castle.

coastline, especially São Jorge da Mina, which was built by Don Diego de Azambuja, a Portuguese, in 1482 as a trading post and is now called the Elmina Castle, at Elmina (figure 23),[3] and Cape Coast Castle, at Cape Coast,[4] gave the new Tabom leader and his community the right forum to make themselves more visible than they have ever been since the nineteenth century.

There is a wide range of literature about the significance of memory to people of African descent, especially in returnee communities. Three major diasporan returnee groups migrated to Ghana during and after the nineteenth century. They include the ex-slaves who left Brazil to resettle in the early 1820s, Caribbean or West Indian blacks who were brought by missionaries and colonial officials to assist with religious evangelism and colonial projects, and African Americans who also arrived on their own volition to support postcolonial reforms, to reconnect with their ancestral roots, and to seek economic opportunities in the tourism sector. Memory played a pivotal role in how the latter returnees, in particular, positioned themselves strategically to reconnect with their ancestral roots and to amass wealth via tourism. As returnees of different stripes and orientations continue to travel to Ghana, the Ghanaian government and other institutions dwell on a variety of historical landmarks that are listed among the World Heritage Sites. They have created convenient policies and an enabling environment to satisfy the needs of diaspora returnees. These institutions also draw from these sites of memory, their historical symbolism, and returnees' interest in material

Figure 24. Luiz Inácio Lula da Silva interacting with Tabom chief Nii Azumah V during his visit to Ghana.

culture to package various incentives to attract more returnees.[5] The Tabom people have also invested their energy and time with the support of the Brazilian embassy in Accra. Their ultimate goal is to meet the needs of the community, partly through the money they generate from the Brazil House, to preserve Brazilian-Tabom history for later generations.[6]

The Tabom leaders' initiatives are not only influenced by economic interests, but also by the need to express the dual identities that underlie what it means to be called a "Ghanaian-Brazilian." This important history that is tied to the horrific experiences that gave rise to the New World and the Black Atlantic has been sustained in other ways since the dawn of the twenty-first century. Broadly speaking, these developments embody the endless nature of reverse migrations. The epigraph to this chapter, for instance, underscores the transformation in relations between Brazil and Africa after the horrific Middle Passage experience that depleted Africa of its working force and skills to develop Brazil and other areas in the New World.[7] It also epitomizes different levels of Brazil's vested interest in Africa. Several historical figures in this book created different levels of opportunities and dialogue to help forge ties between the Tabom and Brazil. While Brazilian president Jânio Quadros and Raymundo de Souza Dantas, the first Afro-Brazilian ambassador to Ghana in the postindependence period, shaped past interactions, more recent collaborations were created by former Brazilian president Luiz Inácio Lula da Silva and Nii Azumah V, the Tabom chief, as illustrated in figure 24. This historic event was showcased in the *Daily Graphic*, a major state newspaper.[8]

Part of the historic speech by Lula during his first meeting with the Tabom people in 2005 is loaded with themes of memory, audacity, dual identity, and yearning for a home. The speech by Lula, the thirty-fifth president of Brazil who held office from 2003 to 2011, forms a magnetic force in the sense that it shows how he personified or made connections between the Tabom people and him when he said, "my brother, our common history symbolizes the capability of human beings to overcome difficulties. ... My presence here has the purpose of bringing to the Tabom people the respect and love of Brazilians."[9] In this speech, it is not clear if Lula is saying he shares a common ancestral origin with the Tabom or if he is indirectly making a connection between his humble beginning and his ascendency to the echelon of politics—his rise from a street vendor to trade union leader to the president of Brazil. Lula's speech calls attention to the returnees' determination and their descendants' commitment to preserving their Brazilian identity and heritage—especially the Tabom people's efforts to restore the Brazil House and other historical monuments in their community.[10] Also, Lula's speech shows aspects of mutual relations between the two groups in their efforts to cement their common ancestral heritage and to forge future ties in tandem.

During the ceremony several prominent people also made various statements emphasizing both the historical and cultural linkages as well as the mutual exchanges between the Tabom and Brazil. One such statement by Nii Azumah V spelled out the relevance of the contributions by the Brazilian government in preserving the Brazil House and the ways in which the historical symbol could solidify memory of their heritage and also impact Accra. He declared,

> At this juncture, may I express my sincere appreciation to the Brazilian Government for the many efforts it has made toward rehabilitating the Brazil House at Jamestown, Old Accra. We are happy about this project, which we believe will go a long way to restore Jamestown to its old beauty, and by and large add to the development of this country. The house will also act as a Documentation Center to provide historical information on the Tabom.[11]

Mãŋtsɛ Nii Azumah V's response, in particular, underscores the pivotal place of Brazil in the Tabom people's ideation, the role of the Brazilian government in the restoration of the Brazil House, and the significance of the Brazilian government to the development and maintenance of ties between the Tabom people and Brazil. The Tabom people hoped that this relationship would lead to improved conditions in the Tabom community and the Gã community in general. Not only do these two important exchanges highlight past dialogue; they also support the ongoing interests in the reconstruction of Brazilian history in Ghana. The Ghanaian government and other foreign institutions, including the United Nations Educational, Scientific and Cultural Organization (UNESCO), have also been drawn into this reverse migration story. The Tabom people's ancestral heritage, especially monuments tied to the Middle Passage, reminds us of the Brazilian-African presence in Ghana from the early nineteenth century. Moreover, the competing forces and overlapping interests embedded in the epigraph provide insight into our understanding of Brazilians' cultural and economic interests in Ghana since the postindependence era. This fledgling dialogue also reflects what the current cross-cultural interactions and exchanges mean to the future of Brazilian history in Ghana.

Further, two years, 1961 and 2007, became symbolic periods in the mutual relations between the Tabom people and the government of Brazil as they forged cultural and historical links. The former era marks the first time Brazil extended or opened diplomatic relations with the new nation of Ghana and established the first major contact with the Tabom community; the latter is emblematic of efforts to restore historical monuments like the Brazil House for tourism. As we shall see later, the 1960s, in particular, were very critical because it was during this period that the Brazilian government appointed Raymundo de Souza Dantas, an Afro-Brazilian, as the first Brazilian ambassador to Ghana to establish both cultural and economic ties between the two countries. In fact, this was the first time Brazil appointed a Brazilian of African descent to represent the nation abroad. In Anani Dzidzienyo's words, this form of political amendment epitomized the "genesis of the problems located in the contradictory signals characterizing Brazilian presence in continental Africa since 1961."[12] It was during this period of diplomatic representation that the first "seed" of Tabom-Brazilian relations was planted. The fledgling relations between the two countries and the Tabom people's mounting awareness of their ancestral homeland in Brazil—especially their plans to visit Brazil—demonstrate how Dantas's visit as well as the diplomatic seed he planted and the exchanges that followed afterward have germinated over the last fifty years.

Not all Ghanaians of Brazilian ancestry have shared these ties or consciousness of another homeland somewhere else or notions of a cultural bond that binds part of the descendant population to Brazil. Mixed feelings about an ancestral homeland in Brazil, particularly evidence of a double consciousness or identity crisis, help to explain why the Tabom people are still confronted with a host of issues, including divisions in the community that have prompted deeper assimilation into Ghanaian culture. Even though things have improved steadily, the squabbles that began after the demise of the early settler group still linger. In fact, they have matured and have taken on different characteristics. The ripple effects of past conflicts over land, such as who should manage the properties they inherited from their forebears, have also stifled unity and progress. While it is not in the scope of this chapter to provide a detailed analysis of the first generation of Brazilian returnees, it is crucial to recognize their legacy, their contributions as they were echoed by Lula, and the implications of their legacy to the history of the current generation of the Tabom people. Their legacy is particularly important to the current dialogue taking place in Ghana between the Tabom people, the government of Brazil, the Brazilian embassy, the government of Ghana, and other entities. This important conversation has carved new channels for reconciling historical linkages along both cultural and economic lines and has created a viable bridge between the past, the present, and the future, despite the divisions and the dimness of their future. On the whole, it underscores the multifaceted dimensions of reverse migrations or diasporas in reverse, part of which intersect with heritage tourism.

In terms of burgeoning tourism in Ghana, the leaders of the Brazilian-African diaspora are conscious of the effects of the Ghanaian government's and tourism industry's treatment of their history. Despite the Tabom story's significance to larger questions about the transatlantic slave trade, identity formation, and heritage tourism as well as broader Ghanaian history, these institutions placed it on the periphery for almost five decades. One of the concerns by Elder William Lutterodt during our interview was that the proximity of Warri House to the Atlantic waters provided an ideal location for building hotels and guest houses for tourists, yet it was not considered by the tourism industry. The old man then declared that, "anybody who is interested in running the museum [now Brazil House] we will give it to him."[13] It is obvious that he is not satisfied with how the Brazil House is advertised or showcased in the tourism industry. In addressing part of this quandary the Tabom people have addressed the marginalization of their history and their contributions to the social history of the Gold Coast over the years. In doing so, I do not minimize the progress the Tabom leadership has made so far and the importance of their mutual relations with the Brazilian government and the Brazilian embassy in Accra. Neither do I ignore how these reciprocal exchanges facilitated the preservation of their history and the repairing of historical monuments in their communities, particularly the opening of the Brazil House for tourism in 2007, two years after Lula's historic visit. Lula's promise to invite a delegation from the Tabom community to visit Brazil has also fueled the Tabom people's interest for almost a decade. Trending developments from the dawn of the twenty-first century provide insight and enhance our understanding of the preservation and the reconstruction of Brazilian-Africans' history in Ghana.

THE BIRTH OF BRAZIL-TABOM RELATIONS IN THE 1960S AND HERITAGE TOURISM

Abaaba sɛ is a Gã word that literally means stepping back to the past. In applying this notion of looking backward or reconnecting with one's ancestral past, it is imperative to trace the origins of mutual relations between the Tabom and Brazil. Brazilian returnees' history in Ghana in the nineteenth century, which began after their migration from Brazil to Nigeria and includes voyages to the Gold Coast, relied heavily on memory.[14] Although Brazilian history in Ghana flourished and gradually evolved, there is no evidence of any major interactions between the Brazilian government and the returnees at the beginning of their settlement in Ghana. Some scholars have noted that a number of Aguda returnees who relocated to Nigeria and other areas attempted to go back to Brazil because of the divisions and religious competitions that developed among them.[15] It is unclear how the Brazilian returnees in general maintained lasting relationships with Brazil in the latter part of the nineteenth century and early twentieth century. For settlements in other areas in West Africa, historian Michael Turner has shown that the first phase of a return to Brazil developed when a number of Brazilian returnees—the first generation of slaves who settled along the coastline of Nigeria, Benin, and other locations—returned to Brazil for trading purposes.[16]

There are no records I know of that show that returnees who settled in Ghana traveled back and forth to Brazil during the nineteenth century, as the Aguda did, or retained any ties with the Brazilian authorities. Despite what looked like the disappearance of contact between Brazil and the returnees in Ghana, especially in the 1800s, a sizable number of returnees visited and maintained relationships with their relatives who settled in Benin, Nigeria, and other countries in West Africa.[17] In the twentieth century, however, the first major attempts at interaction occurred under the leadership of Jânio Quadros, the twenty-second president of Brazil. He came into office in January 1961 and resigned in August the same year. During his tenure, Quadros appointed Dantas as the first black Brazilian ambassador to Ghana on 13 April 1961. Obviously, Dantas's visit contributed to the history of the community. Brazilian historian Anani Dzidzienyo inquires about the challenges that confronted Dantas—not necessarily because he had to work on a different cultural and political turf from 1961 through 1964, but largely because his appointment symbolized a shift from Brazil's long history of marginalization of people of African descent from the national and international arena. Put differently, the appointment of Dantas was an attempt by President Quadros's administration to paint a new picture or image of Brazil—to show their interest in diversity—at least to Afro-Brazilians and to the outside world. The

Chapter Nine

hasty manner in which Dantas was sent to the new independent nation of Ghana was part of the reforms the Brazilian government initiated to improve Brazil's poor record abroad—especially in terms of diversifying their foreign posts to meet these needs. As noted in the epigraph, part of this move was to redeem the image of Brazil from that of a slave nation that once held nearly half of the enslaved Africans to a new nation that was interested in trade partnerships with the societies they once exploited. This problem was a reflection of internal difficulties that were colored by discourse on race and racism on both the local and national levels. Anani Dzidzienyo is of the opinion that Brazil has not done enough to address the race question nor diversified her diplomatic stations in Africa. In Dzidzienyo's opinion,

> Brazilian relations with African countries have been characterized by an inability to reconcile internal race relations with its packaging for overseas consumption.... Brazil's use of history and African culture to present the country and its peoples to newly independent African countries was an innovation.... One Afro-Brazilian Ambassador in nearly half a century is quite a record.[18]

When we analyze the perceptions the Tabom have about Brazil, there is a disconnection between the problems of racial inequalities in Brazil, which scholars such as Anani Dzidzienyo, Michael Hanchard, Abdias do Nascimento, Thomas E. Skidmore, Mieko Nishida, Edward Telles, and others have studied, and the knowledge the Tabom people have about this contentious subject.[19] For instance, during Dantas's interaction with the Tabom people, Nii Azumah III, the Tabom chief from 1936 to 1961, declared,

> It is a fact that none of us here present have ever visited Brazil but that is not important: we continue to consider Brazil as our mother country Mr. Ambassador [Dantas]: for this opportunity of being together in this festive occasion in Ghana . . . We feel it is our duty to offer this durbar [meeting], as you are the legitimate representative of a country we consider, as I already said, our mother country.[20]

What stands out in Nii Azumah III's speech is the manner in which he personified the ties between descendants and Brazil—his use of the word "our mother country" and his description of Brazil as the home of the Tabom people. Indeed, certainly, the term "mother country" is repeated on two occasions in this public announcement, and one cannot help but interrogate the rationale behind this bold assertion. Clearly, the Tabom chief, who was born in Accra, Ghana, in 1877, underscored evidence of his memory of his ancestral past. This has a striking resemblance to what Lula said in his speech when he interacted with the Tabom people for the first time. He declared that "my presence here has the purpose of bringing to the Tabom people the respect and love of Brazilians."[21] Chief Nii Azumah III's parents maintained and passed on their knowledge of Brazil to his generation. In addition to his knowledge of Brazil, Nii Azumah Nelson III's reference provides a glimpse of the gradual transition between the older Tabom and the generations that followed. This raises important theoretical questions about how returnees and their descendants fashioned their identities upon return to Africa and, as in the case of the chief, after their births in Ghana.[22] Based on Nii Azumah III's memory and his attachment to what he described as his "mother country" as well as the oral traditions and the interviews I have conducted for about a decade, I have come to the conclusion that descendants who were born in the nineteenth century retained their memory of Brazil through the assistance of their parents. The same cannot be said of a large segment of the population who did not pass on their history to the subsequent generations from the mid-twentieth century through the dawn of the twenty-first century. This clearly marked line sets the earlier and the later generations apart.

Dantas's role as the first ambassador to Ghana was very important to the development of current relations. Quadros's selection of Dantas sustained ties between Brazil and the independent nation of Ghana. Quadros's short term in office laid a solid foundation for lasting relations between Brazil, the Tabom people, and the Ghanaian government in general. President Quadros's plans to build ties with Ghana were as short-lived as his tenure, which lasted about seven months—from January 31 to August 25, 1961, the shortest Brazilian presidency. Four months after Dantas delivered his speech to the Tabom people, Quadros's term came to an abrupt end. He resigned mainly because of his frustration and impatience with reforms. Three years later there was chaos in Brazil. Political instability there led to military dictatorship, which lasted from 1964 to 1985. Thomas E. Skidmore provides insight about the military regime and how the military juntas ushered in a new era of economic depression and inflation.[23] Over two decades of military rule in Brazil complicated and nearly dissolved the fledgling relationship that had been cultivated between Brazil and the Tabom people. According to *Mãŋtsɛ* Nii Azumah V, Dantas's first visit to Ghana, where he met with Nii Azumah III, the Tabom elders, and members of the Tabom community, marked a new beginning in Brazilian-African and Tabom narratives in Ghana in the twentieth century. Dantas remained in this position until the mid-1960s when the political instability in Brazil led to a period of military dictatorship; thereafter Dantas served in other diplomatic capacities in Togo.

There is limited information about what happened between the Tabom people and the Brazilian embassy during this tumultuous period in Brazilian history. There were no major interactions between the Brazilian government and the Tabom people from 1965 through 1985, when the new leaders in Brazil established a military dictatorship in the country. The tenure of Fortunato Antonio Nelson, who became known as Nii Azumah IV, the Tabom chief from 1961 to 1981, did not bring the Tabom people any closer to Brazil. However, there is ample evidence that the new leader played a major role in the relations between the Brazilian embassy and the Tabom community. He served as the spokesperson for the Tabom people during the reign of his father Nii Azumah III, the former chief, from 1936 to 1961.[24]

In *The Politics of Military Rule in Brazil, 1964-1985*, Skidmore chronicles the genesis of military rule in Brazil and shows how the Latin American nation evolved from an authoritarian to a democratic government by 1985.[25] Skidmore examines the goals of the military, the economic conditions of Brazil over two decades, the military's repression and human rights abuses, and how the military juntas weakened relations between Brazil and other foreign nations. Coincidentally, a year after the Brazilian military juntas began their era of authoritarian rule the new independent nation of Ghana had its first military coup. On 22 February 1966 President Kwame Nkrumah was overthrown. Ghana experienced several different periods of political instability thereafter.[26] The last military takeover in Ghana was on 4 June 1979, led by Flt. Lt. Jerry John Rawlings. The political turbulence came to an end in 2002 when Ghana returned to civilian rule. Evidence of diplomatic relations between Brazil and Ghana during the era of military rule exists, but this information shows that such relations or interactions did not strengthen ties between the Tabom people and Brazil. It took almost forty years for the Tabom people to reestablish lasting ties with Brazil. By and large, the selection of Nii Azumah V as the new Tabom chief in 1998 turned things around. He should be credited for serving as the bridge that linked the Tabom people once again to Brazil. Part of his vision was not only to unite the Brazilian-African diaspora but also to ensure that they became noticeable in Ghana and to excel in heritage tourism.

(RE)CONSTRUCTING AND (RE)ARRANGING TOURISM: THE SIGNIFICANCE OF SITES OF MEMORY

Heritage tourism, which draws heavily from the Middle Passage experience and cultural ties and is sometimes based on economics, has evolved in Ghana in the last three decades. Nonetheless, past policies about sites of memory for heritage tourism largely favored other diasporan returnees who relocated to Ghana in the postindependence era, especially the 1980s. The Ghana Tourist and Monument Board and the Ministry of Tourism and Diasporan Relations mainly focused on how to preserve, remodel, and promote tourism to the Elmina and Cape Coast Castles to generate jobs and revenue for the country. The Ministry of Tourism and Diasporan Relations, in particular, was created around 2001 to showcase Ghana's pivotal role in Pan-Africanism and to channel the cultural interests of diasporan returnees toward various sites of memory where most returnees make claims to a dual identity.[27] The other objective was to direct returnee entrepreneurs to growing commercial activities that have developed at these historical sites since the 1990s.[28] According to scholars in tourism studies, it is vital to underscore the significance of sites of memory in "roots tourism, diaspora tourism, genealogy tourism or simply personal heritage tourism" and their significance to diasporan or returnee communities.[29] Like other returnees in Ghana, descendants of Brazilian-Africans in Ghana are aware of the significance of slave forts and castles in Ghana. The new awareness generated by the Tabom people has led to long-term plans to restore other historical landmarks fixed in their community.

This important undertaking raises a number of questions. How far have the Tabom people come on the restoration of historical sites in their communities? Will this endeavor enhance the process of preserving Brazilian-African history in Ghana when most members of the younger generation have immersed themselves deeply into Ghanaian culture? What is the implication of the opening of the Brazil House, other sites of memory within Tabom communities, and other sprawling tourist sites in Ghana to disciplines such as tourism studies, archaeology studies, social/cultural anthropology, and the study of material culture? What are the implications of these tourist sites to the reconstruction of Ghanaian/African and African diaspora history in the twenty-first century?

By engaging these questions and exploring transnational networks, cross-cultural interactions, and economic exchanges in Brazilian returnees' history in the last fifty years, since the first ambassador was sent to Ghana, we see evidence of interchanging identities, varying textures of memory, and the evolving character of the Brazilian-African diaspora. Primarily, evidence of silences and apathy among the current generation and their determination to travel to Brazil shows fluidity in their history. Contrarily, what the complex narratives demonstrate is that the African diaspora stretches beyond the slave experiences of the New World. Further, the ways in which symbols of slavery such as the Brazil House have reshaped discourse about reverse migrations in Ghana shows the impact of the Middle Passage experience on both memory and identity formation beyond the New World. In other words, the process of remembering and refashioning identity continued through the twenty-first century.

In Ghana there are many archaeological remains that remind us of its central role in the transatlantic slave trade. It is believed that nearly twenty thousand tourists have visited slave forts and dungeons in Ghana annually since the 1990s.[30] This statistic does not include those who have visited the Brazil House since 2007 because there are no figures available. In fact, improper documentation or recording of visitors to the Brazil House has contributed to this problem. The involvements of the Lutterodt family in transforming the Warri House where most of the family members grew up to Brazil House, as well as the initiation of *Mãŋtsɛ* Nii Azumah V as the new Tabom chief in 1998, both of which occurred at the height of global tourism in Ghana, are beginning to address some of these omissions. When Nii Azumah V became more informed about the significance of heritage tourism as an avenue for displaying the Tabom story and developing economic benefits, he prioritized making their neglected past and ancestral history with Brazil visible. To properly link the fledgling relation between the Brazilian government and the Tabom people and place the economic interests of the Tabom people in a historical, commercial, capitalist, and global context, it is imperative to focus on other cultural and economic forces that drove these interactions and shaped new awareness in the Tabom community. These interactions were mainly between returnee communities, tourists, pilgrims, and Ghanaians as well as the Ghanaian government and various tourism institutions.

Transnational structural ties forged between Ghanaians and African American and Afro-Caribbean returnees since the 1980s have some things in common with those of the Tabom people in both cultural and economic terms. Although these returnees and the Tabom share similar migration experiences, they diverge on some historical grounds. For instance the Tabom people's assimilation into Ghanaian cultures—especially their ability to speak Ghanaian languages fluently and participate in local cultural rituals in Accra and other areas in Ghana—set them apart. Additionally, the Tabom people have successfully reconnected with their African roots insofar as they have been completely immersed into local Ghanaian cultures. This achievement did not happen overnight; it occurred through almost a century of assimilation, adjustment, and negotiation with local Gã people and other cultural groups in Ghana. Despite this cultural advantage, their ties to the transatlantic slave trade were ignored in discourse about heritage tourism.

There are various features of tourism in Ghana. Culturally and politically, Ghana has served as an outlet for exploring black culture, black pride, black identity, black liberation, and Pan-Africanism and was once seen as the mecca of African liberation movements for infusing black consciousness in the 1950s.[31] Ghana has other historical significance in areas of tourism. There are several explanations for this. During the transatlantic slave trade about forty-five forts and slave dungeons along the West African coastline were built in Ghana. This unmatched record attracts returnees who travel across the Atlantic Ocean to trace their ancestry in this region.[32] The slave castles and dungeons serve multiple purposes that I cannot include in my analysis. It is imperative to add that for almost six decades various sites of memory in Ghana have become intersections for cultural, emotional, religious, and spiritual points of reunion for returnees and the spirits of their ancestors.[33] Ironically, although the members of the Brazilian-African diaspora were the first group of returnees to settle in Ghana, they were overshadowed by other returnees who actually relocated to Ghana over a century after them.

Since the 1960s, African Americans in particular and returnees in general have used these sacred spaces as sites to reconnect with the spirits of their ancestors, to gain emotional healing for the atrocities that were committed against their ancestors, to find meaning to many unanswered questions about their roots, and as emotional renewal for their battered souls. According to a number of returnees and visitors to Ghana, the dungeons are the location where the hearts and souls of the living and the dead cross paths.[34] At the same time, the historical monuments provide the government of Ghana with revenue through tourism. Indeed, these historical shrines have also become new sites of contestation because they do not only provide historical facts but also constitute stages for political and cultural statements, especially for those among the returnee population who are determined to prevent foreign institutions such as UNESCO from "white washing" what they characterized as past atrocities of the slave trade.[35] It is against this backdrop that tourism in the country evolved. Part of the polemics is about which sites deserve attention and are useful for generating revenue. Knowing well that the Brazilian-African diaspora, like other returnees and Ghanaian institutions, could benefit vastly from the tourism sector, the Tabom people as others have also created a conducive environment for the appropriation and performance of their Brazilian heritage.

THE APPROPRIATION OF AFRICAN HERITAGE: THE GHANAIAN GOVERNMENT, RETURNEES, AND OTHERS

My discussion of the appropriation of African heritage is derived from Paulla Ebron's analysis of the various ways Africans in the diaspora—particularly returnees in Ghana—commodify or look back to symbols of their ancestral past, such as the slave castles and dungeons, and find creative ways of showcasing their transatlantic ties and benefiting from these historical symbols, especially in monetary ways. Beneficiaries include returnees, Ghanaians, and foreign institutions like travel agencies. However, rather than examining the multiple ways different communities, groups, and institutions benefit from sites of memory, most scholars blame Ghanaians and the Ghanaian government for making profit from these sites of memory and sorrow via tourism, revenue collection, and memorabilia that local people sell to tourists.[36] Considering the capital that is needed for economic development in Ghana, this is a justifiable vision. However, such narrow conclusions about who benefits from the historical landmarks do not take into consideration how various returnee groups make profit at these sites of grief. It is obvious that the Tabom people's effort to participate in the commercialization of African heritage and history—especially through revenue from historical sites in Ghana—is not a new phenomenon but a growing trend in the country and other parts of Africa. What we are witnessing within the Tabom community today is another transnational discourse that seeks to enhance tourism in Ghana using one's ancestral ties to the transatlantic slave trade as a point of reference—in some cases, for expressing a sense of entitlement to these historical landmarks.

In terms of discourse about the African diaspora, it cannot be limited to only one side of the Atlantic (the New World). Put in another way, the ways in which people of African origins remember slavery and especially how they construct and reconstruct their identities cannot be restricted to the New World alone. Reverse migrations also show how black identity is contested, appropriated, and constructed in the diaspora, particularly within growing diasporan communities in Ghana where sites of memory and the refashioning of identities work in tandem. In short, diasporan returnees and the Tabom people are now part of this phenomenon and are determined to promote their history on a global scale in capitalist arenas. The Tabom people generally claim that their history has not only been ignored for over half a century in past Ghanaian historiography and Ghanaian public school curricula, but also by the Ghana Tourist and Monument Board and by UNESCO's World Heritage Sites.[37] For example, although the Tabom people and African Americans have unique historical backgrounds and different racialized experiences, they share similar issues connected with slavery. However, in Ghana they have had different access to and visibility around sites of memory.

The economic and cultural representations of slavery I have underscored are relevant to both the Tabom and African Americans; their experiences and interests intertwine on a number of levels. However, one of the striking differences is that the Tabom have no qualms with who renovates Elmina and Cape Coast Castles in the Central Region to make returnees from North America and the Caribbean visible or accommodate their cultural and economic needs. Rather, they are determined to change the angle of the debate to promising sites for future tourism within their own backyard—focusing on the Brazilian-African diaspora along the coast of Otublohum and Swalaba instead of the Central Region and current major sites. The tourism vocabulary and experiences of the Tabom overlap with other returnee communities elsewhere. In Benin, West Africa, where the Aguda people settled in the nineteenth century, there is growing awareness about the significance of Afro-Brazilian heritage in tourism. This, in part, led to the annual enactments and performances of African cultures during events like the Vodum Whydah Festivals.[38] In her recent work about Afro-Cuban returnees in Lagos, Nigeria, Solimar Otero explores various sites of memory, the significance of these historical symbols to tourism, and the activities of vibrant Aguda communities in Nigeria.[39]

The Tabom people have their own ideas about how to preserve and restore their ancestral heritage, their monuments, and their history, which can be traced back to slavery in Brazilian plantations from the sixteenth to the nineteenth centuries.[40] They are responding, in part, to profit-making ventures in the tourism sector that seek to (re-)create a new Brazil in Ghana. This aspect of African diaspora history solidifies existing theories that underscore transnational or cross-cultural networks that are largely shaped by both cultural and economic factors. The Tabom did not make this progress on their own; they received giant support from the Brazilian government and the embassy in Accra.

LULA DA SILVA'S HISTORIC VISIT TO GHANA: CULTURAL AND ECONOMIC FACTORS

The resilience portrayed by the Tabom people in their efforts to preserve their past and strengthen their bonds with Brazil materialized when President Lula da Silva finally accepted an invitation to visit Ghana on 12 April 2005—the first visit by any sitting Brazilian president. During the visit, Lula met with Nii Azumah V, a high-level delegation from the Tabom community, and former president of Ghana John Kofi Agyekum Kufuor, who took keen interest in Ghana's relationship with Brazil as a means of furthering his economic agenda.[41] Lula's visit had three objectives: to solidify the cultural relations between Brazil and the Brazilian-African diaspora as a means of reinforcing the work of former Brazilian president Jânio Quadros and Ambassador Raymundo de Souza Dantas in 1961; to use his interactions with the Tabom people to extend his reforms on diversity back home in Brazil, as he did during his other visits to returnees' places of settlements in West Africa; and to promote economic agreements between Brazil and Ghana in areas including salt production and exports. Although Lula's visit to Accra was brief, he addressed the cultural aspects of his mission when he met with Nii Azumah V and members of the Tabom community. The two leaders acknowledged the lasting ties that bind the Tabom people and the people of Brazil, and they later discussed future cultural and economic cooperation.

During the durbar to welcome Lula, the Tabom people showcased the significance of the Brazilian-African diaspora, particularly the ways in which they have bridged the story of their ancestors with their own experiences as Ghanaians. They highlighted their construction of both Ghanaian and Brazilian identities and their nostalgic feelings for their ancestral roots in Brazil. Both Lula and Nii Azumah V stated the central role of the Brazil House to the survival of Brazilian-African and Tabom history. The gathering also gave the Tabom delegates the opportunity to introduce part of the Tabom population to the Brazilians. Afro-Brazilians such as the famous musician Gilberto Passos Gil Moreira—popularly known as "Gilberto Gil" and Lula's minister of culture from 2003 to 2008—got the opportunity to interact with the Tabom people.[42]

In addition to sparking linguistic, educational, and economic endeavors, Lula's historic visit aided in making the historical cultural sites and monuments, particularly the Brazil House, visible to the public two years later. The Brazil House and the Scissors House were once inhabited and used by the Brazilian returnees in the 1800s for the development of their history and their culture. While the latter site did not survive a 2007 fire outbreak in the area, the former continues to attract local people and foreigners who primarily visit for educational purposes. According to *Mãŋtsɛ* Nii Azumah V, there are future plans to construct "Tabom City" that would include a Tabom clinic, a Tabom library, and Tabom schools.[43] According to Nii Azumah V, to cement the ties between the two groups, President Lula da Silva extended an invitation to the Tabom *mãŋtsɛ*, his elders, and some members of the Tabom community to visit Brazil in August 2005.[44] This was a great opportunity for the Tabom leadership and others in the community. Nonetheless, the promise has not materialized because of various factors beyond the Tabom people's control. This promise had a better chance within the first year, but it dissipated over time. The Tabom *mãŋtsɛ* states that the visit was postponed to a future date because of the Tabom people's participation in the *homowo* festival, an annual cultural celebration by the people in the Gã traditional area in Accra.

Local politics in Brazil and change in government also hindered Lula's promise several times. During the end of Lula's first term in office, he came under enormous pressure and attacks from several fronts. Some of Lula's critics raised questions about various social and racial problems that confronted Brazilians of African descent, most of whom remained on the margins of Brazilian society. One may ask why Lula was interested in inviting the Tabom people to Brazil when he had not been able to meet the promises he made to landless Brazilians and poor working-class Afro-Brazilians during his last political campaign. What was Lula's political vision? Part of this agenda has been addressed by scholars who have interrogated Brazil's motivation for exploring other avenues to redeem Brazil's image as a slave nation and reposition it as in tune with the new global order in the areas of cultural and trade relations. Dzidzienyo notes that, "over the last five decades, Brazil has been traversing the African continent in search of trade and other relations... couched in terms of emphasizing historical and cultural links and ideas."[45]

There is plenty of evidence pointing to the fact that the Brazilian government has a larger agenda beyond cementing and showcasing their shared history and cultures with the Tabom people. To gain even more popularity in the country and to solidify past ties with the Tabom people, the Brazilian government established joint trade and economic programs with the Ghanaian government to enhance salt production in both countries. The economic partnership between Brazil and Ghana cumulated in the Ghana–Brazil Chamber of Commerce and Industry, which was officially opened on 13 April 2005 in Accra during Lula's visit. It was launched by Kufuor, officials from the Ministry of Trade and Foreign Affairs in Ghana, and officials from the Brazilian embassy. The primary goals of this economic partnership were the expansion of transnational economic ties between the two countries in areas of salt production, exports, sugar, paper production, cocoa, shea-nut butter, and bauxite and the exploration of further economic exchanges between the two countries in the twenty-first century.[46] During his tenure, Lula visited several African countries including Nigeria, Guinea Bissau, Senegal, and others to strengthen and create new ties between Brazil and these nations. Lula's ties with the Ghanaian government were remarkable. During the establishment of bilateral cultural and economic cooperation between Ghana and Brazil, President Kufuor of Ghana expressed Ghana's appreciation to the Brazilian president and decorated Lula da Silva with the highest state honor, the Star of Ghana, at a state banquet held in his honor. The citation read, "you are an outstanding democrat.... Your government since its inception forged close cooperation with African countries, as a consequence of its development, Ghanaian–Brazilian relations have also been strengthened further."[47]

If Lula was not successful in carrying out his promise of bringing the Tabom people to Brazil during his tenure, we cannot deny the fact that he was effective in other endeavors that opened the Brazilian-African diaspora to tourism in Ghana. For instance, similar to the attention the first generation received after they were offered vast land by Gã *Mãŋtsɛ* Tackie Komeh I in the early nineteenth century, the history of the Tabom people has been showcased once more locally, nationally, and internationally at the dawn of the twenty-first century.

Chapter Nine

The Opening of the Brazil House

President Lula's and Dantas's visits created new hope for the Tabom people. Through various efforts and the support of the Brazilian embassy in Ghana, the Ghanaian government, the Ghana Tourist and Monument Board, UNESCO, individuals, and organizations, the Brazil House was opened for tourism on 17 November 2007 after over a year of repairs. Several companies and institutions provided funding for the repair works, including M & K Investments (Coral Paints), Ghana; Camargo Correa Construction Company, Brazil; and the Ghanaian and Brazilian governments, who gave money ranging from $30,000 to $100,000.[48] This watershed moment not only marked an important historical event and the birth of tourism within the Tabom community; it symbolized the culmination of decades of attempts to showcase the obscured history of the Brazilian returnee communities in Ghanaian school curriculum and African diaspora history. It is important to add that the Tabom people, especially under the leadership of Nii Azumah V, have made great strides in their daunting efforts. The opening ceremony of the Brazil House was attended by representatives from the Brazilian embassy as well as the Lutterodts, the Tabom chief and his elders, and the Tabom people. Ghana's former minister of tourism and diasporan relations, Stephen Asamoah Boateng, and the former Brazilian ambassador to Ghana, Luis Fernando de Andrade Serra, were also present. Other special guests included Georgina Wood, chief justice of Ghana who grew up at the Brazil House.[49] Her parents handed over the house, which was built in the 1830s by Mama Nassu, to be used for tourism.

There is no doubt that the house was a personal property of the Lutterodts. However, their giving up this house for public use has raised important questions about who now owns the edifice. This success story and progress in the community have been obstructed by lack of coordination and agreement among the Tabom people over which family gets to manage the historical monument. This emerging problem remains a bone of contention and has, in some ways, slowed plans by leaders of the community to transform the Brazil House into a leading tourist spot similar to current tourist destinations as the Elmina and Cape Coast Castles.[50]

Like the interactions between Ambassador Dantas and the Tabom people about five decades earlier, Lula's first visit in 2005 had a tremendous impact on the Tabom community and their ties with Brazil. However, subsequent arrangements between Brazil, the Brazilian embassy in Ghana, and the Tabom people did not always produce the results that they expected. For example, attempts by Tabom leaders and the Brazilian embassy to restore the Portuguese language, an element of Brazilian heritage that has disappeared from the Tabom community since the early 1900s, has not been very successful due to a lack of interest in the Tabom population. Other problems continue because of the difficulty of organizing members of the Brazilian-African diaspora, most of whom are scattered and often assimilated into various regional ethnic groups in Ghana. The influence of English and Ghanaian languages on the Tabom community also makes it difficult for the Tabom people to study Portuguese. Other challenges have been created by Ghanaians.

Both the education systems in Ghana and the Brazilian embassy have to share the blame as well. The former has failed to include the history of the Tabom people in school curricula in Ghana or include the Brazilian returnees' experience in broader Ghanaian historiography. The latter have not yet provided the Tabom people with historical information about slavery in Brazil and its long-term effects on people of Afro-Brazilian descent. Although the embassy contributed a lot to the study of Portuguese at the Ghana Institute of Language in Accra, it has not made any meaningful efforts to explain the complexity of Brazilian history, particularly conversations about race and racial prejudices.[51] Despite these flaws, the Brazilian government and the embassy have aided in stabilizing the Brazilian-African diaspora in Ghana. Lula's achievement does not mean that the Tabom people have no challenges ahead of them. In fact, there is no way of knowing who is actually managing the Brazil House, and with the difficulty in tracing which family group relates to Mama Nassu, the original owner of this important edifice, the answer to how each family group should be involved in managing the Brazil House is uncertain.

WHO OWNS THE BRAZIL HOUSE? MERRY-GO-ROUND RESPONSES, OLD PROBLEMS, AND NEW HURDLES IN THE TWENTY-FIRST CENTURY

The significance of the Brazil House shows the ways in which other returnee communities, especially African Americans, have benefited from the story of the transatlantic slave trade and have transformed their grief into profit.[52] Their strategic interests in heritage tourism and the ways in which they created financially profitable spaces around symbols of slavery fostered new awareness among the Tabom people. It was through this awakening and other parties' existing interests that the restoration of the Brazil House became a priority. The Tabom leaders have partially succeeded in their unyielding efforts to reconstruct and highlight their heritage via tourism, but the blessing is gradually becoming a burden. Like the gift of "Brazilian land" that Gã mãŋtsɛmɛi gave to the Brazilian returnees for farming and housing purposes that later created land disputes, the creation of the Brazil House as a tourist site has ignited division over who owns it. The Lutterodt family voluntarily gave permission for the Warri House to be changed to Brazil House for tourism. By making this bold decision and sacrifice it does not necessarily mean that this property now exists in the Tabom public domain. Over the years, my efforts to find answers to questions about who now owns the Brazil House have not been very successful. I characterize the answers I have been given so far as a roller-coaster academic ride or merry-go-round mainly because of the twists and turns in people's responses: the answers to ownership have not been the same for the Lutterodts, the Brazilian embassy, the Tabom chief, and the Tabom in general. I am not sure about the position of the Ghanaian government.

Various Tabom *we* or family groups make claim to their family ties through Mama Nassu, one of the founding fathers of the Brazilian-African diaspora. Many Tabom people believe he was the leader of the first group of returnees who were given Gã stool land. Nassu is credited for his vision of establishing a permanent edifice, which was known after the 1950s as the Warri House. Yet some of these Tabom people who claim to share blood ties with Nassu do not seem to know or acknowledge those who also share similar lineage with Nassu. In short, aside from the Lutterodts, whoever is able to establish a true lineage with Nassu can also claim the Brazil House. Disagreements over the validity of these diverging claims of ties to Nassu have contributed to existing tensions. Due to the complex nature of inheritance and the difficulty in tracing blood ties to Nassu, the opening of the Brazil House has stirred up new debates and ongoing bickering about who should manage the tourist site.

Recurring themes in my interviews with the Tabom and some of the caretakers and tour guides at the Brazil House show that members of the Brazilian-African diaspora are not the only ones entangled in this contentious matter. The Brazilian embassy is undecided about who should manage the Brazil House. They have made various efforts aimed at avoiding further conflicts between members of various family groups about the future of the Brazil House. They have also expressed interest in managing this historical site on their own. While some Tabom people perceive the daily involvement of the embassy after the Brazil House was opened for tourism as a threat to their own personal interests, others see it as pretentious and paternalistic. Yet for others, the Brazil House is about more than the Tabom people and their ancestors. They see it as a symbol of a successful journey to a distant homeland based on the audacity of hope. These critics also suggest that the embassy should not be given the authority to manage the place. For them, the people who enslaved their ancestors should not have the opportunity to determine the future of the Brazil House. I doubt the Brazilian government and the embassy have made any financial profit from Brazil House. In general, officials at the embassy have also been caught up in this confusion. They have found subtle ways to usurp the authority of the Tabom through their financial contributions to the restoration of the Brazil House, their diplomatic influence, and the maintenance of the status quo. It is also possible that they want to please Afro-Brazilian activists in Brazil, that they feel a sense of entitlement to the historical site, or that they have genuine concerns about the survival of the Brazilian-African diaspora in Ghana and do not know how to express it in a nonthreatening way. Regardless, the embassy has had a long history of support for the Tabom people that deserves praise.

In terms of the broader engagement between the Tabom people and the general public, the Tabom people have received considerable attention and support from the Brazilian government at the local and national levels. Although there was a temporary halt in communication between the Tabom people and the Brazilian government on the national level after the resignation of President Quadros in August 1961 and during the military era from 1964 through 1985, they have consistently maintained positive relations at the local level. Twenty-one years of military dictatorship in Brazil and the military regimes in Ghana that followed the overthrow of Kwame Nkrumah's government in 1966 could not put a brake on the transatlantic relations between Brazil and Ghana. Constructive dialogue continued thereafter. The Brazilian embassy in Ghana facilitated important educational programs in the Brazilian-African diaspora close to the turn of the twentieth century. Further, the embassy has effectively maintained close relations by providing financial resources for the restoration of buildings, streets, historical monuments, and other cultural heritage sites in Tabom communities. The embassy has also highlighted the ex-slaves' social contributions, including their skills in architecture, tailoring, carpentry, and irrigation techniques. The Tabom people and the embassy have what is characterized in recent times as a "love and hate" relationship. Despite what looks like a roller-coaster exchange, they have made great strides in their relations. Nonetheless, some hurdles remain.

Language differences between the Tabom people and the Brazilians also remain a challenge to fluid dialogue. Although most of the embassy representatives speak English, most Brazilians continue to speak Portuguese. To improve communication between Brazil and the Tabom people, the Brazilian government funded a Brazilian lecturer, Marco Aurelio Schaumloeffel, to teach Portuguese at the Ghana Institute of Languages and locations in the Tabom community.[53] After the Brazil House was opened for tourism, the top floor was reserved for providing Portuguese classes for the Tabom people.[54] Additionally, over the years, the Brazilian embassy has created a study-abroad program and sponsored Ghanaian students (who are not necessarily of Brazilian descent) to study in Brazil. These evolving trends suggest that there continue to be positive relationships between the Tabom community and Brazil.

The Brazilian embassy continues to publicize Brazil's connection to the Tabom community and its ongoing contribution to the configuration of the Brazilian-African diaspora story in Ghana. During my first visit to the Brazilian embassy in Accra in 2005, the staff I interviewed seemed passionate about their involvement with the Tabom community and were very supportive of my research.[55] The embassy has demonstrated its vested interest in this community on its website by showcasing the story of the Tabom people and the embassy's Portuguese language program. Moreover, information about the selection of Ghanaians to attend colleges and graduate schools in Brazil, as well as the number of students the embassy has sponsored since the 1990s, is displayed. In addition, the embassy promotes various cultural activities in Ghana. Information about the visits by the former Brazilian president Lula da Silva to Ghana in 2005 and 2007 as well as the programs and festivities that were organized to allow Lula to interact with the Tabom community is especially prominent on the embassy's website. The Brazilian government and the embassy have been successful in depending on cultural and global capitalist interconnections in Ghana since the dawn of the twenty-first century. Various other issues and programs with different dimensions are driving the Brazilian embassy to provide diverse support to the Tabom people. The Tabom people are vigorously pursuing other outlets and have embarked on campaigns to inform Ghanaians about the obscured history of the Tabom people. The Tabom people have other deep interests in the areas of heritage tourism.

Another emerging situation is the performance and commodification of sites of memory. The Tabom youth, in particular, have found new ways to make profit beyond the tourist economy. Although they identify as Tabom, it is very difficult to tell which family group they are part of or whether they are truly members of the Brazilian-African diaspora. Prior to the repairs and the opening of the Brazil House, these young people acted as the "gatekeepers" of these sites of memory. The youth monitored activities of visitors and tourists who entered the Tabom compound to view Brazil Lane, the Warri House, the first Scissors House, and other archaeological remains that some of the local people believe were used as slave dungeons along the shores of Otublohum, Jamestown (Bukom), in Accra. These gatekeepers made their presence known throughout the process. For example, during one of my visits to Otublohum, where the Brazil House stands, to take photographs of the Warri House, several young people approached me and demanded money before I could take photographs. Although I was accompanied by Nii Azumah's assistant and am fluent in the Gã language, the main Ghanaian language spoken by the Tabom community and people in the area, it took a longer time to accomplish my goals that day due to frequent interruptions from the youth.

During the same visit, the youth requested that I take their photographs to show others how they have carried on the skills of their ancestors. At the Scissors House, a location believed to have been inhabited by Brazilian-African returnees who were experts in tailoring and dressmaking, most of the young men started cutting different fibers and clothing materials to show their skills in cloth-making. There was no form of harassment at the Scissors House as in the case of the Warri House. They contested for space and power whenever they saw visitors in their compound. Clearly, the young cloth-makers were performing and enacting their culture as Ebron argues.[56] One may see such visits as harassment, but other members of the community see such interactions as opportunities for disseminating news about the hidden treasures of the Tabom people. They carry on the traditions of cloth-making, encourage tourism, and provide hospitality for tourists and visitors, especially those accompanied by embassy officials. The Brazil House and other sites of memories like the Scissors House remind us of the two centuries of Brazilian-African presence in Ghana. These material cultures signal the dynamic nature of the African diaspora in reverse.

Roots of Silences and Apathy: Obstacles Behind and Ahead

Existing literature underscores how people remember or forget their past intentionally or unintentionally.[57] A similar idea is discussed by Jacques Depelchin. According to Depelchin the construction of academic knowledge and, in the case of reverse migrations, the production of diaspora history largely marginalizes other aspects of slave narratives.[58] Historian Sandra E. Greene was vocal about this important subject when she explained how whispering and silences affected the ways in which Ghanaian history was constructed.[59] Scholars from different disciplines who have written about the challenges confronting African studies and diaspora historiography have raised similar arguments.[60] As Luise White points out, the attempt to mask what has been passed on through oral history and traditions has produced other obstacles.[61] From the postindependence period to present times, the descendants have developed and exhibited interesting characteristics that my study calls "cultural metamorphosis," a critical stage in the history of their community in which part of the population is slowly becoming a "lost generation." In my interviews, this dimension of the Brazilian-African diaspora history becomes even more evident when one examines community members' interest, or lack thereof, in talking about their past.

Documenting gender dynamics in the Brazilian-African diaspora story is particularly challenging, as it is daunting to unearth the voices of women in the Tabom community. Because the history of women and youth has been excluded in various historical accounts, it is difficult to reach any definite conclusion and explore more deeply into how they fashion their identities. Sometimes the Tabom highlight only their Ghanaian identity; other times they identify as both Ghanaians and Brazilians. This section of the population seems to convey the point that they are not interested in discussing the history of their forebears, a past they do not know or do not understand very well.

Other complications have been created by a section of the community's efforts to stop talking about the history of slavery within their families, especially the engagement of returnees in slavery activities in the mid-1800s and the early 1900s.[62] Although one cannot easily divorce him- or herself from biological roots or bloodline, some descendants have made a conscious decision to keep silent about this part of their history. This decision has been shaped largely by the stigma attached to slavery, a lack of interconnected ties between different families of Brazilian ancestry, and divisions that were created during the early years of their assimilation into local cultures. Obviously, part of the contemporary group incorporates the history of their ancestors into their narratives with the aid of oral tradition. However, a number of descendants find no pleasure in associating themselves with the fact that their ancestors were former slaves from Brazil or that their ancestors also sold or had slaves in their homes. Nii Azumah V has attributed these silences in the community about the dark side of their history to the stigma that is attached to domestic and transatlantic slavery.[63]

The position of the Tabom chief on the subject of silences within his community has been confirmed by other research. The consensus is that in the efforts to minimize the role of Ghanaians in the transatlantic slave trade, "the history of the slave trade is largely ignored [by Ghanaians] in order to maintain the coherence of the story of colonialism and independence."[64] Some of these conclusions are debatable. For a number of Tabom people, the strategic erasure of their past with slavery is actually based on matters of positionality. Their families' social and domestic involvements in slavery were more of an attempt by the earlier settlers to draw a distinction between their social status in Ghana and their past social status—once slaves, they later became free wealthy merchants who wanted to dominate their new social environment. Other reasons that are rooted in differences within various segments of the community are beyond the scope of this chapter.[65] In short, the leaders of various family groups neither recovered from the years of land disputes nor had any interest in the future of the community because they chose to identify as Ghanaians. Their attitudes might also reflect a sense that there is no place for their history or that there might not be space for their contributions within broader Ghanaian historiography.

It is also important to understand claims about Ghanaians' replacement of slave narratives with nationalist sentiments. There is a distinction between how the first generation of returnees perceived slavery and how a portion of the current generation distances themselves from this contentious historical subject.[66] The new generations participate in Ghanaian socioeconomic and political life at several different levels and are proud to be Ghanaian. The Tabom people often show pride in their Brazilian heritage whenever a member of their community excels at the national level. For instance, it is believed that a large section of the community, like other Ghanaians, celebrated the victory of Azumah Nelson, a Ghanaian of Brazilian descent, in the boxing arena. Moreover, when Georgina Wood was selected as the first female chief justice in Ghana, the Tabom people gained similar attention and coverage in the media. In fact, the 2006 World Cup soccer match between Brazil and Ghana brought the historical relationship between the Tabom people and Brazil to the forefront. However, such excitement disappeared when it was time to set up interviews with some of them. Although the Tabom were generally very informed and passionate about their historical connections with Brazil, a significant portion of those I interacted with seemed removed from their Brazilian heritage.

Various other factors continue to shape the future of the Brazilian-African diaspora. Land disputes ripped the Brazilian-African and the Tabom communities apart, and lingering problems resulted from unresolved disputes. There is also contestation within their communities over how to choose Tabom chiefs and which family groups they should come from. One tradition, which sustained their communities from the mid-1830s on, was Gã *Mãŋtsɛ* Komeh I's appointment of Azumah Nelson, one of the leaders of the returnees, as the first chief of the community in 1836.[67] The various positions they held as Mãŋtsɛmɛi embodied returnees' movement from slavery to freedom. Five members from the Nelson lineage through the *kyerbi* (the Gã word for patriarchal lineage) have been selected as chiefs since 1839. Descendants have disputed the validity of the claim over inheritance, contending forcefully that such strict tradition served the vested interests of only one family group. As a result of this tension, the "Brazilian throne" remained empty after the death of Nii Azumah IV in 1981 because some Tabom people wanted to select a new chief outside the Nelson pedigree. Others objected to this idea. After nearly two decades of disagreement Nii Azumah V, another descendant from the Nelson family, was initiated to the throne in 1998. This aspect of Tabom history remains a bone of contention.

Other forces have blurred and continue to obscure the historical linkages between the old and the new generations at the dawn of the twenty-first century. These old problems and new hurdles are part of the seeds that were sown in the past—the descendants' decision to protect individual interests in place of communal activities as their ancestors had. According to Nii Azumah V, as the subsequent generations assimilated even more deeply into local cultures and as trading ventures intensified between the end of the 1800s and early 1950s, a great gulf was created between ex-slaves from Brazil who settled in the Ghana and those who settled in other countries in West Africa.[68]

Most of these differences were entrenched in social issues that emerged around this time that the Brazilian-African diaspora evolved.[69]

There are other negative developments that have emerged as a result of these unresolved problems that have carried over from the twentieth century. Clearly, a fraction of the population and the current leadership deserves praise for passing on stories about their Brazilian lineage and for working closely with the Brazilian embassy in Accra to introduce Portuguese language classes in some areas of the Tabom community. However, their failure to create a niche for the younger generation in the Tabom leadership to serve as a bridge between the older and younger group has left a gap that has complicated their future. To add to this, the failure or inability of most of the older generation to pass their history on to the younger generation, and the younger generation's lack of interest in activities like Portuguese classes that the Brazilian embassy coordinates to assist the Tabom, speaks volumes about the growing divide. At the dawn of the twenty-first century, these challenges and hostilities have grown into silences and apathy about their ancestral past that continue to threaten the future of the community, particularly the reconstruction of their history in Ghana.

Certain issues, especially intermarriage that occurred during and after the end of the first generation, lead to a very important subject about silences and marginalization within the Tabom community. These lingering divisions continue to complicate the notion of a dual Brazilian-Ghanaian identity as well as voluntary return to Brazil. These tensions have been colored by the formation of a strategic identity among the Tabom people that takes on different dimensions depending on the particular situation. In a nutshell, descendants decide to be identified as Tabom, Ghanaians, or both depending on different overlapping agendas.

The life experiences of the ex-slaves and the Tabom explain distinctions between how the past and the current generations remembered and showcased their ties to Brazil. Recurring themes are that despite evidence of double consciousness, identity crises, and dissonance of memory, Brazil remained in the psyche of ex-slaves and their offspring in very interesting ways. In Ghana, the emancipated Brazilian-Africans were confronted by stringent colonial ordinances during British colonial rule. The Tabom also encountered unidimensional laws in the postindependence policies that ignored the significance of their ancestral history and larger tourism discourse associated with the transatlantic slave trade. The representation of Africa's past, especially the circulation and production of discourse about the transatlantic slave trade, the Black Atlantic experience, and the appropriation of material culture for historical and capitalist consumption, is the thrust of this chapter. The fact that various groups with connections to the Middle Passage have expressed a sense of ownership or entitlement, showcased historical monuments as cultural commodities for enhancing their dual identities and heritage, and made economic gains from sites of memory does not mean they are given equal coverage. The unidimensional approach to this subject has for a long time benefited returnees from North America and obscured other aspects of the diaspora.[70] The Tabom people are also refashioning, transforming, and repackaging their history in a way that will allow individuals and institutions to see the history of the community through the lens of the Tabom people—based on their Brazilian connections to the transatlantic slave trade. They have basically placed their destiny in their own hands instead of waiting on outside forces to determine their future or make them visible.

Another argument here is that like the Ghana Tourist and Monument Board, past Ghanaian leaders have not fully supported the Tabom community in the area of tourism. Rather, they concentrate on other annual Pan-African cultural programs such as the Pan-African Historical Theatre Festival (PANAFEST), Emancipation Day celebrations, and tourist activities at locations like the Elmina and Cape Coast Castles in the Central Region and new World Heritage Sites in other regions of Ghana. This neglect has increased the problem. Indeed, the Tabom people are no longer depending on or waiting for outside help to showcase their rich history and dual identity. In situating the Brazilian-Tabom narratives in the wider context of tourism and globalization, this chapter maintains that the Tabom community are well informed about the capitalist ventures that are unfolding in the tourist industry in Ghana. In my interview with William Lutterodt, the former custodian of the Warri House (now Brazil House) that his family inherited from their Brazilian ancestor Mama Nassu, not only shows evidence of their Brazilian connections, but it is significant for tourism. Further, during one of our interviews, Nii Azumah V did not hide the Tabom people's economic interests. He blamed the Ghana Tourist Board for making it possible for only the people of Elmina and Cape Coast to benefit from revenues generated from the historical monuments in the area while neglecting equally important historical sites in the Tabom community. Since he was selected as the new Tabom leader in 1998, after nearly two decades of conflict over who should inherit this prestigious position, Nii Azumah V and the elders of the community have turned things around and begun to forge unity among the descendants. As the new chief, he has taken it upon himself to ensure that the history of the community and other aspects of their inheritance are passed on to the next generation for posterity's sake.[71]

The Tabom people's interest in tourism was partly influenced by the success of other returnees from North America and the Caribbean in the tourism industry in Ghana. Indeed, African American and Caribbean returnees also relocated to the "motherland" between the late nineteenth century and the twenty-first century and also contested with the Ghana Tourist and Monument Board and foreign donors to gain some degree of ownership of various sites of memory. Some of these diaspora returnees who believe that they have spiritual ties to slave monuments have made enormous progress in their initiatives.

In general, the Tabom story has not been as visible in the tourism industry as other stories, but they have managed to reverse this trend with the assistance of others. The Brazilian government and embassy have interacted with the community since the 1960s, and the Tabom people and their leaders have served as vehicles for achieving various historical and transnational objectives. The restoration of the Brazil House for posterity and tourism and the Tabom people's interest in visiting Brazil are intertwined. In my attempt to trace the Tabom people's journey to Brazil—their new diaspora migration—and their ongoing attempts to bring their heritage to the forefront of tourism, I am not suggesting that the Tabom people are demanding Brazilian citizenship or are ready to give up their Ghanaian citizenship. Neither am I claiming that they are looking forward to visiting Brazil in order to settle there permanently. Instead, while consciousness of Brazil does not resonate throughout the community, new efforts to showcase the history of the Brazilian-African diaspora in Ghana have gained traction, especially in the tourism industry, through commodification, appropriation, and performance of their ancestral connections to the Middle Passage.

In relation to the Tabom people's commodification and appropriation of the Middle Passage and the material culture that solidifies their story, Paulla Ebron who reminds us,

> There is no better place to explore the contours of performance as an idea and as practice than in the context of Africa, which has been made into an object through a number of performance tropes.... The ways performance becomes a frame of enactment, creative movements of Africa not just for Africa but, most significantly in the performance of Africa for wide-ranging audiences.... The continent becomes an object of significance in various local and global contexts.... Notions of "culture" allows one to observe how Africa becomes a significant site in the performance of place in global context.[72]

The Tabom developed their new "rule for tourism engagement" in response to years of neglect by the Ghanaian government, foreign institutions such as UNESCO, and programs associated with the expansion of World Heritage Sites in Ghana. The Lutterodt family's sacrifice—sharing the Warri House—as well as the Tabom leaders' approach to raising awareness and collaborating with the Ghana Tourist and Monument Board, the Brazilian government, the Brazilian embassy in Accra, and foreign donors with interests in the Brazilian-African diaspora story have been fruitful. The transition from years of neglect to new attention toward the preservation of the Brazilian legacy in Ghana deserves a place in Tabom history, Brazilian history, Ghanaian/African history, the histories of growing transnational communities in the African diaspora, and disciplines like tourism studies that emphasize this important discourse. As Tim Coles and Dallen J. Timothy relate in *Tourism, Diasporas and Space*, the growing trend in global travel toward cultural performance and the institutionalization of tourism for economic gain deserve new interpretations.[73]

The Tabom people, in general, are not familiar with academic claims, tropes, and theories about sites of memory. Nonetheless, part of their interest draws indirectly from claims such as those from Coles and Timothy. The central role of diasporan returnee entrepreneurs in Ghana has not escaped the watchful eyes of the Tabom people. Put directly, the Tabom people are imitating other returnee groups in Ghana. Indeed, one cannot deny the ample evidence that ties the Tabom people to Brazil, but it is obvious that the Tabom people's increasing interactions with and awareness of their ancestral connection to Brazil since the 1980s deserve recognition. Their goals can be summed up as the pursuit of economic opportunities through the Tabom leadership; through the Brazilian government and the Brazilian embassy, the government of Ghana, and the Ghana Tourist and Monument Board; and through foreign institutions such as UNESCO who have expressed some vested interest in the past. Drawing a parallel between the long history of international publicity about the Elmina and Cape Coast Castles within Ghana and the exposure of existing historical landmarks and possible tourist sites in Tabom communities is like comparing apples and oranges. There is a stark difference between these sites of memory. The Tabom people do not only have to compete with two popular tourist locations—the Elmina and Cape Coast Castles—but also with other thriving tourist sites such as Kakum National Park and the Manhia Palace that is the seat of the Asante Kingdom.

The Tabom's restoration of archaeological and historical sites in their community is not isolated from other tourist activities.[74] They have imitated successful tourist institutions and returnee groups in Ghana and solicited financial support to highlight their history with slavery.[75] As a result, they have started advertising the Brazil House through brochures that are distributed at popular tourist sites and hotels and the Accra International Airport. They have furthermore extended invitations to both local and foreign institutions to invest in their community. Nonetheless, considering the international popularity of Elmina and Cape Coast Castles, the dream of the Tabom people to transform their community into a modern tourist spot in the twenty-first century would require a great deal of planning, high-level professional practices, supervision, investment, accountability, and the training of tour guides. It would also require aggressive publicity to encourage visits to their communities. Through social media and other information technology outlets, several school children from public and private schools in Ghana have had various educational tours of the Brazil House since 2007. Students in various study abroad programs who visit Ghana visit this historical landmark as part of their tour of Accra.[76] By and large, the Tabom people's new efforts are also motivated by global forces and deeply colored by economic interests that result from growing investments in tourism in Ghana. Various communities have sought to polish existing sites of memory and repair those in ruin to draw more revenue via the tourist industry.

The current challenges confronting the Tabom leadership over how and which family should manage the Brazil House are not in anomaly; they are an extension of the problems their ancestors had over land distribution. The Tabom people have made individual and collective attempts to visit Brazil in efforts to restore, stabilize, and preserve the memory of their Brazilian past. I contend that their preparation to travel to Brazil was not only fueled by Lula's promise to them, but it was largely influenced by a yearning to showcase their "multiple identities." In general, the experience of return also shows aspects of continuity and change in the history of Ghana/Africa and African diaspora studies beyond the New World.

Chapter 10

Telescoping Lula's Unfulfilled Promise and the Implications of the Tabom's Visit to Brazil: A Hopeless Situation?

> I would like to be a magician and be able to see Brazil once I die.
> —Elder George Nii Aruna Nelson

Throughout the story of reverse migrations, memory has remained as the glue that binds the past with the present and the future. Former Brazilian president Luiz Inácio Lula da Silva rearticulated the central role of memory in the reverse migration story of the Brazilian-African diaspora in Ghana during his speech in 2005. Two traditional Adinkra symbols, *nkyinkyim* and *sankofa*, also emphasize unending journeys and enthusiasm about the unknown. Dissonance of memory and multiple returns, especially in the case of Elder George Nii Aruna Nelson who daydreamed of Brazil throughout his lifetime, as well as the importance of the Tabom and the Brazilian government to the survival of the Brazilian-African diaspora in Ghana cannot be overstated. This concluding chapter furthermore underscores the Tabom people's deep desire to connect with their distant Brazilian heritage—they are interested in visiting Bahia and Rio de Janeiro, Brazil, where most of them believe their ancestors came from. One of Lula's speeches embodied such striking reminder when he acknowledged "the Tabom people, a people whose ancestors in Brazil never forgot their African origins, but on returning to their birthplace [Ghana] continued to cultivate the memory of the Brazilian nation which they helped to found."[1]

Although the Tabom interest in seeing Brazil was influenced by stories that were passed on from past generations, part of the motivation to do so was also shaped by a promise Lula made to the Tabom people during his first visit to the Tabom community in 2005. Some of the Tabom people anticipate a visit to Brazil based on Lula's promise, but the uncertainty about this promise over the last seven years is like having a telescope that is unable to bring distant images into focus. The challenge for the Tabom now is how to remove the fog that has clouded their impending trip. A visit to Brazil could impact Brazilian history in Ghana in unique ways we have not seen before. In resolving this predicament and explaining the Tabom people's fantasy about Brazil, I focus my analysis on the central role of the Brazilian government and embassy in Accra in the Brazilian-African diaspora.

I am not suggesting that the members of the Brazilian-African diaspora are a helpless community that cannot do anything for themselves. Neither am I arguing that the possibility of visiting Brazil rests solely on the promise Lula made in 2005 or the Brazilian embassy's support. I contend that even if the Brazilian government is unable to fund this trip, the records show that they have made enormous contributions and laid a solid foundation for the Tabom people to continue. It is certain that the new generation has a duty to preserve its past in the same way that older members of the community, such as *Mãntse* Nii Azumah V, Elder George Aruna Nelson, Elder William Lutterodt, Cyril Fiscian, and others, have done for posterity. There are successful stories told about the role of the Brazilian government and embassy since their first interactions with the Tabom people over fifty years ago. But there are also contradictions entrenched in their interactions and exchanges with the Tabom people. They have not been courageous enough in addressing problems with racism and racial inequalities in Brazil or been transparent about this dark history in their interactions with the Tabom people. I do not intend to overstate the gravity of racism in Brazil. My argument here is that the Brazilian government has taken advantage of the experiences of the freed Brazilian-Africans' history in Ghana to meet historical, cultural, political, and diplomatic needs, and that these five decades of mutual relations will be incomplete until the Brazilian government explains the roots of prejudice and racial inequalities in Brazil to the Tabom people. The Tabom people may encounter hostility similar to what Afro-Brazilians have encountered since the demise of slavery in Brazil if they are not provided with adequate protection and information regarding racial tensions in the country.

In understanding the pivotal role of the Brazilian government and the embassy, it is important to revisit the origins of the Tabom people's experience in the New World; the African slaves' experience of hardships and subjugation on Brazilian plantations shaped their memories and identity when they resettled in Africa from the nineteenth century.[2] Africans who remained in Brazil after gaining their freedom and those who joined waves of voyages back to Africa were not a homogeneous crowd but were distinct in a variety of ways. I posit that the diversity among them shaped their decisions. For instance, unlike some of the ex-slaves who were not interested in relocating to connect with their distant heritage and preferred to stay in Brazil after gaining their freedom, others established communities and new identities in Nigeria, Benin, and other locations.[3] The irony here is that some of the returnees who made it back to Africa did not forget Brazil despite the agonizing memory of plantation slavery. It remained fresh in their minds for an extensive period. As a result, some of the returnees traveled back and forth between their new locations of settlement in West Africa and Brazil to visit their family members and to trade.

There is no evidence I have come across, however, that shows that the first generation of returnees who settled in the Gold Coast were among these. Unlike some returnees who settled in Nigeria and other areas, those who settled in the Gold Coast did not sustain meaningful relations with Brazil. Paradoxically, over a century after the end of Brazilian slavery, their descendants did the opposite; they have created a new kind of relation with Brazil through historical memory, their imaginations, and a deep yearning to visit. In short, the descendants of victims of slavery on Brazilian plantations continue to reestablish transnational dialogue with Brazil despite the enslavement of their forebears. The Tabom people have maintained this relationship through the support of the Brazilian government and the Brazilian embassy in Accra. Over last fifty years, the Ghanaian government, which did not show any meaningful interest in the Brazilian-African diaspora story before, has now expressed varying vested interests and has strengthened its bilateral economic ties with Brazil.

What is driving the Tabom people to visit Brazil for the first time, and what does this anticipated journey mean? I argue that the few Tabom people who have visited Brazil have already carved a migration route in the African diaspora that others could later follow. Their successful journeys to Brazil and others that might happen later are part of what is termed "multiple belongings" in the African diaspora.[4] Also, the ongoing relationship between the Tabom people and Brazil, especially their plans for future visits to Brazil, is another element of "unfinished migrations" in the diaspora. Moreover, the Tabom people's plans to visit Brazil also cement the bold statement by other scholars that the African diaspora transcends national boundaries and therefore needs more serious academic attention to show how it keeps evolving.

The mutual relationships established between the Tabom leaders, the Brazilian government, and other parties who have shown their vested interest in these continuing reverse diasporic linkages (between Africa and South America) have many objectives: to sustain existing ties between Brazil and the Tabom people, to raise awareness in

Ghanaian society about their Brazilian-Ghanaian roots, to educate the Tabom people about their dual cultural identities, to create a new site for establishing lasting links between Tabom people and other Brazilians of African descent, to facilitate future visits to Brazil, and, most importantly, to raise revenue through heritage tourism. All these overlapping interests linking the Tabom and Brazil have added to the transatlantic current that continues to flow.

The memory of a home in Africa remained in the consciousness of slaves who were dispersed into plantations in Brazil and served in various capacities in the echelon of Brazilian societies. In reverse, the same can be said of the Tabom who have either come close to visiting Brazil for the first time or have not expressed interest in connecting to their Brazilian history. There is no specific way of knowing how many Tabom people have visited Brazil so far. Stories of family members who have visited Brazil are difficult to document. There are scattered stories pointing to family members who have just returned from Brazil, but pursuing this information is like chasing the wind. Nonetheless, Tabom people including Kai Lutterodt and Chief Justice Georgina Theodora Wood have visited Brazil. In my interview with Lutterodt in London in 2011 she underscored the significance of her ancestral homeland to her. Her purpose for visiting Brazil is similar to what most of the Tabom aspire to achieve: to visit the land of their ancestors and connect to their Brazilian heritage. Lutterodt believes that such experiences could aid her identity formation.[5] In the case of Wood, whose story is covered in other parts of the book, she asserts that her visit to Brazil in 2012 enabled her to have a deeper appreciation for the stories her parents shared about Brazilian children when she was raised at her family house, Warri House, which is now the Brazil House.[6]

The life of Elder George Aruna Nelson (a descendant of Chief João Antonio Nelson), who died in Accra on 5 April 2009 at the age of ninety-three, illustrates another dimension of the Tabom experience. In addition, it serves as a microcosm of the discourses of memory, identity, citizenship, and the Tabom's relentless efforts to "inhale" Brazil in the future. Nelson's biography aids in reconstructing his memory of a homeland in Brazil and shows how he negotiated his identity as both a Ghanaian and a Brazilian. Put differently, although Nelson daydreamed about Brazil, he could not set foot on the land where his forebears were enslaved.[7] Before his death, Nelson played a major role in the renovation of the Brazil House.

Although Nelson dreamed of Brazil, not every older person in the Brazilian-African diaspora was interested in visiting Brazil. For instance, in my interview with Elder William Lutterodt, he made it known that although he has a Brazilian heritage, he was not as excited about visiting Brazil as others.[8] Inconsistencies about Tabom people's ties to Brazil are not limited to the older generations. Some of the Tabom youth have also expressed varying degrees of interest about a possible return or visit to Brazil. Together, these stories exemplify the notion of a double consciousness. They also present evidence of other forms of split consciousness affecting Tabom communities, including how to relate to other family groups, dissonance of memory about their Brazilian heritage, and the challenges the Tabom encounter in the preservation and reconstruction of their history. Two of the central questions I have raised in this book are what in the history of these two countries has permitted these historical connections, and how does this mutual relationship inform us about trends in the African diaspora? One thing is certain: the historical umbilical cord that links Brazil and Ghana that is based on memory and the transatlantic slave trade has not been broken in the last three centuries. If this trend continues, it will remain as a unique and unmatched historical development in transatlantic discourse—the creation and preservation of mutual relations between people in Brazil, a former slave Portuguese nation, and the descendants of liberated Brazilian-Africans in Ghana.

Broken Trees and Withering Leaves: The Tabom Yearning to "Inhale" Brazil and the Uneven Process of Returning to Brazil

Former Brazilian president Lula has been identified as one of the Brazilian leaders who have made strides toward addressing racism in Brazil by increasingly enforcing policies such as affirmative action programs for racial equality. Internationally, he was praised for his economic and cultural policies in bridging ties between Brazil and several African nations during his tenure.[9] He has been actively involved in local and international programs since he left office. However, not much is known about the status of the promise Lula made to the Tabom people. Various attempts by the Brazilian government to invite the Tabom people to Brazil did not succeed immediately after Lula's visit in 2005. In fact, during his second presidential campaign some Tabom people expressed concerns about the possibility of their visit. A number of the Tabom people were curious about what would happen if his term in office ended or if he was not reelected for a second term. Lula's reelection in 2006 made these concerns irrelevant. At the same time his reelection did not address all their urgent needs.

The Tabom dream to visit Brazil almost became reality during Lula's second term. However, the invitation, which was coordinated by the Brazilian embassy, ran into several barriers including improper planning and timing. Some of the arrangements went directly against taboos and rituals in Ghanaian cultural traditions. Specifically, the embassy's 2006 proposition failed because it did not take important cultural protocols into consideration. Although the embassy arranged the trip, they only invited Nii Azumah V.[10] Traditionally, a chief in Ghana cannot travel without the company of his linguist and close members of his royal court. More importantly, a leader of such caliber needs sufficient time to consult elders of his circle and his community before leaving his subjects, and the chief has to temporarily assign his position to one of the elders during his absence. The embassy also made the mistake of inviting the chief to visit around the same time the Gã *homowo* celebration was taking place. The Tabom people, especially their leaders, participate in the festivities each year, so they could not travel out of the country at that time. Since this visit, different Brazilian ambassadors in Ghana have made varying attempts to make the trip to Brazil a reality. For example, Nii Azumah V reported that Luis Fernando de Andrade Serra, the former Brazilian ambassador, later paid a visit to the Tabom chief to formulate a more constructive plan to make this dream possible.[11] However, these efforts seem to have gone nowhere.

In order for the Brazilian embassy to accomplish its objective, it would have to give the Tabom leadership advance notice and also make additional provision for a large delegation from the community. I will add that an entourage is significant because of various cultural performances that are needed during the process of leaving Accra and traveling to Brazil. For example, common cultural practices in Ghana that the Tabom have embraced since the early 1900s require the pouring of libations and the performance of various rituals to ask protection from the gods of the land (Ghana) and the spirits of their ancestors to guide the chief, those who are accompanying him, and the community they would leave behind.[12] All these rituals are performed by his linguist and some members of his royal circle. We have yet to know those who would be selected to take this trip if the time comes.

Since Irene Vida Gala took over as an ambassador in 2012 there has not been any new development. Also, although the new ambassador has made some progress in continuing economic partnerships that were initiated by her predecessors, who worked tirelessly to maintain relations between the two countries, she has not yet addressed Lula's promise to the Tabom. Nonetheless, more critical questions remain: How would the "native state" of Brazil embrace the Tabom people? What ties do Afro-Brazilians share with the Tabom after nearly two centuries of separation? What would happen if the two groups converged in Brazil? Who would they meet with in Brazil? Although the answers to these questions are not readily available, it is important to consider how a visit to Brazil would be affected by complex racial issues in Brazil.

Race to Brazil and Racism in Brazil: Confronting the Challenges Ahead, Receding Memory, and Silences

One of the contentious debates in Brazil after Lula won a second term in office is the issue of affirmative action—a program needed desperately in Brazil to close the gap between privileged white citizens and the rest of the population who are mostly nonwhite. According to Brazilian historian João José Reis, there were various petitions for and against affirmative action already in place, and the debate lingered throughout Lula's second term in office.[13] One may wonder why it has taken the Brazilian embassy so long to engage with the Tabom community about growing racial conflicts and social inequalities in their country. If it has taken the embassy this long to address this subject, would that discussion happen in their future engagements with the Tabom people? It may take a long time for us to find answers to these questions. It is possible that the embassy is concerned about backlash or negative responses from the Tabom if it reveals the racial problems in their country.

The flourishing ties between the Tabom people and the Brazilian government and embassy will be incomplete without an honest conversation about Brazil's racial troubles after the end of slavery in 1888—what some refer to as the "black question."[14] Since the mid-1980s there has been a shift in dialogue about race and racial inequalities in Brazil. Racially charged conversations focusing mainly on Brazilian society, economics, and culture as well as matters relating to slavery, historical memory, and heritage tourism have been moved from the margins to the forefront of local, regional, national, and global discourses. My efforts to contextualize the Tabom people's plans to visit Brazil within the possible impact of racism and racial politics do not cover all aspects of this broad subject. Because of the scope of this chapter, I have only included a thumbnail synthesis of racial inequalities in Brazil and its implications to the Tabom people's future visit. This includes social disparities and long history of racial tensions in Brazil and how that is interpreted by the Tabom people. Despite the progress they have made so far in their endeavor, the Tabom fall short in other areas. Ghana's Brazilians are not well informed about racial tensions and economic inequalities in Brazil. The Tabom people are not well informed on this subject. This became visible during my interviews with Nii Azumah V, the current *mãntse*, and the late elder George Aruna Nelson over the years. For example, they gave very defensive responses when I asked questions about racial and economic inequalities in Brazil and why they were looking forward to visiting there in the future. A number of Tabom people, especially Elder Nelson, stated that because their ancestors contributed to the economic success of

Brazil, they deserve a rousing welcome when they are able to visit Brazil. They posit that the entire Tabom group will be embraced by both white and nonwhite Brazilians.[15]

Looking at this from another angle, discussions about racism are perceived as a myth or frivolous among some Tabom people because a number of Tabom leaders claim they have had cordial relations with the Brazilians they have come into contact with so far. Lula amplified this mutual friendship and the sense of brotherhood at the end of a memorable speech delivered before the Tabom community in 2005 in which he reminded his audience about the umbilical cord that binds Brazilians and the Tabom people.[16]

Nii Azuma V's response, which solidified his community's commitment to Lula's broader vision for the Tabom, suggests that the Tabom people were pleased by Lula's support. The Tabom leader's appeal for broader assistance for the Gã *mãŋ* to tackle problems reflects his familiarity with problems in his own backyard. On the other hand, he lacked awareness of problems in Brazil. The late Elder George Aruna Nelson was also not aware of this problem in Brazil. In general, they both seemed to be more concerned about a visit to Brazil than being entangled with complex racial debates that continue to permeate the social, economic, and political landscape of the country.[17]

In general, many members of the Tabom community are not well informed about the existing tensions, identity crises, complex racial and ethnic formations, and racial politics that evolve daily in the former Portuguese slave colony. The Tabom people's knowledge and illusions about Brazil were revealed in other ways during my interviews in Accra. Some members of the Tabom community were reluctant to discuss racial diversity in Brazil and its implications for Afro-Brazilian and white Brazilian relationships. One cannot blame the Tabom people for not knowing about this problem. Most Ghanaians too have not experienced racism in their lifetime as others have. Most Tabom people's perception of racial tensions is framed in a very narrow scope based on their socialization in Ghana. Indeed, their interaction with Brazil so far has been through the lens of their experiences with Brazilians from the embassy, Lula, and prominent Afro-Brazilians such as Gilberto Gil, who interacted with the Tabom people during Lula's visit. Even so, the Tabom people have a responsibility to acquire this knowledge on their own to help them navigate the complex diplomatic exchanges between them and the Brazilian government that began in 1961 and continue today. In spite of its uneven relationship with the Tabom people, the Brazilian embassy has done many things right. They are readily available to provide information and resources that enhance their image in Ghana. It is, however, disturbing that although the embassy officials and their guests have paid regular visits to the community in the last five decades and successfully arranged for the study of a colonial language, Portuguese, they have not initiated any major program to enable the Tabom people to come to terms with the history of slavery in Brazil and how the legacy of slavery continues to shape the future of Afro-Brazilians.

There are other complications. Diversity, or lack of it, within the embassy staff in Ghana reflects another important aspect of racial marginalization in Brazil. With the exception of Ambassador Raymundo de Souza Dantas, who became the first Afro-Brazilian diplomat in Ghana in 1961, subsequent ambassadors have been largely Brazilians of European descent. Anani Dzidzienyo provides an in-depth analysis detailing problems with the lack of diversity in Brazilian diplomatic circles when he says, "Quadros' unprecedented appointment of [a] Black Brazilian ambassador remains a landmark in Brazilian diplomatic relations. . . . There has not been another [black] ambassador representing Brazil in a foreign country since then."[18] As Dzidzienyo contends, it would be interesting to inquire about the racial composition of Brazil's diplomats and staff in other diplomatic posts in Africa.

In Ghana, the lack of diversity within the embassy was very striking during my first visit in 2005 and on subsequent visits. Marco Aurelio Schaumloeffel, who was then the Portuguese language coordinator at the Ghana Institute of Languages, of German descent, and the entire staff in the embassy in Accra (during my first visit) were Brazilians of European ancestry.[19] During my interview with Schaumloeffel at the embassy in Accra, he admitted to racial inequality in Brazil, especially in the education systems that privilege Brazilians of European origin. He also stated that Afro-Brazilians have not been visible in Africa, and in particular were excluded from diplomatic posts in Ghana, confirming some of the arguments raised in academic scholarship regarding myths of racial equality and democracy in Brazil. I asked similar questions during my discussions with Nii Azumah V and Frank C. K. Dugbley, a former Ghanaian official at the Brazilian embassy in Accra.[20] However, both either did not share the same view as Schaumloeffel or did not have any extensive information about this subject. The absence of Afro-Brazilian staff members at the embassy, in addition to Dzidzienyo's conclusion and growing literature on racial politics in Brazil, provides a starting point for the Tabom people to inquire about the lack of racial diversity in such a public diplomatic environment. However, the racial disparity at the embassy does not resonate among a large population of the Tabom community because of their limited knowledge of how notions of racial democracy have marginalized a large population of Brazilians. Recurring themes in contemporary Brazilian literature on race and ethnicity formations are threefold: (1) that white hegemony, white elites, and white scholars have neutralized racial problems; (2) that they have created and perpetuated myths of racial democracy and harmony; and (3) that they have weakened black mobilization and destabilized Afro-Brazilian unity by imposing the notion of *mestizaje*, or racial mixing. In the words of Brazilian historian Thomas Skidmore, "Brazilians see themselves as very different from all other New World societies... yet inequalities and vulnerabilities remain."[21] For Edward Telles, race in Brazil remains a visible marker for creating class and ethnic structures in "which blacks and browns are kept in the lower ranks.... Race and class thus become important signifiers of status conscious society."[22]

Other Brazilian scholars have taken note of how anti–Gilberto Freyre critics are perceived when they interrogate the authenticity of racial equality. Any scholar who debunks or challenges the notion of racial democracy in Brazil is branded "un-Brazilian" or an enemy of Brazilian national racial unity.[23] Considering the recent attention given to aspects of African retentions in the New World, especially in academia, it might be easy for the Tabom people to rely on common historical elements, such as religious and cultural practices like condomblé and capoeira, that tie Africa to Brazil.[24] However, these avenues may not be enough to provide them with the recognition, attention, and reception that the Tabom leader and his people are hopeful of receiving during a future visit. Dzidzienyo has a stern warning to those who think along these lines. He proclaims that, "neither has ... African provenance, such as musical expressions, which have been shifted from the margins to the center of national cultural life in specific Latin American societies, resulted in the transformation of the overall negativity assigned to [people of] African origins."[25]

Racial relations in Brazil have improved to some extent in the twenty-first century. Some of these reforms were a result of the radical approach by Brazilian scholars, intellectuals, and activists such as the late Abdias do Nascimento, Leila Gonzalez, and others. The rise of Afro-Brazilian nationalist movements and the reforms Lula enforced during his tenure made a huge impact.[26] Nonetheless, simmering animosity, stigma, and prejudice against Afro-Brazilians and people of non-European ancestry cements my argument that the Tabom people's dream to visit their ancestors' former home opens up new questions about their unfulfilled desires and fantasy of Brazil. Recent mass public protests by Brazilians during the summer 2014 World Cup soccer tournament in Brazil demanding government attention to social and economic problems affecting its citizens rather than an investment in sports highlights lingering problems. My point is that the mindset of some of the Tabom people and existing racial problems in Brazil may create unexpected problems for Tabom people who visit Brazil. In my opinion, the issue of racial inequality, which is not often raised or addressed by the Brazilian government and those who interact with the Tabom, should be made known to stabilize their mutual relations.

The Brazilian embassy has not fully disclosed this important feature of Brazilian history and social interactions, perhaps because it is concerned that such revelation could taint the image the Tabom people have of Brazil. However, the perception of Brazil within the Brazilian-African diaspora in Ghana is slowly changing. Through his personal initiatives, Nii Azumah V and his people have gained access to reading materials, including academic scholarship that addresses racial and ethnic problems in Brazil, since 2006. These new resources have yielded a great deal of success. The Tabom chief reported being more informed about the controversial subject in Brazil and claimed that he had discussed some of his findings and concerns with officials of the Brazilian embassy. The officials have partly acknowledged racial problems in their country and assured Nii Azumah V that some Brazilian leaders have made efforts to correct the lingering problem. The Tabom chief's new awakening might create some problems for him and his community if they continue to interrogate the embassy about racial issues. One thing is certain: Nii Azumah V continues to share the academic materials with his people to inform them about their ancestral history. But considering the fact that the Tabom are spread throughout various regions of Ghana, Nii Azumah V's new knowledge about Brazil might not go beyond Accra, where he and most of the Tabom currently live.

The Tabom chief is resolute about his vision for his people, and he has been very involved in the progress of the Brazilian-African diaspora since the event during which Nii Azumah V and Lula complimented each other. During Lula's visit the Tabom chief promised that "the [Brazil] House will also act as a Documentation Center to provide historical information on the Tabom."[27] The Tabom chief accomplished this goal when the Brazil House was opened two years after Lula's visit. His plans to include academic materials, video tapes, and other information about Afro-Brazilian history among the list of readings to be housed in the future Tabom City library collections indeed signal a promising future for preserving Brazilian-African diaspora history in Ghana.[28] In most of our interviews he expressed concerns about the fact that most young people of Brazilian origins were apathetic about their dual heritage. In spite of this disappointment, Nii Azumah V contends that he is optimistic that the new generation will continue to depend heavily on oral history, diaries, letters, historical monuments such as the Brazil House and Brazil Lane, and other historical symbols that are yet to be to be repaired to enhance their knowledge about their Brazilian heritage. These landmarks, which still stand in their community, and photographs passed on by the previous generation (some of which I did not have access to) will continue to guide future research to fill the gaps in my book. Indeed, *Mãntse* Nii Azumah V's dedication to the Brazilian-African diaspora and his persistent efforts to restore the history of his forebears have survived numerous obstacles, including squabbles within Tabom communities. Memory continues to play an important role in resolving divisions among the Tabom and sustaining their future.

Chapter Ten

Dwindling Promises and a Disappointing World Cup: Another Unsuccessful Road to Brazil

The 2014 World Cup soccer tournament, which was hosted by Brazil, raised new interests among the Tabom people. Indeed, Ghanaians of diverse status and social background saw this as an opportunity to visit Brazil. In addition, the tournament came at a time when several members of the Brazilian-African diaspora were anticipating that the World Cup could revive the earlier promise that was made to them. However, there were no attempts to use this event to fulfill this promise. According to *Mãntse* Nii Azumah V, although a number of Tabom people were willing to travel to Brazil there was no formal arrangement, support, or special provision by the Brazilian government or the embassy in Accra. Brazilian ambassador Gala did not have anything promising to say to the Tabom people, but she had a lot to say to Ghanaian fans who wanted to travel to Brazil to watch the tournament. One report blazed: "Brazilian Ambassador Warns Fans about Expensive World Cup."[29] This was a missed opportunity for all the parties involved to fulfill this dream. It seems to have become an empty promise. Other disappointments emerged later and created additional disappointments for the Tabom people in the international sports arena. Besides the vagueness of Lula's promise, Ghana's unimpressive performance added another layer of frustration and disappointment as the community kept waiting for a miracle to happen so that they could be flown across the Atlantic waters. In the end, Brazil's own poor performance—the worst ever—provided a tangible reason that alleviated the Tabom people's disappointment at not being able to watch the games live in Brazil.

The lack of proper coordination to bring Tabom people to Brazil shows uncertainty about the future of the promise that was made a decade ago. Looking at it from another angle, it is becoming obvious that Lula's promise was based on an individual interest or efforts from the bottom up, but not on legislation or policy from the top down. Lula had a daunting promise to keep during his tenure. Part of Lula's agenda sought to elevate the image of Brazil as a former slave nation with extensive interest in showcasing the mutual relations they have developed with the offspring of its former slave populations now living in Africa. Lula was determined to meet this colossal responsibility to please the global world and the international diplomatic community. However, he ran out of time.

Darkness and a Fallen Oak Tree: Change or Continuity?

One recurring theme in this book is that memory of a home in Africa remained in the consciousness of slaves who were dispersed into Brazilian plantations as they pursued dangerous voyages back to Africa. I have said the same about descendants who have already visited Brazil for the first time and those still looking for the opportunity to do so in the future. Yearning for Brazil spanned a long time period and different generational groups. The death of Elder George Nii Aruna Nelson, who was the oldest descendant prior to his death on 7 April 2009, provides relevant lessons. He was one of the older community members who were passionate about Brazil but never made it there physically. Nelson wanted to perform tricks as a magician so he could fly to Brazil before he died. As the eulogy shows, the old man played a pivotal role in transforming, sustaining, and disseminating stories about the Brazilian-African diaspora. Part of my analysis also depends on the contribution of Aishatu Nelson to her Brazilian heritage. Both are from the Nelson *we* (family). They have provided relevant information about their ancestors during our interviews. Aishatu took very good care of her grandfather, Elder Nelson, in his old age, especially during the closing stages of his life. It was no surprise that she was selected out of sixty-five grandchildren and thirty great-grandchildren (from twenty children of Elder Nelson) to read a tribute from his offspring during the funeral service. Aishatu read part of the tribute softly and passionately:

> Grandpa, you lived a full and happy life surrounded by those you loved so much, and although we cry and feel great sadness, we know you still remain in our hearts. How we wish you had stayed longer with your grandchildren. . . . We, your grandchildren, have many great and unforgettable memories of our days together; from advice, jokes, revealing the history of our family, and above all, teaching us more about what the Word of God really meant in our lives . . . We had so much from you, Papa Nii this will never be forgotten. . . . Oh Papa Nii, Kpo Yaawo Dzogbann. Rest in peace our great Grandpa and Hero.[30]

Aishatu's tribute revealed a host of issues: the close ties between the old man and the generations that followed him, the acknowledgement that a member of the third generation had passed on the history of their Brazilian heritage, the promise of these young Tabom people that they would never forget Elder Nelson and what he shared about their ancestral past, and an indirect assurance that they would carry the torch of memory and perhaps disseminate similar accounts to the next generation. Indeed, this was a unique case in the community; this trailblazer of Brazilian heritage left a legacy that is worthy of imitation among his descendants. Another element that stands out in the eulogy is the use of Gã words such as "Papa Nii," which means grandfather Nii, the elder's Gã name, and the word *kpo*, which is the Gã word for "sorry." These words were used to express sadness and to explain the pain of his grandchildren's and great-grandchildren's physical separation from him. The sixty-five grandchildren and thirty great-grandchildren dressed in the Ghanaian traditional white outfit as a way of celebrating the long life of the old man rather than mourning his passing. Overall, the tribute epitomized a watershed moment in the history of the Brazilian-African diaspora in Ghana. One question, however, still lingers: How far can the descendants carry on with Papa Nii's legacy?

The old man was a pillar in the Brazilian-African diaspora. There was darkness in the community as one of the "oak trees" fell. His absence has created a vacuum that has not been filled yet. During his lifetime, particularly my last two interviews before his death, he never gave up hope. He continued talking about his lifetime dream to visit Brazil. Papa Nii imagined visiting the ancestral homeland of his grandparents who were once slaves. He was among the Tabom delegation that hosted President Lula, but his wish to visit Brazil was never realized. The funeral of Elder Nelson at the St. Mary's Anglican Church, Asafoatse Nettey Road, Accra, around noon on 10 July 2009 was indeed memorable and historic.[31] Standing before over one thousand mourners and about eight feet from Elder Nelson's casket, Aishatu audaciously read the tribute with her head up while holding her tears. At the cemetery she placed flowers on the old man's grave, and as the grave was covered, Aishatu no longer contained her emotions—she lowered her cheek with pride and wept as she said the final farewell to one of the pillars of the Brazilian-African diaspora.

During interment of Elder Nelson at the Nii Ankrah royal family mausoleum in Accra, it became clear that a tower in the Tabom community who lived for almost a century had fallen. It was the end of an era for one generation and the continuation of an era for another generation. Symbolically, the scene at the cemetery characterized a critical juncture in Brazilian heritage—an intersection between what the elder disseminated about his ancestral past during his lifetime and how this information would aid in the construction of Brazilian history after his burial. How much information Papa Nii took with him to his grave and its impact on the Tabom story may not be known yet. Additionally, Aishatu and those of her generation may have additional knowledge about the Brazilian tree that could have a lasting impact. She and others could become the vehicle for preserving, transporting, and spreading news about their heritage.

The long life and death of Elder Nelson, a trailblazer, was a remarkable journey colored by his determination to embrace both his Ghanaian and Brazilian identities.

The unsuccessful attempt of the late Elder Nelson and other elders of the community to visit Brazil for the first time, which I tie directly to Lula's unfulfilled pledge and the Brazilian embassy's inability to make past promises a reality, has also made it difficult for the younger generation to fathom the reality of a second ancestral homeland in Brazil. My central thesis is that although some of the Tabom are still thinking about Brazil, the notion of a Brazilian homeland is, in general, gradually becoming a myth as they continue to assimilate into larger Ghanaian cultures and as their chances of visiting Brazil seem to be blurred by a lack of financial support and various divisions within the community. In fact, their inability to either pay for the trip on their own or convince the Brazilian government and the embassy in Accra to fund their trip, as during the 2014 World Cup soccer tournament in Brazil, has placed an additional burden on the older members of the community as they try to find ways to make their dream of return a reality.

There were other major cultural differences between the Brazilians and their descendants. Some of these were created by their different historical circumstances and how they constructed and reconstructed their identities. Regarding the issue of citizenship, I in no way suggest that the descendants do not want to be Ghanaian citizens anymore. Rather, the goal of this book is to show that descendants are not homogeneous. They have a variety of views about their past. In short, members of the Brazilian-African diaspora in Ghana hold a range of ideas about their future. Stark diversity within the community is reflected in the ways they identify. I am not suggesting that the Tabom people want to leave Ghana and settle permanently in Brazil. The first generation identified or presented themselves mostly as Brazilians and not the people of the Gold Coast, particularly by the way they dressed in European clothing and their use of Portuguese language. Some of their descendants did the opposite. Court cases such as *Plange v. Brazilians* and *J. E. Maslieno v. J. A. Nelson* have shown a similar trend of deep assimilation into Gã cultures. Most of this transformation occurred via intermarriages. It is imperative to add that although marriage unions stabilized their history to some degree and allowed them to appreciate their dual identities, it did not unite them. The future of the Tabom people continues to oscillate in different historical directions. Despite the success in making the Brazil House and other aspects of their history visible to the Ghanaian public and global heritage tourism, in particular, they still have enormous challenges ahead of them. Some of these challenges are due to their receding memory of their Brazilian heritage and what seems like a fading diaspora as some Tabom continue to grapple with the idea of a *home* in Brazil. Other current challenges are a result of internal movements or the Tabom people's relocation from one point to the other within Ghana. According to Julian Koshie Peregrino-Brimah, the search for jobs and educational demands on the Tabom youth continue to make it difficult for the older generation and the younger ones to spend time together or participate in various family activities including child-naming ceremonies, wedding, parties, and funeral services among others.[32]

The late Elder Nelson, who is now resting in his grave peacefully with his ancestors, served as an example for the community. Those he left behind have imitated his legacy and have focused on the best way to preserve the fragmented histories of the Brazilian-African diaspora. For instance, instead of being entangled in existing debates about rights, access, or who owns historical monuments such as the Brazil House, some members of the community are using various resources in these historical sites as incentives for progress within their community. *Mãntsɛ* Nii Azumah V and the Tabom youth are not the only ones who act as intermediaries between the Tabom people and others outside the community. Despite ambiguity and tension over the Brazil House, the embassy continues to serve as a major actor and a go-between for the Tabom community and the Brazilian government. For the Brazilian embassy in Ghana, the Tabom story embodies a strong diplomatic and transnational enterprise linking the embassy and Ghanaians—hence, their success as a diplomatic station on the African continent—in the context of effectively engaging in this growing diasporan and global discourse. In essence, the mutual relationship between the Tabom people and Brazil exemplifies evidence of a strong cultural umbilical cord binding the two distant groups. These existing networks that tie Brazil and Ghana have allowed the two nations to display their vested interests from multiple angles. They have also allowed the various actors including UNESCO and others to benefit from their synergy. In fact, the performance of culture and the management of identity are visible at the Brazil House as the Tabom people continue to create new avenues to make their history accessible. These efforts have attracted Brazilian citizens, diplomats, tourists, pilgrims, visitors like school children and those involved in study abroad programs, and the general public.

Conclusion

The story of ex-slaves who arrived over a century ago on the shores of Accra on a ship from Brazil remains on the margins of Ghanaian historiography and African diaspora history. *Brazilian-African Diaspora in Ghana* explores this peripheral account and makes this experience a central piece in the reverse migration discourse. This book chronicles the audacious journey to Ghana, showing the complicated future, nuances, and silences in the narratives. It also examines the complexity of reverse migration journeys: the challenges some of the ex-slaves encountered in the nineteenth century when they boarded ships to a *home* in Africa, the difficulty of imagining a distant family over the Atlantic waters, and the challenges of reclaiming a "lost" ancestral root as the tide reversed toward Africa. I attempt to lift the curtain to reveal evidence of double consciousness that oscillates and touches two important geographical points: Ghana and Brazil.

Africa was a place some were traveling to for the first time to reconnect with their heritage and their family since their enslavement. As Alex Haley notes, "in every conceivable manner, the family is a link to our past, a bridge to our future." Indeed, awareness about a homeland did not end with the returnees' physical emigration to Ghana. This notion permeates the consciousness of some Tabom communities in the twenty-first century. Like the ex-slaves who embarked on dangerous passages to their ancestral homeland, the Tabom, the descendants of the ex-slaves, have a deep desire to visit Brazil where their ancestors where once enslaved. The story of the Tabom is not just about an expression of unmatched fortitude in locating an ancestral *home*

Conclusion

somewhere in Brazil—places most of them have heard about, but have not seen. Rather, it is also about preserving the Brazil House, a silent monument of slavery and other historical landmarks in their communities for posterity.[1] Like the *nkyinkyim* and *sankofa* Akan adinkra symbols, the story has no end in sight in part because of the dissonance of memory and the zigzag migratory paths that resonate in their narratives as these returnees and their offspring seek to reconnect with their ancestral roots. The challenges associated with memory and locating an unknown past have larger implications with the study of history in general.[2]

The central tenets of this book include notions of continuities and change and double consciousness associated with the ways in which some of the members of the Brazilian-African diaspora are refashioning multiple identities. The Brazilian-African diaspora in Ghana is one that searched for its past and continues to refashion its identity both through the Middle Passage experience and within a larger Ghanaian culture. Such compartmentalization or modification of an African or diasporic identity suffers "under the weight of many definitions ... or coheres with all other denotations and connotations."[3] While some of the ex-slaves spoke Portuguese and dressed in suits and hats as Europeans to set themselves apart from the Gã people, some Tabom embraced both their Gã or Ghanaian and Brazilian identities.

To a large extent, the Brazilian-African diaspora in Ghana is a story in transition that continues to evolve from one generation to the next. How the Tabom are clamoring for the opportunity to visit their ancestral home in Brazil reflects part of the yearnings of their ancestors. The road to Brazil illuminates dissonance of memory and unending, winding trajectories embedded in this transatlantic history, which provide researchers with plenty of opportunities to further examine other aspects of the Tabom history not covered in or beyond the scope of this book.

This story is grounded not only in the history of identity crises, division, and contentions, but also in how the Tabom have made efforts to reconcile or establish mutual relations among themselves. Furthermore, the narratives of the Brazilian-African diaspora in Ghana are draped in shades of historical developments including the social history of Accra and British colonial rule in particular. These tightly woven intersections do not mean that the social history of Accra and British colonial rule cannot be independent of each other. The converging and diverging points need to be treated separately whenever necessary to highlight the complexity and fluidity in relations between the returnees and towering entities in Ghana such as the Gã mãŋtsɛmɛi and the British Empire from the nineteenth century.

The journey home was not a guaranteed "joy ride." The Brazilian-African diasporic narrative highlights the multiple layers of paradoxes of freedom: first, as stringent British colonial land ordinances seized "Brazilian land," land belonging to the ex-slaves and the Tabom; and second, as some of the ex-slaves were involved in slavery activities to amass wealth and for domestic use. Returning to an ancestral homeland and the process of resettlements in general came with a price; even those that were arranged by philanthropists and various abolitionist groups had their own problems. The interplay between emancipation that began in Brazil in the early nineteenth century, and the paradox of freedom that occurred when colonial restrictions threatened the ex-slaves' liberation resonates in the Brazilian-African diaspora narratives in Ghana. The ex-slaves and the Tabom were not the only ones who were guilty of slavery. Gã mãŋtsɛmɛi, leaders of various ethnic groups, missionaries, merchants, and the people of Ghana invested heavily in slavery for financial gain and to acquire free labor. British officials were guilty, too. At the peak of abolition in Ghana in the early twentieth century, British colonial officials perpetuated slavery as they borrowed slaves from their owners to facilitate war with the Asante people. The British compensated the slave owners after they returned the slaves to their owners.[4] Other Europeans were also determined to deny freedom granted during abolition so they could demand free labor and skills from the ex-slaves to enhance their own plantation systems in the West Indies as well as colonial projects in Ghana.[5]

· · ·

A new approach to studying reverse diaspora migrations as holistic, dynamic, and ongoing phenomena is advanced. Ghana is seen as a key site for applying this alternative vision and expanding our existing knowledge of Atlantic history in part because of its strong ties to the transatlantic slave trade, its heritage tourism, and its contribution to the Pan-African movements from the twentieth century.[6] All this calls for a new discourse that moves beyond the romanticized imagery of returning to the African homeland to a study that traces the unending voluntary journeys back and forth between Africa and Brazil.

The new approach must embrace how the Tabom remember their Brazilian past, how others imagine and construct their Brazilian heritage, why some have traveled to Bahia/Salvador and Rio de Janeiro or aspire to do so in the future, and why some do not associate with their Brazilian ancestry. The illumination of the role of memory—both dissonance of memory and constellations of remembrance—are central to this never-ending course of locating a *home*. These multifaceted migrations across the Atlantic have been journeys of hope to never-before-seen places expressing the search for a *home* entrenched in the cultural memory and imagination of the Tabom. The Tabom people's vigorous attempts to preserve their past history, especially their efforts to visit Brazil, are another turning point in diaspora history. The Tabom leaderships' collective visit to Brazil will happen as soon as the fog overshadowing this trip is cleared.

Conclusion

New challenges confronting the Tabom leadership over which family has to lead the Tabom people and how or which family group has to manage the Brazil House is an extension of the problems their ancestors had over land distribution from the late 1800s to the mid-1900s. Ripples in the pond continue to form bubbles; past conflicts have also created apathy in the community. Furthermore, the involvement of members of the early Brazilian-African settlers in slave trade (after their settlements in Accra) tainted their history, affected their progeny—particularly, creating generations who avoided or denied their "dual" identities, origins, or ancestral ties to Brazil, as well as their lack of interest in ongoing efforts to restore their Brazilian connection. Decades of land disputes and other aspects of the legacy of this dark history have affected the younger generations of Tabom with manifestations of apathy, ignorance, and injury that has contributed to the present-day challenges faced by researchers and the Tabom in reconstructing their history through oral history and traditions and familial and communal interactions.

Part of the fluctuation in their narratives, especially the methodological limitations in my story, is shaped by dissonance of memory as the Tabom attempt to articulate what they remember or express their knowledge or diverse understanding of their family ties to Brazil. Some of the inconsistencies may have been influenced by fantasy and receding memory regarding their distant Brazilian heritage. While yearning for another homeland still permeates Tabom consciousness in the twenty-first century, other creative efforts have led to numerous changes in the Tabom community, such as the creation of Brazil House. The Brazil House is a major site of memory, underscoring its significance, most importantly, for ensuring the survival of Brazilian-African and Tabom history in Ghana.

Many questions have yet to be answered partly because of nuances in the narratives of the ex-slaves and the Tabom. The nuances lie in the rigmarole "dance" embedded in discourse of reverse migrations and disappearing memory, as well as silences within the Brazilian-African diaspora narratives in Ghana. Challenges confronting how the Tabom remember what has been passed on from generations, how they refashion their identities, and how they manage the weight of the past are not in isolation.

Recent study of the life histories of slaves from Madagascar on slave vessels plying the Indian Ocean to plantations in the North American Atlantic world reveals that the descendants of these enslaved Africans also had difficulty remembering their past and tracing their African roots. In *Memories of Madagascar and Slavery in the Black Atlantic*, Wendy Wilson-Falls relates that memory "can be a burden and affect generations of people with its message of trauma, betrayal and loss. Absence in narratives is part of the material that is remembered, because silences, in their way, also record something."[7] John Edward Phillips says it more eloquently when he writes, "History is a conversation the present holds with the past.... History therefore will always be a work in-progress because the 'present' is continually becoming occupied by new generations."[8] The Brazilian-African transatlantic story, like other slavery narratives, is similar to a puzzle that sometimes comes together to form a cohesive piece of art.

Enslaved Africans and their offspring have been engaging in a continuous search for a lost identity in locating the "other home." This hunt for identity has momentous implications for the future history of the Brazilian-Tabom and Atlantic diasporic story. The ever-changing character of the Brazilian-African diaspora is a "kind of voyage that encompasses the possibility of never arriving or returning."[9] The journey continues.

Notes

ABBREVIATIONS

ACS	American Colonization Society Papers, University of Central Arkansas, USA
ADM	Administrative Records, PRAAD, Ghana
CO	Colonial Office, Kew, UK
CVA	Civil Appeal, PRAAD, Ghana
EC	Ecclesiastical, PRAAD, Ghana
FC NB	Furley Collections Notebook, Balme Library, University of Ghana, Legon
FO	Foreign Office, Kew, UK
PRAAD	Public Records and Administration Division, Accra, Cape Coast, and Sekondi, Ghana
RG	Record Groups, PRAAD, Ghana
SC	Special Collections, PRAAD, Ghana
SCT	Supreme Courts Transcripts, PRAAD, Ghana
WO	War Office, Kew, UK
T 70	Treasury Records, Records of the Company of Royal Adventurers of England, Kew, UK

INTRODUCTION

1. CO 97/2, "Ordinances, 1865 to 1883," 19 April 1876; ADM 4/1/1, 4 April 1856, 48; SC 2, 20 September 1858, 4. See also Naaborko Sackeyfio-Lenoch, *The Politics of Chieftaincy: Authority and Property in Colonial Ghana, 1920-1950* (Rochester, NY: University of Rochester Press, 2014); M. E. Kropp Dakubu, *Korle Meets the Sea: A Sociolinguistic History of Accra* (New York: Oxford University Press, 1997); Edward Reynolds, *Trade and Economic Change on the Gold Coast, 1807-1874* (Accra: Sub-Saharan Publishers, 2002); I. van Kessel, *Merchants, Missionaries and Migrants: 300 Years of Dutch-Ghanaian Relations* (Amsterdam: KIT Publishers, 2002); Robin Law, ed. *From Slave Trade to 'Legitimate' Commerce: The Commercial Transition in Nineteenth-Century West Africa* (Cambridge, UK: Cambridge University Press, 1995), 1-56. Interactions between Gã people, Europeans, and other settlers went beyond trade, colonialism, and the spread of religion. As Carina E. Ray demonstrated in *Crossing the Color Line*, colonial officials and missionaries and Gã women were involved in what Ray characterizes as "undesirable [sexual] relations" that created an Afro-European class in Accra. Carina E. Ray, *Crossing the Color Line: Race, Sex, and the Contested Politics of Colonialism in Ghana* (Athens: Ohio University Press, 2015), 56-78.

2. Georgina T. Wood, interview by Kwame Essien, 5 August 2012. See also Antonio Oliz Boyd, *The Latin American Identity and the African Diaspora: Ethnogenesis in Context* (Amherst, NY: Cambria Press, 2010), 258-60.

3. Elder George Aruna Nelson, interview by Kwame Essien, 6 August 2008.

4. In Nigeria, Benin, and Togo the emancipated Brazilian-Africans as well as Afro-Cubans and their offspring are known as the "Aguda." See the following works: Solimar Otero, *Afro-Cuban Diasporas in the Atlantic World* (Rochester, NY: University of Rochester Press, 2010); Kwesi Kwaa Prah, ed., *Back to Africa*, vol. 1, *Afro-Brazilian Returnees and Their Communities* (Cape Town: Center for Advanced Studies of African Society, 2009); José C. Curto and Paul E. Lovejoy, eds., *Enslaving Connections: Changing Cultures of Africa and Brazil during the Era of Slavery* (New York: Humanity Books, 2004); and Michael J. Turner, "Les Bresiliens: The Impact of Former Brazilian Slaves upon Dahomey" (PhD diss., Boston University, 1975). In Liberia, they are called "Americo-Liberians." See the following works: Kenneth C. Barnes, *Journey of Hope: The Back-to-Africa Movement in Arkansas in the Late 1800s* (Chapel Hill: University of North Carolina Press, 2004); Claude A. Clegg III, *The Price of Liberty: African Americans and the Making of Liberia* (Chapel Hill: University of North Carolina Press, 2004); and Ibrahim Sundiata, *Brothers and Strangers: Black Zion, Black Slavery, 1914-1940* (Durham, NC: Duke University Press, 2003). In Sierra Leone they are known as the "Sarro." See the following works: Gibril R. Cole, *The Krio of West Africa: Islam, Culture, Creolization and Colonialism in the Nineteenth Century* (Athens: Ohio University Press, 2013); Nemata Amelia Blyden, *West Indians in West Africa, 1808-1880: The African Diaspora in Reverse* (Rochester, NY: University of Rochester Press, 2000); and John W. Pulis, *Moving On: Black Loyalists in the Afro-Atlantic World* (New York: Garland, 1999). Resettlements in Liberia and Sierra Leone were funded partly by the American Colonization Society and philanthropists in America during and after the period of Reconstruction in the mid-nineteenth century. For African Americans in Ghana, see Kevin K. Gaines, *American Africans in Ghana: Black Expatriates and the Civil Rights Era* (Chapel Hill: University of North Carolina Press, 2006); Kwame Essien, "African Americans in Ghana and Their Contributions to 'Nation Building' since 1985," in *The United States and West Africa: Interactions and Relations*, ed. Alusine Jalloh and Toyin Falola (Rochester, NY: University of

Rochester Press, 2008), chap. 8; and Kwame Essien, "African Americans in Ghana: Successes and Challenges, 1985 through 2005" (MA thesis, University of Illinois-Urbana-Champaign, 2006). For the Caribbean/West Indian returnees in Ghana, see Clifford C. Campbell, "Full Circle: The Caribbean Presence in the Making of Ghana, 1843–1966" (PhD diss., University of Ghana, Legon, 2012); and Jeffrey P. Green, "Caribbean Influences in the Gold Coast Administration in the 1900s," *Ghana Studies Bulletin* 2 (December 1984): 11–16.

5. For Angola, see Roquinaldo Amaral Ferreira, *Cross-Cultural Exchange in the Atlantic World: Angola and Brazil during the Era of the Slave Trade* (Cambridge: Cambridge University Press, 2012); and Mariana P. Candido, *An African Slaving Port and the Atlantic World: Benguela and Its Hinterland* (Cambridge: Cambridge University Press, 2013). For Upper Guinea and Amazonia in Brazil, see Walter Hawthorne, *From Africa to Brazil: Culture, Identity, and an Atlantic Slave Trade, 1600–1830* (Cambridge: Cambridge University Press, 2010). For Jamaica, see Kwasi Konadu, *The Akan Diaspora in the Americas* (New York: Oxford University Press, 2010).

6. Silke Strickrodt, "The Brazilian Diaspora to West Africa in the Nineteenth Century," in *AficAmericas: Itineraries, Dialogues, and Sounds*, ed. Ineke Phaf-Rheinberger and Tiago de Oliveira Pinto (Frankfurt, Germany: Die Deutsche Nationalbibliothek, 2008), 43.

7. Robin Law, "Abolition and Imperialism: International Law and the British Suppression of the Atlantic Slave Trade," in *Abolitionism and Imperialism in Britain, Africa and the Atlantic*, ed. Derek R. Peterson (Athens: Ohio University Press, 2010), 150. See also Frederick Cooper, *From Slaves to Squatters: Plantation Labor and Agriculture in Zanzibar and Coastal Kenya, 1890–1925* (New Haven, CT: Yale University Press, 1980); Sir Reginald Coupland, *The British Anti-Slavery Movement*, 2nd ed. (London: Frank Cass, 1964); Ralph A. Austen and Woodruff D. Smith, "Images of Africa and British Slave-Trade Abolition: The Transition to an Imperialist Ideology, 1787–1807," *African Historical Studies* 2, no. 1 (1969): 69–83.

8. Nelson, interview by Essien, 6 August 2008; and Nii Azumah V, interview by Kwame Essien, 6 August 2008. See also Marco Aurelio Schaumloeffel, "The Influence of the Portuguese Language in Ghana," *Daily Graphic*, 7 May 2004, 7; and Marco Aurelio Schaumloeffel, "Tabon: The Afro-Brazilian Community in Accra," *Daily Graphic*, 3 June 2004, 14.

9. To the best of my knowledge, there is no evidence that shows that the early settlers identified as "Tabom." Furthermore, for various reasons some of their descendants do not identify as Tabom but as Brazilians. For instance, in my interview with Elder William Lutterodt he distanced himself from the the word "Tabom" but held tightly to his identity both as a Brazilian and as a Ghanaian. Lutterodt's strategic way of identifying as a Brazilian may have been influenced by the fact that he is closer to his Brazilian roots with Tabom people, who mostly see themselves as Ghanaians. See also Alcione M. Amos and Ebenezer Ayesu, "'I Am Brazilian': History of the Tabon, Afro-Brazilian in Accra," *Transactions of the Historical Society of Ghana*, n.s., 6 (2002): 35.

10. Nelson, interview by Essien, 6 August 2008.

11. Kwame Essien, "(In)Visible Diasporan Returnee Communities: Silences and the Challenges in Studying Trans-Atlantic History in Ghana." *Ghana Studies* 17 (2014): 63–99; and Kwame Essien, "'Afie ni Afie' (Home Is Home): Revisiting Reverse Trans-Atlantic Journeys to Ghana and the Paradox of Return," *Ìrìnkèrindò: A Journal of African Migration* 7 (June 2014): 47–75.

12. In this context, "returnee" is used in reference to *all* people of African ancestry who returned to Africa to stay temporarily or permanently from the nineteenth century.

13. Although the African American story emerged over a century after Brazilian-African history,

there is more literature on the African American returnees than the latter. In fact, this is consistent with their greater visibility in the tourism industry compared to Brazilian-Africans.

14. For instance in Ghana the Public Land Ordinance of 1876 gave colonial officials permission to use any land they needed in the Gold Coast colony. Also, the Compulsory Labour Ordinance of 1897 demanded free labor from all citizens under what became known as the British Southern Protectorate at the onset of colonial rule.

15. Brazil House is the location in coastal Accra first settled by early returnees. There are other sites of memories associated with the Brazilian-Ghanaian story. They include the Brazilian Road and Scissors House (where the first tailoring shop was established in the 1830s).

16. The following scholars have provided important insight on this subject: Jack P. Greene and Philip D. Morgan, eds., *Atlantic History: A Critical Appraisal* (New York: Oxford University Press, 2009); Jorge Cañizares-Esguerra and Eric R. Seeman, eds., *The Atlantic in Global History, 1500-2000* (Upper Saddle River, NJ: Prentice Hall, 2007); Alison Games, "Atlantic History: Definitions, Challenges, and Opportunities," *American Historical Review* 111, no 3 (2006): 741-57; Bernard Bailyn, *Atlantic History: Concept and Contours* (Cambridge, MA: Harvard University Press, 2005); and Paul Gilroy, *The Black Atlantic: Modernity and Double Consciousness* (Cambridge, MA: Harvard University Press, 1993). See also Ferreira, *Cross-Cultural Exchange in the Atlantic World*, 5-12; and Hawthorne, *From Africa to Brazil*, 1-9.

17. João José Reis, *Divining Slavery and Freedom: The Story of Domingos Sodré, an African Priest in Nineteenth-Century Brazil* (New York, NY: Cambridge University Press, 2015). For works in this genre, see, for example, Ferreira, *Cross-Cultural Exchange in the Atlantic World*; James H. Sweet, *Domingos Álvares, African Healing, and the Intellectual History of the Atlantic World* (Chapel Hill: University of North Carolina Press, 2011); João J. Reis, "Domingos Pereira Sodré: A Nagô Priest in Nineteenth-Century Bahia," in *The Changing Worlds of Atlantic Africa: Essays in Honor of Robin Law*, ed. Toyin Falola and Matt Childs (Durham, NC: Carolina Academic Press, 2009), 387-407; João José Reis, Flávio dos Santos Gomes, and Marcus J. M. de Carvalho, "Rufino José Maria (1820s-1850s): A Muslim in the Nineteenth-Century Brazilian Slave Trade Circuit," in *The Human Tradition in the Black Atlantic, 1500-2000*, ed. Beatriz G. Mamigonian and Karen Racine (Lanham, MD: Rowman & Littlefield, 2010), 65-75; Paul E. Lovejoy, "Narratives of Trans-Atlantic Slavery in the Life Stories of Two Muslims," in *Africa and Trans-Atlantic Memories: Literary and Aesthetic Manifestations of Diaspora and History*, ed. Naana Opoku-Agyemang, Paul E. Lovejoy, and David V. Trotman (Trenton, NJ: Africa World Press, 2008), 7-12. For graphic history, see Trevor R. Getz and Liz Clarke, *Abina and the Important Men: A Graphic History* (New York: Oxford University Press, 2012); Manu Herbstein, *Ama: A Story of the Atlantic Slave Trade* (Accra: Techmate Publishers Ghana Ltd., 2010).

18. *Sankofa* is a Ghanaian Akan word that means "going back."

19. Paul Tiyambe Zeleza, "Rewriting the African Diaspora: Beyond the Black Atlantic," *African Affairs* 104, no. 414 (Jan. 2005): 39-41, 54-57, 63-64.

20. Milton Guran, "The Returnees of Benin, Togo, Nigeria and Ghana: Agudas and Tabom," in Prah, *Back to Africa*, 1:112.

21. Bayo Holsey, *Routes of Remembrance: Refashioning the Slave Trade in Ghana* (Chicago: University of Chicago Press, 2008), 22, 129.

22. Saidiya V. Hartman, *Lose Your Mother: A Journey along the Atlantic Slave Route* (New York: Farrar, Straus and Giroux, 2007), 15.

23. Christopher Adejumo, "Migration and Slavery as Paradigms in the Aesthetic Transformation

of Yoruba Art in the Americas," in *Migrations and Creative Expressions in Africa and the African Diaspora*, ed. Toyin Falola, Niyi Afolabi, and Adérónké Adésolá Adésányá (Durham, NC: Carolina Academic Press, 2008), 91-93.

24. Tim Coles and Dallen J. Timothy, "'My Field Is the World': Conceptualizing Diasporas, Travel and Tourism," in *Tourism, Diasporas and Space*, ed. Tim Coles and Dallen J. Timothy (New York: Routledge, 2004), 1.

25. Kristin Mann, *Slavery and the Birth of an African City: Lagos, 1760-1900* (Bloomington: Indiana University Press, 2007), 22. See also Kristin Mann and Edna G. Bay, eds., *Rethinking the African Diaspora: The Making of a Black Atlantic World in the Bight of Benin and Brazil* (Portland, OR: Frank Cass, 2001), 3-10.

26. See Walter C. Rucker, *Gold Coast Diasporas: Identity, Culture, and Power* (Bloomington, IN: Indiana University Press, 2015), 7-17, 140-43.

27. Paulla A. Ebron, *Performing Africa* (Princeton, NJ: Princeton University Press, 2002), 1.

28. João José Reis, *Slave Rebellion in Brazil: The Muslim Uprising of 1835 in Bahia*, trans. Arthur Brakel (Baltimore, MD: Johns Hopkins University Press, 1993). See also João José Reis, *Death is a Festival: Funeral Rites and Rebellion in Nineteenth-Century Brazil*, trans. H. Sabrina Gledhill (Chapel Hill: University of North Carolina Press, 2003), 306-9.

29. CVA 12/52, *Peter Quarshie Fiscian and Mary A. Fiscian v. Nii Azumah III*, 13 March 1953, 12.

30. For instance, the bond shows how the diplomatic, cultural, and economic partnership between Brazil and Ghana culminated in the Ghana-Brazil Chamber of Commerce and Industry, which officially opened in Accra in 2005 during the historical visit of former Brazilian president Luiz Inácio Lula da Silva, who supported expanding cultural and economic exchanges between the two countries to boost trade and sustain their transatlantic ties. This fledgling relationship led to numerous changes in the Tabom community, including the restoration of the Brazil House.

31. According to Asuah, before the slaves were taken off the shores Gã chiefs gave them a piece of flag to remind them of their old community and heritage. Asuah (Nii Azumah V's assistant), interview by Kwame Essien, 10 January 2009.

32. Nii Azumah V, interview by Kwame Essien, 6 August 2008.

33. Samuel Quarcoopome, "The Brazilian Community of Ghana" (BA thesis, University of Ghana, Legon, 1970), 7-8.

34. Lisa A. Lindsay, "Brazilian Women in Lagos, 1879-1882," in *Shaping Our Struggles: Nigerian Women in History, Culture and Development*, ed. Obioma Nnaemeka and Chima J. Korieh (Trenton, NJ: Africa World Press, 2010), 133-37.

35. Nii Azumah V, interview by Kwame Essien, 6 August 2008.

36. Georgina T. Wood, interview by Kwame Essien, 5 August 2012.

37. The "Black Atlantic" is used here to describe the history of African-descended people in the New World. Literature on the "Black Atlantic" is juxtaposed with Atlantic history in ways that highlight their converging and diverging points.

38. Amos and Ayesu, "'I Am Brazilian'" (a translation of Alcione M. Amos and Ebenezer Ayesu, "Sou Brasileiro, História dos Tabom Afro-Brasileiros em Acra, Gana," *Afro-Ásia* 33 (2005): 35-65); Kwame Essien, "A Abertura da Casa Brasil: A History of the *Tabom* People, Part 1," in Prah, *Back to Africa*, 1:173-92; S. Y. Boadi-Siaw, "Brazilian Returnees of West Africa," in *Global Dimensions of the African Diaspora*, ed. Joseph E. Harris (Washington, DC: Howard University Press, 1982); Kwame Essien, "The African Diaspora in Reverse: The *Tabom* People

in Ghana, 1820s-2009" (PhD diss., University of Texas, Austin, 2010); Samuel Quarcoopome, "The Brazilian Community of Ghana" (masters thesis, University of Ghana, Legon, 1970); and Marco A. Schaumloeffel, *Tabom: The Afro-Brazilian Community in Ghana*, 2nd ed. (published by author, 2008).

39. Mae-ling Jovenes Lokko, *The Brazil House* (Accra: Surf Publications, 2010). See also Mae-ling Jovenes Lokko, "The Brazil House: An Exploration of Accra's Urban Growth through a Critical Geography of Architecture," *Tufts University Art & Art History* 8 (September 2010). Lokko was a graduate student in the Department of Art and Art History at Tufts University in the United States.

40. Schaumloeffel, *Tabom* does not include a comparative study of the Tabom with other returnee communities in Ghana and does not employ a broader historical framework in analyzing the various patterns of migration between Brazil and Ghana. Most of the volumes that have significantly contributed to the field focus mainly on the Aguda. The selected anthologies cover the Tabom and the Aguda in works that emphasize the notion of returning to the motherland. And similar to Schaumloeffel's collaboration with the Brazilian government/embassy, these anthologies are limited in scope. For instance, Prah, *Back to Africa*, vol. 1 is an anthology that examines the African diaspora in reverse. The contributors cover broad themes that focus primarily on the political, economic, and social factors that led to the creation of returnee communities in West Africa. The edited work is narrow in scope and, like others on this subject, it largely ignores the Tabom; only two chapters in fact examine the Tabom story, whereas nine chapters address Aguda history. Curto and Lovejoy, *Enslaving Connections* contains essays presented at a York University conference in 2000. It has twelve chapters that explore transatlantic linkages, covering the Brazilian-African and Cuban-African experience during and after the Middle Passage. The last section highlights returnee settlements in Central Angola, as well as others in (Lagos) Nigeria, (Ouidah) Benin, and (Porto Seguro) Togo. Although part of the broader objective of the anthology is to trace trajectories of return, the volume does not cover the Tabom story. Harris, *Global Dimensions of the African Diaspora* employs a global approach to examine various dispersals and the diasporic tapestry beyond the Atlantic Ocean, as well as the voyages of return that followed. This work attempts to document communities that were created or influenced by people of African descent. Although useful, these accounts by-and-large provide limited coverage that favors select groups: the book covers three black communities in Europe; over five chapters explore the African American presence or influence in Liberia, Sierra Leone, Tanzania, Malawi, and the Congo; and only one chapter explores the Afro-Brazilian returnee experience in Ghana. Given recent studies on various transatlantic connections, this work is outdated.

41. *Brazilian-African Diaspora in Ghana* brings together materials from archival collections in Ghana, Nigeria, Brazil, England, and Italy, including colonial and missionary records, Tabom family letters, and so on. At the British National Archives in Kew, England, I draw from Brazilian consular records, British diplomatic and parliamentary reports, statistical data, and colonial administrative papers, among others. Other sources include the Basel missionary records at the Basel Mission Archives (Mission 21), Basel, Switzerland; documents from district and supreme courts, from land tenure records, and other public records at PRAAD in Accra, Ghana; police reports, drawings, passport photos, and other records from the Arquivo Público da Bahia (Brazil); over fifty interviews conducted since 2005 with Ghanaians of Tabom lineage and Aguda returnees in Lagos, Nigeria, and London, England; and, finally, the biographies of leading Brazilian-Ghanaian figures and a couple of well-known members of the Tabom community from recent and past history. The intention is to marry archival evidence and other relevant records

with oral histories and life experiences of Brazilian-African returnees and their descendants.

42. See Kwame Essien, "'Performance' in Trans-Atlantic Communities in Africa: The Case of Brazilian-Africans and American-Africans in Ghana," in *Pan-Africanism and the Politics of African Citizenship and Identity*, ed. Toyin Falola and Kwame Essien (New York: Routledge; London: Taylor & Francis, 2013).

43. For narratives of returnee communities in Ghana, symbols such as W. E. B. DuBois's tomb at the W. E. B. DuBois Centre in Accra remind us of the role of African American expatriates in both the Pan-African Movements and anti-colonial nationalism. Gaines, *American Africans in Ghana*; Kwame Essien, "African Americans in Ghana."

44. See Kwame Essien, "'Afie ni Afie' (Home Is Home): Revisiting Reverse Trans-Atlantic Journeys to Ghana and the Paradox of Return," *Ìrìnkèrindò: A Journal of African Migration* 7 (June 2014): 47-75.

45. Reis, *Divining Slavery and Freedom*; Ana Lucia Araujo, ed. *African Heritage and Memories of Slavery in Brazil and the South Atlantic World* (Amherst, NY: Cambria Press, 2015); Marcus Wood, *Black Milk: Imagining Slavery in the Visual Cultures of Brazil and America* (New York: Oxford University Press, 2013), 1-47; and Babatunde Sofela, *Emancipados: Slave Societies in Brazil and Cuba* (Trenton, NJ: Africa World Press, 2011).

46. Madam Fatima Okpedu, a freed Brazilian slave who migrated from either Brazil or Nigeria to Accra in search of a home in the late 1800s, was one of the founding mothers of the Brazilian family tree in Accra. She married Chief Alhaji Brimah, a devout Yoruba Muslim, philanthropist, entrepreneur, and community leader in Accra in the early 1900s. Suit no. FAL/1040/10 in the Supreme Court of Judicature in the High Court of Justice Land Division 2 held in Accra on Monday, 9 May 2011, before His Lordship Justice F. K. Awuah, was about a dispute between Okpedu's children (Peregrinos) and Brimah's children from another wife over Chief Brimah's land and assets. This dispute is among numerous court hearings between various Brazilian-Tabom family groups in the twenty-first century.

47. Strickrodt, "The Brazilian Diaspora to West Africa," 57-58.

48. Walter C. Rucker, *Gold Coast Diasporas: Identity, Culture, and Power* (Bloomington, IN: Indiana University Press, 2015), 93-143. See also Walter C. Rucker, *The River Flows On: Black Resistance, Culture, and Identity Formation in Early America* (Baton Rouge: Louisiana University Press, 2006); CO 879/41, Sir. W. B. Griffith, to Marques of Rippon, 15 November 1894, 121; Rebecca Shumway, *The Fante and the Transatlantic Slave Trade* (Rochester, NY: University of Rochester Press, 2011), 25-52.

CHAPTER 1. REVERSE DIASPORA: DISSONANCE OF MEMORY, VOYAGES OF HOPE, AND DEGREES OF RETURN

1. "Slave Trade: Brazil Consular-Bahia, Pará, Pernambuco, Rio de Janeiro and Rio Grande do Sul, Vol. XVI of 1853," FO 84/386. See also FO 84/912. There is extensive literature covering similar themes of slavery and abolition: David Eltis et al., eds., *The Trans-Atlantic Slave Trade: A Database on CD-ROM* (Cambridge: Cambridge University Press, 2000); Phillip D. Curtin, *The Atlantic Slave Trade: A Census* (Madison: University of Wisconsin Press, 1969); Joseph E. Inikori and Stanley L. Engerman, eds., *The Atlantic Slave Trade: Effects on Economies, Societies and Peoples in Africa, the Americas and Europe* (Durham, NC: Duke University Press, 1992); Suzanne

Miers and Igor Kopytoff, eds., *Slavery in Africa: Historical and Anthropological Perspectives* (Madison: University of Wisconsin Press, 1977); Walter Rodney, "African Slavery and Other Forms of Social Oppression on the Upper Guinea Coast of the Atlantic Slave-Trade," *Journal of African History* 7, no. 3 (1966): 431–43; A. J. R. Russell-Wood, *The Black Man in Slavery and Freedom in Colonial Brazil* (New York: St. Martins, 1982); Kátia M. de Queiros Mattoso, *To Be a Slave in Brazil, 1550–1888*, trans. Arthur Goldhammer (New Brunswick, NJ: Rutgers University Press, 1996); and Gilberto Freyre, *The Masters and the Slaves: A Study in the Development of Brazilian Civilization* (New York: Alfred A. Knopf, 1946).

2. Throughout history, "Africa" has meant different things to different people. For instance, according to Ibrahim Sundiata, Africa "in the diasporic imagination represents ... things imaged [or imagined], things recorded and things suppressed." Ibrahim Sundiata, *Brothers and Strangers: Black Zion, Black Slavery, 1914–1940* (Durham, NC: Duke University Press, 2003), 2. For debates about continuity and change in African cultural practices in the New World, see the following selected literature: Ana Lucia Araujo, *Crossing Memories: Slavery and African Diaspora* (Trenton, NJ: Africa World Press, 2011); Ana Lucia Araujo, *Shadows of the Slave Past: Memory, Heritage, and Slavery* (New York: Routledge, 2014); Judith A. Carney and Richard Nicholas Rosomoff, *In the Shadow of Slavery: Africa's Botanical Legacy in the Atlantic World* (Berkeley: University of California Press, 2009); Emmanuel Akyeampong, "History, Memory, Slave Trade and Slavery in Anlo (Ghana)," *Slavery & Abolition* 22, no. 3 (2001): 1–24; Paul Gilroy, *The Black Atlantic: Modernity and Double Consciousness* (Cambridge, MA: Harvard University Press, 1993); Phillip M. Peek, ed., *African Divination Systems: Ways of Knowing* (Bloomington: Indiana University Press, 1991); Melville J. Herskovits, *The Myth of the Negro Past* (Boston: Beacon Press, 1990); and Sidney W. Mintz and Richard Price, *The Birth of African-American Culture: An Anthropological Perspective* (Boston: Beacon Press, 1992).

3. Joseph Miller, "Retention, Reinvention, and Remembering: Restoring Identities through Enslavement in Africa and under Slavery in Brazil," in *Enslaving Connections: Changing Cultures of Africa and Brazil during the Era of Slavery*, ed. José C. Curto and Paul E. Lovejoy (New York: Humanity Books, 2004), 81–121.

4. Kwame Essien, "The African Diaspora in Reverse: The *Tabom* People in Ghana, 1820s–2009" (PhD diss., University of Texas, Austin, 2010).

5. Quoted from Pierre Verger, *Trade Relations between the Bight of Benin and Bahia from the 17th to 19th Century*, trans. Evelyn Crawford (Ibadan: Ibadan University Press, 1976), 533.

6. Ruth Simms Hamilton, ed., *Routes of Passage: Rethinking the African Diaspora*, vol. 1, part 1 (East Lansing: Michigan State University Press, 2007), 2, 11–12.

7. The "Atlantic world" and the "New World" will be used interchangeably to describe both enslaved and emancipated communities in the Americas, Europe, and other parts of the world that were created as a result of the transatlantic slave trade. Essien, "African Diaspora in Reverse," 2.

8. Paul Tiyambe Zeleza, "Rewriting the African Diaspora: Beyond the Black Atlantic," *African Affairs* 104 (2005): 41–42. See also Stephanie J. Shaw, *W. E. B. Du Bois and "The Souls of Black Folk"* (Chapel Hill: University of North Carolina Press, 2013).

9. Nii Azumah Nelson V, interview by Kwame Essien, 6 August 2005. Both Nii Azumah Nelson V and the late Elder George Aruna Nelson use this expression to show their pride in both their Brazilian and Ghanaian heritage as well as their ancestral ties to West Africa and the Afro-Atlantic.

10. Geneviève Fabre and Klause Benesch, eds., *African Diasporas in the New and Old Worlds: Consciousness and Imagination* (Amsterdam: Rodopi, 2004), xiv-xv.
11. *Madam Sarah Clegg vs. Emmanuel Drissu Cobblah*, CVA 40/56, 31 March 1958, 12.
12. Ibid., 17.
13. ACS, reel 147, vol. 296, nos. 1-200.
14. Kenneth C. Barnes, *Journey of Hope: The Back-to-Africa Movement in Arkansas in the Late 1800s* (Chapel Hill: University of North Carolina Press, 2004), chap. 3.
15. John Parker, *Making the Town: Ga State and Society in Early Colonial Accra* (Portsmouth, NH: Heinemann, 2000), xvii-36.
16. Boyd Hilton, "1807 and All That: Why Britain Outlawed Her Slave Trade," in *Abolitionism and Imperialism in Britain, Africa and the Atlantic*, ed. Derek R. Peterson (Athens: Ohio University Press, 2010).
17. See the following abolition documents at Kew: "Regulations for the Guidance of the Commissions Appointed for Carrying into Effect the Treaties for the Abolition of the Slave Trade," FO 84/12; FO 84/679; FO 84/767; FO 84/13; and FO 84/199.
18. Paul E. Lovejoy, introduction to G. Ugo Nwokeji, *The Slave Trade and Culture in the Bight of Biafra: An African Society in the Atlantic World* (Cambridge: Cambridge University Press, 2010), xxiv.
19. David Eltis, "The Volume and Structure of the Transatlantic Slave Trade: A Reassessment," *William and Mary Quarterly* 58 (2001): 17-46. See also David Eltis et al., eds., *The Trans-Atlantic Slave Trade: A Database on CD-ROM* (Cambridge: Cambridge University Press, 2000).
20. H. W. Von Hesse, "A Brief History of Afro-Brazilian Community of Accra" (masters thesis, University of Ghana, Legon, 2014), 46. See also Winslow Robertson, "Yes, They Cared about Architecture: The Significance in Yoruba Traditional and Brazilian-Style Housing" (masters thesis, James Madison University, 2008).
21. Lovejoy, introduction to Nwokeji, *The Slave Trade and Culture in the Bight of Biafra*, xxiv.
22. Part of Francis Zaccheus Santiago Peregrino's story, especially his Pan-African activism, is covered by Marika Sherwood, *Origins of Pan-Africanism: Henry Sylvester Williams, Africa and the African Diaspora* (New York: Routledge, 2010), 258-59.
23. Nwokeji, *The Slave Trade and Culture in the Bight of Biafra*; Verger, *Trade Relations between the Bight of Benin and Bahia*, 314-51; and Pierre Verger, *Bahia and the West African Trade, 1549-1851* (Ibadan: Ibadan University Press, 1964).
24. ACS, reel 147, vol. 296, nos. 1-200.
25. Solimar Otero, *Afro-Cuban Diasporas in the Atlantic World* (Rochester, NY: University of Rochester Press, 2010), 110. She also notes, "Havana's Lagosians and the Cuban Aguda in Lagos were good examples of populations who navigated the waters of slavery, emancipation, and repatriation that developed out of the transnational conceptualization of the Atlantic order in the eighteenth century" (29). See also her chap. 2, "Returning to Lagos: Making the *Oja* Home."
26. Ibid., 104.
27. Toyin Falola, *The African Diaspora: Slavery, Modernity, and Globalization* (Rochester, NY: University of Rochester Press, 2013), 126-210.
28. Alison Games, "Atlantic History: Definitions, Challenges, and Opportunities," *American*

Historical Review 111, no. 3 (2006): 741-57; Alison Games and Adam Rothman, eds., *Major Problems in Atlantic History: Documents and Essays* (Boston: Cengage Learning, 2008), 1-23; Gunvor Simonsen, "Moving in Circles: African and Black History in the Atlantic World," *Nuevo Mundo, Mundos Nuevos* 8 (2008): 1-13; Bernard Bailyn, *Atlantic History: Concept and Contours* (Cambridge, MA: Harvard University Press, 2005); Roquinaldo Amaral Ferreira, *Cross-Cultural Exchange in the Atlantic World: Angola and Brazil during the Era of the Slave Trade* (Cambridge: Cambridge University Press, 2012); and Walter Hawthorne, *From Africa to Brazil: Culture, Identity, and an Atlantic Slave Trade, 1600-1830* (Cambridge: Cambridge University Press, 2010), 1-13.

29. Through my interactions with the members of the Brazilian-Tabom communities from 2005, I was able to have access to private letters and a copy of an obituary of one of the Tabom leaders who died in 2009 at the age of ninety-three years. I interviewed Elder George Nii Aruna Nelson, his children, and grandchild about ten times between 2008 and 2009. My last interview with Elder Nelson was about three months before his death. Also, I had the opportunity to attend his funeral service. However, besides the Nelsons, the Lutterodts, and the Peregrinos, I have not been able to access the private collections of other members of the Brazilian-African diaspora. Further, I have not made very meaningful progress with the other groups partly because of the silences or their lack of knowledge about their history that I talk about in this book. Scholarship about African history in general has not resolved polemics or debates about the limitations of the archives and how ethnography can complement these voids. Whereas some authors underplay the significance of oral history and oral traditions in understanding Africa's past, the use of ethnographic approaches such as by Jan Vansina in his seminal work *Oral Tradition* has contributed immensely to this subject over the years. Jan Vansina, *Oral Tradition: A Study in Historical Methodology*, trans. H. M. Wright (New York: Routledge & Kegan Paul, 1965), 158-59. See also Thomas A. Hale, *Griots and Griottes: Masters of Words and Music* (Bloomington: Indiana University Press, 1998), 1; Luise White, Stephan F. Miescher, and David William Chen, eds., *African Words, African Voice: Critical Practices of Oral History* (Bloomington: Indiana University Press, 2001).

30. Michel-Rolph Trouillot, *Silencing the Past: Power and the Production of History* (Boston: Beacon Press, 1995), 27.

31. Jacques Derrida, *Archive Fever: A Freudian Impression*, trans. Eric Prenowitz (Chicago: University of Chicago Press, 1996).

32. Terry Cook, ed., *Controlling the Past: Documenting Society and Institutions; Essays in Honor of Helen Willa Samuels* (Chicago: Society of American Archivists, 2010).

33. Francis X. Blouin Jr. and William G. Rosenberg, *Processing the Past: Contesting Authority in History and the Archives* (London: Oxford University Press, 2011).

34. Suzanne Schwarz, "Reconstructing the Life Histories of Liberated Africans: Sierra Leone in the Early Nineteenth Century," *History in Africa* 39 (2012): 205.

35. Roquinaldo A. Ferreira, interview by Kwame Essien, 2-3 April 2009, "Black Atlantics: An Urban Perspective, 1400-1900," conference, University of Texas, Austin.

36. James H. Sweet, *Recreating Africa: Culture, Kinship, and Religion in African-Portuguese World, 1441-1770* (Chapel Hill: University of North Carolina Press, 2003), 89-100.

37. João José Reis, *Divining Slavery and Freedom: The Story of Domingos Sodré, an African Priest in Nineteenth-Century Brazil* (New York: Cambridge University Press, 2015); João J. Reis, "Domingos Pereira Sodré: A Nagô Priest in Nineteenth-Century Bahia," in *The Changing*

Worlds of Atlantic Africa: Essays in Honor of Robin Law, ed. Toyin Falola and Matt Childs (Durham, NC: Carolina Academic Press, 2009), 387-407; and João José Reis, Flávio dos Santos Gomes, and Marcus J. M. de Carvalho, "Rufino José Maria (1820s-1850s): A Muslim in the Nineteenth-Century Brazilian Slave Trade Circuit," in *The Human Tradition in the Black Atlantic, 1500-2000*, ed. Beatriz G. Mamigonian and Karen Racine (Lanham, MD: Rowman & Littlefield, 2010), 65-75. See also James H. Sweet, *Domingos Álvares, African Healing, and the Intellectual History of the Atlantic World* (Chapel Hill: University of North Carolina Press, 2011); Ferreira, *Cross-Cultural Exchange in the Atlantic World*; Hawthorne, *From Africa to Brazil*; Kwasi Konadu, *Transatlantic Africa, 1440-1888* (New York: Oxford University Press, 2014); Sandra E. Greene, *West African Narratives of Slavery: Texts from Late Nineteenth- and Early Twentieth-Century Ghana* (Bloomington: Indiana University Press, 2011), 1-17.

38. They include but are not limited to biographies such as Ferreira, *Cross-Cultural Exchange in the Atlantic World*; Sweet, *Domingos Álvares*; Reis, "Domingos Pereira Sodré"; Reis, Gomes, and Carvalho, "Rufino José Maria (1820s-1850s)"; and Greene, *West African Narratives of Slavery*, 1-17.

39. RG 15/1/89, *Nelson v. S. Q. Nelson*, 30 September, 1930, 7.

40. FO 84/920, Letter from Campbell to Lord Clarendon, 28 December 1853. For Brazilian returnees including Francisco de Souza "Chacha," João de Oliveira, and others who became wealthy through their involvements in various slavery activities, see Robin Law, "Francisco de Souza in West Africa, 1820-1849," in Curto and Lovejoy, *Enslaving Connection* ; Robin Law, *Ouidah: The Social History of a West African Slaving "Port," 1727-1892* (Athens: Ohio University Press, 2004); David A. Ross, "The Career of Domingo Martinez in the Bight of Benin, 1833-1864," *Journal of African History* 6, no. 1 (1965): 79-90; and Richard D. Ralston, "The Return of Brazilian Freedmen to West Africa in the 18th and 19th Centuries," *Canadian Journal of African Studies* 3, no. 3 (1969): 581-83.

41. Parker, *Making the Town*, 14.

42. Carlos da Fonseca, *Letters from Brazil* (Brazil: Ministère des Relations Extérieures, 2010).

43. da Fonseca, *Letters from Brazil*, (Ministère des Relations Exterèrieres, 2010), 278.

44. Ibid., 305.

45. Ibid., 177.

46. Ibid. See the beginning of each family's origins and narratives.

47. See Richard Anderson et al., "Using African Names to Identify the Origins of Captives in the Transatlantic Slave Trade: Crowd-Sourcing and the Registers of Liberated Africans, 1808-1862," *History in Africa* 40 (2013): 165-91.

48. Lisa E. Castillo, "Mapping the Nineteenth-Century Brazilian Returnee Movement: Demographics, Life stories and the Question of Slavery," *Atlantic Studies* 13, no. 1 (2016): 25-52.

49. Lisa E. Castillo, "Between Memory, Myths and History: Trans-Atlantic Voyages of the Casa Branca Temple," in *Paths of the Atlantic Slave Trade: Interactions, Identities, and Images*, ed. Ana Lucia Araujo (Amherst, NY: Cambria Press, 2011), 205-10.

50. Lisa E. Castillo and Luis Nicolau Parés, "Marcelina da Silva: A Nineteenth- Century *Candomblé* Priestess in Bahia," *Slavery & Abolition* 31, no. 1 (2010): 1-2.

51. Lisa A. Lindsay, "'To Return to the Bosom of Their Fatherland': Brazilian Immigrants in Nineteenth- Century Lagos," *Slavery & Abolition* 15, no. 1 (1994): 27-35.

Notes

52. Lisa A. Lindsay, "Brazilian Women in Lagos, 1879-1882," in *Shaping Our Struggles: Nigerian Women in History, Culture and Development*, ed. Obioma Nnaemeka and Chima J. Korieh (Trenton, NJ: Africa World Press, 2010), 130-37.

53. Lorenzo D. Turner, "Some Contacts of Brazilian Ex-Slaves with Nigeria, West Africa," *Journal of Negro History* 27, no. 1 (January 1942): 62. See also Ralston, "The Return of Brazilian Freedmen to West Africa," 577-93.

54. See Lorenzo D. Turner Collection, ACMA PM 2003.7064.277, Anacosta Community Museum Archives. Some of Turner's collections housed at the Melville J. Herskovits Library of African Studies at Northwestern University are also of great value to this book.

55. See list provided by Marco A. Schaumloeffel, *Tabom: The Afro-Brazilian Community in Ghana*, 2nd ed. (published by author, 2008), 41.

56. Alcione M. Amos and Ebenezer Ayesu, "'I Am Brazilian': History of the Tabon, Afro-Brazilian in Accra," *Transactions of the Historical Society of Ghana*, no 6 (2002):48-52.

57. ADM 11/1/1502, "Mohammedan Community of Accra, 1902."

58. Elder William Lutterodt, interview by Kwame Essien, 18 July 2012.

59. Lisa Castillo, email communication with the author, 18 April 2012 (we exchanged other emails between 18 April 2012 and 28 July 2013). Others have drawn similar conclusions in their analysis of the Aguda people. For example, Milton Guran relates that assimilation caused some form of rapture in the African-Brazilian identity. The Aguda, as he relates, did not leave their Brazilian names behind when they returned to Africa; rather they brought the surnames of their masters (mostly of Portuguese origins) with them. The "foreign" names served as a social uplift and set them apart from returnees who held on to their Yoruba and other local names. Milton Guran, "The Returnees of Benin, Togo, Nigeria and Ghana: Agudas and Tabom," in *Back to Africa*, vol. 1, *Afro-Brazilian Returnees and Their Communities*, ed. Kwesi Kwaa Prah (Cape Town: Center for Advanced Studies of African Society, 2009), 108-20. In my study of the Tabom people I have identified few Portuguese or Brazilian names: Peregrino, Ribeiro, and Da Costa. Names such as Lutterodt might be tied to Danish or other European settlers in the Gold Coast.

60. The following files provide significant coverage: FO 84/199, FO 84/368, FO 84/679, FO 84/803, FO 84/816, FO 84/848, FO 84/920 and FO 84/950.

61. See, for example, file FO 84/1464, FO 84/920, and FO 84/12, "Regulations for the Guidance of the Commissions."

62. See the following: Nwokeji, *The Slave Trade and Culture in the Bight of Biafra*; Kristin Mann, *Slavery and the Birth of an African City: Lagos, 1760-1900* (Bloomington: Indiana University Press, 2007); Law, *Ouidah*; and Verger, *Trade Relations between the Bight of Benin and Bahia*, to mention just a few.

63. Verger, *Trade Relations between the Bight of Benin and Bahia*, 562-629.

64. Luis Nicolau Parés, "The Nagôization Process in Bahian Candomblé," in *The Yoruba Diaspora in the Atlantic World*, ed. Toyin Falola and Matt D. Childs (Bloomington: Indiana University Press, 2004), 185-208.

65. "The Slave Question," *Lagos Times and Gold Coast Advertizer*, 14 June 1882; "More Massacres-Latest Intelligence from Dahomey," *African Times*, 22 February 1862, 61; "Dahomey," *Africa Times*, 23 January 1863, 75; and "The Fugitive Slaves," *Times of Africa*, 3 July 1897, 2.

66. FO 84/920, "Slave Trade: West Coast of Africa-Consular Reports," January to December

1853.
67. Lisa Earl Castillo, "Mapping the Nineteenth-Century Brazilian Returnee Movement."
68. "Proclamation of Abolition," *Liberian Herald*, 6 April 1853.
69. FO 84/920, Dispatch to Foreign Office, 30 July 1853.
70. FO 84/886.
71. FO 84/920.
72. FO 84/98. See also Verene A. Shepherd, *Saving Souls: The Struggle to End the Transatlantic Trade in Africans* (Kingston, Jamaica: Ian Randle Publishers, 2007), 112-31.
73. FO 84/13. For statements about other illegal activities and the list of vessels and the number of slaves that were imported, see ibid., 64-69 (a). For French, Spanish, Portuguese, and American vessels that violated slave trade laws, see ibid., 64.
74. FO 82/2, Articles 1 through 14. See also FO 84/858.
75. FO 84/1323; FO 84/1180.
76. Robert Conrad, "The Contraband Slave Trade to Brazil, 1831-1845," in *The Atlantic Slave Trade*, vol. 4, *Nineteenth Century*, ed. Jeremy Black (Aldershot: Ashgate, 2006), 339-60.
77. FO 84/846, 8 February 1851, 14-15; and 5 July 1851; FO 84/846, 18 November 1847. See also Dale Torston Graden, *From Slavery to Freedom in Brazil: Bahia, 1835-1900* (Albuquerque: University of New Mexico Press, 2006).
78. FO 84/199. For the estimate of passports that were issued in Bahia from 1820 to 1868, see Verger, *Trade Relations between the Bight of Benin and Bahia*, 563.
79. FO 84/368.
80. FO 84/950, 4 May 1854.
81. Verger, *Trade Relations between the Bight of Benin and Bahia*, 357.
82. FO 84/679.
83. FO 84/1002, Campbell to Clarendon, June 1856.
84. CO 147/159, Moloney to Holland, 20 July 1887.
85. FO 84/102; FO 84/22, 1 January 1823.
86. FO 84/13, 28 August 1821.
87. FO 84/411.
88. FO 84/411.
89. FO 84/803.
90. Verger, *Trade Relations between the Bight of Benin and Bahia*, 457.
91. FO 84/920, Letter from Campbell to Lord Clarendon, 4 May 1854.
92. FO 84/22, 1 January 1823; FO 84/102.
93. Lindsay, "'To Return to the Bosom of Their Fatherland,'" 29.
94. See Lindsay, "Brazilian Women in Lagos," 129-40. See also Ralston, "The Return of Brazilian Freedmen to West Africa"; Ross, "The Career of Domingo Martinez"; and Turner, "Some Contacts of Brazilian Ex-Slaves with Nigeria."
95. Turner, "Some Contacts of Brazilian Ex-Slaves with Nigeria," 60.
96. See Prah, *Back to Africa*, vol. 1.

97. ACS, reel 147, vol. 296, nos. 1-200, contain letters that were exchanged between the freed slaves and officials of ACS as well as those between ACS leaders in the United States and different locations of settlements in Africa.

98. David Eltis et al., eds., *The Trans-Atlantic Slave Trade: A Database on CD-ROM* (Cambridge: Cambridge University Press, 2000).Error! Hyperlink reference not valid.

99. Otero, *Afro-Cuban Diasporas in the Atlantic World*.

100. João José Reis, "Quilombos and Rebellions in Brazil," in *African Roots/American Cultures: Africa in the Creation of the Americas*, ed. Sheila S. Walker (New York: Rowman & Littlefield, 2001), 301-2; Sylviane A. Diouf, *Servants of Allah: African Muslims Enslaved in the Americas* (New York: New York University Press, 1998); Abu Alfa Muhammad Shareef bin Farid, *The Islamic Revolts of Bahia, Brazil: A Continuity of the 19th Century Jihad Movements of Western Sudan* (Pittsburgh: Sankore, 1998); Michael A. Gomez, *Black Crescent: The Experience of Legacy of African Muslims in the Americas* (Cambridge: Cambridge University Press, 2005); and Paul E. Lovejoy, *Transformations in Slavery: A History of Slavery in Africa* (New York: Cambridge University Press, 2000), 23-40, 66-72.

101. Sweet, *Recreating Africa*, 220.

102. Kwasi Konadu, *The Akan Diaspora in the Americas* (New York: Oxford University Press, 2010), 10-12.

103. FO 84/846, Letter from Mr. Hudson to Lord Stanley, Rio Janeiro on 14 August 1851, 1; Hudson to Palmerston, 14 August 1851.

104. Muneer Akolade, interview by Kwame Essien, 3 July 2009. See also *Mary Afua Nelson v. S.Q. Nelson*, 25 November 1931, 107.

105. RG 15/1/89, *Nelson v. S. Q. Nelson*, 30 September 1930, 12.

106. Lisa Yoneyama, *Hiroshima Traces: Time, Space and the Dialects of Memory* (Berkeley: University of California Press, 1999), 27.

107. Pilar Riaño-Alcalá, *Dwellers of Memory: Youth and Violence in Medellín, Columbia* (New Brunswick, NJ: Transaction Publishers, 2006), 11.

108. Judith A. Carney, *Black Rice: The African Origins of Rice Cultivation in the Americas* (Cambridge, MA: Harvard University Press, 2001), 69-177; and Carney and Rosomoff, *In the Shadow of Slavery*; Gomez, *Black Crescent*; and Michael A. Gomez, *Exchanging Our Country Marks: The Transforming of African Identities in the Colonial and Antebellum South* (Chapel Hill: University of North Carolina Press, 1998).

109. Edda L. Fields-Black, *Deep Roots: Rice Farmers in West Africa and the African Diaspora* (Bloomington: Indiana University Press, 2008).

110. Laurent Duboise, *Colony of Citizens: Revolution and Slave Emancipation in the French Caribbean, 1787-1804* (Chapel Hill: University of North Carolina Press, 2004), 171-333; Matt D. Childs, *The 1812 Aponte Rebellion in Cuba and the Struggle against Atlantic Slavery* (Chapel Hill: University of North Carolina Press, 2006).

111. Kim D. Butler, "Clio and the Griot: The African Diaspora in the Discipline of History," in *The African Diaspora and the Disciplines*, ed. Tejumola Olaniyan and James H. Sweet (Bloomington: Indiana University Press, 2010), 21-46; Kim D. Butler, "Defining Diaspora, Refining a Discourse," *Diaspora* 10, no. 2 (2001): 192-206.

112. W. E. B. Du Bois, *The Souls of Black Folk: Authoritative Text, Contexts, Criticism*, ed. Henry Louis Gates Jr. and Terri H. Oliver (Cambridge, MA: Harvard University Press, 1999), ix. See

also Robert Johnson Jr., *Why Blacks Left America for Africa: Interviews with Black Repatriates, 1971-1999* (Westport, CT: Praeger, 1999), xvii.

113. Samuel Boadi-Siaw, "The Afro-Brazilian Returnees in Ghana," in Prah, *Back to Africa*, 1: 146-47.

114. See Otero, *Afro-Cuban Diasporas in the Atlantic World*. Otero's book focuses mainly on Afro-Cuban returnees, the Aguda communities in Lagos, Nigeria. It also examines issues of memory, identity, citizenship, and others. Her work accomplishes a couple of objectives: it provides a new literature from the Spanish speaking diaspora, and it extends the discourse on reverse migrations beyond those of Nemata Amelia Blyden and Kevin K. Gaines that trace these return voyages from Sierra Leone, Ghana, and Nigeria.

115. Curto and Lovejoy, *Enslaving Connections*, 15-16; Solimar Otero, "Orunile: Heaven Is Home, Yoruba and Afrocuban Diasporas across the Atlantic" (PhD diss., Louisiana State University, 2002), 1-4. For returnees from North America and the Caribbean, see Kevin K. Gaines, *American Africans in Ghana: Black Expatriates and the Civil Rights Era* (Chapel Hill: University of North Carolina Press, 2006), 6, 17, 266; Nemata Amelia Blyden, *West Indians in West Africa, 1808-1880: The African Diaspora in Reverse* (Rochester, NY: University of Rochester Press, 2000), 7-15; Sundiata, *Brothers and Strangers*, 9-13.

116. Femi Ojo-Ade, "Afro-Brazilians in Lagos: A Question of Home or Exile?" in Prah, *Back to Africa*, 1: 210-31.

117. Some returnees from North America are of the opinion that these sacred sites are locations for hearing the voices of their ancestors and speaking to the spirits of their forebears. Literature on tourism and its significance to globalization and heritage tourism has increased. For instance, Edmund Abaka explains how material culture or archaeological sites within this community epitomizes visual symbols of collective memory of an ancestral past. Besides the Tabom, returnees from North America who visited or settled in Ghana later drew upon their memory of historical landmarks and sites of grief such as the slave dungeons and forts along the coastline. Anthropologists including Edward M. Bruner make similar arguments in their analyses of African American returnees' claims to the slave castles and dungeons in Ghana. See Edward M. Bruner, "Tourism in Ghana: The Representation of Slavery and the Return of the Black Diaspora," *American Anthropologist* 98, no. 2 (1996): 294.

118. Antônio Olinto, *The Water House*, trans. Dorothy Heapy (New York: Carroll and Graf, 1970).

119. Verger, *Trade Relations between the Bight of Benin and Bahia*, 468.

120. See the following documents: FO 84/920, FO 84/950, FO 84/1002, and FO 84/1031.

CHAPTER 2. HISTORICIZING THE RETURNEE PRESENCE IN GÃ MÃŊ: CHALLENGES AND SILENCES

1. Kwame Essien, "The African Diaspora in Reverse: The *Tabom* People in Ghana, 1820s-2009" (PhD diss., University of Texas, Austin, 2010).

2. Paul Tiyambe Zeleza, "Rewriting the African Diaspora: Beyond the Black Atlantic," *African Affairs* 104 (2005): 41.

3. Tiffany Ruby Patterson and Robin D. G. Kelley, "Unfinished Migrations: Reflections on the African Diaspora and the Making of the Modern World," *African Studies Review* 43, no. 1

(2000): 11–45.

4. Zeleza, "Rewriting the African Diaspora," 63–64.

5. Kim D. Butler, "Clio and the Griot: The African Diaspora in the Discipline of History," in *The African Diaspora and the Disciplines*, ed. Tejumola Olayiyan and James H. Sweet (Bloomington: Indiana University Press, 2010), 23.

6. Michael J. Turner, "Les Bresiliens: The Impact of Former Brazilian Slaves upon Dahomey" (PhD diss., Boston University, 1975), 83.

7. "Hope in Dahomey," *African Times*, 23 December 1862, 66–67.

8. Antônio Olinto, *The Water House*, trans. Dorothy Heapy (New York: Carroll and Graf, 1970).

9. John Parker, *Making the Town: Ga State and Society in Early Colonial Accra* (Portsmouth, NH: Heineman, 2000), 14, 164.

10. Dinah Kuevi, "The History of Otublohum" (BA diss., University of Ghana, Legon, 1979), 13.

11. Rebecca Shumway, *The Fante and the Transatlantic Slave Trade* (Rochester, NY: University of Rochester Press, 2011), 33–47.

12. There are varying statistics about the population of Accra from the nineteenth century. Historian John Parker estimates that there were about 20,000 people in Accra by 1891 while Amon Nikoi suggests a higher figure of about 143,000 by 1910 and 224,771 by 1948. See Parker, *Making the Town*, 7; Amon Nikoi, "Indirect Rule and Government in Gold Coast Colony, 1844-1954: A Study in the History, Ecology and Politics of Administration in a Changing Society" (PhD diss., Harvard University, 1956), 127.

13. EC 6/19, 7, "Digest of Minutes in Basel Mission Periodicals, 1828-1851," 7.

14. EC 6/19, 27.

15. EC 6/19, 10. The relocation of the colonial seat from Cape Coast to coastal Accra (Southern Protectorate) expedited British colonial conquest of the Ashante Kingdom, which was part of the Northern Protectorate. The British defeated the Ashante people in 1901 after the Yaa Asantewaa War. See also T. C. McCaskie, *State and Society in Pre-Colonial Asante* (Cambridge: Cambridge University Press, 1995).

16. Robin Law, interview by Kwame Essien, 2–3 April 2009, "Black Atlantics: An Urban Perspective, 1400-1900," conference, University of Texas, Austin.

17. See Parker, *Making the Town*, 2–10; See also Thorkild Hansen, *Coast of Slaves*, trans. Kari Dako (Legon-Accra: Sub-Saharan Publishers, 2002).

18. Naaborko Sackeyfio-Lenoch, *The Politics of Chieftaincy: Authority and Property in Colonial Ghana, 1920-1950* (Rochester, NY: University of Rochester Press, 2014).

19. George MacDonald, *The Gold Coast, Past and Present: A Short Description of the Country and Its People* (New York: Negro Universities Press, 1969), 199.

20. Parker, *Making the Town*, xix.

21. Quoted from Eric Coleman, "Social History of Accra, 1900-1935: With Special Reference to the Role of the Educated Elite" (BA diss., University of Ghana, Legon, 1980), 1.

22. During the colonial and postcolonial periods, especially at the height of black-nationalism and decolonization campaigns in the mid-twentieth century, Pan-Africanists shared similar opinions about Accra. According to Pauli Murray, Accra was "a nerve center of African Nationalism and political seismograph registering every tremor of the struggle for black nationhood." Pauli Murray, *The Autobiography of a Black Activist, Feminist, Lawyer, Priest and*

Poet (Knoxville: University of Tennessee Press, 1997), 338. Maya Angelou and other African American expatriates also could not resist the central role of Accra (Ghana in general) to the civil rights movements and Pan-Africanism.

23. Parker, *Making the Town*, 8-13, 99.
24. Hansen, *Coast of Slaves*, 9-17.
25. CVA 40/58, 27 January 1958, 31.
26. In court, several descendants claimed that they left their remote farming communities temporarily to pursue other careers as their population increased. Most of them returned to their farmlands when word spread in the city that both members and nonmembers of the community were building houses on family lands that were supposed to be used for farming instead. CVA 40/56, 24 January 1958, 25.
27. RG 15/1/89, 23 April 1931, 15-16.
28. The number of waves of migration covered in this book in no way suggests that these are all the journeys to Accra or the then Gold Coast in general. There were several other journeys that cannot be traced.
29. Roger S. Gocking, *Facing Two Ways: Ghana's Coastal Communities under Colonial Rule* (Lanham, MD: University Press of America, 1999), 70.
30. These documents are part of the archival collections that focus on conflicts between the Tabom people over land in Accra after the demise of the early settlements.
31. CVA 45/49, 16 July 1947, 9.
32. CVA 12/52, *Peter Quarshie Fiscian and Mary A. Fiscian v. Nii Azumah III*, 13 March 1953, 42.
33. Ibid.
34. João José Reis, *Slave Rebellion in Brazil: The Muslim Uprising of 1835 in Bahia*, trans. Arthur Brakel (Baltimore, MD: John Hopkins University Press, 1993).
35. CVA 40/56, *Nii Anyetei Kwao v. Nii Azumah III and others*, 13 March 1953, 42-47.
36. Samuel Quarcoopome, "The Brazilian Community of Ghana" (PhD diss., University of Ghana, Legon, 1970), 4-5.
37. Samuel Boadi-Siaw, "The Afro-Brazilian Returnees in Ghana," in *Back to Africa*, vol. 1, *Afro-Brazilian Returnees and Their Communities*, ed. Kwesi Kwaa Prah (Cape Town: Center for Advanced Studies of African Society, 2009), 151-52.
38. Alcione M. Amos and Ebenezer Ayesu, "'I Am Brazilian': History of the Tabon, Afro-Brazilian in Accra," *Transactions of the Historical Society of Ghana*, n.s. 6 (2002): 35-58.
39. Marco A. Schaumloeffel, *Tabom: The Afro-Brazilian Community in Ghana*, 2nd ed. (published by author, 2008), 19. I interrogate the meaning of these dates and concludes that further studies will be needed to explain these nuances. Essien, "African Diaspora in Reverse."
40. Sackeyfio-Lenoch, *The Politics of Chieftaincy*, 72-93.
41. CVA 45/49, 16 July 1947, 9.
42. FC NB N78, 1840-1841. See also Larry Yarak, email correspondence to Hermann W. von Hesse, 13 January 2016.
43. *Lagos Times*, 13 September 1882.
44. *Lagos Standard*, 19 February 1896.
45. See "Letter from Brazil" (Ministère des Relations Exterèrieres, 2010).

46. Nii Azumah V, interview by Kwame Essien, 15 August 2005.
47. CVA No. 12/52, *Peter Quarshie Fiscian and Mary A. Fiscian v. Nii Azumah III*, 13 March 1953, 41. See also Amos and Ayesu, "I Am Brazilian," 57–58.
48. CVA No. 12/15, *Peter Quarshie Fiscian and Mary A. Fiscian v. Nii Azumah III*, 13 March 1953.
49. Essien, "African Diaspora in Reverse," 144.
50. James H. Sweet, *Recreating Africa: Culture, Kinship, and Religion in African-Portuguese World, 1441–1770* (Chapel Hill: University of North Carolina Press, 2003), 87–188.
51. George Aruna Nelson, interview by Kwame Essien, 6 August 2008; STC 20/7/45, *Isaac Cobblah Fiscian v. Henry Asumah Nelson and Sohby Baksmathy*, 2.
52. CVA 45/49, *Sackey v. Otoo*, 27 August 1914, 80.
53. EC 6/19, 28.
54. CVA 45/49, *Thomas Adu Hammond v. Isaac C. Fiscian and Titus Glover*, 3 September 1949, 57.
55. See G. Ugo Nwokeji, *The Slave Trade and Culture in the Bight of Biafra: An African Society in the Atlantic World* (Cambridge: Cambridge University Press, 2010) and Kristin Mann, *Slavery and the Birth of an African City: Lagos, 1760–1900* (Bloomington: Indiana University Press, 2007).
56. Parker, *Making the Town*, x–xxix.
57. Bridget J. Katriku (chief director of the Ministry of Tourism and Diasporan Relations), interview by Kwame Essien, 8 March 2007. Scholars in various academic fields have also engaged this ongoing story and revealed how various interest groups have benefited from this scheme while others have been challenged by tension that emerged via these interactions and exchanges.
58. Susan Benson, "Connecting with the Past, Building the Future: African Americans and Chieftaincy in Southern Ghana," *Ghana Studies* 6 (2003): 109–33. See also George M. Bob-Milliar, "Chieftaincy, Diaspora, and Development: The Institution of *Nkɔsuohene* in Ghana," *African Affairs* 108 (2009): 541–58.
59. Clifford C. Campbell, "Full Circle: The Caribbean Presence in the Making of Ghana, 1843–1966" (PhD diss., University of Ghana, Legon, 2012).
60. Edmund Abaka, *House of Slaves and "Door of No Return": Gold Coast/Ghana Slave Forts, Castles & Dungeons and the Atlantic Slave Trade* (Trenton, NJ: Africa World Press, 2012).
61. Kuevi, "The History of Otublohum," 9–10.
62. Some of these motivations or petitions that were submitted to Her Majesty's Judiciary Committee through the Council Office of Downing Street, London, sought permission from the queen of England to appoint three Gã citizens as chiefs: Samuel C. Nortey as the acting head of Odoi Kwao *we*; Sarah Clegg as head of Lawrence *we*; and Peter Fiscian as new leader of the Fiscian *we*. See "Privy Council Appeal," ADM 4/1/1, 17 May 1910, 8.
63. Nii Azumah V, interview by Kwame Essien, 20 July 2014.
64. Nii Azumah V, interview by Kwame Essien, 4 July 2007, Accra.

CHAPTER 3. THE SOCIAL HISTORY OF GÃ MÃŊ: COLONIALISM AND THEIR IMPACT ON THE BRAZILIAN-AFRICAN DIASPORA

1. Mary McCarthy, *Social Change and the Growth of British Power in the Gold Coast: The Fante States, 1807-1874* (Lanham, MD: University Press of America, 1983), 154.
2. Sir William Edward Maxwell, "Gold Coast Colony," *Gold Coast Methodist Times*, November-December 1897.
3. CO 98/4, Gold Coast Minutes of Legislative Council, 1881 to 1883, 3.
4. Kwasi Konadu, *The Akan Diaspora in the Americas* (New York: Oxford University Press, 2010), 98. See also Walter C. Rucker, *Gold Coast Diasporas: Identity, Culture, and Power* (Bloomington: Indiana University Press, 2015), 1-6.
5. Lorenzo D. Turner collection, Melville J. Herskovits Library of African Studies, Northwestern University, Evanston, Illinois.
6. Deborah Pellow, *Landlords and Lodgers: Socio-Spatial Organization in an Accra Community* (Chicago: University of Chicago Press, 2008), 44-46, 55. See also Samuel Aniegye Ntewusu, "Settling in and Holding On: A Socio-Economic History of Northern Traders and Transporters in Accra's Tudu; 1908-2008," (PhD diss., University of Leiden, 2011).
7. John Parker, *Making the Town: Ga State and Society in Early Colonial Accra* (Portsmouth, NH: Heinemann, 2000), xviii.
8. Carl C. Reindorf, *The History of the Gold Coast and Asante, Based on Traditions and Historical Facts Comprising a Period of More Than Three Centuries from about 1500 to 1860* (Basel: Basel Mission Depot, 1951), 35.
9. Irene Odotei-Quaye, "Gã and the Neighbors" (PhD diss., University of Ghana, 1972), 53-115.
10. Ibid., 36.
11. John Parker, *Making the Town: Ga State and Society in Early Colonial Accra* (Portsmouth, NH: Heinemann, 2000), 134-46. See also Carina E. Ray, *Crossing the Color Line: Race, Sex, and the Contested Politics of Colonialism in Ghana* (Athens: Ohio University Press, 2015), chap. 1 and 2.
12. ADM 11/1/1086, 10 March 1901.
13. RG 15/1/89, 5.
14. Naaborko Sackeyfio, "The Stool Owns the City: Ga Chieftaincy and the Politics of Land in Colonial Accra, 1920-1950" (PhD diss., University of Wisconsin-Madison, 2008), 8-17.
15. SCT 2/4/19, vol. 8, *Tackie v. Nelson*, 29 September 1892, 1-37.
16. *Gold Coast Chronicle*, 27 April 1987.
17. McCarthy, *Social Change and the Growth of British Power in the Gold Coast*, 148, 154. See also G. E. Metcalfe, *Great Britain and Ghana: Documents of Ghana History, 1807-1957* (London: Thomas Nelson & Sons, 1964).
18. Samuel S. Quarcoopome, "Political Activities in Accra, 1924-1945" (PhD diss., University of Ghana, Legon, 1980), 102.
19. Parker, *Making the Town*, 48.
20. Ibid., 163-65.
21. Reindorf, *The History of the Gold Coast and Asante*, 39.

Notes

22. Kwame Essien, "The African Diaspora in Reverse: The *Tabom* People in Ghana, 1820s-2009" (PhD diss., University of Texas, Austin, 2010), 112.
23. Furley Collection N5 1648-1652, 13 October 1650, University of Ghana, Legon.
24. Odotei-Quaye, "Gã and the Neighbors," 38.
25. Amon Nikoi, "Indirect Rule and Government in Gold Coast Colony, 1844-1954: A Study in the History, Ecology and Politics of Administration in a Changing Society" (PhD diss., Harvard University, 1956), 14.
26. Edward Carstensen, *Governor Carstensen's Diary, 1842-1850* (Legon: University of Ghana, 1965), 4 (26 October 1842).
27. Ibid., 10.
28. CVA No. 997/36, *Thomas Adu Hammond v. Isaac C. Fiscian and Titus Glover*, 3 September 1949, 57.
29. Some local migrants also feel a sense of entitlement to Gã territories partly because of the evidence of long history of intermarriages between the Gã people and the settlers in their coastal communities. However, there is sufficient evidence that the Gã *mãŋ* belongs to the Gã people.
30. S. A. Nunoo, "The History of Ga Wulomo Institution" (BA diss., University of Ghana, Legon, 1981), 2-3.
31. Paulina S. Quist-Therson, "Chieftaincy among the Ga's" (BA diss., University of Ghana, Legon, 1972), 2.
32. George MacDonald, *The Gold Coast, Past and Present: A Short Description of the Country and Its People* (New York: Negro Universities Press, 1969), 195.
33. Margaret J. Field, *Religion and Medicine of the Gã People* (London: Oxford University Press, 1961), 142.
34. Joseph Nii Abekah Mensah, *Traditions and Customs of Gãdangmes of Ghana* (Houston: Strategic Book Publishing, 2013), xxiv-21.
35. Leslie Nii Odartey Lamptey, "The History of Osu (Kinkawe) from the Colonial Period to Date" (BA diss., University of Ghana, Legon, 2006), 8-9.
36. M. E. Kropp Dakubu, "Linguistic Pre-History and Historical Reconstruction: The Gã-Adangme Migrations," *Transactions of the Historical Society of Ghana* 13, no. 1 (June 1972): 93-111.
37. Reindorf, *The History of the Gold Coast and Asante*, 28.
38. Odotei-Quaye, "Gã and the Neighbors," 120-21.
39. The Gã people coined the word "Tabom," which is used in reference to the descendants of liberated Brazilian slaves in Ghana. Carl C. Reindorf's seminal work, *The History of the Gold Coast and Asante*, provides a broad coverage of migrant communities in Accra as well as cross-cultural interactions and exchanges between the Gã people, the Ashante, and Europeans among others. However, this important work does not provide details about the Brazilian-African diaspora in Accra.
40. Dinah Kuevi, "The History of Otublohum" (BA diss., University of Ghana, Legon, 1979), 13.
41. Essien, "African Diaspora in Reverse," 156-68.
42. Parker, *Making the Town*, 10-13. D. K. Henderson-Quartey, *The Ga of Ghana: History & Culture of a West African People* (London: David K. Henderson-Quartey, 2002).

43. Essien, "African Diaspora in Reverse," 156-58.
44. Marco A. Schaumloeffel, *Tabom: The Afro-Brazilian Community in Ghana*, 2nd ed. (published by author, 2008), 41-84.
45. Reindorf, *The History of the Gold Coast and Asante*.
46. Field, *Religion and Medicine of the Gã People*. See also Margaret J. Field, *Social Organization of the Gã People* (London: Crown Agents for the Colonies, 1940); Reindorf, *The History of the Gold Coast and Asante*.
47. Quist-Therson, "Chieftaincy among the Ga's," 2.
48. J. J. Crooks, *Records Relating to the Gold Coast Settlements from 1750 to 1874* (London: Frank Cass, 1973), 118.
49. Eric Nii Annang Akwa, "Chieftaincy among the Ga's: The Paramountcy of the Ga Mantse" (BA diss., University of Ghana, Legon, 1980), 2-8.
50. CVA 45/49, 16 July 1947, 9.
51. Elder George Nii Aruna Nelson, interview by Kwame Essien, 6 August 2008.
52. RG 15/1/89, *Isaac Cobblah Fiscian v. Henry Asumah Kwaku Nelson and Sohby Baksmathy*, 11 November 1945, 29.
53. There are numerous statements by the Tabom referring to constant travels by their parents back and forth from Lagos to Accra as in the case of Ferku. Those who settled in Nigeria, Benin, and Togo are known as the Aguda people. Also, the word "Niger" is used in almost all these references to indicate the Brazilian-Aguda-Tabom connections. Some of this evidence suggests that their ancestors were taken as slaves from Nigeria and not Ghana. See CVA 12/52, *Peter Quarshie Fiscian and Mary A. Fiscian v. Nii Azumah III*, 13 March 1953, 42; RG 15/1/89, *Yawah per J. M. Aryeequaye v. Joseph Edward Maslieno*, 30 September 1930, 22-32. The story about the freed slaves' ties to Nigeria was confirmed by some Tabom including members of the Lutterodt and Peregrino families of Accra in interviews I conducted between 2009 and 2015. The latter continue to travel to Bamgbose-Lagos, Nigeria, to visit family members in the area.
54. Frederick J. D. Lugard, *The Diaries of Lord Lugard*, ed. Margery Perham, 4 vols. (Evanston, IL: Northwestern University Press, 1959-63).
55. *The Gold Coast Aborigines*, 15 October 1898.
56. S. K. B. Asante, *Property Law and Social Goals in Ghana, 1844-1966* (Accra: Ghana Universities Press, 1975), 23. See also Kristine Juul and Christian Lund, eds., *Negotiating Property in Africa* (Portsmouth, NH: Heinemann, 2002).
57. David Kimble, *A Political History of Ghana: The Rise of Gold Coast Nationalism, 1850-1928* (Oxford: Clarendon Press, 1963), 315.
58. Lugard, *The Diaries of Lord Lugard*.
59. "The Dilemma of Our Kings and Chiefs: Government's Unwarranted Intrusion," *Gold Coast Independent*, 10 September 1932, 981.
60. Kimble, *A Political History of Ghana*, 332.
61. Sara Berry, "Privatization and the Politics of Belonging in West Africa," in *Land and the Politics of Belonging in West Africa*, ed. Richard Kuba and Carola Lentz (Leiden: Brill, 2006), 247.
62. CO 95/257, Maxwell to Ripon, 11 May 1895.
63. SCT 2/4/19, vol. 8, *Tackie v. Nelson*, 29 September 1892.

Notes

64. Parker, *Making the Town*, xvii.
65. Sackeyfio, "The Stool Owns the City."
66. Odotei-Quaye, "Gã and the Neighbors," 119.
67. CO 482/1, Letters of Secretary of State to officers/individuals.
68. Africanus B. Hunton, *Letters on the Political Conditions of the Gold Coast*, trans. E. A. Ayandele (London: Frank Cass, 1970), 21. See also Thora Williamson, *Gold Coast Diaries: Chronicles of Political Officers in West Africa, 1900-1919* (London: Radcliffe Press, 2000).
69. Carstensen, *Governor Carstensen's Diary*, 2-3 (26 October 1842).
70. Rebecca Shumway, *The Fante and the Transatlantic Slave Trade* (Rochester, NY: University of Rochester Press, 2011), 24-87.
71. Carstensen, *Governor Carstensen's Diary*, 3-4 (26 October 1842).
72. Edward Carstensen's letters to H. Schumacher and J. Bergenhammer, 30 March, 8 May, and 1 June 1846, in Carstensen, *Governor Carstensen's Diary*, 31-40.
73. See Albert van Dantzing, *Forts and Castles in Ghana* (Accra: Sedco Publishing, 1980); Christopher R. DeCorse, *An Anthropology of Elmina: Africans and Europeans on the Gold Coast, 1400-1900* (Washington, DC: Smithsonian Institution Press, 2001).
74. Edmund Abaka, *House of Slaves and "Door of No Return": Gold Coast/Ghana Slave Forts, Castles & Dungeons and the Atlantic Slave Trade* (Trenton, NJ: Africa World Press, 2012), 40-66.
75. CO 482/1, Letters of Secretary of State to officers/individuals, 1873, 34; and CO 402/1, 4 December 1843, 1.
76. Kimble, *A Political History of Ghana*, 317.
77. Parker, *Making the Town*, 31, 118-23.
78. "Colony or Protectorate?" *Gold Coast Echo*, 13 March 1889, 3. Other commentaries associated the introduction of the Protectorate to the exploitation of resources in the colony. "The Gold Coast Government Prospecting for Gold," *Times*, 13 July 1897, 7.
79. "Government Eating with Both Hands," *Gold Coast Independent*, 26 March 1932, 351.
80. "The Native Ordinances and Our Chiefs," *Gold Coast Independent*, 26 March 1932, 351.
81. CO 879/9, Dr. Gouldsbury's Report of the Journey into the Interior of the Gold Coast, *African*, no. 95, 27 March 1876, 3.
82. Nikoi, "Indirect Rule and Government in Gold Coast Colony," 20.
83. Ibid.
84. Ibid.
85. Carstensen, *Governor Carstensen's Diary*, 4-13.
86. Ibid., 13.
87. "Church's Prayer for Change of Heart in Rulers," *Gold Coast Independent*, 6 August 1932, 831.
88. Parker, *Making the Town*, 117.
89. Quarcoopome, "Political Activities in Accra, 1924-1945," 30-33.
90. Kathryn Firmin-Sellers, *The Transformation of Property Rights in the Gold Coast: An Empirical Analysis Applying Rational Choice Theory* (Cambridge: Cambridge University Press, 1996), 150.
91. Ibid., 146.

92. Naaborko Sackeyfio-Lenoch, *The Politics of Chieftaincy: Authority and Property in Colonial Ghana, 1920-1950* (Rochester, NY: University of Rochester Press, 2014), 2-65. See also J. E. Casely Hayford, *The Truth about the West African Land Question* (London: Negro University Press, 1913), 415.
93. Crooks, *Records Relating to the Gold Coast Settlements*, 58.
94. Parker, *Making the Town*, 10-12.
95. There were a number of European forts and castles in other areas in the Gold Coast. The Portuguese built Elmina Castle in 1481 and named it St. Jorge D' Elmina. It was built to store their goods and protect them from foreign attacks. Thorkild Hansen, *Ships of Slaves*, trans. Kari Dako (Legon-Accra: Sub-Saharan Publishers, 2003), 11. In 1637 the Dutch captured Elmina Castle from the Portuguese. EC 6/19, 1.
96. CO 98/1A, Minutes of Council, 4 April 1829, 8. See also the *West African Herald*, vol. 4, 2nd series, 13 June 1871, 7.
97. Shumway, *The Fante and the Transatlantic Slave Trade*, 64-87.
98. John Mensah Sarbah, *Fanti National Constitution* (London: Frank Cass, 1968), 73.
99. J.A. B. Horton, Letter, No. II to the Right Hon. Edward Cardwell, Her Majesty's Secretary of State for War, 12 September 1869, in Hunton, *Letters on the Political Conditions of the Gold Coast*, 25. See also Sarbah, *Fanti National Constitution*, 73.
100. Hunton, *Letters on the Political Conditions of the Gold Coast*, 22.
101. Shumway, *The Fante and the Transatlantic Slave Trade*, 60-87.
102. "Dutch Return Head of Ghana King," GhanaWeb, 24 July 2009, http://www.ghanaweb.com/GhanaHomePage/NewsArchive/artikel.php?ID=165864.
103. "Sir Brandford Griffith's Letter to Her Majesty the Queen," *Gold Coast Chronicle*, 11 March 1893, 2.
104. Carstensen, *Governor Carstensen's Diary*, 13 (26 October 1842).
105. "Agyemang Prempeh," *Gold Coast Spectator*, 16 May 1931, 1.
106. Asante, *Property Law and Social Goals in Ghana*, 23-31.
107. *The African Herald*, 8 April 1859, 1.
108. Kimble, *A Political History of Ghana*, 317-20.
109. CO 879/67, Gold Coast Correspondence, January 1901-February 1902, Administration of Ashanti and Northern Territories, 7 June 1901, xv. King Prempeh returned to Kumasi in 1924 after twenty-eight years. He was converted to Christianity. Yaa Asantewaa and others died in captivity and were buried in Seychelles. See "Agyemang Prempeh."
110. Edmund Abaka's book *House of Slaves* examines the various transformations that took place in the Gold Coast, especially the ways in which missionaries, colonial officials, and others used the slave castles, forts, and dungeons in Ghana to meet the needs of Europeans. Abaka, *House of Slaves*, 346.
111. *The African Herald*, 13 June 1871, 7. The Dutch also committed atrocities against the people of the Gold Coast, especially the chiefs who resisted European imperialism, as in the case of Nana Badu Bonsu II. Musah Yahaya Jafaru, "The Netherlands Returns Head of Badu Bonsu II, after 170 Years," *Daily Graphic*, 27 June 2009, 47.
112. *Gold Coast Leader*, 26 July 1902.

113. "The Governor's Visit to Cape Coast," *Gold Coast Echo*, 31 January 1889, 3. See also Parker, *Making the Town*, 106.

114. According to De Marees, a European visitor in the Gold Coast, "people of other places in the interior buy many commodities through their slaves ... those slaves buy what the merchants desire, such as linen, woolen cloths ... then send their slaves or blacks with these goods inland in order to sell them there." See Akosua Adoma Perbi, *A History of Indigenous Slavery in Ghana from the 15th to the 19th Century* (Accra: Sub-Saharan Publishers, 2004), 80.

115. ADM 11/1/1086, Dispatch from Governor Nathan, 10 March 1901.

116. CO 96/298/386, Maxwell to Chamberlain, 4 September 1897.

117. Albert Adu Boahen, *Yaa Asantewaa and the Asante-British War of 1900-1901* (Accra: Sub-Saharan Publishers, 2003), 173-75.

118. Kimble, *A Political History of Ghana*, 317.

119. Another letter from British Captain D. Stewart who led a series of battles against the Ashante kingdom related that "While in Kumasi [the capital of the Ashante kingdom] we found out that [the] king was plotting with the Kumasi's against the Government.... The Governor when he asked for the stool did not wait, but went and looked for it himself. During this search, guns were fired ... the people then said they would fight. This palaver was settled and the young men went back to their villages. It started again when the white man attacked Ejisu [Queen Mother Yaa Asantewaa's territory]." CO 879/67, Gold Coast Correspondence, Letter from Captain D. Stewart to Mr. Chamberlain, 31 January 1901, 13.

120. CO 96/270, Confidential dispatch from Maxwell to Chamberlain, 22 February 1896; see also CO 96/378.

121. CO 879/67, Gold Coast Correspondence, Letter from Governor Major Nathan to Mr. Chamberlain, 27 April 1901, 8, 65, 80.

122. "Good Relations with Ashantee: How to Restore and Maintain Them," *African Times*, 23 December 1867, 68.

123. Sackeyfio, "The Stool Owns the City," particularly chap. 2.

124. SCT 2/4/19, vol. 8, *Tackie V. Nelson*, 29 September 1892, 1-10.

125. *Gold Coast Times*, 24 March 1883.

126. ADM 11/1/1086, 19 September 1892, 345.

127. CO 96/671, 3.

128. "Responsibility of the Chiefs," *Gold Coast Independent*, 26 March 1932, 351.

129. Roger S. Gocking, *Facing Two Ways: Ghana's Coastal Communities under Colonial Rule* (Lanham, MD: University Press of America, 1999). See also Roger S. Gocking, *The History of Ghana* (Westport, CT: Greenwood Press, 2005), 37-90.

130. *Gold Coast Chronicle*, 5 April 1895.

131. Quarcoopome, "Political Activities in Accra, 1924-1945," 22-23.

132. CO 96/352.

133. Quarcoopome, "Political Activities in Accra, 1924-1945," 38.

134. Ibid., 48-51.

135. Ibid., 98.

136. "Thought on the Present Discontent," *Gold Coast Methodist Times*, 30 April 1897.

137. See Steven J. Salm and Toyin Falola, *Culture and Customs of Ghana* (Westport, CT: Greenwood Press, 2002).
138. CVA 40/56, 13 March 1953, 42; CVA 40/58, 27 January 1958, 31.
139. *Gold Coast Independent*, 23 July 1932, 810.
140. ADM 1/1, 20 August 1908, 110.
141. CO 97/2, "Gold Coast: Certified Copies of Ordinances, 1865-1883," Miscellaneous-Unlawful Drumming, 35.
142. CO 97/3, "Gold Coast Ordinance for Regulating Towns and Promoting Public Health," 4 November 1892, 43.
143. Parker, *Making the Town*, 141.
144. ADM 1/1, 23 April 1908, 1.
145. McCarthy, *Social Change and the Growth of British Power in the Gold Coast*, 156.
146. ADM 1/1, 16 November 1909, 9.
147. ADM 1/1, 20 August 1908, 1.
148. Ibid.
149. *Gold Coast Chronicle*, 19 September 1892.
150. CSO 11/305, 14 August 1916, 1.
151. ADM 11/1086, 1 February 1890, 512.
152. ADM 4/1, 4 August 1910, 5.
153. FO 84/12, "Regulations for the Guidance of the Commissions Appointed for Carrying into Effect the Treaties for the Abolition of the Slave Trade," 13-18. See also FO 84/1464, 8 February 1851, 9-10.
154. FO 84/93, 7 December 1829. See also FO 84/141, 3 September 1833, 59; and João José Reis, *Slave Rebellion in Brazil: The Muslim Uprising of 1835 in Bahia*, trans. Arthur Brakel (Baltimore, MD: Johns Hopkins University Press, 1993).
155. Gocking, *Facing Two Ways*.
156. FO 84/632, 30 June 1846.
157. CO 96/314, Letter from Brandford C. J. Griffith to Governor Hodgson, 18 April 1898. See also Parker, *Making the Town*, 106, 141-43.
158. Sackeyfio, "The Stool Owns the City." See also Williamson, *Gold Coast Diaries*.
159. Kuba and Lentz, *Land and the Politics of Belonging in West Africa*, 35.
160. Merle L. Bowen, "The Struggle for Black Land Rights in Brazil: An Insider's View on Quilombos and the Quilombo Land Movement," *African and Black Diaspora* 3, no. 2 (2010): 147-68. See also Dale Torston Graden, *From Slavery to Freedom in Brazil: Bahia, 1835-1900* (Albuquerque: University of New Mexico Press, 2006); Rebecca J. Scott, *The Abolition of Slavery and the Aftermath of Emancipation in Brazil* (Durham, NC: Duke University Press, 1988).
161. Even if the Brazilians needed the assistance of Gã *Mãŋtsɛ* Tawiah to confirm that *Mãŋtsɛ* Komeh I gave them the land as a gift, the stringent colonial policies would have made it difficult to grant such petition.
162. *Gold Coast Echo*, 5 November 1888, 4.
163. *Government Gazette*, Dispatch from the Earl of Carnarvon to Governor Freeling, Downing

Street, UK, 28 February 1878, 65.

164. "The Speech of His Excellency the Governor, Re: Land Bill of 1897," *Gold Coast Methodist Times*, 15 November 1897.

165. *Gold Coast Chronicle*, 20 February 1895.

166. Firmin-Sellers, *The Transformation of Property Rights in the Gold Coast*, 32.

167. Kimble, *A Political History of Ghana*, 330.

168. Ibid., 384.

169. Sarbah, *Fanti National Constitution*, vii–xv.

170. Nikoi, "Indirect Rule and Government in Gold Coast Colony," 12–44. See also Lugard, *The Diaries of Lord Lugard*, 234; Frederick J. D. Lugard, *Dual Mandate in British Tropical Africa* (London: Frank Cass, 1965).

171. Quarcoopome, "Political Activities in Accra, 1924–1945," 96.

172. Lisa A. Lindsay, "'To Return to the Bosom of Their Fatherland': Brazilian Immigrants in Nineteenth-Century Lagos," *Slavery & Abolition* 15, no. 1 (1994): 42.

173. Boahen, *Yaa Asantewaa and the Asante-British War*, 173–78.

174. Parker, *Making the Town*, 104–6.

175. Nii Azumah V and Elder George Nii Aruna Nelson, interviews by Kwame Essien, 10 January 2009.

176. Kimble, *A Political History of Ghana*; Gocking, *Facing Two Ways*.

177. Asante, *Property Law and Social Goals in Ghana*, 23. See also Juul and Lund, *Negotiating Property in Africa*, 23–31. See also G. B. Kay, ed., *The Political Economy of Colonialism in Ghana: A Collection of Documents and Statistics, 1900–1960* (Cambridge: Cambridge University Press, 1972).

178. "The Crown Land Ordinance," *Gold Coast Methodist Times*, 30 November 1896.

179. W. Walton Claridge, *A History of the Gold Coast and Ashanti from the Earliest Times to the Commencement of the Twentieth Century*, vol. 2 (New York: Barnes & Noble, 1964), 174–77.

CHAPTER 4. THE EVOLUTION OF LAND IN GÃ MÃŊ AND BRAZILIAN-AFRICAN DIASPORA: PARADOX OF FREEDOM AND THE BIRTH OF CONFLICTS

1. Michael J. Turner, "Les Bresiliens: The Impact of Former Brazilian Slaves upon Dahomey" (PhD diss., Boston University, 1975).

2. "Brazilian-African diaspora" and "colônia de Brazileiros" will be used interchangeably.

3. SCT, *Nelson v. Ammah and Aruna*, 14/10/39, 28.

4. Sir William Edward Maxwell, "Gold Coast Colony," *Gold Coast Methodist Times*, November–December 1897.

5. See *Isaac Cobblah Fiscian v. Henry Asumah Nelson* and *Sohby Baksmathy*; *Yawah v. J. E. Maslieno* and *Mary Afua Nelson v. Samuel Quarshie Nelson*.

6. CVA 40/58, 27 January 1958, 31.

7. *Government Gazette*, 10 March 1897. See also CO 99/10.

8. EC 6/19, 21-22. See also Samuel S. Quarcoopome, "Political Activities in Accra, 1924–1945" (PhD diss., University of Ghana, Legon, 1980), 19–22, 36–38.
9. "Enquiry Held at Dodowa at the Provincial Council Meeting into Gã Stool Succession Dispute," *Gold Coast Independent*, 23 July 1932, 808.
10. EC 6/19, 1-2. See also John Parker, *Making the Town: Ga State and Society in Early Colonial Accra* (Portsmouth, NH: Heinemann, 2000), 8–16.
11. S. K. B. Asante, *Property Law and Social Goals in Ghana, 1844–1966* (Accra: Ghana Universities Press, 1975), 32.
12. Clifford C. Campbell, "Full Circle: The Caribbean Presence in the Making of Ghana, 1843–1966" (PhD diss., University of Ghana, Legon, 2012), 146–84. See also Robert Addo-Fening, "Akyem Abuakwa, c. 1874–1943: A Study of the Impact of Missionary Activities and Colonial Rule on a Traditional State" (PhD diss., University of Ghana, Legon, 1980).
13. EC 6/19, 26.
14. Kathryn Firmin-Sellers, *The Transformation of Property Rights in the Gold Coast: An Empirical Analysis Applying Rational Choice Theory* (Cambridge: Cambridge University Press, 1996), 19.
15. See Gareth Austin, *Labour, Land and Capital in Ghana: From Slavery to Free Labor in Asante, 1807–1956* (Rochester, NY: University of Rochester Press, 2004); Sara S. Berry, *Chiefs Know Their Boundaries: Essay on Property, Power, and the Past in Asante, 1896–1996* (Portsmouth, NH: Heinemann, 2000); and Richard Rathbone, *Nkrumah & the Chiefs: The Politics of Chieftancy in Ghana, 1951–1960* (Oxford: James Currey, 2000).
16. Asante, *Property Law and Social Goals in Ghana*, 22–35.
17. Ibid., 3.
18. Ibid., 34.
19. Ibid., 256–58. See also Kristin Juul and Christian Lund, eds., *Negotiating Property in Africa* (Portsmouth, NH: Heinemann, 2002); Richard Kuba and Carola Lentz, eds., *Land and the Politics of Belonging in West Africa* (Leiden: Brill, 2006); Rathbone, *Nkrumah & the Chiefs*.
20. C. K. Meek, *Land Law and Custom in the Colonies* (London: Oxford University Press, 1949), 192.
21. Asante, *Property Law and Social Goals in Ghana*, 32. See also Polly Hill, *The Migrant Cocoa-Farmers of Southern Ghana: A Study in Rural Capitalism* (Cambridge: Cambridge University Press, 1963).
22. CVA 43/41, 13 January 1940.
23. Samuel S. Quarcoopome, "The Impact of Urbanization on the Socio-Political History of the Gã Mashie People of Accra" (PhD diss., University of Ghana, Legon, 1993), 6.
24. Meek, *Land Law and Custom in the Colonies*, 192–93.
25. Deborah Pellow, *Landlords and Lodgers: Socio-Spatial Organization in an Accra Community* (Chicago: University of Chicago Press, 2008), 2–5.
26. Parker, *Making the Town*, 10–12.
27. FO 84/303, 5 October 1839.
28. RG 15/1/56, *Yawah per J. M. Ayreequaye v. J. E. Maslieno*, 5 August 1930, 37.
29. The following literature traces migrations of Portuguese- and Spanish-speaking emancipated Africans from Brazil and Cuba: Roquinaldo Amaral Ferreira, *Cross-Cultural Exchange in the*

Atlantic World: Angola and Brazil during the Era of the Slave Trade (Cambridge: Cambridge University Press, 2012); Solimar Otero, *Afro-Cuban Diasporas in the Atlantic World* (Rochester, NY: University of Rochester Press, 2010); Kwesi Kwaa Prah, ed., *Back to Africa*, vol. 1, *Afro-Brazilian Returnees and Their Communities* (Cape Town: Center for Advanced Studies of African Society, 2009); José C. Curto and Paul E. Lovejoy, eds., *Enslaving Connections: Changing Cultures of Africa and Brazil during the Era of Slavery* (New York: Humanity Books, 2004); and Turner, "Les Bresiliens."

30. RG 15/1/56, *Yawah per J. M. Ayreequaye v. J. E. Maslieno*, 5 August 1930, 38.
31. Ibid.
32. CO 97/3, "Gold Coast Municipal Ordinances, 1884," 24 September 1890, 8.
33. There are numerous stories about older returnees who returned to Africa so they could be buried there. See also Turner, "Les Bresiliens," 68.
34. Ferreira, *Cross-Cultural Exchange in the Atlantic World*. For Upper Guinea and Amazonia in Brazil, see Walter Hawthorne, *From Africa to Brazil: Culture, Identity, and an Atlantic Slave Trade, 1600–1830* (Cambridge: Cambridge University Press, 2010).
35. Antônio Olinto, *The Water House*, trans. Dorothy Heapy (New York: Carroll and Graf, 1970), 1–7.
36. FO 84/920, "Slave Trade: West Coast of Africa-Consular Reports," January to December 1853.
37. FO 85/95, Letter from Campbell to Hanson, 23 October 1854.
38. Lisa A. Lindsay, "'To Return to the Bosom of Their Fatherland': Brazilian Immigrants in Nineteenth-Century Lagos," *Slavery & Abolition* 15, no. 1 (1994): 22–50. See also Pierre Verger, *Trade Relations between the Bight of Benin and Bahia from the 17th to 19th Century*, trans. Evelyn Crawford (Ibadan: Ibadan University Press, 1976), 506–15.
39. *Gold Coast Echo*, 5 November 1888, 4.
40. FC 84/950, 12 August 1854. See also Turner, "Les Bresiliens," 135.
41. See FO 84/886.
42. Gilberto Freyre, *The Masters and the Slaves: A Study in the Development of Brazilian Civilization* (New York: Alfred A. Knopf, 1946), xxvii, 70.
43. Whereas the *casa grande* depicts colonial Brazil between the sixteenth and the eighteenth centuries, and the ways in which a small group of aristocrats controlled economics and free African slave labor, the *senzala* demonstrates a space for the feeble, the powerless, the marginalized, and the exploited. Freyre's work provides broad insight and details about the living conditions of slaves in the quarters and the contrast with the *casa grande*. The marginalization of people of African ancestry did not end in Brazil after the demise of slavery in 1888. According to Stuart B. Schwartz, after the "Golden Law" was enforced to end slavery nothing major changed afterwards. Stuart B. Schwartz, *Slaves, Peasants and Rebels: Reconsidering Brazilian Slavery* (Urbana: University of Illinois Press, 1992), 1. Postabolition Brazil was characterized by new forms of discrimination as the needs of liberated Africans who decided to remain in Brazil was placed on the periphery while European immigrants and other foreign workers occupied important labor and social ranks in Brazilian societies. Part of the workforce discriminatory practices is covered in numerous articles including George Reid Andrews, *Blacks and Whites in São Paulo, 1888–1988* (Madison: University of Wisconsin Press, 1991), 64, 129, 159–73; Edward E. Telles, *Race in Another America: The Significance of Skin Color in Brazil*

(Princeton, NJ: Princeton University Press, 2004), 16; and Thomas E. Skidmore, *Brazil: Five Centuries of Change* (New York: Oxford University Press, 1999), xiv.

44. Mary C. Karasch, *Slave Life in Rio de Janeiro, 1808-1850* (Princeton, NJ: Princeton University Press, 1987), 321-25.

45. Francisco Vidal Luna and Herbert S. Klein, *Slavery and the Economy of São Paulo, 1750-1850* (Stanford, CA: Stanford University Press, 2003), 1-50. See also Verger, *Trade Relations between the Bight of Benin and Bahia*, 22-37; and Laird Bergad, *The Comparative Histories of Slavery in Brazil, Cuba, and the United States* (New York: Cambridge University Press, 2007).

46. Stuart B. Schwartz, *Sugar Plantations in the Formation of Brazilian Society: Bahia, 1550-1835* (New York: Cambridge University Press, 1985), 440. See also Stuart B. Schwartz, ed., *Tropical Babylons: Sugar and the Making of the Atlantic World, 1450-1680* (Chapel Hill: University of North Carolina Press, 2004).

47. Schwartz, *Slaves, Peasants and Rebels*, 214.

48. Kátia M. de Queirós Mattoso, *To Be a Slave in Brazil, 1550-1888*, trans. Arthur Goldhammer (New Brunswick, NJ: Rutgers University Press, 1996), 102. See also David Barry Gaspar and Darlene Clark Hine, eds., *More than Chattel: Black Women and Slavery in the Americas* (Bloomington: Indiana University Press, 1996); Lisa E. Castillo, "Between Memory, Myth and History: Trans-Atlantic Voyages of the Casa Branca Temple," in *Paths of the Atlantic Slave Trade: Interactions, Identities, and Images*, ed. Ana Lucia Araujo (Amherst, NY: Cambria Press, 2011).

49. João J. Reis, "Domingos Pereira Sodré: A Nagô Priest in Nineteenth-Century Bahia," in *The Changing Worlds of Atlantic Africa: Essays in Honor of Robin Law*, ed. Toyin Falola and Matt Childs (Durham, NC: Carolina Academic Press, 2009), 403-7. See also João José Reis, Flávio dos Santos Gomes, and Marcus J. M. de Carvalho, "Rufino José Maria (1820s-1850s): A Muslim in the Nineteenth-Century Brazilian Slave Trade Circuit," in *The Human Tradition in the Black Atlantic, 1500-2000*, ed. Beatriz G. Mamigonian and Karen Racine (Lanham, MD: Rowman & Littlefield, 2009), 65-75.

50. Zephyr L. Frank, *Dutra's World: Wealth and Family in Nineteenth-Century Rio de Janeiro* (Albuquerque: University of New Mexico Press, 2004), 23.

51. Ibid., 70.

52. Karasch, *Slave Life in Rio de Janeiro*, 126-45.

53. Lorenzo D. Turner, "Some Contacts of Brazilian Ex-Slaves with Nigeria, West Africa," *Journal of Negro History* 27, no. 1 (January 1942): 55-67. See also Richard D. Ralston, "The Return of Brazilian Freedmen to West Africa in the 18th and 19th Centuries," *Canadian Journal of African Studies* 3, no. 3 (1969): 577-93.

54. Verger, *Trade Relations between the Bight of Benin and Bahia*, 3.

55. RG 15/1/89, 7.

56. RG 15/1/56, *Yawah per J. M. Ayreequaye v. J. E. Maslieno*, 5 August 1930, 38.

57. Samuel Boadi-Siaw, "The Afro-Brazilian Returnees in Ghana," in Prah, *Back to Africa*, 1:145-58.

58. Elder George Nii Aruna Nelson, interview by Kwame Essien, 10 January 2009.

59. Irene Odotei-Quaye, "Gã and the Neighbors" (PhD diss., University of Ghana, 1972), 11, 23-38.

60. Naaborko Sackeyfio, "The Stool Owns the City: Ga Chieftancy and the Politics of Land in

Notes

Colonial Accra, 1920–1950" (PhD diss., University of Wisconsin-Madison, 2008), 116–25.
61. CO 96/775, "Native Administration: General Policy" (1942–43).
62. "Direct Taxation in the form of Double Edge Income," *Gold Coast Independent*, 26 March 1932, 351.
63. Sackeyfio, "The Stool Owns the City," 116–25.
64. CVA 40/58, *Madam Sarah Clegg v. Emmanuel Drissu Cobblah*, 12 April 1956, 8.
65. See the list of Brazilian-Tabom chiefs from 1836 in Marco A. Schaumloeffel, *Tabom: The Afro-Brazilian Community in Ghana*, 2nd ed. (published by author, 2008), 41.
66. CVA 12/52, *Peter Quarshie Fiscian and Mary A. Fiscian v. Nii Azumah III*, 13 March 1953, 42.
67. CVA 40/58, 13 March 1953, 43.
68. Ibid.
69. Ibid., 47.
70. CVA 40/58, 24 January 1958, 28.
71. It is uncertain if the Yawah in this case is the same as Ferku's wife due to the limited archival data on this subject.
72. RG 5/1/56, *Madam Yawah v. J. E. Maslieno*, 30 July 1930, 35.
73. Ibid.
74. CVA 45/49, *Sackey v. Otoo*, 27 August 1914, 80.
75. CVA 40/58, 23 January 1958, 21.
76. RG 5/1/56, *Madam Yawah v. J. E. Maslieno*, 30 July 1930, 35.
77. RG 15/1/89, 12 July 1931, 112.
78. Elizabeth Maslieno, interview by Kwame Essien, 28 July 2012.
79. CVA 40/58 27 January, 1958, 30.
80. CVA 40/56, 27 January 1958, 32.
81. CVA 40/58, 1 January 1958, 3.
82. RG 15/1/89, 23 April 1931, 56.
83. CVA 40/58, 1 January 1953, 31.
84. Asante, *Property Law and Social Goals in Ghana*, 152–53.
85. The longest distance from Otublohum (what is known today as Accra's Main Street) or coastal Brazilian settlements in Accra to the agrarian communities—the area now known as Kwame Nkrumah Circle, Adabraka, or Central Accra main post office around Nsawam Road and beyond—is approximately seven to eight miles.
86. CVA 40/58, 27 January 1958, 30.
87. CVA 40/56, 28 January 1958, 34.
88. Nii Azumah V, interview by Kwame Essien, 5 August 2007.
89. RG 15/1/89, 11, 66.
90. RG 15/1/89, *Yawah per J. M. Aryeequaye v. J. E. Maslieno*, 27 February 1931, 56.
91. Sackeyfio, "The Stool Owns the City," 90–112.

CHAPTER 5. ESCAPING SLAVERY INTO COLONIALISM AND SQUABBLES: HOW COLONIAL PROJECTS AND INTERNAL DISPUTES THREATENED BRAZILIAN LAND AND FREEDOM

1. CVA 45/49, 8 March 1949, 10.
2. CVA 45/49, *Thomas A. Hammond v. Isaac C. Fiscian and Titus Glover*, 3 September 1949, 59.
3. It is not clear if King Komeh I or other Gã mãŋtsɛmɛi had given similar Gã stool lands away prior to the arrival of the Brazilians and what the implication might have been to Gã traditions.
4. See "Labor on the Gold Coast," *Times of Africa*, 30 July 1897, 4.
5. Samuel S. Quarcoopome, "Political Activities in Accra, 1924-1945" (PhD diss., University of Ghana, Legon, 1980), 103-4.
6. C. K. Meek, *Land Law and Custom in the Colonies* (Oxford: Oxford University Press, 1949), 279.
7. See Mahmood Mamdani, *Citizen and Subject: Contemporary Africa and the Legacy of Late Colonialism* (Princeton, NJ: Princeton University Press, 1996).
8. SCT 20/7/45, *Isaac Cobblah Fiscian v. Henry Asumah Nelson and Sohby Basmathy*, 32.
9. Abrowee Kojo-Annan, "Impression of the Gold Coast Aborigines Society and the Gold Coast Nationhood," *Gold Coast Independent*, 6 August 1932, 853.
10. ADM 11/1/925, "Ga Manche to Provincial Crown," 14 May 1926. See also Naaborko Sackeyfio, "The Stool Owns the City: Ga Chieftaincy and the Politics of Land in Colonial Accra, 1920-1950" (PhD diss., University of Wisconsin-Madison, 2008), 39-48.
11. Meek, *Land Law and Custom in the Colonies*, 272.
12. "Extracts from the Governor's Dispatch No. 58," *Gold Coast Methodist Times*, 11 March 1896.
13. It is important to emphasize the dream of emancipated Africans. In terms of their determination to own land, their desires were not impeded by the emergence of colonial rule or new land ordinances alone. Internal conflicts that slowly germinated among diverse family groups within the Brazilian-African diaspora in Accra turned them against each other. The squabbles include what Brazilian land should be used for and the role of Brazilian chiefs and the heads of individual family groups in making this decision. All these factors and others contributed to the evolution of Gã *mãŋ* and Brazilian land.
14. FO 84/920, letter from Campbell to Lord Clarendon, 4 May 1854.
15. For the role of the British Crown and Parliament in abolition, see the following documents at the British National Archives, Kew: FO 84/920, "Slave Trade: West Coast of Africa-Consular," January to December 1953; FO 84/1464; FO 84/912; FO 84/336; and FO 84/141.
16. The Brazilians showed solidarity with local communities as long as colonial rule was a direct threat to their survival, but when colonial policies did not have much negative impact on the Brazilian-African diaspora they did not react forcefully.
17. CO 97/2, "Gold Coast: Certified Copies of Ordinances, 1865-1883," 19 April 1876, 1.
18. CO 97/3, "Gold Coast: Certified Copies of Ordinances, 1884-1898," 24 September 1890, 8.
19. CO 97/3, "Gold Coast Ordinance for Regulating Towns and Promoting the Public Health," 4 November 1892, 12.
20. Meek, *Land Law and Custom in the Colonies*, 291.

21. "Mr. Truth on Native Administrative Ordinance," *Gold Coast Independent*, 5 March 1932, 274.
22. "The Preservation and Development of Our Institution," *Gold Coast Independent*, 6 August 1932, 831.
23. Meek, *Land Law and Custom in the Colonies*, 291.
24. RG 15/1/89, 110-11.
25. CVA 45/49, *Thomas A. Hammond v. Isaac C. Fiscian and Titus Glover*, 3 September 1949, 58.
26. RG 15/1/89, 5.
27. RG 15/1/89, 68-72.
28. CVA 40/56, *Madam Sarah Clegg v. Emmanuel Drissu Cobblah*, 21 November 1956.
29. SCT 16/11/45, *J. E. Maslieno v. J. A. Nelson*.
30. *Daily Echo*, 4 February 1938. For another publication, see CVA 40/58.
31. RG 15/1/21, *Isaac Cobblah Fiscian v. Henry A. K. Nelson and Sohby Baksmathy*, 21 February 1946, 73.
32. CVA 45/49, Yawah per *J. M. Aryeequaye v. J. E. Maslieno*, 5 August 1930, 38-39.
33. RG 15/1/21, 15 November 1945, 20. See also Clifford C. Campbell, "Full Circle: The Caribbean Presence in the Making of Ghana, 1843-1966" (PhD diss., University of Ghana, Legon, 2012); Kwame Essien, "(In)Visible Diasporan Returnee Communities: Silences and the Challenges in Studying Trans-Atlantic History in Ghana," *Ghana Studies* 17 (2014): 63-99.
34. RG 15/21, 15 November 1945, 20.
35. RG 15/1/89, 32, 73.
36. RG 15/1/56, 40-41.
37. CVA 40/56, 27 January 1958.
38. CVA 45/49, 9 March 1949, 68.
39. SCT, *Plange v. Brazilians*, 2 April 1921, 3.
40. "The Deportation of Native Kings," *Lagos Times and Gold Coast Advertizers*, 13 July 1881.
41. SCT 2/4/19, vol. 8, *Tackie v. Nelson*, 29 September 1892.
42. CVA 40/58, 27 January 1958, 29.
43. Steven J. Salm and Toyin Falola, *Culture and Customs of Ghana* (Westport, CT: Greenwood Press, 2002).
44. *West African Herald*, 31 March 1871, 5.
45. SCT 2/4/19, vol. 8, *Tackie v. Nelson*, 29 September 1892, 4-10.
46. See "Labor on the Gold Coast."
47. Alcione M. Amos and Ebenezer Ayesu, "'I Am Brazilian': History of the Tabon, Afro-Brazilian in Accra," *Transactions of the Historical Society of Ghana*, n.s. 6 (2002): 55. Like Ferku, the time of Matta's arrival is not known.
48. SCT 2/28/1949, *Nii Azumah III v. Larikie Aruna and Kankle Kofi*, 28 February 1949, 62.
49. SCT 20/7/45, *Isaac Cobblah Fiscian v. Henry Asumah Nelson and Sohby Basmathy*, 12.
50. Kwame Essien, "The African Diaspora in Reverse: The *Tabom* People in Ghana, 1820s-2009" (PhD diss., University of Texas, 2010), 251.
51. Samuel Quarcoopome, "The Brazilian Community in Accra" (PhD diss., University of Ghana,

Legon, 1970), 7-9.
52. Ibid.
53. CVA 45/49, 8 March 1949, 47-48; *Fiscian v. Nelson and Basmathy*, 20 July 1945, 12.
54. CVA 45/49, 8 March 1949, 47-48; *Fiscian v. Nelson and Basmathy*, 20 July 1945, 12. See also Essien, "African Diaspora in Reverse," 252-64.
55. CVA 45/49, 8 March 1949, 47-48; *Fiscian v. Nelson and Basmathy*, 20 July 1945, 18.
56. Ibid.
57. Ibid., 64-65.
58. SCT 16/11/45, *J. E. Maslieno v. J. A. Nelson*, 1.
59. RG 15/1/89, 45.
60. Samuel Aniegye Ntewusu, "Settling in and Holding On: A Socio-Economic History of Northern Traders and Transporters in Accra's Tudu: 1908-2008" (PhD diss., University of Leiden, 2011), 1-38.
61. Nii Azumah V, interview by Kwame Essien, 3 August 2008.
62. SCT 16/11/45, *J. E. Maslieno v. J. A. Nelson*, 11.
63. Elder George Nii Aruna Nelson, interview by Kwame Essien, 6 August 2008.
64. SCT 16/11/45, *J. E. Maslieno v. J. A. Nelson*, 11.
65. CVA 45/49, *Sackey v. Otoo*, 27 August 1914, 80.
66. CVA 45/49, 7 July 1947, 9.
67. SCT 20/7/45, *Isaac Cobblah Fiscian v. Henry Asumah Nelson and Sohby Baksmathy*, 2.
68. Elder George Aruna Nelson, interview by Kwame Essien, 10 August 2008.
69. CVA 45/49, *Thomas A. Hammond v. Isaac C. Fiscian and Titus Glover*, 3 September 1949, 59.
70. CVA 45/49, 8 March 1949, 38.
71. Ibid., 10.
72. Ibid.
73. Ibid., 40.
74. Ibid., 10.
75. CVA 12/52, *Peter Quarshie Fiscian and Mary A. Fiscian v. Nii Azumah III*, 13 March 1953, 42.
76. Ibid.
77. Jeffrey P. Green, "Caribbean Influences in the Gold Coast Administration in the 1900s," *Ghana Studies Bulletin* 2 (December 1984): 11-16.
78. SCT 16/11/45, *J. E. Maslieno v. J. A. Nelson*, 29.
79. Scissors House was one of the historical monuments that was built by a returnee in 1854. See also Essien, "African Diaspora in Reverse," 164.
80. Nii Azumah V, interview by Kwame Essien, 3 August 2008.
81. CVA 40/58, 23 January 1958, 21.
82. SCT 2/4/19, *King Tackie v. Robert Nelson*, 15 September 1892, 21.
83. CVA 45/49, *Cobblah Fiscian v. Na Korley & Family*, 11 March 1949, 22.
84. Essien, "(In)Visible Diasporan Returnee Communities."

CHAPTER 6. (RE-)CREATING BRAZILIAN SLAVERY IN AN ENABLING ENVIRONMENT: THE "GHOST" OF SLAVERY

1. "The Slave Question," *Lagos Times and Gold Coast Advertizer*, 14 June 1882, 2.
2. "The Charge of Slave Selling at Abeokuta," *African Times*, 23 March 1866, 101; *African Times*, 23 November 1864, 3. See also "Stop the Cuban Slave Trade and Africa," *African Times*, 23 December 1862, 67; and J. T. A., *Gold Coast Echo*, 13 March 1889, 3.
3. Nii Azumah V, interview by Kwame Essien, 7 August 2007. See also Alcione M. Amos and Ebenezer Ayesu, "I Am Brazilian: History of the Tabon, Afro-Brazilian in Accra," *Transactions of the Historical Society of Ghana*, n.s. 6 (2002): 52; Sandra E. Greene, *Sacred Sites and the Colonial Encounter: A History of Meaning and Memory in Ghana* (Bloomington: Indiana University Press, 2002), 46. See also Emmanuel K. Akyeampong, *Between the Sea and the Lagoon: An Eco-Social History of the Anlo of Southeastern Ghana, c. 1850 to Recent Times* (Athens: Ohio University Press, 2001), 48.
4. David Eltis, "The British Contribution to the Nineteenth-Century Transatlantic Slave Trade," in *The Atlantic Slave Trade*, vol. 4, *Nineteenth Century*, ed. Jeremy Black (Aldershot: Ashgate, 2006), 163-79.
5. Peter Haenger, *Slaves and Slave Holders on the Gold Coast: Towards an Understanding of Social Bondage in West Africa*, ed. J. J. Shaffer and Paul E. Lovejoy, trans. Christina Handford (Basel: Schlettwein, 2000), 114-15.
6. ADM 1/10/7.
7. *African Times*, 23 November 1864, 3.
8. See J. D. Fage, "Slavery and the Slave Trade in the Context of West African History," *Journal of African History* 10, no. 3 (1969): 393-404; and Gareth Austin, "Human Pawnship in Asante, 1800-1950: Markets and Coercion, Gender and Cocoa," in *Pawnship, Slavery and Colonialism in Africa*, ed. Paul E. Lovejoy and Toyin Falola (Trenton, NJ: Africa World Press, 2003), 187-224.
9. There are numerous newspapers at the British Newspaper Library, Colindale, with coverage on slavery: "Nee Naa and Narkeki Found Not Guilty of Slave Dealing," *African Morning Coast*, 4 January 1939, 1; "The Slave Trade," *African Times*, 23 March 1863, 101; "Dahomey," *African Times*, 23 April 1863, 114-15; and "Slave Ships and Slave Preventing Ships," *African Times*, 23 December 1863, 74.
10. Austin, "Human Pawning in Asante, 1820-1950"; and Beverly Grier, "Pawns, Porters, and Petty Traders: Women in the Transition to Cash-Crop Agriculture in Colonial Ghana," in Lovejoy and Falola, *Pawnship, Slavery and Colonialism in Africa*, 306-8. See also Natalie Swinepoe, "Different Conversations about the Same Thing? Source Materials in the Recreation of a Nineteenth-Century Slave-Raiding Landscape, Northern Ghana," in *Slavery in Africa: Archaeology and Memory*, ed. Paul J. Lane and Kevin C. MacDonald (London: Oxford University Press, 2011), 167-90.
11. Francis Agbodeka, *African Politics and British Policy in the Gold Coast, 1868-1900: A Study in the Forms and Force of Protest* (Evanston, IL: Northwestern University Press, 1971), 56-57.
12. Kwabena Opare-Akurang, "The Administration of the Abolition Laws, African Responses and Post-Proclamation Slavery in the Gold Coast, 1874-1940," in *Slavery and Colonial Rule in Africa*, ed. Suzanne Miers and Martin Klein (London: Frank Cass, 1999), 149-66.

13. Descendants are often reluctant to be open about the element of slavery within their past. Older members of the current generation have provided relevant information about slavery that occurred in the community, perhaps because they were old enough to place it in some kind of perspective. For the younger members, their lack of knowledge about this subject has also contributed to the silences.

14. Joseph C. Miller, *Way of Death: Merchant Capitalism and Angolan Slave Trade, 1730–1830* (Madison: University of Wisconsin Press, 1988); Orlando Patterson, *Slavery and Social Death: A Comparative Study* (Cambridge, MA: Harvard University Press, 1982); Ira Berlin, *Many Thousands Gone: The First Two Centuries of Slavery in North America* (Cambridge, MA: Harvard University Press, 1998); Ira Berlin, *Slaves without Masters: The Free Negro in the Antebellum South* (New York: Pantheon, 1974); Deborah Gray White, *Ar'n't I a Woman: Female Slaves in the Plantation South* (New York: W. W. Norton, 1999); Yuval Taylor, ed., *I Was Born a Slave: An Anthology of Classic Slave Narratives*, vol. 1 (Chicago: Lawrence Hill Books, 1999); and Herbert S. Klein, *African Slavery in Latin America and the Caribbean* (London: Oxford University Press, 1986).

15. CVA 12/52, 15 November 1945, 2.

16. CO 147/159, Moloney to Holland, 20 June 1887.

17. See Thorkild Hansen, *Coast of Slaves*, trans. Kari Dako (Legon-Accra: Sub-Saharan Publishers, 2002). Carstensen's hypocrisy was similar to the position of British colonial officials and missionaries in the Gold Coast. On the other hand, in his subsequent entries, Carstensen predicts how other freed slaves could enhance social developments if they relocated to Africa. He thus offers a gleam of hope that underscores the need for historians to look beyond the dark side of the returnees' past and rather focus on their positive impact in their new environs.

18. Ibid., 188.

19. Ibid., 12–13, 132.

20. Ibid., 87, 171, 258.

21. Ibid., 154.

22. The life of Francisco "Chacha" de Souza, the notorious slave merchant, is one such example.

23. Quoted from George Reid Andrews, *Blacks and Whites in São Paolo, 1888–1988* (Madison: University of Wisconsin Press, 1991), 10. See also Florestan Fernandes, "The Negro Problem in a Class Society," in *Blackness in Latin America and the Caribbean: Social Dynamics and Cultural Transformations*, vol. 2, *Eastern South America and the Caribbean*, ed. Norman E. Whitten Jr. and Arlene Torres (Bloomington: Indiana University Press, 1998), 100.

24. Walter C. Rucker, *Gold Coast Diasporas: Identity, Culture, and Power* (Bloomington: Indiana University Press, 2015), 34–36.

25. See Joseph Miller, "Women as Slaves and Owners of Slaves: Experiences from Africa, the Indian Ocean and the Early Atlantic," in *Women and Slavery*, vol. 1, *Africa, the Indian Ocean World, and the Medieval North Atlantic*, ed. Gwyn Campbell, Suzanne Miers, and Joseph Miller (Athens: Ohio University Press, 2007), 1–40.

26. John Parker, *Making the Town: Ga State and Society in Early Colonial Accra* (Portsmouth, NH: Heinemann, 2000), 62.

27. H. Nii-Adziri Wellington, *Stones Tell Stories at Osu: Memories of a Host Community of the Danish Trans-Atlantic Slave Trade* (Legon-Accra: Sub-Saharan Publishers, 2011), 51, 71.

28. *African Times*, 22 February 1862, 61.

29. EC 6/19, 28. For items or merchandise the Danes exchanged for slaves, see Hansen, *Coast of Slaves*, 122, 168-77.
30. EC 6/3, 57.
31. Pierre Verger, *Trade Relations between the Bight of Benin and Bahia from the 17th to 19th Century*, trans. Evelyn Crawford (Ibadan: Ibadan University Press, 1976), 515. See also Verene A. Shepherd, *Saving Souls: The Struggle to End the Transatlantic Trade in Africans* (Kingston, Jamaica: Ian Randle Publishers, 2007), 6-13; Alberto da Costa e Silva, "Portraits of African Royalty in Brazil," in *Identity in the Shadow of Slavery*, ed. Paul E. Lovejoy (London: Continuum, 2000), 129-36.
32. Antônio Olinto, *The Water House*, trans. Dorothy Heapy (New York: Carroll and Graf, 1970).
33. "On Social Conditions of the Emancipated Slaves at the Eastern District of the Gold Coast," *African Times*, 23 April 1867, 122.
34. Colonial and missionary reports and newspapers covered stories about freed slaves who were reenslaved. See "Many Persons Are Baited into Serfdom," *African Morning Post*, 28 February 1939, 1-4; "Slave Dealer Assisted by Police in Lagos," *African Times*, 23 February 1866, 85.
35. Haenger, *Slaves and Slave Holders on the Gold Coast*.
36. A. A. Opoku, *Riis, the Builder* (Legon-Accra: Institute of African Studies, University of Ghana, 1978).
37. See Inventory of the Historical Archives, Pontificia Università Urbaniana, Rome, Italy: Parocchi Acta, vol. 238 (1872), fols. 250-52; copy of Chausse from Lagos, 1880, fols. 665-68.
38. FO 84/289 and FO 84/303.
39. "Ashantee Defeated the British for the Third Time," *West Africa Herald*, 7 June 1873, 2.
40. FO 84/880.
41. CO 714/64, "The King of Dahomey," Governor Winnieth to Queen Victoria, 5 May 1832, 7. See also Robin Law, "Francisco de Souza in West Africa, 1820-1849," in *Enslaving Connections: Changing Cultures of Africa and Brazil during the Era of Slavery*, ed. José C. Curto and Paul E. Lovejoy (New York: Humanity Books, 2004), 193-205.
42. Verger, *Trade Relations between the Bight of Benin and Bahia*, 209.
43. FO 84/141.
44. FO 84/28. For slave merchants including Domingos José Martins, Joaquim José de Brito, and others who were sentenced for illegal activities including slavery, see Verger, *Trade Relations between the Bight of Benin and Bahia*, 35; 480-90. Other Africans including João de Oliveira, an African who was captured along the Mina Coast and sent to Pernambuco at a young age, later returned to Porto Novo (Benin) after freedom in the mid-nineteenth century to invest in slavery activities in the area. Other freed slaves involved in similar activities traveled between Praya (Praia), a coastal town in Brazil, and Lagos. See also Pierre Verger, *Bahia and the West African Trade, 1549-1851* (Ibadan: Ibadan University Press, 1964), 35, 476-90.
45. The article continued that "it is nonsense to say that slaves are not shipped from Popo and Ahguay. The men and the women are neither bought to be eaten, nor to be employed on the coast, but for shipment to Cuba; and how they find their way there is certain. It seems scandalous if the Quittah Fort is not occupied." "Slave Trade in Quittah, Gold Coast," *African Times*, 23 October 1863, 41.
46. Law, "Francisco de Souza in West Africa," 187-205.

47. Elisée Soumonni, "Lacustrine Village in South Benin as Refuges from the Slave Trade," in *Fighting the Slave Trade: West African Strategies*, ed. Sylviane A. Diouf (Athens: Ohio University Press, 2003), 3-14; Paul E. Lovejoy and David Richardson, "Anglo-Efik Relations and Protection against Illegal Enslavement at Old Calibar, 1740-1807," in Diouf, *Fighting the Slave Trade*, 101-19; and John N. Oriji, "Igboland, Slavery, and the Drums of War and Heroism," in Diouf, *Fighting the Slave Trade*, 121-51.

48. A message from the queen of England that was read by Commodore Wilmont, a British official in Dahomey, sent a stern warning: "Tell the King that I am glad to hear he is well and give him my compliments.... The King must give up the slave trade, or he must prepare to see his ports blocked ... to prevent him from reaching the shores. He cannot live or feed his people without those things. He will not be able to sell his slaves because they cannot be shipped." "Dahomey," *African Times*, 23 September 1864, 37.

49. *African Times*, 30 June 1874.

50. See Paul E. Lovejoy and Jan S. Hogendorn, *Slow Death for Slavery: The Course of Abolition in Northern Nigeria, 1897-1936* (Cambridge: Cambridge University Press, 1993).

51. "Gold Coast," *African Times*, 23 April 1867, 122.

52. "On Social Conditions of the Emancipated slaves in the Eastern District of the Gold Coast," *African Times*, 23 April 1867, 122.

53. Robin Law, *Ouidah: The Social History of a West African Slaving "Port," 1727-1892* (Athens: Ohio University Press, 2004), 155-64.

54. "The Alleged Case of Slave Selling by a British Subject at Abeokuta," *African Times*, 23 January 1866, 73, 101. See also "The Charge of Slave Selling at Abeokuta," 101.

55. J. T. A., *Gold Coast Echo*, 13 March 1889, 3.

56. T. B. Freeman, "Life and Travels on the Gold Coast," *Gold Coast Echo*, 25 September 1888, 4.

57. Edward Carstensen, *Governor Carstensen's Diary, 1842-1850* (Legon: University of Ghana, 1965), 6.

58. Ibid.

59. Thorkild Hansen, *Coast of Slaves*, trans. Kari Dako (Legon-Accra: Sub-Saharan Publishers, 2002), 11-16.

60. EC 6/3.

61. For other reasons why Europeans selected the Gold Coast for agricultural purposes, see Per Hernaes, "A Danish Experiment in Commercial Agriculture on the Gold Coast, 1788-1793," in *Commercial Agriculture, the Slave Trade and Slavery in Atlantic Africa*, ed. Robin Law, Suzanne Schwarz, and Silke Strickrodt (Woodbridge: James Curry, 2013), 116-37; and Robin Law, "There's Nothing Grows in the West Indies but Will Grow Here: Dutch and English Projects of Plantation Agriculture on the Gold Coast, 1650s-1750s," in Law, Schwarz, and Strickrodt, *Commercial Agriculture*, 158-79.

62. EC 6/1.

63. Parker, *Making the Town*, 65, 92.

64. Hansen, *Coast of Slaves*, 13. For coverage on Isert's travels, see Selena Axelrod Winsnes, trans. and ed., *Letters on West Africa and the Slave Trade: Paul Erdmann Isert's Journey to Guinea and the Caribbean Islands in Columbia, 1788* (Accra: Sub-Saharan Publishers, 2007).

65. EC 6/1; EC 6/3.

Notes

66. Haenger, *Slaves and Slave Holders on the Gold Coast*, 173. The approach used by the Basel Mission to expel its members who participated in slavery was consistent with British colonial officials' intolerance for Protestant missionaries in Lagos and other British territories. See Verger, *Trade Relations between the Bight of Benin and Bahia*, 536-38; and Paul E. Lovejoy, *Transformations in Slavery: A History of Slavery in Africa* (New York: Cambridge University Press, 2000), 246-68.
67. EC 6/1, 2, "Article in Digest of Basel Mission Periodicals, 1828-1851."
68. Ibid.
69. Ibid.
70. EC 6/19, 2.
71. Ibid.
72. EC 6/3, 107.
73. Hansen, *Coast of Slaves*, 234.
74. EC 6/3, 13.
75. Hansen, *Coast of Slaves*, 232.
76. Ibid.
77. Ibid., 14.
78. Carstensen, *Governor Carstensen's Diary*, 12.
79. Ibid.
80. See Miers and Klein, *Slavery and Colonial Rule in Africa*; Gwendolyn Midlo Hall, *Slavery and African Ethnicities in the Americas: Restoring the Links* (Chapel Hill: University of North Carolina Press, 2005); Benedetta Rossi, *Reconfiguring Slavery: West African Trajectories* (Liverpool: Liverpool University Press, 2009); and James L. Watson, ed., *Asian and African Systems of Slavery* (Oxford: Blackwell, 1980).
81. Clifford C. Campbell, "Full Circle: The Caribbean Presence in the Making of Ghana, 1843-1966" (PhD diss., University of Ghana, Legon, 2012).
82. Carstensen, *Governor Carstensen's Diary*, 52.
83. Besides using religion as a measure of civilization, Campbell referred to the Christians among the returnees as "Brazilians" and referred to the non-Christians as "Yoruba" to explain the extent to which he was determined to draw distinctions between those who embraced European religions and others who held on to their African beliefs. Verger, *Trade Relations between the Bight of Benin and Bahia*, 550-52.
84. Colonial newspapers served as a vehicle for spreading notions of European civilization and superiority and African savagery and barbarism. For instance a report in the *African Times* echoed these sentiments: "It seems very much like this. We cannot send our civilization to Dahomey and Ashantee for them to look at it with their barbarism, as missionaries can show them the simple truths of Christianity and ask them to compare them with foul teachings of their fetish priests." "Civilizing of Africa: Envoys from Dahomey," *African Times*, 23 May 1866, 124.
85. EC 6/3.
86. According to Kenneth C. Barnes, for most travelers to Liberia "the goal of winning the dark continent for Christianity figured large in the thinking of black Americans about Africa in the late 1800s. Their views of themselves as superior and civilized in comparison to a pagan."

Kenneth C. Barnes, *Journey of Hope: The Back-to-Africa Movement in Arkansas in the Late 1800s* (Chapel Hill: University of North Carolina Press, 2004), 134.

87. Claude A. Clegg III, *The Price of Liberty: African Americans and the Making of Liberia* (Chapel Hill: University of North Carolina Press, 2004), 45.

88. James T. Campbell, *Middle Passages: African American Journeys to Africa, 1787–2005* (New York: Penguin, 2007), xv.

89. Law, "Francisco de Souza in West Africa." See the story of José Maria de Sousa e Almeida of Principe, who also owned slaves during the period of abolition. Catherine Higgs, *Chocolate Islands: Cocoa, Slavery and Colonial Africa* (Athens: Ohio University Press, 2012), 28–29.

90. Carstensen, *Governor Carstensen's Diary*, 19–20.

91. Amos and Ayesu, "'I Am Brazilian,'" 40.

92. Verger, *Trade Relations between the Bight of Benin and Bahia*, 209.

93. *West African Herald*, 3 June 1871, 6.

94. "Slavery in the Gold Coast," *African Morning Post*, 21 May 1935, 4.

95. Patrick Manning, *Slavery, Colonialism and Economic Growth in Dahomey, 1640–1960* (Cambridge: Cambridge University Press, 1982).

96. For works that provide estimates about Chacha's wealth via slavery, see Olatunji Ojo, "Afro-Brazilians in Lagos: Atlantic Commerce, Kinship and Trans-Nationalism," in *Back to Africa*, vol. 1, *Afro-Brazilian Returnees and Their Communities*, ed. Kwasi Kwaa Prah (Cape Town: Center for Advanced Studies of African Society, 2009), 243. See also Law, *Ouidah*, 189–230.

97. SCT 5/4/17, 16 December 1875.

98. RG 15/1/89, 30 April, 1931, 29. See also Catherine Coquery-Vidrovitch, "Women, Marriage and Slavery in Sub-Saharan Africa in the Nineteenth Century," in Campbell, Miers, and Miller, *Women and Slavery*, 1:43–61.

99. Parker, *Making the Town*, 93.

100. See Benedict G. Der, *Slave Trade in Northern Ghana* (Accra: Ghana University Press, 1999).

101. Fatimah L. C. Jackson and Latifa F. J. Borgelin, "How Genetics Can Provide Detail to the Transatlantic African Diaspora," in *The African Diaspora and the Disciplines*, ed. Tejumola Olaniyan and James H. Sweet (Bloomington: Indiana University Press, 2010), 75–79.

102. K. Poku, "Traditional Roles and People of Slave Origins in Modern Ashanti: A Few Impressions," *Ghana Journal of Sociology* 5, no. 1 (1969): 34–38. See also Claire C. Robertson, "Post-Proclamation Slavery in Accra: A Female Affair?" in *Women and Slavery in Africa*, ed. Claire C. Robertson and Martin A. Klein (Madison: University of Wisconsin Press, 1983).

103. SCT 17/5/9.

104. Nii Azumah V, interview by Kwame Essien, 7 August 2007.

105. Akosua Adoma Perbi, "Slaves and Succession to Political Office," chap. 6 of *A History of Indigenous Slavery in Ghana from the 15th to the 19th Century* (Accra: Sub-Saharan Publishers, 2004), 133–51. See also Haenger, *Slaves and Slave Holders in the Gold Coast*, 162–65.

106. SCT 2/4/19, vol. 8, *Tackie v. Nelson*, 29 September 1892.

107. Opoku, *Riis, the Builder*, 173.

108. Irene Quaye, "The Ga and their Neighbours, 1600–1742" (PhD diss., University of Ghana, Legon, 1972), 36.

109. Carl C. Reindorf, *The History of the Gold Coast and Asante, Based on Traditions and Historical Facts Comprising a Period of More Than Three Centuries from about 1500 to 1860* (Basel: Basel Mission Depot, 1951), 144–45.
110. "The Slave Question," 2. See also CO 879/41, February 1900, 22–23; W. Walton Claridge, *A History of the Gold Coast and Ashante from the Earliest Times to the Commencement of the Twentieth Century*, vol. 2 (New York: Barnes & Noble, 1964), 173–77.
111. Haenger, *Slaves and Slave Holders on the Gold Coast*, 169.

CHAPTER 7. CONTRIBUTIONS BY THE BRAZILIAN-AFRICANS AND THE TABOM: IMPACT ON GHANA'S HISTORY

1. Karol K. Weaver, *Medical Revolutionaries: The Enslaved Healers of Eighteenth-Century Saint Dominigue* (Urbana: University of Illinois Press, 2006), 2–6; and James H. Sweet, *Recreating Africa: Culture, Kinship, and Religion in African-Portuguese World, 1441–1770* (Chapel Hill: University of North Carolina Press, 2003), 119–88, 217–26.
2. Elisée Soumonni, "The Afro-Brazilian Communities of Ouidah and Lagos in the Nineteenth Century: A Comparative Analysis," in *Africa and the Americas: Interconnections during the Slave Trade*, ed. José C. Curto and Renée Soulodre-La France (Trenton, NJ: Africa World Press, 2005). For works about creolization or lack thereof, see Melville J. Herskovits, *The Myth of Negro Past* (Boston: Beacon Press, 1990); Sidney W. Mintz and Richard Price, *The Birth of African-American Culture: An Anthropological Perspective* (Boston: Beacon, 1992); Michael A. Gomez, *Exchanging Our Country Marks: The Transforming of African Identities in the Colonial and Antebellum South* (Chapel Hill: University of North Carolina Press, 1998); and Charles Joyner, *Down by the Riverside: A South Carolina Slave Community* (Urbana: University of Illinois Press, 1984).
3. Quoted from Marco A. Schaumloeffel, *Tabom: The Afro-Brazilian Community in Ghana*, 2nd ed. (published by author, 2008), 45.
4. Nina G. Schiller and Georges Fourun, *Georges Woke up Laughing: Long-Distance Nationalism and the Search for Home* (Durham, NC: Duke University Press, 2001).
5. Pierre Verger, *Trade Relations between the Bight of Benin and Bahia from the 17th to 19th Century*, trans. Evelyn Crawford (Ibadan: Ibadan University Press, 1976), 560.
6. Ibid.
7. CO 147/159, Moloney to Holland, 20 June 1887.
8. Edward Carstensen, *Governor Carstensen's Diary, 1842–1850* (Legon: University of Ghana, 1965), 52–53.
9. Ibid., 19–20. See also Edward Carstensen, *Closing the Books: Governor Edward on Danish Guinea, 1842–50*, trans. Tove Storsveer (Legon-Accra: Sub-Saharan Publishers, 2010).
10. Carstensen was in the Gold Coast from 1838 to 1844 and perhaps was aware of the contributions the returnees from Brazil made to the development of Accra. See Thorkild Hansen, *Coast of Slaves*, trans. Kari Dako (Legon-Accra: Sub-Saharan Publishers, 2003), 262–69.
11. Schaumloeffel, *Tabom*, 45.

12. Ama Biney, *The Political and Social Thoughts of Kwame Nkrumah* (New York: Palgrave Macmillan, 2011); Richard Rathbone, *Nkrumah & the Chiefs: The Politics of Chieftancy in Ghana, 1951-1960* (Oxford: James Currey, 2000); A. B. Assensoh, *Kwame Nkrumah of Africa: His Formative Years and the Beginning of His Political Career, 1935-1948* (London: Stockwell, 1989); and Kwame Nkrumah, *Neo-Colonialism, the Last Stage of Imperialism* (London: Thomas Nelson and Sons, 1965).
13. Pierre Verger, *Trade Relations between the Bight of Benin and Bahia from the 17th to 19th Century*, trans. Evelyn Crawford (Ibadan: Ibadan University Press, 1976), 533.
14. Samuel Quarcoopome, "The Brazilian Community of Ghana" (BA diss., University of Ghana, Legon, 1970), 7-8.
15. "The Editorial Notes," *Gold Coast Methodist Times*, November-December 1897, 1.
16. CVA 45/49, 9 March 1949, 57.
17. Nii Azumah V, interview by Kwame Essien, 3 August 2008.
18. Amon Nikoi, "Indirect Rule and Government in Gold Coast Colony, 1844-1954: A Study in the History, Ecology and Politics of Administration in a Changing Society" (PhD diss., Harvard University, 1956), 131.
19. David K. Patterson, "Health in Urban Ghana: The Case of Accra, 1900-1940," *Social Science and Medicine* 13 (1979): 252.
20. "Cattle Plague Accra," *West African Herald*, 31 March 1871, 6; "Small Pox," *West African Herald*, 26 July 1871, 3.
21. David K. Patterson, "Health in Urban Ghana: The Case of Accra, 1900-1940," *Social Science and Medicine* 13 (1979): 251-52.
22. Nikoi, "Indirect Rule and Government in Gold Coast Colony," 131.
23. EC 6/1, 11.
24. EC 6/1, 1825-51, 6.
25. Isaiah 43:20 (New King James Version).
26. EC 6/1, 1825-1851, 8. See also "Second Letter" in Selena Axelrod Winsnes, trans. and ed., *Letters on West Africa and the Slave Trade: Paul Erdmann Isert's Journey to Guinea and the Caribbean Islands in Columbia, 1788* (Accra: Sub-Saharan Publishers, 2007), 47-62.
27. EC 6/1, 1825-51, 6.
28. See Joseph Wuff's account of "climate fever" in the Gold Coast, Hansen, *Coast of Slaves*, 201-44.
29. Ibid., 234-38.
30. EC 6/1, memoir by Johanna Wartz.
31. See Sandra E. Greene, *Sacred Sites and the Colonial Encounter: A History of Meaning and Memory in Ghana* (Bloomington: Indiana University Press, 2002).
32. Nii Azumah V, interview by Kwame Essien, 20 July 2014.
33. Roquinaldo Amaral Ferreira, *Cross-Cultural Exchange in the Atlantic World: Angola and Brazil during the Era of the Slave Trade* (Cambridge: Cambridge University Press, 2012).
34. Sweet, *Recreating Africa*, 220-21.
35. João José Reis, *Slave Rebellion in Brazil: The Muslim Uprising of 1835 in Bahia*, trans. Arthur Brakel (Baltimore, MD: Johns Hopkins University Press, 1993), part 1, part 2, 73-159.

Notes

36. Nii Azumah V, interview by Kwame Essien, 14 August 2005.
37. Ibid.
38. Muneer Akolade (a member of Brazilian Olosun Social Club/Brazilian Gees, Lagos, Nigeria), interview by Kwame Essien, 2 July 2009.
39. Gibril R. Cole, *The Krio of West Africa: Islam, Culture, Creolization and Colonialism in the Nineteenth Century* (Athens: Ohio University Press, 2013), 138.
40. John Parker, *Making the Town: Ga State and Society in Early Colonial Accra* (Portsmouth, NH: Heinemann, 2000), 164. See also Misbahudeen Ahmed-Rufai, "The Muslim Association Party: A Test of Religious Politics in Ghana," *Transactions of the Historical Society of Ghana*, n.s. 6 (2002): 99-114; N. A. Josiah Aryeh, *An Outline of Islamic Customary Law in Ghana* (Accra: Kuno Publishers, 2005).
41. Cole, *The Krio of West Africa*, 138.
42. FO 84/1031.
43. See Inventory of the Historical Archives, Pontificia Università Urbaniana, Rome, Italy: Parocchi Acta, vol. 251 (1883), fols. 236, 101.
44. Bengt Sundkler and Christopher Steed, *A History of the Church in Africa* (Cambridge: Cambridge University Press, 2000), 106.
45. Michael J. Turner, "Les Bresiliens: The Impact of Former Brazilian Slaves upon Dahomey" (PhD diss., Boston University, 1975), 157.
46. Elisée Soumonni, "The Aguda of Benin: From the Memory of Brazil to the Construction of a Community Identity," in *Back to Africa*, vol. 1, *Afro-Brazilian Returnees and Their Communities*, ed. Kwasi Kwaa Prah (Cape Town: Center for Advanced Studies of African Society, 2009), 268.
47. Rev. Cannon Anthony M. Einsuley (the provincial secretary of the Church of the Province of West Africa), interview by Kwame Essien, 20 July 2012, Anglican Headquarters, Accra.
48. John S. Pobee, *The Anglican Story in Ghana: From Mission Beginnings to Province of Ghana* (Accra: Amanza, 2009), 93-108.
49. Verger, *Trade Relations between the Bight of Benin and Bahia*, 533.
50. Nii Azumah V, interview by Kwame Essien, 1 August 2007.
51. Quoted from A. R. Gomda, "A Slice of Brazil in Accra: The Nelsons, Lutterodts, Peregrinos, Fiscians et al," *Daily Guide*, 4 June 2011, 8.
52. Elder George Aruna Nelson, interview by Kwame Essien, 10 January 2009. See also Schaumloeffel, *Tabom*, 88-92.
53. Nancy Ellen Lawler, *Soldiers, Airmen, Spies, and Whisperers: The Gold Coast in World War II* (Athens: Ohio University Press, 2002), 25-80. See also David Killingray, *Fighting for Britain: African Soldiers in the Second World War* (Woodbridge: James Curry, 2010); Judith Byfield et al., eds., *Africa and World War II* (Cambridge: Cambridge University Press, 2015).
54. Samuel Boadi-Siaw, "The Afro-Brazilians in Ghana," in Prah, *Back to Africa*, 1:155.
55. CVA 40/56, 27 January 1958, 30.
56. *Osagyefo* in the Akan language means the savior or messiah. See Kwame Essien, "African Americans in Ghana and Their Contributions to 'Nation Building' since 1985," in *The United States and West Africa: Interactions and Relations*, ed. Alusine Jalloh and Toyin Falola (Rochester, NY: University of Rochester Press, 2008); "Kwame Nkrumah Is Our Shepherd, We Shall Not

Want," *Ghanaian Times*, 14 September 1962, 2; "Placards Go Up: Sunyani Protests; Osagyefo Must Be Life President," *Ghanaian Times*, 13 September 1962, 3; "Osagyefo Africa's Defender of Faith," *Ghanaian Times*, 13 September 1962, 2; and "We Are behind You, Osagyefo," *Ghanaian Times*, 13 September 1962, 2.

57. See James T. Campbell, *Middle Passages: African American Journeys to Africa, 1787-2005* (New York: Penguin, 2007); and Kevin K. Gaines, *American Africans in Ghana: Black Expatriates and the Civil Rights Era* (Chapel Hill: University of North Carolina Press, 2006). Returnees who settled in Ghana had the opportunity to make contributions to reforms in the new independent nation, but they had problems with assimilation and acceptance. Other Africans who also settled voluntarily elsewhere had similar challenges. Isidore Okpewho asserts, "For the new African diaspora, the experience of exile has been both beneficial and troubling. Whether we arrived here as highly skilled professionals or struggling students, many of us have been able to realize the goals of our voluntary expatriation in ways that have both benefited the host society ... and improved the fate of relatives we left back home in our native lands." Isidore Okpewho, "Introduction: Can We 'Go Home Again'?," in *The New African Diaspora*, ed. Isidore Okpewho and Nkiru Nzegwu (Bloomington: Indiana University Press, 2009), 9.

58. Clifford C. Campbell, "Full Circle: The Caribbean Presence in the Making of Ghana, 1843-1966" (PhD diss., University of Ghana, Legon, 2012); and Jeffrey P. Green, "Caribbean Influences in the Gold Coast Administration in the 1900s," *Ghana Studies Bulletin* 2 (December 1984): 11-16.

59. Elder George Aruna Nelson, interview by Kwame Essien, 6 August 2008.

60. Alcione M. Amos and Ebenezer Ayesu, "I Am Brazilian: History of the Tabon, Afro-Brazilian in Accra," *Transactions of the Historical Society of Ghana*, n.s. 6 (2002): 39.

61. Gomda, "A Slice of Brazil in Accra," 8.

62. Emmanuel Doe Ziorklui, *Ghana: Nkrumah to Rawlings, a Historical Sketch of Some Major Political Events in Ghana from 1957-81*, vol. 1 (Accra: Ghana Publishing Corporation, 1998), 312. See also John Westwood, *J. J. Rawlings: From School Days at Achimota to Castle* (Accra: Blue Savana, 2001); Kevin Shillington, *Ghana and the Rawlings Factor* (London: Macmillan, 1992).

63. Sam Nelson, interview by Kwame Essien, 14 August 2005.

64. Georgina T. Wood, interview by Kwame Essien, 26 July 2012.

65. Elder William Lutterodt, interview by Kwame Essien, 1 August 2012.

CHAPTER 8. BRAZILIANS TOGETHER, BRAZILIANS APART: THE FAMILY TREES AND THE PROCESS OF BECOMING GÃ

1. CVA 12/52, 28 February 1949, 62. See also CVA 45/49, 9 March 1949, 57.
2. LS 214/1956, *Clegg v. Cobblah*, 1 April 1957, 2. See also RG 15/1/1121, *Odoi Kwao v. Nii Azumah III*.
3. Tabom traditions hold that the Nelsons are the only family group that could serve as chiefs within the community.
4. CVA 40/58, 27 January 1958, 32.
5. Kwame Essien, "The African Diaspora in Reverse: The Tabom People in Ghana, 1820s-2009"

Notes

(PhD diss., University of Texas, Austin, 2010).

6. FO 84/846.
7. Elder George Aruna Nelson, interview by Kwame Essien, 6 August 2008.
8. Cliff Ekuful, "The D-Day Is Here: Ghana Brazilians Divided in Loyalty," *Ghanaian Times*, 27 June 2006, 1.
9. Gina M. Pérez, *The Near Northwest Side Story: Migration, Displacement, and Puerto Rican Families* (Berkeley: University of California Press, 2004), 9-13.
10. James H. Sweet, *Recreating Africa: Culture, Kinship, and Religion in African-Portuguese World, 1441-1770* (Chapel Hill: University of North Carolina Press, 2003), 87-101.
11. CVA 40/58, 27 January 1958, 32.
12. CVA 40/56, *Jemima Nassu Ore v. The Basel Mission*, 10 October 1957, 42.
13. Division within the community also added to gradual integration, which would have a lasting impact on the Brazilian-Tabom history in Ghana.
14. CVA 40/58.
15. Essien, "African Diaspora in Reverse," 11-112.
16. RG 15/1/89, 23 April 1931, 15-16.
17. CVA 29/55, 23 January 1958, 23.
18. CVA 45/49, *Samuel Q. Nelson v. S. Ammah and Yawa Aruna*; CVA 947/1920, 3 August 1949, 40.
19. CVA 12/52, 13 March 1953, 4, 44.
20. CVA 40/58, 27 January 1958, 32.
21. Nii Azumah V, interview by Kwame Essien, 8 August 2007.
22. CVA 45/49, 23 March 1940, 41.
23. David Eltis et al., eds., *The Trans-Atlantic Slave Trade: A Database on CD-ROM* (Cambridge: Cambridge University Press, 2000).
24. Fatimah L. C. Jackson and Latifa F. J. Borgelin, "How Genetics Can Provide Detail to the Transatlantic African Diaspora," in *The African Diaspora and the Disciplines*, ed. Tejumola Olaniyan and James H. Sweet (Bloomington: Indiana University Press, 2010), 75-100.
25. Dr. A. Olowun Toyin Peregrino-Brimah, interview by Kwame Essien, 15 July 2014. See also A. R. Gomda, "A Slice of Brazil in Accra: The Nelsons, Lutterodts, Peregrinos, Fiscians et al," *Daily Guide*, 4 June 2011, 8-9; Antonio Oliz Boyd, *The Latin American Identity and the African Diaspora: Ethnogenesis in Context* (Amherst, NY: Cambria Press, 2010), 267-81.
26. Gomda, "A Slice of Brazil in Accra," 8.
27. Marika Sherwood, *Origins of Pan-Africanism: Henry Sylvester Williams, Africa and the African Diaspora* (New York: Routledge, 2010), 141-68, 258-59. See also Les Switzer, ed., *South Africa's Alternative Press: Voices of Protest and Resistance, 1880s-1960s* (Cambridge: Cambridge University Press, 1997), 23-135.
28. Elder William Lutterodt, interview by Kwame Essien, 18 July 2012.
29. Ibid.
30. Elder William Lutterodt, interview by Kwame Essien, 18 July 2012.
31. Dr. Lutterodt won the Queen Elizabeth II Diamond Jubilee Medal award in Regina,

Saskatchewan, Canada, on 22 March 2013. The award was in honor of his outstanding and exceptional contributions to his community. See "Dr. Alfred Luterrodt Honoured," *Diasporan News*, 18 May 2013, http://www.ghanaweb.com/GhanaHomePage/NewsArchive/artikel.php?ID=274356.

32. Elder William Lutterodt, interview by Essien, 18 July 2012.
33. Sherwood, *Origins of Pan-Africanism*, 258–59. See also Kwaku Larbi Korang, *Writing Ghana, Imagining Africa: Nation and African Modernity* (Rochester, NY: University of Rochester Press, 2003).
34. Sherwood, *Origins of Pan-Africanism*, 259.
35. Ibid., 141–42.
36. Letter from Manu Herbstein to Chief Amida Peregrino-Brimah (son of Brimah), 9 June 1993. This letter was provided by Segun Peregrino-Brimah during our first interview on 25 July 2011. In the letter Herbstein expresses his appreciation to Peregrino for his contribution to the black freedom struggle in South Africa.
37. Segun Peregrino-Brimah, interview by Kwame Essien, 25 July 2011, Peregrino House, Accra, Ghana.
38. WRG 8/1/35, "Nigerians in Ghana." According to A. Olowun Toyin Peregrino-Brimah, although some Yoruba migrants relocated to the Gold Coast voluntarily, the British brought a large number of them as laborers to build the James Fort. A. Olowun Toyin Peregrino-Brimah, interview by Kwame Essien, 5 May 2015.
39. *Lagos Times and Gold Coast Advertizer*, 9 February 1881, 3; *Times of Africa*, 10 October 1895, 3.
40. CO 267/184, 12 June 1844. Correspondence between colonial officials in both the Gold Coast and Nigeria also provides evidence of how they aided the settlements. For example, Sir George Denton and Lord Lugard, who were both stationed in Nigeria, worked effectively with Mr. Chamberlain, another British official, to train colonial troops to assist the Crown in battles with the Ashante Kingdom. CO 879/62, Gold Coast Telegraphs from 6 April–31 December 1900, Relating to Ashanti War, No. 13, Letter from Sir George Denton (Lagos) and Mr. Chamberlain, 14 April 1900, 5–8.
41. Samuel Aniegye Ntewusu, "Settling in and Holding On: A Socio-Economic History of Northern Traders and Transporters in Accra's Tudu, 1908–2008," (PhD diss., University of Leiden, 2011), 1–38.
42. ADM 11/1/1502.
43. Thorkild Hansen, *Coast of Slaves*, trans. Kari Dako (Legon-Accra: Sub-Saharan Publishers, 2002), 11–16.
44. ADM 11/1/1502.
45. Ibid.
46. Alhaji Farouk Brimah, "Brief Biography of Alhaji Chief Brimah I" (unpublished manuscript, 11 January 1998), 2. This document is held at the Peregrino House in Accra. I received copies from A. Olowun Toyin Peregrino-Brimah and his siblings during my interview.
47. A. Olowun Toyin Peregrino-Brimah, interview by Kwame Essien, 1 August 2015.
48. Segun Peregrino-Brimah, interview by Kwame Essien, 15 July 2015. Segun is a Yoruba word that means "victory."

Notes

49. Segun Peregrino-Brimah, interview by Kwame Essien, 3 July 2014.
50. CVA 12/52, Jemima Nassu & Ors v. Basel Mission Factory, 13 March 1953. See also SCT 2/4/59, *Jemima Nassu & Ors v. Basel Mission Factory*, 29 April 1915.
51. According to Larry Yarak, Sokoto got into trouble with "colonial" laws later. Van der Eb, a Dutch governor in Elmina in the early 1840s, accused Sokoto of stealing after he purchased stolen items. Larry Yarak's email exchanges with Hermann W. von Hesse, 6 April 2015.
52. Carlos da Fonseca, *Letters from Brazil* (Brazil: Ministère des Relations Extérieures, 2010).
53. The British officials introduced the Native Jurisdiction Ordinance at different times to meet a particular need. John Parker, *Making the Town: Ga State and Society in Early Colonial Accra* (Portsmouth, NH: Heinemann, 2000), 102.
54. One of the Tabom served as a bishop in the Anglican Church in Accra.
55. Since the mid-twentieth century Ghanaian leaders and chiefs have used honorary titles such as *Nkɔsuohene* (development chief) and *nkɔsuohenemaa* (development queen mothers) to attract returnees from North America and the Caribbean, including Rita Marley, the widow of the legendary reggae musician Bob Nesta Marley. Although "honorary" chief in the Brazilian-African diaspora context and what later became known as development chiefs from the end of the twentieth century are similar, the former is permanent and more deeply integrated into local Ghanaian cultures than the latter.
56. Elder George Nii Aruna Nelson, interview by Kwame Essien, 6 August 2008.
57. SCT 17/4/3, 8 May 1876.
58. See Roger S. Gocking, *Facing Two Ways: Ghana Coastal Communities under Colonial Rule* (Lanham, MD: University Press of America, 1999). See also David E. Apter, *The Gold Coast in Transition* (Princeton, NJ: Princeton University Press, 1955).
59. Nii Azumah V, interview by Kwame Essien, 7 August 2007. Marco A. Schaumloeffel, *Tabom: The Afro-Brazilian Community in Ghana*, 2nd ed. (published by author, 2008), 41-84.
60. Nii Azumah V, interview by Kwame Essien, 10 January 2009.
61. CVA 40/58, *Nii Anyetei Kwao v. Nii Azumah III and others*, 13 March 1953, 43.
62. CVA 40/56, *Madam Sarah Clegg v. Emmanuel Drissu Cobblah*, 10 October 1957,, 17.
63. Schaumloeffel, *Tabom*, 62-63, 127.
64. Elder George Aruna Nelson, interview by Kwame Essien, 7 January 2009. For the succession of Tabon chiefs, see Schaumloeffel, *Tabom*, 41; Alcione M. Amos and Ebenezer Ayesu, "I Am Brazilian: History of the Tabon, Afro-Brazilian in Accra," *Transactions of the Historical Society of Ghana*, n.s. 6 (2002): 50-52.
65. RG 15/1/89, 23 April 1931, 15.
66. Emmanuel K. Akyeampong, *Drink, Power and Cultural Change: A Social History of Alcohol in Ghana, c. 1800 to Recent Times* (Portsmouth, NH: Heinemann, 1996), 12-15. See also Steven J. Salm and Toyin Falola, *Culture and Customs of Ghana* (Westport, CT: Greenwood Press, 2002), 128.
67. The linguist during my first interaction with the Tabom was the late Samuel Nelson, who was a former minister for sports in the 1980s.
68. Gocking, *Facing Two Ways*, 70.
69. SCT 17/4/12; Samuel Quarcoopome, "The Brazilian Community of Ghana" (PhD diss.,

University of Ghana, Legon, 1970), 8-11.
70. RG 15/1/89, 23 April 1931, 56.
71. See Jean Allman, ed., *Fashioning Africa: Power and the Politics of Dress* (Bloomington: Indiana University Press, 2004).
72. This is not the same as the use of inheritance in the selection of Brazilian-Tabom chiefs to lead the Brazilian-African diaspora.
73. RG 15/1/89, 30 April 1931, 26.
74. Nii Azumah V, interview by Kwame Essien, 14 August 2005. See also Schaumloeffel, *Tabom*, 114-16.
75. Albert Adu Boahen, *Yaa Asantewaa and the Asante-British War of 1900-1901* (Accra: Sub-Saharan Publishers, 2003).
76. Harry N. K. Odamtten, "Dode Akabi: A Reexamination of the Oral and Textual Narrative of a 'Wicked' Female King," *Journal of Women's History* 27, no. 3 (Fall 2015): 61-85.

CHAPTER 9. FADING DIASPORA AND RECEDING MEMORY: HOW THE BRAZILIAN GOVERNMENT AND THE TABOM ARE PRESERVING THE BRAZIL HOUSE AND CRISSCROSSING THE ATLANTIC IN FULL CIRCLE

1. Kwame Essien, "'Performance' in Trans-Atlantic Communities in Africa: The Case of Brazilian-Africans and American-Africans in Ghana," in *Pan-Africanism and the Politics of African Citizenship and Identity*, ed. Toyin Falola and Kwame Essien (New York: Routledge; London: Taylor & Francis, 2013), 101-18. See also Katharina Schramm, *African Homecoming: Pan-African Ideology and Contested Heritage* (Walnut Creek, CA: Left Coast Press, 2010); Joann Merritt Schofield-Childs, *Take Me Home to Afrika: An Autobiography of a Returnee* (published by author, 2011); and Seestah Njinga Imahkus, *Ababio: A 21ˢᵗ Century Anthology of African Diaspora Returnees to Ghana, Cape Coast* (Ghana: One Africa Tours and Specialty, 2009).
2. Paulla A. Ebron, *Performing Africa* (Princeton, NJ: Princeton University Press, 2002).
3. The word Elmina has Portuguese origins in "Mina," which refers to land of gold. David Birmingham, "The Regimento da Mina," in *Portugal and Africa* (Basingstoke: Macmillan, 1999), 25-32; and P. E. H. Hair, *The Founding of the Castelo de São Jorge da Mina: An Analysis of Sources* (Madison: University of Wisconsin-Madison, African Studies Program, 1994). See concerns raised about scholars' failure to contextualize the use of the word "Mina" in its proper historical, cultural, and geographical context. Kwasi Konadu, *The Akan Diaspora in the Americas* (New York: Oxford University Press, 2010), 6-15.
4. The Cape Coast Castle was built by the Swedes in 1652 as a trading post. See Edmund Abaka, *House of Slaves and "Door of No Return": Gold Coast/Ghana Slave Forts, Castles & Dungeons and the Atlantic Slave Trade* (Trenton, NJ: Africa World Press, 2012).
5. George M. Bob-Milliar and Gloria K. Bob-Milliar, "Mobilizing the African Diaspora for Development: The Politics of Dual Citizenship in Ghana," in Falola and Essien, *Pan-Africanism and the Politics of African Citizenship and Identity*, 119-36; George M. Bob-Milliar, "Chieftaincy, Diaspora, and Development: The Institution of Nkɔsuohene in Ghana," *African Affairs* 108 (2009): 541-58.

6. Nii Azumah V, interview by Kwame Essien, 6 August 2005.
7. Walter Rodney, *How Europe Underdeveloped Africa* (Dar es Salaam: Tanzania Publishing House, 1973).
8. Sheila Sackey, "Prez Lula Ends Visit," *Daily Graphic*, 14 April 2005.
9. Marco A. Schaumloeffel, *Tabom: The Afro-Brazilian Community in Ghana*, 2nd ed. (published by author, 2008), 133-36.
10. Nehemiah Owusu Achiaw, "Brazilian President's Official Visit: Government Honors Lula da Silva," *Daily Graphic*, 14 April 2005, 24.
11. Schaumloeffel, *Tabom*, 133-36.
12. Anani Dzidzienyo, "The Challenges of Africa and Brazil: Looking Ahead by Reconsidering the Record," in *Back to Africa*, vol. 1, *Afro-Brazilian Returnees and Their Communities*, ed. Kwesi Kwaa Prah (Cape Town: Center for Advanced Studies of African Society, 2009), 19.
13. Elder William Lutterodt, interview by Kwame Essien, 5 August, 2012.
14. SCT 2/4/59, *Jemima Nassu and Ors v. The Basel Mission*, 31 March 1915, 249.
15. Michael J. Turner, "Les Bresiliens: The Impact of Former Brazilian Slaves upon Dahomey" (PhD diss., Boston University, 1975), 146-48; S. Y. Boadi-Siaw, "Brazilian Returnees of West Africa," in *Global Dimensions of the African Diaspora*, ed. Joseph E. Harris (Washington, DC: Howard University Press, 1982), 299.
16. Ibid. See also Lisa A. Lindsay, "'To Return to the Bosom of Their Fatherland': Brazilian Immigrants in Nineteenth-Century Lagos," *Slavery & Abolition* 15, no 1 (1994): 29-33.
17. SCT 2/4/59, *Jemima Nassu and Ors v. The Basel Mission*, 17 June 1915, 391-92.
18. Dzidzienyo, "The Challenges of Africa and Brazil," 16. Dzidzienyo remarked that "although Marcus Vinicius Moreira Marinho and other younger Afro-Brazilians have been recruited to perform different roles in Divisão da Africa over the years, Brazil still has a long way to go." Drawing from Dantas's personal notes in his diary (Missáo Condenada: Diário in *Africa Difícil*) Dzidzienyo notes that although Dantas made significant contributions and did well during his tenure, he did not receive enough support from the Brazilian government to accomplish his mission in Ghana and elsewhere. He characterized this is a "condemned mission ... and a nightmare" (19-20).
19. For an overview, see the following literature: Anani Dzidzienyo and Suzanne Oboler, eds., *Neither Enemies nor Friends: Latinos, Blacks, Afro-Latinos* (New York: Palgrave Macmillan, 2005); Femi Ojo-Ade, ed., *Home and Exile: Abdias Nascimento, African Brazilian Thinker and Pan-African Visionary* (Trenton, NJ: Africa World Press, 2014); Edward E. Telles, *Race in Another America: The Significance of Skin Color in Brazil* (Princeton, NJ: Princeton University Press, 2004); Mieko Nishida, *Slavery and Identity: Ethnicity, Gender, and Race in Salvador, Brazil, 1808-1888* (Bloomington: Indiana University Press, 2003); Michael George Hanchard, *Orpheus and Power: The "Movimento Negro" of Rio de Janeiro and São Paulo, Brazil, 1945-1988* (Princeton, NJ: Princeton University Press, 1998); Michael George Hanchard, *Racial Politics in Contemporary Brazil* (Durham, NC: Duke University Press, 1999); Rebecca L. Reichmann, ed., *Race in Contemporary Brazil: From Indifference to Inequality* (University Park: Pennsylvania State University Press, 1999); Hendrick Kraay, ed., *Afro-Brazilian Culture and Politics: Bahia, 1790s to 1990s* (Armonk, NY: R. M. E. Sharpe, 1998); Eduardo Silva, *Prince of the People: The Life and Times of a Brazilian Free Man of Color*, trans. Moyra Ashford (London: Verso, 1993); Abdias do Nascimento, *Brazil, Mixture or Massacre? Essays in the Genocide of a Black People*, trans. Elisa

Larkin Nascimento (Dover, MA: Majority Press, 1989); Thomas E. Skidmore, *Brazil: Five Centuries of Change* (New York: Oxford University Press, 1999); Carl N. Degler, *Neither Black nor White: Slavery and Race Relations in Brazil and the United States* (New York: Macmillan, 1971).

20. Quoted in Schaumloeffel, *Tabom*, 63.
21. Ibid., 133-36.
22. See Paul Gilroy, *The Black Atlantic: Modernity and Double Consciousness* (Cambridge, MA: Harvard University Press, 1993).
23. Skidmore, *Brazil*, 109-12. See also Thomas E. Skidmore, *The Politics of Military Rule in Brazil, 1964-1985* (New York: Oxford University Press, 1988).
24. Schaumloeffel, *Tabom*, 63-67.
25. Skidmore, *The Politics of Military Rule in Brazil*, 36-38.
26. Emmanuel Doe Ziorklui, *Ghana: Nkrumah to Rawlings, a Historical Sketch of Some Major Political Events in Ghana from 1957-81*, vol. 1 (Accra: Ghana Publishing Corporation, 1998), 312. See also John Westwood, *J. J. Rawlings: From School Days at Achimota to Castle* (Accra: Blue Savana, 2001).
27. Abaka, *House of Slaves*, 339-53.
28. Bridget J. Katriku (chief director of Ministry of Tourism and Diasporan Relations), interview by Kwame Essien, 8 March 2007.
29. Dallen J. Timothy and Victor B. Teye, "American Children of the African Diaspora: Journeys to the Motherland," in *Tourism, Diaspora and Space*, ed. Tim Coles and Dallen J. Timothy (New York: Routledge, 2004), 111.
30. Ibid., 116.
31. According to Pauli Murray, Ghana was the "gateway to Africa south of the Sahara, a nerve center of African Nationalism and a political seismograph registering every tremor of the struggle for black nationhood." Pauli Murray, *The Autobiography of a Black Activist, Feminist, Lawyer, Priest and Poet* (Knoxville, TN: University of Tennessee Press, 1997), 338.
32. See Edward M. Bruner, "Tourism in Ghana: The Representation of Slavery and the Return of the Black Diaspora," *American Anthropologist* 98, no. 2 (1996): 295-96.
33. Ibid., 294-304.
34. Jazz legend Louis Armstrong, Richard Wright, Dr. W. E. B. Du Bois, Maya Angelou, and other prominent African Americans as well as returnees from the Caribbean such as Rita Marley, the widow of reggae maestro Bob Nesta Marley, from Jamaica have also established cultural ties with Ghana since the 1960s. See Kwame Essien, "African Americans in Ghana and Their Contributions to 'Nation Building' since 1985," in *The United States and West Africa: Interactions and Relations*, ed. Alusine Jalloh and Toyin Falola (Rochester, NY: University of Rochester Press, 2008); and Kevin K. Gaines, *American Africans in Ghana: Black Expatriates and the Civil Rights Era* (Chapel Hill: University of North Carolina Press, 2006).
35. Brempong Osei-Tutu, "Ghana's 'Slave Castles,' Tourism, and the Social Memory of the Atlantic Slave Trade," in *Archaeology of Atlantic Africa and the African Diaspora*, ed. Akinwumi Ogundiran and Toyin Falola (Bloomington: Indiana University Press, 2007), 192-93. See also Brempong Osei-Tutu, "African American Reactions to the Restoration of Ghana's 'Slave Castles,'" *Public Archaeology* 3 (2004): 195; "Ghana Sees Profits in Memory of Slave Trade," *Detroit Free Press*, 7 June 1996, 1A; and Seestah Njinga Imahkus, *Returning Home Ain't Easy but*

It Sure Is a Blessing (Cape Coast: One Africa Tours and Speciality, 1999).

36. Bayo Holsey, *Routes of Remembrance: Refashioning the Slave Trade in Ghana* (Chicago: University of Chicago Press, 2008), 151-73. See also Saidiya V. Hartman, *Lose Your Mother: A Journey along the Atlantic Slave Route* (New York: Farrar, Straus and Giroux, 2007).

37. Nii Azumah V, interview by Kwame Essien, 5 August 2005.

38. Peter Sutherland, "Ancestral Slaves and Diasporic Tourists: Retelling History by Reversing Movements in a Counternationalist Vodun Festival from Benin," in *Africanizing Knowledge: African Studies across Disciplines*, ed. Toyin Falola and Christian Jennings (New Brunswick, NJ: Transaction, 2002), 69-71, 79.

39. Solimar Otero, "Orunile: Heaven Is Home, Yoruba and Afrocuban Diasporas across the Atlantic" (PhD diss., Louisiana State University, 2009), 115-17, 146-53.

40. See Gilberto Freyre, *The Masters and the Slaves: A Study in the Development of Brazilian Civilization* (New York: Alfred A. Knopf, 1946).

41. Nehemiah Owusu Achiaw, "Brazilian President's Official Visit: Government Honors Lula da Silva," *Daily Graphic*, 14 April 2005, 24.

42. Those present at the gathering included Paulo Américo V. Wolowski, the Brazilian ambassador to Ghana, and Benedicta da Silva who later became the minister of social promotion. During his tenure, Lula surrounded himself with several Brazilians of African heritage. He appointed Dr. Joaquim Bardoza Gomez to the supreme court, Matilda Ribeiro as the head of the secretariat for the promotion of racial justice, and others.

43. Nii Azumah V, interview by Kwame Essien, 4 November 2006.

44. The first and perhaps the last time Brazil welcomed a royal delegation from Ghana was in 1978 when the then *Asantehene* (Asante King) Otumfuo Nana Opoku Ware II visited Brazil with a delegation during the reign of Brazilian president Ernesto Geisel's military regime. Memory of the Asante Kingdom (Ghana) is pervasive in Afro-Brazilian public discourse. In his study of the Akan presence in the Americas, Kwasi Konadu showcased the history of the Asante Kingdom through the theme song for the 1983 carnival in Brazil. One of the lyrics of "Negrice Cristal" was "viva o rei Osei Tutu," which translates "Long live to King Osei Tutu," one of the great kings of the Ashanti people. Konadu, *The Akan Diaspora in the Americas*, 11.

45. Dzidzienyo, "The Challenges of Africa and Brazil," 21.

46. There has been progress in ties between the Tabom and Brazil. Beginning in the 1990s, the Tabom leaders created new dialogue with the Brazilian government and embassy in Accra, the Ghanaian government, UNESCO, and other parties of similar interests, which led to the first restoration of a site of slave memory in a Tabom community—the opening of the Brazil House for tourism in 2007. Other ongoing collaborations have brought the companies Queiroz Galvao, JBS Friboi, Sabo, and Stafanini in Brazil and their Ghanaian counterparts to elevate existing mutual relations. Some of these meetings took place in São Paulo and Rio de Janeiro, Brazil, from 29 March to 3 April 2014 to explore areas of mutual interests: construction, energy, oil and gas, agriculture, and others. Collaboration between Ghana and Brazil in the area of construction led to the modification of major highways in central Accra near Kwame Nkrumah Circle to improve traffic and transportation in the area. The total project, which is estimated to cost 74.88 million Euros, is funded jointly by the two nations.

47. Achiaw, "Brazilian President's Official Visit," 24.

48. Mae-ling Jovenes Lokko, *The Brazil House* (Accra: Surf Publications, 2010), 72-73.

49. Georgina T. Wood, interview by Kwame Essien, 26 July 2012.
50. Nii Azumah V, interview by Kwame Essien, 30 July 2009.
51. Marco Schaumloeffel, interview by Kwame Essien, 20 January 2005. In 2003, Marco A. Schaumloeffel was appointed by the Ministry of External Relations in Brazil to teach Portuguese language at the Ghana Institute of Language and in the Tabom community among others. Schaumloeffel is currently an attaché of the Brazilian government in the Caribbean.
52. There is growing literature about the African American experience in Ghana, especially those who have invested heavily in the tourism sector. Essien, "'Performance' in Trans-Atlantic Communities in Africa," 107–12. See also Edmund Abaka, *House of Slaves and "Door of No Return": Gold Coast/Ghana Slave Forts, Castles & Dungeons and the Atlantic Slave Trade* (Trenton, NJ: Africa World Press, 2012).
53. Marco A. Schaumloeffel, interview by Kwame Essien, 20 January 2005. See also Marco A. Schaumloeffel, "The Influence of the Portuguese Language in Ghana," *Daily Graphic*, 7 May 2004, 7. As part of these initial efforts to make the Tabom story public, Schaumloeffel published a number of articles in the local newspapers. After his numerous interactions with the Tabom people he later provided a useful handbook, *Tabom: The Afro-Brazilian Community in Ghana* (2008), a project he completed for the Brazilian government and the embassy in Accra to meet part of their diplomatic and cultural needs.
54. Nii Azumah V, interview by Kwame Essien, 15 July 2014.
55. Frank C. K. Dugbley (staff of the Brazilian embassy, Accra), interview by Kwame Essien, 14 January 2005; and Marco A. Schaumloeffel, interview by Kwame Essien, 20 January 2005.
56. Ebron, *Performing Africa*, 1.
57. Michel-Rolph Trouillot, *Silencing the Past: Power and the Production of History* (Boston: Beacon Press, 1995), 14–20.
58. Jacques Depelchin, *Silences in African History: Between the Syndromes of Discovery and Abolition* (Dar es Salaam: Mkuki na Nyota Publishers, 2005), xi.
59. Sandra E. Greene, "Whispers and Silences: Explorations in African History," *Africa Today* 50, no. 2 (2003): 41–54.
60. John Edward Phillips, ed., *Writing African History* (Rochester, NY: University of Rochester Press, 2006), 254, 267.
61. Luise White, Stephan F. Miescher, and David William Chen, eds., *African Words, African Voices: Critical Practices in Oral History* (Bloomington: Indiana University Press, 2001), 3–10.
62. SCT 2/4/50, *Millers v. Victoria Van Hein*, 12.
63. Nii Azumah V, interview by Kwame Essien, 1 August 2008.
64. Holsey, *Routes of Remembrance*, 129.
65. Nii Azumah V, interview by Kwame Essien, 1 August 2008.
66. Holsey, *Routes of Remembrance*, 128–29.
67. Schaumloeffel, *Tabom*, 40–42.
68. Nii Azumah V, interview by Kwame Essien, 27 July 2008.
69. Nii Azumah V, interview by Kwame Essien, 15 August 2005. Various factors help explain similarities and differences between the earlier and contemporary generations, especially their overlapping but yet robust and stringent ways they identified and why the history of the Tabom

people has not become a part of Ghanaian historiography and public school curriculum. These include a lack of continuity in past relationships between the returnees in Ghana and Brazil, evidence of transforming identities, the correlation between intermarriages with the local people and assimilation and the conversion of Tabom Muslims to Christianity, and degrees of acculturation. Others include the failure of the Ghana Tourist and Monument Board to preserve Brazil House and the first Scissors House as well as their lack of interest in the Tabom people's historical past and particularly their contributions to Ghana's history.

70. In her book *Routes of Remembrance: Refashioning the Slave Trade in Ghana*, anthropologist Bayo Holsey demonstrates how diasporan returnees congregate at the Elmina and Cape Coast Castles for a vast array of reasons—especially how the Ghana Tourist and Monument Board and the Ghanaian government benefit from such ongoing interactions. It is this one-dimensional focus by Ghanaians and tourist institutions that the Tabom people are trying to reconfigure in order to showcase their historical heritage, landmarks, and dual heritage or identity. On the other hand, Holsey's book does not show how diasporan returnees from North America (African Americans) and the Caribbean (Jamaicans, etc.) are also making economic gains from these historical spaces. This type of approach is common in other literature. For instance, in her thought-provoking book *Lose Your Mother: A Journey along the Atlantic Slave Route*, Saidiya Hartman demonstrates how communities like Salaga, a former slave-trading market in northern Ghana, have developed new strategies to attract tourists from the diaspora to their community while at the same time ignoring investments by diasporan communities in the tourism sector.

71. The historical memory of diasporan blacks (other returnees) about the transatlantic slave trade intersected with the history of the Tabom people. This is part of what influenced the Tabom people to create routes between a homeland (Ghana) and a hostland (Brazil), a term Kim Butler coined. Kim D. Butler, "Defining Diaspora, Refining a Discourse," *Diaspora* 10, no. 2 (2001): 192-206.

72. Ebron, *Performing Africa*, 1-2.

73. Coles and Timothy, *Tourism, Diaspora and Space*, 1-5.

74. Parallels can be drawn between the Tabom and the people of Loiza in Puerto Rico, a United States territory, who also transformed their deteriorating community into a "capital of [African] tradition for economic gains"; the Tabom people do not want their rich Brazilian heritage to remain on the margins. They both "opened their doors to the recognition of the [transatlantic] African tradition . . . as a means of survival." See Samiri Hernández Hiraldo, "If God Were Black and from Loiza: Managing Identities in a Puerto Rican Seaside Town," trans. Mariana Ortega-Brena, *Latin American Perspectives* 33, no. 1 (January 2006): 66; Samiri Hernández Hiraldo, *Black Puerto Rican Identity and Religious Experiences* (Gainesville: University Press of Florida, 2006), 4-6.

75. Nii Azumah V, interview by Kwame Essien, 14 August 2005.

76. Oko (tour guide at the Brazil House), interview by Kwame Essien, 15 July 2014.

CHAPTER 10. TELESCOPING LULA'S UNFULFILLED PROMISE AND THE
IMPLICATIONS OF THE TABOM'S VISIT TO BRAZIL: A HOPELESS SITUATION?

1. Marco A. Schaumloeffel, *Tabom: The Afro-Brazilian Community in Ghana*, 2nd ed. (published by author, 2008), 133-36.
2. See João José Reis, *Slave Rebellion in Brazil: The Muslim Uprising of 1835 in Bahia*, trans. Arthur Brakel (Baltimore, MD: Johns Hopkins University Press, 1993). According to João José Reis, besides the relentless efforts by slaves become free the 1835 rebellions in Bahia were mainly provoked by attempts by Brazilian authorities to impose Catholicism upon African slaves who practiced Islam. Retribution for revolts included five years of forced labor, 150 lashes (43); deprived leisure (45); death sentence and repatriation to Africa (47); new laws for regulating the congregation of slaves—Article 113 of the 1830 Criminal Code characterized the gathering of more than twenty slaves as illegal (205); and imprisonment for five to eight years (206).
3. According to Michael J. Turner, "Afro-Brazilians who were able to leave Brazil in the period between 1850-1875 had been able to make the greatest financial progress and economic success on the African coast." "Les Bresiliens: The Impact of Former Brazilian Slaves upon Dahomey" (PhD diss., Boston University, 1975), 83. See also Emmanuel K. Akyeampong, *Between the Sea and the Lagoon: An Eco-Social History of the Anlo of Southeastern Ghana, c. 1850 to Recent Times* (Athens: Ohio University Press, 2001).
4. Paul Tiyambe Zeleza, "Rewriting the African Diaspora: Beyond the Black Atlantic," *African Affairs* 104 (2005): 39-41, 54-57.
5. Kai Lutterodt, interview by Kwame Essien, 20 June 2011, London.
6. Georgina Wood, interview by Kwame Essien, 5 July 2012.
7. Elder George Nii Aruna Nelson, interview by Kwame Essien, 10 January 2009.
8. Elder William Lutterodt, interview by Kwame Essien, 18 July 2012.
9. Schaumloeffel, *Tabom*, 133-36.
10. Nii Azumah V, interview by Kwame Essien, 15 June 2014.
11. Nii Azumah V, interview by Kwame Essien, 10 January 2009.
12. A similar ritual was performed during my first interview with the Tabom leader.
13. João José Reis (Thinker Scholar at the University of Texas, Austin), interview by Kwame Essien, 29 November 2006.
14. Josildeth Gomes Consorte, "The Black Question in Brazil: An Inside Issue Denied," in *Routes of Passage: Rethinking the African Diaspora*, ed. Ruth Simms Hamilton, vol. 1, part 2 (East Lansing: Michigan State University Press, 2007), 1-12.
15. Sam Nelson, interview by Kwame Essien, 14 August 2005. .
16. Schaumloeffel, *Tabom*, 133-36.
17. Elder George Nii Aruna Nelson, interview by Kwame Essien, 10 January 2009. The general Ghanaian experience with racism during the colonial era is minimal compared to blacks in South Africa during the apartheid period and racial discrimination in the African diaspora. It is reasonable to argue that the Tabom people are not conscious about this subject or not aware of its lasting impact on Afro-Brazilian history. For older people like George Aruna Nelson, he preferred to satisfy his curiosity about his ancestral homeland in Brazil than engage in the

dialogue about race and racism.

18. Anani Dzidzienyo, "The Challenges of Africa and Brazil: Looking ahead by Reconsidering the Record," in *Back to Africa*, vol. 1, *Afro-Brazilian Returnees and Their Communities*, ed. Kwesi Kwaa Prah (Cape Town: Center for Advanced Studies of African Society, 2009), 22.

19. Marco A. Schaumloeffel, interview by Kwame Essien, 20 January 2005. Part of this analysis is also based on my visit to Rio de Janeiro in Brazil where I observed that almost all administrative positions are held by Brazilians of European descent. Recent scholarship in Brazil has been devoted to the reality of racial inequalities in the country.

20. I interacted with Frank Dugbley on two more occasions.

21. Thomas E. Skidmore, *Brazil: Five Centuries of Change* (New York: Oxford University Press, 1999), xiv.

22. Edward E. Telles, *Race in Another America: The Significance of Skin Color in Brazil* (Princeton, NJ: Princeton University Press, 2004), 16.

23. Gilberto Freyre was a Brazilian sociologist who argued forcefully that Brazil is a color-blind society. Anani Dzidzienyo and Suzanne Oboler, eds., *Neither Enemies nor Friends: Latinos, Blacks, Afro-Latinos* (New York: Palgrave Macmillan, 2005), 137-39.

24. See Luis Nicolau Parés, *The Formation of Condomblé: Vodun History and Ritual in Brazil* (Chapel Hill: University of North Carolina Press, 2013); and J. Lorand Matory, *Black Atlantic Religion: Tradition, Transnationalism, and Matriarchy in the Afro-Brazilian Candomblé* (Princeton, NJ: Princeton University Press, 2005).

25. Anani Dzidzienyo, "Coming to Terms with the African Connection in Latino Studies," *Latino Studies* 1 (2003): 164.

26. Michael George Hanchard, *Orpheus and Power: The "Movimento Negro" of Rio de Janeiro and São Paulo, Brazil, 1945-1988* (Princeton, NJ: Princeton University Press, 1998); Femi Ojo-Ade, ed., *Home and Exile: Abdias Nascimento, African Brazilian Thinker and Pan-African Visionary* (Trenton, NJ: Africa World Press, 2014).

27. Schaumloeffel, *Tabom*, 133-36.

28. Nii Azumah V, interview by Kwame Essien, 15 August 2005.

29. Ambassador Gala was also quoted as saying, "I hear some people say 11,000 dollars will be ok but I doubt it would be.... You go to Brazil and you marvel at the tourist attraction and the big hotels. You can't just go and see only football matches.... I'm sure you will love to go to the beaches and all that is not going to be easy.... The standard of living in Brazil has risen more than three times in the past year that should tell you how high it is to go there." See "Brazilian Ambassador Warns Fans about Expensive World Cup," Ghana Soccer Net, 11 March 2014, http://ghanasoccernet.com.

30. From the funeral program of Elder George Nii Aruna Nelson, 10 July 2009, 16-17.

31. Several of the members of the Nelson family including Tabom chiefs Nii Azumah III and Nii Azumah V were all members of the Anglican Church.

32. Julian Koshie Peregrino-Brimah, interview by Kwame Essien, 14 May 2015.

CONCLUSION

1. The following Brazilian diplomats at the embassy in Accra played a major role to showcase the Brazilian-African diaspora in Ghana during the 1960s: Raimundo de Souza Dantas, Luíz Garrido Cavadas, Carlos Norberto de Oliveira Pares, Sem Funcionário, Helder Martins de Moraes, Paulo Américo Veiga Wolowski, and Irene Vida Gala. Rubem Guimarães Coan Fabro Amaral, Minister Counsellor, Embassy of Brazil in Accra, e-mail to author, 5 March 2015.

2. See the introduction to Geoffrey Cubitt, *History and Memory* (Manchester, UK: Manchester University Press, 2007). See also Pier Martin Larson, *History and Memory in the Age of Enslavement: Becoming Merina in Highland Madagascar, 1770–1822* (Portsmouth, NH: Heinemann, 2000), 38–39; and Michael Lambek, *The Weight of the Past: Living with History in Mahajanga, Madagascar* (New York: Palgrave MacMillan, 2002).

3. Michelle M. Wright, *Physics of Blackness: Beyond the Middle Passage Epistemology* (Minneapolis: University of Minnesota Press, 2015), 1.

4. Peter Haenger, *Slaves and Slave Holders on the Gold Coast: Towards an Understanding of Social Bondage in West Africa*, ed. J. J. Shaffer and Paul E. Lovejoy, trans. Christina Handford (Basel: Schlettwein, 2000), 114.

5. Edward Carstensen, *Governor Carstensen's Diary, 1842–1850* (Legon: University of Ghana, 1965), 12–31.

6. Kwame Essien, "'Performance' in Trans-Atlantic Communities in Africa: The Case of Brazilian-Africans and American-Africans in Ghana," in *Pan-Africanism and the Politics of African Citizenship and Identity*, ed. Toyin Falola and Kwame Essien (New York: Routledge; London: Taylor & Francis, 2013), 96–98, 179–80, and 207–9.

7. Wendy Wilson-Fall, *Memories of Madagascar in the Black Atlantic* (Athens: Ohio University Press, 2015), 153.

8. John Edward Phillips, ed., *Writing African History* (Rochester, NY: University of Rochester Press, 2006), 4.

9. Paul Tiyambe Zeleza, "Rewriting the African Diaspora: Beyond the Black Atlantic," *African Affairs* 104 (2005): 63–64.

Bibliography

ARCHIVES

Arquivo Publico da Bahia, Bahia, Brazil

British Newspaper Library, Colindale, England

Inventory of the Historical Archives, Pontificia Universitas Urbania, Rome, Italy

National Archives of London, Richmond, England

National Archives of Nigeria, Ibadan, Nigeria

Public Records and Administration Division; Accra, Cape Coast, and Sekondi, Ghana

The University of Ghana-Balme Library, Accra, Ghana

PUBLICATIONS

Abaka, Edmund. *House of Slaves and "Door of No Return": Gold Coast/Ghana Slave Forts, Castles & Dungeons and the Atlantic Slave Trade*. Trenton, NJ: Africa World Press, 2012.

Addo-Fening, Robert. "Akyem Abuakwa, c. 1874–1943: A Study of the Impact of Missionary Activities and Colonial Rule on a Traditional State." PhD diss., University of Ghana, Legon, 1980.

Adejumo, Christopher. "Migration and Slavery as Paradigms in the Aesthetic Transformation of Yoruba Art in the Americas." In *Migrations and Creative Expressions in Africa and the African Diaspora*, ed. Toyin Falola, Niyi Afolabi, and Adéronké Adésolá Adésànyá, 66–81. Durham,

NC: Carolina Academic Press, 2008.

Afolabi, Niyi. *Afro-Brazilians: Cultural Production in a Racial Democracy*. Rochester, NY: University of Rochester Press, 2009.

———, ed. *Marvels of the African World: African Cultural Patrimony, New World Connections and Identities*. Trenton, NJ: African World Press, 2003.

Agbodeka, Francis. *African Politics and British Policy in the Gold Coast, 1868-1900: A Study in the Forms and Force of Protest*. Evanston, IL: Northwestern University Press, 1971.

Ahmed-Rufai, Misbahudeen. "The Muslim Association Party: A Test of Religious Politics in Ghana." *Transactions of the Historical Society of Ghana*, n.s. 6 (2002): 99-114.

Akwa, Eric Nii Annang. "Chieftancy among the Ga's: The Paramountcy of the Ga Mantse." BA diss., University of Ghana, Legon, 1980.

Akyeampong, Emmanuel K. *Between the Sea and the Lagoon: An Eco-Social History of the Anlo of Southeastern Ghana, c. 1850 to Recent Times*. Athens: Ohio University Press, 2001.

———. *Drink, Power and Cultural Change: A Social History of Alcohol in Ghana, c. 1800 to Recent Times*. Portsmouth, NH: Heinemann, 1996.

———. "History, Memory, Slave-Trade and Slavery in Anlo (Ghana)." *Slavery & Abolition* 22, no. 3 (2001): 1-24.

Allman, Jean, ed. *Fashioning Africa: Power and the Politics of Dress*. Bloomington: Indiana University Press, 2004.

Amos, Alcione M., and Ebenezer Ayesu. "'I Am Brazilian': History of the Tabon, Afro-Brazilian in Accra." *Transactions of the Historical Society of Ghana*, n.s. 6 (2002): 35-58.

———. "Sou Brasileiro, História dos Tabom Afro-Brasileiros em Acra, Gana." *Afro-Ásia* 33 (2005): 35-65.

Anderson, Richard, Alex Borucki, Daniel Domingues da Silva, David Eltis, Paul Lachance, Philip Misevich, and Olatunji Ojo. "Using African Names to Identify the Origins of Captives in the Transatlantic Slave Trade: Crowd-Sourcing and the Registers of Liberated Africans, 1808-1862." *History in Africa* 40 (2013): 165-91.

Andrews, George Reid. *Blacks and Whites in São Paolo, 1888-1988*. Madison: University of Wisconsin Press, 1991.

Apter, David E. *The Gold Coast in Transition*. Princeton, NJ: Princeton University Press, 1955.

Araujo, Ana Lucia. *Crossing Memories: Slavery and African Diaspora*. Trenton, NJ: Africa World Press, 2011.

———. *Shadows of the Slave Past: Memory, Heritage, and Slavery*. New York: Routledge, 2014.

Aryeh, N. A. Josiah. *An Outline of Islamic Customary Law in Ghana*. Accra: Kuno Publishers, 2005.

Asante, S. K. B. *Property Law and Social Goals in Ghana, 1844-1966*. Accra: Ghana Universities Press, 1975.

Assensoh, A. B. *Kwame Nkrumah of Africa: His Formative Years and the Beginning of His Political Career, 1935-1948*. London: Stockwell, 1989.

Austen, Ralph A., and Woodruff D. Smith. "Images of Africa and British Slave-Trade Abolition: The Transition to an Imperialist Ideology, 1787-1807." *African Historical Studies* 2, no. 1 (1969): 69-83.

Austin, Gareth. "Commercial Agriculture and the Ending of Slave-Trading and Slavery in West

Africa, 1780s-1920s." In *Commercial Agriculture, the Slave Trade and Slavery in Atlantic Africa*, ed. Robin Law, Suzanne Schwarz, and Silke Strickrodt, 243-53. Woodbridge: James Curry, 2013.

———. "Human Pawning in Asante, 1820-1950: Markets and Coercion, Gender and Cocoa." In *Pawnship, Slavery, and Colonialism in Africa*, ed. Paul E. Lovejoy and Toyin Falola, 187-224. Trenton, NJ: Africa World Press, 2003.

———. *Labour, Land and Capital in Ghana: From Slavery to Free Labour in Asante, 1807-1956*. Rochester, NY: University of Rochester Press, 2004.

Ayittey, George B. N. *Indigenous African Institutions*. New York: Transnational Publishers, 1991.

Bailyn, Bernard. *Atlantic History: Concept and Contours*. Cambridge, MA: Harvard University Press, 2005.

Barnes, Kenneth C. *Journey of Hope: The Back-to-Africa Movement in Arkansas in the Late 1800s*. Chapel Hill: University of North Carolina Press, 2004.

Bellagamba, Alice, Sandra E. Greene, and Martin A. Klein, eds. *African Voices on Slavery and the Slave Trade: The Sources*. Vol. 1. Cambridge: Cambridge University Press, 2013.

Benson, Susan. "Connecting with the Past, Building the Future: African Americans and Chieftaincy in Southern Ghana." *Ghana Studies* 6 (2003): 109-33.

Berlin, Ira. *Many Thousands Gone: The First Two Centuries of Slavery in North America*. Cambridge, MA: Harvard University Press, 1998.

———. *Slaves without Masters: The Free Negro in the Antebellum South*. New York: Pantheon, 1974.

Berry, Sara S. *Chiefs Know Their Boundaries: Essays on Property, Power, and the Past in Asante, 1896-1996*. Portsmouth, NH: Heinemann, 2000.

———. "Privatization and the Politics of Belonging in West Africa." In *Land and the Politics of Belonging in West Africa*, ed. Richard Kuba and Carola Lentz, 241-63. Leiden: Brill, 2006.

Biney, Ama. *The Political and Social Thoughts of Kwame Nkrumah*. New York: Palgrave Macmillan, 2011.

Birmingham, David. *Portugal and Africa*. Athens: Ohio University Press, 1999.

Black, Jeremy, ed. *The Atlantic Slave Trade*. Vol. 4, *Nineteenth Century*. Aldershot: Ashgate, 2006.

Blouin, Francis X., Jr., and William G. Rosenberg. *Processing the Past: Contesting Authority in History and the Archives*. Oxford: Oxford University Press, 2011.

Blyden, Nemata Amelia. *West Indians in West Africa, 1808-1880: The African Diaspora in Reverse*. Rochester, NY: University of Rochester Press, 2000.

Boadi-Siaw, S. Y. "Brazilian Returnees of West Africa." In *Global Dimensions of the African Diaspora*, ed. Joseph E. Harris, 280-312. Washington, DC: Howard University Press, 1982.

———. "The Afro-Brazilian Returnees in Ghana." In *Back to Africa*, vol. 1, *Afro-Brazilian Returnees and Their Communities*, ed. Kwesi Kwaa Prah, 145-58. Cape Town: Center for Advanced Studies of African Society, 2009.

Boahen, Albert Adu. *Yaa Asantewaa and the Asante-British War of 1900-1901*. Accra: Sub-Saharan Publishers, 2003.

Bob-Milliar, George M. "Chieftaincy, Diaspora, and Development: The Institution of *Nkɔsuohene* in Ghana." *African Affairs* 108 (2009): 541-58.

Bob-Milliar, George M., and Gloria K. Bob-Milliar. "Mobilizing the African Diaspora for

Development: The Politics of Dual Citizenship in Ghana." In *Pan-Africanism and the Politics of African Citizenship and Identity*, ed. Toyin Falola and Kwame Essien, 119-36. New York: Routledge; London: Taylor & Francis, 2013.

Bowen, Merle L. "The Struggle for Black Land Rights in Brazil: An Insider's View on *Quilombos* and the *Quilombo* Land Movement." *African and Black Diaspora* 3, no. 2 (2010): 147-68.

Boyd, Antonio Oliz. *The Latin American Identity and the African Diaspora: Ethnogenesis in Context*. Amherst, NY: Cambria Press, 2010.

Brana-Shute, Rosemary, and Randy J. Sparks, eds. *Paths to Freedom: Manumission in the Atlantic World*. Columbia: University of South Carolina Press, 2009.

Braziel, Jana Evans, and Anita Mannur, eds. *Theorizing Diaspora: A Reader*. Malden, MA: Blackwell, 2003.

Brubaker, Rogers, and Frederick Cooper. "Beyond 'Identity.'" *Theory and Society* 29 (2000): 1-47.

Bruner, Edward M. "Tourism in Ghana: The Representation of Slavery and the Return of the Black Diaspora." *American Anthropologist* 98, no. 2 (1996): 290-304.

Butler, Kim D. "Clio and the Griot: The African Diaspora in the Discipline of History." In *The African Diaspora and the Disciplines*, ed. Tejumola Olaniyan and James H. Sweet, 21-46. Bloomington: Indiana University Press, 2010.

———. "Defining Diaspora, Refining a Discourse." *Diaspora* 10, no. 2 (2001): 189-219.

———. *Freedom Given, Freedom Won: Afro-Brazilians in Post-Abolition Sao Paolo and Salvador*. New Brunswick, NJ: Rutgers University Press, 1998.

Byfield, Judith, Carolyn A. Brown, Timothy Parsons, and Ahmad Alawad Sikainga, eds. *Africa and World War II*. Cambridge: Cambridge University Press, 2015.

Campbell, Clifford C. "Full Circle: The Caribbean Presence in the Making of Ghana, 1843-1966." PhD diss., University of Ghana, Legon, 2012.

Campbell, Gwyn, ed. *The Structure of Slavery in Indian Ocean Africa and Asia*. Portland, OR: Frank Cass, 2004.

Campbell, Gwyn, Suzanne Miers, and Joseph C. Miller, eds. *Women and Slavery*. Vol. 1, *Africa, the Indian Ocean World, and the Medieval North Atlantic*. Athens: Ohio University Press, 2007.

Campbell, James T. *Middle Passages: African American Journeys to Africa, 1787-2005*. New York: Penguin, 2007.

Candido, Mariana P. *An African Slaving Port and the Atlantic World: Benguela and Its Hinterland*. Cambridge: Cambridge University Press, 2013.

Cañizares-Esguerra, Jorge, and Eric R. Seeman, eds. *The Atlantic in Global History, 1500-2000*. Upper Saddle River, NJ: Prentice Hall, 2007.

Carney, Judith A. *Black Rice: The African Origins of Rice Cultivation in the Americas*. Cambridge, MA: Harvard University Press, 2001.

Carney, Judith A., and Richard Nicholas Rosomoff. *In the Shadow of Slavery: Africa's Botanical Legacy in the Atlantic World*. Berkeley: University of California Press, 2009.

Carstensen, Edward. *Closing the Books: Governor Edward on Danish Guinea, 1842-50*. Translated by Tove Storsveen. Legon-Accra: Sub-Saharan Publishers, 2010.

———. *Governor Carstensen's Diary, 1842-1850*. Legon: University of Ghana, 1965.

Castillo, Lisa E. "Between Memory, Myths and History: Trans-Atlantic Voyages of the Casa Branca

Temple." In *Paths of the Atlantic Slave Trade: Interactions, Identities, and Images*, ed. Ana Lucia Araujo, 205-10. Amherst, NY: Cambria Press, 2011.

———. "Mapping the Nineteenth-Century Brazilian Returnee Movement: Demographics, Life Stories and the Question of Slavery," *Atlantic Studies* 13, no. 1 (2016): 25-52.

Castillo, Lisa E., and Luis Nicolau Parés. "Marcelina da Silva: A Nineteenth-Century *Candomblé* Priestess in Bahia." *Slavery & Abolition* 31, no. 1 (2010): 1-27.

Childs, Matt D. *The 1812 Aponte Rebellion in Cuba and the Struggle against Atlantic Slavery*. Chapel Hill: University of North Carolina Press, 2006.

Claridge, W. Walton. *A History of the Gold Coast and Ashanti from the Earliest Times to the Commencement of the Twentieth Century*. Vol. 2. New York: Barnes & Noble, 1964.

Clegg, Claude A., III. *The Price of Liberty: African Americans and the Making of Liberia*. Chapel Hill: University of North Carolina Press, 2004.

Coates, Ta-Nehisi Paul. "Ghana's New Money." *Time*, August 21, 2006, 2.

Cohen, Robin. *Global Diasporas: An Introduction*. London: UCL Press, 1997.

Cole, Gibril R. *The Krio of West Africa: Islam, Culture, Creolization and Colonialism in the Nineteenth Century*. Athens: Ohio University Press, 2013.

Coleman, Eric. "Social History of Accra, 1900-1935: With Special Reference to the Role of the Educated Elite." BA diss., University of Ghana, Legon, 1980.

Coles, Tim, and Dallen J. Timothy. "'My Field Is the World': Conceptualizing Diasporas, Travel and Tourism." In *Tourism, Diasporas and Space*, ed. Tim Coles and Dallen J. Timothy, 1-29. New York: Routledge, 2004.

———, eds. *Tourism, Diasporas and Space*. New York: Routledge, 2004.

Conrad, Robert. "The Contraband Slave Trade to Brazil, 1831-1845." In *The Atlantic Slave Trade*, vol. 4, *Nineteenth Century*, ed. Jeremy Black, 339-60. Aldershot: Ashgate, 2006.

Consorte, Josildeth Gomes. "The Black Question in Brazil: An Inside Issue Denied." In *Routes of Passage: Rethinking the African Diaspora*, ed. Ruth Simms Hamilton, 1, pt. 2:1-12. East Lansing: Michigan State University Press, 2007.

Cook, Terry, ed. *Controlling the Past: Documenting Society and Institutions; Essays in Honor of Helen Willa Samuels*. Chicago: Society of American Activists, 2011.

Cooper, Frederick. *From Slaves to Squatters: Plantation Labor and Agriculture in Zanzibar and Coastal Kenya, 1890-1925*. New Haven, CT: Yale University Press, 1980.

Cooper, Frederick, Thomas Cleveland Holt, and Rebecca Jarvis Scott. *Beyond Slavery: Explorations of Race, Labor, and Citizenship in Postemancipation Societies*. Chapel Hill: University of North Carolina Press, 2000.

Coquery-Vidrovitch, Catherine. "Women, Marriage, and Slavery in Sub-Saharan Africa in the Nineteenth Century." In *Women and Slavery*, vol. 1, *Africa, the Indian Ocean World, and the Medieval North Atlantic*, ed. Gwyn Campbell, Suzanne Miers, and Joseph C. Miller, 43-61. Athens: Ohio University Press, 2007.

Coupland, Sir Reginald. *The British Anti-Slavery Movement*. 2nd ed. London: Frank Cass, 1964.

Crooks, J. J. *Records Relating to the Gold Coast Settlements from 1750 to 1874*. London: Frank Cass, 1973.

Cubitt, Geoffrey. *History and Memory*. Manchester, UK: Manchester University Press, 2007.

Curtin, Phillip D. *The Atlantic Slave Trade: A Census.* Madison: University of Wisconsin Press, 1969.

Curto, José C., and Paul E. Lovejoy, eds. *Enslaving Connections: Changing Cultures of Africa and Brazil during the Era of Slavery.* New York: Humanity Books, 2004.

Dakubu, M. E. Kropp. *Korle Meets the Sea: A Sociallinguistic History of Accra.* New York: Oxford University Press, 1997.

———. "Linguistic Pre-History and Historical Reconstruction: The Gã-Adangme Migrations." *Transactions of the Historical Society of Ghana* 13, no. 1 (June 1972): 87–111.

da Fonseca, Carlos. *Letters from Brazil.* Brazil: Ministère des Relations Extérieures, 2010.

Dantzing, Albert van. *Forts and Castles in Ghana.* Accra: Sedco Publishing, 1980.

Davies, Carole Boyce, ed. *Encyclopedia of the African Diaspora: Origins, Experiences, and Culture.* Vol. 1. Santa Barbara: ABC-CLIO, 2008.

DeCorse, Christopher R. *An Archaeology of Elmina: Africans and Europeans on the Gold Coast, 1400–1900.* Washington, DC: Smithsonian Institution Press, 2001.

Degler, Carl N. *Neither Black nor White: Slavery and Race Relations in Brazil and the United States.* New York: Macmillan, 1971.

Depelchin, Jacques. *Silences in African History: Between the Syndromes of Discovery and Abolition.* Dar es Salaam: Mkuki na Nyota Publishers, 2005.

Der, Benedict G. *Slave Trade in Northern Ghana.* Accra: Ghana University Press, 1999.

Derrida, Jacques. *Archive Fever: A Freudian Impression.* Translated by Eric Prenowitz. Chicago: University of Chicago Press, 1996.

Diedrich, Maria, Henry Louis Gates Jr., and Carl Pederson, eds. *Black Imagination and the Middle Passage.* New York: Oxford University Press, 1999.

Diouf, Sylviane A., ed. *Fighting the Slave Trade: West African Strategies.* Athens: Ohio University Press, 2003.

———. *Servants of Allah: African Muslims Enslaved in the Americas.* New York: New York University Press, 1998.

Drescher, Seymour, and Stanley L. Engerman, eds. *A Historical Guide to World Slavery.* New York: Oxford University Press, 1998.

Du Bois, W. E. B. *Souls of Black Folk.* New York: Penguin, 1996.

———. *The Souls of Black Folk.* Edited by David W. Blight and Robert Gooding-Williams. Boston: Bedford/St. Martin's, 1997.

———. *The Souls of Black Folk: Authoritative Text, Contexts, Criticism.* Edited by Henry Louis Gates Jr. and Terri H. Oliver. Cambridge: Harvard University Press, 1999.

Dubois, Laurent. *A Colony of Citizens: Revolution and Slave Emancipation in the French Caribbean, 1787–1804.* Chapel Hill: University of North Carolina Press, 2004.

Dunbar, Ernest, ed. *The Black Expatriates: A Study of American Negroes in Exile.* New York: Dutton, 1968.

Dzidzienyo, Anani. "The Challenges of Africa and Brazil: Looking Ahead by Reconsidering the Record." In *Back to Africa*, vol. 1, *Afro-Brazilian Returnees and Their Communities*, ed. Kwesi Kwaa Prah, 13–25. Cape Town: Center for Advanced Studies of African Society, 2009.

———. "Coming to Terms with the African Connection in Latino Studies." *Latino Studies* 1 (2003): 160–67.

Dzidzienyo, Anani, and Suzanne Oboler, eds. *Neither Enemies nor Friends: Latinos, Blacks, Afro-Latinos*. New York: Palgrave Macmillan, 2005.

Ebron, Paulla A. *Performing Africa*. Princeton, NJ: Princeton University Press, 2002.

Edwards, Brent Hayes. *The Practice of Diaspora: Literature, Translation, and the Rise of Black Internationalism*. Cambridge, MA: Harvard University Press, 2003.

Eltis, David. "The British Contribution to the Nineteenth-Century Transatlantic Slave Trade." In *The Atlantic Slave Trade*, vol. 4, *Nineteenth Century*, ed. Jeremy Black, 163–79. Aldershot: Ashgate, 2006.

———. "The Volume and Structure of the Transatlantic Slave Trade: A Reassessment." *William and Mary Quarterly* 58 (2001): 17–46.

Eltis, David, Stephen D. Behrendt, David Richardson, and Herbert S. Klein, eds. *The Trans-Atlantic Slave Trade: A Database on CD-ROM*. Cambridge: Cambridge University Press, 2000.

Essien, Kwame. "A Abertura da Casa Brasil: A History of the *Tabom* People, Part 1." In *Back to Africa*, vol. 1, *Afro-Brazilian Returnees and Their Communities*, ed. Kwesi Kwaa Prah, 173–92. Cape Town: Center for Advanced Studies of African Society, 2009.

———. "'Afie ni Afie' (Home Is Home): Revisiting Reverse Trans-Atlantic Journeys to Ghana and the Paradox of Return." *Ìrìnkèrindò: A Journal of African Migration* 7 (June 2014): 47–75.

———. "African Americans in Ghana: Successes and Challenges, 1985 through 2005." MA thesis, University of Illinois-Urbana-Champaign, 2006.

———. "African Americans in Ghana and Their Contributions to 'Nation Building' since 1985." In *The United States and West Africa: Interactions and Relations*, ed. Alusine Jalloh and Toyin Falola, 141–73. Rochester, NY: University of Rochester Press, 2008.

———. "The African Diaspora in Reverse: The *Tabom* People in Ghana, 1820s–2009." PhD diss., University of Texas, Austin, 2010.

———. "The History of African American Business in Ghana, 1990–2007: The Case of Jerry John Rawlings." PhD portfolio, University of Texas, Austin, 2008.

———. "(In)Visible Diasporan Returnee Communities: Silences and the Challenges in Studying Trans-Atlantic History in Ghana." *Ghana Studies* 17 (2014): 63–99.

———. "'Performance' in Trans-Atlantic Communities in Africa: The Case of Brazilian-Africans and American-Africans in Ghana." In *Pan-Africanism and the Politics of African Citizenship and Identity*, ed. Toyin Falola and Kwame Essien, 101–18. New York: Routledge; London: Taylor & Francis, 2013.

Fabre, Geneviève, and Klause Benesch, eds. *African Diasporas in the New and Old Worlds: Consciousness and Imagination*. Amsterdam: Rodopi, 2004.

Fage, J. D. "Slavery and the Slave Trade in the Context of West African History." *Journal of African History* 10, no. 3 (1969): 393–404.

Falola, Toyin. *The African Diaspora: Slavery, Modernity, and Globalization*. Rochester, NY: University of Rochester Press, 2013.

Falola, Toyin, Niyi Afolabi, and Adérónké Adésolá Adésànyá, eds. *Migrations and Creative Expressions in Africa and the African Diaspora*. Durham, NC: Carolina Academic Press, 2008.

Falola, Toyin, and Matt D. Childs, eds. *The Changing Worlds of Atlantic Africa: Essays in Honor of Robin Law*. Durham, NC: Carolina Academic Press, 2009.

———, eds. *The Yoruba Diaspora in the Atlantic World*. Bloomington: Indiana University Press, 2004.

Falola, Toyin, and Christian Jennings, eds. *Africanizing Knowledge: African Studies across the Disciplines*. New Brunswick, NJ: Transaction, 2002.

Falola, Toyin, and Amanda Warnock, eds. *Encyclopedia of the Middle Passage*. Westport, CT: Greenwood Press, 2007.

Fernandes, Florestan. "The Negro Problem in a Class Society." In *Blackness in Latin America and the Caribbean: Social Dynamics and Cultural Transformations*, vol. 2, *Eastern South America and the Caribbean*, ed. Norman E. Whitten Jr. and Arlene Torres, 99–145. Bloomington: Indiana University Press, 1998.

Ferreira, Roquinaldo Amaral. *Cross-Cultural Exchange in the Atlantic World: Angola and Brazil during the Era of the Slave Trade*. Cambridge: Cambridge University Press, 2012.

Field, Margaret J. *Religion and Medicine of the Gã People*. London: Oxford University Press, 1961.

———. *Social Organization of the Gã People*. London: Crown Agents for the Colonies, 1940.

Fields-Black, Edda L. *Deep Roots: Rice Farmers in West Africa and the African Diaspora*. Bloomington: Indiana University Press, 2008.

Firmin-Sellers, Kathryn. *The Transformation of Property Rights in the Gold Coast: An Empirical Analysis Applying Rational Choice Theory*. Cambridge: Cambridge University Press, 1996.

Florentino, Manolo Garcia, and José Roberto Góes. "Slavery, Marriage and Kinship in Rural Rio de Janeiro, 1790–1830." In *Identity in the Shadow of Slavery*, ed. Paul E. Lovejoy, 137–62. London: Continuum, 2000.

Frank, Zephyr L. *Dutra's World: Wealth and Family in Nineteenth-Century Rio de Janeiro*. Albuquerque: University of New Mexico Press, 2004.

Freyre, Gilberto. *The Masters and the Slaves: A Study in Development of Brazilian Civilization*. New York: Alfred A. Knopf, 1946.

Fyfe, Christopher. *A History of Sierra Leone*. Oxford: Oxford University Press, 1964.

Gaines, Kevin K. *American Africans in Ghana: Black Expatriates and the Civil Rights Era*. Chapel Hill: University of North Carolina Press, 2006.

———. *Uplifting the Race: Black Leadership, Politics, and Culture in the Twentieth Century*. Chapel Hill: University of North Carolina Press, 1996.

Games, Alison. "Atlantic History: Definitions, Challenges, and Opportunities," *American Historical Review* 111, no. 3 (2006): 741–57.

Games, Alison, and Adam Rothman, eds., *Major Problems in Atlantic History: Documents and Essays*. Boston: Cengage Learning, 2008.

Garvey, Amy Jacques, ed. *The Philosophy and Opinions of Marcus Garvey: Or Africa for the Africans*. Fitchburg, MA: Majority Press, 1986.

Gaspar, David Barry, and Darlene Clark Hine, eds. *More than Chattel: Black Women and Slavery in the Americas*. Bloomington: Indiana University Press, 1996.

Gates, Henry Louis, Jr. *In Search of Our Roots: How 19 Extraordinary African Americans Reclaimed their Past*. New York: Crown Publishers, 2009.

Getz, Trevor R. *Slavery and Reform in West Africa: Toward Emancipation in Nineteenth-Century Senegal and the Gold Coast*. Athens: Ohio University Press, 2004.

Getz, Trevor R., and Liz Clarke. *Abina and the Important Men: A Graphic History*. New York: Oxford University Press, 2012.

Gilroy, Paul. *The Black Atlantic: Modernity and Double Consciousness.* Cambridge, MA: Harvard University Press, 1993.

Gocking, Roger S. *Facing Two Ways: Ghana Coastal Communities under Colonial Rule* Lanham, MD: University Press of America, 1999.

———. *The History of Ghana.* Westport, CT: Greenwood Press, 2005.

Gomez, Michael A. *Black Crescent: The Experience of Legacy of African Muslims in the Americas.* Cambridge: Cambridge University Press, 2005.

———, ed. *Diasporic Africa: A Reader.* New York: New York University Press, 2006.

———. *Exchanging Our Country Marks: The Transforming of African Identities in the Colonial and Antebellum South.* Chapel Hill: University of North Carolina Press, 1998.

———. *Reversing Sail: A History of the African Diaspora.* Cambridge: Cambridge University Press, 2005.

Gordon, Edmund T., and Mark Anderson, "The African Diaspora: Toward an Ethnography of Diasporic Identification." *Journal of American Folklore* 112, no. 445 (1999): 282-96.

Graden, Dale Torston. *From Slavery to Freedom in Brazil: Bahia, 1835-1900.* Albuquerque: University of New Mexico Press, 2006.

Green, Jeffrey P. "Caribbean Influences in the Gold Coast Administration in the 1900s." *Ghana Studies Bulletin* 2 (December 1984): 11-16.

Greene, Jack P., and Philip D. Morgan, eds., *Atlantic History: A Critical Appraisal.* New York: Oxford University Press, 2009.

Greene, Sandra E. *Sacred Sites and the Colonial Encounter: A History of Meaning and Memory in Ghana.* Bloomington: Indiana University Press, 2002.

———. *West African Narratives of Slavery: Texts from Late Nineteenth- and Early Twentieth-Century Ghana.* Bloomington: Indiana University Press, 2011.

———. "Whispers and Silences: Explorations in African History." *Africa Today* 50, no. 2 (2003): 41-53.

Grier, Beverly. "Pawns, Porters, and Petty Traders: Women in the Transition to Cash-Crop Agriculture in Colonial Ghana." In *Pawnship, Slavery, and Colonialism in Africa,* ed. Paul E. Lovejoy and Toyin Falola, 306-8. Trenton, NJ: Africa World Press, 2003.

Guran, Milton. "The Returnees of Benin, Togo, Nigeria and Ghana: Agudas and Tabom." In *Back to Africa,* vol. 1, *Afro-Brazilian Returnees and Their Communities,* ed. Kwesi Kwaa Prah, 108-20. Cape Town: Center for Advanced Studies of African Society, 2009.

Haenger, Peter, *Slaves and Slave Holders on the Gold Coast: Towards an Understanding of Social Bondage in West Africa.* Edited by J. J. Shaffer and Paul E. Lovejoy. Translated by Christina Handford. Basel: Schlettwein, 2000.

Hair, P. E. H. *The Founding of the Castelo de São Jorge da Mina: An Analysis of Sources.* Madison: University of Wisconsin-Madison, African Studies Program, 1994.

Hale, Thomas A. *Griots and Griottes: Masters of Words and Music.* Bloomington: Indiana University Press, 1998.

Hall, Gwendolyn Midlo. *Slavery and African Ethnicities in the Americas: Restoring the Links.* Chapel Hill: University of North Carolina Press, 2005.

Hamilton, Ruth Simms, ed. *Routes of Passage: Rethinking the African Diaspora.* Vol. 1, part 1. East

Lansing: Michigan State University Press, 2007.

Hanchard, Michael George. *Orpheus and Power: The "Movimento Negro" of Rio de Janeiro and São Paulo, Brazil, 1945-1988*. Princeton, NJ: Princeton University Press, 1998.

———. *Racial Politics in Contemporary Brazil*. Durham, NC: Duke University Press, 1999.

Hansen, Thorkild. *Coast of Slaves*. Translated by Kari Dako; illustrations by Birte Lund. Legon-Accra: Sub-Saharan Publishers, 2002.

———. *Ships of Slaves*. Translated by Kari Dako; illustrations by Birte Lund. Legon-Accra: Sub-Saharan Publishers, 2003.

Harris, Joseph E. *Africans and Their History*. New York: Penguin, 1987.

———, ed. *Global Dimensions of the African Diaspora*. Washington, DC: Howard University Press, 1982.

Hartman, Saidiya V. *Lose Your Mother: A Journey along the Atlantic Slave Route*. New York: Farrar, Straus and Giroux, 2007.

Hasty, Jennifer. "Rites of Passage, Routes of Redemption: Emancipation Tourism and Wealth of Culture." *Africa Today* 49, no. 3 (2002): 47-76.

Hawthorne, Walter. *From Africa to Brazil: Culture, Identity, and an Atlantic Slave Trade, 1600-1830*. Cambridge: Cambridge University Press, 2010.

Hayford, J. E. Casely. *The Truth about the West African Land Question*. London: Negro University Press, 1913.

Henderson-Quartey, D. K. *The Ga of Ghana: History & Culture of a West African People*. Published by author, 2002.

Herbstein, Manu. *Ama: A Story of the Atlantic Slave Trade*. Accra: Techmate Publishers Ghana Ltd., 2010.

Hernaes, Per. "A Danish Experiment in Commercial Agriculture on the Gold Coast, 1788-1793." In *Commercial Agriculture, the Slave Trade and Slavery in Atlantic Africa*, ed. Robin Law, Suzanne Schwarz, and Silke Strickrodt, 116-37. Woodbridge: James Curry, 2013.

Herskovits, Melville J. *The Myth of the Negro Past*. Boston: Beacon Press, 1990.

Higgs, Catherine. *Chocolate Islands: Cocoa, Slavery and Colonial Africa*. Athens: Ohio University Press, 2012.

Hill, Polly. *The Migrant Cocoa-Farmers of Southern Ghana: A Study in Rural Capitalism*. Cambridge: Cambridge University Press, 1963.

Hilton, Boyd. "1807 and All That: Why Britain Outlawed Her Slave Trade." In *Abolitionism and Imperialism in Britain, Africa and the Atlantic*, ed. Derek R. Peterson, 63-83. Athens: Ohio University Press, 2010.

Hiraldo, Samiri Hernández. *Black Puerto Rican Identity and Religious Experience*. Gainesville: University Press of Florida, 2006.

———. "'If God Were Black and from Loiza': Managing Identities in a Puerto Rican Seaside Town." Translated by Mariana Ortega-Brena. *Latin American Perspectives* 33, no. 1 (January 2006): 66-82.

Holsey, Bayo. *Routes of Remembrance: Refashioning the Slave Trade in Ghana*. Chicago: University of Chicago Press, 2008.

Hochschild, Adam. *King Leopold's Ghost: A Story of Greed, Terror, and Heroism in Colonial Africa*.

Boston: Houghton Mifflin, 1998.

Hunton, Africanus B. *Letters on the Political Conditions of the Gold Coast.* Translated by E. A. Ayandele. London: Frank Cass, 1970.

Hutton, Patrick. "Recent Scholarship on Memory and History." *History Teacher* 33, no. 4 (2000): 533–48.

Imahkus, Seestah Njinga. *Ababio: A 21ˢᵗ Century Anthology of African Diaspora Returnees to Ghana, Cape Coast.* Ghana: One Africa Tours and Specialty, 2009.

———. *Returning Home Ain't Easy but It Sure Is a Blessing.* Cape Coast: One Africa Tours and Speciality, 1999.

Inikori, Joseph E., and Stanley L. Engerman, eds. *The Atlantic Slave Trade: Effects on Economies, Societies and Peoples in Africa, the Americas, and Europe.* Durham, NC: Duke University Press, 1992.

Jackson, Fatimah L. C., and Latifa F. J. Borgelin. "How Genetics Can Provide Detail to the Transatlantic African Diaspora." In *The African Diaspora and the Disciplines*, ed. Tejumola Olaniyan and James H. Sweet, 75–100. Bloomington: Indiana University Press, 2010.

Jalloh, Alusine, and Toyin Falola, eds. *The United States and West Africa: Interactions and Relations.* Rochester, NY: Rochester University Press, 2008.

Jayasuriya, Shihan de Silva, and Richard Pankhurst. *The African Diaspora in the Indian Ocean.* Trenton, NJ: African World Press, 2003.

Johnson, Robert, Jr. *Why Blacks Left America for Africa: Interviews with Black Repatriates, 1971–1999.* Westport, CT: Praeger, 1999.

Joyner, Charles. *Down by the Riverside: A South Carolina Slave Community.* Urbana: University of Illinois Press, 1984.

Juul, Kristine, and Christian Lund, eds., *Negotiating Property in Africa.* Portsmouth, NH: Heinemann, 2002.

Karasch, Mary C. *Slave Life in Rio de Janeiro, 1808–1850.* Princeton, NJ: Princeton University Press, 1987.

Kay, G. B., ed. *The Political Economy of Colonialism in Ghana: A Collection of Documents and Statistics, 1900–1960.* Cambridge: Cambridge University Press, 1972.

Kea, Ray A. *Settlements, Trade, and Polities in the Seventeenth-Century Gold Coast.* Baltimore, MD: Johns Hopkins University Press, 1982.

Kessel, I. van. *Merchants, Missionaries and Migrants: 300 Years of Dutch-Ghanaian Relations.* Amsterdam: KIT Publishers, 2002.

Killingray, David. *Fighting for Britain: African Soldiers in the Second World War.* Woodbridge: James Curry, 2010.

Kimble, David. *A Political History of Ghana: The Rise of Gold Coast Nationalism, 1850–1928.* Oxford: Clarendon Press, 1963.

Klein, Herbert S. *African Slavery in Latin America and the Caribbean.* London: Oxford University Press, 1986.

Klein, Herbert S., and Stanley E. Engerman. "Shipping Patterns and Mortality in the African Slave Trade to Rio de Janeiro, 1825–1830." In *The Atlantic Slave Trade*, vol. 4, *Nineteenth Century*, ed. Jeremy Black, 181–98. Aldershot: Ashgate, 2006.

Konadu, Kwasi. *The Akan Diaspora in the Americas*. New York: Oxford University Press, 2010.

———. *Transatlantic Africa, 1440-1888*. New York: Oxford University Press, 2014.

Korang, Kwaku Larbi. *Writing Ghana, Imagining Africa: Nation and African Modernity*. Rochester, NY: University of Rochester Press, 2003.

Koser, Khalid, ed. *New African Diasporas*. London: Routledge, 2003.

Kraay, Hendrick, ed. *Afro-Brazilian Culture and Politics: Bahia, 1790s to 1990s*. Armonk, NY: R. M. E. Sharpe, 1998.

Kuba, Richard, and Carola Lentz, eds. *Land and the Politics of Belonging in West Africa*. Leiden: Brill, 2006.

Kuevi, Dinah. "The History of Otublohum." BA diss., University of Ghana, Legon, 1979.

Lacy, Leslie Alexander. *The Rise and Fall of a Proper Negro: An Autobiography*. New York: Macmillan, 1970.

Lambek, Michael. *The Weight of the Past: Living with History in Mahajanga, Madagascar*. New York: Palgrave MacMillan, 2002.

Lamptey, Leslie Nii Odartey. "The History of Osu (Kinkawe) from the Colonial Period to Date." BA diss., University of Ghana, Legon, 2006.

Lamptey, T. M. "History of Osu: From the Earliest Times to 1854." BA diss., University of Ghana, Legon, 1972.

Larson, Pier Martin. *History and Memory in the Age of Enslavement: Becoming Merina in Highland Madagascar, 1770-1822*. Portsmouth, NH: Heinemann, 2000.

Law, Robin. "Abolition and Imperialism: International Law and the British Suppression of the Atlantic Slave Trade." In *Abolitionism and Imperialism in Britain, Africa and the Atlantic*, ed. Derek R. Peterson, 150-74. Athens: Ohio University Press, 2010.

———. "Francisco de Souza in West Africa, 1820-1849." In *Enslaving Connections: Changing Cultures of Africa and Brazil during the Era of Slavery*, ed. José C. Curto and Paul E. Lovejoy, 187-212. New York: Humanity Books, 2004.

———. *From Slave Trade to "Legitimate" Commerce: The Commercial Transition in Nineteenth-Century West Africa*. Cambridge: Cambridge University Press, 1995.

———. *Ouidah: The Social History of a West African Slaving "Port," 1727-1892*. Athens: Ohio University Press, 2004.

———. "There's Nothing Grows in the West Indies but Will Grow Here: Dutch and English Projects of Plantation Agriculture on the Gold Coast, 1650s-1750s." In *Commercial Agriculture, the Slave Trade and Slavery in Atlantic Africa*, ed. Robin Law, Suzanne Schwarz, and Silke Strickrodt, 158-79. Woodbridge: James Curry, 2013.

Law, Robin, Suzanne Schwarz, and Silke Strickrodt, eds. *Commercial Agriculture, the Slave Trade and Slavery in Atlantic Africa*. Woodbridge: James Curry, 2013.

Lawler, Nancy Ellen. *Soldiers, Airmen, Spies, and Whisperers: The Gold Coast in World War II*. Athens: Ohio University Press, 2002.

Lawrence, Benjamin N. *Locality, Mobility, and "Nation": Periurban Colonialism in Togo's Eweland, 1900-1960*. Rochester, NY: University of Rochester Press, 2007.

Lindsay, Lisa A. "Brazilian Women in Lagos, 1879-1882." In *Shaping Our Struggles: Nigerian Women in History, Culture and Development*, ed. Obioma Nnaemeka and Chima J. Korieh, 129-40.

Trenton, NJ: Africa World Press, 2011.

———. "'To Return to the Bosom of Their Fatherland': Brazilian Immigrants in Nineteenth-Century Lagos." *Slavery & Abolition* 15, no. 1 (1994): 22-50.

Lokko, Mae-ling Jovenes. *The Brazil House*. Accra: Surf Publications, 2010.

Lovejoy, Paul E., ed. *Identity in the Shadow of Slavery*. London: Continuum, 2000.

———. "Narratives of Trans-Atlantic Slavery in the Life Stories of Two Muslims." In *Africa and Trans-Atlantic Memories: Literary and Aesthetic Manifestations of Diaspora and History*, ed. Naana Opoku-Agyemang, Paul E. Lovejoy, and David V. Trotman, 7-12. Trenton, NJ: Africa World Press, 2008.

———. *Transformations in Slavery: A History of Slavery in Africa*. New York: Cambridge University Press, 2000.

Lovejoy, Paul E., and Jan S. Hogendorn. *Slow Death for Slavery: The Course of Abolition in Northern Nigeria, 1897-1936*. Cambridge: Cambridge University Press, 1993.

Lovejoy, Paul E., and David Richardson. "Anglo-Efik Relations and Protection against Illegal Enslavement at Old Calibar, 1740-1807." In *Fighting the Slave Trade: West African Strategies*, ed. Sylviane A. Diouf, 101-19. Athens: Ohio University Press, 2003.

Lugard, Frederick J. D. *The Diaries of Lord Lugard*. Edited by Margery Perham. 4 vols. Evanston, IL: Northwestern University Press, 1959-63.

———. *Dual Mandate in British Tropical Africa*. London: Frank Cass, 1965.

MacDonald, George. *The Gold Coast, Past and Present: A Short Description of the Country and Its People*. New York: Negro Universities Press, 1969.

Mamdani, Mahmood. *Citizen and Subject: Contemporary Africa and the Legacy of Late Colonialism*. Princeton, NJ: Princeton University Press, 1996.

Mamigonian, Beatriz G., and Karen Racine, eds. *The Human Tradition in the Black Atlantic, 1500-2000*. Lanham, MD: Rowman & Littlefield, 2010.

Mann, Kristin. *Slavery and the Birth of an African City: Lagos, 1760-1900*. Bloomington: Indiana University Press, 2007.

Mann, Kristin, and Edna G. Bay, eds. *Rethinking the African Diaspora: The Making of a Black Atlantic World in the Bight of Benin and Brazil*. Portland, OR: Frank Cass, 2001.

Manning, Patrick. *Slavery, Colonialism and Economic Growth in Dahomey, 1640-1960*. Cambridge: Cambridge University Press, 1982.

Matory, J. Lorand. *Black Atlantic Religion: Tradition, Transnationalism, and Matriarchy in the Afro-Brazilian Candomblé*. Princeton, NJ: Princeton University Press, 2005.

Mattoso, Kátia M. de Queirós. *To Be a Slave in Brazil, 1550-1888*. Translated by Arthur Goldhammer. New Brunswick, NJ: Rutgers University Press, 1996.

McCarthy, Mary. *Social Change and the Growth of British Power in the Gold Coast: The Fante States, 1807-1874*. Lanham, MD: University Press of America, 1983.

McCaskie, T. C. *State and Society in Pre-Colonial Asante*. Cambridge: Cambridge University Press, 1995.

Meek, C. K. *Land Law and Custom in the Colonies*. Oxford: Oxford University Press, 1949.

Mensah, Joseph Nii Abekah. *Traditions and Customs of Gãdangmes of Ghana*. Houston: Strategic Book Publishing, 2013.

Meriwether, James H. *Proudly We Can Be Africans: Black Americans and Africa, 1935-1961*. Chapel Hill: University of North Carolina Press, 2002.

Metcalfe, G. E. *Great Britain and Ghana: Documents of Ghana History, 1807-1957*. London: Thomas Nelson & Sons, 1964.

Miers, Suzanne, and Martin Klein, eds. *Slavery and Colonial Rule in Africa*. London: Frank Cass, 1999.

Miers, Suzanne, and Igor Kopytoff, eds. *Slavery in Africa: Historical and Anthropological Perspectives*. Madison: University of Wisconsin Press, 1977.

Miller, Joseph C. "Retention, Reinvention, and Remembering: Restoring Identities through Enslavement in Africa and under Slavery in Brazil." In *Enslaving Connections: Changing Cultures of Africa and Brazil during the Era of Slavery*, ed. José C. Curto and Paul E. Lovejoy, 81-121. New York: Humanity Books, 2004.

———. *Way of Death: Merchant Capitalism and Angolan Slave Trade, 1730-1830*. Madison: University of Wisconsin Press, 1988.

———. "Women as Slaves and Owners of Slaves: Experiences from Africa, the Indian Ocean and the Early Atlantic." In *Women and Slavery*, vol. 1, *Africa, the Indian Ocean World, and the Medieval North Atlantic*, ed. Gwyn Campbell, Suzanne Miers, and Joseph Miller, 1-40. Athens: Ohio University Press, 2007.

Mintz, Sidney W., and Richard Price. *The Birth of African-American Culture: An Anthropological Perspective*. Boston: Beacon Press, 1992.

Mitchell, Michele. *Righteous Propagation: African Americans and the Politics of Racial Destiny after Reconstruction*. Chapel Hill: University of North Carolina Press, 2004.

Morrow, Curtis J. *Return of the African-American*. Huntington, NY: Kroska Books, 2000.

Moses, Wilson J. *Afrotopia: The Roots of African American Popular History*. Cambridge: Cambridge University Press, 1998.

Murray, Pauli. *The Autobiography of a Black Activist, Feminist, Lawyer, Priest, and Poet*. Knoxville: University of Tennessee Press, 1997.

Nascimento, Abdias do. *Brazil, Mixture or Massacre? Essays in the Genocide of a Black People*. Translated by Elisa Larkin Nascimento. Dover, MA: Majority Press, 1989.

Neale, Caroline. *Writing "Independent" History: African Historiography, 1960-1980*. Westport, CT: Greenwood Press, 1985.

Nikoi, Amon. "Indirect Rule and Government in Gold Coast Colony, 1844-1954: A Study in the History, Ecology and Politics of Administration in a Changing Society." PhD diss., Harvard University, 1956.

Nishida, Mieko. *Slavery and Identity: Ethnicity, Gender, and Race in Salvador, Brazil, 1808-1888*. Bloomington: Indiana University Press, 2003.

Nkrumah, Kwame. *Neo-Colonialism, the Last Stage of Imperialism*. London: Thomas Nelson and Sons, 1965.

Nnaemeka, Obioma, and Chima J. Korieh, eds. *Shaping Our Struggles: Nigerian Women in History, Culture and Development*. Trenton, NJ: Africa World Press, 2011.

Ntewusu, Samuel Aniegye. "Settling in and Holding On: A Socio-Economic History of Northern Traders and Transporters in Accra's Tudu: 1908-2008." PhD diss., University of Leiden, 2011.

Nunoo, S. A. "The History of Ga Wulomo Institution." BA diss., University of Ghana, Legon, 1981.

Nwokeji, G. Ugo. *The Slave Trade and Culture in the Bight of Biafra: An African Society in the Atlantic World*. Cambridge: Cambridge University Press, 2010.

Odamtten, Harry N. K. "Dode Akabi: A Reexamination of the Oral and Textual Narrative of a 'Wicked' Female King," *Journal of Women's History* 27, no. 3 (Fall 2015): 61-85.

Odotei-Quaye, Irene. "Gã and the Neighbors." PhD diss., University of Ghana, 1972.

Ogundiran, Akinwumi, and Toyin Falola, eds. *Archaeology of Atlantic Africa and the African Diaspora*. Bloomington: Indiana University Press, 2007.

Ojo, Olatunji. "Afro-Brazilians in Lagos: Atlantic Commerce, Kinship and Trans-Nationalism." In *Back to Africa*, vol. 1, *Afro-Brazilian Returnees and Their Communities*, ed. Kwasi Kwaa Prah, 232-60. Cape Town: Center for Advanced Studies of African Society, 2009.

Ojo-Ade, Femi. "Afro-Brazilians in Lagos: A Question of Home or Exile?" In *Back to Africa*, vol. 1, *Afro-Brazilian Returnees and their Communities*, ed. Kwesi K. Prah, 210-31. Cape Town: Center for Advanced Studies of African Society, 2009.

———, ed. *Home and Exile: Abdias Nascimento, African Brazilian Thinker and Pan-African Visionary*. Trenton, NJ: Africa World Press, 2014.

Okpewho, Isidore. "Introduction: Can We 'Go Home Again'?" In *The New African Diaspora*, ed. Isidore Okpewho and Nkiru Nzegwu, 3-30. Bloomington: Indiana University Press, 2009.

Okpewho, Isidore, and Nkiru Nzegwu, eds. *The New African Diaspora*. Bloomington: Indiana University Press, 2009.

Olaniyan, Tejumola, and James H. Sweet, eds. *The African Diaspora and the Disciplines*. Bloomington: Indiana University Press, 2010.

Olinto, Antônio. *The Water House*. Translated by Dorothy Heapy. New York: Carroll and Graf Publishers, Inc.,, 1970.

Opare-Akurang, Kwabena. "The Administration of the Abolition Laws, African Responses and Post-Proclamation Slavery in the Gold Coast, 1874-1940." In *Slavery and Colonial Rule in Africa*, ed. Suzanne Miers and Martin Klein, 149-66. London: Frank Cass, 1999.

Opoku, A. A. *Riis, the Builder*. Legon-Accra: Institute of African Studies, University of Ghana, 1978.

Opoku-Agyemang, Naana, Paul E. Lovejoy, and David V. Trotman, eds. *Africa and Trans-Atlantic Memories: Literary and Aesthetic Manifestations of Diaspora and History*. Trenton, NJ: Africa World Press, 2008.

Oriji, John N. "Igboland, Slavery, and the Drums of War and Heroism." In *Fighting the Slave Trade: West African Strategies*, ed. Sylviane A. Diouf, 121-51. Athens: Ohio University Press, 2003.

Osei-Tutu, Brempong, "African American Reactions to the Restoration of Ghana's 'Slave Castles.'" *Public Archaeology* 3 (2004): 195-204.

———. "Ghana's 'Slave Castles,' Tourism, and the Social Memory of the Atlantic Slave Trade." In *Archaeology of Atlantic Africa and the African Diaspora*, ed. Akinwumi Ogundiran and Toyin Falola. Bloomington: Indiana University Press, 2007.

Otero, Solimar. *Afro-Cuban Diasporas in the Atlantic World*. Rochester, NY: University of Rochester Press, 2010.

———. "Orunile: Heaven Is Home, Yoruba and Afrocuban Diasporas across the Atlantic." PhD diss., Louisiana State University, 2009.

Bibliography

Ottley, Roi. *New World A-Coming: Inside Black America*. New York: Houghton Mifflin, 1943.

Palmer, Colin A. "Defining and Studying the Modern African Diaspora." *Journal of Negro History* 85, nos. 1/2 (winter-spring 2000): 27-32.

Parés, Luis Nicolau. *The Formation of Condomblé: Vodun History and Ritual in Brazil*. Chapel Hill: University of North Carolina Press, 2013.

———. "The 'Nagôization' Process in Bahian Candomblé." In *The Yoruba Diaspora in the Atlantic World*, ed. Toyin Falola and Matt D. Childs, 185-208. Bloomington: Indiana University Press, 2004.

Parker, John. *Making the Town: Ga State and Society in Early Colonial Accra*. Portsmouth, NH: Heinemann, 2000.

Patterson, David K. "Health in Urban Ghana: The Case of Accra, 1900-1940." *Social Science and Medicine* 13 (1979): 251-52.

Patterson, Orlando. *Slavery and Social Death: A Comparative Study*. Cambridge, MA: Harvard University Press, 1982.

Patterson, Tiffany Ruby, and Robin D. G. Kelley. "Unfinished Migrations: Reflections on the African Diaspora and the Making of the Modern World." *African Studies Review* 43, no. 1 (2000): 11-45.

Peek, Phillip M., ed. *African Divination Systems: Ways of Knowing*. Bloomington: Indiana University Press, 1991.

Pellow, Deborah. *Landlords and Lodgers: Socio-Spatial Organization in an Accra Community*. Chicago: University of Chicago Press, 2008.

Perbi, Akosua Adoma. *A History of Indigenous Slavery in Ghana from the 15th to the 19th Century*. Accra: Sub-Saharan Publishers, 2004.

Pérez, Gina M. *The Near Northwest Side Story: Migration, Displacement, and Puerto Rican Families*. Berkeley: University of California Press, 2004.

Peterson, Derek R., ed. *Abolitionism and Imperialism in Britain, Africa and the Atlantic*. Athens: Ohio University Press, 2010.

Philips, John Edward, ed. *Writing African History*. Rochester, NY: University of Rochester Press, 2006.

Pobee, John S. *The Anglican Story in Ghana: From Mission Beginnings to Province of Ghana*. Accra: Amanza, 2009.

Poku, K. "Traditional Roles and People of Slave Origins in Modern Ashanti: A Few Impressions." *Ghana Journal of Sociology* 5, no. 1 (1969): 34-38.

Prah, Kwesi Kwaa, ed. *Back to Africa*. Vol. 1, *Afro-Brazilian Returnees and Their Communities*. Cape Town: Center for Advanced Studies of African Society, 2009.

Pulis, John W. *Moving On: Black Loyalists in the Afro-Atlantic World*. New York: Garland, 1999.

Quarcoopome, Samuel. "The Brazilian Community of Ghana." BA diss., University of Ghana, Legon, 1970.

———. "The Impact of Urbanization on the Socio-Political History of the Gã Mashie People of Accra." PhD diss., University of Ghana, Legon, 1993.

———. "Political Activities in Accra, 1924-1945." PhD diss., University of Ghana, Legon, 1980.

Quaye, Irene. "The Ga and Their Neighbours, 1600-1742." PhD diss., University of Ghana, Legon, 1972.

Quist-Therson, Paulina S. "Chieftancy among the Ga's." BA diss., University of Ghana, Legon, 1972.

Ralston, Richard D. "The Return of Brazilian Freedmen to West Africa in the 18th and 19th Centuries." *Canadian Journal of African Studies* 3, no. 3 (1969): 577-93.

Rathbone, Richard. *Nkrumah & the Chiefs: The Politics of Chieftancy in Ghana, 1951-1960*. Oxford: James Currey, 2000.

Ray, Carina E. *Crossing the Color Line: Race, Sex, and the Contested Politics of Colonialism in Ghana*. Athens: Ohio University Press, 2015.

Reichmann, Rebecca L., ed. *Race in Contemporary Brazil: From Indifference to Inequality*. University Park: Pennsylvania State University Press, 1999.

Reindorf, Carl C. *The History of the Gold Coast and Asante, Based on Traditions and Historical Facts Comprising a Period of More than Three Centuries from about 1500 to 1860*. Basel: Basel Mission Depot, 1951.

Reis, João José. *Death Is a Festival: Funeral Rites and Rebellion in Nineteenth-Century Brazil*. Translated by H. Sabrina Gledhill. Chapel Hill: University of North Carolina Press, 2003.

———. *Divining Slavery and Freedom: The Story of Domingos Sodré, an African Priest in Nineteenth-Century Brazil*. New York: Cambridge University Press, 2015.

———. "Domingos Pereira Sodré: A Nagô Priest in Nineteenth-Century Bahia." In *The Changing Worlds of Atlantic Africa: Essays in Honor of Robin Law*, ed. Toyin Falola and Matt Childs, 387-407. Durham, NC: Carolina Academic Press, 2009.

———. "Quilombos and Rebellions in Brazil." In *African Roots/American Cultures: Africa in the Creation of the Americas*, ed. Sheila S. Walker, 301-13. New York: Rowman & Littlefield, 2001.

———. *Slave Rebellion in Brazil: The Muslim Uprising of 1835 in Bahia*. Translated by Arthur Brakel. Baltimore, MD: John Hopkins University Press, 1993.

Reis, João José, Flávio dos Santos Gomes, and Marcus J. M. de Carvalho. "Rufino José Maria (1820s-1850s): A Muslim in the Nineteenth-Century Brazilian Slave Trade Circuit." In *The Human Tradition in the Black Atlantic, 1500-2000*, ed. Beatriz G. Mamigonian and Karen Racine, 65-75. Lanham, MD: Rowman & Littlefield, 2010.

Reynolds, Edward. *Trade and Economic Change on the Gold Coast, 1807-1874*. Accra: Sub-Saharan Publishers, 2002.

Riaño-Alcalá, Pilar. *Dwellers of Memory: Youth and Violence in Medellín, Columbia*. New Brunswick, NJ: Transaction Publishers, 2006.

Richards Sandra L. "What Is to Be Remembered: Tourism to Ghana's Slave Castle-Dungeons." *Theatre Journal* 57 (2005): 617-37.

Robertson, Claire C. "Post-Proclamation Slavery in Accra: A Female Affair?" In *Women and Slavery in Africa*, ed. Claire C. Robertson and Martin A. Klein, 220-42. Madison: University of Wisconsin Press, 1983.

Robertson, Winslow. "Yes, They Cared about Architecture: The Significance in Yoruba Traditional and Brazilian-style Housing." MA thesis, James Madison University, 2008.'

Rodney, Walter. "African Slavery and Other Forms of Social Oppression on the Upper Guinea Coast of the Atlantic Slave-Trade." *Journal of African History* 7, no. 3 (1966): 431-43.

———. *How Europe Underdeveloped Africa*. Dar es Salaam: Tanzania Publishing House, 1973.

Rodrigues, José Honório. "Influence of Africa on Brazil and Brazil on Africa." *Journal of African History* 3, no. 1 (1962): 49-67.

Ross, David A. "The Career of Domingo Martinez in the Bight of Benin, 1833-1864." *Journal of African History* 6, no. 1 (1965): 79-90.

Rossi, Benedetta. *Reconfiguring Slavery: West African Trajectories.* Liverpool: Liverpool University Press, 2009.

Rucker, Walter C. *Gold Coast Diasporas: Identity, Culture, and Power.* Bloomington: Indiana University Press, 2015.

———. *The River Flows On: Black Resistance, Culture, and Identity Formation in Early America.* Baton Rouge: Louisiana University Press, 2006.

Russell-Wood, A. J. R. *The Black Man in Slavery and Freedom in Colonial Brazil.* New York: St. Martins, 1982.

Sackeyfio, Naaborko. "The Stool Owns the City: Ga Chieftancy and the Politics of Land in Colonial Accra, 1920-1950." PhD diss., University of Wisconsin-Madison, 2008.

Sackeyfio-Lenoch, Naaborko. *The Politics of Chieftaincy: Authority and Property in Colonial Ghana, 1920-1950.* Rochester, NY: University of Rochester Press, 2014.

Safran, William. "Diasporas in Modern Societies: Myths of Homeland and Return." *Diaspora* 1, no. 1 (1991): 83-99.

Said, Edward. *Orientalism.* New York: Vintage Books, 1979.

Salm, Steven J., and Toyin Falola. *Culture and Customs of Ghana.* Westport, CT: Greenwood Press, 2002.

Sansone, Livio, Elisée Soumonni, and Boubacar Barry, eds. *Africa, Brazil and the Construction of Trans-Atlantic Black Identities.* Trenton, NJ: Africa World Press, 2008.

Sarbah, John Mensah. *Fanti National Constitution.* London: Frank Cass, 1968.

Schaumloeffel, Marco A. *Tabom: The Afro-Brazilian Community in Ghana.* 2nd ed. Published by author, 2008.

Schiller, Nina G., and Georges Fourun. *Georges Woke up Laughing: Long-Distance Nationalism and the Search for Home.* Durham, NC: Duke University Press, 2001.

Schofield-Childs, Joann Merritt. *Take Me Home to Afrika: An Autobiography of a Returnee.* Published by author, 2011.

Schramm, Katharina. *African Homecoming: Pan-African Ideology and Contested Heritage.* Walnut Creek, CA: Left Coast Press, 2010.

Schwartz, Stuart B. *Slaves, Peasants and Rebels: Reconsidering Brazilian Slavery.* Urbana: University of Illinois Press, 1992.

———, ed. *Tropical Babylons: Sugar and the Making of the Atlantic World, 1450-1680.* Chapel Hill: University of North Carolina Press, 2004.

Schwarz, Suzanne. "Reconstructing the Life Histories of Liberated Africans: Sierra Leone in the Early Nineteenth Century." *History in Africa* 39 (2012): 175-207.

Scott, Rebecca J. *The Abolition of Slavery and the Aftermath of Emancipation in Brazil.* Durham, NC: Duke University Press, 1988.

Scott, William R. "Black Nationalism and the Italo-Ethiopian Conflict, 1934-1936." *Journal of Negro History* 63, no. 2 (April 1978): 118-34.

Shareef bin Farid, Abu Alfa Muhammad. *The Islamic Revolts of Bahia, Brazil: A Continuity of the 19th Century Jihaad Movements of Western Sudan.* Pittsburgh: Sankore, 1998.

Shaw, Stephanie J. *W. E .B. Du Bois and "The Souls of Black Folk."* Chapel Hill: University of North Carolina Press, 2013.

Shepherd, Verene A. *Saving Souls: The Struggle to End the Transatlantic Trade in Africans.* Kingston, Jamaica: Ian Randle Publishers, 2007.

Sherwood, Marika. *Origins of Pan-Africanism: Henry Sylvester Williams, Africa, and the African Diaspora.* New York: Routledge, 2010.

Shillington, Kevin. *Ghana and the Rawlings Factor.* London: Macmillan Press, 1992.

Shumway, Rebecca. *The Fante and the Transatlantic Slave Trade.* Rochester, NY: University of Rochester Press, 2011.

Silva, Alberto da Costa e. "Portraits of African Royalty in Brazil." In *Identity in the Shadow of Slavery*, ed. Paul E. Lovejoy, 129-36. London: Continuum, 2000.

Silva, Eduardo. *Prince of the People: The Life and Times of a Brazilian Free Man of Color.* Translated by Moyra Ashford. London: Verso, 1993.

Simonsen, Gunvor. "Moving in Circles: African and Black History in the Atlantic World." *Nuevo Mundo, Mundos Nuevos* 8 (2008): 1-13.

Skidmore, Thomas E. *Brazil: Five Centuries of Change.* New York: Oxford University Press, 1999.

———. *The Politics of Military Rule in Brazil, 1964-1985.* New York: Oxford University Press, 1988.

Skinner, Elliot P. *African Americans and U.S. Policy toward Africa, 1850-1924: In Defense of Black Nationality.* Washington, DC: Howard University Press, 1992.

Smallwood, Stephanie E. *Saltwater Slavery: A Middle Passage from Africa to American Diaspora.* Cambridge, MA: Harvard University Press, 2007.

Soumonni, Elisée. "The Afro-Brazilian Communities of Ouidah and Lagos in the Nineteenth Century: A Comparative Analysis." In *Africa and the Americas: Interconnections during the Slave Trade*, ed. José C. Curto and Renée Souloudre-La France, 231-42. Trenton, NJ: Africa World Press, 2005.

———. "The Aguda of Benin: From the Memory of Brazil to the Construction of a Community Identity." In *Back to Africa*, vol. 1, *Afro-Brazilian Returnees and Their Communities*, ed. Kwasi K. Prah, 261-73. Cape Town: Center for Advanced Studies of African Society, 2009.

———. "Lacustrine Village in South Benin as Refuges from the Slave Trade." In *Fighting the Slave Trade: West African Strategies*, ed. Sylviane A. Diouf, 3-14. Athens: Ohio University Press, 2003.

Strickrodt, Silke. "The Brazilian Diaspora to West Africa in the Nineteenth Century." In *AficAmericas: Itineraries, Dialogues, and Sounds*, ed. Ineke Phaf-Rheinberger and Tiago de Oliveira Pinto, 37-68. Frankfurt: Die Deutsche Nationalbibliothek, 2008.

Sundiata, Ibrahim. *Brothers and Strangers: Black Zion, Black Slavery, 1914-1940.* Durham, NC: Duke University Press, 2003.

Sundkler, Bengt, and Christopher Steed. *A History of the Church in Africa.* Cambridge: Cambridge University Press, 2000.

Sutherland, Peter. "Ancestral Slaves and Diasporic Tourists: Retelling History by Reversing Movements in a Counternationalist Vodun Festival from Benin." In *Africanizing Knowledge: African Studies across Disciplines*, ed. Toyin Falola and Christian Jennings, 65-84. New Brunswick, NJ: Transaction, 2002.

Sweet, James H. *Domingos Álvares, African Healing, and the Intellectual History of the Atlantic World.* Chapel Hill: University of North Carolina Press, 2011.

———. *Recreating Africa: Culture, Kinship, and Religion in African-Portuguese World, 1441-1770*. Chapel Hill: University of North Carolina Press, 2003.

Swinepoe, Natalie. "Different Conversations about the Same Thing? Source Materials in the Recreation of a Nineteenth-Century Slave-Raiding Landscape, Northern Ghana." In *Slavery in Africa: Archaeology and Memory*, ed. Paul J. Lane and Kevin C. MacDonald, 167-90. London: Oxford University Press, 2011.

Switzer, Les, ed. *South Africa's Alternative Press: Voices of Protest and Resistance, 1880s-1960s*. Cambridge: Cambridge University Press, 1997.

Taylor, Yuval, ed. *I Was Born a Slave: An Anthology of Classic Slave Narratives*. Vol. 1. Chicago: Lawrence Hill Books, 1999.

Telles, Edward E. *Race in Another America: The Significance of Skin Color in Brazil*. Princeton, NJ: Princeton University Press, 2004.

Thiong'o, Ngũgĩ wa. *Decolonising the Mind: The Politics of Language in African Literature*. Portsmouth, NJ: Heinemann, 1986.

Thornton, John K. *Africa and Africans in the Making of the Atlantic World, 1400-1800*. 2nd ed. Cambridge: Cambridge University Press, 1999.

Timothy, Dallen J., and Victor B. Teye. "American Children of the African Diaspora: Journeys to the Motherland." In *Tourism, Diaspora and Space*, ed. Tim Coles and Dallen J. Timothy, 111-23. New York: Routledge, 2004.

Trouillot, Michel-Rolph. *Silencing the Past: Power and the Production of History*. Boston: Beacon Press, 1995.

Turner, Lorenzo D. "Some Contacts of Brazilian Ex-Slaves with Nigeria, West Africa." *Journal of Negro History* 27, no. 1 (January 1942): 55-67.

Turner, Michael J. "Les Bresiliens: The Impact of Former Brazilian Slaves upon Dahomey." PhD diss., Boston University, 1975.

Vansina, Jan. *Oral Tradition: A Study in Historical Methodology*. Translated by H. M. Wright. New York: Routledge & Kegan Paul, 1965.

Verger, Pierre. *Bahia and the West African Trade, 1549-1851*. Ibadan: Ibadan University Press, 1964.

———. *Trade Relations between the Bight of Benin and Bahia from the 17th to 19th Century*. Translated by Evelyn Crawford. Ibadan: Ibadan University Press, 1976.

Vinson, Ben. "Introduction: African (Black) Diaspora History, Latin American History." *Americas* 63 (2006): 1-18.

Von Eschen, Penny M. "Race against Empire: Black America and Anticolonialism, 1937-1957." PhD diss., Columbia University, 1994.

———. *Race against Empire: Black Americans and Anticolonialism, 1937-1957*. Ithaca, NY: Cornell University Press, 1997.

Von Hesse, H. W. "A Brief History of Afro-Brazilian Community of Accra." Master's thesis, University of Ghana, Legon, 2014.

Watson, James L., ed. *Asian and African Systems of Slavery*. Oxford: Blackwell, 1980.

Weaver, Karol K. *Medical Revolutionaries: The Enslaved Healers of Eighteenth-Century Saint Dominique*. Urbana: University of Illinois Press, 2006.

Weisbord, Robert G. *Ebony Kinship: Africa, Africans, and the Afro-American*. Westport, CT: Greenwood Press, 1973.

Wellington, H. Nii-Adziri. *Stones Tell Stories at Osu: Memories of a Host Community of the Danish Trans-Atlantic Slave Trade.* Legon-Accra: Sub-Saharan Publishers, 2011.

Westwood, John. *J. J. Rawlings: From School Days at Achimota to Castle.* Accra: Blue Savana, 2001.

White, Deborah Gray. *Ar'n't I a Woman: Female Slaves in the Plantation South.* New York: W. W. Norton, 1999.

White, Luise, Stephan F. Miescher, and David William Chen, eds. *African Words, African Voices: Critical Practices in Oral History.* Bloomington: Indiana University Press, 2001.

Whitten, Norman E., Jr., and Torres, Arlene, eds. *Blackness in Latin America and the Caribbean: Social Dynamics and Cultural Transformations.* Vol. 2, *Eastern South America and the Caribbean.* Bloomington: Indiana University Press, 1998.

Williamson, Thora. *Gold Coast Diaries: Chronicles of Political Officers in West Africa, 1900–1919.* London: Radcliffe Press, 2000.

Wilson-Fall, Wendy. *Memories of Madagascar in the Black Atlantic.* Athens: Ohio University Press, 2015.

Winsnes, Selena Axelrod, trans. and ed. *Letters on West Africa and the Slave Trade: Paul Erdmann Isert's Journey to Guinea and the Caribbean Islands in Columbia, 1788.* Accra: Sub-Saharan Publishers, 2007.

Wright, Michelle M. *Physics of Blackness: Beyond the Middle Passage Epistemology.* Minneapolis: University of Minnesota Press, 2015.

Yoneyama, Lisa. *Hiroshima Traces: Time, Space and the Dialects of Memory.* Berkeley: University of California Press, 1999.

Zeleza, Paul Tiyambe. "Rewriting the African Diaspora: Beyond the Black Atlantic." *African Affairs* 104 (2005): 35–68.

Zelizer, Barbie. "Reading the Past against the Grain: The Shape of Memory Studies." *Critical Studies in Mass Communication* 12, no. 2 (1995): 213–39.

Ziorklui, Emmanuel Doe. *Ghana: Nkrumah to Rawlings, a Historical Sketch of Some Major Political Events in Ghana from 1957–81.* Vol. 1. Accra: Ghana Publishing Corporation, 1998.

Index

A

Abeokuta, 101, 159, 162
Abokobi, 164, 181-83
abolition movement, 24, 82, 159, 161; campaigns, 6, 20, 162, 166; abolitionists, 5, 18-25, 41, 82, 101, 124, 277
Aborigines' Rights Protection Society, 78, 123
Accra: Dutch, 36, 71, 153, 169, 173, 176; postcolonial, xxi, 230; precolonial, 5, 64, 77, 178, 190, 221; strangers in, xxv, 12, 33-36, 42-44, 156, 173, 199-213
Accra Town Council Bill, 181
Act of Parliament 51, 20
Adabraka, 43, 121, 129
Adinkra symbols, 3, 4, 259, 276
African Americans, xxii, xxx, 46, 228, 230, 240-42, 247, 255
Africanists, xxiv, 9, 47, 211
agrarian skills, 35, 46, 95-98, 106-9, 113-19, 129, 177-79, 221-22; activities, 95, 108, 147-48; nonagrarian activities, 106-7, 110-12, 117, 130, 148
Aguda, xix, xxiv-xxx, 5-9, 14-19, 24-26, 185-88, 235, 242-43
Ahikwa, Otu, 60
Akabi, Naa Dode, 224

Akan, 81, 95, 106, 171, 177-79, 203, 224, 276
Akua v. Nelson, 189
akutso, 33, 59
Akwamu people, xxxiv, 48, 54, 59-61, 65, 89
Akwandor, 43, 121, 137, 139, 145, 147
Alata people, 49, 59, 212
American Colonization Society, xxix, 5, 166, 168
Amponsah, Kofi Acquah, 206
Anacostia Community Museum Archives, 16, 19
Anglican churches, 187, 188, 272
Angola, xix, xxx, 10, 25, 101, 184
Ankrah, Kwaku, 49, 144, 169, 173, 272
Apenteng, Nii Kofi *we*, 60
appropriation, xxxi, 229, 241, 254-56
archival records, xxxii, 12, 106, 144, 155
Arquivo Publico da Bahia, xxvi, 14, 17, 18, 25
Asafoatse, 60, 272
Asante: Empire, 61, 66, 75, 76; Kingdom, 74, 75, 224, 257; kings, 66, 72, 73; leaders, 67, 73, 76, 84; people, 61, 71, 73-76, 83, 88, 153, 227
Asantehene, 84
Asantewaa, Yaa, 73, 75, 88, 224
Atlantic Ocean, 35-37, 92, 240

359

Atlantic world, xxv, xxiv, xxx, 4, 6, 10, 20-21, 27-30, 86, 166, 169, 278
Azumah, Nii, III, 42, 107-8, 135-36, 142, 177, 195-96, 218-19, 236-38

B

Back-to-Africa movement, xxix, 5, 24, 166
Bahia, xix, xxvi, xxxvii, xxxi, 10, 16-23, 38, 52, 82, 97, 102, 103, 124, 161, 184, 186-88, 197, 220, 259
Basel Mission, 34, 142, 164-68, 172, 181-82, 215
Benin, xix, xxv, xxvii, xxx, xxxiv, 7-14, 19-22, 26, 32, 37, 58-59, 91, 101, 154, 159, 169, 184-88, 200, 216, 223-35, 242, 261; Bight of, 23, 28-32, 36-37, 46, 88, 103, 114, 116, 144, 160-62, 168-70, 178-79, 185, 201-2, 222
Bight of Biafra (Bight of Bonny), 20, 30
Bonsu, Badu, II, 72
Brazil House, xxiii-xxxvi, 14, 17, 48, 190-93, 203-9, 219, 227-33, 239, 240, 244, 246-51, 255-58, 262, 269, 273-74, 276-78
Brazilian-Ghanaians, xix, 17, 28, 229
Brazilian Olosun Mosque, 184, 185
Brazilians: chief, xx, 5, 17, 31, 45, 49, 55, 73, 88, 91, 100, 146, 177, 196, 200, 205, 216, 220, 237; Embassy, xxix, xxxv, 12, 209, 219, 227, 231; family tree, 39, 202; government, xxiii, xxxv, 12, 19, 208, 227, 232, 235; heritage, 14-17, 42, 143, 155, 170, 184, 203, 216-18
Brimah, Alhaji (chief), 142, 143, 210, 212-14
Brimah, Alhaji Farouk, 214

C

calabashes, 44, 58
Cape Coast Castle, 73, 76, 229-30, 239, 242, 246, 255, 257
caretakers, 112, 114, 115, 248
Caribbean, xx, xxii, xxviii, xxx, 24, 32, 48, 52, 146, 166, 168, 187, 190, 210, 228, 230, 242, 255
casa grande, 102
cassava, 102, 112, 115, 123, 138, 147, 175, 178-79
Catholics, 25, 26, 184-88

chartered companies, 158, 159, 161
Chief Brimah, 17, 142, 143, 212-14
Christianborg Castle, 71, 157, 166
Christians, 29, 38, 163,165, 184, 186-88, 221; gospel, 156, 187; missionaries, xvii, 164, 165, 181, 187
citizenship, xx, xxvi, 5, 6, 11, 256, 262, 273
civilization, 19, 51-53, 68-69, 102, 166-67, 176, 186
colonialism, 54, 62, 96; African intellectuals on, 63; land ordinances, 95; policies, 77-79, 87-89, 92-96, 113, 116, 120, 124-30, 136-38; rule, 98, 118, 123, 124; scheme, 70
compensation, 127-31, 181, 208, 219
Compulsory Labour Ordinance of 1897, xxxiii, 46, 84, 117, 125, 177, 178, 205
confiscation of land, 56, 125
continuity of history, xxxii, 5, 23, 32, 108, 195, 202, 258, 271
Crown Land Bill of 1896, 126
Cuba, xxviii, xxx, 5, 7, 10-11, 162, 183, 188, 228

D

Da Costa, 12
Dahomey, 22, 26, 59, 159-62
Daily Echo, 129
Danes, 36, 43, 65, 69, 71-72, 156-57, 163-66, 213
Dantas, Iodine de Souza, 220
Dantas, Raymundo de Souza, 196, 220, 231, 233, 235-37, 243, 246, 267
de Andrade Serra, Luis Fernando, 229, 246, 264
de Azambuja, Don Diego, 230
Denkyira, 60
Densu River, 181
de Souza, Francisco "Chacha," 160, 161, 170, 206, 207
double consciousness, 4, 27, 195-97, 233, 254, 263, 275-76
drumming, 50, 79, 80
dual heritage, 4, 269
dual identity, xxii, 28, 57, 104, 217, 232, 239, 255
Du Bois, 27, 28, 210
Dutch West India Company, 58, 173

Dzase, 49, 60
Dzidzienyo, Anani, 233–36, 245, 267–68

E

Earl of Clarendon, 19, 23
economic activities, xxiii, 65, 77, 102, 190, 197, 231–33, 255–58
Elmina Castle, 66, 73, 103, 230
Emancipation Day celebrations, 46, 47, 255; laws, 20
Emillia, 22–23
England: abolitionist, xxxi, 18–24, 101, 124; colonial officials, xvii, 51, 153; consulate, 19, 22; crown, 67; Empire, 68, 276; naval patrol, 20, 21; royal naval patrol, 22, 160; ordinance, 79; Parliament, 18, 20, 21
ethnicity, xxvi, xxxii, 14, 221, 267; groups, 54, 61, 65, 220, 247, 277
ethnography, 9, 10
enslavement. *See* slavery
entrepreneurs, 129, 130, 190, 239, 257
European suits xxix, 190, 221, 222, 276
Ewe people, 61, 65, 83, 169
exile, 4, 43, 66, 72, 77, 84, 89, 132–35

F

Fante, xxxiv, 65, 71, 80, 83, 87
Fatuma, 98, 99, 201
Ferku, xx, xxxiii, 10–11, 92–93, 97–104, 116–17, 140, 212
Fernandes, Florestan, 158
Ferreira, Roquinaldo A., 10,
festivals, 45–46, 60, 79–80, 200, 243–44, 255
Fiscian, Cyril, 12, 190, 260
Fiscian, Isaac Cobblah, 38, 108, 128, 137, 144, 145, 190
Fiscian, Nathaniel Kassum, 190
Fiscian, Peter Quarshie, 42, 108
Fiscian family, 12, 38, 40–42, 108–10, 128, 137–39, 144–47, 190
Fonafor Valley, 43, 121
Fort Creyecoeur, 11
Fredensborg, 157, 163
Freye, Gilberto, 102, 268
Fulani community, 213

G

Gã: becoming, 56, 195, 201, 219; *mãntsɛmɛi*, xxviii, xxxii–xxxiv, 5, 31, 35–36, 44–45, 49–61, 64; middlemen, 58, 69, 112; nationalism, 61, 80, 89; paramountcy, 48–49, 59, 60, 65, 79, 105, 213, 217, 218, 220; Gã-Tabom identities, 220
Gala, Irene Vida, 264, 270
Gazette, 126
Gbese, 59
gender roles, xxviii, 75, 140, 223
genealogy, xxvi, 18, 155, 239; DNA, 170, 202
geographical boundaries, 4, 146
Gezo, 160
Ghanaian-Brazilians. *See* Brazilian-Ghanaians
Ghana Tourist and Monument Board, 238, 242, 246, 255–57
globalization, xxvi, xxvii, 255
global tourism, xxx, xxxvi, 149, 227, 240
Glover, John, 41
Gold Coast Echo, 67, 74, 101, 162
Gold Coast Independent, 67, 69, 77, 126
Gold Coast Methodist Times, 51–52
"Golden Stool," 73, 75
Growther, Francis, 81

H

Haley, Alex, 3, 6, 275
Hausa, 188, 203, 213
Headmen, 51, 56, 75
Henriqueta, 22
heritage tourism, xxiii, xxvi–xxvii, xxx, 208, 228, 234–40, 262–65, 273–77
Holland, 20, 36, 40, 51, 65, 71–73, 83, 211–13
Homowo, 45, 50, 60, 78–80, 200, 220–24, 264

I

Illorin, 214
indirect rule, 36, 62, 66–70, 75, 78, 96, 122, 126; Lugardian principle of, 87
irrigation technology, xxxv, 48, 175, 183, 184, 186–88, 197–98, 212
Islam, 33, 38, 184–88; faith of, 11, 184, 185
Island of São Tomé, 21

J

Jaase, 64
James Fort, 71
Jamestown, 23, 60, 232, 250
J. E. Maslieno v. J. A. Nelson, 129, 139, 144, 273

K

Kakum National Park, 257
Keta, 163, 169
Kinkã, 33
Kogen af Ashanti, 163
Konadu, Kwasi, 25, 52
Kongensteen, 157
Kufuor, John Kofi Agyekum, 193, 243-45
Krio diaspora, 186
Kyarcha, Naa, 206

L

Laaburg Gallei, 163
Labadi, 60
land: interfamily conflicts over, 108, 117, 133-35, 142; intrafamily conflicts over, 117, 128, 131, 133, 139, 142; landownership, xxxiii, 34-35, 42, 55, 85, 93-98, 104-8, 117-26; landowning members, 57, 64, 120, 127; and its ripple effects, 27, 48, 75, 89, 92-93, 131, 149, 172; rural-to-urban migration, 58
lawsuits, xxxiv, 111, 119, 131, 138
Lebanon, 51
Letters from Brazil, 12, 14, 16, 180, 223
Lindsay, Lisa A., xxix, 24
linguists, 4, 134, 221, 264
Lugard, Frederick J. D., 36, 68
Lula da Silva, Luiz Inácio, 175, 231, 243, 244, 245, 250, 259
Lutterodt, Alfred, 206-8
Lutterodt, William, 17, 193, 203-7, 234, 255, 260, 262
Lutterodt family, 204, 207-8, 228, 240, 248, 256

M

Madam Sarah Clegg v. Emmanuel Drissu Cobblah, 5, 108, 111
Manhia Palace, 257
manumission, xxviii, xxxii, 5, 20, 82-83, 101-3, 106, 199
marriage unions, xxxiii, 9, 17, 92, 98, 116, 211-15, 273
Martins, Domingo, 159
merchants, xxxiv, 20-21, 26, 160, 165, 172, 221; European, 36, 129, 130
Methodist churches, 38, 52, 168, 187-88, 221, 252
Mfantsi Amabuhu Fekuw, 87
Ministére des Relations Extérérieres (Ministry of External Relations), 12
Ministry of Tourism and Diasporan Relations, 46, 238-39
Moloney, Alfred, 156, 176
monuments, 232-34, 241, 249, 254, 269, 276
Morton, 12, 190-92, 201

N

Nagô, 10
Nathan, Matthew, 74, 79
National Archives of Ghana, 43, 139
native courts, 94, 108-12, 121-22, 130-33, 136-40
Native Jurisdiction Ordinance of 1883, 77, 117, 122, 217
Native Prisons Ordinance of 1888, 122
negroes, 22, 25, 153, 160-69, 176, 186
Nelson, Abiana, 17, 188
Nelson, Alasha, 17
Nelson, Antonio João, xix-xx, 17, 55, 84-85, 107-9, 125-26
Nelson, Azumah, xxviii, 140, 192, 220, 237, 253
Nelson, Azumah, Nii, V, 123, 133-39, 148, 187, 204, 216-22
Nelson, George Aruna, xiv-xxi, 43, 104, 144, 189-90, 197, 217, 259-66
Nelson, Henry Asumah Kwaku, 137
Nelson, Sam, 192
Nelson family, 128
Nikoi, Amon, 68
Nkrumah, Kwame, 43, 46, 178, 190-92, 211, 238, 249
"Note System," 58
Nungua, 60

O

odonkor, 170–73
Odotei-Quaye, Irene, 59
Okpedu, Fatima, 17, 142–43, 210, 214
Olinto, Antonio, 29, 32, 101
Onim, 5, 16
Osu, 35, 60
Otero, Solimar, 7, 9, 243
Otublohum, xxiii–xxxiv, 33–35, 88, 144, 147, 250

P

Pan-African Festival (PANAFEST), 46–47, 255
Pan-Africanism, 209–10, 239–40
Patterson, Tiffany Ruby, 32
Peregrino, Francis Amida, 203, 210
Peregrino, Francis J., 209
Peregrino, Francis Zaccheus Santiago, 6–8, 190, 209–11
Peregrino-Brimah, Emmanuel Issah-Modulpe, 188
Peregrino-Brimah, Olowun Toyin, 214
Peregrino-Brimah, Segun, 215
Peregrino House, 205
Pernambuco, 14, 20–22, 161
philanthropists, 172, 277, 282
Plange family, 12, 17, 136, 142, 189, 210, 273
Prempeh, Agyeman, I, 72–73, 84
protectorates, 66–67, 74–76, 88, 125, 160
Pontificia Universitas Urbaniana, 26
Portuguese language, xxix, 27, 59–60, 98, 246, 250–54, 267, 273
Public Land Ordinance of 1876, xx, xxxiv, 55, 86, 117, 120–21, 125
public protests, 63, 268

Q

Quadros, Jânio, 231, 235–37, 243, 249, 267
Quarcoopome, Samuel, 39, 78, 96, 137, 179
queen mothers, xxviii, 48, 56

R

Rawlings, Jerry John, 192–93, 238
Reindorf, Carl C., 59, 173
Reis, João Jose, xxiv, 10, 103, 184–86, 265
Ribeiro, Harry Francisco, 191–92
Ribeiro, Miguel Augustus, 191–92
Ribeiro family, 12, 38, 111, 129, 142, 200–201, 218, 221
Riis, Andre, 160, 164
Rio de Janeiro, xii, xix, 14–22, 103, 120, 160, 259, 277

S

Salvador da Bahia, xix, 12, 14, 20, 185, 197, 277
sankofa, xxvi, 3–4, 259, 276
São Jorge da Mina, 103, 230
Sarbah, John Mensah, 87
Sarro, xix, xxx, 9, 186, 200
Schiedt, Frederikgave, 165
Schwartz, Stuart B., 102, 308
Scissors House, xxix, 147, 190, 224, 250–51
Sempe, 59
Seychelles, 73
Shango, 183, 188–89
Sierra Leone, xxx, 7–10, 24, 32, 73, 106, 166–67, 186–87
sites of memory, xxxi, 204–8, 228–29, 238–39, 241–43, 250, 255–58
slavery, 24, 171, 200; demise of, 24, 82, 83, 93, 260; and monetary gain, xxx, 50, 170, 228; revolts, xxi, 27, 52, 82, 166, 184–86; trauma and, 158, 278; travel paths of, 5, 14–16; unmatched fortitude and, xvii, 3, 240, 263, 275
Sociedade Protertora dos Desalidos (Society for the Protection of the Disenfranchised), 12
Sodre, Domingos Perreira, xxiv, 10, 103
Sokoto, Mama, 12, 17, 38, 40, 91–92, 146–47, 215
South America, xxv, 32, 168, 201, 261
Spectator, 210
Stool Property Protection Ordinance of 1940, 95, 122
St. Xavier Fort, 71. *See also* Christianborg Castle
Supiano, Naa, 207
Supreme Court of the Gold Coast, xxxiv, 56, 112, 121, 129, 135–42, 149
Swalaba, xxix, 37, 114–15, 147, 190, 242
Swedes, 43, 71, 94
Sweet, James H., xiii, 10, 178, 184
Switzerland, 48, 94, 160, 166, 183, 286
Syria, 51, 111, 130

T

Tabom: ancestral heritage, xxxii, 64, 171, 197, 232-33, 243; family tree, 39, 155, 195, 199-202, 215-16; tudo bom, xxi; women, 224; youths, xxviii, 192, 250-51, 263, 273-74
Tabom City, 244, 269
Tackie v. Nelson, 64, 76, 108, 133, 134-35
tailoring (profession), xxiii, xxix, 24, 104, 116
Tawiah, Tackie, 55-57, 64, 71-75, 89, 132-35, 140, 148, 213
taxation, 58, 75, 78, 105
Teshie, 60, 157
Town Council Ordinance of 1896, 75
Trans-Atlantic Slave Trade Database, 202
Trouillot, Michel-Rolph, 9-10
Turner, Lorenzo Dow, 16, 19, 24, 52, 97
Turner, Michael J., 32, 91, 186-87, 235

U

United Nations Educational, Scientific, and Cultural Organization (UNESCO), 208, 233, 241-46, 256-57, 274
Ussher Fort, 35, 71, 190

V

Verger, Pierre, 18, 23-24, 103

W

Warri House, xxiii, xxix, 193, 207-9, 228-29, 240-51, 255-56, 262. *See also* Brazil House
water (well) drilling, 37, 144, 156, 177, 180, 183, 217
waves of migrations, xxxii, 31, 39, 198
Wharton, Henry, 34
Whydah, 21, 26, 32, 37, 160-61, 243
Williams, Henry Sylvester, 210
World Cup soccer, xxxvi, 253, 268, 270, 273
World Heritage Sites, xxvii, 230, 242, 255-56
Wood, Georgina Theodora, xiv, xix, 193, 206-7, 246, 253, 262
Wuff, Joseph, 157

Y

Yawah, xxxiii, 92, 98, 142, 212, 224
Yawah v. J. E. Maslieno, 92, 98, 100, 116, 133, 140-42
Yoruba, 9-11, 16-17, 20-26, 49-50, 142, 184, 203, 211-15
Yoruba-Brazilians, 7, 209

Z

Z-path, 4
Zeleza, Paul T. xxv, 32
Zimmerman, Johannes, 164